W9-CCZ-076

GENDER MATTERS IN GLOBAL POLITICS

Fully revised and updated, this second edition of *Gender Matters in Global Politics* is a comprehensive textbook for advanced undergraduates studying feminism and International Relations, gender and global politics, and similar courses. It provides students with an accessible but in-depth account of the most significant theories, methodologies, debates and issues.

This textbook is written by an international line-up of established and emerging scholars from a range of theoretical perspectives, and brings together cutting-edge feminist scholarship in a variety of issue areas.

Key features and benefits of the book:

- Introduces students to the wide variety of feminist and gender theory and explains the relevance to contemporary global politics.
- Explains the insights of feminist theory for a range of other disciplines including International Relations, International Political Economy and Security Studies.
- Addresses a large number of key contemporary issues such as human rights, trafficking, rape as a tool of war, peacekeeping and state-building, terrorism and environmental politics.
- Features detailed pedagogical tools and resources – seminar exercises (available on the Companion Website), text boxes, photographs, suggestions for further reading, web resources and a glossary of key terms.
- Contains new chapters on environmental politics and ecology; war; terrorism and political violence; land, food and water; international legal institutions; peacebuilding institutions and post-conflict reconstruction; citizenship; art, aesthetics and emotionality; and new social media and global resistance.

This text will enable students to develop a sophisticated understanding of the role that gender plays in processes and practices of global politics.

Laura J. Shepherd is Associate Professor of International Relations at UNSW Australia. She teaches and researches in the areas of gender politics, International Relations and critical security studies.

 A range of further resources for this book is available on the Companion Website: www.routledge.com/cw/shepherd

GENDER MATTERS IN GLOBAL POLITICS

A feminist introduction to International Relations

Second edition

Edited by
Laura J. Shepherd

LONDON AND NEW YORK

First published 2015
by Routledge
2 Park Square, Milton Park, Abingdon, Oxon OX14 4RN

and by Routledge
711 Third Avenue, New York, NY 10017

Routledge is an imprint of the Taylor & Francis Group, an informa business

© 2015 selection and editorial material, Laura J. Shepherd;
individual chapters, the contributors

The right of Laura J. Shepherd to be identified as author of the editorial material,
and of the authors for their individual chapters, has been asserted in accordance
with the Copyright, Designs and Patent Act 1988.

All rights reserved. No part of this book may be reprinted or reproduced or utilised in any form or by any electronic, mechanical, or other means, now known
or hereafter invented, including photocopying and recording, or in any information storage or retrieval system, without permission in writing from the publishers.

Trademark notice: Product or corporate names may be trademarks or registered
trademarks, and are used only for identification and explanation without intent to
infringe.

British Library Cataloguing in Publication Data
A catalogue record for this book is available from the British Library

Library of Congress Cataloging-in-Publication Data
Gender matters in global politics : a feminist introduction to international
relations / edited by Laura J Shepherd. – Second edition.
pages cm
Includes bibliographical references and index.
ISBN 978-0-415-71520-1 (hardback) – ISBN 978-0-415-71521-8 (paperback) –
ISBN 978-1-315-87981-9 (e-book) 1. International relations. 2. Feminism.
3. Feminist theory. I. Shepherd, Laura J.
JZ1253.2.G46 2014
327.101–dc23
2013050051

ISBN: 978-0-415-71520-1 (hbk)
ISBN: 978-0-415-71521-8 (pbk)
ISBN: 978-1-315-87981-9 (ebk)

Typeset in Adobe Garamond
by Cenveo Publisher Services

CONTENTS

PART 5: INTERNATIONAL INSTITUTIONS

PART 6: IDENTITIES, ORDERS, BORDERS

PART 7: INFORMATION, COMMUNICATION, TECHNOLOGY

LIST OF FIGURES

NOTES ON CONTRIBUTORS

Anna M. Agathangelou is Associate Professor of Political Science and Women's Studies at York University, Toronto, and is the co-director of Global Change Institute, Nicosia, Cyprus. Her publications include *The Global Political Economy of Sex: Desire, Violence and Insecurity in Mediterranean Nation-States* (Palgrave Macmillan 2006), and *Transforming World Politics: From Empire to Multiple Worlds* (Routledge 2009), co-authored with L.H.M. Ling (New School).

Dibyesh Anand is a Reader in International Relations in the Department of Politics and IR at the University of Westminster. His research areas include majority–minority relations in China and India, the Tibet issue, and China–India relations. He is the author of *Geopolitical Exotica: Tibet in Western Imagination, Tibet: A Victim of Geopolitics, Hindu Nationalism in India and the Politics of Fear* and several articles on security, identity and Asian politics. He is currently working on a project on the China–India border dispute and Chinese public diplomacy around Tibet.

Monika Barthwal-Datta is Lecturer in International Security in the School of Social Sciences, University of New South Wales (UNSW), Sydney, in Australia. She currently teaches and researches in the areas of critical approaches to security, food security and the international politics of South Asia. She is the author of *Understanding Security Practices in South Asia: Securitization Theory and the Role of Non-State Actors* (Routledge 2012) and has a forthcoming work entitled *Food Security in Asia* (Routledge forthcoming).

Soumita Basu is Assistant Professor of International Relations at the South Asian University, New Delhi, India. Her primary areas of research are feminist International Relations, the United Nations, critical security studies and food politics. She co-edits the 'conversations' section of the *International Feminist Journal of Politics*.

Roland Bleiker is Professor of International Relations at the University of Queensland, in Australia. His publications include *Popular Dissent, Human Agency and Global Politics* (Cambridge University Press 2000), *Divided Korea: Toward a Culture of Reconciliation* (University of Minnesota Press 2005/2008) and *Aesthetics and World Politics* (Palgrave 2009/2012). He is currently working on a collaborative project that examines how images – and the emotions they generate – shape responses to humanitarian crises.

Katherine E. Brown is a Lecturer at the Defence Studies Department of King's College London. Her research is engaged with issues of gender, religion and global security politics. Her work addresses the gendered nature of terrorism, counterterrorism and political Islam, with particular reference to the UK and Pakistan. Her work is concerned with the development of critical feminist understandings of the religion–security nexus. She is also interested in the role of emotions in security politics, particularly humour. She has published widely with an interdisciplinary focus, including in *Antipode* (2013), *Interventions* (2010) and *The British Journal of Politics and IR* (2008).

Terrell Carver is Professor of Political Theory at the University of Bristol, UK. He has published extensively on gender, sex and sexuality in a feminist and international frame, including 'The Machine in the Man', in *Rethinking the Man Question* (Zed Books 2008), 'Men in the Feminist Gaze: What does this mean in IR?', *Millennium: Journal of International Studies* (2008) and 'International Relations', in the *Routledge International Encyclopedia of Men and Masculinities* (2008).

Cynthia Cockburn is a feminist researcher and writer, living in London. She is a Visiting Professor in the Department of Sociology, City University London, and an Honorary Professor in the Centre for the Study of Women and Gender, University of Warwick. Her research is action oriented and designed to contribute to social movements, particularly the movement for peace and justice. She is active in Women in Black against War and the Women's International League for Peace and Freedom. Her most recent book is *Antimilitarism: Political and Gender Dynamics of Peace Movements* (Palgrave Macmillan 2012).

Juanita Elias is Assistant Professor in the Department of Politics and International Studies at the University of Warwick. Her research and teaching interests are in the areas of international political economy, gendered approaches to international politics, and southeast Asian political economy. She is the author of *Fashioning Inequality: The Multinational Corporation and Gendered Employment in a Globalising World* (Ashgate 2004) and the co-author of *International Relations: The Basics* (Routledge 2007) and *The Global Political Economy of the Household in Asia* (Palgrave 2013). Her research also appears in journals such as the *Review of International Studies, Third World Quarterly, Men and Masculinities, Economy and Society* and *New Political Economy*.

Lucy Ferguson is Visiting Researcher at the Gender Unit, Instituto Complutense de Estudios Internacionales, Universidad Complutense de Madrid, in Spain. Her research is concerned with the gendered political economy of global development, with a particular interest in social reproduction and the tourism industry. She has worked as a gender consultant at the United Nations World Tourism Organization (UNWTO) and recently established Equality in Tourism, an organization dedicated to promoting gender equality in the tourism industry. Current research interests include the political economy of feminist knowledge transfer and gender and infra-structure in contemporary development.

Emma A. Foster is a Lecturer in International Politics and Gender in the Department of Political Science and International Studies at the University of Birmingham. Emma's research interests include queer ecology and international sustainable development policy and her current research focuses on gender and eco-sexual normativity in international environmental policy. Emma has published on this topic in a variety of journals, including *Globalizations* (2011) and *Gender, Place and Culture* (2013).

M. I. Franklin is Professor of Global Media and Politics at Goldsmiths, University of London, UK, and Co-Chair of the Internet Rights and Principles Dynamic Coalition at the UN Internet Governance Forum (www.internetrightsandprinciples.org). A former Chair of the ISA Feminist Theory and Gender Studies Section, she has been a recipient of research funding from the Social Science Research Council (USA) and Ford Foundation. Her latest book is *Digital Dilemmas: Power, Resistance and the Internet* (Oxford University Press 2013).

Caron Gentry is a Lecturer in the School of International Relations at the University of St Andrews. Having written on women's involvement in politically violent groups with articles in various journals, her publications also include (with Laura Sjoberg) *Mothers, Monsters, Whores: Women's Violence in Global Politics* (Zed Books 2007) and the edited volume, *Women, Gender, and Terrorism* (University of Georgia Press 2011).

Rosemary Grey is a PhD candidate in the Faculty of Arts and Social Sciences at the University of New South Wales, in Australia, and a sessional lecturer in the Faculty of Law. Her research is on gender issues in international criminal law, focusing on the prosecution of sexual and gender-based violence in the International Criminal Court. During her candidature Rosemary has spent time as a visiting PhD scholar at the Centre for International Governance and Justice at the Australian National University, in Canberra in Australia, and has interned with the International Bar Association in The Hague, the Netherlands.

Penny Griffin is a Senior Lecturer in International Relations at the University of New South Wales. Her work explores the processes, practices and effects of the contemporary global political economy with a view to understanding how these shape and are shaped by identity politics. She has published *Gendering the World Bank* (Palgrave Macmillan 2009) (BISA International Political Economy Group book prize winner 2010), in the journals *Men and Masculinities, New Political Economy, Review of International Political Economy, British Journal of Politics and International Relations, Australian Journal of International Affairs, Globalizations* and in the *International Studies Encyclopedia* (Oxford Blackwell) and the *Encyclopedia of Power* (SAGE).

Lucy Hall is a Doctoral Researcher at the University of New South Wales, in Australia. Her research focuses on the ways in which gender is invoked, ignored and configured in the development and implementation of the Responsibility to Protect (R2P) with specific reference to conflict induced internal displacement. Lucy previously worked for the International Institute for Humanitarian Law, and was seconded to the United Nations High Commissioner for Refugees (UNHCR), where she specialized in training and developing state capacity in relation to refugee law and internal displacement policy, with an emphasis on the gendered impact of forced displacement.

Lene Hansen is Professor of International Relations in the Department of Political Science, University of Copenhagen, Denmark. Her current research interests include the role of images in international security, gender and security and concepts and theories of security. Her publications include *Security as Practice: Discourse Analysis and the Bosnian War* (Routledge 2006), *The Evolution of International Security Studies*, co-authored with Barry Buzan (Cambridge University Press 2009) and articles in *International Studies Quarterly, European Journal of International Relations, Review of International Studies, Millennium* and *Security Dialogue*.

Denise M. Horn is Assistant Professor at Northeastern University, Boston, USA. Her research interests include transnational activism, feminist International Relations theory, democratization and civil society. She has published widely on these topics, and is author of *Women, Civil Society and the Geopolitics of Democratization* (Routledge 2010) and *Democratic Governance and Social Entrepreneurship: Civic Participation and the Future of Democracy* (Routledge 2013).

Krista Hunt teaches gender and global politics at York University, UK, and the University of Toronto, Canada. Her teaching and research focus on unlearning privilege in global and local contexts. Courses include gender and development, women and environments, violence and security, and topics in women and politics. She co-authored *Engendering the War on Terror: War Stories and Camouflaged Politics*, edited with Kim Rygiel (Ashgate 2007) and is currently working on a learning project called Teach.Learn.Change (www.teachlearnchange.org).

Kimberly Hutchings is Professor of International Relations at the London School of Economics (LSE). Her interests include feminist political and international theory, international ethics and the work of Kant and Hegel. She is the author of *Kant, Critique and Politics* (1996), *International Political Theory: Re-thinking ethics in a global era* (1998), *Hegel and Feminist Philosophy* (2003), *Time and World Politics: Thinking the present* (2008) and *Global Ethics: An Introduction* (2010).

Emma Hutchison is a Postdoctoral Research Fellow in the School of Political Science and International Studies at the University of Queensland, Australia. Her current key research projects examine trauma and emotions in world politics, as well as how disaster images shape humanitarian practices. Her research has appeared and is forthcoming in a range of scholarly journals, such as the *Review of International Studies, International Political Sociology, International Relations, Global Society* and the *European Journal of Social Theory*.

Adam Jones is Professor of Political Science at the University of British Columbia Okanagan in Kelowna, Canada. He is author of *Gender Inclusive: Essays on Violence, Men, and Feminist International Relations* (Routledge 2009) and author or editor of a dozen other books on genocide and human rights, gender and IR, and transitional mass media. He serves as executive director of Gendercide Watch (www.gendercide.org).

Suzanne Levi-Sanchez is a Visiting Research Collaborator at the Woodrow Wilson School at Princeton University. Her research focuses on ethnographic methodologies and political anthropology, with specific reference to Iran, Tajikistan and Afghanistan. Her PhD dissertation, 'Border (In)Security: The Case of Badakhshan', analyses the intersection of increasing border controls with cross-border cooperation.

Valentine M. Moghadam is Professor of Sociology and Director of the International Affairs programme at Northeastern University, Boston, US. Her areas of research include globalization, transnational social movements and feminist networks, and gender and social change in the Middle East and North Africa. Among her many publications are *Modernizing Women: Gender and Social Change in the Middle East* (Lynne Rienner Publishers 1993, 2003, 2013), *Globalizing Women: Transnational Feminist Networks* (Johns Hopkins University Press 2005) and *Globalization and Social Movements: Islamism, Feminism, and the Global Justice Movement* (Rowman & Littlefield 2009, 2013).

Donna Pankhurst is Professor of Peacebuilding and Development at the Department of Peace Studies, University of Bradford, UK. In recent years she has researched in Africa on conflict, post-conflict settlements and peacebuilding, particularly with a focus on gender issues. Publications include *Gendered Peace: Women's Struggles for Post-Conflict Justice and Reconciliation* (Routledge 2007).

Swati Parashar is a Lecturer in Politics and International Relations at the School of Social Sciences, Monash University, Australia. She teaches and researches in the areas of feminist International Relations, critical security studies, gender, war and political violence. Her recent publications include *Women and Militant Wars: The Politics of Injury* (Routledge 2014), 'What Wars and "War Bodies" know about International Relations', *Cambridge Review of International Affairs* (2013), 'Gender, Jihad, and Jingoism: Women as Perpetrators, Planners, and Patrons of Militancy in Kashmir', *Studies in Conflict & Terrorism* (2011), 'Feminist IR and Women Militants: Case Studies from South Asia', *Cambridge Review of International Affairs* (2009).

V. Spike Peterson is Professor of International Relations at the University of Arizona, US, with courtesy appointments in the Department of Gender and Women's Studies and Institute for LGBT Studies. Her research pursues two interweaving threads: informalization, global householding, and global insecurities in the context of critically analysing global political economy; and long histories and current queering of states/nations.

Jindy Pettman, former Professor of International Relations at the Australian National University, has published numerous articles investigating transnational feminisms, nationalism and the gendered politics of peace and war, in Asia and the Pacific in particular. She is author of *Worlding Women: A Feminist International Politics* (Routledge 1996) and a founding editor of the *International Feminist Journal of Politics*.

Nadine Puechguirbal is currently the Coordinator for the UN Action against Sexual Violence in Conflict, a network of 13 UN entities chaired by the Special Representative of the Secretary-General on Sexual Violence in Conflict. She was formerly the Senior Gender Advisor for the UN Department of Peacekeeping Operations in New York; and worked as the Senior Gender Adviser for the UN Stabilization Mission in Haiti (MINUSTAH) between 2004 and 2008. Dr Puechguirbal is a Senior Fellow and Visiting Professor at the UN-affiliated University for Peace (UPEACE) in Costa Rica where she teaches yearly on international peace studies.

Christina Rowley is a Research Associate at the University of Bristol, UK. Her research is located at the intersection between IR, security, gender, culture and American studies. She has published on US identity and US foreign policy, insecurity and *Buffy the Vampire Slayer*, teaching gender, and the gendered politics of science fiction, among other topics. She is co-founder and co-editor of the Popular Culture and World Politics book series (Routledge) (for more information, see www.pcwp.net).

Laura J. Shepherd is Associate Professor of International Relations at the University of New South Wales, Australia. She works at the intersection of gendered global politics, critical approaches to security and International Relations theory. Laura is the author/editor of five books, including *Gender, Violence and Security: Discourse as Practice* (Zed 2008) and *Gender, Violence and Popular Culture: Telling Stories* (Routledge 2013). Laura has published many scholarly articles in journals such as *International Studies Quarterly, International Feminist Journal of Politics, Review of International Studies* and *Journal of Gender Studies*.

Laura Sjoberg is Associate Professor of Political Science at the University of Florida, with an affiliation with the Center for Women's Studies and Gender Research. Her research focuses on gender and international security, with an empirical interest in the representation of women's violence in global politics. She is author or editor of eight books, including, most recently, *Gendering Global Conflict: Towards a Feminist Theory of War* (Columbia University Press 2013). Dr Sjoberg currently serves as the homebase editor of the *International Feminist Journal of Politics*.

Jill Steans is Senior Lecturer in International Relations Theory at the University of Birmingham, UK. She is the author of a number of books and articles on gender in International Relations and international political economy, including *Gender and International Relations* (Polity Press 2013).

Barbara Sullivan is Senior Lecturer in the School of Political Science and International Studies, University of Queensland, Australia. She teaches and researches in the area of gender politics, feminist political theory, prostitution and trafficking. She has published in a range of political science and criminology journals as well as in two recent comparative politics texts: *Gendering the State in the Age of Globalization: Women's Movements and State Feminism in Post Industrial Democracies*, edited by Melissa Haussman and Birgit Sauer (Rowman & Littlefield 2007) and *The Politics of Prostitution: Women's Movements, Democratic States and the Globalisation of Sex Commerce*, edited by Joyce Outshoorn (Cambridge University Press 2004).

Sophie Toupin is currently working for Media@McGill, a hub for research, scholarship and public outreach on media, technology and culture at McGill University in Montreal, Canada. In 2012–2013 she was a research associate at the Five College Women's Studies Research Centre in Amherst, Massachusetts, in the US. Her research interests focus on the relationship between feminist online and offline practices within social movements and feminist and queer hacker culture.

Jacqui True is Professor of Politics and International Relations at Monash University, Australia. She has published extensively on gender mainstreaming and global governance, critical international political economy, and feminist methodologies. Her book *The Political Economy of Violence against Women* (Oxford University Press 2012) won the American Political Science Association's 2012 biennial prize for the best book in human rights and the British International Studies Association 2013 IPEG book prize.

Heather M. Turcotte holds a joint appointment with the Political Science Department and the Women's Gendered Sexuality Studies programme at the University of Connecticut. Dr Turcotte's current research examines how the US is made into a geographical site of justice through the mystification of its own role in the production of global violence. By reading against the grain of naturalized knowledge, her work offers a decolonial reading of US imperialism and considers a plurality of transnational justice frameworks. Her research has been published in *Alternatives: Global, Local, Political* and *International Studies Review* and she is currently working on a book manuscript entitled, *Petro-Sexual Politics: U.S. Legal Expansions, Geographies of Violence and the Critique of Justice*. Dr Turcotte is also the chair of the New England Women's Studies Association and co-chair of the Anti-White Supremacy Taskforce within the National Women's Studies Association.

Marysia Zalewski is Professor of Gender/International Relations in the School of Social Sciences at the University of Aberdeen, UK. She specialises in critical approaches to feminist and gender theory, masculinity studies and contemporary approaches particularly aesthetics. She has published widely in the areas of critical approaches to methodology and theory, feminist theory, masculinities, gender mainstreaming and human rights. Her latest book is *Feminist International Relations: Exquisite Corpse* (Routledge 2013).

ACKNOWLEDGEMENTS

The production of this second edition of *Gender Matters* was prompted by Craig Fowlie and Nicola Parkin at Routledge, and has benefited from editorial assistance from Peter Harris. I am grateful to the team for their support of, and their belief in, this project. You are a dream to work with. We might leave it a couple of years before we start thinking about a third edition, however ...

I appreciate the support I have received from colleagues and the Faculty of Arts and Social Sciences at UNSW Australia, and the research assistance of Caitlin Hamilton, who compiled the first cut of this manuscript for me to work on and who puts up with my font obsession. Cait, you are a star. A thousand thanks.

I am once again grateful to and made humble by the contributors to this volume; as with the first edition, I have learned so much through engaging with each chapter. I appreciate the commitment and enthusiasm that everyone has shown for producing new work or revising existing work and the patience that everyone has shown as I have let the occasional deadline slip by unacknowledged. Thanks, everyone.

I am also grateful more generally to the community of brilliant and supportive scholars of which I am a part, including but not limited to the British International Studies Association Gendering International Working Group and the Feminist Theory and Gender Studies section of the International Studies Association. The latter maintains a Facebook group (come join us!) and, when I posted that I was considering a request from Routledge to put together a second edition, I received wonderful feedback on the first edition, generous offers to write for the second edition, and excellent suggestions for content. It was in large part this engagement that inspired me to proceed – so thank you. It continually inspires me to belong to such a vibrant – and growing – community and I know that the interactions I have with my colleagues make me a better scholar and a better educator. Thank you.

Laura J. Shepherd
UNSW Australia
December 2013

FOREWORD

Cynthia Enloe

Just last week I was in Tokyo, a good place from which to look out on international politics – especially if you have Japanese feminists as your guides.

It was a week chock-full of conversations (over coffee, green tea and *sake*) and adventures (via Tokyo's amazing subway system). What was striking was how present World War II remained in the minds of these smart, alert Japanese feminist analysts of today's international politics. What these Japanese activist thinkers – Ruri, Hisako, Fumika, Mina, Risa, Naoko, Kunika, Amane, Kaori and others – explained to me was this: Japanese government and non-governmental organizations cannot possibly take meaningful international steps in today's complicated world – in peacekeeping, for instance, or in the delivery of humanitarian aid – if they, together with ordinary Japanese citizens, do not first deal honestly and fully with their country's role in the last global war.

The past is the present if denial of embarrassing parts of that past is serving as the foundation of today's actions.

They were very specific about this. They were continuing to do research on where women were in all phases of Japanese colonialism during the 1910–1945 era and during the conflict we simplistically call World War II. That meant, they said, uncovering myriad roles that Japanese women, including 'ordinary housewives', played in supporting patriotic mobilizations, creating images of women in colonized Manchuria, Korea and Taiwan, legitimizing the Emperor and pretending that the imperial military's brothel system was just a myth. As they spoke, I thought of all the new investigations that feminist researchers are doing in other countries also revealing where women were – and what they were thinking and what they were doing – in those crucial colonizing, militarized years of the 1930s and 1940s. What were diverse British women, Russian, Italian, German, Turkish, American, South African and Australian women doing to promote or to resist those ideas and practices that facilitate violence and cement unequal relations between societies? And why is it that it is only now, six decades after the alleged end of World War II, that we are beginning to acknowledge those gendered realities?

What my generous Japanese feminist hosts were exposing was how dependent colonizers and militarizers are on women, thus also on their abilities to manipulate notions of both masculinity and femininity. What they were also showing me was how much effort goes into post-war denial and myth making.

By their careful digging – and their often courageous writing and speaking – these contemporary Japanese feminist investigators were demonstrating how much of the entire dynamics of international politics we all will miss if we do not take seriously the full range of international experiences of diverse women. By 'taking seriously' my hosts did not mean universally admiring. They were open to finding whatever their research exposed: yes, women who took risks to make their societies and their society's international relations more fair and less violent, but also women who (for multiple reasons) were complicit in narrowing the definition of 'patriot', or who took pride in their government's overseas exertions of power or who profited in some way from the spread of racist or xenophobic stereotypes.

My Japanese feminist friends – Ruri, Hisako, Fumika, Mina, Rui, Kuniko, Amane, Kaori, Naoko, and Risa – would, I think, find the book you are now to plunge into exciting. They would see that the contributing authors whom editor Laura Shepherd has brought together here are on an investigatory journey similar to their own. The writers here are also urging us to be courageous, to ask questions that may make us quite uncomfortable, to absorb evidence that more conventional commentators prefer to dismiss and to be ready to be surprised.

17 December 2013

GLOSSARY

Aboriginal Beings or things that are native to a specific region or territory.

Activism Action in protest against or support for a political cause.

Advocacy Offering information and opinion in favour of a political cause. See also 'lobbying'.

Aesthetics The study of what is pleasing, often visually and aurally, through the senses and to the imagination (the nature of beauty, taste).

Agency The capacity to act.

Anarchy The absence of political authority. In International Relations, the international system is assumed to be anarchic, because there is no legitimate authority higher than the sovereign state.

Anti-foundationalism The belief that there is no basic or foundational belief (e.g. in God, rationality, senses) from which to create a system of values or meanings.

Autonomy The capacity to act independent of external constraints.

Balance of power The mechanism by which the international system is assumed to seek equilibrium, with (groups of) states forming and dissolving alliances in order to 'balance' the waxing and waning powers of other (groups of) states.

Bonded labour Also known as 'debt bondage'.

Capitalism An economic system in which one section of society owns the means of production and exploits the labour of the remainder to generate profit.

Cartography The study of maps.

Citizenship The claim to rights and acceptance of responsibilities as a citizen of a particular nation-state.

Civil society Any actors or groups of actors that are assumed to be separate from the state.

Civilian An individual who is not involved in military or paramilitary activity. Also used informally to describe non-members of a particular organisation or institution.

Collective security A formal agreement between states that any attack on one member of the group will be perceived, and responded to, as an attack against all.

Colonialism The practice of extending authority over, controlling or coercing external territories.

Communism An economic system in which property and the means of production are owned collectively and society is organised for the common advantage of all.

Communitarianism Belief system that emphasises the importance of the community in political life, in contrast to 'cosmopolitanism'.

Comparative advantage The idea that every actor (region, state, bloc) can produce some type of goods or service at a lower cost than any other actor.

Complex interdependence The neoliberal idea that states working through various institutions and organisations will become embedded in a variety of relationships that will in turn increase the extent to which the states are connected.

Constructivism The theoretical position that sees reality as intersubjectively constituted rather than existing objectively.

Cosmopolitanism Belief system that envisions humanity as a single community, with shared interests, in contrast to communitarianism.

Cultural relativism The idea that values and beliefs are dependent on the social context rather than universally determined.

Cyberspace The totality of computer-mediated virtual existence.

Cyborg A humanoid hybrid of organic (biological) and inorganic (technological) materials.

Decolonisation The process by which former colonies achieve self-determination (self-governance).

Deconstruction Proceeding from the assumption that reality is socially constructed, a range of techniques that allow an analyst to unpack or 'deconstruct' the way meaning – and therefore reality – is constructed.

Demography The study of population and their characteristics.

Deregulation Reducing or removing regulations governing practice or behaviour, usually used to describe policies that lessen governmental control of industries and corporations.

Digital divide The increasing gap between those that have access to information and computer technologies and those that do not.

Dimorphism The guiding assumption that beings or things can be divided into two forms or shapes.

Discipline A subject-specific area of study in academia, e.g. International Relations. Can also be used as a verb in a Foucauldian analysis, to describe the ways in which boundaries between beings and things are created and maintained.

Discourse A system of linguistic and non-linguistic signifiers that produce meaning.

Discursive Pertaining to discourse.

Emancipation Freedom from tyranny or oppression, the production of autonomy.

Empire A political unit governed by a single political authority spread over several territories.

Empiricism The belief that reality can be objectively identified through experiential data.

Empowerment Increased capacity for action.

Environmental sustainability The ability of a process or practice to continue without having a negative long-term effect on the environment.

Epistemic Relating to epistemology. An 'epistemic community' is a group of people who accept or espouse one particular epistemology; it is also more generally used to describe a group of people who share a particular theory or set of ideas.

Epistemology Theory of knowledge, beliefs about how we know what we know.

Essentialism The belief that beings or things have innate characteristics that are largely unchanging.

Ethnic cleansing The mass killing of a particular ethnic group, and/or the forced movement of people out of a territory or homeland.

Ethnography The study of people and society.

Export processing zone (EPZ) An area of a state where trade regulations (and sometimes certain other standards and safeguards) are reduced or removed to encourage overseas investment.

Export-oriented industrialisation (EOI) An economic development policy that seeks to exploit a state's comparative advantage by increasing exports in that area and thus speed up industrialisation.

Femininity Characteristics and modes of behaviour associated with being female.

Feminisation Either the attribution of feminine characteristics to that which is not usually considered feminine in an effort to delegitimise it (e.g. the feminisation of an enemy), or the disproportionate effect on women of a particular political process (e.g. the feminisation of poverty).

Flexibilisation The process of making trade and industry less regulated and more dynamic.

Foundationalism The belief that there are basic or foundational beliefs (e.g. in God, rationality, senses) from which to create a system of values or meanings.

Fundamentalism Belief in and adherence to a strict set of principles, often derived from a single authoritative text that is religious in nature.

Gender gap The idea that men and women vote differently on different issues.

Gender mainstreaming Ensuring that all institutional policies and practices are formulated with attention paid to the impact they will have on individuals as a result of their gender.

Geopolitical A combination of geographical and political factors.

Global governance The institutions and organisations that manage or regulate international behaviour (despite there being no legitimate political authority higher than the sovereign state according to many theories of IR).

Global politics The totality of political interactions, relationships and transactions (broadly conceived) occurring in the world.

Globalisation A short-hand way of explaining the increasing interconnectedness of states and other actors in areas of trade, culture and governance.

Governance The process of exercising political authority.

Great Power A state that has the capacity to exert influence in global politics.

Hegemon A state that exerts influence in global politics through coercion, persuasion or compulsion.

Hermeneutics A word that can relate to either a methodology for interpreting meaning in texts, or more generally, the philosophy of interpretation.

Heterogenous Comprised of many different elements.

Heteronormative Practices that privilege heterosexual behaviours or beings.

Homogenous Comprised of many identical elements.

Human rights The rights that human beings are assumed to hold by virtue of their humanity.

Human security The idea that security should be sought on behalf of human beings rather than on behalf of states.

Humanitarian intervention Military, economic or political interference in the domestic affairs of a sovereign state aimed at alleviating human insecurities or suffering. Many scholars use a narrower definition confining HI to the use of military force for human protection purposes.

Hypermasculinity The exaggeration of characteristics or modes of behaviours that are associated with being male.

Iconography The study of representations (beings or things) that carry symbolic meaning, or the representations themselves.

Ideology A belief system or set of ideas through which proponents make sense of the world. According to Marxist theory, a belief system aimed at perpetuating the status quo to benefit the few at the expense of the many.

Imperialism Attitudes or policies in international relations that seek to extend one state's economic or political control or influence over other states.

Intelligibility The ability to be known and understood.

Interdisciplinary An approach that bridges disciplinary divides or draws on different subject-specific knowledges.

Internally displaced person(s)/IDP(s) Individual or community that has been forcibly or voluntarily relocated (usually as a result of conflict) but remains within the boundaries of their home state.

International organisation An institution made up of state members, e.g. United Nations, World Bank, World Trade Organisation.

International Relations The academic discipline devoted to studying global politics. Written in lower case ('international relations'), the policies and practices of global political actors.

International system The location of international relations, assumed to be comprised of but greater than the sum total of state actions.

International/domestic divide The assumption in International Relations that politics at the international and domestic level are analytically and practically separate.

Interpretivism Theory that is based on an analyst's interpretation of a given phenomenon, event or dataset, in contrast to 'empiricism'.

Intersectionality The notion that different markers of identity (e.g. race, class, gender, sexuality) interconnect to produce different forms of exclusion and inequality.

Intersubjectivity Collective or social meaning or opinion; where meaning and opinion is formed in negotiation or coincidence between autonomous subjects.

Intertextuality The idea that all texts necessarily refer to and draw meaning from other texts.

Levels of analysis Also known as 'images of analysis'. The neorealists division of international relations into three discrete areas of study: the individual (state leaders), the state and the international system.

Liberalism A political theory that emphasises human capacity for positive behaviour and the autonomy of the individual human subject. Also, an economic theory that prioritises trade freed from state preferences (free trade) and market activity freed from government regulation.

Lobbying Action in support of or protest against a particular political idea or policy.

Maquiladora A manufacturing operation or factory at the US–Mexican border built to take advantage of the free trade agreements between the two states.

Marginalise To metaphorically push to one side or ignore.

Marketisation The application of market rules and economistic logics to a previously non-market enterprise such as a national industry.

Masculinisation Either the attribution of masculine characteristics to that which is not usually considered masculine in an effort to legitimise it (e.g. the masculinisation of a leader), or the disproportionate representation of men in a particular political process (e.g. the masculinisation of governance).

Masculinity Characteristics and modes of behaviour associated with being male.

Materiality Substance or physical form.

Media Modes or channels of communication, e.g. television, radio, newspapers, advertising, etc.

Mediate Either to negotiate between two or more parties to reach a peaceful resolution to a conflict or dispute, or to act as a link or conduit between two or more different symbols or concepts.

Metaphor A figure of speech in which a term or phrase is linked to something to which it is not usually or otherwise linked in order to suggest a resemblance, e.g. 'Her office was a pigsty' (her office is not literally a pigsty, but the metaphor suggests that it shares the characteristics of a pigsty, i.e. her office is dirty, smelly and/or untidy). NB If the figure of speech makes a comparison using 'like' or 'as', it is a simile, not a metaphor, e.g. 'Her office was like a pigsty'.

Methodology The study of methods, usually research methods, and/or a description of the actual methods use to conduct research.

Militarisation The process by which beings or things become associated with the military or take on military characteristics.

Militarism The belief that the most appropriate solution to a problem or response to an event is the military one.

Militia An armed force not under the control of the official state military.

Modernity Era associated with the privileging of rationality, progress and scientific method, and the belief in the legitimate authority of those.

Multinational corporation (MNC) Industry or business that conducts activities and has assets in more than one state.

Multiplicity The recognition of many beings or things.

Narrative The communication (recounting, telling) of a sequence of events, or things that have happened so as to establish a meaningful connection between them (story, sequence).

Nation A grouping of people who are assumed to share language, custom, territory and history.

Nationalism A belief system that prioritises the interests of the nation.

Neoliberalism A political and economic theory that adds to classical Liberalism a central concern for economic growth.

Neologism New word.

Neorealism A theory of International Relations that attempts to rework classical Realism and produce a rigorous and testable account of why states behave as they do in the international system. Also known as structural Realism, not to be confused with 'structuralism'.

Non-governmental organisation An institution or group that is not part of any government and is therefore assumed to have political autonomy.

Non-state actors Any actors in International Relations other than sovereign states.

Normative Pertaining to what should be (rather than what is).

Objectivity Where meaning and existence are assumed to exist independently from individual bias or belief.

Ontology The study of the nature of being and what exists to be known.

Paradigm Set of guiding beliefs and assumptions about a given matter.

Patriarchy Literally means 'rule of the father', now generally extended to mean the power and authority of masculinity.

Performativity The theoretical idea that discourse constitutes the objects and subjects of which it speaks.

Positivism A set of beliefs about knowledge that values empiricism (the belief that reality can be objectively identified through experiential data), progressivism (the belief that social and political science should further progress the aims and knowledge of humanity), secularism (the belief that science and politics should be separate from religious beliefs) and unity of scientific method (where both social and natural sciences should use the same methodology).

Postcolonialism A theoretical approach that is rooted in the difficult experiences of constructing cultural and individual identity during and after colonial rule.

Postpositivism A theory of knowledge that critiques the foundational assumptions of positivism, without disregarding the need for coherent and valid theories of meaning and reality.

Poststructuralism A theory that builds on a critique of structuralist linguistics, materialism and positivist approaches; in opposition to singularity and fixity of meaning, poststructuralism emphasises multiplicity and fluidity.

Praxis Action, practice or mode of behaviour (plural 'praxes').

Privatisation Abdicating state authority over enterprises or industries that were previously managed by the state.

Public/private divide The assumption that social life can be separated into two discrete realms, characterised by formal political phenomena and informal social phenomena.

Radical Concerned with the root cause of a phenomenon, also used to mean extreme or drastic.

Rationalism The belief that reason is the foundation of knowledge (rather than experience or intuition).

Rationality That which is reasonable, in contrast to that which is emotional or uncontrolled.

Realism In International Relations, a theory that explains state behaviour by assuming that the international system is anarchic and that states will pursue self-interested policies aimed to ensure their own survival.

Reflectivism The belief that rationalism is a flawed and partial way to understand meaning and reality and that instead attention should be paid to the interpretative, experiential and intuitive.

Reification The process of misunderstanding an abstraction as a physical being or thing, e.g. writing about the state as an actor is a reification.

Relations of constitution (constitutive relations) The signifiers and chains of connotation that produce meaning and make a being or thing what it is.

Representation Three meanings: 1. The act of standing in for an individual or collective to advance their interests (e.g. the UK is represented at the United Nations); 2. The act of symbolising or signifying a being or thing (e.g. the Union Jack is a representation of the UK); 3. The symbol or signifier itself (e.g. the Union Jack).

Semiotics The study of signs and symbols.

Signifier Something that carries or conveys meaning, a symbol.

Sovereignty Independence from external interference, political autonomy.

Spatiality Of or relating to space.

Stakeholder An individual or collective who has an interest in or will be affected by a particular policy or practice.

Standpoint Perspective. Also used to describe a branch of feminism that emphasises the legitimacy and authority of experience and argues that women have unique access to a particular kind of knowledge and experience by virtue of their femininity.

State A notionally autonomous political entity that has a population and a territory.

State-centric An approach to International Relations that assumes the analytical primacy of the state.

Structural adjustment policies (SAPs) A much-critiqued set of standards and guidelines implemented by the World Bank from the 1970s to the 1990s aimed at alleviating poverty in lesser-developed countries.

Structural violence Harm or suffering caused by systemic problems and inequalities in society.

Structuralism A theory of International Relations that draws on Marxist and neo-Marxist works and argues that the (capitalist) structure of the international system is unequal and unjust.

Subjectivity Where meaning and existence are assumed to be dependent on individual bias or belief.

Supranational Above the state.

Sustainable development Modernisation or industrialisation that occurs with minimal long-term damage done to the natural environment.

Technocratic A belief in the primacy of technical or technological solutions.

Text Any collection of signifiers and representations, most frequently used to describe a written document but also includes films, adverts, flags, buildings, cartoons, songs, etc.

The personal is political Feminist slogan aimed at drawing attention to the interrelationship of private and public spheres.

Transnational corporation (TNC) See 'multinational corporation'.

Universalism The belief that some codes or rules should apply to all people, irrespective of their cultural context.

PART 1 THEORY/PRACTICE

CHAPTER 1

Feminist International Relations: Making sense …

Marysia Zalewski

▌ LEARNING OUTCOMES

Upon completion, readers should be able to:

- Begin to see how gender works at different levels of international politics.
- Start to understand why it matters theoretically and politically to ask 'where are the women' and 'what work is masculinity doing'?
- Begin to understand why it is necessary to use feminist theory to adequately understand the complexities of international politics.

▌ INTRODUCTION: MAKING SENSE?

> For an explanation to be useful, a great deal of human dignity has to be left on the cutting room floor.
>
> (Enloe 1996: 188)

There was much excitement when tennis player Andy Murray won the Wimbledon men's singles championship in July 2013. 'We've been waiting 77 years for this' – or so it was announced with much regularity by media commentators. Although doubt on this was raised by many, exemplified by Chloe Angyal's tweet, 'Murray is indeed the first Brit to win Wimbledon in 77 years unless you think women are people' – which was retweeted 9,425 times (the 'retweet' count the day after Murray won). In the same month I read about the turmoil in Cairo. Randa, a young woman from Cairo had been dressing as a teenage boy as she thought this may help prevent her being an automatic target for violence; 'if you are female you are viewed as someone who is worthy of punishment' (*The Guardian* 2013). I also read about another young woman – Malala Yousafzai and the speech she gave at the United Nations in New York.

I do not know how one can think seriously or adequately about any of these instances without the conceptual and theoretical help of feminist theory (and, of course, there are countless other similar instances, in their different hues, witnessed and experienced daily). To be sure it is possible (and usual) to think about these events not so seriously especially perhaps the first one given there is no 'obvious' violence here, gendered or otherwise. The second one not so obviously given the abhorrent violence many women are facing in the streets of Cairo today (time of writing July 2013). Even so, all manner of justifications are offered to rationalise these incidences of violence, from the individual and/or culturally induced psychologies of the male perpetrators in Egypt (usually laced with a racist edge), to the more amorphous 'shrug of the shoulders' type response implying that human nature (perhaps particularly male?) is what it is – and these things will happen (like rape in war).

In this chapter, I aim to illustrate, if briefly, why it matters to think seriously about events like these whether locally, nationally or globally. My claim is that using the insights and tools of feminist theory are absolutely necessary to make adequate sense. I borrow the idea of making sense from Cynthia Enloe's *Bananas, Beaches and Bases: Making Feminist Sense of International Politics*, first published in 1989. That Enloe chose this title is extremely important, calling her book 'Applying Feminism to International Politics' (or something similar) would have implied a vastly different and much less interesting or radical book. Rather than recycling knowledge, the idea of making sense is fundamentally concerned with how we produce, construct and contain knowledge about our international political world(s). What issues do we count as important to take into account when investigating international politics? What kind of knowledges do we regard as legitimate and authoritative? What concepts or categories – theoretical, methodological, philosophical, epistemological – do we regard as appropriate to use?[1] What international (or any) stories become credible? Whose lives and what kind of lives count as important? Although feminism is often assumed to be simplistically 'only' about women's lives and experiences, it is more appropriate to think of feminism as primarily concerned with the kinds of question just raised, questions which are fundamentally about 'how we organize life, how we accord it value, how we compel the world' (Butler 2004a: 205).[2] Feminist scholars implicitly and explicitly work with these kinds of question often starting and sometimes staying with women's lives, but usually using the multifaceted and intersectional prism of gender to tell the ensuing narratives. This minimally implies that feminist scholars will present very different accounts of international politics than those conventionally provided.

A number of approaches have been used to tell these varying feminist accounts or 'stories'[3] about international politics, each with its own method of dealing with the constraints of creating the landscape of international politics through feminism. Some scholars work with the ontological, political and disciplinary parameters of the discipline of International Relations (IR) through which to create feminist IR. J. Ann Tickner's early work might be included in this genre as her work, for example on security, is constituted in response to the failure of discipline of IR to properly acknowledge the importance of gender (1992). More recently Tickner engages the tension between remaining committed to insisting that feminist scholarship is both credible and necessary to IR, while simultaneously recognising that the parameters of IR are antithetical to the political and ethical demands of feminism (2001, 2006, Tickner and Sjoberg 2011). Christine Sylvester's earlier work similarly worked with IR's frame in order to demonstrate the latter's abject failure in regard to gender (1994). Her more recent work, albeit still responsive to IR's frame, is more dismissive of IR's authority or necessity (2007a, 2008, 2012).

A significant book in the development of feminist IR is V. Spike Peterson and Anne Sisson Runyan's *Global Gender Issues* (2013 [1993]). This offers not only an accessible and exceedingly informative feminist account of how gender matters in international politics; it also offers an innovative conceptual tool to students and scholars still unconvinced. Using the metaphor of a 'lens', Peterson and Runyan demonstrate that seeing the world of international politics through an alternative (gendered) focus, facilitates the ability to 'see' depictions (realities) of international politics alternative to those conventionally offered. They include a picture to illustrate how the 'gender–lens' metaphor works: it shows two giant-like (in size) white men (with miserable expressions!) each wearing a Western-style man's suit, a shirt and tie and both are wearing spectacles. In front of one of the men is a 'normal' sized white woman (i.e. not giant sized) standing on a ladder, wearing an apron, a scarf on her head and carrying a bucket (one is led to assume she is a 'cleaning lady'). She is shown on top of the ladder reaching up to clean the spectacles the two men are wearing and working on the second lens of the first man's glasses having, we assume, wiped the first lens clean. The second man's spectacles are still completely darkened. The attached caption explains this is a 'graphic depiction of how lenses affect fields of visions and how women at the bottom of the world politics hierarchy are struggling to make elite men see the world more clearly' (Peterson and Runyan 2013 [1993]: 20).

Global Gender Issues and the idea of gender as a lens is such an interesting example of feminist work in IR; epistemologically, methodologically and politically. Politically, the link with what we can still call radical feminism[4] is clear, we can see this in the insistence that it is crucially important to centralise women's lives, particularly given women's ongoing place on many of the 'bottom rungs' of significance or international care (Enloe 1996). Without this concentrated focus on women, we will not see these 'other' worlds of international politics as they are methodologically obscured when we fail to see through gender(ed) lenses. Moreover, epistemologically the lens approach reveals one of the persistent paradoxes that infuses feminism (within IR and further afield), which can be illustrated through these two questions. Are feminist scholars producing better truths, indeed more *complete* truths that would imply the empirical, theoretical and ethical *necessity* of feminist scholarship in a field of study (IR) given the latter insists it is producing rigorous and useful knowledge about the world of international politics? Or are feminist scholars simply producing an *alternative* set of stories that may be deemed ultimately *unnecessary* in the generic pursuit of useful knowledge about international politics?[5]

These are just a few examples of the wide range of work that might be regarded as 'feminist IR', a field in which there is a vast range of contemporary research; readers are directed to the footnotes and references (and the other chapters in this book) for further reading.[6] What I want to do in the rest of this chapter is focus on two of the main questions that feminist scholars continue to prioritise: where are the women? And, what work is masculinity doing? I am intentionally not starting with a rigid definition of feminism even though I think it is the case that most students who want to know about feminism and International Relations think an early and 'clear' definition will help. But there is a deep violence in reducing something to a single feature (Žižek 2008: 52), indicating that definitions may not be as useful, or as innocent as they promise, especially if they are meant to *importantly* capture the meaning of something. It is clearly impossible to include all the complexities and complications of something in a single sentence (or two) which begs an important question – what gets left *out* to make the definition workable (or make sense)? Conversely, the idea of 'capturing meaning' suggests that only specific things get counted *in*; the question begged here is, what gets counted in or assumed, and on what basis and to what effect? However, defining something is perhaps perceived to be particularly important and necessary when the thing being defined is understood to be controversial or particularly challenging.[7] This, I think, is the case with feminism. In the context of the study of international politics and indeed more generally (academically and popularly), feminism remains the focus of a wide array of seemingly contradictory questions and criticisms. Is feminism still relevant; or it is old hat? Is it more necessary than ever in our deeply inequitable societies? Is it overly theoretical or a-theoretical? Is it too political? Is it too reactionary? Is it too Western? Isn't it just about women or women's issues? What about men? What about other categories?[8] These questions indicate some of the political and theoretical complexities inflecting contemporary feminism that suggests starting with a narrow definition will not be very helpful in constructively understanding how feminist work makes sense of international politics. My preference is to defer commencing with a tight definition, and thus risk (violently) closing off the potential of feminism right at the beginning. It is more helpful to work with the central questions posed by feminist scholars in international politics and to explore what kind of knowledges or stories this work produces, and to consider where this work might take us; intellectually, empirically, politically. I will start with the radical[9] question – where are the women?

WHERE ARE THE WOMEN?

> Paying serious attention to women can expose how *much* power it takes to maintain the international political system in its present form.
>
> (Enloe 1989: 3; emphasis in original)

When, why and how do we notice women in international politics? The feminist purpose, broadly speaking, of 'noticing women' is to focus on what women are doing (or not) to see how this matters politically. To return to the example I opened with, it seems to have been very easy for many to 'forget' that Virginia Wade had won the Wimbledon singles championship in 1977. It requires some deployment (however implicit) of feminist-inspired concepts and principles to 'remember' this victory, or to agree that women matter, or to reject traditional assumptions that 'women's version' of what 'men do' is less interesting or valuable. The 'women's version' may be 'different' but this begs the (feminist inspired) question, what is the norm or standard to which women's difference is being measured and so often found wanting? But let me move to discuss, albeit briefly, the other two examples I opened with.

Placing women in international politics

There have always been some women in important international political roles, Hillary Clinton, Margaret Thatcher and Benazir Bhutto, for example. But focusing on women in these places tends to do little to change how we think about what international politics is, or to what gets counted as important to analyse internationally, or how we think international politics actually works. It is often more fruitful to look more closely at 'ordinary' women as this helps to illustrate the ubiquitous presence of women in international politics. When we take this task seriously, the answer to the questions about what international politics is and what work gender is doing begins to change, though perhaps not always with immediate or conventionally visible effects. However, it is not that ordinary women are *not* noticed in international politics, but oftentimes this is as victims in need of rescue (usually by the West); here the women of Afghanistan are a recurrent example, as also, of late, are the women in Egypt, which is the example to which I will now turn.

It is perhaps unsurprising that the turmoil in the 'Greater Middle East' region has attracted a lot of international attention as it is always perceived to be something of a pressure cooker region for global politics and which 'the West' has a great interest in. The recent violence against women in the streets of Cairo and especially Tahrir Square has clearly not gone unnoticed or unreported, even if this most often appears in the 'women's pages' of newspapers, or on social networking sites. The reasons for such violence, which includes a rabid increase in 'everyday' sexual harassment and increasing incidences of sexual violence and rape, are manifold. But Randa's comment about women being a target for punishment is particularly shocking, perhaps because it makes some sense, if a contradictorily irrational one. Why would the ordinary women of Cairo be seen as deserving of punishment by the (we assume) ordinary men of Cairo *just* for being female?

Deploying feminist insights, these violent gendered acts reveal less about women as victims and more about the precarious and contradictory nature of security, though perhaps especially for women. Women 'out of place' regularly emerge as 'asking for it', when they are patently not. Yet the bold assertion by one Egyptian man that 'Women contribute 100% to their rape because they put themselves in that position', suggests otherwise (Kirollos 2013). The point is not the veracity of the claim that women are rightfully in one place rather than another (in Tahrir

Square as opposed to staying at home), rather that this solidly held perception of 'women's place' at times of heightened political tension is readily exploited as a conduit through which to wreak vengeance for subjective feelings of wounded masculinity experienced by the ordinary men of Cairo. At least this is one way to make better sense of the violence against women in Cairo and the stated reasons: 'Violence against women, always feels legitimate to the man who enacts it. That is why it is so readily excused, even by its victims; that is why it is so easily repeated' (Kramer 2000: 8). Making feminist sense of this begins to start unravelling the complex interconnections between gender and the international, not least in helping to unmoor conventional rationales for violence committed by 'other' men from their usual orientalist and colonialist frames; although significantly it is often these kinds of unstated reasons that continue to justify international political and militarised interventions.

What feminist sense can we make of Malala Yousafzai in the context of international politics? Malala Yousafzai is the Pakistani girl who, aged 15, was shot by the Taliban on her way to school for her outspoken campaign for education for girls. She survived the bullet wound to her head, was treated in a hospital in Birmingham, England, and has since become something of a global media star feted for her inspiring bravery in the face of such danger. On her sixteenth birthday (declared as 'Malala Day') she addressed the United Nations in New York passionately and persuasively arguing the case for female education worldwide. 'One child, one teacher, one pen and one book can change the world. Education is the only solution' (BBC News 2013b). Across the Atlantic, Sarah Brown[10] hosted a simultaneous event at the Southbank Centre in London sponsored by a children's charity, *Plan UK*. British schoolchildren watched Malala's speech on a big screen prompting tears and rapturous applause: 'She is just my idol, I look up to her so much', one 13-year-old girl said (quoted in Topping 2013).

The intelligence and bravery of Malala are indeed striking and admirable. Her perceptive comment that the Taliban are 'afraid of women' gets right to the heart of the feminist-inspired question about women's place being of paramount international political significance. What is it about keeping women in place that matters so much politically, locally and globally? So much that a 15-year-old girl on her way to school can be shot? So much that women in a public square are so readily understood to be 'asking for it'? But it is also Malala's new 'place' on the international political scene that bears feminist enquiry. 'One extraordinary' woman intrepidly emerging from a mass of 'ordinary' women (and think of the way women from the 'Greater Middle East region' are regularly depicted by the media) but *also* so eagerly requisitioned by powerful Western political institutions is significant.

Drawing on Judith Butler's work in *Precarious Life* (2004b), in the context of Afghan women, Synne Dyvik claims that the individualist representation of the 'heroic Afghan woman' serves to reify the collective representation of Afghan women as hapless victims in need of saving (2010). Butler's insights about stories which fit comfortably within a Western neoliberal frame are important here. Think of how Malala's new place at the heart of Western liberalism comfortably affirms Westernised senses of agency 'in terms of a subject' and how this 'accords with our ideas of personal responsibility' (Butler 2004b: 5). This might give us further feminist pause for thought about how this feeds ongoing justifications for interventions into the 'Greater Middle East' region (and elsewhere) all couched in the implicit superiority of Western rationality and individualism. To start to get to these ways of thinking, it is important to keep asking that question of seemingly little importance to IR, 'where are the women?' to help continue the unravelling of heavily policed conventional boundaries and foundations and to offer different ways to think about what is important and what is normal and how much work assumptions about the latter are doing.

As such the focus on women does so much more than simply supply better information 'about women' (in/and international politics), though our understanding of the ways wars are waged or alliances are built (or destroyed), or how international corporations trade internationally or how nations and citizens are secured (or insecured), are made immensely more complex and intricate when we ask, 'where are the women?'. Asking this question impels us to tell the story(ies) of international politics in very different ways. It impels us (if we *stay* with it, empirically and conceptually) to reconsider how conventional methodologies and epistemologies, rather than facilitating the collection of 'good knowledge', make invisible much of what 'goes on' – or to put it another way – shows us how 'discursive power functions by concealing the terms of its fabrication' (Brown 2001: 122). Further, the placing of women and questions about women centre stage is something feminist work encourages as it begins to open up ways to rethink why activities traditionally associated with women or femininity seem irrelevant or insignificant in the context of international politics. There are two results here we might note: first, we get new, more complex images of what happens in international politics and thus what international politics is (about). Second, we get a better sense of how important women are in international politics – in so many ways – which really begs the question, how is it so easy to leave them out?

But feminists tend not to linger very long at the conventional centre of international politics. It is important to turn our attention away from the centre and look at some of the work women do that is not typically regarded as political or politically interesting. Cynthia Enloe's scholarship serves as an exemplar in this context, theoretically and empirically illustrating how the 'personal is international' (1989). International politics would not function without the work of diplomatic and loyal wives (indicating there is a politics to love and heterosexual expectations); or nimble fingered and thus poorly paid workers (suggestive of 'natural' female aptitudes as opposed to learned skills); or sex workers serving the military (further reinforcing particular ideas about militarised (heterosexual) masculinity); or as markers and symbols of the nation, bearers of the nation's children and ideologies, as tourists, flight attendants, chamber maids, colonised women, film stars and fashion models. The list of the ways in which women – especially when involved in traditional gendered/feminised activities – are integral to the practices of international politics is endless. If we leave women's activities unexamined we end up with a devastatingly weak and inadequate understanding of how international politics works.

Let me move to the second question that feminist scholars ask about international politics (and gender): what work is masculinity doing?

WHAT WORK IS MASCULINITY DOING?

> Far from being just about men, the idea of masculinity engages, inflects, and shapes everyone.
>
> (Berger et al. 1995: 7)

If we take a quick glance at the contemporary international political scene it still appears to be overwhelmingly populated by men as well as still being highly masculinised. However, thinking about this perception through feminism does not necessarily lead to the conclusion that either men or masculinity are monolithic and all powerful. If we take the feminist opportunity to closely reflect on the varying and contradictory ways that masculinities are woven through the theories and practices of international politics a more complicated picture, of both gender and international politics, emerges. Indeed, keeping a sharp focus on masculinity[11] can help to dispel the idea that masculinity *is* all powerful, or that men are the only people important enough to take notice of. This exposes some of the frailties around masculinity (often expressed as a form of felt 'injury'), as well as the accompanying fragility of the boundaries holding gender categories and practices in place. Moreover, concentrating on masculinity signals quite clearly that the whole of international politics is gendered, a point more easily, if wrongly missed when the gender focus remains on women (Zalewski and Parpart 2008: 1).[12]

In this section, I will look briefly at popular culture given this is a prime transmitter of cultural values and beliefs (see Chapters 28, 29 and 30). I want to look at a small selection of the popular genre of 'post-Apocalyptic'/'disaster'-type films, many of which dabble with some of the more visible international political concerns of twenty-first-century Western publics; climate change, terrorism ('ordinary, cyber and bio') at least as filtered through the hegemonic cinematic lens of the US. Here I will look at one of the ways masculinity emerges in *Children of Men*,[13] *The Road*[14] and *Taken*.[15]

Where's the daddy?

Masculinity and the boundaries keeping gender in place are ever fragile hence much work goes into securing them. Tracking this through 'Hollywood movies' in this post-*post*-9/11 atmosphere, we can trace some stunning re-assertions of the very traditional masculinised place of 'fatherhood'. Why does this matter for our thinking about international politics? Typical of this genre, these three films exhibit something of an internationalised 'moral panic' about what will happen if 'we' (read 'the West') 'don't mend our ways'. They draw stark attention to some of the consequences of not taking seriously the mistakes of *now*, imagining for us a future which might be unforgiving and unliveable in; as if this was not already a reality for many. The normative work of gender is easily missed in the mire of these 'big' concerns. The three films I refer to here all invoke some form of international political issues: human trafficking in *Taken*, and the ensuing degradations of everyday life in something of a post-apocalyptic future in *Children of Men*, if not at the same horrific level as in *The Road*.

Taken, although a film with little critical acclaim, is nevertheless popular, certainly with some of my own students. And although gender streams through this film like a torrent, it appears as barely noticeable. A conventionally packaged contemporary 'trafficking tale' centring around two teenage girls 'taken' while on vacation in Paris – one a 'good girl' (virginal), the other 'not so good' (sexually active). The 'good girl' is saved in the end by her (real) father (played by Liam Neeson) but the blatant reinscription of the rightful place of 'real fathers' is easily absorbed without noticing. As a beleaguered ex-husband, with income and professional status (and ability to 'buy stuff') paling in comparison to the new husband (stepdad), Liam Neeson's valiant rescue of his virginal daughter successfully re-secures his (and 'the') rightful fatherly place.

The Children of Men is also a story of rescue and heroism, if a more depressed and subdued version than the 'Liam Neeson' one. This is a dystopian film in which human beings can no longer procreate and where violence, degradation, filth and fear pervade the London streets on which most of the action takes place. The central character is Theo, a depressed former social justice activist, who ultimately leads the miraculously pregnant woman (women stopped having babies 18 years ago) to safety and in doing so loses his own life. But it is Theo's own fatherly redemption in 'giving life' (and assuaging his own guilt) that secures the most significant filmic moment (Ahmed 2010). As Žižek notes, the most important thing in this film is what is happening in the background;[16] and gender emerges very clearly if we look closely at the background. In *The Road*, as in so many of these films, the actions of individuals, especially men, are paramount. They are also saturated with narratives of heroic rescue/sacrifice in the face of horrific circumstances. In *The Road*, the post-apocalyptic future is very bleak, the possibilities of a liveable-in future filmically sensed only through the dignified, masculinely inflected heroism of the father figure (played by Viggio Mortensen) in the face of vicious and relentless instances of violation, greed, exploitation. The gendered making of sense in these films silently but powerfully offers blatant, if simultaneously subtle, reassertions of masculinity through the figure of the 'father'.

CONCLUSION

By beginning with questions about women, gender, masculinity, femininity, questions not usually at the centre of international political analysis, and by very closely analysing the kinds of story that emerge – feminism emerges as an important theoretical resource in studying and creating knowledge about international politics. The important question is not how to choose the 'best' theory or narrative, rather it is a case of making visible the functions and workings of gender in their varied manifestations – minimally as masculinity and femininity. We do not tend to 'see' gender and we certainly radically underestimate the work it does.[17] Investigating how gender functions – through the figure of woman, the activities of women and the ways in which masculinity helps to make sense – to provide normative clues as to appropriate behaviours and lives is necessary if the future is to be 'safe'. This all begins to illustrate the staggering significance of gender in the construction and daily enactment of international politics.

Questions for further debate

1. Is feminism just about women? (And why/how does this question matter?)
2. What is the relationship between gender and feminism? (Can we study gender without feminism?)
3. Why are feminists interested in masculinity? (How is masculinity connected to men?)
4. What does feminism *do* to the study of international politics? (How do we know where to look for the answer to this question?)
5. What would IR look like if it were feminist? (How biased does this feel?)

Sources for further reading and research

Gordon, A. (2001) *Ghostly Matters: Haunting and the Sociological Imagination*, Minneapolis: University of Minnesota Press.

Men and Masculinities Special Issue: Men, Masculinity, and Responsibility (2013) co-edited by Penny Griffin, Jane L. Parpart & Marysia Zalewski, 16: 1.

Weston, K. (2002) *Gender in Real Time: Power and Transience in a Visual Age*, London: Routledge.

Zalewski, M. (2006) 'Distracted Reflections on the Production, Narration and Refusal of Feminist Knowledge in International Relations', in B. Ackerly, M. Stern and J. True (eds) *Feminist Methodologies for International Relations*, Cambridge: Cambridge University Press: 42–61.

Zalewski, M. and Runyan, S. A. (2013) 'Taking Feminist Violence Seriously in Feminist International Relations', *International Feminist Journal of Politics*, published online 26 March 2013.

Notes

1 See Ackerly, Stern and True (2006), Shaw and Walker (2006), Stern and Zalewski (2009), Zalewski (2013) and Zalewski and Parpart (2008).

2 See also Weston (2002) and Wiegman (2004) in regard to feminism as a complex critical (and contested) theory that necessarily implies that 'feminism' is not to be read as singular.

3 See Clare Hemmings on 'feminist stories' (2011).

4 Although I do not want to typologise feminism too much, the legacy and continuing contested impact of what we can call radical feminism (see Crow 2000; Jaggar 1983) is too important not to mention.

5 It is not in the remit of this chapter to resolve this paradox – but readers are reminded that it remains extremely significant. When teaching Peterson and Runyan's work to undergraduates, one student looked at me quizzically and said, 'when I come to this class I put my gender lenses on, but when I go to my other IR class, I take them off again.' My response to him was something on the lines of, Well, no, you don't actually take them off at all ... The visual logic of lenses (as potentially optional or removable) indicates that although the metaphor is methodologically and pedagogically innovative, and perhaps sometimes politically necessary for feminists; if taught too tightly within or through IR's disciplinary epistemological and political parameters, it potentially leaves space for gender to be, once again, discarded from the intellectual landscape of significance.

6 For other approaches to the study of feminism and international politics, see, for example, Ackerly et al. (2006) Parpart and Zalewski (2008), Peterson and Runyan (2013), Steans (2013), J. Ann Tickner (2001), Tickner and Sjoberg (2011) and Zalewski (2013).

7 Although definitions are always problematic; see Diane Elam (1994: 4).

8 See Wendy Brown (2005), Janet Halley (2006), Mary Hawkesworth (2004), Adam Jones (1996) and V. S. Peterson (2012).

9 The word 'radical' here can be taken both to infer 'radical feminism' and simultaneously a more generic understanding of 'radical' given that a central and persistent focus on women is still very much out of keeping with traditional and commonplace practice.

10 She is the wife of a former British Prime Minister Gordon Brown; he was at the event in New York.

11 I do mean to imply a singularity to masculinity, indeed, the opposite is the case as there are many differing masculinities. But, rather than using the double-barrelled masculinity/masculinities throughout, for ease, I will use the word 'masculinity'.

12 For more discussion of man, men and masculinities, see Connell (1995, 2002b), Hooper (2001), Kegan Gardiner (2002), Wiegman (2001) and Special Issue of *Men and Masculinities* (2013).

13 *Children of Men*, Dir. Alfonso Cuaro, based on the novel by P. D. James, Universal Pictures, 2006.

14 *The Road*, Dir. John Hillcoat, Dimension Films, 2010.

15 *Taken*, Dir. Pierre Morel, Europa Corp., 2008.

16 Žižek on *Children of Men*; http://www.youtube.com/watch?v=pbgrwNP_gYE.

17 See Kronsell on the problems of 'studying silences' (2006).

CHAPTER 2

Ontologies, epistemologies, methodologies

Lene Hansen

LEARNING OUTCOMES

Upon completion, readers should be able to:

- Define ontology, epistemology and methodology.
- Understand the ontological, epistemological and methodological approaches that feminists working on international relations adopt.
- Locate feminist work on the larger terrain of International Relations.

INTRODUCTION

All academic approaches make three sets of decisions: about *ontology*, that is the question of what exists, what should be studied, and what the basic nature of that which is studied is; about *epistemology*, that is the question of what we can know and how to achieve this knowledge; and *methodology*, that is the concrete steps and techniques that allows one to carry out an analysis. Because ontologies, epistemologies and methodologies have fundamental implications for how research agendas are put together, what is considered important to study and how studies are conducted, it is crucial to examine the way in which they have been adopted by feminists working in the field of International Relations (IR).

To say that ontologies, epistemologies and methodologies are *decisions* rather than given once and for all is also to say that there are different ways in which ontology, epistemology and methodology can be chosen. These decisions may be either explicitly discussed or they may be implicitly assumed – but even if studies do not go into detailed discussions of ontologies, epistemologies and methodologies, they still have to make assumptions about them since they are the 'motor' that makes the analytical engine run. Many IR feminist writings do, however, discuss ontology and epistemology, probably because the dynamic of academic disciplines is one where non-mainstream approaches have to invest energy on laying out their ontologies and epistemologies, precisely because they challenge taken-for-granted assumptions.

Since ontology, epistemology and methodology are so significant to the study of gender and world politics, this chapter provides an overview of how the main approaches to gender in the discipline of IR – most label themselves as feminist, others as doing gender analysis – define them. Since debate over ontology and epistemology is a main feature of IR, the chapter will also show how feminist approaches are located on the broader terrain of IR.

CONNECTING ONTOLOGICAL AND EPISTEMOLOGICAL ASSUMPTIONS

At the level of ontology, there are two main questions as feminism and IR are brought together: how to theorise the state and international relations; and how to theorise gender.

The state is the main analytical entity in IR, even for those who criticise its privileged status. So while sharing a concern with the state and its relations to other states and non-state actors, the ontological assumptions that IR theorists make about the state vary greatly. They disagree over the extent to which the state should be seen as the only significant actor in global politics, whether one should have a critical and normative approach to the state or try to objectively explain its behavior, and finally, whether states are doomed to acting in a 'Realist' manner (driven by their own interests and power politics) that makes conflicts and war inevitable, or whether states are more 'Idealist' or 'Liberal' and thus able to cooperate, build lasting international institutions, and solve their disagreements peacefully.

Turning to gender, feminist approaches to IR have adopted three different ontologies, first, as given through biological gender; second, as biological gender mediated through social understandings of masculinity and femininity; and third, of both social and biological gender as socially and performatively constituted (see Figure 3.2). These gender ontologies have been coupled to three epistemological perspectives that correspond to Sandra Harding's division of feminist epistemologies into empiricist, standpoint and poststructuralist (or postmodern), a division that has been institutionalised in feminist IR debates (Keohane 1989; Sylvester 1994; Weber 1994). Empiricist feminism belongs to what Robert Keohane has labelled rationalist approaches to IR, that is, positivist analysis that builds causal theories about the behaviour of states, international institutions and transnational actors. Because 'empiricism' is a somewhat problematic term, and 'rationalism' is the common term in IR, this chapter will refer to 'rationalist feminism' rather than

- **Ontology:** What exists? What should be studied?

- **Epistemology:** What can we know? How can we gain knowledge?

- **Methodology:** What techniques should we adopt? What material should we examine and how?

Figure 2.1 Ontology, epistemology, methodology.

'empiricist'. Standpoint feminism comes out of a post-Marxist tradition, and hence has affinities to Critical Security Studies, Human Security and neo-Gramscian International Political Economy. Poststructuralist feminism is both a part of IR Poststructuralism and has influenced this approach in significant ways (see Figure 2.1).

The rest of this chapter will present the state and gender ontology, epistemology, and methodology of rationalist, standpoint and poststructuralist feminism as well as the criticism most often levied against each perspective. Yet before we do so, there are a few general points that should be clarified. First, ontology is about making *assumptions*, they are analytical abstractions, they define what one takes as a given and they cannot therefore be tested or proven wrong. Ontologies therefore cannot be said to be true or false, but we can discuss what the consequences are of making different ontological choices.

Second, the ontologies and epistemologies described in this chapter are analytical distinctions and have an 'ideal-type' character. In reality, feminist studies frequently cross boundaries, particularly between standpoint and poststructuralist feminism, and work with a wide variety of methodologies. Third, choices at one level have consequences for the others and ontology, epistemology, and methodology have therefore to go together. If, for instance, one works with an IR ontology of the state as being a utilitarian actor driven by self-help, and a positivist epistemology that stresses causal relationships between particular variables and state behaviour, then one will usually adopt a methodology of quantitative, statistical analysis or of comparative case studies. Usually, there is also a connection between the ontologies of state and gender, so that if the state is seen as the given unit of IR, gender tends to be seen as a biological variable, whereas if the state is seen as the product of social practices, gender is too.

Fourth, that said, we should be cautious not to assume that there are only a limited number of fixed ontology-epistemology-methodology combinations, or that there is one feminist approach that is superior to all others. IR feminists have, in fact, been quite open minded about the combinability and coexistence of different epistemologies and methodologies, because different ontology-epistemology-methodology constellations might tell us different things and provide different ways of being critical. A feminist rationalist analysis can, for instance, search for the variables explaining the likelihood of rape being adopted as a tool of war, while a standpoint feminist analysis casts light on the way in which wartime rape victims narrate their experiences, and a poststructuralist shows how competing discourses link the rapes to different foreign policies to be pursued. But one might also think strategically about the coexistence of multiple IR feminisms. IR is a field made up of a variety of approaches, and since it is very unlikely that one perspective is going to convince or conquer all others, we would want to have feminists represented in as many IR camps as possible.

RATIONALIST FEMINISM

Rationalist feminism for the most part assumes that the state is the central actor that defines international relations, both as an empirical practice and as a discipline, and that the state can be treated as a utilitarian actor concerned with its own survival. The key ambition for rationalist IR is to explain the way in which states and international institutions behave, that is, the conditions that determine such central questions as whether states go to war, how they trade or form alliances. It is important to note that rationalists may be Realists as well as Liberals, and that there is a strong quantitative rationalist tradition in the fields of Conflict Resolution and Peace Research that seek to find the causes of war so that they might be avoided in the future. This tradition breaks ontologically and normatively with rigid realist understandings of conflicts and war as inevitable. The influential 'democratic peace' literature that argues that democracies do not go to war with one another is a case in point. The ontology of gender in rationalist feminism treats the division of women and men as fairly unproblematic biological empirical categories. Combining the ontologies of state and gender, the research agenda that appears is one where gender is a variable that may impact state behaviour, or inverting the question, where state type or foreign policy might impact men and women differently.

Empiricism in its original formulation stresses that theories should be tested (and falsified) against empirical evidence. Compared to experimental sciences such as biology and chemistry, IR has virtually no possibilities of running controlled laboratory experiments. This means that rationalist IR has had to adopt other methodologies, usually quantitative ones in which statistical material that comprises a very large number of observations can be coded and tested in an infinite number of combinations (the advent of computer technology provided a huge leap forward for this kind of research) or carefully selected case studies that control for dependent and independent variables.

Putting ontology, epistemology and methodology together, we can identify two main rationalist feminist research agendas. First, there are quantitative feminists whose research ties in with the quantitative Peace Research tradition of tracing the causes of war. These researchers ask how gender impacts state behaviour, for instance whether there is a correlation between the level of gender equality in a given country, on the one hand, and this country's likelihood of going to war, on the other (Caprioli 2000; Caprioli and Boyer 2001; Regan and Paskeviciute 2003).

A more indirect causal relation between gender and foreign policy is examined by works on the so-called 'gender gap' in foreign policy attitudes (Togeby 1994; Eichenberg 2003). Survey data and election and referenda results have often shown that women are more sceptical of EU integration and that they have less 'Realist' views of foreign policy: that they are more reluctant to support war and more susceptible to withdraw support when casualties occur. Adopting the methodologies of quantitative analysis, the explanatory power of gender may then be correlated with a number of other possible explanatory variables like income, ethnicity, education, rural/urban residency and level of political participation (party membership for example). Studies that come to the conclusion that gender makes a difference thus also raise the question as to *why* that may be the case: are women more peaceful than men or are their different views a product of socialisation and/or a particular (disadvantaged) location within society? Most quantitative studies leave that question open, but it takes us back to classical discussions within Feminist theory of whether gender is biologically determined or whether it is a politically produced identity that women come (or are forced) to embrace.

A second body of rationalist research shifts from quantitative methodologies to comparative case studies, a methodology that is common in influential American journals such as *International Security* and *International Organization*. Among the works in this tradition is Valerie M. Hudson and Andrea den Boer's study of how sex-selective abortion in China and India lead to a disproportionate larger number of male children being born. This, the authors hold, might cause these countries to adopt aggressive foreign policies in the attempt to usurp their male surplus population (Hudson and den Boer 2004). Conventional constructivists self-identify as positivists to different extents, but their shared concern with the causal explanation of state behaviour provides enough of a link to rationalist IR to include them in this category. Gender analysis from this perspective also adopts case study methodology in the study of how gendered norms impact foreign policies such as, for instance, the evacuation practices adopted by humanitarian organisations operating in war zones (Finnemore and Sikkink 1998; Carpenter 2003).

Rationalist scholarship has been criticised for making state behaviour the object of analysis: to study gender becomes 'only' a matter of discovering the impact of gender variables on how states respond, not of uncovering the structural disadvantages that women face and the ways in which these are linked to dominant understandings of masculinity and femininity (see Chapters 1 and 3). Some quantitative feminists, most prominently Mary Caprioli (2004a), have responded to this criticism arguing that there is indeed a prominent space for rationalist analysis in Feminist IR and that it does have critical potential. First, some studies turn the causal interest around asking what explains women's status rather than state behaviour. Caprioli (2004b) asks, for example, whether democracy and human rights ensure women's security (defined through measures of fertility rates, rape, birth attended by health staff, economic and political inequality, and education). Second, quantitative analyses allow feminists working in other traditions to document their assumptions in more rigorous ways. Third, knowledge about correlations might provide the platform from which better to target practices that one seeks to redress.

STANDPOINT FEMINISM

Moving from rationalist to standpoint feminism ontology, epistemology and methodology change. Beginning with the ontology of the state, standpoint feminism has an explicitly critical understanding of the state as a set of patriarchal practices that support, yet silence the structural disadvantages that women face. Crucial to standpoint feminism's criticism of the patriarchal state is the historical separation of the public and the private sphere, with women being located in the latter while men would be the governors of the public as well as the patriarchal family. In order to bring out the implications of the patriarchal state, one should, holds standpoint feminism, shift the study from abstract states to how real living women are impacted by economic and security structures within and across state boundaries. This involves a double shift of focus from mainstream IR and rationalist feminism in that it moves from states to gender and from abstract structures to concrete individuals. Standpoint feminists argue further that one should focus in particular on marginalised women as these are particular disadvantaged, yet systematically overlooked. Combining ontology and epistemology, marginalised women are seen as having knowledge that is different from that of men's (and privileged women's), and which is essential to getting a full, and more objective, picture of global politics.

This critical reading of the state – domestically and in international relations – also reflects a change in gender ontology from the one of biological sex in rationalist feminism. Standpoint feminism maintains women as a particular subject defined by physical bodies, yet understands the meaning that these bodies hold to be constituted through socially powerful understandings of femininity and masculinity. Masculinity and femininity are deployed to produce and reproduce the proper ways to be women and men, both at the general level of heroic and just warriors defending women and children (and hence the nation) (Elshtain 1987) and concretely for instance in male peacekeepers' constructions of masculinity and femininity (Higate and Henry 2004). Standpoint feminism is careful to point out that one should not take femininity and masculinity to be uniform constructions that are identical across time and place or assume that women are inherently peaceful and men violent. Studies have for instances pointed to women as agents of violence (Alison 2004) or to the gender-mixed messages of the Abu Ghraib scandal, particularly the role of – and media obsession with – the female guard Lynndie England (Enloe 2004b). Crucially however, standpoint feminists still maintain the understanding that there is a concrete living female subject who can be referred to and who should be at the centre of the analysis.

Epistemologically, the social constructions of femininity and masculinity mean that women have historically been considered less suited for scientific careers. The construction of the male as rational implies that 'scientific', positivist forms of knowing are privileged, while other more narrative, hermeneutic and contextual forms of knowledge are constituted as feminine and inferior. In this view, the epistemologies adopted by rationalist feminist scholars are therefore not simply one choice among many, but a masculine one that silences other, feminine forms of knowledge. Some standpoint feminists take the view that women have a particular form of knowledge that is more emotional, concrete, dialogical, aesthetic and narrative (Stec 1997: 140). Others hold that it is problematic to essentialise a particular form of knowledge. Regardless of the view on this issue, standpoint feminism calls for bringing attention to the forms of knowledge that women have by uncovering and studying their experiences as this provides a prism onto how global politics is felt and constituted by real living embodied beings.

Methodologically, the concern with how subjects 'document their own experiences in their own terms' (Tickner 2005: 19) means that there is a preference for an 'ethnographic style of individually oriented story-telling typical of anthropology' (Tickner 1997: 615) and other hermeneutic and interpretative methodologies. Some even go as far as saying that proper feminist research cannot be conducted unless extensive fieldwork and interviews are carried out (Jacoby 2006: 158). Standpoint feminists also pay attention to the interaction between researcher and research subject, not only as part of establishing a situation that is conducive to the gathering of empirical material, but because 'the researcher cannot simply disappear from the text' (Jacoby 2006: 162; see also Cohn 2006). However, the concern with the structural inequalities women face means that studies often include quantitative material as well as secondary sources such as court transcripts, media coverage (including interviews), parliamentary debates, commission reports and even fiction.

The attraction of an epistemology of experience is that it allows for a focus on those subjects who are marginalised by state-centric understandings of international relations. There are, however, also difficulties connected to choosing experience as an epistemology through which to uncover the meaning of gender in IR (Dietz 2003: 403–405). Standpoint feminism has been attacked for assuming a single coherent female subject, and diversity feminism that understands identity as informed not only by gender but by ethnicity, class and race was developed in response. This opened for a bigger variety of, in Donna Haraway's words, situated knowledges or group-based experiences, but it also created the problem of how to assess multiple experiences. More importantly, 'experience' is a concept that promises a direct link to the everyday lives of (marginalised) subjects and to a deeply subjective, narrative and often emotional form of knowledge. Yet, this subject is simultaneously constituted through a gendered structure: it is only conceivable as a 'gendered experience' if gender is already accepted as an identity frame of reference. Individual experiences have, in short, to correspond to a feminist idea of what 'women' are and what they might say, write or feel. Since 'experience' is simultaneously presented as an expression of the feelings of the individual and derived from a given identity structure the researcher is required/empowered to make decisions about which experiences are more genuinely feminist than others.

POSTSTRUCTURALIST FEMINISM

Beginning with ontology, poststructuralists agree with standpoint feminists that the public/private distinction has had fundamental consequences for women's political, economic, and cultural marginalisation. Women were to reside in the private due to their fragile, emotional, short-sighted, everyday oriented and irrational nature, while men were decisive, rational, responsible and long-term planners. These constructions of femininity and masculinity legitimised the public–private distinction, but were also simultaneously upheld and reproduced by discourses and practices that kept these understandings in place.

If feminist are to 'bring gender in', it is not, argue poststructuralists, sufficient to point to women as marginalised bodies, it requires a reworking of the political assumptions and 'identity solutions' that the modern state entails (Walker 1992). One has to reconstruct the way in which the state has offered a particular powerful solution to questions of citizenship, belonging, identity, order and power, questions that evolve around the public–private gendered split. Even if the public individual may have shed its explicit link to male bodies – women can be politicians, bank directors and presidents – the expectation of how the proper public person acts and reasons is one that concurs with the masculinity assumptions previously reserved for men. Linking feminist poststructuralism to poststructuralism as a general IR approach, poststructuralists such as David Campbell (1992) and Roxanne Lynn Doty (1996) have traced the continued significance of gendered discourse in the construction of national identity, security policies and development thinking.

Standpoint feminism does, as noted earlier, point to the significance of socially constituted understandings of femininity and masculinity, yet it maintains women as a referent object with a real-world existence based on biological gender. Poststructuralist feminism follows instead Judith Butler's view of gender as performative, as 'always a doing, though not a doing by a subject who might be said to preexist the deed' (Butler 1990: 25; see also Chapter 3), hence there is no extra-discursive biological gender that stands apart from the social constitution of femininity and masculinity.

Putting epistemology and gender ontology together poststructuralist feminist analysis is concerned with how discourses, often competing ones, construct subjects, how this delineates or legitimises particular courses of action, and how certain subject positions are silenced as a consequence (Kronsell 2006). As there is no 'woman' subject constituted outside of discourse, there are also no 'lived experiences' that can be taken as authentic statements of what (marginalised) women really think, feel or want. This does not imply that poststructuralists are uninterested in what women – or men – say, but rather that they treat statements about lived experience as texts and discourses through which subjects constitute themselves with identities, goals, interests and desires (Scott 1992). Since discourses are shared structures of meaning, women 'speaking experience' are thus simultaneously speaking to those structures in place and potentially reworking or deconstructing them. To poststructuralists, the ontological and epistemological emphasis on discourse also means that the idea of 'the authentic' experience is itself a particular discursive construction rather than something that can be uncovered 'in reality'. Poststructuralists have also warned against depicting women as marginalised 'victims' insofar as this subject position entails an understanding of women as passive, subdued, and to be pitied rather than as proper political agents (Aradau 2008; Penttinen 2008). In effect, this concurs with classical constructions of femininity as fragile, passive, and reliant on masculine protection.

Poststructuralism's discursive ontology and epistemology imply methodologically that most deconstruct texts to show the complex relational constructions of identity that govern world politics. Yet, there are also many feminist poststructuralists who include ethnographic field work and interviews, one of the most well known being Carol Cohn's study of defence intellectuals during the Cold War, discussed in Chapter 3 (Kronsell 2006; Penttinen 2008). The difference between standpoint feminism and poststructuralism is thus not in terms of what kind of

Feminist IR perspective	State ontology	Gender ontology	Epistemology	Methodology	Familiar IR perspective
Rationalist	Empirically open, state may be liberal and/or norm driven	Variable based on biological gender	Positivist–causal connections between state action and gender	Large-scale quantitative or causal qualitative analysis (comparative case studies)	Quantitative Peace Research/Conflict Resolution Conventional Constructivism
Standpoint	Patriarchal	Biological gender mediated through social construction of feminity and masculinity	Experience – combines structure and individual/everyday	Fieldwork, narrative analysis, interviews, hermeneutic, quantitative documentation	Critical Security Studies, Human Security, neo-Gramscian IPE
Poststructuralist	Patriarchal	Biological gender constituted in discourse	Discursive	Discourse analysis, texts and fieldwork, interviews	Poststructuralism

Figure 2.2 Ontology, epistemology and methodology in practice.

material is studied, but whether it is used to uncover women's experiences or the constitution of 'women' in discourse.

The most important criticism levied against poststructuralist feminists from within the feminist camp is that its deconstruction of the gendered subject undermines a critical feminist project. If 'women' are not a subject that can be referred to, but 'only' constituted in discourse, it becomes difficult if not impossible to speak of the structural inequalities that women face (see Figure 2.2). And, if we cannot speak of women as 'victims', what alternative vocabularies should we use? The reply from poststructuralist feminism is that discourses do indeed silence and legitimate and hence a discourse analysis needs to critically engage the subject positions that are closed off by particular discourses.

CONCLUSION

This chapter has shown that there are different ontologies, epistemologies and methodologies in feminist IR, hence also that there are different ways of being critical. All feminist approaches share a concern with the way in which the state impacts women's security, economic standing, health and political status: rationalist feminism interrogates the consequences of state type or foreign policy behaviour for women, standpoint feminism has a critical view of the state as a patriarchal structure, and poststructuralist feminism deconstructs the subject constructions that are linked to the state and which have implications for domestic as well as foreign policy.

Situating feminist IR on the broader landscape of IR we find that while standpoint is the dominant feminist perspective, it belongs to a group of critical perspectives that remain marginalised within IR as a whole, particularly in the American context (Tickner 1997: 614; see also Dietz 2003; Caprioli 2004a). Rather than seeing the battlefield as feminist it is more fruitful to think of it as feminists engaging not only each other, but also those in their own 'home IR camp' (Sylvester 2007b). Precisely because of rationalism's privileged IR status, rationalist feminism may be an important strategic player in the fight to have gender become an integral part of IR. The broader field of feminist world politics is, in short, well advised to maintain its multi-ontological, multi-epistemological, and multi-methodological identity.

Questions for further debate

1. Is it important to discuss epistemology?
2. What may a feminist foreign policy look like? What strategies could be adopted to make the state more feminist?
3. What would you consider the strengths and difficulties of interviews as a research methodology?
4. Why do you think that critical IR approaches are more common in feminist IR than in IR as a whole?
5. How can one create dialogue across different IR perspectives? How could non-feminist IR become more concerned with gender?

Sources for further reading and research

Ackerly, B. A., M. Stern and J. True (eds) (2006) *Feminist Methodologies for International Relations*, Cambridge: Cambridge University Press.

Caprioli, M. (2004) 'Feminist IR Theory and Quantitative Methodology', *International Studies Review*, 6: 253–69.

Sylvester, C. (1994) *Feminist Theory and International Relations in a Postmodern Era*, Cambridge: Cambridge University Press, especially Chapter 1, 'The Palette of Feminist Epistemologies and Practices'.

Tickner, J. A. (2001) *Gendering World Politics: Issues and Approaches in the Post-Cold War Era*, New York: Columbia University Press.

Tickner, J. A. (2005) 'What Is Your Research Program? Some Feminist Answers to International Relations Methodological Questions', *International Studies Quarterly*, 49: 1–22.

CHAPTER 3

Sex or gender? Bodies in global politics and why gender matters

Laura J. Shepherd

LEARNING OUTCOMES

Upon completion, readers should be able to:

- Articulate their own theory of gender.
- Explain what it means to understand gender as a noun, a verb and a logic.
- Explain why feminist scholars argue that we should pay attention to representations and practices of bodies in global politics.

INTRODUCTION

The title of this textbook can be read in two ways. It is ambiguous, and deliberately so, as it seeks to draw attention not only to the subject matter of the book – 'gender matters' in global politics – but also to an epistemological belief espoused by its contributors: that gender *matters* in global politics.[1] As Jindy Pettman argues, 'it should be possible to write the body into a discipline that tracks power relations and practices which impact so directly and often so devastatingly on actual bodies' (1997: 105). If this is the case, and in this book various contributors argue that it is, then it behoves us to delve deep into the meaning of the body and explore the implications of studying gender in a global political context. This chapter, then, explores why and how gender matters, and interrogates various conceptions of the body in global politics through the discussion of some key gendered narratives of international relations (and International Relations as an academic discipline). In the second section, I present two accounts of bodies in global politics: bodies in social movements and bodies as scientists. I conclude with a summary of Judith Butler's work on the performativity of gender and the implications of such theory for the study and practices of global politics.

EVERYONE HAS A THEORY OF GENDER

To understand what I mean by the claim that 'everyone has a theory of gender', it is necessary to unpack what I mean by both theory and gender. Theory is often represented, especially by those who see it as a tool, as 'objective' and 'value free'. A 'theory' is supposed to explain and predict things about the world (see Smith and Baylis 2005: 1–12) and it is supposed to be 'scientific'. This has important implications for the study and practices of global politics, because International Relations as an academic discipline is usually described as a 'social science'. However, theory need not be seen as a tool or device. Rather than retaining a commitment to theory as a something that can be applied to the world as it exists independent of our interpretation of it, we can see theory as practice and 'theorising [as] a way of life, a form of life, something we all do, every day, all the time' (Zalewski 1996):

> This is relevant to International Relations scholars because it means that first, we are *all* theorising (not just the 'theorists') and second, that the theorising that counts or that matters, in terms of affecting and/or creating international political events, is not confined either to policy makers or to academics.
>
> (Zalewski 1996: 346; emphasis in original)

'Theorising', in this context, means that the way we think about the world is constitutive of that world. How we think we might be able to 'solve' certain problems of global politics, whether we think certain issues are problems in the first place and who gets to make these decisions: all of these affect and effect how we perceive the world we live in and therefore our responses to it. These responses in turn affect and effect our social/political reality; this is what is meant by 'constitutive'. On this view, theory is a *verb* rather than a tool to be applied, and is something that informs our everyday lives. If we think of gender as something we are 'theorising' daily, we can perhaps begin to see why gender matters. Ideas about appropriate and inappropriate gendered behaviours are wide ranging, influential and sometimes unconscious, but because they affect and effect how we behave in the world, they are of interest to the scholar of global politics.

An example might help clarify the issue. Look at the image in Figure 3.1. Can you make sense of those signs? If so, then you have a theory of gender. You have a theory, or an understanding, of what the signs signify and of their social importance, because in order to make sense of the signs you have to accept that there are two types of person and that each type of person is represented by one or the other figure in the sign. (Furthermore, the difference between the two types of person is predicated on their bodies, a point to which I return later.) If you recognise yourself as part of the group signified by the picture on the right, you would certainly not (apart from in

Figure 3.1 Can you make sense of these signs?
Photograph: Author.

exceptional circumstances) go through the door on the left, and vice versa. As Butler says, '[d]iscrete genders are part of what "humanizes" individuals within contemporary culture; indeed, we regularly punish those who fail to do their gender right' (1999: 178). We know what the signs mean, and even though they bear no necessary relevance to the way we look, today or ever, they order the way we act in the world.

If we accept that gender is the social meaning attached to the shape of our bodies, we can begin to understand why it is that feminist IR scholars insist that gender is not something we add to the study of world politics, but rather is integral to its functioning. That is, you cannot ignore (or abstract) the ways that gender informs and affects the practices of world politics. Gender is, on this view, not only a noun (i.e., an identity) and a verb (i.e., a way to look at the world, as in the phrase 'gendering global politics') but also a logic, which is produced by and productive of the ways in which we understand and perform global politics. This chapter wants to explore further the issue of gender and the body, and to suggest that the relationship between sex and gender is not as straightforward as it is commonly represented:

> [T]he genital area accounts for only 1 percent of the surface area of the body. But – 1 percent or not – genitals carry an enormous amount of cultural weight in the meanings that are attached to them, and I would argue that they constitute nearly 100 percent of what we, as both cultural members and as producers of cultural knowledge, come to understand and assume about the body's sex and gender.
>
> (Valentine and Wilchins 1997: 215)

We in the Anglophone world conventionally share an ontological assumption of the duality of gender: humans (and most other living things, for that matter) come in either 'M' or 'F'. This is best described as a commitment, most often unconscious, to *dimorphism*: the assumption that human beings can be easily and unproblemati- cally divided into two (*di*) distinct categories based on their physical forms (*mor- phism*). This essential separation informs the ways in which we think about the body and also the ways in which we think about a host of social and political events and relationships that we conceive of as being 'to do' with the body – for example, marriage ceremonies, parenting, sports, even eating. Because the separation occurs at a subconscious level, we are not even aware most of the time that our preconcep- tions about bodies are influencing how and what we eat, what sports we think we should or should not learn at school and who other people should and should not sleep with. The crucial insight of this book is that these assumptions about bodies are intrinsically, inherently related to the study and practices of global politics, because *global politics is studied and practiced by gendered bodies.*

It is very comforting to think of the body as something that we cannot change,[2] something that does not affect our social or political lives, or even not to think of it at all. Conventional contemporary theories of International Relations do not speak much of bodies because the individual does not matter – only collectives of indi- viduals, known as 'nations' feature, and only then insofar as they are assumed con- gruent with the state (hence 'nation-state'). Admittedly, in classical realist theory, representations of state behaviours draw heavily on ideas relating to 'human nature' (Morgenthau 1952: 963). Classical realism claims as its antecedents theorists of 'human nature' such as Thucydides, Machiavelli and Hobbes, and appeals to logics of 'human nature' to explain self-interest and rationality as 'evidenced' by the uni- tary state. However, the 'human nature' under discussion is, on closer inspection, the nature of 'man' (see Morgenthau 1973: 15–16). 'Men' feature, then, but only inasmuch as they are abstract universalised individuals; men as bodies do not enter into discussion. This is largely due to the conventional understanding of the body as *natural* rather than social or political. However, as Chris Weedon explains, '[t]he appeal to the "natural" is one of the most powerful aspects of *common-sense* think- ing, but it is a way of understanding social relations which denies history and the possibility of change for the future' (1997: 3; emphasis in original).

Formulating a politics of the body, or a perspective on global politics that takes the body seriously, requires that we think carefully about how the body manifests in our understandings of international relations. 'Formerly, the body was domi- nantly conceptualized as a fixed, unitary, primarily physiological reality. Today, more and more scholars have come to regard the body as a historical, plural, cultur- ally mediated form' (Bordo 2003: 288). This claim is a useful starting point for thinking about the body in global politics: how and in what ways is the body medi- ated? How have our understandings of 'appropriate' bodies changed over time? How do variously located practices of global politics mediate and situate bodies differently? As Michel Foucault argues, 'the body is … directly involved in a politi- cal field; power relations have an immediate hold upon it; they invest it, mark it, train it, torture it, force it to carry out tasks, to perform ceremonies, to emit signs' (1977: 26). If this is the case, then we need to understand the ceremonies and signs, and acknowledge that our understanding is affected by the bodies that carry and are carried by them. This is not a politics of aesthetics, that is, how the body *looks* in specific circumstances. In this volume, we do investigate how bodies are represented, but also interrogate the political practices through which bodies come to matter at all in global politics.

OF SCIENCE AND SOCIAL MOVEMENTS

In the previous section, I outlined a way to conceptualise or think of theory, particularly in relation to a 'theory of gender', as a performance, a series of representations (see Figure 3.2).

While these concepts are discussed further in the concluding section of this chapter, there are numerous carefully crafted accounts of the ways in which gender, when marked on (and performed by) specific bodies, matters in global politics. Christine Sylvester argues that 'men' and 'women' as social subjects are just collections of the stories that have been told about men and women, and that we behave in accordance with these stories: 'Boys don't cry', 'That's not ladylike' and so on (1994: 4).[3] For the study of global politics, this means we have to pay attention to the stories that are told about men and women as well as attending to the positioning and marking of bodies, both male and female. (Analyses of masculinity in global politics – accounts of 'men being men' – are an integral part of studies of gender; an important function of this book as a whole is to remind its readers that 'gender is not a synonym for women' [Carver 1996].) Following this logic, I offer two accounts of bodies in global politics in this section: bodies in social movements and bodies as scientists. I have chosen these two accounts as they map on to and serve to problematise the description of International Relations as a 'social science', as discussed already. This section also makes an analytical contribution to the discussion, as I demonstrate how, in two different contexts, narratives about the body and representations of the body function in political space.

- Many theorists argue that sex is biological (that is, 'natural') and gender is social (or 'cultural'). Such theories accept that gendered behaviours are largely a product of socialisation, i.e., they are constructed through interaction with society and vary according to social and historical context. This is one way to think about gender and is generally known as a *constructivist* account.

- Some scholars claim that there are gendered social behaviours that issue directly from biological sex – for example, women are inherently more peaceful than men, mothering comes naturally to women, men are usually more aggressive than women and so on. This is known as an *essentialist* account of gender as it rests on the assumption that there is an 'essence' of man/woman that determines behaviour in spite of socialisation.

- In this chapter, I draw on Judith Butler's work to argue that gender is *performative*. On this view, the sexed body is as much a product of discourses about gender as discourses about gender are a product of the sexed body. This can be seen as a *discursive* account. As I explain here, such an approach encourages us to look at gendered behaviours as 'representations of gender'. Importantly, unlike the essentialist account, the discursive account does not seek to find a 'doer behind the deed' of gendered behaviours – the 'doer' is at once produced by and productive of their representations.

Figure 3.2 Gender: a conceptual summary.

Bodies in social movements

The following account of social movements *begins* with the body, in particular the female body, and behaviours appropriate to it. Symbols of motherhood, which represented both the women at Greenham Common Women's Peace Camp in the United Kingdom during the early 1980s who campaigned for the removal of US nuclear weapons from the Greenham Common military base, and the Mothers of the Plaza de Mayo in Argentina from 1977 onwards, who congregated in the Plaza to protest the illicit arrest and capture of their (biological and symbolic) relatives, had profound implications for the social movements and for the study and practices of gender in global politics. (Although these were both local social movements, both attracted the attention of and, in the case of the latter, support from the international community. Besides, problematising the divide between politics designated international and that designated domestic is an important analytical contribution of feminist scholarship in IR.) I identify three discursive practices, common to both groups but enacted in different ways, through which the women reaffirmed their identities as mothers. The first of these is biologically determined separatism. Second, I discuss the question of boundaries and political space and, third, the role of 'the child' as metaphor and physical embodiment of vulnerability informing the politics enacted by these groups.

Both movements were explicitly 'women only': the Mothers of the Plaza de Mayo from its inception and the Greenham Common Women's Peace Camp from a year after the protestors set up camp in 1981. Despite the cultural, political and temporal differences in the context of the movements, the accounts offered in explanation for their separatism are startlingly similar. From Greenham, the opinion that 'women-only actions offered a more complete guarantee of nonviolence' (Liddington 1989: 235) echoes the statements made five years previously by women on another continent: 'We endure the pushing, insults, attacks by the army ... But the men, they never would have stood such things without reacting' (Mariá Adela Antokoletz, cited in Arditti 1999: 35). In terms of the Mothers' protest, it was both justified and justifiable: the junta in power at the time, influenced by the Catholic family-oriented values of a traditional Argentine way of life, was less likely to 'disappear' mothers than fathers. This was in keeping with the gender expectations of the time that idealised motherhood and the family in the hope of rebuilding society in an image pleasing to the eyes of the regime. While it could be argued that by virtue of their femininity and in the voicing of a public protest, both movements offered resistance to the discourses of gender that construct properly passive female subjects, I interpret this separatism with a degree of gender scepticism. In maintaining a 'women-only' ethos, both movements conserved rather than challenged gendered expectations about feminine passivity. However, the Greenham women also articulated a desire for greater equality of participation and less hierarchical social organisation, which they suggested would be best achieved through single-sex arrangements. This was represented in contemporary media coverage as threatening to family values at best and at worst as providing a sanctuary for 'lesbians, one parent families, and lost causes' (Newbury resident quoted in the *Daily Mail*, cited in Cresswell 1994: 50).

The question of boundaries is the second element of the discursive construction of motherhood common to both groups. In addition to declaring themselves women only, both groups self-consciously transgressed metaphorical and physical boundaries and used these transgressions to frame their protests. Both movements were comprised of women who would not 'sit still and keep at home' (Rowbotham 1972: 16) as women were expected to do, leaving the realm of formal politics to masculine/ised subjects. Instead they used their weapons of protest – their bodies, their *female* bodies – in a carefully articulated statement of female agency. Initially, the Mothers of the Plaza de Mayo organised their protests in socially sanctioned 'women's spaces', 'using feminine/maternal public parks and tea houses as places to make plans and exchange information' (Radcliffe and Westwood 1996: 157), but in taking their protest to the steps of the government buildings in the Plaza de Mayo, the Mothers altered the social and spatial impact of the movement. Through associating themselves with the Plaza de Mayo, which is deeply significant in Argentine history and politics, the Mothers achieved recognition and a public space for their political protest. This, however, is not the same thing as saying that the Mothers 'moved in' to that public space; it should be remembered that the Plaza de Mayo was occupied by the Mothers just once a week. In contrast, the peace camp at Greenham Common was a permanent fixture. The women involved in the camp inhabited an altogether more liminal space. They had left their fixed houses for tenuous settlements on common land; the mothers at Greenham Common Women's Peace Camp *did* 'move in' to that public space, both with and without their children by their sides in a confrontational bid to challenge notions of home and security in the shadows cast by missile silos. The permanence of their move is reaffirmed in the memories recorded by the women who lived there: 'women who have been there ... say they will never be the same' (Elshtain 1995: 241). The women's refusal to return 'home' at the end of each day was interpreted as the challenge to public order that it intended. Instead of questioning that order, however, the widespread response in UK media coverage of the events was to question the behaviour of the women. 'The question of women's roles as mothers was used frequently as a stick of castigation with which to beat the Greenham women: if they were so fond of children, why were they not at home with them?" (Young 1990: 68).

Finally, the third discursive practice that helped construct the collective identity of 'mother' for the women in question was a commitment to child-centred politics. While the Mothers of the Plaza de Mayo searched for their *niños desaparecidos*, the disappeared children from their past in the present, the Greenham Common Women's Peace Camp was dedicated to ensuring a better life for the children of the future in the present. The same key terms resonate in both cases: both movements sought to offer children protection, to provide them with security and to honour a notion of maternal care. The symbols used to denote this child-centred commitment are also similar. The Association of the Mothers of the Plaza de Mayo adopted a white headscarf, symbolising a baby's nappy, as their emblem of collective identity. As one mother suggested, 'a gauze shawl, a diaper ... will make us feel closer to our children' (cited in Bouvard 1994: 74). The whiteness signifies peace as well as life, in a tacit refusal to don the black *mantilla* worn as part of traditional mourning dress in Argentina. The symbolic function of the baby's nappy reinforces the notion of maternal care mentioned earlier, as well as evoking thoughts of birth, thus life, and hope. The nappies and toys pinned to the fence at Greenham Common were among the many symbols of 'mundane' domesticity deployed in contrast to the high-powered high politics of a nuclear base in the nuclear age. These symbols sought to idealise motherhood and legitimise the presence of the protestors. This is by no means an unproblematic view, but a culturally intelligible narrative nonetheless; the children of tomorrow represented by a soft toy pinned to a hard wire fence being protected, cared for, *mothered* by the women at the Peace Camp, who felt 'a special responsibility to offer them [the children] a future – not a wasteland of a world and a lingering death" (cited in Liddington 1989: 227).

Despite surface similarities between two social movements that drew on representations of and myths about motherhood to inform their protests, the dynamics of the two movements were radically different. Later media coverage of the Mothers describes them in positive language, with words such as 'courage' and 'inspiration' (Fisher 1998) validating the Mothers' struggle and reporters acknowledging that the Mothers became 'world icons of courageous demands for accountability, the assertion of human rights' (Omang 2006). References to Greenham Common frame the women's efforts in a wholly different light, describing the Camp as a 'debacle' and denying the protest any efficacy or legitimacy (Vuillamy and Hinsliff 2001; see also Petitt 2006). The Camp was variously represented as 'a criminal activity, a witches' coven, a threat to the state, the family and the democratic order' (Young 1990: 2). In widening their protest from 'acceptable' women-as-mothers protecting the children of the future to 'deviant' women questioning the gender order that assisted in the construction of the missiles that sparked their protest, Greenham Common Women's Peace Camp lost the focus of its collective identity and the legitimacy this identity afforded their protest. In contrast, the Mothers of the Plaza de Mayo maintained a conservative representation of motherhood, restricting their protest to the recovery of the disappeared and denouncing the authority of the military regime. These two different performances of body politics in global politics had very different effects.

Bodies in science

A second set of significant bodies emerge as visible through the feminist interrogations of weapons technology and strategic culture. In 1987, Carol Cohn published an analysis of 'nuclear strategic thinking' evidenced in the 'almost entirely male world' of 'distinguished "defence intellectuals"' (Cohn 1987: 678–79). This article remains one of the most significant accounts of the impact of gender, gendered language and bodily images on the study and practices of global politics. Cohn also draws our attention to the complex intersections of race, gender and class (referring to 'white men in ties discussing missile size' [Cohn 1987: 683] in a typically snappy turn of phrase).

In earlier analysis of the development of nuclear technology, the gendered imaginings used to make sense of the new weaponry are obvious, and function to inscribe a link between violence and masculinity that feminist scholarship has long sought to problematise. When the first fusion device was tested in the United States of America in 1952, the telegram reporting its success to authorities – describing an explosion about a thousand times more powerful than the bomb that destroyed

Hiroshima in 1945 – read 'It's a boy!' (Easlea 1983: 130; see also Cohn 1987: 701).[4] Admittedly, that was back in the 1950s; surely we can expect to see contemporary defence experts refusing to deploy the gendered metaphors employed by their ancestors? On the contrary, Cohn reports that defence intellectuals continue to construct their language, which Cohn names 'techno-strategic discourse', using a gendered framework. Cohn witnessed a country without tested nuclear capacity being referred to as a nuclear 'virgin' (Cohn 1987: 687). Similarly, phrases such as 'more bang for the buck', 'the Russians are a little harder than we are' and the assertion that 'you're not going to take the nicest missile you have and put it in a crummy hole' all contribute to the ongoing masculinisation of nuclear weapons technology (Cohn 1987: 683–84). One recent example is worth quoting at length:

> At one point, we re-modelled a particular attack, ... and found that instead of there being 36 million immediate fatalities, there would only be 30 million. And everybody was sitting around nodding, saying, 'Oh yeah, that's great, only 30 million,' when all of a sudden, I heard what we were saying. And I blurted out, 'Wait, I've just heard how we're talking – Only 30 million! Only 30 million human beings killed instantly?' Silence fell upon the room. Nobody said a word. They didn't even look at me. It was awful. I felt like a woman.
>
> (cited in Cohn and Ruddick 2003: 14)

Feeling 'like a woman' compromised this interviewee's masculinity, but also his professionalism: the underlying assumption is that women (irrational, emotional creatures) have no place in the hard-headed world of defence strategy. Crucially, Cohn's research draws attention to the ways in which gender functions in security by not only interrogating the actions of physical bodies but also by asking what work gender is doing to organise and make sense of security discourses. The rationality employed and deployed by the communities in which Cohn has conducted her research is literally dis-embodied, amounting to the denial of human experience in the narratives of the defence intellectuals: 'it is not only impossible to talk about humans in this language, it also becomes in some sense illegitimate to ask the paradigm to reflect human concerns' (Cohn 1987: 711–12). It is precisely these 'human concerns' to which Cohn wishes to draw our attention, facilitated by a nuanced and convincing analysis of the ways in which bodies, and particularly masculine bodies, delimit the domain of nuclear weapons technology.

PROBLEMATISING 'BODIES THAT MATTER'[5]

Earlier, I illustrated how (certain) bodies matter in global politics and, more importantly, how certain *performances of gender* produce and are produced by (further, legitimise and are legitimised by) political practices on a global scale. In this section, I challenge the ways in which the valuable political interjections described above are still framed in reference to a narrative of dimorphism. This framing is in part due to what Butler identifies as a 'matrix of intelligibility' (1999: 24). Put simply, this means that in order to be recognisable to others and ourselves, our gender must be performed within particular cultural and historical boundaries. 'The cultural matrix through which gender identity has become intelligible requires that certain kinds of "identities" cannot "exist" – that is, those in which gender does not follow from sex and those in which the practices of desire do not "follow" from either sex or gender' (Butler 1999: 23–24). Taking such a perspective on gender matters in global politics demands that we ask, how are various performances of gender congruent with or disruptive of the limits of intelligibility in a given cultural context? Seen in this light, the tales offered earlier describe actors that both remain within the boundaries (the scientists and the Mothers of the Plaza de Mayo) and contest those boundaries (the Greenham women). The last were seen as less 'successful' and more threatening precisely because they transgressed appropriate behavioural limits.

The question then becomes: How are these limits set? Who gets to decide that 'boys don't cry' or that to 'throw like a girl' is an insult? Gender does not 'read' from sex in any straightforward way. I would suggest that sex is as much a fiction as gender – that the foundational narrative of dimorphism on which our 'matrix of intelligibility' is so heavily dependent is itself contestable. Moreover, we frequently amend the bodies to fit the dominant (dimorphic) theory of gender, and not vice versa. At the moment of gendering – when an infant human is named as a 'boy' or a 'girl' – medical intervention is sometimes required to align the body with one side or the other of a dichotomous gender framework, so as not to disrupt the 'matrix of intelligibility'. Interestingly, medical experts tend to focus on the importance of socialisation in such cases, arguing that it is a matter of whether the child is raised (read: trained to perform) as a boy or girl. 'Of course, at normal [sic] births, when the infant's genitals are unambiguous, the parents are not told that the child's gender is ultimately up to socialization' (Kessler 1990: 17). This would suggest that sex, as well as gender, is dimorphically constructed.

Throughout this section, I have used the term 'performance' to describe the ways in which gender manifests in social/political life. This is a concept most closely associated with the work of Judith Butler (see Figure 3.3), and refers to the identifiable linguistic and non-linguistic practices that constitute our understanding of gender. It does *not* mean that pre-formed individuals are free to perform gender as they wish; rather, the 'matrices of intelligibility' constitute the limits of sex (Butler 1993; see also Segal 1997).

One way to think about performativity is through the gender classification of a child at birth, as mentioned earlier:

> Consider the medical interpellation which ... shifts an infant from an 'it' to a 'she'; or a 'he' and in that naming, the girl is 'girled' ... But that 'girling' of the girl does not end there; on the contrary, that founding interpellation is reiterated by various authorities and throughout various intervals of time to reenforce or contest this naturalized effect.
>
> (Butler 1993: 7–8)

The 'reiteration' to which Butler refers is the continuing construction of identity through what she terms 'performativity'. In this way, bodies themselves take on the gendered characteristics appropriate to their designated 'sex' from birth and throughout life gender is performed repeatedly. Crucially, in order to have a 'liveable' life, an infant must be 'shifted from an "it" to a "she" or a "he"'. There are variations within the discursive construction of gender and it is therefore more

'What continues to concern me most is the following kinds of questions: what will and will not constitute an intelligible life, and how do presumptions about normative gender and sexuality determine in advance what will qualify as the "human" and the "liveable"? In other words, how do normative gender presumptions work to delimit the very field of description that we have for the human? What is the meaning by which we come to see this delimiting power, and what are the means by which we transform it?'

(Butler 1999: xxii)

Judith Butler's works on gender theory, political philosophy and ethics have been highly influential across a range of subject disciplines. It is specifically her work on the performativity of gender that is of interest here, not least because it can usefully be employed as an analytical frame to great effect in the study of global politics. David Campbell (1992), for example, draws on her theory of performativity in *Writing Security*, his exploration of US foreign and security policy. Lene Hansen (2000) uses Butler's work to critique the 'Copenhagen School' of security theory and Maria Stern (2006) draws on Butler to interrogate the concept of *in*security.

Figure 3.3 The work of Judith Butler.

appropriate to recognise and interrogate multiple masculinities and femininities, as do the authors in this book, rather than some fixed or essential notion of what constitutes a 'man' or 'woman'. However, performances of gender, where gendered subjects are 'tenuously constituted in time ... through a *stylized repetition of acts*' (Butler 1999: 179; emphasis in original), despite the variants, must be congruent with culturally and historically specific gender narratives in order to be recognised as legitimate – the 'matrix of intelligibility' I discussed earlier. Crucially, on this view, 'gender is always a doing, though not a doing by a subject who might be said to preexist the deed ... There is no gender identity behind the expressions of gender; that identity is performatively constituted by the very "expressions" that are said to be its results' (Butler 1999: 33).

This chapter has provided an overview of one way in which it is possible to conceptualise sex and gender,[6] and introduced you to some illustrations to show how and why gender matters in global politics. This book encourages you to develop a 'feminist curiosity' (Enloe 2007: 1) about the study and practices of global politics. Challenging the assumptions of conventional theories and approaches, unsettling that which was previously taken for granted, even (perhaps especially) such things as 'human nature' and the body – these are among the ways in which a feminist curiosity works.

Questions for further debate

1. Why should the study of global politics attend to the practices of bodies? In other words, why is 'gender' a useful category of analysis?
2. What additional examples of bodily actions in global politics can be included alongside those mentioned here? What do these practices tell us about the relevant 'matrices of intelligibility'?
3. Why might people be resistant to the idea that gender matters in global politics?
4. Is it helpful to imagine the possibility of a 'third gender'?
5. Are you persuaded that there is a significant difference between sex and gender?

Sources for further reading and research

Blackless, M., A. Charuvastra, A. Derryck, A. Fausto-Sterling, K. Lauzanne and E. Lee (2000) 'How Sexually Dimorphic Are We? Review and Synthesis', *American Journal of Human Biology*, 12(1): 151–66.

Butler, J. (1993) *Bodies That Matter: On the Discursive Limits of 'Sex'*, London: Routledge.

Feinberg, L. (1993) *Stone Butch Blues*, Ann Arbor, MI: Firebrand Books.

Grosz, E. (1994) *Volatile Bodies: Towards a Corporeal Feminism*, Bloomington, IN: Indiana University Press.

Zalewski, M. (2000) *Feminism After Postmodernism: Theorising Through Practice*, London: Routledge.

Notes

1 An 'epistemology' is a theory of knowledge. Ontology, epistemology and methodology are discussed fully in Chapter 2.

2 Of course, the body can be shaped and adorned according to, or in transgression of, social norms, but the physical form cannot be re-gendered except through recourse to complex sex reassignment therapies including hormone treatments and surgery.

3 Cynthia Weber calls these stories 'unconscious ideologies', which she describes as 'the foundations of our ideological and political thinking that we place beyond debate' (2005a: 4). She suggests, and I agree with her, that drawing these common-sense accounts of gender back *into* debate can be profoundly unsettling as it can threaten our own ideas about being in the world (see also Peterson and True 1998).

4 The nuclear weapon dropped on Hiroshima on 6 August 1945 was named 'Little Boy'.

5 This subheading is borrowed from Judith Butler's 1993 text of the same name.

6 In this chapter, I have not discussed various other ways in which to conceptualise this relationship, which are explored in sophisticated detail in a range of political writing. In addition to the suggested readings, see, for example, Connell (1995), Fuss (1989), Lloyd (2005) and Oakley (1972).

CHAPTER 4

Postcolonial theories and challenges to 'first world-ism'

Anna M. Agathangelou and Heather M. Turcotte

LEARNING OUTCOMES

Upon completion, readers should be able to:

- Explain how geography informs feminist and IR knowledge formations.
- Distinguish between 'first world-ism' and postcolonial feminisms.
- Evaluate the utility of examining IR through an approach of feminisms of critical geographies.

INTRODUCTION

The discipline of International Relations (IR) is often considered to be a site of examination into global power relationships, and a place from which to develop theories, methods and practices that provide insight to the materiality[1] of global politics. The discipline itself has been (and continues to be) a geopolitical site of intense power struggles and negotiations. Various theories and methods of IR have produced explicit analyses of the relationships of global power within IR's own frameworks of knowledge production. In particular, the works of critical, feminist and postcolonial theorists have shifted the orientation of IR scholarship to consider the different configurations and effects of international politics when attentive to various objects, subjects and power relations circulating within critical geographies (Chowdhry and Nair 2002; Grovogui 2002; Sylvester 1994; Turcotte 2011; Walker

1993). These interventions heed the exclusions of canonical IR theories and teachings, and question its role in shaping global places, scales, networks and spatial relations. What kinds of political strategy and theoretical framework are currently being drawn on to understand world politics and the discipline of IR?

In this chapter, we argue that the critiques of postcolonial feminists and critical feminisms has contributed knowledge frameworks and material insights into hegemonic power relations and, in particular, global violence. More specifically, such work has raised questions about the 'geopolitical', in order to transform IR's contentious emphasis on geographical and territorial realms of power. Mainstream IR constructions of global violence are explained through static constructions of geography that territorialise where violence is and who are the victims, perpetrators and protectors. Take, for example, the discourses of 'women's rights as human rights', which are focused on the abuse of 'women' in the 'Third' and 'Second World' regions of 'Africa', 'Asia', 'Latin America', 'Middle East', and 'Eastern Europe'. In these discourses, the regions of the 'US', 'Canada' and 'Western Europe' are territories of protections and rights; the geographical destinations of migration and asylum are Northern states. In short, geographical location conditions one's relationship and access to rights and state protections (for further discussion of human rights, see Chapter 7). Such discourses often elide the power relationships and structures of inequality that make rights claims possible through the regulation of national and international 'citizenship'.

Multiple processes have redrawn static boundaries worldwide: unequal migration patterns of people and labour, often forced, from the Global South to the Global North and from rural areas to urban; a proliferation of borderland territories; an increased number of export free trade zones; and refugee camps within and between states. Territories marked as the 'Global North' and 'Global South' are built on histories of struggle and contestation and geographies of segregation. In other words, the mobility of bodies (people and knowledge) troubles and conditions the perceived geographical immobility. Homogeneous and static constructions of geography, which contain known subjects and objects of study, rely on histories of segregation to reconstruct the world (Agathangelou 2004, 2012). Such histories represent gender, race, sexuality, religion and nation as separate moments and entities, which propagate violent inequalities through the knowledge claims of global power and forms of justice. What are the ways in which First World discourses of women's rights as human rights necessitate the violence and 'victimisation' of Others within the Global South? How does geography inform and become informed by international relations and frameworks of decolonial justice? Why is geography a crucial concern for feminist theorisations, methods, pedagogies and praxes of global and gender politics?

The frameworks of geopolitics within the mainstreams of IR, including feminist IR, rely on geographical separations of land, people and knowledge. This process of *geopolitical segregation* is presented as naturalised, even when violence is foundational to its consolidation (Agathangelou 2004, 2010; Turcotte 2011). This geographical segregation, although foundational to the remaking and reshaping of spatial relations (including assumptions about global (im)mobility, or restrictions to accessing resources and justice) becomes visible when read through aboriginal, postcolonial and feminist lenses. Such lenses enable us to enquire into the convergences of segregation and also investigate the disruptions that are made possible through the many struggles of marginalised people. More concretely, these enquiries have opened the space for us to engage with First World feminisms (i.e., in their multiple permutations but mostly realist, liberal and even some radical ones) and the different projects they articulate, to see how such feminisms move across, create possibilities and even collude in creating spaces of violence, by sustaining projects of segregation.

In reading and articulating the creative and compelling ways feminists contest the violences of segregation and the challenges that emerge from their interventions, we articulate a feminism that draws on historical insights of spatiotemporal relations and reconfigures geography beyond its epistemic and material cartographic role to foster social relations that disrupt dominant geopolitical asymmetries of power. We take geopolitics as a critical geography of multiple engagements of time, space and place within various sites of world politics, including relations of knowledge production. By pushing the theoretical realms of geopolitics into unconventional sites, such as IR and feminist knowledge production, we engage and critique the knowledge terrains of the personal and systemic within International Relations. Geopolitics relies on the theoretical and material segregations of people's lives, land, bodies and knowledge to maintain structures of power (Agathangelou 2012). Feminism is a geopolitical structure and it too relies on these same histories of segregation. What would it mean to account for these segregations within feminism? What are the stakes to attending to segregations as well as the tensions within them specifically for the emergence and formation of world-making projects of decolonial justice?

We centre people as major participants within global politics (Tétreault and Lipschutz 2005), being attentive to the exclusion of gendered analyses of the state (Enloe 1983, 1989; Hooper, 1999; Peterson 1992) and considering the varied relationships and positionalities of the 'Other' (Inayatullah and Blaney 2004; Ling 2002; Walker 1993) as systemic moments of power within International Relations. In so doing, we suggest that the analytical frames of global power within IR generally, and feminist IR more specifically, require theoretical articulations that embody accountable political interventions in world politics on multiple scales. Such analyses can provide a deeper understanding of problems in our everyday lives within the multiple communities we inhabit, and they can bring our communities in closer proximity to one another to address global violence and inequalities. Because power is always circulating within the material and epistemic realms of IR, we address the major logics and intelligibilities within formulations of IR knowledge to argue that processes of geopolitical segregation are constitutive of these formulations.

In other words, IR, as a 'coherent' field of study, discipline and practice, imagines and produces itself through geopolitical segregation. We connect these segregations explicitly by engaging with the ways we, as IR and/or feminist scholars, are conditioned to generate global politics and geopolitical sites as if they are separated moments and relations without historical specificities or connections to the field, its development and its contemporary practices. Our articulation of feminisms of critical geographies works to: (1) describe and articulate the critique of First World feminism(s)[2] and the contingent challenges and disruptions made possible by post-colonial feminists; (2) highlight the contributions of feminisms' various theoretical approaches that could allow us to construct a more nuanced landscape of practices and vision of transnational feminisms and feminist social relations (Kuokkanen 2008; Mohanty 1991a; Shohat 2002); (3) conceptualise varied possibilities for the emergence of an open-ended feminist framework attentive to the geopolitics in which feminisms emerge, struggle and engage; and (4) imagine possible solidarities praxis for decolonial, feminist, anti-racist and anti-capitalist International Relations.

FIRST WORLD FEMINISM(S) AND GEOPOLITICAL SEGREGATION

More than a decade ago several theorists called for an end to neglecting imperialism in IR and for recognising that knowledge and representation is an important form of a power (Darby and Paolini 1994) in understanding world politics. Since then many scholars have critiqued the provincial and Eurocentric aspects of the discipline by drawing on postcolonial thinking and practices (Barkawi and Laffey 2001; Krishna 1993; Ling 2002). This disruption of the discipline's dominant epistemologies by critical theorists and feminist scholars, and particularly Marxist and scholars of the Global South (Chowdhry and Nair 2002), prepared the ground for our critique by expanding the theoretical and methodological terrains of IR. These works not only explore the interconnected relevance of gender, race, ethnicity, sexuality, class, nationality and regionality but they also engage with the ways in which knowledge production plays a significant role in shaping political praxis and the formation of colonial and imperial projects. These works continue to play an imperative part in constituting, founding and shaping the conditions of possibility within global politics, as well as the representations of postcolonial and Western identities. Postcolonial critiques highlight that our understandings of the international and the relations of identity formations are limited (Inayatullah and Blaney 2004; Ling 2002; Rupert 1995). Postcolonial theorisations have highlighted the significance of international geographies by suggesting that the constitution of geographical sites as social relations depends on violence (Mama 1995; Mamdani 1996; Mbembe 2001; Mudimbe 1994) as well as world-making projects of decolonial justice (Agathangelou 2013). More specifically, some IR scholars argue that the formations and constitution of colonial globalities (Muppidi 2004), one of which is the discipline of International Relations, depend on violently segregating the world (Agathangelou 2004; Rai 2007; Smith 2006).

Geopolitical segregation is a substantive set of imperial strategies that produce distinct divisions and locales of world politics, including the discipline and practice of IR (realist, neoliberalism, critical, feminist, postcolonial). Oftentimes it pits intellectual communities against one another and distributes them unevenly and asymmetrically to each other[3] within 'their own' cordoned-off territory because of a scramble for resources, claims to expertise and/or to merely legitimise positions of power within an asymmetrical IR world order. We consider such segregation frameworks – although useful maybe on a short-term basis – as turning into strategies that become complicit with the desires and even violent fantasies of imperialism (see also Agathangelou and Ling 2009) (see Figure 4.1). Such frameworks feed imperial projects that consolidate global space, feminist theory and subject formation 'anew' within the borders of IR, which make capital's crossings and violations possible. Segregation is a logic and practice that regulates, elides and spectacularises bodies (people, land, knowledge) through gender, racial, ethnic, sexual, national and global orders within the frameworks of IR, albeit with many tensions and myriad contradictions. Geopolitical segregation, then, is a means to solidify the conditions of power that regulate, control and exploit bodies as central to imperial reformations of political practice and knowledge formations. The subjects of IR and IR subjects themselves are negotiated through their divided geographies of power within the discipline in the name of projects that centralise profit and fear as their goals (Agathangelou and Ling 2009).

The segregation and division of different sites within IR mystifies their co-constitutive histories, unequal divisions of labor and makes difficult the raising of questions about its political praxes through the naturalisation – the canonisation – of IR, feminist theory and postcolonial world politics. Therefore, it is crucial to consider geopolitical bodies (the state, the physical bodies of individuals, regions, knowledges) generally, and the geopolitical bodies of IR (scholars, researchers, policymakers) more specifically, as constantly forming through their struggles (Agathangelou 2013), flows, movements, migrations and 'transnational connectivities' (Grewal 2005). Through the description of the multiple worlds that we occupy, and the articulation of critical spatial and temporal frames that make it possible for

---

Materiality

The concept of materiality is a contested one and its genealogy bears a much longer discussion.

We define materiality in this chapter as the practices of the 'social' (i.e., international, global, corporeal, transnational etc.) as 'practices' that breathe life and meaning into gendered, sexualized, racialized, classed being and relations, rather than assertions of specific sorts of practices (i.e., economic, systemic, structural etc.) that are accorded causal priority in shaping social relations (i.e., gendered, racialized, classed, sexualized etc.). In addition, materiality here refers also to the production, including epistemological articulations toward the formation of a shifting and dynamic change of socio-ontologies of gender, sexuality, race, class that disrupt the dominant formations of property relations including its dominant being.

Geopolitical segregation

The concept of geopolitical segregation builds on theoretical and experiential understandings of different kinds of people, land and knowledge that are seemingly disconnected or in relationship to one another, but only through the power dynamics of hierarchical comparison.

Geopolitical suggests political geographies that can be mapped onto certain spaces and bodies of the world. Segregation suggests separate, not imbricated or co-constituted. Put together, we argue, the concept suggests a substantive set of imperial strategies that produce distinct divisions and locales of world politics, including the people, discipline and practice of IR (e.g., realist, neoliberalism, critical, feminist, postcolonial as separate knowledge sites of IR).

Figure 4.1 On materiality and geopolitical segregation.

us to 'see' that the knowledge and practice of 'global' politics are historically entangled within an imperial project of geopolitical segregation is crucial. It allows us to recognise that some are called to be complicit (i.e., appropriating their struggle for justice to the struggle for more profits and capital formation) and others to actively participate in protecting the interests of first world-ism and its contingent identified interests even with a high cost, privileged subjects consequently impeding possibilities of transformative 'transnational' and 'global' analyses and practices for a just feminist world (see Figure 4.2).

Global feminist practices can redraw the political boundaries of academic knowledge to secure whiteness and first world-ism as structures of privilege within feminist *and* IR frameworks. Gender mainstreaming and the expansion of Anglo-American feminist framing of IR produces feminist objects to be found and studied for data that often support Anglo-American feminist ideals and projects. Such theories and practices continue to deepen the polarisations between different modes and people who embody feminist work; it further generates imperial feminist praxes that foreclose possibilities of solidarity.[4] The theories and methods of some First World feminisms, women of colour feminisms, Third World feminisms, feminisms of the Global South and transnational feminisms from varied geopolitical constituencies articulate their opposition to gender essentialisms and the racial, class and heteronormative privileging and the colonising practices of International Relations through their own locations and oppositional histories (see, for example, Grewal and Kaplan 1994; Imam 1997; Nnaemeka 2005; Spivak 1988). Yet, many of these scholars and the knowledges produced with these critical frameworks – both from the Global South and the Global North[5] – are relegated to the margins and asymmetrically located on the varied knowledge matrices of the academy (see also Agathangelou and Ling 2002). Pointing to the decolonial struggles and world-making projects that rupture segregation in the everyday as a process and productive strategy of violence is fundamental to the imaginary and formation of an international that is decolonial and just.

Cyprus Roars

I am Cyprus and I am in deep pain
My womb is in shambles
My head and shoulders ache all my body cells, one by one, are injured
Male doctors unceasingly excavate my pain
I cannot speak of my dead sisters/their beatings all the rapes,
My anguish
I cannot speak of my colonizers and all my struggles for justice
At times, I can hardly remember all the stories I had to tell
When I was an active witness to myself to a world of abject poverty
all the sexual violence
When my memories overflow/wanting me to tell
I am Cyprus/and I can be silent no longer

(Agathangelou 2000: 12)

Figure 4.2 *Cyprus Roars.*

Underlying much of world politics has been the violent division of the world into domestic and international, the centre and the periphery, the developed and the underdeveloped worlds, the masculine from the feminine, the state territorial space from the anarchic and violent world. Many of these segregations and divisions of the places that people live and relate with on a daily basis have been detrimental to our lives. Segregation has extensively contributed to experiences with violation, and many times death (Agathangelou 2010), even when the international discourses have been about change, development, and peace and world order. Numerous scholars from the Global South have questioned the relevance of Anglo-Saxon feminist ideas for women in the Third World arguing that such theories presume a unified category of a 'poor woman of the Third World' (Chang 2000; Mohanty 1991b; Okeke 1996; Rowley 2003) and argue that feminism itself is a bourgeois ideology of the First World that privileges gender oppression and struggles against patriarchy at the expense of many other structural struggles (Narayan and Harding 2000; Shohat 1998; Waller and Rycenga 2000).

However, as feminists from the First and Third World have engaged one another and tensions have emerged, a move by some to understand gender, racial, national and class-based violences and oppressions in specific, local and historical contexts also have emerged in productive and contested ways. As Mohanty (1991a) explains understanding feminism in only gendered terms assumes that definitions and practices of identities of 'womanhood' are not connected to racial, class, nation or sexuality; rather, it is precisely these imbrications of identity that form the ideologies of womanhood. Third World feminism(s)' critiques of First World feminism(s) embody within them two simultaneous deconstruction projects: (1) First World feminism(s), while not a unified project, has been built on systemic underpinnings of imperialism; (2) Third World feminism(s), while not a unified project, has been built on anti-imperial connections. Drawing on these contradictions and tensions in the formations of First and 'Other' feminisms necessitates an articulation of feminist projects grounded in the histories, cultures and experiences of women from different spatial formations. It is not enough to merely focus on 'gender relations'; we need understand how the 'dominant' notions of 'womanhood' and 'manhood' are also intertwined with multiple scales such as constructions and geographies of power along racial, ethnic, class, sexual, regional and international dimensions.

Explicit attention to spatially racialised and class critiques of white First World feminisms by black feminists, women of colour and African diasporic scholars offer invaluable theoretical insights because such work reveals the naturalisation of spatial whiteness within hegemonic feminisms, as well as the investments that many feminists have in this neoimperial project (Magubane 2001; Nnaemeka 1998). Such theorisations are not a move to occupy whiteness or First World privileges, neither are they simple inversions of power (Spivak 1988); rather, they problematise the trajectories of violence produced through the geographical assumptions of First World feminisms.[6] Such work raises questions about the representations of localised and globalised geographies through the attention to global structures of slavery, colonialism, imperialism and capitalism that challenge First World feminists' hierarchical and segregated representations of feminism, gender violence and feminist justice (Busia 1993; Chukukere 1995; Magubane 2004; Mama 2007). Bringing together the insights of feminists who are attentive to the complexity of geopolitics reveals how the consolidation of Western identity formation depends on the division of the world into spaces that seem to be disconnected from each other (Turcotte 2008). As numerous postcolonial scholars argue, the West needs 'a rest' in order to make itself. Feminisms of critical geographies question these processes of geopolitical segregation by suggesting that feminists: (1) recognise how significant segregation is as an imperial practice and technology in the formation and constitution of social relations of power; (2) form relations (i.e., bringing supposedly dissimilar phenomena of feminism next to each other); and (3) draw and build on the histories of work put forth by women of colour, Third World, postcolonial, transnational, global and First World feminisms to highlight the complexities and complicities of feminist engagements.

FORCED INCAPACITATIONS AND THE GEOPOLITICS OF FEMINISMS

The divisions of the world outlined earlier became intensified beginning in the 1970s and the early 1980s. Much of the world, and especially under stringent conditions (e.g., militarisations, forced mobilities, imprisonments, theft of their lands and labour), has been forced to restructure its socioeconomic, political relations, ecologies and bodies. What many have come to articulate as 'globalisation' is really the dramatic demands made by newer neoimperial and capitalist regimes desiring the shifts of capital in the hands of very few in the world by forcing personal, local, national, regional and transnational restructurings (see Chapters 15–18). Out of these contestations and restructurings, dominant institutions such as the UN and feminists have carved out space in which to critique the privileges and violences of 'globalisation' by accounting for the ways familiar colonial intelligibilities and practices continue to work (Agathangelou 2004; Conway 2008). Feminist interventions into the frameworks of globalisation also disrupt new articulations of imperialism that have been consolidated into a (neo)liberal 'global' order (Aguilar and Lacsamana 2004). Within these dramatic restructurings and geopolitical changes, much feminist work has focused on assessing and understanding 'globalisation' and its effects on many peoples and women in particular. Critics of globalisation focus on the devastating effects of neoliberalism, its contingent projects such as structural adjustment, the privatisation of basic resources, decreased wages, decreased social resources to support social welfare and the poor, the militarisation of everyday life and the effects of these policies on the most impoverished populations in the Global South (see, for example, Gibson-Graham 1996; Kuokkanen 2008; Naples and Desai 2002). However, globalisation has also generated the possibility of 'unintended consequences' such as the transnational feminist networks (Alvarez 2000; Moghadam 2005). Organising in contexts outside the Global North has enabled feminists in various spaces to critique the 'imperial march' and the 'Europology' of Western feminisms and articulate it as 'an elaboration of what is a distinctly European phenomenon into a human universal' (Oyewumi 2003: 1–3). The 'Europology' critique in Africa and Latin America (see, for instance, Lavrin 1998), emerged out of the experience of women's revolutionary challenges to colonialism, capitalism, imperialism and the counter-revolutionary insurgencies that took place from the 1960s to 1980s and within post-revolutionary transitions to neoliberalism (Alvarez 2000; Mama 1995, 1997).

It is imperative to highlight that the academy is not separate from these histories of movements and systemic restructurings. Feminism is also formed through feminists' own participation in revolutionary organisations for decolonial justice. Theory and practice are not separate; they are consistently making one another. The academy develops in relationship to the larger social formations. As black and post-colonial scholars (McKittrick 2006) with substantial histories of their own enter the metropolitan academy, they too are marked by their geopolitical origins both in the three-world schema (Wallerstein 1979) and in their negotiated feminist-black-postcolonial epistemic structure within feminism and IR. Postcolonial scholars arrive in the metropolitan academy and are expected to enter as 'outsiders' to its institutional politics as if the organisation of the academy is not already part of a global structure formed through the imbricate power relationships of the Global North and Global South. Such processes foster IR and feminism's appropriations of the geopolitical intellectual labors of postcolonial scholars and spaces of the Global South. The delinking of these relationships contributes to a silencing of knowledge as political practice making way for a neoliberal restructuring knowledge that positions us within mythical discourses of post-revolutionary, post-racial, post-feminist, and so forth.

Postcolonial scholars are often left to negotiate between the colonial erasures of the academy and the politics of survival within an 'insider–outsider' epistemic structure (for example, see Alexander 2005; Kincaid 1988; Lorde 2001). Many black and postcolonial feminists are supposed to be represented through the academy but always as 'contained units' of social relations and called on to perform Otherness. In this sense, the academy mystifies violence through conditioning scholars to perform as embodiments of their geopolitical 'homes,' (Grewal 2001; Mohanty 2003b) and through demarcating which type of body produces what type of knowledge. In other words, academic geopolitics defines and legitimises academic citizenry. The simultaneous homogenisation and segregation of scholars and scholarship within academia – either as a feminist of colour who is often immediately marginalised into one universal category of the Third World and/or as a feminist who embodies a personal experience from Other global territories considered 'out there' and separate from US political arrangements – is a systemic relationship that divides feminists (of colour, postcolonial, white, transnational, global) through the multiple geopolitical divisions of the international system and situates us in opposition to one another.

These sets of entangled social power relations are global, systemic, collective and personal, and their connections are often elided within IR, which sustains segregated and hegemonic geopolitical agendas that compete for legitimacy within IR frameworks. For example, feminist IR focuses on making women 'visible' and 'equal' within a masculinist geopolitical Order, while postcolonial IR focuses on the explicit connections of historical and contemporary racisms and classisms resulting from imperial and colonial projects. Considering postcolonial and feminist knowledges through feminisms of critical geographies provides 'new' grammars for political claims that refuse individualised readings of global politics by relinking the historical layers of personal and structural conditions that make geopolitics and feminism possible. Feminist IR and IR are in need of nuanced frameworks for addressing international, transnational and global questions that account for feminist slippages in the quest to eradicate gender violence and promote decolonial justice. Indeed, the meanings of local, national, transnational, international and global feminisms are put into question. It is not enough to argue for a feminist vanguard without putting pressure on its constitution and formation within a broader context of human geography.

FEMINISMS OF CRITICAL GEOGRAPHIES: SOLIDARITIES AND POSSIBILITIES

A postcolonial gendered framework of global politics explores global relations of power transnationally to complicate and desegregate existing taxonomies of thought within larger structures of historical, political, economic and social relations. It requires explicit attentiveness to transnational formulations of race, gender, class and sexuality that can complicate the 'discursive colonizations' (Mohanty 1991a) of geopolitical bodies and dismantle segregated frameworks of 'technologies of Empire' (Agathangelou et al. 2007). In particular, postcolonial gendered frameworks reveal how complicities and segregations within feminism and postcolonial theories continue to deterritorialise and reterritorialise global bodies within an imperial geopolitical logic (Grewal 2005). It is our aim here to push the conceptual and methodological underpinnings of gender and the postcolonial transnationally, while also attending to the problematic appropriations of these signifiers of geopolitics (see Figure 4.3).

A framework of feminisms of critical geographies makes two important interventions within hegemomic feminist and postcolonial approaches within IR. First, it problematises the politics of 'gender mainstreaming' within academia, activist and policy arenas (see Chapter 19) by asking, What are the ways in which such practices regulate bodies through discourses of development, security and rights? The ways in which logics and practices of mainstreaming reproduce colonial, racist and gender asymmetrical relations are too often overlooked. Second, it challenges masculinist objectives within postcolonial frameworks that too often centre nationalist narratives, which are 'premised on a rescued masculinity' (Morrison 1992, cited in Alexander 1994: 14) that polices gender, sexuality, race and ethnicity for national interests (Alexander 1994, 2005). The challenge of feminisms of critical geographies is to further open up global questions of violence and justice. What does it mean to think about feminist justice, to imagine a world in which women, queer communities, people of colour and the working class are not marginalised, exploited and killed in the name of a feminist global order? How do we frame projects of solidarity among feminists in an imperial context that thrives on segregation? How do we transform the politics of geopolitical containment that dictates (im)possibility through racist heteronormative patriarchies of representation? What are the ways in which we can concretise feminisms of critical geographies?

The Homeland, Aztlán/*El otro México*

... 1,950 mile-long open wound
    dividing a *pueblo*, a culture,
    running down the length of my body,
      staking fence rods in my flesh,
    splits me   splits me
       me raja   me raja

        This is my home
        This thin edge of
         barbwire.

        But this skin of the earth is seamless.
        The sea cannot be fenced,
      el mar does not stop at borders.
To show the white man what she thought of his
         arrogance,
     Yemaya blew that wire fence down ...
                       (Anzaldúa 1987)

Figure 4.3 Excerpt from 'The Homeland, Aztlán/*El otro México*'.

Considering these questions requires an engagement with geopolitical questions about feminist epistemologies of spatiality in which the knowledges of black-postcolonial-Third World feminisms are already in relationship to first world feminisms due to the organisation and social structures of the interstate system, or what we call here worldism. If spaces of IR and feminisms continue to take this interrelationship as mystified and/or rendered invisible through mainstream epistemologies, then dominant technologies of imperialism will continue to prevail. However, if feminisms and IR draw out the bodily movements (people, land, knowledge) of postcolonial feminisms and Third World historically situated subjects and expose these segregations as part and parcel of larger hegemonic histories and practices of the political economy of social relations and knowledge, then multiple modes of solidarity become possible. Feminisms of critical geographies signals worldism and geopolitical segregation as a way to disrupt dominant theorisations and methods to world problems and issues elided within hegemonic interdisciplinary studies and to 'renovate our engagements' (Alexander 2005) with who we are as subjects and movements 'international', 'transnational' and 'feminist'. It is our hope that such renovations work to dismantle structures of apartheidism within global knowledge movements and relations and create the space for deeper theorisations of gender justice.

Segregation is more than just a mere level of interpretation. It is as much about the global divisions of labor as it is about the global struggles to co-constitute the world in less violent and less segregationist manners. It is in these varied and complicated spaces of feminisms (thought and practice), which are attentive to the historic specificities and systemic connectivities of geopolitics, that justice and feminist solidarities become a possibility. The task of feminisms of critical geographies is not to be responsible for 'solving' the problems of global inequality and gender violence; rather, it is to open up the theoretical and material frames of justice that support and build multiple epistemic and ontological communities of survival and transformation. It is through the opening up of commitments to one another and negotiations of our complicities that we can continue to intervene in geopolitical foreclosures that pit us against one another in the various power struggles of global politics.

Questions for further debate

1. Some critical feminists and postcolonial theorists have argued that geography shapes feminisms and informs the ways feminists (i.e., depending on the location one occupies) understand the world and within it global power. Do you agree and/or disagree? Why?
2. According to feminist, aboriginal, and postcolonial feminist scholarship segregation is foundational to asymmetries, inequalities and racisms in global politics. Do you agree and/or disagree? Why?
3. What are the ways in which segregation continues to shape the formation of global politics?
4. How has critical feminist and postcolonial scholarship intervened in segregated logics and practices? How has such scholarship been complicit in strategies of global segregation?
5. Through the framework of desegregation that feminisms of critical geographies offer, can you think of examples of how you experience global segregation, how you participate in it and ways that you have intervened in disrupting it?

Sources for further reading and research

Agathangelou, A. M. (2010) 'Bodies of Desire, Terror and the War in Eurasia: Impolite Disruptions of (Neo) Liberal Internationalism, Neoconservatism and the "New" Imperium', *Millennium – Journal of International Studies*, 38(3): 1–30.

Chowdhry, G. and S. Nair (2004) *Power, Postcolonialism and International Relations: Reading Race, Gender and Class*, London: Routledge.

Grovogui, S. N. (1996) *Sovereigns, Quasi-Sovereigns, and Africans*, Minneapolis: University of Minnesota Press.

Mama, A. (1995) *Beyond the Masks: Race, Gender and Subjectivity*, New York: Routledge.

Turcotte, H. (2011) 'Contextualizing Petro-Sexual Violence', *Alternatives: Global, Local, Political*, 36(3): 200–20.

Notes

1 Materiality refers to the practices of the 'social' (i.e., international, global, corporeal, transnational, etc.) as 'practices' that breathe life and meaning into gendered, sexualised, racialised, classed being and relations, rather than assertions of specific sorts of practices (i.e., economic, systemic, structural, etc.) that are accorded causal priority in shaping social

relations (i.e., gendered, racialised, classed, sexualised, etc.). In addition, materiality here refers also to the production of gender, sexuality, race and class.

2 First World feminism(s) is not a unified project even when several feminists within it assume and articulate a universal set of epistemological assumptions (i.e., West, free, secular, white) against which everything else is measured and described.

3 See Agathangelou (1997), where she argues that knowledges produced in the North American context draw extensively on the works of Third World theorists to constitute their theoretical frameworks as global analytics while sustaining the work they used as either 'case studies' and/or descriptive data to support their 'global' analytical frames.

4 For further examples of such critiques, see Arat-Koç (2007), Carney (2003), DeFrancicso et al. (2003), *Incite! Women of Color Against Violence* (2006) and Mohanty (2003a, 2006).

5 For instance, black peoples from all over the world including many who are the descendants of slaves and many who are now migrating through the colonial pathways of geopolitical economic possibility are interpolated as people of colour, even when their class location in their nations of origin could mitigate against their being located within an axis of power that relegates them to the margins of first world-ism.

6 As Imam explains, Western theories 'should be criticized not *because* they are Western, but to *the extent* that, having developed in cultural, historical, class, racial and gender realities in the West, they misrepresent African realities and obscure analysis of Africa' (1997: 17). Imam suggests there is a significant relationship *and* disconnect between the epistemic and material formulations and experiences of geography, which needs further feminist examination and conversation (see also Turcotte 2011).

PART 2 ETHICS AND SUBJECTIVITY

CHAPTER 5

Ethics

Kimberly Hutchings

LEARNING OUTCOMES

Upon completion, readers should be able to:

- Understand and explain feminist critiques of mainstream paradigms in international ethics.
- Assess the strengths and weaknesses of different strands of feminist international ethics.
- Apply feminist ethical insights to international ethical issues such as war and human rights.

INTRODUCTION

The word 'ethics' has two related meanings, both of which are important for this chapter. The first is the familiar meaning of ethics as a set of substantive moral values, beliefs and practices. In this sense, ethics is about the distinctions we make, on an everyday basis, between right and wrong, asking ourselves questions such as, Is it ethical to buy fruit originating from an oppressive regime? The second meaning of ethics is more specialised, and refers to the philosophical study of the ways in which we justify our claims about right and wrong, asking questions such as, How do I know buying the fruit is or is not ethical? The purpose of this chapter is to explore how substantive international ethical issues *and* questions about the basis of ethical claims in an international context are affected by being looked at from a gender perspective.

KNOWING RIGHT FROM WRONG

Michael Walzer, one of the best known contributors to international ethical theory, made a distinction in his work between 'thick' and 'thin' morality in the international sphere (Walzer 1994). 'Thick' morality referred to moral values, beliefs and practices that were firmly located in the traditions of particular political communities, and which derived their legitimacy from community history and identity. 'Thin' morality referred to moral values, beliefs and practices that had resonance for all humanity regardless of community or culture, and derived their legitimacy from universally valid moral principles. In general, mainstream international ethical theory falls into one or other of the 'thick' or 'thin' categories. It either makes moral claims that are legitimated in relation to particular historical contexts, or that are held to be universally true across boundaries of culture and power. Another way in which this distinction is labelled is as the distinction between *communitarian* and *cosmopolitan* versions of international ethics (Brown 1992; Dower 2007: 53–119).

What do 'thick' and 'thin' theories have to say about questions of the responsibility of rich states to redistribute their wealth to poor states? Or about the obligation to intervene in countries where there are mass violations of human rights? A 'thick' response to the first question might argue that the kinds of obligation of justice we have to our fellow nationals are much stronger than those we owe to strangers. In other words, our moral obligations are relative to our national identity, therefore we are not required, as a matter of justice, to redistribute our wealth to poorer states, although we may wish to do so on grounds of charity or benevolence. A 'thick' response to the second question might be that the whole notion of 'human rights' is a Western construction that does not reflect the moral values inherent in other cultures and communities, that nations have a right to self-determination and that there should therefore be a strong presumption against intervention. In contrast, a 'thin' response to the question of international distributive justice might argue that because the welfare of all human beings matters equally, regardless of nationality, then there is an obligation on the rich to give to the poor until the point at which they become globally disadvantaged by doing so. Similarly, 'thin' responses to the second question typically argue that there are certain human rights that are universally fundamental, and that the obligation to protect those rights ought not to stop at state borders (see Figure 5.1).[1]

What is striking about these traditions, whether they take 'culture' or 'humanity' as the key ethical reference point, is that none of them explicitly refers to gender as being relevant either to moral issues of justice and rights or to the grounds and nature of moral judgement. However, if we examine these supposedly gender-free theories a little more closely it is not difficult to identify gendered logics at work. From a gendered perspective, to locate morality in culture is to run the risk of embracing cultural values that are strongly patriarchal and heteronormative, and have traditionally defined women and homosexual men as morally inferior. Once one starts to

Both of these approaches to thinking about international ethics have their roots in western philosophical traditions (Brown 2002: 38–56). Communitarianism is grounded in the ethical valuation of community that can be traced back to thinkers such as Hegel and Herder. It involves giving priority to the national/cultural or state community as both moral agent and object of moral concern in international ethics. Cosmopolitanism can be traced back to the enlightenment thinking of philosophers such as Kant and Bentham.

Strands of cosmopolitanism have set the agenda for contemporary international ethics because of their explicit universalism and there are many debates within cosmopolitanism itself, in particular, between 'deontological' and 'utilitarian' versions of moral universalism. Simply put, deontological theories regard certain principles or values as having an absolute moral status (lying is *always* wrong), whereas utilitarians assess principles and values on the basis of their consequences in particular circumstances, so that the same moral principle might have a different moral status if circumstances change (lying might be justified if it increases overall utility in a particular context).

What both deontological and utilitarian theories have in common is that they both give moral priority to individuals rather than collectives, and that they have an essentially liberal concept of the rational and disembodied moral agent (see Robinson (1999) for a useful feminist critique of communitarianism and cosmopolitanism).

Figure 5.1 Communitarianism and cosmopolitanism.

think about this then it becomes difficult to see how feminist analysis could be satisfied with the 'thick' communitarian response to how to deal with international ethical issues. For this reason, 'thin' responses to questions about ethical judgement seem more promising from a feminist point of view, since they appear to avoid the trap of embracing sexist or homophobic values as a given. However, feminist analysis has shown that the apparently gender neutral constructions of deontological or utilitarian moral theory are in practice based on a model of what it means to be human that takes male bodies and masculine characteristics (obviously not the same thing) as the norm. For thinkers such as Kant and Bentham, the human is never captured, empirically or ideally, in the pregnant or emotional human being. The way in which moral problems and solutions are formulated by 'thin' universalist moral theories tend to marginalise what is regarded as feminine. For instance, the most famous moral theory addressing the question of distributive justice of the last 30 years, John Rawls's *Theory of Justice*, did not include any consideration of justice within the family. He associated justice entirely with the masculine-dominated public sphere (Okin 1989; Rawls 1971).[2] Similarly, theories of human rights have traditionally focused on ways in which individuals are vulnerable to abuse by the state (for example, being tortured or persecuted), but paid much less attention to the ways in which individuals are vulnerable to abuses located in the private realm (for example, domestic violence including sexual violence) (Donnelly 1993).

Feminist analysis has not confined itself simply to the critique of mainstream 'thick' and 'thin' ethics, but has sought to show how bringing a gendered perspective into moral theorising can change what we privilege as being of moral significance and how we ground and justify our moral claims. The most prominent development of feminist ethical theory was prompted by the work of Carol Gilligan, *In A Different Voice: Psychological Theory and Women's Development*, and has been labelled the 'ethic of care' in contrast to 'thin' morality's 'ethic of justice' (Gilligan 1982). Gilligan was a social psychologist investigating theories about what we should count as appropriate mature moral reasoning in response to moral dilemmas. At the time she was writing, the predominant view was that the height of moral maturity was signified by a capacity for the moral agent to detach him or herself from the context of the specific moral dilemma, and make a judgement in terms of what general moral rules ought to apply to any similar situation. In empirical work, social psychologists had found that men were more likely to exhibit these kinds of characteristic. Women, in contrast, were more likely to make contextual judgements relating to the specific patterns of responsibility and obligation in which they were caught. Gilligan pointed out that the rational, detached, autonomous characteristics supposedly significant of moral maturity clearly reflected the priorities of the 'thin' tradition of moral theory and the privileging of masculine over feminine. She then argued that the supposedly inferior modes of moral reasoning more typical of women (ethic of care) were, in fact, equally reflective and sophisticated to those of an ethic of justice and should be taken as equally significant of moral maturity. For her, the ethic of care and the ethic of justice were both essential to adequate moral reasoning.

Gilligan's work inspired a whole literature on the idea of a feminist ethic of care (Browning-Cole and Coultrap-McQuin 1992; Card 1991; Held 1995, 2006). In broad terms, those feminists trying to take forward the idea of an ethic of care have sought to ground ethical value in the relations and responsibilities associated with caring practices, often exemplified by the relation between mother and child (Held 1993; Noddings 1984; Ruddick 1989). The feminist critics of the ethic of care, in contrast, tend to come from two different kinds of perspective, which in some ways (although not in all) echo the 'thin' and 'thick' positions in mainstream ethics described earlier. Some feminists have argued that care ethics risks reproducing gender stereotypes and undermining the grounds for the critique of the relegation of women to the private sphere, and have therefore sought to rework an ethic of justice along feminist lines (Benhabib 1992; Nussbaum 2000). Others have argued that care ethics is as universalising as the ethic of justice and effectively excludes the ethical significance of the experiences of different women in different social, cultural and political contexts. These critics return to the question of difference (although not simply cultural difference) as foundational to ethics (Hekman 1995; Larrabee 1993). These debates are reproduced, as we shall see later, in the specific context of feminist international ethics.

GENDERING INTERNATIONAL ETHICS

In this section, I will explore the development of feminist international ethics in terms of three trajectories: 'care ethics', 'justice ethics' and 'postmodern ethics' (Hutchings 2000, 2007a).

International feminist ethics of care

In her book, *Maternal Thinking: Towards a Politics of Peace*, Ruddick draws on the idea of an ethic of care as a central part of her argument for a feminist moral orientation in the context of international politics (Gilligan 1982; Ruddick 1989). The book involves a rejection of realist arguments as to the tragic inevitability or structural necessity of war and communitarian claims to the special ethical status of the collective group or nation. In addition it develops a critique of traditional moral justifications for war – in both utilitarian and deontological variants – as well as a positive characterisation of how a different kind of moral judgement and political practice is possible in relation to war. There are essentially two stages to Ruddick's argument. In the first stage she develops a feminist approach to moral judgement through the idea of 'maternal thinking', in the second stage she explores the implications of 'maternal thinking' for making moral judgements about war.

'Maternal thinking', according to Ruddick, 'is a discipline in attentive love', a discipline which is rooted in the demands of a particular relation of care, that between mother and child, and which reflects a particular range of metaphysical attitudes, cognitive capacities and virtues (Ruddick 1989: 123). Ruddick claims that the implication of maternal thinking is not just the rejection of the possible moral justifications for war, but also the active embracing of peace politics (Ruddick 1989: 141–59):

> The analytic fictions of just war theory require a closure of moral issues final enough to justify killing and 'enemies' abstract enough to be killable. In learning to welcome their own and their children's changes, mothers become accustomed to open-ended, concrete reflection on intricate and unpredictable spirits. Maternal attentive love, restrained and clear sighted, is ill adapted to intrusive, let alone murderous judgements of others' lives.
>
> (Ruddick 1989: 150)

From the standpoint of maternal thinking, the appropriate stance to take in ethical judgement is to attempt to build on particular experiences of the practice of care to help to identify with and take responsibility for the needs and suffering of others. Ruddick frequently cites the example of the Argentinian Mothers of the Plaza de Mayo (see Chapter 3), whose movement gradually grew to embrace concerns with children across the world who had suffered harm: 'This is not transcendent impartiality but a sympathetic apprehension of another grounded in one's own particular suffering' (Ruddick 1993: 123). This is not just a matter of 'feeling for' another's pain, but assuming an attitude of responsibility for it and therefore trying to do something about it. In addition, however, maternal thinking is sensitive to the specific contexts in which ethical dilemmas are embedded and the importance of appreciating the ethical weight of the perspectives of all parties to any dispute or conflict. For Ruddick, ethical judgement has to be on a case-by-case basis, but without ready-made principles of adjudication.

In her books, *Globalizing Care: Ethics, Feminist Theory and International Relations* (1999) and *The Ethics of Care: A Feminist Approach to Human Security* (2011), Robinson follows Ruddick in arguing for an approach to international ethics derived from 'care'. Her 'critical' care approach develops an international ethics that encompasses not only questions about the morality of war but also about international human rights, global distributive justice and security. Unlike Ruddick,

Robinson does not rely on a concept of 'maternal thinking' but more generally on the idea of care as an everyday practice and moral orientation, embedded in a number of actual contexts. Moreover, Robinson places more emphasis than Ruddick on the significance for care ethics of the broader political, social and economic context of the international sphere and the ways in which particular patterns of advantage and disadvantage, power and oppression, sameness and difference are institutionalised within it:

> An ethics of care is not about the application of a universal principle ('We all must care about all others') nor is it about a sentimental ideal ('A more caring world will be a better world'). Rather it is a starting point for transforming the values and practices of international society; thus it requires an examination of the contexts in which caring does or does not take place, and a commitment to the creation of more humanly responsive institutions which can be shaped to embody expressive and communicative possibilities between actors on a global scale.
>
> (Robinson 1999: 47–48)

Feminist critiques of an international ethics of care typically come from two perspectives: there is the 'justice' critique, which identifies problems for feminism with care ethics' abandonment of reliance on universal principle; then there is the 'postmodern' critique which argues, contrary to the justice critics, that the ethic of care remains too close to the logic of traditional ethical paradigms in the context of international politics, because it treats the feminist standpoint for judgement in an overly universalised way. Both critiques worry about the incapacity of an ethics based on an idea of care to further the goals of feminism, goals broadly conceived as those of redressing gendered inequalities of power across the international arena. Nevertheless, the arguments of justice and postmodern critics against care ethics are distinct. This will become clearer as we look at these alternative approaches in more detail.

Feminist international justice

As mentioned already, there is a longstanding feminist critique of the masculine bias of 'thin' accounts of morality in the Western tradition. Most feminist theorists take this critique seriously, but they respond to it constructively in different ways. In the case of feminist justice ethics, the response is not to abandon the universal terms of traditional moral theory, but to make them genuinely inclusive and universal. On this view, the problem with, for example, Rawls's theory of justice, is not that he thinks about justice in the wrong way but that he fails to include women's work within his thinking. The way to put this right, it is argued, is to extend the scope of his analysis and add women and the family in, but this does not involve abandoning the universal pertinence of his principles of justice. Underlying this kind of move is the concern, shared by many feminists, that to abandon the universal status of certain moral principles of justice and rights is to fall into the trap of 'thick' ethics, which will undermine the possibility of criticism of 'cultures' with moral norms that devalue women and the feminine (Benhabib 1992, 2002). But if feminists are to articulate justice ethics in a way that also does not discriminate against women and the feminine, then they clearly need to find a way of grounding moral claims in terms of justice and rights that does not rely on masculine biased accounts of moral reasoning as well as being able to be valid universally, across boundaries of culture and power.

One example of a feminist moral theory that develops this kind of universal account of ethics is the argument put forward by Martha Nussbaum in her book *Women and Human Development* (2000). Here, Nussbaum finds the grounds for certain (limited) universal ethical values and claims in a set of human 'capabilities' that she argues are foundational for the flourishing of any human life. She then uses the example of the lives of women in developing countries as a way to exemplify how the capabilities approach can be used as a kind of yardstick to critique existing practice in different national contexts and to provide fundamental principles for progress, in particular progress for women. In her argument, Nussbaum puts forward a robust defence of feminist moral universalism, but she also argues that her specific form of feminist justice ethics allows considerable space for the importance of the virtues of care and empathy and for cultural sensitivity and difference (Nussbaum 2000: 7, 70–71).

At present, according to Nussbaum, women in developing countries are particularly likely to experience their lives as subordinated to others, including the demands of patriarchal cultures and of exploitative conditions of work. For this reason, a focus on 'care' she argues is dangerous unless it is framed by an ethic of justice which limits the kinds and degrees of responsibility that carers (usually women) should be obliged to carry. 'Thick' approaches to morality, she argues, allow local norms that subordinate and harm women. Nevertheless, her particular version of moral universalism is, she claims, less prone to problems associated with other kinds of justice ethics because it does not so much elaborate a substantive set of moral principles that all must follow, but rather specifies 'human capabilities' that are inherently enabling rather than prescriptive, and that can be the ongoing subject of debate. The capabilities that Nussbaum outlines as of universal ethical significance are as follows (Nussbaum 2000: 78–81):

1. Life – ability to live out a natural life span.
2. Bodily health – ability to have good health including reproductive health, adequate nourishment, shelter.
3. Bodily integrity – freedom of movement, security from physical violation, sexual and reproductive autonomy.
4. Senses, imagination, thought – ability to use all of these fully in an educated way.
5. Emotions – ability to be attached to others, to have a capacity for love and affection.
6. Practical reason – to be able to reflect rationally, identify one's own conception of the good life and plan for it.
7. Affiliation – ability to live with others in personal relationships and social communities.
8. Other species – ability to live in relation to nature.

9. Play – ability to enjoy recreation.
10. Control over one's material and political environment – ability to participate in political choices, ability to hold property, to work on equal terms with others.

It becomes clear very quickly that the capabilities approach is ethically very demanding, in that it requires the institutionalisation of equality across a range of domains even to live up to threshold conditions. For example, the capability to live in affiliation with others is, in Nussbaum's view, fatally undermined by status-based discrimination on grounds of 'race, sex, sexual orientation, religion, caste, ethnicity, or national origin' (Nussbaum 2000: 79). Critics of Nussbaum have argued that her capabilities approach ends up being closer to traditional universalist moral theories than she herself admits. Although her argument claims to make room for 'care' and 'culture', it seems that the universalisation of certain fundamental rights trumps either of these as a source of value in Nussbaum's account. From the point of view of care feminism, Nussbaum does not pay enough attention to the distinctive virtues of care and ends up subsuming women under the more general category of humanity in a way that emphasises the masculinised norms of the Western public sphere. For postmodern feminists, Nussbaum's arguments have been accused of reifying the figure of the 'third world woman', and thus replaying a colonial move in which the situation of women is used as a means of setting up other (non-Western) cultures as backward and inferior (Ackerly 2008; Mohanty 2003b; Mohanty, Russo and Torres 1991; see also Chapter 4).

Feminist postmodern ethics

Postmodern feminists insist on the ethical significance of the fact that all women are not the same, either in virtue of being *women* or in virtue of being *human*. As has already been noted, they are suspicious of both care and justice ethics precisely because those approaches are grounded on the universalisation of either 'feminine' or 'human' qualities and attributes. This is not simply a theoretical dispute. For postmodern feminists, the prescriptive implications of care in relation to peace and of justice in relation to human rights and development have been shown to be ethically problematic for women who do not fit with standard Western liberal assumptions about either women or humans. Many feminists from the developing world have supported wars in the pursuit of struggles for decolonisation and national liberation and deny that there is a necessary connection between feminist ethics and pacifism. Similarly, many feminists in the developing worlds are wary of the liberal language of global human rights and economic development and argue that it reflects the moral priorities of an earlier Western history and is insufficiently sensitive to context. It seems, therefore, as if postmodern feminist ethics may take us back to Walzer's 'thick' morality, and the cultural specificity of both the ways we defend our moral judgements and the judgements that we make. However, this is not the case. For postmodern feminists, 'context' is not equivalent to a monolithic account of 'culture'. For postmodernists, culture and identity, like all other facets of social and political life, are sites of power relations and struggles. There is therefore always a *political* dimension to ethics, and this, according to postmodernists, is the dimension that care and justice feminists, in different ways, neglect.

For postmodern ethics it is ethical principles of respect for difference and radical democracy that are fundamental to feminism. Although they share with care and justice feminisms a commitment to challenging gendered relations of power, for postmodernists specific questions about what moral values should guide human conduct at a global level could not be satisfactorily answered until the world has changed in such a way that the voices of those currently most excluded from moral debate can be heard (Hutchings 2004; Jabri 1999; Mohanty 2003b; Spivak 1999). In the meantime, moral priority must be given to those ethical values that do most to support struggles to change the world to include the excluded, and that do least to further repress the voices of the least powerful actors in current world politics. The problem with this ethical project is that, as postmodernists themselves point out, any explicitly articulated universal ethical claim in international ethics always carries its own exclusions with it, intended or unintended. This is typified by the Universal Declaration of Human Rights, which, for example, in speaking of all human beings' fundamental right to marriage and family life, necessarily excludes those human beings who do not fit with heterosexual norms, or with the assumption of a humanity split into two genders (Butler 2004a: 102–30).

One of the feminist ethical theorists who has attempted to address what postmodern ethics implies in an international context is Judith Butler. Focusing on the concept of universal human rights, Butler has shown how the concept of the human in human rights, by setting up a norm of what it means to be human, consistently operates so as to situate certain categories of people as 'less than' human, rendering their lives in crucial respects 'unliveable' and 'ungrievable' (Butler 2004a: 225–27; 2004b: 18–49). Thus she directly challenges Nussbaum's claim that it is through an inclusive account of what it means to be human that a genuinely universal international ethics can be articulated as a yardstick for the judgement of practice. At the same time, Butler does not advocate the abandonment of the idea of universal rights, but rather argues that the meaning of 'universal' should always be open to challenge and renegotiation, and that we should never assume that our claims to universality actually live up to their promise (2004a: 33):

> There are no obituaries for the war casualties that the United State inflicts, and there cannot be. If there were to be an obituary, there would have to have been a life, a life worth noting, a life worth valuing and preserving, a life that qualifies for recognition.
> (Butler 2004b: 34)

This quotation, in which Butler reflects on the 2003 war following the US and allied invasion of Iraq, recalls Ruddick's argument about the ease with which militarist and just war theorists dismiss the value of enemy lives and suggests some overlap between postmodern and care ethics in the emphasis on the problems of exclusion inherent in both 'thin' and 'thick' moralities. Unlike Ruddick, however, it is not clear that postmodern ethics could ever endorse pacifism as such, or the idea that there is a definable set of virtues that are morally superior (see Figure 5.2). Somewhat paradoxically, postmodern ethics is universalist in its orientation towards

Contemporary discussions of the ethics of war tend to be carried out in relation to the framework of Just War theory, which has its origins in Christian thinking about war and peace during the Roman Empire. In the twentieth century, Just War theory was secularised and incorporated into international law. Below is an account of some of the key criteria that Just War theory uses to decide on whether a war is just *ad bellum* (in terms of the reasons for going to war in the first place) and *in bello* (in terms of the ways war is conducted once it has started) (see Peach (1994) and Sjoberg (2006) for feminist re-workings of traditional Just War theory):

Justice ad bellum

1. Just cause – e.g., self-defence by a state in response to unprovoked aggression (the only uncontested just cause in international law); protecting the innocent (the reason given for recent humanitarian interventions).
2. Legitimate authority – war must be carried out by an actor that has the legitimate right to use violence. States (e.g., UK) or state-based organisations (e.g., UN) are the only legitimate authorities recognised in international law. However, many national groups have argued that they have the legitimate authority to pursue a project of self-determination through violence.
3. Last resort – all reasonable alternatives to the use of war should have been exhausted.

Justice in bello

1. Proportionality – the violent means used in war should not outweigh in their effects the good that their use is supposed to bring about.
2. Discrimination – only combatants may be targeted not civilians.

Figure 5.2 Just War theory.

giving moral priority to the excluded in general, but sees this universalism as always failing. For postmodern ethics, ethical priorities will differ depending on context, so that there is (and ought to be) no feminist consensus on the ethics of war or the nature of fundamental human rights.

CONCLUSION

It is clear from the discussion in this chapter that feminist ethical theories give different accounts of how we justify our moral views and also have different implications for questions of moral right and wrong in international politics. Nevertheless, all of the theories have in common dissatisfaction with standard moral theories of a 'thin' or 'thick' kind. In addition, whatever their differences, feminist ethical theories share the view that taking account of gender shifts our ethical horizons when we try to think about issues to do with the ethics of war, human rights or distributive justice. There are feminists that believe war can never be just from a feminist perspective and feminists that believe that it can. But if you examine the arguments feminists make for and against the morality of war then you find a *different* set of reference points than you find in traditional debates over Just War theory. Typically, these reference points take the gendered underpinnings and effects of war as relevant to our judgement of it, and draw on specifically feminist values to make their case one way or the other (Hutchings 2011; Peach 1994; Sjoberg 2006). In the case of human rights, whether feminists end up endorsing the notion of ethical universals or not, the lens of gender opens up the limitations of mainstream accounts of the 'human', criticising false claims to the universality of certain types of vulnerability, and thereby pushing for ideas of human rights to be reworked in ways that accommodate the lives of those gendered feminine in the international sphere (Ackerly 2008; Mackinnon 2006; Peterson 1990; Robinson 2003). In relation to distributive justice, whether feminists are for or against international development discourses, they transform mainstream ethical debates by foregrounding the way that divisions of productive and reproductive labour, and the remuneration, or lack of it, of different kinds of labour, is fundamentally gendered. This can lead not only to the broadening of theories of distributive justice to include recognition of unpaid caring labour, but also draws attention to the ethical value in the virtues and practices inherent in what is often dismissed as 'women's work' (Held 2006; Robinson 1999, 2006, 2011).

Questions for further debate

1. Is the issue of abortion morally equivalent in the UK and in India?
2. In what ways is communitarianism gendered?
3. Is Nussbaum's account of human capabilities genuinely universal?
4. Assess the strengths and weaknesses of the feminist ethic of care.
5. Are postmodernists just ethical relativists?

Sources for further reading and research

Butler, J. (2004b) *Precarious Life: The Powers of Mourning and Violence*, London: Verso.

Held, V. (ed.) (1995) *Justice and Care: Essential Readings in Feminist Ethics*, Boulder, CO: Westview Press.

Mohanty, C. T. (2003) *Feminism without Borders: Decolonizing Theory, Practicing Solidarity*, London and Durham, NC: Duke University Press.

Robinson, F. (2011) *The Ethics of Care: A Feminist Approach to Human Security*, Philadelphia, PA: Temple University Press.

Sjoberg, L. (2006) *Gender, Justice and the Wars in Iraq: A Feminist Reformulation of Just War Theory*, Lanham, MD: Rowman & Littlefield.

Notes

1 All these examples do actually occur in the literature. For an overview of the debates in which we find these 'thick' and 'thin' arguments, see Brown (2002: 115–211).

2 It is worth noting that Rawls himself did not see his theory of justice as directly translatable to the international sphere. In his theory of international justice, *Law of the Peoples*, Rawls concedes some ground to 'thick' arguments and the rights of peoples to collective autonomy, although arguing for certain universal human rights (Martin and Reidy 2006).

CHAPTER 6

Environmental politics and ecology

Emma A. Foster[1]

■ **LEARNING OUTCOMES**

Upon completion, readers should be able to:

- Demonstrate an understanding of the policy implications related to gendering 'nature'.
- Identify and problematise the essentialism and universalism that underpins the logic of environmentalism.
- Consider new ways to conceptualise gender and ecology.

INTRODUCTION

> The earth is my sister: I love her daily grace, her silent daring, and how loved I am, how we admire this strength in each other, all that we have lost, all that we have suffered, all that we know: we are stunned by this beauty, and I do not forget: what she is to me, what I am to her.
>
> (Susan Griffin 1978)

'No Compromise in the Defense of Mother Earth!' (*Earth First!* motto)

Ecologism and environmentalism[2] are social/political movements that have as their main objective the protection of the natural environment. As such, ecologists and environmentalists (also known as 'greens'), to varying degrees, seek to challenge existing economic, political and social organisation, typified by industrialisation, urbanisation and economic growth, in favour of more environmentally friendly ways of living. It is commonly believed that the movement originated in the 1960s, with the publication of the marine biologist Rachel Carson's seminal work *Silent Spring* (1962). By the 1970s environmental concerns became prominent within international politics (discussed at more length later in this chapter) as questions were being raised by highly regarded scientists and professionals about the rate of economic growth and population growth in relation to the finite resources of the Earth. Overall, environmentalism/ecologism and environmental politics are predominantly concerned with the relationship between humankind and the natural environment.

The opening quotations demonstrate the gendered symbolism attached to conceptions of the 'natural' environment which work to make sense of our relationship with the 'natural' environment as gendered bodies. In other words, both the self-proclaimed ecological feminist Susan Griffin and the radical environmental movement *Earth First!* gender nature as female; as a sister and mother, respectively. In fact, with regards to the latter it is not uncommon in a variety of cultures, both Western and non-Western, for nature to be referred to as Mother Earth/Nature. Further, the gendered sentiments outlined here offer a relational understanding of feminised nature. First, as a female sibling, who should be mutually respected and who has suffered a shared oppression/exploitation with embodied women and, second, as a mother who needs to be protected by her sons, in other words by embodied men.

In this chapter, I explore how feminising the natural world has impacted on the environmental movement and contemporary international environmental policy. First, I discuss the link made between women and nature. Second, I engage with UN environmental policies and how these have explicitly and implicitly been informed by the women–nature nexus. Third, I outline how women have been targeted specifically as saviours, problems and victims in relation to environmental degradation (Bretherton 1998; Foster 2011). Finally, I consider an environmental politics whereby these gendered categories are questioned, through the gender, environment, development (GED) approach, and destabilised, through the concept of queer ecology (Sandilands 1997, 2005, 2008).

THE WOMAN–NATURE NEXUS AND ENVIRONMENTAL POLICY

As indicated earlier, nature or the environment has long been personified as feminine, most often in a maternal form as a mother. The Roman and Greek civilisations worshipped the female deities *Terra* and *Gaia* (respectively), both of which are considered early personifications of Mother Earth, with the latter being reimagined in 1970s radical green philosophy through what was termed the Gaia hypothesis (Lovelock 1979). In addition, the personification of nature as a mother or a goddess can be seen in non-Western cultures, such as the *Pachamama* in Andean culture and *Bhumi* in Hindu culture. As such, this idea of Mother Earth has been entrenched into the popular imaginary.

Given the cultural currency of the Mother Earth concept, many ecologists and environmentalists have embraced the personification as a framework to pursue their objectives. As already mentioned the radical environmentalist group *Earth First!* use the idea of defending mother earth as their primary 'mission statement' and the radical ecologist James Lovelock put forward the Gaia Hypothesis in 1979 (see Figure 6.1).

However, the group of environmentalists who embraced this metaphor most emphatically were, perhaps unsurprisingly, the ecological feminists.

Ecofeminism

Ecological feminism, also referred to as ecofeminism, is a fractured and diverse movement and as such it is more accurate to talk of ecofeminisms (plural). Indeed, ecofeminism appears to replicate the divisions within feminism, largely forming around three different strands: liberal, radical and socialist. Liberal ecofeminists simply seek to challenge and revise laws and regulations that concern 'women' and the 'environment'. Radical ecofeminists (also labelled affinity ecofeminists to mark their affinity with nature), consider women to hold a privileged standpoint and relationship with the natural world that is founded in a biological and essential relationship with 'nature', most notably because of the processes of childbirth and motherhood. In light of this, radical ecofeminists point to masculine driven social, political and economic traditions (patriarchy) as foundational and accountable for current environmental degradation (for example, Collard and Contrucci, 1988). Similarly, socialist or social ecofeminists (for example, Mies and Shiva, 1993) recognise patriarchy as foundational to environmental ills. However, they tend to focus on economic inequalities, highlighting both capitalism and patriarchy as the dual systems that depend on the joint exploitation of the environment and women. As such, socialist/ social ecofeminists regard the relationship between women and nature to have been generated from their joint oppression and exploitation under systems of patriarchal capitalism and, thus, extend their analysis to include issues of class and ethnicity.

Overall, despite their differences, Sachs (1997) has noted three ways in which ecofeminisms overlap:

* the focus on women's relationship with nature
* the connections between the domination of women and the domination of nature
* the role of women in solving ecological problems.

Generally, ecofeminisms, as well as other ecological movements, have celebrated the link between women and nature. However, this link is arguably problematic for a number of reasons, three of which I shall recount here.

The entire range of living matter on Earth from whales to viruses and from oaks to algae could be regarded as constituting a single living entity capable of maintaining the Earth's atmosphere to suit its overall needs and endowed with faculties and powers far beyond those of its constituent parts ... [Gaia can be defined] as a complex entity involving the Earth's biosphere, atmosphere, oceans, and soil; the totality constituting a feedback of cybernetic systems which seeks an optimal physical and chemical environment for life on this planet (Lovelock 1979: 9).

Figure 6.1 The Gaia Hypothesis.

First, the supposed relationship between nature and women has historically led to women being excluded from the public sphere. Underpinned by the legacy of Cartesian dualism, which informs the basis of stratified binaries used in language, 'woman' and her relationship to nature (and the body) has been constructed as subordinate to man and his relationship to culture (and the mind). For example, women have historically been thought of as too close to nature (read: primitive and emotional) to participate in politics and the public sphere more broadly. As such, to re-invoke these ideas, even in the affirmative way that ecofeminists do, tends to solidify this link which has been used to exclude women from certain types of political, economic and social participation. Second, the links drawn between femininity, motherhood and nature work to suggest that women have essential characteristics (for a good summary of essentialist understandings of gender refer to the introduction of this edition). In other words, it suggests that women are naturally more caring due to their biological/reproductive role as mothers, and therefore best placed to 'save the natural world' from environmental degradation or destruction (Braidotti et al. 1994). Essentialism is problematic as, by casting gendered behaviour as natural/biological, gendered bodies are constrained and constructed to behave in particular ways at the risk of marginalisation. Moreover, a behaviour that is constructed as biological is rendered immutable and, therefore, the social relations that have been derived from these discourses of natural gendered behaviour, whereby women, by and large, have been subordinated, are also considered to be part of the natural order.

Finally, essentialism works to over generalise the experiences of women, which leads to the final critique, of universalism. The argument that women have a special bond with the natural world disregards other identity intersections such as culture, age, sexuality, class and geographical location. Further, this implies that men do not have the same propensity to care for the natural world (Leach 1992). The essentialism, universalism and gender dichotomies that underpin the logic of ecofeminist thinking, and environmentalism/ecologism more generally, are demonstrative of heteronormativity (i.e., the privileging of heterosexuality in society). This is because the gender roles ascribed through ecological thought tend to reproduce notions of maternal, passive, heterosexual femininity and aggressive, protective, heterosexual masculinity. The feminised Earth, after all, is personified as a mother (or sister) and, as such, constructed in a relational role within a heterosexual family unit (Sandilands 1997).

Despite these concerns, gendered assumptions, harking back to ideas about Mother Earth and earth mothers, have arguably informed environmental politics and policies (for a good summary of ecofeminism and policy, see Buckingham 2004), in part due to the entrenchment of these ideas within many cultures across the world. As such, the next sections turn to look at international environmental policy and gender.

International environmental policy

In light of growing environmental concerns during the 1960s, the first international conference tasked with finding strategies to mitigate environmental degradation was held in 1972. The 1972 UN Conference on the Human Environment (more commonly known as the Stockholm Conference) led to the creation of the United Nations Environment Programme (UNEP), which was the body charged with coordinating international environmental efforts, and the production of the Stockholm Declaration and the Plan of Action. The Stockholm Declaration and the Plan of Action, although non-binding, led to environmental concerns being placed higher up the international agenda and influenced later international negotiations on environmental issues.

What the Stockholm Conference failed to do was reconcile the (inter)national desire for economic development with environmental sustainability (Rich 1994: 82). As a result, the UN set up the World Commission on Environment and Development (WCED) – also known as the Brundtland Commission – to address this problem. The Brundtland Commission produced a document entitled *Our Common Future* (1987), which outlined the concept of sustainable development. Sustainable development is defined as 'development that meets the needs of the present without compromising the ability of future generations to meet their own needs' (1987: 43). This new concept, although thought to be unachievable by many ecologists and environmentalists who feel that economic development and environmental sustainability cannot be reconciled, informed perhaps the most important UN environmental conference and multilateral agreement on environmental degradation to date – namely the United Nations Conference on Environment and Development (UNCED, also known as the Rio Earth Summit) and *Agenda 21*.

Agenda 21[3] remains the guiding plan of action for securing sustainable development and is based around four key chapters. Since 1992, *Agenda 21* and UNCED have been reviewed in subsequent conferences – in New York in 1997 (Rio +5), in Johannesburg in 2002 (World Summit on Sustainable Development), and, most recently, in 2012 at Rio +20 (which, in light of the economic crisis, turned its attention to green banking). What is interesting about *Agenda 21*, unlike the Stockholm Plan of Action which preceded it, was that it focused on gender and dedicated an entire chapter to the role of women in sustainable development.

Women and environmental policy

Underpinned by the Women, Environment, Development (WED)[4] approach and based in ecofeminist rhetoric, women's involvement in the preparatory process leading up to UNCED was fairly substantial. An international women's meeting was held in Miami in 1991, entitled the *World Women's Congress for a Healthy Planet*, and was attended by representatives from all over the world, from a number of disciplines and organisations. This produced the document *Women's Action Agenda 21*, which 'outlined what needs to be done in order to avert the global environmental holocaust' (Braidotti et al. 1994: 2). In addition, parallel to UNCED, women organised the separate forum *Planeta Femea*. Here, they presented a summary of the *Women's Action Agenda 21*. This document highlighted that women are the main victims of poverty and environmental degradation, that industrialisation has affected the health of women and their families, that free market capitalism is the root of environmental damage and that the relationship between developmental and environmental crises was a consequence of militarism, nuclear threat, growing economic inequalities, violation of human rights and the subordination of women (Braidotti et al. 1994: 5).

Critics (ibid.) have argued that the WED and ecofeminist activities prior to and during UNCED were problematic in that they upheld dualistic gender binaries and universaled 'women's concerns', along the normalised lines of earth mothers, mothers and peace (see Figure 6.2). This is notable through the separation between the 'male-stream' and 'female' derived *Agenda 21* documents and conferences surrounding the sustainable development debate.

These discourses, which normalise the women/nature relationship, typified through WED and the ecofeminist approach outlined earlier, rather than being absented from *Agenda 21*, were in fact granted a form of legitimacy. However, how much that had to do with the efforts of the women lobbyists and how much it was due to the uptake of normalised discourses of gender is questionable. It is also important to note that, even though *Agenda 21* explicitly notes that women should be involved in environmental decision making, and even in the context of wider gender mainstreaming efforts in the UN (see Chapter 19) women continue to be underrepresented in the higher echelons of environmental policymaking organisations like the UN Framework Convention on Climate Change (UNFCCC) (WEDO 2013).

In addition, throughout the *Agenda 21* document women (along with children) are considered to be the main victims of environmental degradation. Alongside these gendered constructions, a further construction of women, as exacerbating environmental problems, primarily through reproduction, and consequently population growth, was also implicitly highlighted and received direct attention in subsequent conferences such as the 1994 International Conference on Population and Development (ICPD – also known as the Cairo Conference).

Involved in the processes leading up to the 1992 UN Conference, Rosi Braidotti et al. commented:

As the UNCED process unfolded the two of us who attended the global forum ... became convinced that even though the women participating had achieved an unprecedented common position critical to the dominant development model and visions for the future, at *Planeta Femea* they did not always avoid the dangers of reproducing patterns of domination, dualism and the reversal of old hierarchies in the process (1994: 5).

And that:

[T]here was a masked tendency to emphasize commonalities between women, resulting in an implicitly essentialist position – women as closer to nature than men – as the basis for a collective decision. Some women did see themselves as better environmental managers than men, and as privileged knowers about the environment, but this position was not propagated in a naive way, rather there was a more or less tacit assumption that women see themselves as nurturers of the planet, as people who 'care' (1994: 104).

Figure 6.2 Gender essentialism at UNCED.

SUBJECTS AND/OR OBJECTS OF ENVIRONMENTAL POLICY

To frame the debate on the construction of women in environmental policymaking it is useful to think about whether women are considered subjects or objects of policy (Bretherton 1998: 88). An object of policy can be read as someone or something which policy is made for – which the policy targets. A subject of policy is regarded as someone who engages in the policymaking process. Within *Agenda 21* women are constructed simultaneously as both subjects and objects of policy, and these constructions have been based on a number of essentialist and problematic gendered assumptions.

Women and nature: a privileged episteme?

In his introductory comments at the Rio Earth Summit, Maurice Strong (the then Executive Director of UNEP) commented on the 'special relationship' women have to the environment (Bretherton 1998: 89). Strong reinforced the idea that women have a better understanding of, and higher propensity to care for, the environment than men. As such, this belief informed the *Agenda 21* document insofar as it called on women to be involved in decision-making processes related to the environment. Therefore, this supposed special knowledge (or privileged episteme) women were considered to have about the natural world was used to justify the inclusion of (some) women as subjects of policy.

The special position or vital role inscribed on female bodies throughout the UN sustainable development discourses can be read in a number of ways. One reading of 'special' concerns a fundamental assumption that women have a privileged knowledge of the natural world due to their 'natural' inclination towards motherhood or their specific forms of labour which have traditionally led them to work closer to the land. For example, throughout the sustainable development discourses, women's participation is called for on the basis that they have particular knowledge regarding environmental issues and can, thus, offer technical insights.

In addition, women are considered to have knowledge of the implications of unsustainable environmental practices due to their assumed investment in future generations. Women's bodies are constructed as an interface between present and future generations through their reproductive capacity to bear children. Although this is not explicit, the absence of 'men's' concerns in the statements shown in Figure 6.3 indicates something generally 'female/maternal' about the desire to sustain future generations. In sum, the narrative implies that it is mothers who can best understand and care for the environment as they are biologically programmed to care and nurture; mothers are at the forefront of (pro)creating future generations.

It is often noted as evidence in support of women's privileged knowledge and propensity to care for the environment that women tend to be heavily involved in grassroots environmental activism. The most oft-cited example of this is the Chipko movement, a largely female-populated movement that sought to prevent deforestation in India. However, it has since been interpreted 'not as evidence of women's closeness to nature but as a struggle for material resources in the context of

Women have a vital role in environmental management and development. Their full participation is therefore essential to achieve sustainable development (UNCED 1992).

To increase the proportion of women decision makers, planners, technical advisers, managers and extension workers in environment and development fields (UNCED 1992).

Young people and women around the world have played a prominent role in galvanizing communities into recognizing their responsibilities to future generations (Rio +5 1997).

We are committed to ensuring that women's empowerment, emancipation and gender equality are integrated in all the activities encompassed within Agenda 21, the Millennium Development Goals and the Plan of Implementation of the Summit (Johannesburg Declaration 2002).

Figure 6.3 Examples of UN policy that highlight women as subjects of policy.

gender-ascribed natural resource dependence; and women's limited opportunities to out-migrate as compared with men' (Leach 2007: 75). Further counter narratives dismissing and problematising the 'privileged episteme' argument suggest that 'women' do not present a special episteme vis-à-vis the environment and that gender differentiation regarding ecological knowledge is marginal or inconclusive (Momsen 2004: 113–16). Indeed, as Leach notes '[w]omen's roles in managing and using natural resources are exaggerated if men's roles are ignored; indeed women's relationship with the environment may appear "special" only because men's does not appear at all' (1992: 16).

Reproduction, population and sustainable development

The link between environmental degradation and population growth is made by many responsible for, and/or foundational to, the UN response to population and sustainable development. Many ecologists/environmentalists understand population growth to be a key contributor to environmental harm as too many people will mean the Earth's carrying capacity will be surpassed, leading to resource shortages and pollution (Ehrlich and Ehrlich 1990: 38). Contrariwise, critics such as Frank Furedi (1997: 143) critically point out that the constructed link between environmental degradation and population growth is oversimplistic and works to reinvent a Malthusian[5] paranoia.

The 1994 ICPD, echoing *Agenda 21*, highlighted the 'common-sense' notion that population regulation is necessary to relieve and avoid environmental trauma. The directives outlined at the ICPD, and subsequent population and development conferences focus on gender relations, or rather the central role women have to play in the reproductive process. With regards to the focus on women, directives typified by the ICPD have indeed been open to much criticism, principally for ignoring the roles of men in issues of reproduction (Morrell 2005: 84) and for placing too much responsibility on to 'women's roles', to such an extent that 'she' becomes a scapegoat for the apparent ills of population growth (Bretherton 1998). The latter is particularly true in relation to women of the Global South who are often constructed as 'over-libidinous' and 'over-reproductive' in this context. In addition, the policy informing agreements related to population growth and sustainable development are premised on very normalised and Western-centric understandings of gender, family models and heterosexual relations (Foster 2011). In this construction, women, particularly women of the Global South, are rendered objects of policy.

Victims of environmental degradation

International environmental policy often perpetuates the view that women are disproportionately affected by environmental degradation. The view that women are the main victims of environmental degradation is premised on a number of factors. For instance, poverty is considered a key factor in preventing successful attempts towards adaptation in response to environmental crises/natural disasters. Women make up a high proportion of those in poverty and, as such, women are considered to be disproportionality affected by these disasters. In addition, women are often regarded as the primary caregivers of a family and therefore responsible for the collection of fuel and production of food. These subsistence activities are undermined by environmental degradation as 'the fuel wood gatherer [has to walk] ever-further to fulfil her roles in a deforesting landscape' (Leach 2007) and climate change may affect subsistence farming. This view of women as victims of environmental degradation is embedded in *Agenda 21* (see Figure 6.4) and continues to be influential in contemporary environmental policy.

However, this construction of women as victims has been problematised considerably within feminist scholarship. It is arguable that the construction of women as victims undermines women's agency as it is transferred to (male) protectors (for a good discussion of the victim/protector binary see Chapter 21). In fact, the discourse of 'saving Mother Earth' present in many environmental narratives indicates that the feminised victim needs to be protected by the masculine guardian (Collard and Contrucci 1988). In addition, the 'women as victims' logic is problematic, taking the example outlined earlier, because victimisation operates, in environmental discourses and policies, through stereotypical understandings of 'third world womanhood'. However, women in developing countries, like women in developed countries or women in general, cannot be universalised as having the same experiences and the same objectives. Neither can they be considered to share the same relationship with the natural environment (Foster 2011). Finally, another problem with the victimisation of women in relation to environmental degradation is that it

Countries should take urgent measures to avert the ongoing rapid environmental and economic degradation in developing countries that generally affects the lives of women and children in rural areas suffering drought, desertification and deforestation, armed hostilities, natural disasters, toxic waste and the aftermath of the use of unsuitable agro-chemical products (*Agenda 21* 1992).

Figure 6.4 Example of UN policy that highlights women as objects of policy.

undermines the complex ways in which men and women, and gender relations more broadly, are affected by environmental degradation through patterns of migration, public health and changes to the economy.

GENDER, ENVIRONMENT AND DEVELOPMENT AND QUEER ECOLOGY

As we have seen, environmentalism, ecologism and international environmental politics are saturated by gendered discourses. Given these discourses are so prolific in shaping environmentalism/ecologism, and given these discourses are contradictory in the sense that they both privilege and undermine femininity, it is important at this juncture to consider more useful ways to understand the relationship between humans and the natural world which mitigate some of the problems outlined above.

The GED approach works as a corrective to the criticisms directed at the WED approach. Rosi Braidotti (1994) noted above for her concerns regarding the essentialism informing WED and Melissa Leach (1992, 2007) are the main proponents of the GED approach which seeks to apply 'the perspectives of gender analysis … in the environmental domain' (2007: 74). Consequently, GED scholars focus on both men and women and the natural world from a perspective that men, women, gender relations and the natural world are dynamic and ever changing. Moreover, this approach focuses on how the differences between women, based on age, income, geographical location, ethnicity among other identity intersections, shapes subsequent relations to the natural environment; thereby undermining the universalising tendencies of WED and highlighting how other factors, such as changes to one's economic or kinship position, may alter relationships with the environment.

The GED approach is a practical approach to understanding the human–nature relationship. Another, more theoretical approach, to understanding the natural environment without drawing on gender normative constructions is queer ecology. Queer ecology is a form of analysis that looks at the relationship between the organisation of sexuality and ecology. Queer ecologists argue that the exploitation of nature is located within heteronormativity as concepts of 'love' and care are restrained to heterosexual kinship ties. This being the case, the main reasons human's wish to preserve (some of) the natural world is based in their desire to sustain themselves and future generations – (re)produced through (hetero)sex. Queer ecologists, by the same token, note that undermining heteronormative ethics of care would work to extend that care to those not biologically related or even species related. For example, queer ecologist Catriona Sandilands has linked HIV/AIDS to the notion of localised environmental damage. She notes that, care for those suffering from HIV/AIDS, unlike the maternal care essentialised through environmentalism/ecologism, is often undertaken by those who share an affinity with the HIV/AIDS sufferer, rather than by biological family members (2005). This form of care is denaturalised and undermines biological links and gendered assumptions. Sandilands argues that this form of care can be transposed to localised environmental illness/degradation.

CONCLUSION

Environmentalism has become increasingly prominent within international policy-making activity. The environmentalism adopted at international level, namely in the 'watered-down' concept of sustainable development, has brought with it gender logics that feminise the Earth and make assumptions about the relationships women (as a homogenised/coherent group) and men have with the natural environment. It has been argued here that these gender logics are problematic, even though they are used to, sometimes, justify women as subjects of policymaking. I concluded by recounting some feminist responses to environmental politics which work to undermine gender logics in the form of GED and queer ecology. Perhaps, returning to Susan Griffin's poem, quoted at the beginning of this chapter, rather than thinking of the Earth as a sister, there may be ecological advantages to queering the love and solidarity recounted here.

Questions for further debate

1. What is the value, if any, of associating women with nature in relation to environmental politics and policymaking?
2. What are the problems with emphasising the woman–nature link in environmental theory and practice?
3. How useful is a GED framework for understanding issues of gender and the environment?
4. How far is a queer ecology approach useful for re-contextualising relations between humans and the natural environment?
5. What do you think a *Queer Agenda 21* would look like?

Sources for further reading and research

Bretherton, C. (1998) 'Global Environmental Politics: Putting Gender on the Agenda?', *Review of International Studies*, 24(1): 85–100.

Foster, E. A. (2011) 'Sustainable Development: Problematising Normative Constructions of Gender within Global Environmental Governmentality', *Globalisations*, 8(2): 135–49.

Leach, M. (2007) 'Earth Mother Myths and Other Ecofeminist Fables: How a Strategic Notion Rose and Fell', *Development and Change*, 38(1): 67–85.

Mies, M. and V. Shiva (1993) *Ecofeminism*, London: Zed Books.

Sandilands, C. (1997) 'Mother Earth, the Cyborg and the Queer: Ecofeminism and (More) Questions of Identity', *NWSA Journal*, 9(3): 18–40.

Notes

1 I would like to extend thanks to Roxana Raileanu, Safiyya Saeed and Paula Stoleru for their research assistance relating to this chapter.

2 Throughout this chapter I have used the terms ecologism and environmentalism interchangeably. However, it is important to note that, although they share much commonality, ecologism more often seeks radical changes in order to preserve the natural environment whereas environmentalism tends to be more reformist and conservative in its environmental agenda.

3 This chapter is largely focused on the overarching multilateral environmental negotiations relating to sustainable development in general. However, it is important to note that there have been many international negotiations and agreements that are focused on specific environmental problems such as the Convention on International Trade in Endangered Species of Wild Fauna and Flora (1973), the Montreal Protocol (1987) on Ozone Depletion, the Basel Convention (1989) on Hazardous Waste, the Biodiversity Convention (1992) and various negotiations and agreements on climate change, which has dominated the international environmental agenda since the 1990s, most notably the Kyoto Protocol (1997) and Copenhagen negotiations (2009).

4 The women and development (WED) approach is a feminist approach to development. Feminist approaches to development include, the women in development approach (WID), the women and development approach (WAD), and the gender and development approach (GAD) – among others. The WED approach, unlike the others listed, sought to look at the environment and development specifically in the context of increasing concerns about environmental degradation in the 1980s and 1990s.

5 Malthusianism is a theory derived from the work of Thomas Malthus. Malthus, working at the end of the eighteenth century, argued that population growth would lead to food shortages. Malthus was one of the first thinkers to problematise population growth.

CHAPTER 7

Body politics: Gender, sexuality and human rights

Jill Steans

▌ LEARNING OUTCOMES

Upon completion, readers should be able to:

- Explain how debates over universalism versus cultural relativity intersect with discussions about human rights.
- Account for the major conventions and documents relating to the protection of women's human rights.
- Present a compelling argument about whether the language of human rights and human rights convention is useful to LGBT activist groups and individuals.

▌ INTRODUCTION

In distinctive ways, all the contributors to this book interrogate conceptions of the body embedded in gendered narratives in International Relations (the academic discipline) and 'international relations' (concrete policies and practices in world politics). This chapter also focuses on the body, this time in relation to international human rights discourse and practice. The chapter is centrally concerned with *language*, specifically, the tension between claims made in the name of specific cultural, ethnic, religious or national groups and claims made in the name of individuals, which employ the liberal language of autonomous subjects. The chapter employs the term 'body politics' in two usages, which are set out in the first section. The second section concentrates on the politics surrounding women's human rights and the right to bodily autonomy and control over sexuality and reproductive choice specifically. In the third section, this discussion of contestation in regard to sexuality and human right is extended to Lesbian, gay, bi-sexual and transgender (LGBT) issues.

BODY POLITICS

The 'body' might refer to a physical, corporeal body. In contemporary social and political theory, the work of Michel Foucault on the body as a site of politics – of intervention, discipline, regulation and resistance – has become increasingly influential. The appropriation of Foucault's ideas by feminists is not uncontroversial. Nevertheless, many contemporary feminist theorists regard Foucault's conception of the body as a cultural construct and his treatment of the relations between power, sexuality and the body, as helpful in developing a critique of essentialist conceptions of sex and gender (Butler 1993). As Laura Shepherd argues (in Chapter 3), the body has conventionally been understood as natural, but is interwoven with and constitutive of systems of meaning, signification and representation. That is to say, the body is social and, moreover, is a plural and culturally mediated form.

The term 'body' might also be employed in analogy to describe a political and territorial entity – a nation-state – or more specifically to describe the 'sovereign' (government) and the citizens of a politically defined entity, as in the 'body politic', or in a less precise sense to describe any collective founded on seemingly common understandings of how social relations between its constitutive members should be organised.[1] The term 'body politics' can thus be used in relations to struggles around conceptions and meanings of gendered and sexualised bodies and, here, 'the body' can refer to either a collective – national, cultural or religious – entity or an individual, autonomous body, as in liberal rights discourse.

Insofar as gender is constructed it follows that there can be no 'essence' to gender or, put another way, the gendered body is not 'natural'. Instead, gender is better understood in terms of ideology or discourse that serves to legitimise certain forms of social organisation and also to justify political interventions. As will be elaborated presently, the gendered body is very much a site of intervention and regulation by the state. At the same time, gender is necessarily fluid and changing. Indeed, a major point of disagreement among contemporary feminist theorists is the degree to which gender is 'fixed' within the broader political and legislative framework of any given state or within the social structures and social practices of any given society.

Contestation over the meaning of gender and gendered bodies is not confined within the boundaries of discrete political and cultural entities, such as states and nations, but is increasingly internationalised. Non-governmental organisations (NGOs) and human rights activists in varied contexts, often contest claims made in the name of nation, culture or religion communities, arguing such claims might and often do violate the rights of individual members of those same groups. This is evident in regard to women's rights and is increasingly manifest in struggles for

LGBT rights. Even in countries in which human rights discourse is not securely embedded in domestic legal systems or prominent in public discourse, human rights conventions and regimes are invoked by NGOs and sometimes individual activists to challenge discriminatory practices and hold states to account. Increasingly NGOs and advocacy groups are not only framing their demands in the language of human rights, but are often directly involved in monitoring and – sometimes – implementing human rights conventions in specific countries.

And yet, even as human rights appear to be gaining near universal acceptance, it is important to recognise that human rights are constructed rather than 'natural' or 'God given', and thus human rights are not 'universal' by their very nature (see Figure 7.1). Claims that people are bearers of human rights continue to be contested, along with issues regarding the proper relationship between the individual and the state and the role of international law in regard to the practice of sovereign, bounded states. As Seyla Benhabib (2004) has noted, our fate as late-modern individuals is, it seems, to be caught up in a permanent tug of war between the vision of the universal and the attachments of the particular; these struggles are played out in the realm of human rights.

Struggles for human rights and contestation of specific rights serves to cast doubt on the liberal, Enlightenment narrative of human rights as, in some sense, an inevitable consequence of the gradual unfolding of an historical trend from 'barbarism', subjugation and ignorance to civilisation, liberty and enlightenment. As will be argued presently, the human rights agenda has advanced and been rolled back at different times in history and in different national contexts. Furthermore, it is similarly evident that human rights are not a 'gift' bestowed by progressive states on 'backward' peoples, but are rights attained in concrete struggles in which the stakes can be very high indeed.

THE BODY, SEXUALITY AND REPRODUCTIVE RIGHTS

The domain of human rights is a particularly interesting context in which to explore the tension between variously constructed 'bodies', conceived of as bounded, autonomous and sovereign. In regard to women's bodies, the 'tug of war' between the universal and particular, frequently plays out as a struggle between the liberal construct of 'woman' as an autonomous subject and 'woman' as, in some sense, a repository of group identity. While many cultures have systems of duties and obligations that are akin to rights, in many non-Western countries and societies, the good of the collective is often privileged over the rights of the individual. However, the language of 'rights' and human rights largely privileges a liberal conception of the autonomous individual. This is far from being solely a philosophical or theoretical debate; women's bodies are fought over, often fiercely, in various arenas or *sites* in world politics.

It is an oversimplification to describe the women's human rights agenda as a wholly Western project (see Figure 7.1), since many non-Western countries and NGOs have played an important role in the development of human rights generally and women's human rights specifically. However, it is fair to say that Western

The notion that human rights are universal – possessed by all people regardless of age, class, race, religion, culture or gender – is sometimes contested on the grounds that 'human rights' are a historically and culturally specific construct. Some feminists have claimed that the language of human rights is actually unhelpful when making claims on behalf of women, because historically the so-called 'universal' subject in rights discourse was male/masculine. Thus, human rights cannot accommodate gender difference either conceptually and on a practical level; human rights are an inadequate tool with which to promote women's needs within certain gender determined lifestyles. The counter-claim is that human rights have proved to be a dynamic and flexible instrument that has been used effectively in struggles to empower women.

Cultural relativists argue that there are no transcendent, or universal, standards from which to make moral claims and the liberal human rights agenda is actually a Western project and Western imposition – a form of neocolonial or neo-imperialist domination. In response to this charge, since the late 1970s feminists have become much more attentive to the importance of cultural differences among women. Indeed, some feminists argue that Westerners and Western women specifically cannot speak for 'women' in non-Western countries because 'women' is not a single or universal category. Yet the doctrine of cultural relativism is not unproblematic; it rather glosses over key questions concerning who speaks for 'culture' and ultimately privileges differences between cultures over values that cultures share in common.

Rather than representing culture as comprised of fixed and authentic sets of values, dispositions and behaviours that give people their 'way of life', culture might be conceived as discursively constructed, unstable and changing. Cultural differences can thus – potentially – be 'negotiated' in the interests of creating a world in which all people are free to deliberate and develop values to help them live more equitable lives. This process of negotiation is sometimes presented as an attempt to rescue human rights as an inter-subjectively negotiated universal project. Alternatively, negotiation can be presented as aiming to achieve social change at the local level, by forging locally appropriate strategies to promote women's human rights in diverse contexts (Ackerly 2001). From this perspective, the use of human rights discourse by activists represents an attempt to move beyond the dichotomies of universal and particular; rights provide universal aspirations and standards, but rights claims remain embedded in highly specific local contexts.

Figure 7.1 Human rights and cultural difference.

countries and most particularly European countries have been major players in this effort. Since the establishment of the Commission on the Status of Women (CSW or Commission) in 1946, the United Nations has been active in promoting the women's rights agenda. Over its lifetime, the CSW has worked to extend rights commonly enjoyed by men – the right to vote, the right to own property – to women and struggled to realise equal rights in marriage, divorce and inheritance. The CSW has also addressed discrimination in relation to citizenship and nationality law.

The culmination of the Commission's work is the Convention on the Elimination of Discrimination against Women (CEDAW 1979).[2] CEDAW goes beyond the particular needs of women, demanding changes in traditional gender roles that are deemed to perpetuate inequality and discrimination. Where women were previously regarded as, if not the actual possessions of men, then subject always and everywhere to male authority, women's equality with men is now widely accepted around the world; in principle at least. Thus CEDAW constitutes a significant moment in instituting a public and international discourse of women's rights. Hitherto, women's status, position and problems were regarded as a 'private' matter.

CEDAW has also served to challenge the notion that the family is sacrosanct in both international and domestic systems of law.

Nevertheless, in the present age, one can still find plenty of examples of discrimination on the grounds of gender and many instances of *institutionalised* gender discrimination. That gender inequality and discrimination is still pervasive around the world, attest to the power of gendered discourse in reproducing gender and gender inequality in practice. Even as CEDAW has been lauded as a landmark convention, something akin to an international Bill of Rights for women, it actually provides only a few rights based on the specific life experiences of women. The convention also enjoys a somewhat paradoxical position as one of the most widely adopted international conventions in existence and also one that is characterised by a high number of reservations. Many provisions in CEDAW remain contested. Moreover, the USA, a country that is regarded and self-identifies as a champion of human rights, has not as yet ratified CEDAW.

After CEDAW, the most significant milestone in the development of women's human rights occurred at the Fourth United Nations Conference on Women in Beijing in 1995;[3] significant because of the high degree of publically stated consensus on the women's human rights agenda among both state delegates and NGOs. However, the Beijing Platform of Action (BPfA) and the language embodied in the BPfA, was contested before, during and after the conference. The widespread public commitment to women's human rights and a solid consensus among NGOs and human rights activists notwithstanding, ahead of the gathering, some 40 per cent of the entire text of the BPfA was bracketed (contested); the so-called 'Holy Brackets'. At Beijing, a 'Holy alliance' comprised of some States and religious organisations sought to roll-back the language of 'gender' and 'equality', insisting that sex roles were founded in nature and were complementary. This conservative alliance insisted that the language of equity ('fairness') and complementarity be adopted, rather than the language of autonomy and 'equality'. Neoconservative organisations from the USA aligned with the Holy See and conservative Islamic states to actively roll back key planks of the international women's rights agenda, in the interest of rescuing the traditional – read patriarchal – family.

At the Beijing +5 review, held in New York in 2000, the dispute was eventually settled in favour of retaining the 'Cairo language' (language previously used and agreed at the International Conference on Population and Development, held in Cairo in 1994). Human rights organisations hailed this outcome as a 'victory' for women. However, states retain considerable discretion in deciding what constitutes 'appropriate measures' to eliminate discrimination and in how they implement the BPfA. Post-Beijing, the gap between the public commitment on the part of states to women's human rights and the actual implementation of concrete and effective measures to institutional women's human rights in domestic systems of law was – and remains – striking.

In 2013, at the fifty-seventh annual meeting of the CSW, delegates reaffirmed their commitment to eliminate violence against women and girls. Once again, the Vatican, now in alliance with 16 countries including Syria, Iran and Russia, put forward a number of amendments to roll back specific rights in relation to marriage and in women's ability to control their sexual and reproductive health, including a proposed ban on access to abortion for survivors of rape. Once again, the language in the text was a site of contention.

It would be misleading to suggest that it is only conservative states and organisations that have contested key planks of the women's human rights agenda. However, reclaiming the family as a site of male power and dominance is a common objective of all fundamentalist religious groupings (Christian, Jewish, Islamic and so on). Conservative states also continue to oppose specific categories of women's rights, in the name of defending the greater good of the family (Buss and Herman 2003). Moreover, women's bodies often serve as a repository of group identity, serving to reproduce the boundaries of cultural groups and, indeed, nation-states. Hence, women's bodies are a key site of political and legislative interventions. For example, women's rights in regard to the right to nationality and statehood and ostensibly 'private' decisions regarding marriage (whom one is allowed to marry) and, especially, sexuality and reproduction, have all proved to be contentious historically and many of these rights are contested today.

It is because measures like CEDAW and the BPfA are open to varying interpretations and permit a wide measure of discretion in implementation, that women's human rights remain a significant site of political struggle between states and different organised activist groupings; struggles that take place in both international forums and domestic/local settings (Joachim 2003). NGOs and transnational advocacy networks have been extremely important in shaping the women's human rights agenda. NGOs and other activist groups have fought against potential or actual 'roll-back' and, where opportunities have arisen, have driven the women's human rights project forward.

That is not to say that non-state actors and transnational movements are always of one mind and speak with one voice on human rights issues. The women's human rights agenda at the UN has been periodically dogged by disagreement and conflict, especially between organisations and activists from the West or 'global North' and organisations and activists from the global South. This is because in practice human rights activists and women's groups and feminist organisations from the West/North have tended to reproduce a dominant discourse on the West/North as 'advanced' and the global South as – somewhat – backward and regressive, thereby reproducing unequal power relations between the West/North and South. From time to time, furtherance of the women's human rights project has also been impeded by differences over the individualistic language of rights, which is not always appropriate or strategically helpful to women in non-Western societies. Activists from some countries in the global South desire social and political change that is favourable to women, but do not necessarily reject all cultural values from their own countries or the more collectivist conception of the 'common good' that prevails in many non-Western societies (see Figure 7.2).

LGBT RIGHTS

While Beijing (and subsequent reviews) was concerned with women's human rights specifically, it is evident that many of the same issues that were contested and fought

Since the end of the UN Decade for Women in 1985, there has been a proliferation of NGOs organised around the promotion and protection of women's human rights. Post-Beijing, networks to promote the implementation of CEDAW have grown exponentially, aided by advances in information and global communications technologies. Moreover, gender 'mainstreaming' efforts have institutionalised the link between (selected) NGOs, relevant UN bodies and individual governments/states (Bunch 1995; Chinkin 1999; Joachim 2003). These institutionalised linkages have potentially strengthened the capacity of NGOs to have an impact on policy formulation, lawmaking and the implementation and monitoring of women's human rights at both international and national/local levels.

Outside these formalised or institutionalised relationships, NGOs increasingly have embraced the human rights agenda since it can be a useful political tool for activists. In so far as governments make public commitments to rights at the UN and elsewhere, NGOs can subsequently hold governments to account for their actions – or failure to act with respect to human rights violations.

NGOs are sometimes portrayed as representatives of grassroots women or as conduits of civil society (particularly in the liberal literature), but the role of NGOs is not uncontroversial. There are a number of issues that arise concerning the legitimacy of NGO claims to represent or speak for civil society. For example, there is an accreditation process for NGO participation at the UN and while there must necessarily be some limits on numbers, the criteria and decisions on who to include and exclude can be politically motivated, as was the case at the Beijing women's conference. Some so-called NGOs are actually so closely connected with government that they are scarcely independent entities. Moreover, as noted earlier, if not entirely excluded women and women's groups – particularly those from countries outside the affluent West – are marginalised in international forums, often simply lacking the resources to participate.

Figure 7.2 Feminist organising and human rights.

over before, during and after the conference, are highly pertinent to LGBT rights. Indeed, at the Beijing women's conference, the Holy See objected to what it characterised as a 'homosexual agenda' in regard to rights relating to sexuality and sexual orientation. The Holy See objected on the grounds that the 'traditional' or heteronormative family model was threatened by demands from homosexuals for equal rights in marriage and so must be defended. A deal was eventually bartered that strengthened prohibitions outlawing violence against women, but at the expense of Lesbians or, more properly, at the expense of all people in relationships and living in family units that did not conform to the heterosexual 'norm'.

LGBT rights raise issues of 'body politics' as acutely as do women's rights and are equally contested. Obviously LGBT expressions of identity confound rigid views of gender as falling neatly into binaries of male/female. LGBT expressions of identity also challenge heterosexual normative values and arrangements that underpin societies and that are, very often, supported by the state. Moreover, just as women's bodies are often controlled and regulated in the interests of producing and reproducing collective identities, homosexuality and LGBT rights might be articulated as 'alien' to indigenous societies – a Western imposition, if you will. For example, in recent history a number of prominent African leaders have denounced homosexuality as 'un-African' and a 'colonial imposition'. There is evidence to contest both propositions.

Foucault produced major works on *The History of Sexuality* in which he demonstrated how the homosexual body (his argument applies to transgender and intersex bodies) has been a site of intervention, regulation and disciplinary practices throughout history. In Western, bourgeois societies from the eighteenth century onwards, sex and sexuality increasingly came to be seen as 'private' matters, but only in the sense that they were activities confined to the realm of the private, patriarchal family and engaged in to reproduce human society, rather than matters of private choice, less still pleasure. Historically, the state and social and medical institutions that deal with sexual health and psychological well-being have engaged in disciplinary practices that, one way or another, serve to reproduce the idea of homosexuality, bi-sexuality and transgender expression of identity as 'deviant'. Even as Western societies have ostensibly undergone period of 'sexual liberation', homosexual and bi-sexual practice are still regarded as deviant from 'the norm'.

There is undoubtedly still prejudice and discrimination against LGBT people, yet recent developments in regard to gay marriage in many states and countries around the world attest to growing acceptance of homosexual practices and lifestyles. This has actually been the case throughout history: in different societies and cultures throughout the world at different times. The 'homosexual' is, in Foucault's terms, an 'invention'; a product of changes in Western knowledge/constructions of what is 'normal' and 'abnormal'. At the same time, the right to freely express one's sexuality and engage in non-heterosexual sexual practices continues to be contested by certain political and social constituencies across the world.

Contestation and struggles around gay rights are often represented in the media and in public discourse as polarised along Western and non-Western lines. This is misleading. Historically, there has been much variation in attitudes towards homosexuality, bio-sexuality and transgender people across countries and societies. This remains the case today. For example, while homosexuality is criminalised in many African countries, South Africa has actually played a leading role in promoting gay rights in recent decades.

The Beijing women's conference and the outcome of the Beijing +5 review was a setback for gay rights, but there have been notable advances in gay rights since the early 1990s. Particularly significant developments include a statement on gay rights to the General Assembly of the UN in 2008, supported by the European Union, and a resolution proposed by South Africa in 2011, which was subsequently passed by the UN Human Rights Council. The latter aimed to challenge discrimination based on sexual orientation and gender identity, in countries throughout the world. The current UN High Commissioner for Human Rights, Navi Pillay, and the present-day UN General-Secretary Ban Ki-Moon have publically and consistently supported LGBT rights, despite opposition from many African and Arab states. There have also been parallel developments that support LGBT rights in individual states, notably in relation to gay marriage.

Unfortunately, this does not mean that LGBT people no longer face discrimination. According to the International Lesbian, Gay, Bisexual, Trans and Intersex Association (ILGA), in 2010, 76 countries still prosecuted people on the grounds of their sexual orientation and seven had legislation in place that punished same-sex acts with death (although death sentences are not usually enforced). LGBT people are frequently the target of repressive legislation and subjected to social opprobrium and physical violence.

In drawing this section of the chapter to a conclusion, it is necessary to note here that the promotion of LGBT rights on the part of non-state actors, such as human rights NGOs and LGBT activists, is rarely a wholly conflict free endeavour (see Figure 7.3). As with the promotion of women's rights, there can be manifest disagreements among actors from the West and the global South, although in this case disagreements are more often about tactics and strategy rather than the substance of LGBT rights claims. For example, campaigns waged by Western human rights organisations and LGBT rights groups can, in certain circumstances, play into the hands of conservatives who cast the entire LGBT agenda as a 'Western imposition' or 'neocolonial project' and thereby actually make it harder for locally based, grass roots organisations to realise better conditions for LGBT people.

CONCLUSION

A number of key points emerge from the discussion in this chapter. First, as already discussed in Chapter 3, women's human rights and LGBT rights are good examples of how discourses and practices centred on the body are relevant in the study of International Relations. While conventionally constructed as 'private matters', the

---

Russia serves as a good example of how gender and sexuality is policed in the name of a greater good. As a state that positioned itself as the ideological vanguard of progressive social and political change, the Soviet Union professed women's equality with men. The criminal code outlawing homosexuality was repealed in 1917 (homosexuality was recriminalised during the Stalinist era). In reality, there was a gap – if not, indeed, a gulf – between rhetorical commitment to gender and sexual equality and the reality of lived experienced. In the 1920s and 1930s, legislation was enacted to 'emancipate' women, but they continued to be regarded as sex objects or bearers of children for husbands, families and the state and also bore an exhausting 'double burden' of paid work and unpaid labour.

In 1992 the principle of sexual equality was reaffirmed in the Russian Federation's constitution, but continuing widespread discrimination evidenced the largely rhetorical nature of this commitment. Indeed, the UN Committee on CEDAW has repeatedly pressed for the enactment of specific legislation in Russia to combat sexual discrimination. The subservient role of Russian women, along with high levels of domestic violence, rape and sexual harassment, have been attributed to conservative social attitudes and religious orthodoxy, but women's rights are also subordinated to state interests. In 2012 the Russian parliament adopted a law restricting abortions as a way of tackling a demographic crisis that, political leaders held, posed a threat to Russian security.

Since 1992 Russia has ostensibly reaffirmed some gay rights, but here too there is a gulf between the formal legal position and everyday experience. In recent years LGBT people have faced growing restrictions on their rights. Laws have been passed prohibiting dissemination of information about LGBT issues to minors, thereby curtailing the publication of gay lifestyle magazines and gay pride celebrations. In 2013 the LGBT 'Bok o Bok' film festival was affected by the ban. The state claims to act in accordance with public opinion; there is manifest hostility towards LGBT people in Russia. However, the interests of the state are undoubtedly at play. In 2003 the ban on gays serving in the military was lifted, but this was in the context of Russia's looming demographic crisis. The ban on public expressions of LGBT identity is part of a wider clampdown on 'foreign influence' in a country in which the state controls all media output.

Figure 7.3 Gender, sexuality and the Russian state.

state routinely intervenes in the interest of regulating social relations in the private realm. Women's human rights and LGBT rights demonstrate how the boundaries between what is considered 'public' and 'private' and 'domestic' and 'international' shift and change over time. In relation to sexuality and reproductive rights particularly, struggles and contestation over language and meaning are germane to international politics.

Neither the women's human rights agenda, nor LGBT rights is a solely Western project. Human rights discourse has been evoked in a number of countries, with different political regimes and diverse ideological, religious and cultural sensibilities, to bring pressure to bear on governments to act in specific cases of human rights violations. However, women's bodies particularly are central to 'boundary-drawing' and 'identity-fixing' practices and so claims made in the name of women's human rights can never be fully entangled from claims made in the name of specific cultural, ethnic, religious or national groups. Evidence drawn from across the world suggests that commitment to women's human rights is often more rhetorical than real. Women's rights are still apt to be subordinated to other categories such as class and nation. LGBT rights might be – and frequently are – cast as 'alien' to 'authentic' cultural values and practices.

In respect to both women's rights and LGBT rights, the human rights agenda bears testimony to the continuing strategic and political necessity of making claims in the name of specific identities while also utilising a universal idiom to speak about injustice. In some contexts, human rights discourse and instruments also furnish activists with useful tools for advancing their goals. However, it is equally evident that human rights is not a 'gift' to be conferred by benevolent elites, but an outcome of tough battles fought over time, in which there are advances and setbacks and in which the specific character of the struggles is shaped by both international, national and local contexts. At a time when human rights talk is seemingly everywhere and the widespread acceptance of human rights notwithstanding, human rights continue to be violated and specific categories of rights continue to be disputed. LGBT rights and women's rights remain among the most contested and among the most violated.

Questions for further debate

1. Can a case be made for gender-specific rights (such as maternity pay for women)? Can such provisions be reconciled with the principle of equality under the law?
2. Should feminists support political or military interventions, if there is an ostensive commitment to put an end to human rights violations?
3. Susan Okin has argued that multiculturalism is potentially or actually incompatible with women's human rights. Is she right?
4. Do you agree that the language of human rights and human rights conventions provide a useful tool for activists seeking to 'empower' women or 'liberate' LGBT people?

Sources for further reading and research

Ackerly, B. (2001) 'Women's Rights Activists as Cross-Cultural Theorists', *International Feminist Journal of Politics*, 3(3): 311–46.

Benhabib, S. (2004) *The Rights of Others*, Cambridge: Cambridge University Press.

Bunch, C., R. Raj and E. Nazombe (eds) (2002) *Women at the Intersection: Indivisible Rights, Identities and Oppressions*, New Jersey: Centre for Women's Global Leadership.

Joachim, J. (2003) 'Framing Issues and Seizing Opportunities: The UN, NGOs and Women's Rights', *International Studies Quarterly*, 47(2): 247–74.

Special Forum Section (2007) 'Negotiating Difference/Negotiating Rights: The Challenges and Opportunities of Women's Human Rights', *Review of International Studies*, 33(1): 5–103.

Notes

1 Political philosophers from Aristotle to Thomas Carlyle have represented the body politic as an organic or natural entity. Carlyle, for example, regarded government as the 'skin' of the body that protected the health of the 'body' from attacks or invasions from pernicious maladies. Today, the notion that politically constituted bodies are 'natural' or 'organic' is apt to be regarded as rather old fashioned, but the term is still occasionally employed in the looser sense described here.

2 CEDAW demanded the abolition of discriminatory customs and practices and inequities in marriage and divorce; articulated an international standard for what was meant by 'equality' between men and women, granted formal rights to women, and also promoted equality of access and opportunity and in so doing recognised that rights could be meaningless unless attention was paid to the economic, social and cultural context in which they were claimed.

3 The Beijing Platform for Action (BPfA) affirmed the liberal principles of 'freedom of choice for individual women' and proclaimed that it was 'the duty of governments to promote and protect human rights of women, by building on previous agreements and ratifying and implementing relevant human rights treaties'. The BPfA also imposed on states 'regardless of their political, economic, and cultural systems' an obligation 'to promote and protect all human rights' and 'to address the violation of women's human rights' in varied contexts.

CHAPTER 8

Trafficking in human beings

Barbara Sullivan

LEARNING OUTCOMES

Upon completion, readers should be able to:

- Demonstrate how the problem of human trafficking has been constructed in recent world politics.
- Show how trafficking is defined in international law.
- Analyse some of the gendered consequences of anti-trafficking campaigns.

INTRODUCTION

Human trafficking emerged as an important issue in world politics in the 1990s. A wide range of feminist and human rights organisations argued that trafficking – in particular, sex trafficking and the forced labour of women and girls in prostitution – was a growing international problem, a form of 'modern slavery' that needed urgent and international attention. In 2000 the United Nations General Assembly adopted a new anti-trafficking protocol – the *Protocol to Prevent Suppress and Punish Trafficking in Persons, Especially Women and Children*. In the wake of this, many governments (led by the US government), and regional organisations (such as the Council of Europe) have developed extensive regimes designed to prevent trafficking, prosecute traffickers and protect victims. Significant state and non-state resources are now devoted worldwide to anti-trafficking campaigns.

There has been increasing recognition over the last decade that trafficking is not confined to *sex* trafficking. Women and girls may be trafficked and subject to forced labour for other purposes, for example, domestic or agricultural work. There has also been increasing recognition that men and boys may also be victims of trafficking. Consequently, the language used to discuss trafficking has shifted in recent times – from a focus on 'sex trafficking' to the more gender-neutral formulation of 'people trafficking' or 'trafficking in human beings'. However, it is clear that *gender matters* in the trafficking arena. It is still *sex* trafficking that tends to be the primary object of concern and anti-trafficking campaigns have gendered consequences with negative impacts on some women, especially migrant women and sex workers.

WHAT IS TRAFFICKING?

Horrifying accounts by the victims of trafficking are now widely reported by researchers, non-government organisations and mainstream media. However, the current global concern with trafficking did not really begin until the 1980s and 1990s. The issue was initially raised in the feminist movement in the USA and was part of a broader concern about violence against women – including rape, domestic violence, pornography and prostitution. Radical feminists argued that prostitution was always non-consensual and thus, a form of rape; consequently, all prostitution was an abuse of women's human rights and sex trafficking was part of this (Barry 1979).

This radical feminist construction of prostitution and trafficking owed a considerable debt to abolitionist positions first elaborated more than 100 years ago (Weitzer 2007: 467). In the late nineteenth and early twentieth centuries feminists and others looked to abolish prostitution although, as is still the case today, there were a variety of reasons for this stance. Today, religious abolitionists argue that prostitution is contrary to god's law while feminist abolitionists regard prostitution as rape and an abuse of women's human rights. All abolitionists oppose any form of legal or tolerated prostitution; they claim that there is a direct and causative relationship between legal prostitution and trafficking. However, this claim is also disputed in the academic literature (O'Brien 2011).

Between 1901 and 1949 a number of international agreements were addressed to the trafficking issue (see Doezema 2002). Initially, the main problem was seen in terms of 'white slavery' and the fear that European women were being abducted and transported around the world where they were forced to prostitute themselves with non-white men. So, from the very beginning, debates about trafficking were framed within wider concerns about prostitution, the sexual activity of women and (white) racial concerns about 'other' cultures.

The focus on white women was eventually set aside and the language of anti-trafficking came to reflect a general concern about 'sex slavery' and the forced prostitution of women and girls. From 1933 onwards, all international agreements on trafficking also had an explicitly abolitionist agenda (Doezema 2002). They condemned the recruitment for prostitution and required states to punish 'any person who, in order to gratify the passions of another person, procures, entices or leads away, *even with her consent*, a woman or girl of full age for immoral purposes to be carried out in another country' (*1933 International Convention for the Suppression of the Traffic in Women*, cited in Doezema 2002: 23; emphasis added).

What this brief history suggests is that the problem of trafficking was constructed in a particularly gendered and raced way in the first half of the 20th century. Kempadoo (2005: x) says that the trafficking debate emerged from a 'racialized social panic'. Women were seen to have a 'vulnerable sexuality' that was readily exploited by men; trafficking always involved prostitution and women's consent was irrelevant. Thus international law did not envisage trafficking occurring outside prostitution – for example, in agriculture, manufacturing or domestic labour. It also erased the possibility of women being active agents in their own lives, for example by migrating to undertake lucrative paid work in the sex trade.

In the 1980s and 1990s radical feminists began to renew the earlier abolitionist campaign against prostitution and trafficking (see Jeffreys 1997). They called for a new international agreement as part of their opposition to prostitution and trafficking. At this time, gender issues – and women's human rights – were also assuming a new importance in the work of international and development organisations. So a path was already open for anti-trafficking concerns to become established. Some new contestations also opened up in this period as sex workers and their allies argued that prostitution should be regarded as a form of labour, as 'sex work'. From this perspective, there was an important distinction to be drawn between trafficking and sex work; trafficking involved forced labour but sex work could be undertaken voluntarily (as a rational decision about how best to earn a living). Not all migration for sex work involves violence, coercion and trafficking (Saunders 2005).

Fundamental disagreements about the nature of trafficking and sex work were also reflected in debates about the form of a new international anti-trafficking agreement in the 1990s. The definition of trafficking that was finally agreed on and incorporated in the *Protocol to Prevent, Suppress and Punish Trafficking in Persons, Especially Women and Children* (2000) was said to represent a 'compromise' between these opposing positions. Trafficking is defined as:

> The recruitment, transportation, transfer, harbouring or receipt of Persons, by means of threat or use of force or other forms of coercion, of abduction, of fraud, deception, of the abuse of power or of a position of vulnerability or of the giving or receiving of payments or benefits to achieve the consent of a person having control over another person, for the purposes of exploitation. Exploitation shall include, at a minimum, the exploitation of the prostitution of others or other forms of sexual exploitation, forced labour or services, slavery or practices similar to slavery or servitude or the removal of organs.
>
> (UN Protocol, Article 3(a))

For those without legal training (and even for those with!) this is not a very clear definition. It has some abolitionist elements but does not define trafficking wholly in terms of prostitution or negate the consent of sex workers who have migrated for sex work (but who have not been subject to forced labour).

The United Nations Office of Drugs and Crime (UNODC), which is the UN body with responsibility for the *Protocol*, says that three distinct elements must be present for an activity to be seen as trafficking under the *Protocol*:

1. Actions that involve recruiting or moving someone (recruitment, transportation, transfer etc.).
2. Means by which those actions are carried out (threat or use of force or other forms of coercion, abduction, fraud, abuse of power, etc.).
3. Purpose (forced labour, exploitation including sexual exploitation, removal of organs).

If these three elements are present then trafficking has occurred (and any 'consent' offered by victims is invalidated).[1]

This suggests that trafficking is a distinct crime that can be separated from other crimes such as 'people smuggling' where migrants pay a third party to transport them into another country ('people smuggling' is the object of a separate UN Protocol). UNODC has said there are three features of trafficking that distinguish it from migrant smuggling. First, the smuggling of migrants involves people who have consented to the smuggling process; trafficking victims have either never consented or their consent has been nullified by the coercion, deception or violence of the trafficker. Second, the process of migrant smuggling ends with the arrival of the migrants at their destination; for trafficking victims arrival at the destination begins a new phase of exploitation. Third, smuggling is always transnational whereas trafficking may not be; it can occur across national boundaries or between regions within a country. In many respects, then, the crime of trafficking has been constructed in international law as feminine – with a 'gendered emphasis on passivity, ignorance and force' (Agustín 2005: 98). Smuggling, by the same token, has all the agency and freedoms often associated with masculinity.

In practice, it may be hard to distinguish between people trafficking and migrant smuggling. Citing Liz Kelly's work, Maggy Lee claims:

> [T]here are both overlaps and transitions from smuggling to trafficking, and … trafficking is best understood as a 'continuum' which involves varying degrees of force, exploitation and positions of vulnerability. All this suggests that a discrete categorisation of 'trafficking' and 'smuggling' may be artificial and unhelpful, and may draw attention away from the broader context of exploitation and complex causes of irregular migration.
>
> (Lee 2007: 11)

Laura Agustín has recently argued that a major problem with the trafficking debate – and with most attempts to define the crime of trafficking – is that it ignores the voices of migrant women themselves (Agustín 2005: 96). From fieldwork with migrant women working in the sex industry in Europe, she concludes that:

> [W]omen migrants are actively engaged in using social networks to travel, often aware of the sexual nature of the work, and, like other migrant workers, variably able to resist the economic, social and physical forms of compulsion they face. Their status as 'illegal' migrants, without permission to work in Europe, is, for them, the single overarching problem to solve, and their irregular status, not sex, is the heart of the issue.
>
> (Agustín 2005: 98)

This statement calls attention to two more aspects of how the trafficking problem has recently been constructed in international law. The UN trafficking *Protocol* (2000) is attached to the *Convention Against Transnational Organised Crime*. So trafficking is not primarily regarded as an issue of migration, poverty, or inequality; it is a crime perpetrated by transnational criminal networks. This also means that trafficking is constructed as a direct threat to the peace and security of nation-states, legitimising both increased surveillance of borders and tighter immigration controls.

WHAT IS THE INCIDENCE AND WHO ARE THE MAIN VICTIMS OF TRAFFICKING?

There are widely varying – and often contradictory – estimates of the number of trafficked human beings around the world. One of the main problems here is the use of varying definitions of trafficking and/or of estimation methods that rely on conjecture rather than evidence. Some activists and researchers regard all transportation and migration for sex work as trafficking – even if the women concerned have actively sought out third parties to facilitate their migration and employment (including in sex work). So there is a tendency to conflate trafficking with sex trafficking (that is, to not 'count' other forms of trafficking involving forced labour) *and* to regard all migration for sex work as forced trafficking. There has also been a tendency to construct, rely on and/or repeat often wild 'guesstimates' of the incidence of trafficking. Many of the claims made in this area are 'unsubstantiated and undocumented, and are based on sensationalist reports, hyperbole and conceptual confusion' (Kempadoo 2005: xiv). This means that debates about trafficking often take on the appearance of a 'moral panic' rather than an evidence-based exploration of the issues involved (see Weitzer 2007).

In the 2013 Trafficking in Person (TIP) Report, for example, the USA Department of State says 'social scientists estimate that as many as 27 million men, women and children are trafficking victims at any given time' (no source is cited for these data). Figures like these have been criticised by academic researchers (Di Nicola 2007) and are contradicted by the United Nations office charged with monitoring trafficking worldwide (UNODC) which says that '2.4 million people are trafficking victims at any given time' (i.e., less than a tenth of the USA figure). The UNODC data are based on research conducted by the International Labour Organization (ILO 2005), which reviews the whole issue of forced labour, and does not simply focus on trafficking. The ILO estimates that:

- 12.3 million people are in forced labour around the world. They suggest that 'forced labour is a truly global problem, affecting substantial numbers of people in both developed and developing countries and in all regions of the world' (ILO 2005: 12).
- 40–50 per cent of the victims of forced labour are children (ILO 2005: 15).
- The majority of victims (64 per cent) are in forced labour involving economic exploitation – for example, in agriculture, manufacturing or other economic activities.

- 11 per cent of victims (1,390,000) are in forced labour involving commercial sexual exploitation (ILO 2005: 12).
- A majority (56 per cent) of the victims in forced labour involving economic exploitation are women and girls; 98 per cent of the victims in forced labour involving commercial sexual exploitation are women and girls.
- 20 per cent (2.45 million) of all victims of forced labour were trafficked; 43 per cent of these were in forced labour involving commercial sexual exploitation (ILO 2005: 10–14).

So this study suggests that forced labour is a significant problem in the world today and, while trafficking is part of this problem, it is clearly not the largest part. The study also indicates that more human beings are subjected to forced labour for economic exploitation than for sexual exploitation although – in both categories – women and children are most vulnerable.

WHAT CAUSES TRAFFICKING?

There has been much recent debate about the causes of trafficking particularly as a way of developing better means for addressing and preventing trafficking. A wide range of issues have been suggested as 'root causes' of trafficking including: poverty, limited educational opportunities, patriarchal social structures (limiting the economic opportunities of women), social and economic marginalisation, failed and corrupt governments, family breakdown, and historical precedents of bonded labour.

Many authors call attention to *poverty* as an important factor affecting the vulnerability of individuals to trafficking. Poor people clearly have fewer income and migration options and are less able to negotiate or challenge oppressive work conditions. They may be 'pushed' into moving away from their home communities (or sending their children away) in order to survive and/or in search of better economic opportunities. So, it is perhaps not surprising that the main 'trafficking flows' in the world today follow general migration paths – between poorer and wealthier regions of the world, and between developing and wealthier countries (see Chapter 23). UNODC says that the main countries of *origin* for trafficking victims include those in Eastern Europe, West Africa, central and Southeast Asia. The main *destination* countries for trafficking include those in Western Europe, North America, Japan and the Middle East (Israel, Saudi Arabia and the United Arab Emirates).

However, the link between poverty and human trafficking is complex. When the countries reported most frequently as countries of origin and destination for trafficking are compared against the United Nations Human Development index, the main countries of origin are in the middle of this scale. So it is not the poorest people in the world who are most likely to be targeted as victims of trafficking; trafficking victims (like migrants generally) are individuals with at least some resources. But this still calls attention to the role of global inequalities in the causes of trafficking. Migration is encouraged by the widening gap between the 'haves' and the 'have nots' in the world, the demand for unskilled or semi-skilled labour in industrialised countries (especially for jobs that are 'dirty' and low paid), and the possibilities offered by increasing globalisation. For some migrants this will result in the extreme coercion and exploitation of trafficking (see GAATW 2010 for an excellent analysis of the relationship between globalisation and trafficking).

Gender is also clearly an important factor in trafficking vulnerability. As Kempadoo (2005: ix) reminds us 'women are disproportionately represented among the poor, the undocumented, the debt-bonded, and the international migrant workforce'. Right around the world, discrimination and misogyny deeply affect women's lives and limit their economic opportunities. One way that women negotiate a 'highly gendered and racialized world order' (Kempadoo 2005: xi) is to migrate in search of better paid work. However, 'most legal migration channels are strongly biased toward work that is traditionally done by men, while two very common areas of migration for women, domestic and entertainment work, have very little protection under labor laws' (Marshall and Thatun 2005: 52). So, in processes of migration women tend to be more vulnerable to traffickers.

The situation of migrant women working in the sex industry is similar in many ways to the situations faced by other migrant women (Kempadoo 2005: xi) especially those who have to negotiate a lack of legal work status or who end up employed in underground, unregulated and/or informal economies within industrialised countries. It is the demand for cheap, flexible, wage labour in these countries – together with restrictive immigration laws and policies – that are probably the main 'causes' of people trafficking in the world today. Empirical evidence indicates that attempts to restrict immigration assist trafficking rather than hindering it (Marshall and Thatun 2005: 50). This means that much of what is currently being done by governments and international organisations in the name of combating trafficking may actually be contributing to the problem.

CONCERNS ABOUT ANTI-TRAFFICKING

In the last decade, significant state and non-state resources have been applied to the worldwide development of a powerful anti-trafficking campaign. The main dimensions of this campaign are evident in the positions adopted by powerful institutions and organisations such as the Office to Combat and Monitor Trafficking in the USA State Department, the UNODC, IOM and Council of Europe. At this point, it is not at all clear if this anti-trafficking campaign is well targeted or likely to succeed in the way its proponents hope. However, some serious concerns have recently been raised about anti-trafficking campaigns. Some have argued that the focus on trafficking has displaced broader concerns about the welfare of migrants and about labour conditions in general. Moreover, as suggested earlier, a range of authors have questioned the framing of the trafficking problem and the figures cited to support claims about its incidence. In a recent special edition of *Dialectical Anthropology* (Vol. 37, Issue 2, June 2013), several papers point to major problems in anti-trafficking campaigns including that detailed ethnographic work around the world provides almost no evidence to support the characterisation of trafficking on which anti-trafficking campaigns are based.

Anti-trafficking campaigns can have a negative impact on women's human rights

There are various ways that anti-trafficking campaigns impact negatively on women's human rights. In the first place, they may have the effect of limiting women's mobility – for example by forcing them to stay home or denying the right to emigrate. The Global Alliance Against Trafficking in Women found that immigration officers in industrialised countries have 'stereotyped young women travellers from certain countries, such as Brazil and Nigeria, as potential sex workers or victims of trafficking and used this as an excuse to impede their entry' (GAATW 2007: 17). Of course, the effects of measures like these impact more heavily on women who are poor than on women who are better off and better educated.

Sex worker organisations have also documented the impact of anti-trafficking campaigns – the 'violence and terror' – on the human rights of women who support themselves via sex work (Kempadoo 2005: 149; see also Murphy and Ringheim 2002). This particularly pertains to police raids on brothels and the public shaming of sex workers by officials engaged in anti-trafficking activities in some countries (see Scarlet Alliance 2008). But sex workers in many countries have reported the detrimental effects of anti-trafficking campaigns on their lives and work (see Empower Foundation 2012; see also the website for the Global Network of Sex Work Projects).

The problematic representation of women and gender difference in anti-trafficking campaigns

Despite the complexity of trafficking scenarios, and the many factors which cause human beings to be trapped in forced labour (see earlier), anti-trafficking campaigns often focus on sex trafficking telling powerful and emotional stories about female victims. These are stories which construct – and reconstruct – women as innocent and powerless, as 'naturally' vulnerable and endangered by the world (see Hesford 2005; see also Andrijasevic 2007). Anti-trafficking campaigns focused in this way are often sexually charged but are more unlikely to undermine the power and agency of real women. They may, for example, lead the viewer to the conclusion that women are easily trafficked; or that women who choose to migrate and engage in sex work cannot ever be trafficking victims; or that trafficking will be prevented if women just stayed home and did not seek work abroad.

Anti-trafficking campaigns maintain a problematic focus on sex trafficking and have a tendency to conflate sex trafficking with migration for sex work

Most anti-trafficking efforts continue to focus on sex trafficking and to ignore the other ways that human beings are trafficked and subject to forced labour. Far less attention is paid to the situation of women and girls trafficked for forced labour outside prostitution (for example, domestic labour) or to the trafficking of men and boys. This means that sex trafficking is often the only sort of trafficking that gets 'noticed', policed and counted. As discussed already, there is also an ongoing tendency to discuss all migration for sex work in terms of trafficking, ignoring the important differences between forced labour in the sex industry and other forms of relatively un-coerced labour in the sex trade (which arguably, is the normal lot of workers in many occupations). In some countries, most notably the USA, the campaign against trafficking has become the platform for a renewed abolitionism and opposition to all prostitution. This is evident in law, public policy and education material produced by the USA government in recent years. In 2003 the USA government began to require non-government organisations applying for funds addressed to anti-trafficking or HIV/AIDS prevention to sign an 'anti-prostitution pledge' which meant they could not also support the legalisation or decriminalisation of prostitution. Although the anti-prostitution pledge was struck down by the USA Supreme Court in June 2013, it had a significant and negative impact on sex worker communities around the world for more than a decade.

Anti-trafficking agendas have become attached to state security interests

In the last decade, anti-trafficking campaigns have been absorbed into state security agendas more concerned with border security and terrorism. A recent report by the Global Alliance Against Trafficking in Women (GAATW 2010) traces out in detail many of the interconnections here. It says:

> Globalisation fosters conditions that push women to migrate in search of work opportunities, which can often add to their financial and personal wellbeing. However security policies and thinking have made that movement more dangerous. Security policies typically include tighter border controls and restrictive immigration policies, increasing the likelihood that migrants will ask agents to help with clandestine movement (thus also increasing the vulnerability to trafficking). The fight against trafficking has taken on an even greater security orientation because of the 'War on Terror' and policies that conflate trafficking with terrorism and transnational organised crime.
>
> (GAATW 2010: 5)

In this regard it is notable that the United States government, while pursuing both 'homeland security' and an international 'war on terror', is also committed to rallying the world to defeat human trafficking. Via its annual Trafficking in Persons (TIP) Reports the US State Department has brought strong pressure on other countries in relation to their anti-trafficking laws and policies. This includes the threat of significant sanctions such as withdrawing US aid and opposing applications for financial assistance to international institutions such as the IMF and World Bank. As suggested earlier, these security developments have gendered consequences and may not always operate to advance the human rights of women, especially those of poor and migrant women.

The weakness of human rights protections for trafficking victims and migrant workers generally

The current protections offered to trafficking victims are often minimal. The trafficking *Protocol* (2000) requires countries to introduce law enforcement measures designed to prosecute and punish traffickers. However, many of the measures designed to protect trafficking victims and uphold their human rights are not obligatory for countries that sign the Protocol (see GAATW 2007: 5). Trafficking victims are often immediately deported (as illegal migrants) or are confined within shelters and detention centres. In many wealthy countries, such as the USA, UK and Australia, protection and assistance for trafficking victims is conditional on cooperation with law enforcement officials; so there is no clear right to protection and assistance and involuntary repatriations can occur at any time, back to the country of origin. The interlinking of trafficking and migrant labour suggests the need for strong human rights protections for migrant workers in general. There is a specific UN convention addressed to upholding the rights of migrant workers generally (the *International Convention on the Protection of the Rights of All Migrant Workers and Members of Their Families*) but this has not been ratified by a single industrialised country receiving large numbers of migrants. As Dottridge (in GAATW 2007: 12) has recently argued:

> While efforts are nominally made to protect people from being trafficked, the main emphasis of most governments when it comes to migrants is to 'control' and limit immigration and does not involve assisting or protecting migrants. Indeed, the narrow focus on trafficking seems in many countries to act as a justification for not taking action to end *all* the abuse to which migrant workers in the informal sectors of the economy are subjected.

CONCLUSION

The forced labour of human beings remains an issue of significant magnitude right around the world today. The recent focus on human trafficking calls our attention to this bigger problem and to the way that women, men and children may be subjected to forced labour. There are gendered patterns in human trafficking and forced labour; there are also key vulnerabilities related to race, age, economic inequality and globalisation. It is important to keep this bigger picture in mind and to recognise some of the dangers associated with simplistic 'solutions' associated with anti-trafficking campaigns.

Questions for further debate

Imagine you are a young woman who needs to financially support herself and her family:

1. Why might you be tempted to migrate from your home in search of work?
2. What work would you be willing to do? What work would you *not* be willing to do? What sort of working conditions would be unacceptable?

3. In your migration and search for work, how would you seek to protect yourself from being trafficked and/or subjected to forced labour?

4. If, despite your best efforts, you found yourself in a situation where you were being forced to labour, where would you look for assistance? (Police? Health workers? Anti-trafficking groups?)

5. What factors would make you more or less vulnerable to being trafficked or subjected to forced labour?

Sources for further reading and research

Agustín, L. M. (2006) 'The Conundrum of Women's Agency: Migrations and the Sex Industry', in R. Campbell and M. O'Neill (eds) *Sex Work Now*, Cullompton: Willan Publishing, 116–40.

Andrijasevic, R. (2007) 'Beautiful Dead Bodies: Gender, Migration and Representation in Anti-Trafficking Campaigns', *Feminist Review*, 86: 24–44.

Blanchette, T. G., A. P. Silva and A. R. Bento (2013) 'The Myth of Maria and the Imagining of Sexual Trafficking in Brazil', *Dialectical Anthropology*, 37(2): 195–227.

Saunders, P. (2005) 'Traffic Violations. Determining the Meaning of Violence in Sexual Trafficking Versus Sex Work', *Journal of Interpersonal Violence*, 20(3): 343–60.

Weitzer, R. (2007) 'The Social Construction of Sex Trafficking: Ideology and Institutionalization of a Moral Crusade', *Politics & Society*, 35(3): 447–75.

Note

1 For those under the age of 18, the second element does not need to be established; the case will be regarded as trafficking if there has been recruitment (or transportation, etc.) and any forced labour or 'exploitation'.

PART 3 VIOLENCE AND SECURITY

CHAPTER 9

War

Swati Parashar

LEARNING OUTCOMES

Upon completion, readers should be able to:

- Understand the gendered order that produces war and is in turn produced by it.
- Identify the relationship between war and gendered bodies, particularly the images of women's bodies.
- Understand, evaluate and further research different feminist approaches to the study of war and its impact on women's lives.

INTRODUCTION

War encapsulates the destructive and violent potential of human nature and has been part of the historical evolution of every society. It remains the single most theorised and researched activity in Politics, International Relations and cognate disciplines. Visit any music and video shop or a bookstore in your town or city in any part of the world, and you will find at least one section devoted to war. Switch on your TV and the news media is focused on the wars of our time; the more exciting films are based on a war theme, and 'History' and 'Discovery' channels are obsessed with World War stories of the twentieth century. At the time of writing this chapter, civil wars in Syria and Nigeria are constantly in the news, along with spectacular and unexpected acts of political violence such as the Boston bombings.[1]

The last is not just one odd incident but part of a larger social, political and military culture, where war making has not only become easier but also incorporates a wider audience across a much larger terrain. Mary Kaldor (1999) developed the concept of 'new wars' making a distinction from old wars where territory, geopolitics and strategic doctrines dominated; war had certain rules and participants were easily identifiable. Kaldor's 'new wars' include conflicts over ideology; they are highly decentralised and there are no rules or ethics, with violence and brutality knowing no limits. This might adequately capture for us the story and motivations of contemporary wars, although it is possible to distinguish one 'new war' from another (Chan 2011).

Vivienne Jabri, describing what she terms as the 'matrix of war', argues:

> Practices constitutive of global war are best understood in terms of a matrix, incorporating states and their bureaucracies, as well as non-state agents, and targeting at once states, particular communities and individuals.
>
> (Jabri 2006b: 47)

Wars have become more sophisticated, more theatrical and in many ways we are living within wars. We think we 'know' wars and acts of collective violence associated with wars are accepted as a given. In this vein, Christine Sylvester articulates the need to question the nature and character of the collective violence that is the defining feature of wars. She suggests that 'war is a politics of injury: everything about war aims to injure people and/or their social surroundings as a way of resolving disagreement or, in some cases, encouraging disagreement if it is possible to do so' (2012: 3–4). War as 'politics of injury' is a deeply gendered activity in how it is imagined, strategised, performed and also in its impact, representation and storytelling. Femininity and masculinity are invoked in specific ways and men and women perform a variety of roles in wars which either entrench gender hierarchy and uphold gender subordination or transform gender relations in significant ways.

WAR AND THE GENDERED ORDER

He strives for supremacy
Under heaven
Intact,
His men and weapons
Still keen
His gain
Complete.
This is the method of
Strategic attack.

(Sun-Tzu, *The Art of War*)

The history of most wars demonstrate the social and political nurturing of a special kind of 'militarised masculinity' (Enloe 2000b) that privileges the idea of honour and nationalism reclaimed or preserved in a violent contest between the 'self' and 'other'. Since ancient times, the purpose of going to war has been to test the limitless possibilities of valour, courage and aggression associated with the male half of the population. The rewards of war are gendered in how they attain for the male warriors: territory, resources, women, slaves and supremacy over their enemies. The prevailing gendered order and norms thus create and nurture conditions under which war is imagined and performed and specific roles are determined of men and women. Feminist scholars have unpacked this gendered order and have explained how war is a patriarchal imagining, from the time its inevitability is propounded by its supporters to its very end when post-war reconstruction, rehabilitation and development are put in place. Feminists have suggested that the gender hierarchy that is part of mainstream society extends to the social order produced by war (Elshtain 1987; Enloe 1983).

It is commonly assumed that aggression is part of masculinity and men are inclined towards violence and wars; femininity is passive, emotional, and women are naturally inclined towards peace and nonviolence. As a social institution, there-fore, war upholds its own gendered order where there is a clear division of labour between the sexes; the majority of war's combatants are thought to be men while women are presented as victims on whom the injuries are inflicted or for whose honour wars are fought. This narrative has been used throughout history to exclude women from wars' activities and narratives or to make them the raison d'être of wars. For example, in the ancient Indian war epic, *Mahabharata* (Great War), war's gendered imaginings and its strict sexual division of labour was suitably demon-strated. The war was fought between members of the same clan and extended family, over territory, nationalism and also to avenge the dishonouring of the central female character, Draupadi (Uberoi 2005).[2] The other Indian epic, *Ramayana* (Story of Ram) is also about war fought between protagonists who wanted to estab-lish their military prowess over each other, but also over the abduction, and dishon-ouring of the female character, Sita (Narayan 2006).[3]

This scene from the *Mahabharata* demonstrates the gendered order that pro-duces war (see Figure 9.1). The female character, Draupadi, is being disrobed as she helplessly prays to the divine incarnation, Krishna, who comes to her rescue to protect her honour; to her right are her five emasculated husbands (Pandavas) defeated in a game of dice; to her left are the evil cousins (Kauravas) who want the war at any cost.

WAR'S STRATEGIES/WARRING BODIES

If the motives of war are to produce and uphold the militarised patriarchal social order, war uses a number of gendered strategies in the pursuit of its objectives. Women are 'othered' in dramatic and violent ways as part of war strategies.

Women as repositories of cultural identities

Women become the upholders of social and cultural values of the warring sides in any war and women's bodies and their gendered identities become the territories on

Figure 9.1 Scene from the *Mahabharata*.

Image: Wikimedia Commons.

which wars are waged and ideologies played out. Nira Yuval-Davis (1997) effectively shows the linkages between gender and nationalism and how women's bodies become cultural symbols of the nation (see also Chapter 25). Physically eliminating the enemy is not always possible or desirable and in many wars of recent times, emasculating the enemy by raping 'their' women is considered a viable war strategy. It not only serves as a tool to emasculate the enemy (as they fail to protect their women) and target ethnic purity and solidarity by impregnating the women, but also causes social upheaval in the post-war environment. The social trauma from war time rape is long lasting as raped women and children born to them are stigmatised and socially ostracised, left alone to fend for themselves.

Bina D'Costa has analysed the rape of 300,000 Bangladeshi women in the 1971 Liberation War. She argues that the women 'were raped by members of the Pakistan

Army in a strategic attempt to target Bengali ethnic identity' (D'Costa 2011: 19). Gender is thus at the core of the nationalist narrative of the Bangladesh War where 'women were targeted by the political project of the Pakistani government to create a "pure" Muslim state' (ibid: 139). Wartime rape and sexual violence are discussed further in Chapter 14.

Women as victims/survivors

The changing nature of war has meant that more women are now part of the war matrix as victims and survivors. Modern warfare makes no distinction between civilians and combatants and attacks by unmanned drones, land mines, improvised explosive devices, suicide bombs and random shootings result in deaths and injuries to a large number of women and children. In fact, warring sides choose 'soft targets' to attack the enemy and often label the death and injuries (experienced by unarmed women and children) as 'collateral damage'. Areas frequented by women and children, including schools, places of worship, historical religious shrines and markets are subjected to a great degree of violence. One estimate says that approximately 10 per cent of violent deaths in the Iraq war since 2003 have been women.[4] In Afghanistan, the number of targeted killings has increased and even the United Nations Assistance Mission in Afghanistan acknowledged in 2012 that targeted killings of women by anti-government elements were a worrisome development. While writing this chapter, news came in that Lieutenant Islam Bibi, who had survived death threats from her own brother to rise through the ranks, and served as the most senior female police officer in Afghanistan's Helmand province, was shot dead by the Taliban on 3 July 2013.

Displacement by war particularly affects women and children and many end up in refugee camps for internally displaced people. Up to 80 per cent of all refugee and asylum seekers are estimated to be women and children. They are vulnerable not only to material hardship, but also to the possibility of exploitation and trafficking. Women as caregivers and those responsible for obtaining food, water, and basic needs for families suffer extreme hardship when life is disrupted by war. In addition, deaths of male members of the society lead to forced widowhood on women. In Iraq, nearly 2 million women as widows have become the primary wage earners in the family.

Disappearances are common in war time situations when men and boys are picked up by the armed forces, on charges of treason and anti-state activities. Women are left behind to grieve and to also provide for their families. Women whose husbands have gone missing experience many of the same problems as widows, although without official recognition of their status. They are regarded as neither wives nor widows (sometimes half-widows) and are denied the legal support that widows are entitled to. This further affects their rights to property, inheritance, guardianship of children and the prospect of remarriage. However, many women have turned their grief and suffering into a window of opportunity to fight for human rights and to push for greater accountability and transparency. Ironically, even in the most conservative of societies, they attain access to public spaces and jobs as they become breadwinners and activists. Women as survivors of wars have challenged gender norms in significant ways.

Parveena Ahangar, head and spokesperson of Association of Parents of Disappeared Persons (APDP), is an international human rights activist for the parents of missing children in Kashmir (see Figure 9.2). After her 16-year-old son, Javed Ahangar, was forcibly taken by the Indian Army on 18 August 1990 and could not be traced, Parveena became a full-time human rights activist organising, advocating and seeking justice for the families of the disappeared. She works with other women whose family members have disappeared, putting pressure on the authorities to provide information and respond to legal notices about the disappearances. The women in the APDP mourn and sing songs as part of their emotional and psychological healing.

Women in many other parts of the world have responded to wars and conflicts by different kinds of activism. In Sri Lanka, a camphor campaign for missing relatives was organised in the months of October, November and December 2012 in Colombo, Raddoluwa and Trincomalee. Family members (mostly women) of the disappeared persons, gathered to protest in front of the United Nations office in Colombo and to pay tribute at the Monument of the Disappeared in Raddoluwa (see Figure 9.3). These women have been pushed to become the main breadwinners of the families, in the absence of missing menfolk.

Figure 9.2 Kashmiri human rights activist Parveena Ahangar.

Photograph: Author.

Figure 9.3 Protest in front of UN offices, Colombo, Sri Lanka, 2012.

Photograph: Dushiyanthini Kanagasabapathipillai. Reproduced with kind permission.

Women as combatants and perpetrators

Although the dominant images of women associated with wars have been as grieving widows and mothers, selfless nurses and anti-war activists, since ancient times women have been participating in wars as combatants and supporters in different capacities. 'Women in combat support roles, furthermore, have had little trouble fitting into military organisations, and have held their own when circumstances occasionally placed them in combat (especially in guerrilla wars). They can fight; they can kill' (Goldstein 2001: 127). While women have participated in modern nationalistic wars since the mid-nineteenth century (with anti-state subversive movements in Europe and Russia and anti-colonial wars in Asia and Africa), the state-controlled armed forces in the West opened to women in the 1970s to 'restore legitimacy to the armed forces which in many countries were going through a deep crisis of public consensus' (Addis et al. 1994: xiii).

The inclusion of women in armed combat in different roles is either scripted through an appeal to women's empowerment or to traditional feminine notions of sacrifice, nation and motherhood (Haq 2007; Parashar 2009, 2011a). Women's participation in and support for combat roles, in both states and non-state militaries, is a growing phenomenon and yet is dependent on gender norms that vary from culture to culture. The reasons why Tamil women fought in the war in Sri Lanka were very different from women who contributed to the anti-colonial war in Algeria, to the militant resistance in Kashmir or to the Maoist resistance in Nepal (see Figures 9.4 and 9.5). A number of women continue to participate in war mongering and violent activities of right-wing vigilante groups, even advocating the use of extreme violence and rape against women perceived as the 'enemy' (Bacchetta 2004; Sarkar 1996; Sen 2008).

HOW DO FEMINISTS UNDERSTAND AND STUDY WAR?

Feminists have been reluctant to 'own wars' in the same way as they have owned other social institutions.[5] Christine Sylvester reminds us, 'Feminists understudy war relative to other trans-historical and trans-national institutions, such as the family and religion' (Sylvester 2005). Feminist scholarship, although recognising the significance of the concept of 'militarised masculinity' in understanding the gendered order of wars, also grapples with the dilemma of advancing this concept further and looking at the fluidity of gender roles in wars. Some feminists have argued that wars and conflicts are direct manifestations of militarism traditionally identified with masculine values (Chenoy 2002; Enloe 1983, 2000b). Radical feminists have rejected the idea of women fighting in men's wars claiming special affinity of women with peace (Tickner 2001: 58). Other writings have acknowledged that women are disproportionately affected by wars and conflicts and yet they also experience moments of empowerment and agency in their war experiences. The roles and experiences of women in/of wars are diverse and dramatic and affect their physical and emotional being in very intimate ways (Parashar 2009, 2011b; Sylvester 2005, 2011a, 2012).

Feminist scholarship in the last decade has included war and violent conflict in its scope of research inquiry and theorising, although this has been mediated through the concepts of security and militarisation. In many existing and emerging new works feminists have critiqued 'realist' understandings of wars and the over emphasis on state actors at the cost of common people and their experiences. War and the violence it unleashes is not an extraordinary experience for millions of people forced to live 'inside' wars. The focus on ordinary people and their everyday experiences of war alone make it possible to unravel the gendered stories. There is greater scrutiny of how women participate in these wars and internalise, question and displace patriarchy at the same time.

On 21 May 1990, South Asia awoke to a tragedy with implications far beyond the region. The former Prime Minister of India, Rajiv Gandhi, while on a campaign in the state of Tamil Nadu was assassinated at Sriperumbudur in a suicide bomb attack. The 'human bomb' in this case was a woman who had a suicide vest attached to her torso. It was later discovered that Dhanu, the assassin, was a member of the Liberation Tigers of Tamil Elam (LTTE), the Tamil militant group waging a war against the Sri Lankan State from 1983 to 2009 when they were defeated by military forces and a majority of their leadership killed.

The LTTE had a large number of female cadres who fought alongside their male counterparts and supported the armed resistance in other ways. In the early 80s when they were recruited, women served in supportive roles such as cleaning, nursing, cooking, intelligence and other logistical and administrative duties. The armed resistance itself and women's participation in it were not without paradoxes. The strict control that the LTTE exercised and the disciplinary impositions made on its cadres, on one hand, were balanced by a greater degree of social and cultural freedom experienced by women who were part of it, as also those in the larger Tamil society, on the other. They were not just pure victims or agents but women who systematically broke down the barriers in a highly patriarchal and militarised society for which they also paid a considerable price (Alison 2008; Balasingham 1993; de Mel 2007; de Soyza 2011; Parashar 2009).

Figure 9.4 Liberation Tigers of Tamil Elam (LTTE).

Figure 9.5 Women in the LTTE.
Photograph: Roger Parton.
Reproduced with kind permission.

Through analysing personal narratives, oral histories, open-ended interviews, discourse analysis of primary data such as military doctrines, UN Resolutions, cease-fire orders and peace treaties, feminist scholarship has focused on a range of gendered experiences of war for both men and women. There is also increasing engagement with emotions, not just of people within wars but also of those studying it. Feminist researchers have highlighted the difficulties and challenges of 'doing' research on topics that include war, violence, death and destruction of great magnitude, when their sensibilities are affected during the field work as also during the writing of the research (Sylvester 2011b). This is in the spirit of understanding how the study of wars can work in tandem with the feminist axiom that the 'personal is political'.

An important argument that feminists continue to make is that war's stakeholders are many and the experiences are multiple and gendered for both men and women. If there is a certain kind of masculinity deployed to preserve the conditions that perpetuate wars, women's bodies become the gendered turf for many wars. Despite this close association with wars, women and men are represented in familiar gendered categories, as grieving mothers and widows and as aggressive and violent male combatants. There is little engagement with those who challenge these gender norms; like men who are opposed to war (Rowe 2013) and women who are committed to it (Parashar 2009, 2014). Feminists have mapped the exclusions and silences that have kept women's experiences out of war narratives and have emphasised that war stories need to be retold. Excluding women's experiences of war implies that they are excluded from peace and development initiatives in the post-war moment. Most importantly, lack of gendered understandings of war makes post-war reconstruction and rehabilitation difficult with short-sighted policies in place. In her study of female soldiers in Sierra Leone, Megan MacKenzie points out that the policies in the post-conflict period will be effective only when the gendered experiences of female soldiers are taken into account. She argues that, 'post-conflict policies have the potential to inscribe and enforce exploitative and patriarchal forms of gendered order post armed conflict' (2012: 3). MacKenzie also shows how flawed

DDR programmes can be in the absence of gender input, disempowering women in many ways (2012: 63–84).

CONCLUSION

Feminists across disciplines see women's multiple roles in wars, the complex gender dynamics that give rise to militarised masculinities, gendered nationalism, gender mobilisation strategies, and differential effects of war on different groups of women and men. Nonetheless, many of these studies emphasise the exclusion of women and their politics from war, presenting women as 'acted upon rather than as actors themselves … Their gender is often subverted by their political role or used to discredit them as capable international players' (Hunt and Rygiel 2006: 1).

The impact of this exclusion is the absence of women from formal peace talks and conflict resolution processes. This is based on the widely held belief that men alone participate in wars and armed resistance and thus 'sacrifice' their lives and freedom for their ethnic, political or religious group/community. Women perform multiple roles in wars and political violence, including as armed guerrilla fighters, militants and support systems. However, their experiences are only documented in public memory as 'worst sufferers and victims'. The message from such situations is that stakeholders in peace must have served and sacrificed in the war and it is usually men who are recognised in their war roles. Increasingly, feminist scholarship and activism has challenged this notion of what women 'do'/'are' in wars and articulated that women's voices are critical in not just engendering and sustaining a conflict but also in its resolution.

There is another gendered aspect to this exclusion of women in resolutions to end wars and conflict. 'Peace' deals are waged on women's bodies as we witnessed in the case of the Nizam-e-Adl resolution negotiated between the Taliban and the government of Pakistan in February 2009. Under the 'peace for Sharia' deal the Taliban agreed to stop its armed campaign in the Swat region of North West Pakistan, and surrender its arms in exchange for the legal enforcement of Sharia laws. Sharia courts would interpret civil rights according to Islamic strictures and women would be veiled and pushed into a life of invisibility, violence and abuse. This deal subsequently collapsed because the Taliban refused to disarm but it highlighted how wars – and, also indeed, peace – are waged on women's bodies.

Questions for further debate

1. How are women's and men's experiences of war different or similar? Is it justified to claim that women are disproportionately affected by wars?
2. Women should be included as fighters in the armed forces of nation states. Do you agree? Discuss with examples.
3. Do male and female combatants have different needs for rehabilitation and reintegration when the war ends? Discuss with special reference to UN Resolution 1325.

4. Do women guerrilla fighters and combatants challenge patriarchal gender norms? Is it possible to study the lives of these women beyond the binaries of victimhood and agency?

5. How do women's bodies become repositories of culture, honour and nationalism in war times?

Sources for further reading and research

Cohn, C. (ed.) (2013) *Women and Wars*, Cambridge: Polity Press.

Elshtain, J. B. (1987) *Women and War*, New York: Basic Books.

Enloe, C. (1983) *Does Khaki Become You?*, London: Pluto Press.

MacKenzie, M. (2012) *Female Soldiers in Sierra Leone: Sex, Security, and Post-Conflict Development*, New York: New York University Press.

Sylvester, C. (2013) *War as Experience: Contributions from International Relations and Feminist Analysis*, London: Routledge.

Notes

1 The Boston bombings occurred during the Boston Marathon on 15 April 2013. Improvised explosive devices in the form of two pressure cooker bombs exploded near the finishing line killing three people and injuring 264 others. The suspects were identified two days later as Chechen brothers Dzhokhar and Tamarlan Tsarnaev. Tamarlan was killed in an encounter with the FBI; Dzhokhar was captured after a long chase and is now awaiting trial for waging war on the USA.

2 *Mahabharata* is a popular story in India of a fratricidal war between the Kauravas and Pandavas, the children of two brothers of the Kuru clan who ruled in the north of India in the eighth and ninth century BCE. Although the original epic was written in Sanskrit, several English translations are available. Uberoi (2005) has narrated the story in an effective manner. She has captured the main reasons for going to war and especially the episode of the disrobing and dishonouring of Draupadi, the wife of the five Pandava brothers, the oldest of whom had wagered her in a game of dice with the Kauravas.

3 Sita was the wife of divine incarnate Ram. She was abducted by the demon Ravan when along with her husband, Ram and his brother, Lakshman, she was living in the forest, banished from the kingdom of Ayodhya (north India). Sita's abduction led to a bitter war between Ram and Ravan's forces and when she was rescued, she was forced to sit through fire to prove her chastity to Ram. There are multiple versions of *Ramayan* and the story differs in each version. R. K. Narayan's 2006 Penguin classic is the adaptation of Kamban's *Ramayan* from South India.

4 For more details on the casualties in the Iraq war, see *Iraq: The Human Cost*; http://web.mit.edu/humancostiraq/ (accessed 21 June 2013).

5 Carolyn Nordstrom, Christine Sylvester, Jean Elshtain, Cynthia Enloe, Bina D'Costa, Laura Sjoberg, Caron Gentry, Megan MacKenzie, Cami Rowe, Miranda Alison are notable exceptions whose works have focused on different aspects of wars.

CHAPTER 10

Militarism

Cynthia Cockburn

LEARNING OUTCOMES

Upon completion, readers should be able to:

- Perceive the mutual shaping of gender and war.
- Trace the gender relations in successive time phases of the continuum of war.
- Imagine effective gender strategies for opposing militarism and war.

INTRODUCTION

As discussed in Chapter 9, the relationship between gender and war can be described in at least two contrasting ways. It is often represented as a somewhat casual, contingent, kind of relationship, in which 'men and women' stand in for 'gender', and significance is accorded to 'who does what' in war. Alternatively the gender/war relation may be given much more explanatory importance, to the extent of positing a two-way causality. War may be seen as actually shaping the gender relations of a given society, while, in turn, a certain gender order may be seen as predisposing a society to war (Cockburn 2007, 2010; Goldstein 2001; Reardon 1996).

THE 'SEXUAL DIVISION OF WAR': INTERESTING BUT INSUFFICIENT

Statistically speaking, there is a 'sexual division of war', just as there is a sexual division of labor, in which men and women characteristically play different roles. In all armies, men are the majority of combatants. They undergo a brutalizing training and are expected to kill. More men than women die in combat, while women are more commonly numbered among civilian casualities, dying of disease, malnutrition, sexual violence, and accident. Then again, among refugees UN statistics consistently show women to comprise a significantly higher proportion of adult refugees displaced by armed conflict, so that a characteristic role for women in war is looking after the young, elderly, and sick in extreme conditions. Although figures are impossible to verify, it is also clear that large numbers of women are raped and subjected to other kinds of sexual torture during war (see Chapter 14). Some of the reports of human rights organizations (such as Amnesty International and Human Rights Watch) are descriptive of this gender specificity in various features of war, laying down valuable groundwork for a gender analysis.

Sex-disaggregated statistics do reveal something interesting about probable divergences and contrasts in the experiences and attitudes of women and men in relation to armed conflict. For example, commercial opinion polls often confirm the belief that women are, in general, in some societies, less favourably disposed to war than men. Polls in the UK for instance found that throughout the run-up to the US and British invasion of Iraq in early 2003 one clear-cut demographic pattern was that women were much more hostile to the war, a difference that at its greatest saw almost twice as many men as women approving the government's plans. Yet such statistics, if we read them with attention, also tell us that some women, even if it is a minority, are as much or more inclined to support war as are some men. And indeed, qualitative knowledge reveals many women actually supporting masculine war projects. In England as the First World War broke out some women participated in a 'white feather' campaign. If they saw an able-bodied man of draft age on the streets not wearing a soldier's uniform, they shamed him by giving him a white feather to signify cowardice. Today, in the profoundly patriarchal culture of India's Hindu extremist organizations, women are cast as the selfless wife and mother. But during the massacre of Muslims in Gujarat in 2002 these right-wing women were out on the streets chiding the men for 'wearing bangles' – in other words not being man enough to kill and rape Muslim women. They thus acted in defiance of the stereotype 'women are inclined to be peaceful' yet remained within the bounds of patriarchal relations. Women antiwar activists, it may be noted, by contrast conform to that stereotype while defying patriarchal power and especially its affinity to militarism and nationalism (see Figure 10.1).

Statistics seldom reveal a 100-to-zero per cent difference between the positioning of men and women in the sexual division of labor, life, or war. There are always those 5 per cent, 10 per cent, or 15 per cent of one sex or the other who are 'exceptions'. A useful example is the minority of women among the masculine ranks of military personnel (Carreiras 2006). The proportion of women in Western militaries has shown a marked upward trend in recent years. Women climbed from around 2 per cent to around 20 per cent of the US Army between 1973 and 2008, while in political and ethnic insurgencies in the last few decades, for example in Nicaragua, Chiapas (Mexico) and Sri Lanka, rebel militias have included a significant proportion of women among combatants.

Such figures, at one reading, indicate that women can be similarly positioned to men. But when some men or some women show up like this as a minority statistic, defying a gender stereotype, it does not mean that gender counts for nothing in

The relationship between gender and war may be conceptualized in different ways. It may be seen as involving a certain gender specificity of location, experience and role in militarized societies and in armed conflict. From this perspective, quantitative information will be relevant, although the distinctive differences between men and women thus revealed will never be complete and the exceptions will be informative.

A more profound understanding of 'gender and war' may be achieved through, first, conceptualizing gender as an enduring relation of power, closely intersected with ethno-national and economic power relations, and, second, visualizing war as social, systemic and as a phased continuum. Within a sociological framework of this kind, a study of institutions, processes and cultures reveals patriarchal gender relations to be both cause and consequence of war.

Figure 10.1 Conceptualizing gender and war.

explaining war. On the contrary, the situation of the minority sex in any of these roles and situations is seldom equivalent to that of the majority, and the qualitative difference throws light on both gender and war. For instance, women may have the right to join the military, but when they choose to do so their experience is very different from that of men. For one thing, women soldiers characteristically experience sexual harassment and rape by their male comrades and superiors. (See Figure 10.2 for an autobiographical account by a young woman soldier of her service in Iraq, evidence that being a woman soldier does not yield the same experience as being a male soldier.)

Instances such as those just examined suggest that to fully understand the relationship of gender and war we need to know more than the statistical distributions of wartime roles between men and women. Much more meaningful is the expression of the gender *relations* in war, the qualitative relation between masculinity and femininity, as sets of ideals and values, qualities, motivations and vectors, mapped onto the bodies and behaviours of men and women respectively in complex and sometimes contradictory ways. When we see things this way, the minority experiences revealed in the statistics, instead of negating the significance of gender and stating 'one sex can do whatever the other can do', turn out to be hiding a

Kayla Williams was promoted to sergeant during her tour of duty with the US Army in Iraq. She thought of herself as a capable and well-adapted soldier like any other: 'I do fifty-five push-ups in under a minute. Tough, and proud to be tough. I love my M-4, the smell of it, of cleaning fluid, of gunpowder: the smell of strength. Gun in your hands, and you're in a special place' (Williams 2005: 15).

Ninety-one per cent of all army career fields were open to Williams, and like the male soldiers in her unit, she had encounters with a dangerous and violent enemy in the war zone of Iraq. But it was encounters with her male colleagues that stuck fast in her memory so that six months after her return she was still having difficulty convincing herself, as she put it: 'I am not a slut.' She wrote: 'A woman soldier has to toughen herself up. Not just for the enemy, for battle, or for death. I mean toughen herself to spend months awash in a sea of nervy, hyped-up guys who, when they're not thinking about getting killed, are thinking about getting laid. Their eyes on you all the time, your breasts, your ass – like there is nothing else to watch … It was like a separate bloodless war within the larger deadly one' (Williams 2005: 13, 22).

Figure 10.2 On being a female soldier.

profound qualitative difference. Gender relations are much more than 'who does what' and they permeate militarization and war, through and through.

PATRIARCHAL GENDER RELATIONS AND A SOCIOLOGICAL TAKE ON WAR

Perceiving gender as a relation reveals it to be consistently a relation of power, that is to say, of asymmetry, inequality and domination. It calls for the notion of a sex/gender system with continuity over time and expression in institutions and cultures. In the contemporary world and far back in the past those societies of which we know have all, to differing degrees and in different ways, been characterized by the supremacy of men and masculinity, the subordination of women and femininity. The term commonly used to describe such a gender order is 'patriarchy', its meaning now extended beyond 'rule of the father' to rule by men more generally, both in the public and private realm. Patriarchy's persistence over at least 5,000 years and its variations from region to region have been widely mapped and discussed, and are mentioned elsewhere in this volume (see also Lerner 1986). Social structures and their institutions are adaptively reproduced from one generation to the next in the main by cultural means – most importantly in the case of patriarchy by the cultural shaping, in continually changing circumstances, of hegemonic masculinity in a form adequate to power, and particularly to the deployment of coercive power. It must have authority over subordinate (and sometimes rebellious) masculinities, while femininity too must be appropriately shaped, taking a form that assures female compliance and cooperation with the patriarchal project. Thus women sign up to the 'patriarchal bargain' (Kandiyoti 1988), while men, to different degrees in different social classes and ethnic groups, benefit from the 'patriarchal dividend' (Connell 1987). From this perspective, we can see that the hierarchical and complementary gender relations of a patriarchal order, in which men and masculinity are authoritative, combative and prone to coercion, while women and femininity are submissive, supportive and nurturing, are particularly fitted to the needs of militarist and nationalist societies and cultures.

The cultural processes through which patriarchal gender relations are generated – upbringing and schooling, recreation, media, employment – in most societies include immersion in militarization and war, either fictively or in reality. War – the experience of war, remembering war, fearing war, and preparing for war – shapes masculinities and feminities. To see the influence exerted on each other by gender and war it helps to study war with a sociologist's lens. While the hegemonic international relations analysis of war focuses on the macro-level concerns of statehood, sovereignty, security and the balance of power, sociologists stress that war, despite its deadliness, involves human relationships. As Brian E. Fogarty puts it, 'warfare is a distinctly social enterprise' (Fogarty 2000: 21). People participate in war as groups. They do so in the understanding that they are willing if necessary to kill and die for some social purpose. In these circumstances, it is implicitly agreed that war is not murder. And (whether they are observed or not) there are 'rules' of warfare – such as the Geneva Conventions. Many feminist sociologists by now have added a gender perspective to this sociological understanding of war.

War, besides, is systemic. It may be imagined as a set of interacting or interdependent entities (government ministries, arms manufacturing firms, training academies, fighting units), functionally related, with inputs and outputs, and information flows within and across its open borders. The system has products (bombs, battleships, bullets), and influential ideologies (expressed in values, attitudes and cultures). War seen systemically in this way readily opens up to a gender analysis. Its institutions can be seen as loci of several dimensions of power, among which is that of gender. A military training academy, for instance, is likely to be, simultaneously, a site of economic power and its class relations, of ethno-national, racialized, relations, and of patriarchal gender relations. These and other dimensions of power are interwoven, they are intersectional, each working with, in and through the others. We can see overlaps and information flows between the war system and other social systems – education, the arts, sport, for instance – and the significance in all of them of gender, as of other, power relations.

So, war as relational, war as systemic – and a third qualifier also is important here: the idea that actual wars are only phases in a sequence of conditions linked together as a *continuum*. This is particularly clear to the organizations and networks of the movement that opposes war, which now span the globe and are linked by electronic communications. Some of them, rather than seeking to end or prevent particular wars, address militarist thinking and the build up of nuclear arsenals. They seek to prevent wars breaking out, and strive for demobilization after war. Thus they inevitably see 'war' as part of a continuum. The spiralling cycle leads from militarism (as a persisting mindset, expressed in philosophy, newspaper editorials, church sermons), through militarization (processes in economy and society that signify preparation for war), to episodes of 'hot' war, and thence to ceasefire and standoff, followed perhaps by an unsteady peace with sustained military investment, beset by sporadic verbal and physical violence, prefiguring a further twist to the spiral (Cockburn 2004).

Many mainstream commentaries reflect this perception of a phased cycle or continuum of war. They show, for example, how high military expenditure in the West was maintained despite the end of the Cold War. They suggest that in contemporary civil wars some participants have a vested interest not in winning war but rather in continued conflict and in the long-term institutionalization of violence. Some have pointed out that the age of industrial warfare has ended, and the new paradigm of war fought among civilians has increased the continuum effect. Seeing war as processual in this way assists a gender perspective, allowing for the various cultures and subcultures of militarization and war to come to light, and the part of masculinity and femininity in them. International Relations theory approaches war very differently from feminist sociology. It reveals other aspects of war that are certainly important to know, but it does not readily reveal gender at work.

SEEING GENDER AND WAR AS MUTUALLY PRODUCTIVE

Just as, at first sight, it seems counter-intuitive to think of war as social, so it seems counter-intuitive to see violence as productive. But the violence of war does indeed produce social relations in certain forms that endure long after a given episode of fighting has ended. For example, the wars involved in the disintegration of Yugoslavia in the 1990s are commonly held to have been 'caused by' ethnic enmities among and between Serb, Croat and Bosnian Muslim segments of the population of Yugoslavia. Yet the ethnic distinctiveness of Serb, Croat and Bosnian Muslim may just as easily be seen as produced, and intentionally produced, *through* the violence (Zarkov 2007). The productiveness in the case of the gender/war relation was likewise mutual, working in both directions simultaneously. Prior to war, the social order of Yugoslavia, although in other ways considerably modified by the ideology and administrative measures of the League of Communists, had continued to be a male-dominated gender order and heavily militarized. It had been producing masculinity and femininity in a form conducive to war (see Figure 10.3). During the 1990s the convulsion of armed conflict then deepened gender divisions in such a way that in this present period, dubiously deemed 'post-war', feminists find themselves obliged to struggle for women's rights (and simultaneously for a restoration of inclusion, unity and peace) in a gender order that is more hierarchical, undemocratic and divisive than it was before the wars began.

Maintaining preparedness for war

Masculinities in many societies, even in times that appear to be 'peaceful', are socially constructed through activities such as competitive sports and computer games in a form that is readily adaptable to serve well in war conditions. James McBride suggests that, in the USA, football is an allegory or metaphor for war, sharing its pursuit of male territorial gains. 'Football, like war,' he writes, 'is a form of male aggression, consciously played out in a variety of cultural practices' (McBride 1995: 4). He notes that domestic violence by men against women surges during significant football events and at the onset of wars. With its male-bonding rituals, McBride writes, 'the game of football reinscribes war and the concomitant values of the warrior as a template for the identity of football enthusiasts – the vast majority of men in America' (McBride 1995: 86).

In the patriarchal gender orders that prevail in our societies, gender is a relation of power. It intersects with other significant dimensions of power such as those of economic class and that of ethno-national relations. They shape each other and often achieve their effects, including militarization and war, through the self-same institutions and cultural processes.

Patriarchal gender relations, in which men and masculinity are constituted as sharply contrasted to women and femininity, and as both superior and complementary to them, are highly favourable to militarist and nationalist interests. This is particularly the case where hegemonic masculinity is shaped as authoritative, competitive and aggressive, and where women value, or tolerate, these qualities in men. Such gender relations predispose societies to war, while militarization and war violence in turn produce them. In such an analysis, the transformation of gender relations is necessary if peace is to be achieved and sustained.

Figure 10.3 Militarism and patriarchy.

An elite group of men continually engaged in readying the USA for war are the defence intellectuals who debate and plan the country's nuclear weapons policy. Carol Cohn, a feminist social scientist, was shocked to find, during participant observation among such a group, that these articulate, charming, humorous, and decent men routinely discussed the most horrific possibilities of vaporized cities and mangled bodies in light-hearted, abstract and euphemistic terms, revealing an 'astounding chasm between image and reality' in their techno-strategic language (Cohn 1990: 34; see also Chapter 3). The linking thread in the discourse of this nuclear 'priesthood', as she terms them, was sexism. It was their masculinity that enabled them to distance themselves from the actual death and destruction implied in their work, inescapable to anyone engaged with everyday human care and concern.

It is not only masculinity, however, that keeps a society trapped on the continuum of war. Femininity plays its part, too. Painful examples of women, deeply embedded in conventional patriarchal gender relations, urging their men to fight, and even to rape enemy women, were given earlier. Many less dramatic but quietly pervasive processes have been observed in which civilian women are induced to play an unquestioning part in support of societal militarization.

Taking a country into war

The moment of entry into war can be especially revealing of the causal effect of gender. Italian fascism and German National Socialism were able to draw on a radicalized masculinity emerging from World War I, to reconstruct a sense of national community and prepare for World War II. More recently, it has been suggested that patriarchal masculinity was at the root of the erroneous political decision to take the USA into war against the Communist regime in Vietnam. Robert Dean found the policymakers of the time to have been 'a small and strikingly homogenous group', strongly formed by their shared class and gender belonging. He shows how those foreign policy decisionmakers 'incarnated an imperial masculinity tied to patterns of class and education'. They shared a background in exclusive male-only institutions, such as boarding schools, Ivy League fraternities and secret societies, elite military service, and metropolitan men's clubs, 'where imperial traditions of "service" and "sacrifice" were invented and bequeathed to those that followed'. They served to imbue men with a particular kind of manhood, indoctrinate them in an 'ideology of masculinity', ritually creating 'a fictive brotherhood of privilege and power' (Dean 2001: 4–5). These were the patriarchal gender relations that, intertwined with those of economic class and nationalism/imperialism, disposed a group of men to lead their country into a doomed war.

Training men to fight

In certain widespread and influential male subcultures, the masculinity fostered and rewarded is aggressive and violent. We see this in computer games, in certain forms of music, in popular film, and in the fascination knives and guns hold for men and boys. These cultures predispose young males to see themselves as potential fighters and to consider armed conflict normal, even a fulfilment of their manhood. John Horne made a study of masculinity in war and politics over 100 years from 1850. He proposes that to fully understand war we need to explore 'the dense associative life of men' (Horne 2004: 27). It is through hard cultural *work*, the shaping and manipulation of that sociality, that military managers create their armies. Those destined to be leaders are educated in an authoritative masculinity in officer training courses, while those destined to be the rank-and-file are subjected to acquisition of a different masculinity in the disciplinary torture of 'boot camp', where drill sergeants prepare their recruits for war by reinforcing their racism, misogyny, and homophobia, annihilating any vestige of the feminine in them.

War fighting

A feature of many if not most wars is mass sexual violence inflicted by men on women – and on some men (see Chapters 13 and 14 for fuller discussions of this issue). It occurs in phases of fighting that afford particular opportunity for it, such as invasions, occupations and the imposition of state terror on political insurgencies. Many authors have explored the relationship of so-called 'peacetime' rape and war rape. Rape in both circumstances may be opportunistic and 'recreational', a product of the deep misogyny among men (and, unfortunately, among many women, too, it must be said) characteristic of societies in both conditions. However, we are now more alert to situations where military commanders make deliberate use of mass rape by their soldiers to demoralize enemy communities, a strategy that is the more effective the more these are known to value female chastity as a property of masculine honour (Seifert 1995).

Negotiating peace

Declarations of peace usually involve a victorious and a defeated side. While this provokes a crisis for the defeated, it can also be a demanding moment for the victor, for he must ensure that the defeated enemy is not totally reduced. Patriarchy as a generalized system of masculine authority demands at least a partial restitution of the defeated male's masculine dignity. This imperative is apparent in the fact that in contemporary armed conflicts there is a clear reluctance to remove responsibility for the negotiation of peace from the hands of the men who made war, even though they may, due to their part in the conflict and by experience and training, be inappropriate for the task. The passing of UN Security Council Resolution 1325 of 2000, on *Women, Peace and Security*, which among other things calls for women to be included in peace negotiations, recognizes this problem. The Resolution can be seen as an interestingly anti-patriarchal measure introduced, under organized pressure by women, by the most masculine and authoritiative body (the Security Council) in the United Nations system.

Recovery from defeat

After the ignominious withdrawal from Saigon in 1975, the shock to the US psyche of the defeat of its massive military power by a small guerrilla force brought about a kind of national trauma, felt as a collapse of manly pride and self-respect. This postwar period has interested several gender researchers. James Gibson and Susan Jeffords, for example, analyse novels and films of the period, and dwell in particular on the characteristic 'lone hero' of postwar culture. Rambo and others like him are hyper-masculine warriors with a vicious and insatiable appetite for destruction, 'the epitome of masculine power and self-development, and combat as the only life worth living' (Gibson 1994: 32). These authors see such cultural productions as part of a strategy of remasculinization, invoking a masculine bond across class and colour, excluding women from the masculine realm, and taking revenge on the state and the anti-war movement, both despised as effeminate and effeminizing. Jeffords is emphatic that we should not perceive and respond to war as merely the antithesis of peace. Rather, we should see the discourse of warfare as the primary vehicle for the stiffening of masculine resolve in American society (Jeffords 1989).

Constituting citizenship as masculine and military

In some cultures, the link between masculinity and war is highly explicit and is not dependent on an imminent war. Since Mustafa Kemal Ataturk brought the modern Turkish state into being in 1923, Turkey has seen itself as not merely a nation but a 'military nation'. The Turkish man has been visualized before all else as a soldier. Ayse Gul Altinay shows the two-way productiveness of gender and militarization in Turkey through analyzing the militarizing role given to schools and the educating role given to the military. She suggests 'that the practice of compulsory military service has created a major gender difference administered by the state, and that the decision-makers were well aware of the gender implications of this practice from the very beginning' (Altinay 2004: 7).

Others have suggested that the modern national armies of nineteenth-century Europe were both made by and makers of gender relations. One study has pointed to a connection between male suffrage and conscript armies in the making of citizenship. When working-class men got the vote it enabled them to enter for the first time into relations of notional equality with men of other classes, while simultaneously male citizenship was being constructed crucially around military service in the new conscript armies. Increasingly, these authors say, masculinity was 'virilized', differentiated ever more emphatically from femininity (Dudink and Hagemann 2004: 11). Modern armies were 'established through strongly gendered discourses' and were at the same time 'co-producers of a universalising discourse of sexual difference'. As such they became 'the pillars of social and political order' (Dudink and Hagemann 2004: 17).

CONCLUSION

In the instances examined in this chapter, and many more from different periods and different places, gender relations may be seen as both cause and consequence of war. War shapes gender relations in a particular mode, while, in turn, those gender relations act as a motor of war. A logical implication is that the strategies of movements that seek to end militarization and war must include a transformation of gender relations.

Questions for further debate

1. In what ways might the gender relations of more and less militarized societies be expected to differ?
2. Women may achieve a greater degree of agency through the demands made of them in wartime. Can this shift postwar gender relations in a direction that does not predispose to further war?
3. The great majority of conscientious objectors are male. Is this an effect only of the gendered conscription policy of most nation states?
4. When women encourage their menfolk and nation to engage in war does this contradict patriarchal gender relations?
5. Must an effective movement against militarism, nationalism and patriarchy necessarily be anti-homophobic?

Sources for further reading and research

Anonymous (2005) *A Woman in Berlin*, London: Virago.
Cockburn, C. (2007) *From Where We Stand: War, Women's Activism and Feminist Analysis*, London and New York: Zed Books.
Enloe, C. (2000) *Maneuvers: The International Politics of Militarizing Women's Lives*, London and Berkeley, CA: University of California Press.
Whitworth, S. (2004) *Men, Militarism and Peacekeeping: A Gendered Analysis*, London and Boulder, CO: Lynne Rienner.
Woolf, V. (1997) *Three Guineas*, Harmondsworth: Penguin Books.

CHAPTER 11

Terrorism and political violence

Caron Gentry and Laura Sjoberg

LEARNING OUTCOMES

Upon completion, readers should be able to:

- Recognize the gendered binary that exists between state and non-state actors and its dependency upon the Westphalian notion of state sovereignty and monopoly on violence.
- See the label of terrorism is beholden to gendered ideals of rationality and legitimacy.
- Understand the ways in which 'non-state' politically violent actors are gendered in discourses of terrorism and counterterrorism.

INTRODUCTION

It is well known within International Relations and the subfield of Terrorism Studies, that a universally agreed definition for 'terrorism' is elusive and undecided. Most scholars (English 2009; Hoffman 2006; Jackson 2005; Richardson 2006; Schmid and Jongman 2006) would argue that terrorism is a value-laden term, a pejorative, used to discredit and delegitimize those who are labelled 'terrorists'. Feminist scholarship reveals how power hierarchies are created through binaries, such as masculinities and femininities (Peterson and Runyan 2010; Steans 2006; Tickner 1992). One such binary is key to understanding how terrorism is approached as a subject. States are always seen as the legitimate, heroic, rational actor (masculinized) and terrorist actors as illegitimate, horrifically violent and irrational (feminized or devalorized). Feminists would thus note that 'terrorist' is also a heavily gendered term used to devalorize politically violent actors, replicating the Westphalian binary of masculinized/legitimate states with the monopoly on violence against feminized/ illegitimate non-state actors without access to sanctioned forms of violence.

Using gender analysis helps to see the gender biases in the concept of 'terrorism' that are at the apex of its definitional concerns, political problems and moral ambiguities. The first section of this chapter examines the definitional problem of terrorism, not just for inconsistencies but also for how what or who is included (and excluded) in common definitions and how these inclusions/exclusions are gendered. In the second section, we problematize terrorism by looking for its gendered implications. The next section points out one of the important elements of using gender analysis to theorize terrorism: understanding how people identified as terrorists are gendered in media and scholarly discussions of their actions. The final section discusses genderings in counterterrorism theory and practice.

WHAT IS TERRORISM?

Alex Schmid and Albert Jongman have tried to highlight the various aspects of the definition issue in relation to the concept of terrorism. For the second edition of their book, *Political Terrorism* (2006), they surveyed scholars and policymakers for a definition of terrorism. Schmid and Jongman received 109 different responses. They then coded these definitions and came up a list of ten terms that showed up with the most frequency. These are:

• violence, force	83.5 per cent
• political	65 per cent
• fear, terror emphasized	51 per cent
• threat	47 per cent
• psychological effects and anticipated reactions	41.5 per cent
• victim–target differentiation	37.5 per cent
• systematic, organized action	32 per cent
• method of combat, strategy, tactic	30.5 per cent
• extranormality	30 per cent
• coercion	28 per cent

Thus, most scholars would emphasize that terrorism is *violence* most often directed at *non-combatants* used to emphasize a *political* position and intended to spread *fear and terror*. While no part of these characteristics determines that a 'terrorist' must be a non-state actor, many scholars limit the use of the term to non-state actors, meaning it distinguishes both a method of violence and a type of actor (see Hoffman 2006; Richardson 2005) (see Figure 11.1).

In her classic article, Carole Pateman (1980) traces how women have been constructed as 'disordered beings'. She defines disorder as:
- civil disorder: riot, breakdown of law and order
- personal: internal malfunction of an individual; disordered imagination; disorder of health.

She outlines how women's 'threatening nature' has been attributed to engendering vice; bringing a state to ruin; making women hostile and contrary to civilization; and are, overall, subversive forces. Through ancient and modern gendered constructions of individuals and society, women are seen as biologically weak and unable to handle the weight of civic and political responsibilities. This means they are unable to grasp the full ideas of justice. Men, by way of contrast, constructed as rational beings, are able to handle the responsibilities of public life.

Ann Tickner (1992) critiques Morgenthau for transposing the rational man onto the state: that in the Westphalian system, IR scholars have granted masculine characteristics to states. These include rationality, logic, and assertiveness. But this assertion of states as rational actors rests on the notion that an opposite force/actor exists. In some work, participation in international organizations is seen as irrational (see Kenneth Waltz's use of Rousseau's stag hunt (1959: 167–70)).

For the purposes of this chapter, how can the rational/irrational binary be seen in the tensions between states and non-state politically violent groups? Can one apply Pateman's criticism of 'disordered' women to 'disordered' terrorists?

Figure 11.1 The disorder of women, the disorder of terrorist organizations.

Defining terrorism is as controversial among policy institutions as it is among scholars and policymakers. The 'official' definition of the United Nations General Assembly (UNGA) includes intentional and unlawful causing of death, bodily harm, property damage and/or economic loss with the purpose of intimidating populations or compelling government or intergovernmental organization action. While this definition is fairly straightforward, other parts of the United Nations and even other resolutions of the UNGA, have different definitions. Even within a country such as the United States, multiple government agencies hold multiple definitions. Each definition is subjective (see Jackson 2005), context based (see Hoffman 2006) and politically beholden to the purposes of those defining it (see Jackson et al. 2009).

Perhaps because of these difficulties, there is a trend towards characterizing terrorism (as a 'weapon of the weak', as 'one person's freedom fighter is another's terrorist' and as 'new' and Islamic) rather than defining it. Through gender lenses, each of these characterizations brings with it a history and a set of problems. Characterizing terrorism as a 'weapon of the weak' is based on a Westphalian notion that a state both does *and should* have a monopoly on the legitimate use of force in politics. This implies a divide between the (legitimate) state and the (illegitimate) non-state, which feminist scholars (see, e.g., Tickner 1992) have criticized as not only false but insidious, hiding the violence of states towards their marginalized citizens, including women. 'The weak', then, are opposed to 'the strong' legitimate states, and are by definition delegitimized and devalorized by the reification of a gendered notion of sovereignty. Suggesting that 'one person's terrorist is another's freedom fighter', while acknowledging the subjectivity of the definition of terrorism, does little to deconstruct the use of the label. Many people are accused of and punished for 'terrorism' only to be later recognized as heroes or freedom fighters (see Figures 11.2 and 11.3).

Perhaps the most insidious of these shortcut characterizations, through gender lenses, is also one of the most influential: the 'new terrorism' thesis espoused by Bruce Hoffman (1999, 2002) and Walter Laqueur (1996, 2000). In a nutshell, 'new terrorism' proponents argue that terrorism used to be about few deaths for a big audience and a political cause, and now focuses on large-scale attacks and mass casualties with an ideological or fundamentalist religious cause. While most 'new terrorism' theorists do not explicitly say it, the effect (and some argue intent) of their understanding of terrorism is to associate a bigger, badder, terrorism with Islam. Both the empirical validity of the 'new terrorism' thesis and the normative problems with this association have been widely critiqued in the literature (see Githens-Mazer and Lambert 2010; Jackson 2005; Puar and Rai 2002; Tuastad 2003), but tend to have salience as a shortcut to understanding terrorism. Critics of this idea suggest that its salience in academia and in government comes from longstanding prejudices against Muslims and the Arab world, which is often referred to as Orientalism.

The word 'Orientalism' was first used by Edward Said (1978) to describe a Western perspective towards Muslim populations that assumes that all people associated with Islam are fundamentally unable to progress and adhere to Western standards of morality and civilization. The prejudiced assumptions include: that Muslims are less intelligent and incapable of learning; that Muslim men are more violent, controlling and hypersexualized than Western men; that Muslim women are more submissive and therefore helpless than Western women; and that all Muslims are religiously fundamentalist (see Akram 2000; Nader 1989; Said 1978). Postcolonial feminist scholars have identified the association between Islam and

Figure 11.2 Nelson Mandela and F. W. de Klerk.
Image: Wikimedia Commons.

It may be surprising to some that former president of South Africa, Nelson Mandela, and one of the iconic images for peace and reconciliation, was once considered a terrorist by the South African apartheid government. Mandela had been a leader of a political party, the African National Congress (ANC), that advocated the violent overthrow of the apartheid regime. In 1964 Mandela was found guilty of counts relating to guerrilla activity and sentenced to life in prison on Robbin Island. Mandela's leadership of the movement against apartheid *from prison* paired with immense pressure from the international community to change the government of South Africa, led to the end of apartheid. President de Klerk legalized the ANC and freed Mandela, effectively changing his classification from 'terrorist' to 'political leader' very quickly. In 1994, Mandela was elected to be the first post-apartheid South African president and is now seen as a hero for his activism in the face of danger.

By way of contrast, Augusto Pinochet, the fascist dictator of Chile from 1973 to 1990, was a state leader when he committed acts that would likely have otherwise been defined as terrorism, including but not limited to targeting, kidnapping and torturing civilians to maintain his control over his country. Pinochet also participated in Operation Condor, identifying left-wing activists for both the United States and other South American juntas who injured or killed them. Pinochet was protected internationally from any charges that might link to terrorism due to his status as a former leader of a sovereign state.

If a 'terrorist' can become a 'freedom fighter' and then a state leader and a hero, why can a state leader not become a terrorist? Is terrorism a method, a style of violence, or does it also depend on the identity or ideology of the actor?

Figure 11.3 Who is a terrorist? The cases of Nelson Mandela and Augusto Pinochet.

terrorism as both racist and sexist, a fundamental problem with terrorism theories and counterterrorism policies (see Nayak 2006).

It is therefore easy to see that none of these shortcut characterizations, not least the association of terrorism and Islam, solves either the definitional or political problems with the word 'terrorism'. Yet, many scholars want to study and teach about terrorism, and many students want to learn about it. This conundrum often creates a 'we know it when we see it' sort of attitude towards labelling terrorists (see Richardson 2006: 19). The things we 'know' as terrorism tend to focus on causing fear by deliberately targeting non-combatants, something that has been on the wrong side of theoretical and jurisprudential laws of war for centuries if not millennia (see Bellamy 2008). Perhaps because of this 'knowledge', it is easy to associate terrorism with normative wrong (and even monstrosity) and counterterrorism with normative right (and even heroism).

Yet this association does not always tell the whole story. For example, in the 2004 Beslan school siege by Chechen 'terrorists', 334 hostages were killed, including 186 children. Doubtless, the Chechens who seized the school did something normatively wrong. Still, the impulse to hold the Chechens *as 'terrorists'* wholly responsible for the deaths seems empirically and normatively problematic. It was actually Russian security forces who both escalated the confrontation and killed some of the hostages. Certainly, the Russian 'counterterrorists' share some of the empirical and normative blame for the deaths. This analysis also does not take into account the political context of Russian forces being responsible for mass killings and endemic sexual violence, among other atrocities, in Chechnya. While that in no way takes the blame from the Chechens, it shows a more complicated picture than the evil 'terrorists' wronging the legitimate 'counterterrorists'.

GENDERING TERRORISMS

Feminist scholars have expressed concerns that a number of things that technically fit most definitions of terrorism are selectively left out of being labelled as terrorism. For example, 'many feminists in social work and psychology have demonstrated the parallels between domestic violence and terrorism', where domestic violence victims 'face violence or the threat of violence to inculcate fear and to coerce or intimidate them into compliance' (Sjoberg 2009: 71). For nearly four decades, couples and family therapy scholars have argued that a particular form of domestic abuse, a situation in which violence escalates and is meant to control and intimidate the spouse, is related to the ideological system and structure of patriarchy. Because it is related to ideology, which espouses political goals, and is a form of violence meant to create terror, these scholars call this form of abuse 'patriarchal terrorism' (see Dobash and Dobash 2004; Gentry 2013; Johnson 1995).

This is one of the first gendered things that one sees in the concept of terrorism – the 'you know it when you see it' definition excludes some things that would qualify under most of the explicit definitions. We argue that the normally excluded elements usually happen to women, who are assumed to be by definition irrelevant to the study (and practice) of terrorism. Women are underrepresented in the study of terrorism, as scholars and as subjects. Many recent books and journal articles understood to be the 'state of the art' in terrorism studies omit women altogether, while others cast them in traditional, one-dimensional gender roles. As we will discuss later, this has a significant influence on who is identified as a 'terrorist'.

That impact is because the omission of women from terrorism studies accompanies and is accompanied by the omission of values, character traits, ways of knowing, and methods of analysis associated with femininity. Scholars who study terrorism usually only use analytical tools associated with masculinity – objective 'scientific' research into terrorists' autonomous 'rational' behaviour. This work ignores the feminist realization that all knowledge is both *perspectival* and *political* – including knowledge about what terrorism is and how terrorism works. As a result, it often pays inadequate attention to the political context of 'terrorist' actors, their interdependence, the role of emotion in triggering and reacting to their behaviour and often neglects personalized and politicized ways of studying them.

In addition to leaving out these 'parts' of the 'whole' of studying terrorism, the gender blinders on terrorism studies often causes scholars to stop short of studying a particular – and particularly important – context in which acts of terrorism are committed. It is important to pay attention to the fact that terrorism and insurgency *take place in a gendered world* (Sjoberg 2011: 237) (see Figure 11.4). Each person engaging in, or reacting to, actions classified as terrorism, lives in a community structured by gender hierarchy within a gendered state in a gender-hierarchical international system. Thus, if terrorism studies fails to account for the complexities of gender, it provides an incomplete account of the factors that go into producing and countering political violence.

Just days after the 9/11 attacks, posters were placed in New York depicting Osama bin Laden as being sodomized by the Empire State Building with the caption: 'The Empire Strikes Back.' Puar and Rai (2002) argue that this is a demonstration of the United States' affronted masculinity asserting itself against the masculinity of not just bin Laden but the whole of Al Qaeda and potentially all of Islam. In their fascinating article, they create links between images such as the poster in New York with the activities of the War on Terror. For instance, it is well known that torture took place in Abu Ghraib, a prison in Iraq taken over by US forces to hold terrorist suspects during the war in Iraq. Much of this torture was sexualized and used to emasculate Iraqi men. Rape and forced masturbation were common. This extra-normative violence targeted the deeply held beliefs about sexuality in Iraqi culture and was meant to shame the violated men and women.

What are other examples of how political violence uses gender norms regarding societal position and sexuality to undermine and demoralize the opposing side?

Figure 11.4 Sexuality, new terrorism and counterterrorism activities.

Gendered terrorists

One of the shortcut assumptions usually made about terrorism is that terrorists are men. Gender stereotypes that assume women's innocence and non-violence make the idea of a female terrorist seem like an oxymoron. Therefore, when women work with organizations usually understood as 'terrorists' or commit acts usually understood as acts of 'terrorism', governments, media outlets and even scholars are often confused. Although women have entered a number of personal and professional spheres that were previously reserved for men, including soldiering, the idea that women are capable of violence, which is *by definition* morally wrong, still seems to be outside the boundaries of femininity (see Sjoberg and Gentry 2007).

Still, no matter which definition of terrorism is used, there is a large and growing number of female terrorists both currently active and historically documented. There have been female suicide bombers in Palestine, Syria, Iraq, Yemen, Kenya, Afghanistan, Chechnya, Sri Lanka, India and Pakistan, to name a few. Women have committed acts classified as terrorist for organizations as diverse as the right-wing Ku Klux Klan (United States) and the left-wing Shining Path (Peru); the Red Army Faction (a Marxist-Leninist group in West Germany) and Al Qaeda (a global Islamist movement); the Liberation Tamil Tigers of Elam (a Tamil independence movement in Sri Lanka) and the Chechen separatist movement. Women have engaged in bombings, aeroplane hijackings, support operations, militant fighting, intelligence gathering and other activities for these and many other organizations generally understood as terrorist. Several organizations labelled terrorists have explicit policies including women and seeking women's rights (such as the LTTE, or the FARC (Revolutionary Armed Forces of Colombia) in Colombia), and others, though more conservative on gender rights issues, have recruited for women (such as Al Qaeda). All of these, however, still face challenges to the full integration of women (see Alison 2008; MacDonald 1988; Ness 2008; Parashar 2009; Tétreault 1994).

Although women have been involved in many if not most movements classified as terrorist in recent history, the shortcut idea of what a terrorist is remains male. When women commit terrorism, they are often distanced both from regular or normal femininity and from agency in their actions. They are sometimes characterized as products of femininity gone awry, a move that allows the preservation both of the idea of the purity of femininity and of the masculinism of terrorists. As our previous work has discussed, women terrorists are often characterized with gender-essentialist narratives about motherhood, monstrosity or sexuality. In each of these narratives, women are compelled to violence by flaws in their femininity: by the need to avenge either infertility or the harm of children, by insanity, by hypersexuality or by Lesbianism (Sjoberg and Gentry 2008a). While there is virtually no evidence that these motivations play any (much less a dominant) role in women's terrorism, they are often the features of accounts of women's terrorism. Women's terrorism is frequently characterized as *psychological* rather than political, and *involuntary* rather than agential.

The stereotypical (new) 'terrorist', then, becomes a *hypermasculine* man, politically motivated but religiously inspired, aggressive, dominant, and violent without the restraint that would come from civilization, from being bounded by a state, from being strong. Seeing that women are 'terrorists' suggests that the idea of terrorism needs to be rethought. Terrorism has been theorized largely as if it is the enterprise of men; theorizing it as the enterprise of men and women changes how we think about how *people* (men and women) commit terrorism (see Parashar 2009; Sjoberg and Gentry 2008).

Particularly, recognizing women as terrorists suggests that it is important to question the personal/political divide. While the literature characterizes 'terrorists' as politically motivated and 'female terrorists' as psychologically motivated, seeing terrorism as something that both men and women do suggests that politically violent actors have both personal and political motivations. Recognizing women as terrorists also helps to see past the rational/emotional divide. 'Terrorists' are often assumed to be rational actors, while 'women terrorists', even when rational, are seen as 'rationally' driven by emotional concerns (e.g., Bloom 2011; Pape 2005). Seeing terrorism as something both men and women do suggests that strategic and emotional considerations play a role in decisions to commit political violence. Understanding that women commit acts of terrorism also helps to interrogate traditional notions of terrorist decision making. 'Terrorists' are often seen as decision makers, while 'female terrorists' are seen as without agency in their violence. Seeing terrorism as something women and men do helps us understand that terrorists are never fully independent in their decision making, but maintain agency in their decisions; they are, to different degrees, relationally autonomous (see Hirschmann 1989).

Gendered counterterrorisms

The construction of counterterrorism is entirely dependent on how the activity of terrorism is perceived. As the new terrorism thesis has shaped the perspective of policymakers and academics alike many counterterrorism policies reflect these influences. For instance, it is argued that many of the events of the 'War on Terror' are owed to new terrorism and its relationship with Orientalism (see Tuastad 2003). Such a fundamentally flawed and biased perspective has influenced counterterrorism policy for the past 15 years. Often counterterrorism policies can be examined for constructions of gender and race as illustrated in Figure 11.4. These racialized and gendered conceptions of all people associated with Islam have allowed for problematic international and domestic counterterrorism policies to emerge. Despite the fact that only one out of 498 terrorist attacks in Europe was conducted by radical Islamist actors in 2006 (and four out of 583 in 2007) (Europol 2009), the key agenda in Western and global counterterrorism is combatting radical Islamist groups such as Al Qaeda (see Cortright and Lopez 2007; Githens-Mazer and Lambert 2010; Romaniuk 2010). Nonetheless, the influence of new terrorism can be seen in a case study of the United Kingdom's domestic counterterrorism policies.

The UK's CONTEST counterterrorism strategy

The UK's counterterrorism strategy is known as CONTEST, which is based on a rule of law and criminal prosecution approach. Its strategic framework is broken into four sections: **p**ursue (to stop attacks), **p**revent (to stop radicalization), **p**rotect (to strengthen protection against attacks) and **p**repare (to mitigate any attack's impact). The most widely contested and heavily criticized strategy is that of **p**revent. The focus of **p**revent is to stop radicalization, reduce support for terrorism and to discourage people from becoming terrorists.

Radicalization is defined as 'a process of personal development whereby an individual adopts ever more extreme political or politic-religious ideas and goals, becoming convinced that the attainment of these goals justifies extreme methods' (Volintiru 2010: 7). It is a relatively new and contested notion within terrorism studies particularly because the 'process' by which a person radicalizes is unknown and unverifiable (see Githens-Mazer and Lambert 2010). Further, the language of radicalization is problematic. Radicalization is synonymous with irrationality, fanaticism, and extremism – discourse that removes credibility, legitimacy and political agency from the subject. Models of radicalization are often conflated with 'jihad' and radical Islam and are thus tied to the new terrorism thesis (see Borum 2011; Sedgwick 2010). Further, just because a person is 'radicalized' does not necessarily imply that they are violent or will become violent (Githens-Mazer and Lambert 2010).

The connection to new terrorism is clear in **p**revent's focus and discourse. **P**revent's objectives include challenging the ideology behind violent extremism, disrupting extremists and supporting vulnerable individuals and communities – all of which is tied in the original document to Islam (Home Office 2009). CONTEST focuses on the radical Islamic threat, particularly Al Qaeda, to the UK and argues that this is the most pressing, in spite of the historical threat from the nationalist Irish Republican Army and the growing threat from the far-right English Defence League (EDL). Thus it advocates for allying with the Muslim community in order to marginalize extremist voices. Yet, this is problematic as it has led to Muslims feeling monitored and manipulated by the police and community services (see Vertigans 2010). Also, it is gendered. The UK has assumed that men are more likely to be radicalized and have begun to target women for introduction into the community (see Brown 2013). It is assumed that because women are more submissive in these communities, the women are also not involved in the planning or implementation of political violence.

These assumptions pose significant problems. As mentioned earlier, by being focused on Muslim communities and radical Islamic violence, the UK government fails to notice or recognize other threats. Second, in trying to ally with the Muslim community, the strategy is backfiring as the communities feel further marginalized as a bias of radicalization has been essentially levelled at everyone, not just a few. Third, some scholars argue that counter-radicalization is not a remit of counterterrorism and conflates social services (allying with a community) and security operations (Richards 2011).

CONCLUSION

Looking at terrorism *and* terrorism studies through gender lenses reveals that we miss many of the important dimensions about what terrorism is, who commits acts classifiable as terrorism and how and why counterterrorism works (or does not work) if we neglect its gendered dimensions. We, with other scholars of gender and terrorism, suggest that understanding terrorism as a *gendered phenomenon* in a *gendered world* increases the accuracy and sophistication of our understanding of the idea of 'terrorism'.

Questions for further debate

1. Is the term 'terrorism' helpful and accurate? What are its intellectual and political implications? Can you define 'terrorism' usefully?
2. Can states be 'terrorists'?
3. What does a 'terrorist' look like? Can people go from being 'terrorists' to 'lawful citizens'? Are terrorists gendered masculine or feminine?
4. How do constructions of masculinity and femininity impact counterterrorism policies? How are gender norms and ideals written into counterterrorism? Is this helpful or harmful?
5. How (if at all) does gender analysis improve understanding, seeing or reacting to terrorism?

Sources for further reading and research

Åhäll, L. and Laura J. Shepherd (eds) (2012) *Gender, Agency and Political Violence (Rethinking Political Violence)*, Harmondsworth: Palgrave Macmillan.

Gentry, C. E. (2009) 'Women as Agents of Violence', Feminist Theory and Gender Studies Section, International Studies Association Compendium Project, London: Blackwell.

MacDonald, E. (1988) *Shoot the Women First*, London: Arrow Books.

Puar, J. K. and A. S. Rai (2002) 'Monster, Terrorist, Fag: The War on Terrorism and the Production of Docile Patriots', *Social Text*, 20(3): 117–38.

Sjoberg, L. and C. Gentry (eds) (2011) *Women, Gender, and Terrorism*, Athens, GA: University of Georgia Press.

CHAPTER 12

The 'war on terrorism'

Krista Hunt

LEARNING OUTCOMES

Upon completion, readers should be able to:

- Understand how the war on terror is gendered, as well as racialized, classed and sexualized.
- Think critically about the official 'war stories' being told about the War on Terrorism.
- Learn about people and organizations that are resisting war and the stories that justify violence.

INTRODUCTION

Although the 'malestream' discipline of International Relations continues to examine the war on terror as if gender does not matter, when we look at it using gendered lenses (Peterson and Runyan 1999), we see that gender figures prominently in this conflict. Yet in order to examine gender, we must also look through the lenses of race, class, nationality, sexuality, and religion. In 'making feminist sense' (Enloe 1989) of the war on terror, this chapter will examine some of the gendered war stories that have been constructed and deconstructed since 9/11, the ways that gender has been reinforced and refigured in the ensuing war on terror, and how gender is used to camouflage the patriarchal and imperialist politics of war. As you will see, feminists who study the war on terror detail the centrality of gender to this conflict and argue that we cannot separate our understanding of the war from an understanding of how it is gendered.

GENDERED WAR STORIES

War stories are the narratives told about war: why we go to war, who our enemies are, what we are fighting for, and how wars will be won (Hunt and Rygiel 2006: 4; see also Cooke 1996). Following Miriam Cooke (1996), Hunt and Rygiel argue that war on terror stories are always gendered, typified by hypermasculine war heroes and commanders in chief, grieving mothers, dutiful military wives, and barbaric (and eventually emasculated) enemies. In almost all cases, official war stories – the ones told by those in positions of power (state leaders, elites, mainstream media) – are based on a gendered logic of protection (Young 2003). According to Young, the logic of protection is characterized by a 'gallantly masculine man [who] faces the world's difficulties and dangers in order to shield women from harm … [who] can only appear in their goodness if we assume that lurking outside the warm familial walls are aggressors, the "bad" men, who wish to attack them' (2003: 224). In the war on terror, this logic of protection is typified by the post-9/11 war story that 'the fight against terrorism is also a fight for the rights and dignity of women' (L. Bush 2001). According to U.S. President George W. Bush, '[t]he central goal of the terrorists is the brutal oppression of women – and not only the women of Afghanistan … that is the reason this great nation, with our friends and allies, will not rest until we bring them all to justice' (G. W. Bush 2001d). The Bush administration's rallying cry to save Afghan women from the arch-evil Taliban/Al Qaeda exemplifies the time-honored war story of good men and nations fighting bad men in order to protect racialized women (see Figure 12.1). This war story serves to reinforce patriarchal power and justify violence abroad to a frightened and uncritical public 'at home.'

If looking at the war on terror through gender lenses means 'pay[ing] attention to the stories that are told about men and women as well as attending to the positioning and marking of bodies' (Shepherd, this volume; see Chapter 3), then

---

'The terrorists' directive commands them to kill Christians and Jews, to kill all Americans, and make no distinction among military and civilians, including women and children … In Afghanistan, we see al Qaeda's vision for the world. Afghanistan's people have been brutalized – many are starving and many have fled. Women are not allowed to attend school. You can be jailed for owning a television. Religion can be practiced only as their leaders dictate. A man can be jailed in Afghanistan if his beard is not long enough … Our war on terror begins with al Qaeda, but it does not end there. It will not end until every terrorist group of global reach has been found, stopped and defeated … This is not, however, just America's fight. And what is at stake is not just America's freedom. This is the world's fight. This is civilization's fight. This is the fight of all who believe in progress and pluralism, tolerance and freedom' (Bush 2001a).

Figure 12.1 George W. Bush's war story.

examining the gendered dimensions of the war on terror also requires paying attention to the ways in which those gendered stories and gendered bodies are also positioned and marked by race, class, sexuality, nationality, religion, and so on. Many feminists analyzed the Bush administration's war story about saving Afghan women as being reminiscent of colonial stories about 'saving brown women from brown men' (Spivak 1988: 297; see also Abu-Lughod 2002; Enloe 2004a; Hunt 2002; Thobani 2001) (see Figure 12.2). Without recognizing the ways in which gender, race, nationality, and religion intersect with each other, we would not be able to understand the imperial power dynamics that produce white, Western men and women as saviours of brown Afghan women from the Taliban regime.

If we simplify our perspective and only focus on gender, we might read Bush's war story as one that calls on American women to help rescue their 'sisters' in Afghanistan and/or powerful men trying to protect 'victimized' women in another part of the world from misogynist men. What we would ignore is the way that this war has constructed different kinds of man and woman based on race, religion, and nationality. Specifically, we would not see the way that this 1) positions white Western women as liberated compared to their oppressed Afghan sisters; 2) provides an historical, colonial justification for conquest and invasion that are all too familiar to previously colonized people; 3) reinforces resistance to women's rights and feminism by some Afghan women and men who see it as a Western imposition; 4) obscures the reality that white Western women are still being oppressed by the very same patriarchal powers that purport to be liberating Afghan women; 5) serves to divide and conquer women and inhibit transnational dialogue and solidarity. In other words, when we examine how race, class, nationality, religion, and sexuality intersect with gendered war stories, we become aware of how gendered stories are used to forward problematic political agendas while simultaneously silencing other key issues.

'And it's really interesting to hear all this talk about Afghani women. Those of us who have been colonized know what this saving means. For a long time now, Afghani women, and the struggles they were engaged in, were known here in the West. Afghani women became almost the poster child for women's oppression in the Third World. And, rightfully so, many of us were in solidarity. Afghani women of that time were fighting against and struggling against the Taliban. They were condemning their particular interpretation of Islam. Afghani women, Afghanistan women's organizations were on the front line of this. But what (did) they become in the West? In the West, they became nothing but poor victims of this bad, bad religion, and of (these) backward, backward men. The same old colonial construction. They were in the frontline, we did not take the lead from them then, where we could see them more as victims, only worthy of our pity and today, even in the United States, people are ready to bomb those women, seeing them as nothing more than collateral damage. You see how quickly the world can change. And I say that we take the lead from Afghani women. They fought back against the Taliban, and when they were fighting back they said that it is the United States putting this regime in power. That's what they were saying. They were saying, look at U.S. foreign policy!' (Thobani 2001).

Figure 12.2 Excerpt from Sunera Thobani's speech at the 'Women's Resistance: From Victimization to Criminalization' conference, Ottawa, 1 October 2001.

REINFORCING AND REFIGURING STORIES ABOUT GENDER

While many war stories reinforce traditional gender dynamics: hypermasculine firefighters rushing into the World Trade Center to save helpless victims; defiant politicians such as President Bush and New York City Mayor Guiliani declaring that they would 'smoke out of their holes' the terrorists (G.W. Bush 2001a); the overwhelmingly male military forces being deployed to Afghanistan and Iraq; and depictions of barbaric, ruthless, suicidal terrorists that could be hiding anywhere in our multicultural midst. When we look through a gendered lens at war on terror stories, we also see that gender is reconfigured.

Remember this picture (see Figure 12.3)? In May 2003, this was one in a series of photos released by Western media outlets depicting the torture and humiliation of male prisoners at Abu Ghraib prison in Iraq. Although there were photos of men abusing both male and female prisoners, the pictures of Private Lynndie England abusing male prisoners were most widely circulated (Brittain 2006: 86). Pictures depicting women abusing 'the enemy' resonated most deeply. When the media released these pictures, many commentators predicted a serious blow to the Bush administration and public perception about the war on terror. Pictures of American 'liberators' torturing defenceless Iraqi prisoners for kicks certainly challenged the official war story about who the 'good guys' and the 'bad guys' were. Instead, however, these abuses were individualized as a case of 'a few bad apples' rather than

Figure 12.3 Abu Ghraib prisoner abuse.
Image: Wikimedia Commons.

dealing with the systemic problems of violence and abuse by and against military personnel.

These pictures also challenged conventional assumptions about gender, which served to obscure dominant power relations. As Zillah Eisenstein argues, the representation of a female soldier acting as the torturer serves as a 'gender decoy' for imperial war: 'As decoys they create confusion by participating in the very sexual humiliation that their gender is usually victim to. This supposed gender swapping and switching leaves masculinist/racialized gender in place' (Eisenstein 2007: 37). Such images challenge conventional assumptions about who is fit to fight wars; female soldiers torturing 'the enemy' (and enjoying it!) challenge essentialist ideas that women are less violent than men. In this way, such pictures reinforce the story that American women are fully liberated since a few of them have made it into the masculinized ranks of the military. However, the focus on England's gender and working-class background also provides an explanation that the abuses at Abu Ghraib were in no way representative of the U.S. military, but rather a case of 'a woman, doing improper things' (Brittain 2006: 88). As gender decoy, Lynndie England can be seen as one of a few bad apples deflecting attention away from the ways that the war on terror was also a 'war of terror' (Eisenstein 2007: 37; Shepherd 2008b: 220).

Gender is also confused when American women feminize Iraqi men. According to Eisenstein (2007: 34):

> Men who are tortured and sexually degraded are 'humiliated' *because* they are treated like women; they are forced to be women – sexually dominated and degraded. Men who are naked and exposed remind us of the vulnerability usually associated with being a woman. The brown men at Abu Ghraib are then constructed as effeminate and narrate a subtext of homosexuality. They were made to feel like and be like women or fags while being tortured by females. The brown men at Abu Ghraib remained male, but not men; and the white women guards were female but not women. The trick is that there is no clear demarcation between being female and being a woman. The two are connected but not determinant.

While challenging assumptions about gender, these pictures play into assumptions and fantasies about racialized enemies. Historically and currently, the imperial war story that Western powers are embarking on a mission to liberate brown women depends on fighting (and killing) brown men. As Brittain argues, 'images of Arab men being broken, subdued, shamed and disciplined by a white woman allow for the realization of the "American dream" of the total demasculation and humiliation of Arab men'; a demasculation that has been connected by more than one commentator to the lynching of black men in U.S. history (Brittain 2006: 89). The feminization of the racialized enemy in war symbolizes defeat, which is further reinforced when that defeat comes at the hands of a 'liberated' white woman. Here, gender is refigured by the female soldier, but also reinforced because she is the exception.

Finally, these pictures serve to silence the abuse of different groups of women by 'the good guys', thereby maintaining the official war story that the war on terror will liberate Afghan and Iraqi women, as well as protect the rights of 'liberated' women back home. While our attention is focused on female soldiers abusing male prisoners, the abuse of female Iraqi prisoners by male soldiers at Abu Ghraib (Eisenstein 2007: 40; Shumway 2004) is rendered out of sight. Further, it deflects attention from reports that Pentagon officials were aware of 112 sexual assaults against female soldiers by their fellow soldiers in Afghanistan and Iraq over an 18-month period (Brittain 2006: 90; Eisenstein 2007: 40; Weiser 2004). And beyond the theater of war, these pictures serve to obscure the fact that the so-called women's liberators – the Bush administration – continue to wage a war on women's reproductive rights at home and abroad (Eisenstein 2007: 119–20) (see Figure 12.4).

CHALLENGING OFFICIAL WAR STORIES

Telling official war stories depends on silencing and/or delegitimizing those that challenge dominant versions, and by virtue of that, the war itself. In the U.S. and elsewhere, critics were being separated from the post-9/11 patriotic herd with the

---

The U.S. administration's hardline agenda to limit women's reproductive rights is visible domestically and internationally. To begin, the U.S. continues to stall efforts to ratify the United Nations Convention on the Elimination of All Forms of Discrimination Against Women (CEDAW), which is considered 'the most comprehensive and detailed international agreement which seeks the advancement of women' (Feminist Majority Foundation). The irony that the United States is the only industrialized nation that has not ratified CEDAW cannot be overstated, especially when that country is the self-proclaimed arbiter of democracy and human rights.

It also cannot be ignored that the U.S. currently shares its opposition to the convention with the governments of Iran (a member of the 'axis of evil') and Sudan (DAW). Next, on his first day in office, Bush reinstated the 'Global Gag Rule', making U.S. foreign aid only available to family planning clinics that abstain from providing abortions or counselling women about abortion. At the Asia Pacific conference on regional population control in December 2002, the U.S. argued that the global consensus on reproductive rights 'promoted abortion and underage sex' and tried to convince other states to 'dismantle sex education, undermine condom use in HIV/AIDS prevention, and water down policies intended to prevent and treat unsafe abortion' (Planned Parenthood 2003). Showing his desire to reinstate conservative values regarding sexuality, Bush continued to promote abstinence as the Christian way to prevent pregnancy and the transmission of STDs. Domestically, Bush forwarded this agenda by banning 'partial birth abortion' and supporting anti-choice attempts to dismantle *Roe v. Wade*.

With respect to Afghan women, Bush has done little to ensure they receive proper health care, much less reproductive rights. In August 2002 Bush withdrew $2.5 million dollars in emergency funds for programs supporting women in Afghanistan, arguing that on further study, there is no real emergency (Planned Parenthood). However, UNICEF and the U.S. Center for Disease Control report that: 'Afghan women suffer from one of the highest levels of maternal mortality in the world, with almost half of all deaths among women aged 15 to 49 coming as a result of pregnancy and childbirth' (UNICEF 2002). Instead of funding family planning clinics that would help prevent these unnecessary deaths, the U.S. State Department has decided to fund 'non-family planning programs' in Afghanistan (Marshall 2003). The Bush administration's antifeminist position on reproductive rights has led the International Women's Health Coalition (IWHC) to characterize the White House as 'conducting a stealth war against women' with devastating effects being felt 'by women and girls worldwide' (Marshall 2003).

Figure 12.4 War on women's rights.

charge of 'You are either with us or you are with the terrorists.' In the media, feminist journalists remarked that 'virtually the only female faces in the media at the
moment are the victims; women are cast as passive' (Bunting, cited in Hunt 2002:
117). When images and voices of women did not support the very narrow roles
allocated by the official war story – mother of U.S. soldier killed in Iraq now an
outspoken anti-war activist; 9/11 widows and families opposing the war; Afghan
women's rights activists challenging both fundamentalism and orientalism –
dominant powers attempted to silence them.

In Canada, the case of Sunera Thobani provided an early example of how dissent
would be handled. On October 1, 2001, Professor Thobani gave a speech to a
group of Canadian feminists (see Figure 12.2). In the speech, Thobani critiques the
framing of the conflict as one of unprovoked terrorism, stating that the 'path of US
foreign policy is soaked in blood' and that the impending war on terror would not
lead the world towards peace, democracy or justice (Thobani 2001). She argues that
'there will be no emancipation for women anywhere on this planet until the
Western domination of this planet is ended' (Thobani 2001). The reaction to her
critiques of the impending war on terror was swift, with politicians and media
publicly attacking her; she received hate mail, was told she should be fired from her
academic post, and was even subject to a hate-crimes investigation by the Royal
Canadian Mounted Police (RCMP) (Thobani 2003: 403). Significantly, the
response was racially motivated with detractors calling for her to go back to where
she came from. As Thobani argues, 'by repeatedly reconstructing my status as a
non-White, immigrant woman, the media reiterated – in a highly intensified
manner – the historically racialized discourse of who "belongs" to the Canadian
nation, and hence has a right to "speak" to it' (2003: 401). What Thobani's case
highlights is the reality that 'elite ideas are widely disseminated and popularized
through the media, and during times of war, being able to hold onto the allegiances
of populations can be crucial to the success of the global ambitions of national
elites' (2001: 404). Thus, the media response to Thobani sent 'a very direct and
clear message to others about the costs of challenging elite "truth" claims and of the
dangers of voicing dissent' (401). Ironically, while the symbol of women became the
justification for war in Afghanistan and Iraq, women's voices that challenged official
war stories were silenced and accused of supporting the terrorists.

The silencing of dissent went far beyond attempts to discredit Thobani.
Numerous academics, activists, and public figures were challenged for asking
'unpatriotic' questions (Hunt 2005; Thobani 2003). Even the American public was
put on notice, with White House spokesperson Ari Fleischer issuing the following
statement after TV personality Bill Maher criticized the government's handling of
the war: 'There are reminders to all Americans that they need to watch what they
say, watch what they do, and this is not a time for remarks like that; there never is'
(Hunt 2005: 157). Although there was little space in the mainstream media for
dissent, critics found other spaces to challenge the official war story, including alternative and online forums. Silenced war stories included ones about the U.S. role in
empowering the Taliban during the Cold War and their oil interests in Afghanistan
(Hawthorne and Winter 2003); Afghan women's rights organizations that argue
that war on terror will not liberate them (RAWA); the anti-women policies of the

Bush administration (Eisenstein 2007); the situation of Afghan and Iraqi women during the war on terror (Enloe 2004a); and the abuses of Muslim men in Western countries (Rygiel 2006; Sharma 2006). What became clear from feminist analyses is that stories about women are acceptable when they serve the patriotic mission and reinforce dominant ideas about other people; when they do not, there is an attempt by different actors to silence women's stories.

By looking through a gender lens, we begin to see how gender is both reinforced and refigured in the service of patriarchal and imperial power. In the case of the Bush administration, official war stories served to justify imperial war by appealing to racist and colonialist fantasies about liberating Muslim women, as well as to avoid responsibility for the torture of prisoners at Abu Ghraib. In the case of Sunera Thobani, we see how those who dare to challenge official war stories are denounced and discredited as traitors and enemies. What this tells us is that while war stories are powerful enough to gain consent for war, they are also fragile enough that critics must be silenced. If we are to think critically about the war on terror (or any war for that matter), we must begin to ask questions about the war stories we are told and why they have been so easy for so many people to believe.

VISUAL WAR STORIES

Stories about the war on terror have not only been told through the written word, but often, and perhaps more powerfully, through visual representations of this war (see Figure 12.5). Think of the images of planes crashing into the Twin Towers, played over and over and over. Think of the images of tortured and humiliated prisoners at Abu Ghraib, and their female captors. Think of the images of blue *burqa* clad Afghan women that continue to circulate in the Western media. One could argue that these photos have left more of a lasting impression on their target audience than any given story in the news. In part, this is because people often uncritically perceive pictures as being a transparent reflection of reality. You know the cliché – 'pictures don't lie.' Another cliché is that 'a picture is worth a thousand words.' Implicit in this statement is that you need no words, because the picture says it all. It is also because many official war stories have been exposed as fabrications.

It is, however, dangerous to assume that pictures are straightforward reflections of 'what happened,' since pictures always come from a particular lens. For instance, imagine a picture taken of a group of U.S. soldiers storming into a building. The perspective we see is what the photographer shows us: the soldiers rushing into a building. What we do not know from the picture is what kind of building it is; whether or not there are people inside; if there are people, whether they are civilians or combatants; what happens after the soldiers go inside; and so on. In other words, we are only able to see part of what is going on, from the perspective of the photographer, who only made the soldiers visible. What we are limited from seeing is the context for the raid – did someone fire on the soldiers? Do they suspect insurgents are hiding there? Is this a routine operation? Is this a drill? Did they make a mistake and raid the home of a civilian family? Did the soldiers follow the Geneva Convention in their treatment of the people in that building? In other words, the

Since most people know about wars through the media, it is essential to examine the media and the stories they tell through a critical lens. Embedded media was instituted in Iraq based on the U.S. Department of Defense recognition that the media 'shape public perception of the national security environment … which can affect the durability of our coalition' (U.S. Department of Defense 2003). This is especially important given that the U.S. Department of Defense has a policy of 'embedding' media with its troops. Embedded media as a concept was instituted in Iraq. According to the DOD, in order to 'tell the factual story', journalists must 'live, work, and travel as part of the units with which they are embedded to facilitate maximum, in-depth coverage' (2003).

As I have argued elsewhere, 'this use of the media was a clear attempt to manufacture consent for the war' (Hunt 2006: 52). In other words, the policy of embedding journalists in conflict zones is an attempt to control the message and to tell particular stories from a particular lens (the war story that military officials decide to tell) in order to gain popular support for the war. However, that is not to say that if journalists were not embedded that their stories would be any more objective; rather, they would produce another particular story as seen through another particular lens (the war story that they and the particular media outlet decides to tell).

Therefore, it is necessary for us to look critically at the media not because they are often embedded, but because they – like everything – are always embedded in some political position. This acknowledgement of inevitable subjectivity requires us to see said stories as arguments, ones that try to shape our own perspectives. War stories are never simply information that transparently reflects what is reported to have happened. As such, we need to start asking critical questions of the stories we are told. Beyond a doubt, the most important question to ask is invariably the one that no one else seems to be asking.

Figure 12.5 Embedded media.

decision to take that picture limits us from seeing what else is going on, as well as the context for that situation. By virtue of taking a picture of 'A', 'W, X, Y and Z' are necessarily out of focus. Further, that photographer likely had instructions about what to photograph from editors back home ('Get shots of soldiers in action rooting out the terrorists and those that harbor them'). And once those photographs were submitted, editors then made decisions about which pictures were going to be published, what stories they would accompany, and what descriptive text would be written to explain the photos (*Soldiers Storm Taliban Stronghold*, for example). As you can see, there are layers of different people's and organization's perspectives shaping each and every photo you see in the news. Undoubtedly, then, these pictures do political work. The picture of U.S. soldiers storming a Taliban stronghold (whether or not it was a Taliban stronghold, whether it was a combat situation or a drill) is sold by the photo agency and then sold to us by the news agency in order to confirm the official war story that Coalition forces are 'rooting out the terrorists and those that harbor them.'

However, if editors choose to use that picture alongside a story about how civilians in combat zones are being mistreated by such raids, that picture would do different political work, and may confirm or challenge the official war story and our own opinion about the war. Add to that all that the perspective(s) you bring to the news you see, hear, and read, and you have many partial perspectives constructing how you see the war and thereby what you think about it. For example, a war veteran might see a fellow soldier risking his life; an exiled Afghan woman might see a group of colonial invaders; and a feminist scholar might see a display of militarized masculinity. Therefore, pictures are not reflections of what happened; they are pieces of what happened that then go through a process that shapes the way they are seen. And these pictures – like all war stories – can both reinforce and/or challenge official, state-sanctioned war stories.

Questions for further debate

1. How does U.S. President George W. Bush's speech (see Figure 13.1) construct a war story about 'good guys and bad guys'? Why do you think this story was so widely accepted as justification for the ongoing war on terror?
2. Although the abuses of male prisoners at Abu Ghraib jail by female soldiers circulated widely in the media, why did the reports of male soldiers raping female prisoners or female soldiers get not nearly as much coverage?
3. Are there sources that people can go to get the 'truth' about the war on terror? If so, how do we decide on the validity/reliability of sources?
4. How can people challenge war stories in their daily lives?
5. Through an analysis of the relevant web-based resources (see the Companion Website), compare and contrast the organizations' campaigns in response to the war on terror. How do they define the problem? What sort of political action are they campaigning for? How could you get involved in, interact with, protest and/or challenge these campaigns?

Sources for further reading and research

Agathangelou, A. and L. Ling (2004) 'Power, Borders, Security, Wealth: Lessons of Violence and Desire from September 11', *International Studies Quarterly*, 48: 517–38.

Eisenstein, Z. (2007) *Sexual Decoys: Gender, Race and War*, London: Zed Books.

Hawthorne, S. and Winter (eds) (2003) *After Shock: September 11 2001 Global Feminist Perspectives*, Vancouver: Raincoast.

Hunt, K. and K. Rygiel (eds) (2006) *Engendering the War on Terror: War Stories and Camouflaged Politics*, London: Ashgate.

Young, I. (2003) 'Feminist Reactions to the Contemporary Security Regime', *Hypatia*, 18(1): 223–31.

CHAPTER 13

Genocide and mass violence

Adam Jones

LEARNING OUTCOMES

Upon completion, readers should be able to:

- Analyse the ambiguities in the UN Genocide Convention.
- Explain why it is useful to examine genocide through gendered lenses.
- Account for several of the ways in which gender informs our understanding of genocidal violence (including the ways in which gender makes visible certain types and perpetrators of violence while obscuring others).

INTRODUCTION

A man mobilizes his neighbors to assassinate their 'enemies'; other men, and some women, answer his call eagerly or reluctantly. Younger men, deemed 'subversive' as a group, are the first targeted for murder; females, especially younger women, are sexually attacked and abused. Against this backdrop of violent upheaval, in an isolated rural region a peasant woman bleeds to death in childbirth, as her mother had before her. And, on the other side of the world, in a silo deep underground, two men stand ready to turn keys that, in combination, will launch a nuclear missile capable of obliterating entire populations.

What do these fragmentary scenarios have to do with gender in mass conflict – and with the concept of 'genocide', developed by Raphael Lemkin in the 1940s to denote the destruction of human groups? This chapter introduces readers to genocide as a theoretical tool and social-historical phenomenon. It explores the complex interweaving of genocide with gendered roles, expectations, and behaviors. It draws in particular on the literatures of comparative genocide studies and feminist International Relations. In 'gender' and 'genocide,' we confront two essentially contested concepts, and one should be careful to define one's terms. I discuss definitional issues surrounding 'genocide' later, including my preferred usage. Throughout, I adopt Joshua Goldstein's use of gender 'to cover masculine and feminine roles and bodies alike, in all their aspects, including the (biological and cultural) structures, dynamics, roles, and scripts associated with each gender group' (Goldstein 2001: 2).

FEMINIST IR AND COMPARATIVE GENOCIDE STUDIES: SOME PARALLELS

Most feminisms have an 'epistemological foundation in the realm of women's experiences', use this to demonstrate 'that women and the feminine constitute historically underprivileged, under-represented, and under-recognized social groups and "standpoints"', and make the explicitly *normative* claim that 'this should change in the direction of greater equality' (Jones 1996: 406). (Poststructural feminisms claim to transcend these claims and distinctions, although not always persuasively, in my view.) In similar fashion, genocide scholars seek not just to understand genocide, but to suppress it and if possible banish it from human affairs, as Atlantic slavery was cancelled as a legal and widespread institution in the nineteenth century. In this respect, they share a core commonality with feminist IR, melding both an analytical and an activist/normative dimension.

Both genocide studies and feminist IR therefore seek to establish normatively grounded *prohibition regimes* in the domestic and international practice of states and peoples (although prohibition regimes can also be conceptualized as *promotional* regimes, i.e., as campaigns to instill positive norms, as opposed to merely banning an abusive or atrocious practice). A stimulating line of IR analysis focuses on the role of norms and regimes in shaping and constraining behavior by states and non-state actors (Nadelmann 1990). The international legal ban on genocide, generally ineffectual though it has been to this point, is an example of a nascent prohibition regime. Many feminist-inspired regimes have advanced much further. Although numerous chasms still yawn, attempts to confront the legacy of discrimination against females throughout history, in the spheres of political, social, and economic rights, have enjoyed greater success – thanks to the efforts of generations of feminists and their supporters – than the slapdash and perfunctory attempts to confront the scourge of genocide. Feminism and feminist IR (including, for present purposes, the related field of development studies) may offer significant guidance to scholars and activists working to entrench an anti-genocide regime.

The concept of genocide was the brainchild of a Polish-Jewish jurist named Raphael Lemkin, who in the 1920s and 1930s sought a language to convey the vulnerability of social minorities (especially ethnoreligious collectivities) to destruction at the hands of their own rulers. The plight of such groups had been the subject of considerable discussion and debate in the later nineteenth century, particularly in the context of Ottoman depredations, both real and imagined, against Christian populations of the empire. This had even produced occasional interventionist actions, as with the brief flurry of trials of alleged mass murderers of Armenians after the First World War had ended and the Ottoman Empire disintegrated. But none of this had been codified in international law: domestic constraints on homicide, the killing of individuals, were unmatched by a general prohibition of states' violence against entire groups, including (especially) their 'own' populations. Lemkin experimented in the 1930s with terms such as 'vandalism' and 'barbarity', before settling – in US exile; he had fled Poland when the Nazis invaded in 1939 – on the word *genocide*. The neologism combined the Greek *genos* (race, tribe) with the Latin-derived suffix *-cide* (killing). Although subsequent discussion of genocide has heavily emphasized the mass-killing dimension, Lemkin referred to the 'destruction' of a collectivity in a wider, social-civilizational context (for a recent exploration, see Shaw 2007). Not only murdering members of groups, but also destroying their cultural foundations and scattering their populations far and wide, could qualify as genocide.

Lemkin's relentless lobbying of the new United Nations resulted in one of the most rapid adoptions of a new norm and prohibition regime in the history of international relations. Lemkin first published the term 'genocide' in his otherwise obscure 1944 volume *Axis Rule in Occupied Europe* (Lemkin 1944), which for most of its length analyzed Nazi occupation policies and their pseudo-legal buttressing in the German-conquered territories. Just four years later, in December 1948, the United Nations Convention on the Prevention and Punishment of the Crime of Genocide (hereafter, the Genocide Convention) was unanimously adopted by the General Assembly. By 1951, the required number of states had signed on and ratified it into domestic legislation – although a key player, the United States, would hold out until 1984. Genocide became a crime under international law (see Figure 13.1).

'The lack of clarity about which groups are, and are not, protected has made the Convention less effective and popularly understood, than should be the case. The 1948 Convention enumerates groups protected as "a national, ethnical, racial or religious group", without defining such terms. Differing views have been expressed as to what extent the terms "national" or "ethnical" groups include minorities. The Nazi policy was also to exterminate the sexual minority group of homosexuals. *It is recommended that the definition [of genocide] should be extended to include a sexual group such as women, men, or homosexuals*' (Whitaker 1985; emphasis added).

Whitaker's was the only substantial UN attempt to rethink the Genocide Convention of 1948, in particular its controversial limiting of protected groups to 'national, ethnical, racial, and religious' ones alone. Strikingly, Whitaker recommended the addition of gender/sexual groups, among others. He recognized not only that homosexuals constituted a vulnerable minority, but that males as well as females could be targeted for genocidal violence on the basis of their gender or sex.

Figure 13.1 Whitaker on the UN Genocide Convention.

The 1948 Genocide Convention remains the foundational legal definition of genocide – it was integrated word-for-word into the Rome Statute of the new International Criminal Court (1998), for example. It is a fascinating and vexing document. At its heart is the following interpretation and injunction:

> The Contracting Parties,
>
> Having considered the declaration made by the General Assembly of the United Nations [...] that genocide is a crime under international law, contrary to the spirit and aims of the United Nations and condemned by the civilized world,
>
> Recognizing that at all periods of history genocide has inflicted great losses on humanity, and
>
> Being convinced that, in order to liberate mankind from such an odious scourge, international co-operation is required,
>
> Hereby agree as hereinafter provided:
>
> *Article I:* The Contracting Parties confirm that genocide, whether committed in time of peace or in time of war, is a crime under international law which they undertake to prevent and to punish.
>
> *Article II:* In the present Convention, genocide means any of the following acts committed with intent to destroy, in whole or in part, a national, ethnical, racial or religious group, as such:
>
> (a) Killing members of the group;
> (b) Causing serious bodily or mental harm to members of the group;
> (c) Deliberately inflicting on the group conditions of life calculated to bring about its physical destruction in whole or in part;
> (d) Imposing measures intended to prevent births within the group;
> (e) Forcibly transferring children of the group to another group.

Article III of the Convention declares punishable not just the act of genocide, but also 'conspiracy to commit genocide', 'direct and public incitement to commit genocide', attempted genocide, and 'complicity in genocide'.

A number of problems arise with the Convention's text. Among those most relevant to the study of gender and genocide are: Why does the Convention protect only national, ethnic, racial, and religious groups? (And how meaningful are these concepts in a world where easy concepts of 'race', 'nation', and 'ethnicity' have been challenged by critical scholarship, including feminist scholarship?) How does one ascertain an 'intent to destroy [a group], in whole or in part', and what 'part' is sufficient to constitute genocidal destruction? What is the threshold for 'serious bodily or mental harm' as a genocidal strategy? Article II(d) – 'prevent[ing] births within the group' – seems the aspect of the Convention that is most directly gendered but what are its implications for women and men? And – pushing at the outer limits of the Convention's language – how might the emphasis on crimes committed 'in time of peace' as well as 'in time of war', and by indirect means ('deliberately inflicting ... conditions of life calculated' to destroy the group), be adapted to an analysis of structural and institutional forms of violence, and their specifically gendered dimension?

GENOCIDE AND GENDER: THE HISTORICAL RECORD AND CONTEMPORARY ANALYSIS

A chapter of this nature offers no space to provide a systematic overview of the connections between gender and genocide, and the diverse implications of those connections. I want to suggest, however, that the subject can be approached from both a *historical* and a *humanitarian* direction, reflecting the twin underpinnings – empirical and normative – of both genocide studies and feminist International Relations. (For present purposes, I subsume the international-legal component under the 'humanitarian' rubric.)

Until relatively recently, explorations of gender and mass conflict, including genocide, focused overwhelmingly on the component of anti-female victimization and discrimination. Within these parameters, a heavy emphasis was placed on sexual violence against women and girls, including trafficking for the purposes of sexual enslavement. The prominence of this approach reflects a number of factors. Rape and sexual assault were foundational themes of second-wave feminism: the benchmark work, Susan Brownmiller's *Against Our Will*, appeared in the mid-1970s (Brownmiller 1975). In parallel with the anti-pornography and 'Take Back the Night' movements of the 1980s, feminist analysis and activism alike were particularly sensitive to sexual atrocity, and thus well prepared to highlight the mass sexual atrocities inflicted in the first half of the 1990s – the largescale rapes in Bosnia (1992–95), and the truly horrific sexual attacks against Tutsi women during the Rwandan genocide of 1994.

When war and genocide broke out in the Balkans and East Africa in the 1990s, the ancient and enduring character of sexual attacks on women was immediately recognized and widely discussed in media and policy circles. Feminist analyses – as well as cultural traditions – had primed the public, and analysts across a broad spectrum, to view rape as a longstanding 'weapon of war' and of male terrorism against women (see Chapter 14). Violation of women's physical and psychological integrity, feminists noted, had been classed for millennia as the legitimate or tacitly tolerated 'spoils' of war. In the twentieth century alone, the Balkans and Rwandan examples were preceded by rape on a huge scale in the infamous 'Rape of Nanjing' by Japanese forces (1937–38); by the depredations of Soviet soldiers on German territory at the end of the Second World War (1945); and by the Bangladesh war and genocide of 1971, which Brownmiller details in *Against Our Will*.

Feminist critiques aimed to crystallize another conceptualization of sexual violence: as *a crime against the female victim*. While this may seem self-evident, international law, in particular, approached sexual violence only circuitously. It deployed euphemisms such as 'family honor and rights' (as in the 1907 Hague Convention) to displace the primary victim and diffuse her victimization through the patriarchal family and wider social collectivity. Spearheaded by the legal scholar Catharine MacKinnon, feminist academic and legal framings of sexual assault gradually percolated into domestic and international legislation and case law alike. Feminist mobilizations, including substantial street demonstrations in the Americas and

Europe, produced a sea change in the understanding of sexual violence, and the sanctions devised to confront it. Of greatest significance were verdicts of the *ad hoc* tribunals for Yugoslavia and especially the ICTR in Rwanda, which declared that the mass rape of Tutsi women *constituted* genocide under Article II(b) of the Genocide Convention. (This lists 'serious bodily or mental harm to members of the group' as a genocidal strategy.)[1]

While the ancient practice of rape and sexual enslavement of females established itself as the paradigm for studies of gender and conflict, it was not the only female-focused debate in academia and the policy sphere. The high representation of females in many populations of refugees and the 'ethnically cleansed' generated substantial attention among UN bodies and nongovernmental organizations. The transformations of women's roles in wartime, and the additional burdens placed on them, were searchingly examined. Women's agency in postconflict peacebuilding grew in importance as the genocidal outbreaks of the first few years of the 1990s gave way to humanitarian interventions and reconstruction initiatives.

Implicit in much of this analysis, however, was an 'absent subject' (Jones 1994): the males also swept up in these conflicts, and their universe of gendered experience. The male as 'soldier–rapist' was a well-established motif – the necessary counterpart to the highlighted female rape victim. The male was rarely considered, however, as gendered victim of conflict. Some notice was paid to the men who were often the indirect targets of the rape of women, their inability to protect 'their' women serving as a devastating demonstration of their emasculation. A more literal emasculation of males also figured, as it had throughout history. Sexual atrocities against men and boys, including rape, castration, and mutilation, ran rampant in the Balkans conflicts and in Rwanda (Sivakumaran 2007); recent research has detailed the prevalence of such atrocities, notably the systematic rape of males, in conflicts including those in Uganda and the Democratic Republic of the Congo (e.g., Storr 2011).

Such atrocities are often underpinned by a practice that, like rape, extends back to the dawn of the historical record, yet remarkably had received no sustained attention whatever until the 2000s: the gender-selective ('gendercidal') killing of males, especially men of a perceived 'battle age', between roughly 15 and 55 years old. Ancient sources from the Hebrew bible to Homer and Thucydides describe the imposition of ruthlessly gendered strategies on conquered populations. First, and worst, was usually the wholesale massacre of community males; there followed the kidnapping, enslavement, and forced sexual concubinage of children and women. The phenomenon has also been standard (although not ubiquitous) in the wars and genocides of the twentieth and twenty-first centuries. All the so-called 'classic' genocides – by Ottoman Turks against Armenians and other minority Christians during and after the First World War (1914–23); by Nazis against European Jews between 1941 and 1945; and against Tutsis and moderate Hutus in Rwanda in 1994 – to a significant degree followed the pattern of an initial targeting of community men, followed by the 'root-and-branch' extermination of remaining members of the population (Jones 2000).

One of the most notorious instances of the selective slaughter of a community's menfolk was the Nazi massacre on June 10, 1942 at the Czech village of Lidice, an act of vengeance following the assassination of the leading Nazi, Reinhard Heydrich,

Figure 13.2 The phenomenon of separating and selectively slaughtering a community's menfolk is as old as recorded history.

Photograph: Author.

in Prague (see Figure 13.2). One hundred and seventy-three civilian men were rounded up and summarily executed, in scenes captured in the above bas-relief at the Lidice memorial. Such gender-selective slaughters of males often expand subsequently to include children and women: indeed, dozens of Lidice's women died of hunger, disease, and abuse in the Nazis' Ravensbrück concentration camp, while 88 of the children were murdered in the Chelmno death camp.

The gendercidal targeting of males thus frequently serves as a harbinger and trigger of the subsequent, generalized slaughter. In many other cases, the selective massacre of males largely *bounded* and *delimited* the strictly murderous dimension of the military/genocidal enterprise. Genocides such as those in the Belgian Congo's 'Rubber Terror' against native African populations from 1890 to 1910; under Joseph Stalin in the communist USSR in the 1930s; in Bangladesh in 1971; and in the Balkans in the 1990s all evinced this trend. By the best available estimate, men constituted over 90 per cent of those killed, and striking gender disparities were often evident in post-genocide population surveys (e.g., Conquest 1968: 711–12; Hochschild 1998: 232) (see Figure 13.3).

These practices of gender-selective massacres and other atrocities against males – no less prevalent and institutionalized in the historical record than the rape and sexual exploitation of women – help to account for phenomena that feminist scholars and activists discerned in the 1990s: The refugee and 'cleansed' populations heavily weighted towards women (and children, and the elderly); the disproportionate burden of postconflict peacebuilding. Men not detained, incarcerated, or murdered very likely had fled, perhaps into protracted exile. Indeed, one empirical challenge in the aftermath of war and genocide is to establish the demographic impact of gendercidal massacres of males, because males may be still alive, but dislocated in isolated regions or foreign countries. Approaching the question of gendered victimization in genocide in an inclusive way thus enables us to understand

'No territory-wide census was taken in the Congo until long after the rubber terror was over. But Daniel Vangroenweghe, a Belgian anthropologist who worked in a former rubber area in the 1970s, found persuasive demographic evidence that large numbers of men had been worked to death as rubber slaves or killed in punitive raids – and he discovered the evidence in the [Belgian] regime's own statistics. No other explanation accounts for the curious pattern that threads through the village-by-village headcounts taken in the colony long before the first territorial census. These local headcounts consistently show far more women than men. At Inongo in 1907, for example, there were 309 children, 402 adult women, but only 275 adult men ... At nearby Iboko in 1908 there were 322 children, 543 adult women, but only 262 adult men. Statistics from numerous other villages show the same pattern. Sifting such figures today is like sifting the ruins of an Auschwitz crematorium. They do not tell you precise death tolls, but they reek of mass murder' (Hochschild 1998).

Figure 13.3 Gendercide through forced labour: Belgian Congo, 1890–1920.

not only a wider range of gendered experience, but points of connection among experiential realms. To delve deeper, however, we must move beyond the political-military crises that are the familiar stuff of International Relations and of comparative genocide studies, to examine underlying institutions and the *structural* forms of violence that often sustain them. These rarely enter into mainstream analyses of international relations, but have been central to feminist critiques; the inquiry is relevant to little appreciated male vulnerabilities as well.

GENDERCIDAL INSTITUTIONS

The concept of 'structural' violence – inflicted indirectly, and usually mediated by the institutions that buttress day-to-day life in a society – is associated with the peace studies school of Johan Galtung and others. Feminists, however, have made a distinctive contribution by emphasizing the gendered vulnerabilities of females, not only adult women, but also young and even infant girls. The mass slaughter of innocent females or 'gynocide', as Mary Daly originally labeled it (Daly 1990), extends as far as the womb, with female fetuses overwhelmingly more likely to be aborted than males. Indeed, this was the main subject of Mary Anne Warren's 1985 text *Gendercide*, which offered a more gender-inclusive term than Daly's 'gynocide' (see Warren 1985). This was the language I deployed in exploring the gender-selective massacre of civilian males. But I have also examined the operations of 'gendercidal institutions' including female infanticide/neonaticide/foeticide (see also Hudson and den Boer 2004), girls' nutritional and educational deficit, maternal mortality (see further later), 'honour' killings, and witch-hunts such as those in early modern Europe (see Figure 13.4). In none of these cases did gender alone determine outcomes – most obviously, variables of age and class/caste were prominent in the mix. It is vital to recognize that such variables *always* operate in tandem with gender to produce outcomes; but gender remains central to the equation.

The framing of gendercidal institutions may also be extended to men and masculinities. Military conscription/impressment, capital punishment, and above all

Few events in the early modern period seem as bizarre to contemporary observers as the witch-hunts that swept Europe and the colonized world from the fifteenth to the eighteenth centuries. In a wave of hysteria fuelled by religious conflict, epidemics and natural disasters, economic crisis, political rivalries, and grassroots vendettas, tens of thousands of innocents were accused of being in league with the Devil – and tried, tortured, and generally condemned to death for their 'crimes'. Men are an underappreciated category of victims of these hunts and trials – they constituted a majority in France, for example. Europe-wide, however, women accounted for 75–80 per cent of those targeted. Indeed, when females are targeted for such 'gendercidal' attacks, it is often on the basis of their supposed complicity with subversive and supernatural forces. The notorious *Malleus Maleficarum* ('The Hammer of Witches'), published by Catholic authorities in the late fifteenth century, declared that 'All wickedness is but little to the wickedness of a woman ... Women are by nature instruments of Satan – they are by nature carnal, a structural defect rooted in the original creation' (quoted in Katz 1994: 438–39). Widows were particularly vulnerable, their marginal and impoverished status in society giving rise to all manner of nefarious accusations. These were generally made by members of their own community, and usually by other women, who sought to blame widows as 'witches' for the sickness, infertility, and child mortality that afflicted their households.

Witch-hunting remains epidemic today, particularly on the continent of Africa (see Gendercide Watch 2000). In Tanzania in the late 1990s, the *Sunday Telegraph* reported that:

> Lynch mobs have killed hundreds ... whom they accuse of witchcraft as black magic hysteria sweeps East Africa. Most of the usually elderly victims have been beaten or burnt to death by gangs of youths. Some old women have been singled out simply because they have red eyes – regarded as a sign of sorcery by their assailants. The condition is actually caused by years of toiling in smoky kitchens cooking family meals (Harris 1999).

Police estimated that as many as 5,000 Tanzanians – women and men alike – were lynched or burned alive between 1994 and 1998 alone. Witch-hunts are also widespread in Latin America and Southeast Asia.

In Papua New Guinea in February 2013, 'hundreds of bystanders watched as a woman accused of witchcraft was being burned alive'. This followed 'a series of gruesome deaths ... [including] the burning at the stake in February of a young mother in front of large crowd ... the decapitation of a retired school teacher in the autonomous region of Bougainville ... and the kidnapping and torturing with [a] hot iron of six women and one man in the Southern Highlands' (Lloyd 2013). All were accused of 'sorcery', which is actually a crime under the Papuan legal code.

Figure 13.4 A gendercidal institution? Witch-hunts then and now.

forced/*corvée* labour – perhaps the most destructive of all human institutions – have disproportionately targeted males, sometimes to the point of exclusivity, with casualty counts that likewise may dwarf those inflicted by more traditional forms of violence and conflict.

These observations bear on the reconfiguration of concepts of 'security' in international relations as a field of study. As feminists have stressed, a highly militarized and masculinized 'realist' conception of security has prevailed in both academic and policy circles (Enloe 2007: 47). It is questionable whether a great deal has changed at the policy level, but academic and public debate is increasingly dominated by exponents of 'human security,' which emphasizes the vulnerabilities of ordinary individuals and points out the paradox that a highly 'secure' state may in fact drastically undermine the security of its own population. At certain points, human *insecurity* may be so largescale and systematic that it merits the 'genocide' designation, and should activate humanitarian intervention based on the principle of 'a responsibility to protect' (International Commission on Intervention and State Sovereignty [ICISS] 2001). There is no reason that structural and institutional vulnerabilities should not be factored into this mix, though the recipe for 'intervention' may differ from that of a militarized and time-bound crisis. I return to this subject in the conclusion.

GENDERING PERPETRATORS

Recent feminist contributions, dating roughly from the late 1990s, have significantly transformed the schematic early image of male perpetrators and female victims, at least in academic discussions. Among these contributions is a reworked understanding of gender and the *perpetration* of violence, including mass violence. This touches on one of the central preoccupations of comparative genocide studies over the past two decades: Who *are* the perpetrators? What motivates and mobilizes them? And what role does gender play in the process?

Like so much in genocide studies, the debate over genocidal perpetrators revolves around the case study of the Jewish Holocaust. The centrality of the Holocaust has lessened in recent years, in part because of the primacy of the Rwandan genocide for a new generation of scholars and students. It nonetheless underpins the field historically, and for most ordinary individuals, the Holocaust remains the iconic genocide. How was it possible for a modern European state to impose industrialized death on millions of innocent civilians? And how could such extraordinary atrocities be inflicted by otherwise 'ordinary' individuals?

The debate crystallized with the publication of two works derived from the same set of archives: Christopher Browning's *Ordinary Men* (Browning 1998) and Daniel Jonah Goldhagen's *Hitler's Willing Executions* (Goldhagen 1997). The archives in question recorded in meticulous detail the actions of Reserve Police Battalion 101, an adjunct killing squad deployed as the Holocaust exploded on the Eastern Front in summer 1941. The members of the battalion were not the fanatical Nazis of SS ranks, but mostly older reservists, 'the "dregs" of the manpower pool available' (Browning 1998: 165). Mobilized for behind-the-lines service as Nazi forces raced across Soviet-occupied eastern Poland and the western reaches of the USSR, they were promptly drafted to serve as executioners of Jewish civilians. At first, in the typical pattern, overwhelmingly younger able-bodied men were targeted for massacre by close-up rifle fire. Then, rapidly, the genocide expanded to include Jewish children, women, the elderly, the incapacitated. There was little official consequence to absenting oneself from the killing operations, although the fear of losing the solidarity of one's peers in conditions of mortal risk does seem to have been a factor (Browning 1998: 170). A few members excused themselves from the mass killing; others were traumatized by the close-up intimacy of the slaughter, emerging from the murder sites spattered with blood and brains and seeking oblivion in alcoholic binges. The horror was immeasurably greater for the victims, of course – some 2 million Jews died in this 'Holocaust of bullets' in 1941–42 (see Figure 13.5) – but it was the prospect of undermining the psychological well-being of these 'ordinary

Figure 13.5 A German police officer shoots Jewish women still alive after a mass execution of Jews from the Mizocz ghetto.
Image: United States Holocaust Memorial Museum.

men' that led the Germans to develop gas vans as a more hands-off method of mass murder, and finally to construct the network of industrial death camps, gas chambers, and crematoria on Polish soil.

What can one say of the gendering of these perpetrators' actions? First, that it was largely absent from Browning's and Goldhagen's accounts. Goldhagen did offer, in passing, one of the most trenchant summaries of the genocidal character of gender-selective executions of males, and an unusually nuanced depiction of the incremental (although rapid) escalation of the killing campaign, from gendercidal to root-and-branch variants.[2] Implicit in this was a gendered understanding of 'legitimate' victims in war, versus other population groups traditionally deemed 'harmless' and meriting special protection; and how a brutal targeting of the former category may acclimatize perpetrators to broader 'root-and-branch' genocides against traditionally 'defenseless' groups, notably children, women, and the elderly/disabled. Without an understanding of how gender contributed to these imputed identifications, we cannot understand the special measure of anxiety and outright trauma apparently experienced by German troops commanded to kill not only massively but indiscriminately. Browning, for his part, hinted at the male bonding that underpinned the solidarity of Reserve Police Battalion 101's members, including the drinking binges (alcohol commonly serves both as a spur to masculine solidarity and a salve for its violent excesses). But strikingly for someone who titled his book *Ordinary Men*, Browning accorded no meaningful role to gender as such.[3] Instead, he relied heavily on the famous psychological experiments of Stanley Milgram and Philip Zimbardo et al. (Milgram 1974; Zimbardo 2007), along with the ideological and racist-propagandistic influences to which Goldhagen ascribed primacy in explaining the conduct of his 'ordinary Germans'. Goldhagen's and Browning's fundamental indifference to gender was typical of the large majority of genocide scholars, although a substantial literature did develop on the theme of women and the Jewish Holocaust (surveyed in Pine 2004).

Feminist comparative analyses of mass violence, by contrast, have placed special emphasis on gendered constructions of masculinity to explain atrocious behavior. (While essentialist concepts of males' greater biological/psychological disposition to violence figured in some early treatments, this line of argument has mostly been left to sociobiologists; see, for example, Peterson and Wrangham 1997.) The most influential psychoanalytical treatment is Klaus Theweleit's *Male Fantasies* (Theweleit 1987a, 1987b) which offered an extraordinarily detailed account of one set of predecessors of Reserve Police Battalion 101 – the right-wing Freikorps paramilitaries who terrorized alleged 'communists' after the First World War. As the Police Battalion forces waged war on 'world Jewry', the Freikorps had battled inundation by a 'Red Tide' (at once communist and essentially female/feminine), seeking to preserve a militarized imperviousness to the enveloping female body, and the realm of sentiment and emotion that it symbolized.

The interplay of plural masculinities (Connell 2002b) with a psychologically distanced, emotionally neutered stance toward violent atrocity has remained a touchstone in feminist analyses. Carol Cohn's study of 'Sex and Death in the Rational World of Defense Intellectuals' (1987) remains perhaps the signal North American contribution of the era. Based on up-close observations of the US defense establishment, Cohn signaled its obsessions with paternalistic (implicitly patriarchal) claim staking, masculine potency, and emotional disengagement. Touring a nuclear weapons facility, for example, Cohn was invited to 'pat the missile':

> (f) What is all this patting? Patting is an assertion of the intimacy, sexual possession, affectionate domination. The thrill and pleasure of 'patting the missile' is the proximity of all that phallic power, the possibility of vicariously appropriating it as one's own. But patting is not only an act of sexual intimacy. It is also what one does to babies, small children, the pet dog. The creatures one pats are small, cute, harmless – not terrifyingly destructive. Pat it, and its lethality disappears.
>
> (Cohn, 1987: 695–96)

Cohn conceded her *own* liability to seduction by this apparatus of euphemistic language wedded to absolute destructive power. Thus, even this relatively early stage of feminist thinking about international relations and mass violence destabilized some of the essentialist conception advanced, for example, by Sara Ruddick in *Maternal Thinking* (Ruddick 1989). Such treatments went some distance to unsettle the 'Beautiful Soul' concept of femininity that operated in tandem with the 'Just Warrior' image of men and masculinity. These terms are drawn from Jean Bethke Elshtain's classic *Women and War* (Elshtain 1987). Elshtain pointed instead to evidence, and constructed identities, that disrupted easy gender distinctions: Pacifist males, for example, were contrasted with bellicose females, such as those in England during the First World War who handed out white feathers (symbolizing cowardice) to men not wearing military uniforms in public. Figure 13.6 demonstrates that masculinities can be both plural and mercurial. Along with a license to kill and inculcation with pervasive homophobia, the state grants militarized males the right – even the obligation – to express love, compassion, and tenderness in ways that might otherwise be viewed as effeminate. Here, in a Pietà-like sculpture commemorating the battles on the Turkish peninsula of Gallipoli, a Turkish soldier is depicted cradling a wounded British soldier, and returning him to his front lines. It is based on an apparently factual incident from the trenches in 1915.

As the genocide and ethnic conflict of the 1990s captured the attention of scholars and mass publics, feminist-inspired accounts paid increasing attention to women as perpetrators and supporters of violent and genocidal enterprises. The exemplary works in the Zed Books 'Women and Violence' series (especially Cockburn 1998; Jacobs, Jacobson and Marchbank 2000; Moser and Clark 2001) highlighted cases such as the Hindu extremist movement in India, in which women were prominent as leaders and followers (Mukhta 2000; see also Sen 2006). The dramatic impact of the events in Rwanda in 1994 should also not be overlooked. For the first time in recorded history, women played an active role at every level of

Figure 13.6 Masculinities are plural and mercurial.

the genocidal enterprise, from the leaders planning and administering the killing, to nuns supervising mass executions and ordinary female villagers wading through piles of victims to strip the dead of their valuables (see African Rights 1995). After Rwanda, it seemed reasonable to argue that 'if women anywhere can participate in genocide on such a scale, and with such evident enthusiasm and savagery, then ... they are capable of such participation everywhere' (Jones 2004: 127; see also Sjoberg and Gentry 2007). Nonetheless, males – many of them eager aggressors, many others coerced and conscripted – still constituted an overwhelming majority of the direct murderers in Rwanda, and one should be cautious about drawing excessive parallels between male and female perpetrators.

An intriguing question to guide comparative research in the future is *how* men and women are mobilized to participate in genocide and mass killing. Feminist analyses of militarized and masculinised concepts of 'security' and insecurity are highly relevant here (see, for example, Weber 1999). My own research on the Rwandan and other cases suggests how contextual features such as economic crisis and widespread unemployment served to magnify the existential vulnerabilities of Hutu males, and to increase the appeal of genocidal killing of Tutsis. The gendered nature of genocidal propaganda offers some fascinating insights into the mobilization process. Out-group males (typified by the 'Eternal Jew' of Nazi imagery) are generally depicted as dirty, dangerous, subversive, and sexually predatory – thus 'priming' populations for the gendercidal extermination of males in the early stages of a genocidal campaign. Propaganda campaigns against out-group women are much smaller in scale and narrower in their range of gendered motifs; but in Rwanda, for instance, Hutu propaganda depicted Tutsi women as a sexually seductive 'fifth column' in league with the Hutus' enemies, including foreign peacekeepers (see Taylor 1999). The extraordinary savagery of the sexual violence against Tutsi women during the genocide, and the eager complicity of many Hutu women in it, suggested that the propaganda had effectively exploited gendered desires and vulnerabilities to mobilize male and female perpetrators alike.

HUMANITARIAN CHALLENGES

In our approach to gender and genocide, if it is advisable to move beyond analysis and on to engagement with the public and policy spheres, then it remains to sketch some of the ways in which a gender lens may assist in forging effective strategies of humanitarian intervention, including legal interventions and postwar peacebuilding.

The influence of gender frameworks on the drafting of international law, and the crafting of legal institutions at both international and domestic levels, has grown exponentially in the past two decades. Although the gap between theory and practice remains large, the gendered vulnerabilities of females – in armed conflicts and otherwise – are now generally recognized. An issue which a couple of generations ago would hardly have registered in international discourse, such as the mass and frequently mutilative rapes of Congolese women, are now front and centre in the humanitarian equation (although with no effective halt to the crisis). The gamut of daily human rights abuses that women confront in most parts of the world has been meticulously dissected by feminist scholars and activists, and ideas of 'women's rights' have moved from a derided marginalization to a recognition as essential elements of any coherent human rights framework (see Chapter 7). The quest to realize the promise of these new understandings will engage us for decades if not centuries hence, but all prohibition regimes that eventually achieve a high degree of acceptance and obedience must begin as 'catalyzing ideas' and nascent campaigns. It can at least be said that rights-based and violence-focused initiatives by feminists and their allies have enjoyed greater success than most such campaigns. The rapidity with which they have entrenched themselves is remarkable.

No one confronting the enduring and pervasive phenomenon of male violence against women can overlook men as agents whose actions cause and explain female victimization, or the hecatombs of casualties thus inflicted. It is increasingly recognized, however, that this depiction has left a great deal of males' gendered experience out of the equation – not least, from both analytical and humanitarian perspectives, the gender-selective victimization of males in war and genocide. Guided both by normative concern for 'absent subjects', and assisted by a newly plural conception of 'masculinities' (Connell 2002b), some ground has been broken in extending feminism's nuanced and empathetic stance on gender and victimization to the civilian males who often constitute a majority of victims of the most extreme and annihilatory violence.

This has been central to my own work on the gender-selective killing of men of imputed 'military age', and attendant atrocities such as selective detention/incarceration and torture. I have explored the humanitarian implications of this framework in detail elsewhere (Jones 2001), but consider one example only. In a 1994 article for *Ethnic and Racial Studies*, I noted the gender-selective evacuation policies of the United Nations at the town of Srebrenica in Bosnia-Herzegovina (underway at the time I wrote in May 1993) (see Figure 13.7). Serb forces besieging Srebrenica had refused to allow 'battle age' males to leave on evacuation convoys. Remarkably, UN field workers 'accommodate[d] themselves to the blatantly discriminatory rules laid down by Serb occupiers leaving behind large numbers of trapped, desperate, and wounded males who feared execution or incarceration when Srebrenica fell to the Serbs' (Jones 1994: 131). The year after the article was published, Srebrenica *did* fall, with notorious results – namely, the wanton slaughter of 8,000 Bosnian Muslim men and boys in Europe's worst massacre since the Einsatzgruppen atrocities of the Second World War, often in mass executions reminiscent of the Nazi 'Holocaust of bullets' against Jews on the Eastern Front in 1941–42.

Would a more forceful intervention in 1993 have staved off the massacres of 1995? Did a form of tunnel vision prevent humanitarian workers from perceiving the needs of Bosnian Muslim men? In a series of articles for leading IR journals, and subsequently in an important book (Carpenter 2006), Carpenter found extensive empirical support for the idea of a one-sided framing of gender and humanitarian intervention. If such interventions are indeed guided by broad humanitarian concern, and seek to avoid arbitrarily excluding substantial categories of victims, Carpenter's kind of critical and cautionary investigation will be of considerable relevance.

Figure 13.7 Exhumed remains of a Bosnian Muslim victim of the Srebrenica massacre of July 1995 being carried to the cemetery for reburial.

The study of gender-selective killing and other mass violence can be usefully extended, as noted, to the structural and institutional realm – and concepts of 'humanitarian intervention' extended thereby. We are still too readily guided by a fixation on time-bounded 'crises' that spawn debates over largescale but usually short-term military intervention. This mindset underpinned the best-known attempt to entrench a 'responsibility to protect' civilian populations afflicted by conflict and state repression worldwide. But it is worth reading the report issued by the Canadian-sponsored International Commission on Intervention and State Sovereignty (ICISS 2001) through a lens of gendered structural violence. The commission discerned 'two broad sets of circumstances' that it felt could justify military interventions. One was 'large scale "ethnic cleansing," actual or apprehended, whether carried out by killing, forced expulsion, acts of terror or rape' (ICISS 2001: 32). The mention of rape is significant in the gender equation, of course; but from another angle, perhaps more interesting still was the other set of specified circumstances: one characterized by *large scale loss of life, actual or apprehended, [inflicted] with genocidal intent or not, which is the product either of deliberate state action, or state neglect or inability to act, or a failed state situation* (emphasis added).

Consider the widespread scourge of maternal mortality. This kills hundreds of thousands of women annually, frequently in an agony that parallels the worst human-devised tortures. This is a death toll comparable to some estimates of the Rwandan genocide's, and it is repeated *every year*. Even in poor countries, regimes have the capacity to reduce or virtually eliminate the threat. Revolutionary Cuba, for example, brought maternal care to women in rural areas and poor urban neighborhoods; today its maternal mortality rate is lower than that of the US. Most regimes, however, prefer to spend scarce resources on mansions and Mercedes limousines rather than on primary health care, especially for women. Now let us revisit the ICISS justifications for military intervention. 'Large scale loss of life', for example, certainly obtains. Is it 'the product ... of deliberate State action'? In the sense just specified, it clearly is; but note that the ICISS does not require evidence of intentional action; cases of 'State neglect' also qualify. Therefore, according to ICISS requirements, the crisis of maternal mortality would appear to justify largescale military intervention.

I am not, of course, suggesting that military interventions should be mounted in such cases. Rather, I seek to highlight the guiding and rather narrow assumptions of the 'humanitarian intervention' debate, and how a gender perspective attuned to a structural as well as an event-driven perspective might helps to destabilize these assumptions. Surely, a good deal of our nonmilitary humanitarian resources (aid, suasion, etc.) should be directed towards addressing institutional expressions of violence that inflict more casualties than all but the worst political-military genocides. Although some may consider this at the outer limits of 'responsible' thinking on policy issues, interpretations of gender and mass violence – notably the core feminist contributions – have always been driven to push against boundaries and upset traditional mindsets. The struggle continues.

Questions for further debate

1. What is genocide, and what are the difficulties and ambiguities of the United Nations Genocide Convention?
2. What is 'gendercide', and what is the role of gendercidal institutions?
3. What role do rape and sexual assault play in genocide?
4. How have males generally been depicted in gendered analyses of mass conflict? What, if anything, has been absent from standard formulations?
5. How are women and men mobilized to participate in genocide and other forms of mass violence? Additionally, how do distinctions of class, ethnicity, and sexual orientation destabilize easy generalizations about these gendered experiences?

Sources for further reading and research

Chalk, F. and K. Jonassohn (1990) *The History and Sociology of Genocide*, New Haven, CT: Yale University Press.

Lentin, R. (ed.) (1997) *Gender and Catastrophe*, London: Zed Books.

Moser, C. O. N. and F. C. Clark (eds) (2001), *Victims, Perpetrators or Actors? Gender, Armed Conflict and Political Violence*, London: Zed Books.

Stiglmayer, A. (ed.) (1995) *Mass Rape: The War against Women in Bosnia-Herzegovina*, Lincoln, NE: University of Nebraska Press.

Warren, M. A. (1985) *Gendercide: The Implications of Sex Selection*, Totowa: Rowman & Littlefield.

Notes

1 Also relevant is Article II(d), 'preventing births within the group.' Not only are raped women often too traumatized to resume normal sexual relations, but if they are impregnated or infected with disease as a result of the rape (which is often gang rape), births deemed to be 'within the group' may be prevented for the duration of the pregnancy or ailment. When the infection is the HIV virus, rape is a death sentence (Article II(a)). These themes are prominent in the current highly incisive feminist commentary, and widespread activism, surrounding the atrocious mass rapes in Congo. This builds on earlier analyses of the Balkan and Rwandan conflicts, as the widespread coverage in mainstream media reflects prior feminist mobilizations.

2 'Even if ... the initial order was to kill "only" teenage and adult Jewish males – the order was still genocidal and clearly was understood by the perpetrators as such ... The killing of the adult males of a community is nothing less than the destruction of that community' (Goldhagen 1997: 153). On the step-by-step escalation of the killing: 'First, by shooting primarily teenage and adult Jewish males, they would be able to acclimate themselves to mass executions without the shock of killing women, young children, and the infirm. ... By generally keeping units' initial massacres to smallish numbers (by German standards) of a few hundred or even a thousand or so, instead of many thousands, the perpetrators would be less likely to become overwhelmed by the enormity of the gargantuan bloodbaths that were to follow. They also could believe that they were selectively killing the most dangerous Jews, which was a measure that they could conceive to be reasonable for this apocalyptic war. Once the men became used to slaughtering Jews on this sex-selective and smaller scale, the officers could more easily expand the scope and size of the killing operations' (Goldhagen 1997: 150).

3 The one meaningful passage focuses on masculine role expectations in shaping concepts of soldierly strength and weakness – in an intriguing way: 'Most of those who did not shoot [Jewish civilians] only reaffirmed the "macho" values of the majority – according to which it was a positive quality to be "tough" enough to kill unarmed, noncombatant men, women, and children – and tried not to rupture the bonds of comradeship that constituted their social world' (Browning 1998: 185).

CHAPTER 14

Sexual violence in war

Donna Pankhurst

LEARNING OUTCOMES

Upon completion, readers should be able to:

- Explain what a gendered analysis of violence in wartime can reveal.
- Problematise dominant representations of conflict-related sexualised violence.
- Provide an account of the international political and legal responses to the prevalence of conflict-related sexualised violence.

INTRODUCTION

In most textbooks, the key defining feature of war is the absolute (and occasionally relative) number of casualties. This is a challenging criterion because data are almost always hard to establish, let alone verify, and are generally highly contested, as recently demonstrated in international disputes about deaths in the Iraq war (Davies 2006). In recent wars, there has been a tendency for civilian deaths to exceed military casualties, and women and children have become the major casualties in war where once they were the minority (Cockburn 2001: 21; Giles and Hyndman 2004: 3, 4–5). Many authors cite a figure of 90 per cent of today's war casualties being civilians in support of this claim (although the original source is rarely acknowledged). Such a conclusion has sometimes led to the elision that women are victimised by war to a greater extent than men, because the majority of adult civilians are women, and when the populations of civilian women and children are added together, they outnumber male combatants. Furthermore in the post-war context women survivors generally outnumber men and so it is also often said that women as a group bear a greater burden for post-war recovery (see, for example, Turshen 2001a: 58), and that is before we begin to assess the effects of those acts of sexual violence from which women survive.

Actually it is evident that more men than women die directly from violence across the world in general, as well as directly from war (Pearce 2006), although when serious disease is included in the effects of war (as, for example, in Beaumont, 2006; Stewart et al. 2001: 93) the gender differential does emphasise greater suffering on the part of women. We may come to the rather more sophisticated conclusion that:

> [O]ver the entire conflict period interstate wars, civil wars and internationalised civil wars on average affect women more adversely than men ... we also find that ethnic wars and wars in 'failed' states are much more damaging to women than other civil wars.
>
> (Plümper and Neumayer 2003: 3)

Thus some texts appear to over-emphasise the relative burdens, or costs of war paid by women as a gender compared with men, perhaps out of concern for women as 'innocent' victims, and in attempts to redress a historic neglect of their plight. Women's deaths, and their multiple roles in war, are no longer ignored in the way they once were, but controversy remains when assessing the relative burdens of women and men in war, where the focus is on death and disease (Human Security Commission [HSC] 2005: 11; Pankhurst 2007: 2–3).

Feminists have identified other features of war that appear to be commonplace besides death and disease. A political and social backlash against women is common in the aftermath period, as is widespread sexual violence against women both during and in the aftermath (always on a much larger scale than that against men, and almost always perpetrated by men).

For some authors sexual violence against women is presumed to be ubiquitous in war and almost self-explanatory; it is wartime and therefore men will behave in this way (this is perhaps one of the 'stories about men' to which Shepherd alludes in Chapter 3). For others there is a further explanation besides men's bestial nature that gives such acts of violence political meaning. Militarised cultures and military and political leaders encourage, orchestrate and even command such acts in order to achieve two broad political outcomes. First is that of undermining the morale of the enemy communities, particular the male fighters who find themselves unable to protect their women. This is the 'rape as a weapon of war' thesis which can be found in commentaries and analyses of wars in all parts of the world and throughout history. Second is that of boosting the morale of combatants who are also said to regard rape as a reward, and also tend to bond more closely as fighters, when such violent acts against women have a collective element (see Chapters 9, 10 and 13).

In addition, less orchestrated rape occurs during wars where there are no clear frontlines or endings. Perpetrators act on their own initiative, but this may still be described as 'mass rape'. Examples are found in Sierra Leone, Peru, and East Timor. Such violent acts are conducted in a political atmosphere of impunity, and where there is an expectation that such an act broadly serves a political cause.

Rape in refugee camps is also often very high. Some of the violence is committed by enemy forces, but sometimes rape is committed by men who are employed to provide protection to camp members, such as UN peacekeepers and even humanitarian workers, who still on the whole remain unprosecuted even when vulnerable women and girls provide evidence to and seek redress from the relevant authorities (see Higate 2007; Nordstrum 1998: 83; Rice and Sturcke 2008). So there seems to be something about the nature of war itself that leads to sexual violence against women and children.

It is also common for assaults on women to increase in the aftermath of war (sometimes to an even higher level than during it). This may be from 'enemy' men on retreat, with two infamous examples often quoted as Berlin in 1945 and Nanking in 1937 (Anon, 2002; Seifert 1999: 147). To complicate matters further, sexual violence against women by men on the same side in the conflict tends to increase during and certainly in the aftermath of war, including violence from intimate partners who have returned from a front line and even sometimes from those who never left. In this chapter, we review the different explanations given for, and consequences of, this sexual violence.

RAPE AND SEXUAL VIOLENCE: DEFINITIONS AND STATISTICS

> In recent years, mass rape in war has been documented in various countries, including Cambodia, Liberia, Peru, Bosnia, Sierra Leone, Rwanda, the Democratic Republic of Congo, Somalia and Uganda. A European Community fact-finding team estimated that more than 20,000 Muslim women were raped during the war in Bosnia. At least 250,000, perhaps as many as 500,000 women were systematically raped during the 1994 genocide in Rwanda, according to reports from the World Bank and UNIFEM. Most recently in Darfur, Western Sudan, displaced people have described a pattern of systematic and unlawful attacks against civilians by a government-sponsored Arab militia and the Sudanese military forces.
>
> (IRIN 2008a)

Rape and sexual violence in different contexts are defined differently. In international law, rape need not include penile penetration, but is defined as:

> The invasion of any part of the body of the victim or of the perpetrator with a sexual organ, or of the anal or genital opening of the victim with any object or any other part of the body by force, coercion, taking advantage of a coercive environment, or against a person incapable of giving genuine consent.
>
> (International Criminal Court, cited in IRIN 2008b)

In recent times, international law has changed to recognise rape as a form of torture, and as a war crime – initially through the International Criminal Tribunal for

Rwanda, but subsequently in other ad hoc post-conflict tribunals and the International Criminal Court (Walsh 2007). However, just as data about deaths caused by war are difficult to obtain and verify, and are often contested, so too are those on the incidence of rape and sexual violence. Where public displays of mass rape such as those in Bosnia and Rwanda occur, eye-witness accounts can help but estimates still vary widely. For other types of rape that are less public, even such estimates are very difficult to make. Women often choose not to seek redress even where an appropriate legal framework exists which perhaps reinforces a tendency to under-estimate the frequency.

The consequences of rape and sexual violence in these contexts other than death are often extreme and very long term. Disease is a common outcome and in post-conflict societies medical facilities, particularly those dealing with trauma, are usually scarce and tend not to be geared to the needs of women. In addition, women who were raped by 'enemy' men, particularly those who bore children as a result, often find themselves excluded from aid and other support (Turshen 1998: 9) and are commonly abandoned or divorced by husbands, family and even their community. In recent wars, it is not uncommon for children to be both 'perpetrators' and 'victims' of sexual violence, with boy conscripts (and a smaller number of girls) being forced to commit acts of sexual violence (sometimes on relatives) and young girls (and some boys) being victims of sexual violence. The long-term effects of such experiences rarely receive attention, in spite of having been known about for a long time (Nordstrum 1997; Plunkett and Southall 1998; Watson 2007).

Not the same everywhere

Not all wars have all these features. Some do not appear to have much rape at all, but they are in the minority, and it is difficult to explain the variation. It may be that strict military discipline, and an ideology which inhibits such behaviour contribute where the most extreme forms of organised rape are absent. For instance Nazis did not rape Jewish women in this kind of public, organised way; and neither have Israeli forces in occupied territories, nor Pol Pot's forces in (at least parts of) Kampuchea.

Even in the most infamous and dramatic examples it seems that not all men behaved in the same way. There are variations in the extent and type of violence; the degrees of sanction and direction by political and military leaders, and in the degree to which men engage in such acts with determination or reluctance. We have evidence in a few examples where research was undertaken with men. For instance, Enloe examines an interview with a man who had been involved in an attack on women in Bosnia. The account describes how a group of soldiers were instructed to commit gang rape on a woman and then kill her. One of the participants shares his ambivalence – even bewilderment – about the experience, and evidently did not experience the feelings of pleasure, bonding or triumph that were expected, and did not consider that his co-perpetrators did either (Enloe 2004a: 114–17).

If we read with care some narratives of war whose key intention is to illustrate the prevalence of extreme violence committed by men against women, it is also possible to see counter-narratives in the comments by male witnesses and reluctant participants. This may be seen in accounts given to the Peers Inquiry into the My Lai atrocities committed on Vietnamese civilians by US military forces. For instance, '[m]ost people in our company didn't consider the Vietnamese human ... A guy would just grab one of the girls there and ... they shot the girls when they got done' (from Peers Inquiry tapes, highlighted in BBC News 2008). Note that this soldier says that 'most', not all, behaved in this way. He was giving evidence against his fellow soldiers.

EXPLANATIONS FOR SEXUAL VIOLENCE IN WAR

Rape as a weapon of war

The type of rape most commonly associated with war is that of mass rape, committed in public by many men. It has a long history (perhaps as long as that of human warfare) in all regions of the world (Copelon 1998: 63) and does not seem to be on the decline. In many of these dramatic moments the women were killed or died of wounds shortly after being raped many times. In recent wars the presence of HIV/AIDS increases the likelihood that women die as a result. Such acts may be part of a military and/or political strategy in advance or retreat. The perpetrators may be soldiers or citizens. 'Rape, when used as a weapon of war, is systematically employed for a variety of purposes, including intimidation, humiliation, political terror, extracting information, rewarding soldiers, and "ethnic cleansing"' (Amnesty International USA 2005). This common 'explanation' suggests that there is a planned, intended outcome of sexual violence and rape. It is found in commentaries of many other wars pre-dating feminist analysis, with a particular emphasis on punishment and terrorisation of 'the enemy'. As such it is cast as being part of combatants' armoury and therefore an important part of the study of warfare. Such 'purposes' are not thought to be about sex per se (other than that of 'rewarding' soldiers), although there is still the vexed question, in the case of penile rape, of the connection between the violent act and sexual arousal (Turshen 1998: 12).

Rewarding soldiers

Collective acts of sexual violence are sometimes intended to 'galvanise the troops'. It is said to makes them feel positive, bonded as a group, and to constitute an effective outlet for their 'natural' urges which dissipates 'inappropriate' frustration and aggression when it is deemed unsuitable for military conduct. This persuasive analysis is seen as a key part of a broader strategy of 'militarism' (see Chapter 10), which has been identified and researched most notably by Cynthia Enloe (1989, 1993, 1998, 2000b, 2004a) and picked up by many other writers (for example, Cockburn 2001: 22; De Abreu 1998: 92–3; Elshtain 1987; Seifert 1995: 58; Turshen 1998: 12). Through a methodological approach that asks the question, 'Where are the women?' in many different sites of interest to analysts of war and international relations, Enloe has helped to reveal the ways in which military, security and governmental structures rely on specific types of relationship between, and behaviour patterns of, both men and women.

A further type of reward for soldiers is to be found in the material gain to be had through threatening or extending sexual violence against women (Turshen 2001a: 55, 60). In Africa at least, Turshen suggests that '[s]ystematic rape and sexual abuse are among the strategies men use to wrest personal assets from women' (Turshen 2001a: 55). Such material gain may include women's labour (de Abreu 1998: 92–94; Pillay 2001: 38; Turshen 2001a: 61); or land (Turshen 2001a: 62–63) or other property (Turshen and Twagiramariya 1998: 109) where women feel they have no choice but to give men whatever they request when faced with rape and other forms of assault and threat of further violence. She suggests that this motivation might be restricted to societies where gender relations are so unequal that women are not legally autonomous individuals (that is, where colonial and customary legal codes have combined) (Turshen 2001a: 65). Perhaps an additional context is one of poverty, where relatively small amounts of property have great significance, or contexts where access to property is highly transferable.

The incidence of rape tends to be higher with irregular, undisciplined armies, in wars where there is not a sharp division between military and civilian personnel (Turshen 1998: 12). In some general sense, men having 'licence' to act violently and in a sexual way towards women itself is thought to constitute a 'reward' or right without any expected political outcome or indeed encouragement. This kind of 'explanation' still begs the question of why it would be an activity chosen by men, particularly when it is committed against women from their own community, rather than 'enemy' women.

Absence of social constraints

A more general and highly pervasive assumption made by journalists and academics about men's violence against women during wars is that sexual violence is an inevitability if social constraints on men's behaviour are removed (Goldstein 2001; HSC 2005; Turshen 2001b: 59), and has no other real 'purpose'. The assumption is that men will behave like this simply because their social dominance means they can. This 'constraints removed' thesis is also said to explain partner violence both at 'the front' and at home. Men's sexually violent urges are seen as being biologically and socially driven to such an extent that men have no control over them, almost having the tag 'natural' (Goldstein 2001: 365). This biosocial connection between violence and sex also has resonance with some explanations for rape in non-war settings, where men are assumed to be violent against women when they are not socially restrained or believe they will not be 'caught' (Cowburn 2005: 226–27; Gavey 2005: 42; Pankhurst 2007). This thinking harks back to an old feminist school of thought that 'all men are potential rapists' (Brownmiller 1975). It is exemplified here: 'even without official encouragement most wars involve a dramatic erosion in the norms that restrain anti-social behaviour in times of peace ... there is often little to deter *individuals* from acting out their *violent desires*' (HSC 2005: 109; emphasis added). This approach ignores, or at least downplays, the testimonies of men who claim to commit such acts only under duress (Enloe 2004b: 117) and does not allow for the variety in men's attitudes and behaviour.

Masculinity as a root cause

In contrast to a biosocial explanation, an increasing number of writers use the term 'masculinity' to describe patterns of male behaviour, and assume that this changes along with major social and political change. Several writers have argued that at times of socio-political tension prior to conflict, as well as during conflict itself, some types of masculinity come to be celebrated and actively promoted to a greater degree than others (El Bushra 2000: 76, 80; Cockburn 1998: 207, 2001: 20). In some conflict situations, the more violent aspects of masculinity are played out in all aspects of men's lives to an extreme degree, in what Hague calls a 'hetero-national masculinity', with reference to the Serb and Bosnian Serb military (Hague 1997: 55).

Rather than changes in masculinity somehow being inevitable with war, some writers emphasise that this change is consciously sought and promoted by political leaders as part of the purposeful strategy of rape as a weapon of war. Encouraging men to be more aggressive with the rise of nationalist or ethnic consciousness is here intended both to gain political support for the cause and to undermine 'the other' (see Figure 14.1). Egotistical, aggressive, dominant behaviours are common features of such cultural definitions of masculinity, as is men's dominance over women (Byrne 1996: 33). This manipulation of masculinity is often asserted in the literature but is rarely accompanied by analysis of how it happens. Women play key roles in affirming and encouraging all aspects of masculinities, as one of the main institutions for promoting one or other set of behaviours and values is that of the family, where women play a leading role in educating young people and indeed in encouraging adults to favour one or other set of attributes. In some cases, this leads women to put great pressure on male relatives, including sons, to embrace violence, to 'be brave', fight, stand up for the honour of your family/nation etc. – in effect 'be a real man' (Munn 2008; Pillay 2001: 41).[1]

The effects of conflict-related poverty and economic change have left men in northern Uganda feeling no longer able to 'be a man' in the same way as in the past. Dolan usefully distinguishes between the lived experience of men, which may be highly varied in peace time, but which in wartime often becomes closer to being uniform, and the lived expectations of men, that is, what they hope to be, which could always be the same. Such an example may be seen to exemplify a situation where a hegemonic masculinity, as a set of idealised identities, behaviours and roles, is imagined and aspired to, but which is not achieved by most men. Men commit new forms of violence against women because their masculinity (that is, their 'proper' role in society) has been thwarted, and men are failing to achieve what they want or need to (Dolan 2002: 77–79): that which others might describe as the ideals of a hegemonic masculinity.

Figure 14.1 Linking economics and violence.

The type of behaviour such processes encourage or engender are described as 'hyper-masculinity' by some (Boesten 2007); aggression and uncontrolled virility being key features, but also accompanied by some rejection of modernity embodied in a sense of a 'return to the warrior' or to the 'essence' of a key group. Such ideology is also often accompanied with an undermining of women's rights by the state (Turshen 2001b). Masculinity here is explicitly not seen as being in crisis, as is sometimes suggested, but in the ascendancy and in a primary dominant phase. Used in this way the concept does not allow us to see easily or understand what happens to individual men (why they change) or the variety of men's responses. Segal (1990: 121–22) highlights interesting examples of men who seem to personify a particularly violent form of hyper-masculinity, and yet who do not fit the corresponding stereotype in all their behaviour. She highlights Nazi camp supervisors in Auschwitz, Treblinka and Dachau who were gentle to their wives and a British army veteran of the Falklands war who was 'completely without bravado' (ibid.).

Frustration–aggression and men's trauma

Other commentators squarely attribute precisely the same violent behaviour to the psychological damage experienced by men (Krog 2001: 212; Sideris 2001a: 57, 59–60). While many people take the view that emotional and psychological factors affect men's war and post-war behaviour (IRIN 2004), it is surprisingly difficult to draw strong conclusions from actual research in this area (Jones et al. 2002) and research suggests that no society in the world responds adequately to support men thought to be suffering in this way (Gabriel and Neal 2002). When one considers the findings from non-war contexts about the importance of childhood trauma in causing violent behaviour later in life, and the high numbers of soldiers in today's wars who start their combat lives as children, the problem seems enormous. Yet the psychological effects of war (or childhood poverty, trauma or other experiences) on men do not appear in many people's explanations for why men commit violence against women, or as a priority in post-war reconstruction and rehabilitation efforts.[2]

The existence of 'posttraumatic stress disorder' is still debated in the medical literature and profound questions remain about what would constitute a 'cure', although there is increasing research in this area (Gabriel and Neal 2002; Jones et al. 2002). Richards' work (1995) on Sierra Leonean 'warboys' highlights child abuse through several generations as a major cause of their extremely violent behaviour. In the analysis of some post-conflict settings, the psychological dimension does appear, but with reference to the whole community, rather than to men in particular. Hamber comments:

> In South Africa, the entire discourse of nation building was imbued with the pseudo-psychological construction on national healing, incorrectly implying that nations have collective psyches. The problematic results were that individual needs such as long-term healing and the desire for justice were, to a degree, subordinated to the collective drive to 'reconcile'.
>
> (Hamber 2003: 14)

Ignatieff (1998) also warns against assuming there is a national psyche, and Arendt's warnings about conceptualising a 'sick society', rather than sick people, are also pertinent here; she sees this as being more likely to make people see violence as natural (and inevitable) rather than being politicised (Arendt 1970: 75). In any case, research in non-war settings into how men's attitudes to rape can change suggests that the social context (and social attitudes towards rape in particular) has to change as well as individual men's proclivity (Gavey 2005: 45). Perhaps it is not just the fact of war that causes men to behave in this way. This analysis does not lead to very optimistic or feasible strategies for future change. On the positive side, it does reinforce the view that such behaviour is not in any simple way biologically determined, and therefore the 'constraints removed' thesis is less compelling, if one considers it to be founded on a biological or biosocial argument. Furthermore the fact that not all men behave in the same way, even when they have been through similar experiences, brings further into doubt that the correlation between participation in war, and violence against women, signifies a simple causal relationship.

PROSECUTION AND LEGAL FRAMEWORK

Until relatively recently, women's rights in the post-war context seem to have been breached almost with complete impunity. In contexts where transitional systems of justice are used as part of a process to rebuild the rule of law, women's human rights are not given priority. For instance, police forces tend to operate with a strong gender bias, even where post-war reform and political change mean that men are no longer subject to arbitrary arrest and torture (Kandiyoti 2007). It is not uncommon for there to be immense post-war social pressures on women not to report abuse by men, particularly if the men are members of key political movements, the government, or where there is a shortage of men available for marriage. Where rape was widespread during war, and is not effectively prosecuted afterwards, it is extremely difficult to bring prosecutions for rape in the post-war setting, an issue that remains as much of a problem as when it was highlighted over a decade ago in the UN. Children's rights have been taken more seriously over the last decade, with the plight of former child soldiers receiving a great deal more attention and increasing international support, although there is still a long way to go and the focus still remains on boys' war experience rather than girls'. Many experiences of girls, such as sexual abuse by peacekeeping forces in Mozambique (Nordstrum 1997: 15–19), remain hidden.

Nonetheless the definition and prosecution of gender-based violence in conflict have moved ahead enormously over the last decade:

> The legal advances made in the *ad hoc* tribunals have intersected with decisions in national and regional jurisdictions to produce a consistent body of international jurisprudence that has established and re-affirmed rape as a war crime, a crime against humanity and an element of genocide.
>
> (Walsh 2007: 50)

Much has also been learned about the actual processes required for women to access such justice frameworks in the post-war context, and Walsh particularly highlights the lessons learned from the International Criminal Court for Yugoslavia. The International Criminal Court now has a sophisticated framework which recognises lessons from the difficulties experienced by women in the past and she suggests that it is important to acknowledge this great, and largely unexpected, success but also to keep in mind that for many women the ability to access such justice requires support from their nation state and the 'legal literacy' and knowledge of processes available to them (see Chapter 20).

For instance in over a decade of work by the International Criminal Tribunal for Rwanda we can see the attempts and failures to prosecute gender-based violence that was such a key part of the genocidal violence. Women survivors were treated very poorly in the justice processes, and a low priority was given by the court to the prosecution of such crimes. The ways in which some were asked to give evidence resulted in personal and material suffering on their return home, although it seems that some positive lessons have been learned about this in establishing the Sierra Leone post-conflict legal framework (Nowrojee 2007).

CONCLUSION

So what does all this mean for the study of international relations? First, it remains an important challenge to international relations to identify the circumstances under which mass rape is sometimes taken very seriously at the international level and sometimes downplayed and ignored.

Second, in the study of warfare, there are significant gaps in our knowledge and understanding of the political effectiveness of a common military strategy; that of organised sexual violence against women. Such gaps spill over into our understanding of what it takes to recover from conflict and build lasting peace, when one considers the experience of ex-combatants (men, women and children) and of civilians (men, women and children).

Third, seeking explanations for wartime sexual violence against women reveals how clumsy an explanatory tool is 'masculinity'. As described here, it is alternately said to be in the ascendancy or in crisis to explain the same phenomena. These phenomena may include men's behaviour (for example, increased sexual violence against women), people's beliefs (what is acceptable and desirable in terms of behaviour) and ideology (whether consciously promoted by agents or not), but authors often do not specify or indeed switch between these without making it clear. Furthermore, assertions about such phenomena are themselves rarely based on empirical research. Nonetheless 'masculinity' seems to many authors still to hold considerable explanatory potential in explaining the likelihood of states, movements and other non-state actors becoming engaged in organised violence, although a debate is growing about its deficiencies and it is certainly becoming rather more common to refer to *masculinities* (see Pankhurst, 2007).

Fourth, asking questions about men's specific sexual violences facilitates a greater insight into children's experiences of violence at the hands of adult men during wars, and the ways in which these tend to be eclipsed. Such an analysis presents challenges for how International Relations might be forced to change its scope if children are to be seen as actors rather than simply victims (Watson 2006: 248).

To sum up, sexual violence committed by military and civilian men against women and girls is a common feature of war and its aftermath across the world. In many places it is openly seen as part of a military and political strategy, and should therefore be taken very seriously by students of international relations. Explanations for its variety, causes and implications remain contested and complex, however, with much potential for further theoretical, conceptual and (perhaps of most significance) empirical work remaining.

Questions for further debate

1. What does a gender analysis of violence in wartime reveal?
2. How useful is the term masculinity in explaining why men do and do not commit rape and other forms of sexual violence during wars and in their aftermath?
3. Why is rape and sexual violence more prevalent in some wars than others?
4. How do the explanations for rape in non-war settings compare with the explanations for that which takes place in war?
5. What are the key international instruments available to reduce wartime rape and what are the key inhibitors that restrict their effectiveness?

Sources for further reading and research

Cockburn, C. (2001) 'The Gendered Dynamics of Armed Conflict and Political Violence', in C. Moser and F. C. Clark (eds) *Victims, Perpetrators Or Actors? Gender, Armed Conflict and Political Violence*, London: Zed Books.

Copelon, R. (1998) 'Surfacing Gender: Reconceptualizing Crimes Against Women in Time of War', in L. A. Lorentzen and J. Turpin (eds) *The Women and War Reader*, London: New York University Press.

Pillay, A. (2001) 'Violence Against Women in the Aftermath' in S. Meintjes, A. Pillay and M. Turshen (eds) *The Aftermath: Women in Post-conflict Transformation*, London: Zed Books.

Seifert, R. (1995) 'War and Rape. A Preliminary Analysis', in A. Stiglmayer (ed.) *The War Against Women in Bosnia-Herzegovina*, London and Lincoln, NE: University of Nebraska Press.

Turshen, M. (2001) 'The Political Economy of Rape: An Analysis of Systematic Rape and Sexual Abuse of Women During Armed Conflict in Africa', in C. Moser and F. C. Clark (eds) *Victims, Perpetrators Or Actors? Gender, Armed Conflict and Political Violence*, London: Zed Books.

Notes

1 Some writers are keen to avoid blaming women entirely for this phenomenon, stressing that this role has to be weighed against the role of other key institutions such as political parties, nationalist movements and age groups (El Bushra 2000).
2 In the case of South Africa, some action research has led to a rethinking about the nature of posttraumatic stress disorder and the ways in which it might be treated (Hamber et al. 2000: 35) but these findings have not been widely taken up.

PART 4 POLITICAL ECONOMY

CHAPTER 15

International/global political economy

V. Spike Peterson

█ **LEARNING OUTCOMES**

Upon completion, readers should be able to:

- Distinguish between empirical and analytical gender and explain how they differently matter for analyzing the global political economy.
- Describe productive, reproductive, and virtual economies, major trends within and the gendering of each, and how their interaction produces the global political economy.
- Understand how 'feminization' constitutes symbolic and material devalorization of ideas, qualities, identities, and practices and how this matters for multiple, intersecting inequalities.

INTRODUCTION

Globalization is understood in many ways, but in this chapter the objective is to describe the *political economy* of globalization. This means that we will not simply describe 'political' decision making or 'economic' phenomena at the global level, but consider how political *and* economic dimensions of globalization interact and are co-determined. For example, we typically think of government officials and policymakers as 'political' agents, and think of bankers and business owners as 'economic' agents. But the government cannot maintain power and implement policies without economic resources, and businesses require the legal and physical infrastructure that governmental power makes possible. Through a political economy lens, we examine how states and markets – or politics and economics – are never categorically separate but continuously interactive and mutually determining.

Some scholars use international political economy (IPE) and global political economy (GPE) interchangeably. IPE is typically preferred by those who see it as a subfield of IR, and GPE by those who emphasize transnational processes and transdisciplinary perspectives. I prefer GPE and will use it throughout this chapter. A distinction that does matter in this chapter concerns the difference between gender as empirical and gender as analytical.

When gender is used empirically it typically refers to embodied male–female sex difference (the dimorphism discussed in Chapter 3). In this sense, we examine how women and men differently shape, and are differently affected by, globalization processes. For example, women appear to be entering the paid work force in ever increasing numbers, while men are in many places facing un- or underemployment as a result of neoliberal globalization. As we will see throughout this chapter, research based on empirical gender provides important data for analyzing GPE – especially in terms of revealing who does what kind of work, under what conditions, and with what compensation and status. But we will also see the importance, and pervasive influence, of gender understood analytically. This refers to how gender operates discursively – as a governing code that *conceptualizes* gender as differentiating hierarchically between masculinized and feminized identities, qualities or characteristics (the gender 'logic' discussed in Chapter 3).

The claim here is that gender pervades language and meaning systems, 'ordering' how we think (and hence shaping how we act) by privileging that which is associated with masculinity (not all men or only men) over that which is associated with femininity. Research based on analytical gender reveals how important gender coding is systemically, and in GPE in particular it reveals how gendering constitutes valuing. As we will see throughout this chapter, ideas, skills, work and activities that are masculinized are more likely to be valued than those that are feminized: they are more likely to be seen as 'real' work and be taken seriously in terms of both symbolic status *and* material compensation (see Figure 15.1).

GENDER MATTERS IN ECONOMIC THEORY

Mainstream approaches ignore how gendered bodies and gendered codes shape how we think about and practice 'economics.' Orthodox theory focuses on the formal (recorded, regulated) economy and male-dominated 'productive' activities, thereby excluding women's domestic, reproductive, and caring labour. Similarly, 'women's work' and feminized qualities are devalued: deemed economically irrelevant, characterized as subjective, 'voluntary', 'natural' and 'unskilled', and either poorly paid or not paid at all. At the same time, most economists assume that social reproduction occurs through heteronormative families and non-conflictual intra-household

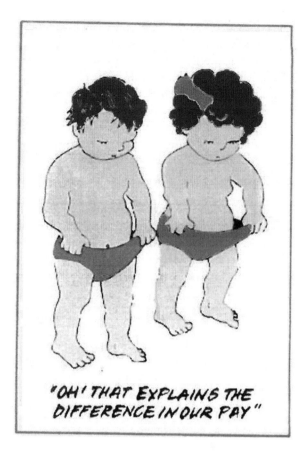

Figure 15.1 Gender and pay.
Image: Leeds Postcards.

dynamics; alternative household forms and the rising percentage of female-headed and otherwise 'unconventional' households are rendered deviant or invisible.[1]

Feminist research addresses and attempts to 'correct' these biases and omissions in several ways. A familiar starting point is 'adding women', which may seem methodologically simple but often produces surprising results. For example, Esther Boserup's pioneering research (1970) on *women's* experiences in non-industrialized countries revealed the often deleterious effects of modernization policies and undercut orthodox claims that development benefitted everyone. Subsequent 'women in development' (WID) studies documented both how policies and practices marginalized women *and* how women's exclusion jeopardized development objectives (see Chapters 16, 17, and 18).

Numerous later and ongoing studies demonstrate how a focus on women and gender *improves* our knowledge of economics more generally. For example, feminists produce more accurate accounts of intra-household labour and resource allocation; move beyond quantitative indicators to enhance measurements of human well-being; and document the centrality of 'women's work' to development, long-term production of social capital, and more accurate national accounting. And women in the global south especially demonstrate the importance of local, indigenous and colonized people's agency in identifying problems and negotiating remedies (see Hawkesworth 2006; Moghadam 2005; Mohanty 2003b).

While WID's focus on empirical gender prompted policies to *include* women in development, this failed to address significant problems: the devaluation of feminized labour, the structural privileging of men and masculinity, and the depoliticization of women's subordination in the family and workplace. As feminists queried underlying *assumptions* (Elson 1991), the liberal, modernist inclinations of WID approaches lost ground to more constructivist, critical starting points of gender and development (GAD) orientations. Understanding gender analytically enabled GAD scholars to problematize the meaning and desirability of 'development', interrogate the definition of work and how to 'count it', examine gender ideologies to explain unemployed men's reluctance to 'help' in the household, challenge constructions of feminism imposed by western elites, and criticize narratives of victimization for denying agency and resistance (see, for example, Benería 2003b; Bergeron 2009; Rai 2002).

In the twenty-first century, feminists continue to expose masculinist bias and its effects on the theory/practice of political economy, and to expand the evidence corroborating – and complicating – early feminist critiques. Their research extends from more obviously gender-differentiated effects of microeconomic phenomena to less visible, indirect effects of macroeconomic policies and global financial markets. Feminists are also engaged in examining alternatives (Bennholdt-Thomsen et al. 2001; Dickinson and Schaeffer 2001) and generating economic visions that include ethical, more humane concerns. In particular, many feminists abandon masculinist models and priorities in favor of a more relevant and responsible model of 'social provisioning' (Power 2004). The remainder of the chapter draws on this and additional research to provide a 'big picture' analysis of GPE that takes both empirical and analytical gender seriously.

GENDER MATTERS IN GPE[2]

Since approximately the 1970s, economic restructuring has been propelled by neoliberal policies favored by geopolitical elites (see Chapter 18 for a further discussion of development institutions and neoliberal policies). Deregulation has permitted the hypermobility of ('footloose') capital, induced phenomenal growth in crisis-prone financial markets, and increased the power of private capital interests. Liberalization is selectively implemented: powerful states continue to foster their interests while developing countries have limited control over protecting domestic industries, goods produced, and jobs provided. Privatization has entailed the loss of nationalized industries in developing economies and a decrease in public sector employment and provision of social services worldwide. While the results of restructuring are complex, uneven, and controversial, evidence increasingly suggests expanding inequalities, indeed a *polarization* (gap between top and bottom) of resources within and between countries (see Figure 15.2).

Globalization is a gendered process that reflects both continuity and change. Men, especially those who are economically, ethnically, racially and geopolitically

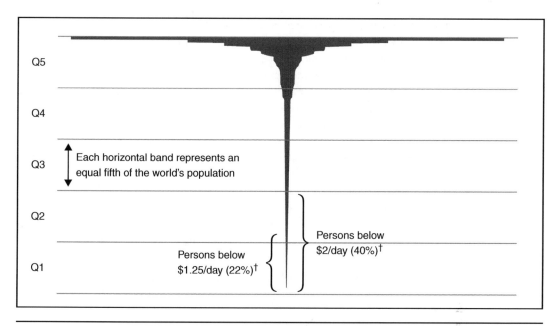

Figure 15.2 Global income distributed by percentiles of the population.
Source: Ortiz and Cummins (2011).

privileged, continue to dominate institutions of authority and power worldwide. Masculinist assumptions and objectives continue to dominate economic and geo-political thinking, with the effect of policymaking that is top-down, formulaic, and over-reliant on growth and quantifiable indicators – rather than focused on provi-sioning, human well-being and sustainability. But globalization is also *disrupting* gendered patterns by altering conventional beliefs, roles, livelihoods, and political practices worldwide. While some changes are small and incremental, others chal-lenge our deepest assumptions (e.g., male breadwinner roles) and most established institutions (e.g., heteropatriarchal families/households). Feminists argue that not only are the benefits and costs of globalization unevenly distributed between men and women, but that masculinist bias in theory/practice exacerbates inequalities manifested in differently constructed but intersecting hierarchies of race/ethnicity, class, and nation.[3]

To make better sense of how these hierarchies *intersect*, I argue that devaloriza-tion of feminized qualities – constituted by the governing code, or logic, of gender – systemically affects how we 'take for granted' (normalize and depoliticize) the devalorization of feminized qualities, bodies, identities, *and* activities. This has obvious relevance for analyzing GPE, where assessments of 'value' are key. In effect, casting subordinated individuals as feminine devalorizes not only the (empirical gender) category of 'women' but also sexually, racially, culturally, and economically marginalized 'men' (e.g., 'lazy migrants', 'incompetent natives', 'effeminate gays'). That is, while structural hierarchies *vary* by reference to the 'difference' emphasized and modalities of power involved, they typically *share* a common feature: the devalorization of feminized qualities attributed to those who are subordinated (lacking reason, agency, control, skills, etc.). Moreover, when we understand gender analytically, not only gendered *bodies* but also concepts, styles, 'ways of knowing', music, hobbies, skills, jobs, and nature, etc., can be feminized – with the effect of reducing their legitimacy, status, and value. This devalorization is simultaneously ideological (discursive, cultural) and material (structural, economic). Consider again how 'women's work' – whether done by women *or* marginalized men – is poorly paid, or frequently not paid at all; and we hardly notice, in part because the depreciation of feminized activities is so taken for granted.

Oppressions differ, as do attempts to explain and/or justify them. Hence, feminization is not the only 'normalizing' ideology in operation. I argue, however, that what distinguishes feminization and renders it so *ideologically* powerful is the unique extent to which it invokes a deeply internalized and naturalized binary – the dimorphism of 'sex difference' – which is then 'available' to naturalize diverse forms of structural oppression. To clarify: even as sex and gender are increasingly ambiguous to some, most people most of the time take a categorical, essentialized distinction between male and female completely for granted: as biologically 'given', reproductively necessary, and psychosocially 'obvious'. Yet history indicates not only that sex difference itself is *produced* – through contingent, socially constructed practices and institutionalizations – but that it is inextricable from masculinism as a system of asymmetrical power. That is, the deeply sedimented *concept* of sex difference and historically institutionalized *practices* of gender hierarchy are mutually constituted. As one effect, the 'naturalness' of sex difference is generalized to the 'naturalness' of masculinist (not necessarily *male*) privilege, so that both aspects become normalized 'givens' of social life (Peterson and Runyan 2010).

The point of arguing that feminization devalorizes is neither to explain how different inequalities are historically produced, nor to claim that gender hierarchy is the 'primary' oppression overshadowing race or class or sexuality. The point is rather to suggest how gender operates *across* hierarchies: if the sex binary normalizes gender hierarchy such that feminized qualities are deemed 'naturally' inferior, then those who are attributed such qualities can be rendered 'naturally' inferior as well. This does the political work of making the limited options and precarious lives of subordinated groups seem somehow inevitable rather than unconscionable.

A FEMINIST GPE FRAMEWORK – REPRODUCTIVE, PRODUCTIVE AND VIRTUAL ECONOMIES

To provide a 'big picture' analysis that genders GPE, I move beyond a narrow definition of economics and develop an alternative analytical framing of reproductive, productive, and virtual economies, abbreviated as 'RPV'. This refers not to conventional but Foucauldian economies: mutually constituted (therefore coexisting and interactive) systemic sites through and across which power operates. These sites involve conceptual and cultural dimensions that are inextricable from – are indeed mutually constituted by – material effects, social practices, and institutional structures. Here I review only major trends in each economy, emphasizing how they are gendered but also how gendered inequalities intersect with other hierarchies.

The productive economy

I begin with what is most familiar: the 'productive economy' understood as 'formal' – regularized and regulated – economic activities identified with primary, secondary and tertiary production. Restructuring variously complicates these sectoral distinctions, especially as information and communication technologies (ICTs) alter what is produced and how.

The first trend is a dramatic decline in world prices of and demand for (non-oil) primary products. This has been devastating to 'third world' economies where primary production dominates: unemployment problems are exacerbated, ability to attract foreign investment is reduced, and debt dependency may be increased. In response, countries may encourage foreign investment by advertising the availability of 'cheap' labour and unregulated, non-unionized worksites. Or they might experience people migrating elsewhere in search of work.

Second, 'de-industrialization' is most prominent in advanced economies and major cities. It involves two shifts: first, from traditional material-based manufacturing (refrigerators) to informational and knowledge-based manufacturing (computer games), and second, a decline in previously well-paying (masculinized) jobs, manifested variously through outsourcing, downsizing, loss of skilled and often unionized positions, growth in low-wage, semi- and un-skilled jobs, and relocation of production to lower wage areas. Like agricultural production in the past, manufacturing remains important but declines in value relative to the higher status and earnings of ICT-based work.

In overlapping ways, job security is additionally eroded for all but elite workers due to a third trend, 'flexibilization' (see Chapter 18). This characterizes how production processes shift: to spatially dispersed networks (the global assembly line, subcontracting), to increasingly casualized (non-permanent, part-time) and informalized (unregulated, non-contractual) jobs, to small batch, 'just in time' (short-term rather than long-term) production planning, and to avoidance or prohibition of organized labour. These changes tend to increase un- and under-employment (especially of men) and coupled with erosion of union power translate into a decline in 'real' incomes and household resources.

Fourth, the most significant job growth is in services, which accounts for 50–70 per cent of the workforce in advanced economies and is increasing rapidly in developing countries. This growth is due in part to the shift from material- and labour-intensive to ICT-based production. For instance, the material and labour costs of producing microchips are only a fraction of the knowledge-based (research and development) costs. Polarization of incomes is exacerbated insofar as service jobs tend to be either skilled and high-waged (professional-managerial jobs; read 'masculinized') or semi-, un-skilled, and poorly paid (personal, cleaning, retail, and clerical services; read: 'feminized'). Hence, this shift also favors countries with developed technology infrastructures and relatively skilled workers.

The fifth trend is *feminization* of employment, understood simultaneously as a material, embodied transformation of labour markets (increasing proportion of women in paid work) and a conceptual characterization of deteriorated and devalorized labour conditions (less desirable, meaningful, safe, or secure). As flexibilization becomes the norm, employers seek workers who are perceived to be undemanding (unorganized), docile but reliable, available for part-time and temporary work, and willing to accept low wages. Gender stereotypes depict women as especially suitable for these jobs and gender inequalities render women especially desperate for access to income. In short, as more jobs are casual, irregular, flexible and precarious (read: feminized), more women – *and* devalorized men – are doing them (Peterson 2012).

In general, elite, educated, and highly skilled women benefit from this trend, and employment in any capacity arguably benefits women in terms of access to income and the personal and economic empowerment this affords. Women, however, continue to earn 30–50 per cent less than men worldwide, and most women are entering the workforce under adverse structural conditions: available work is often tedious, physically demanding, and sometimes hazardous, with negative effects on women's health and long-term working capacity.

Sixth, globalization increases flows of people: to urban areas, export-processing zones, seasonal agricultural sites, and tourism locales. Migrations are not random. They are shaped by colonial histories, geopolitics, capital flows, state policies, labour markets, cultural stereotypes, skill attributions, kinship networks, and identity markers. Consistent with structural vulnerabilities and the nature of 'unskilled,' poorly valued jobs that are most frequently available, migrant worker populations are especially marked by gender, class and race/ethnicity. Moreover, being on the move – for work, recreation, or escape – affects personal and collective identities and cultural reproduction. Not least, traditional family forms and divisions of labour are disrupted, destabilizing men's and women's identities and gender relations more generally. Shifting identities have complex effects on imagined communities, whether expressed in anti-immigrant racism, nationalist state building, ethno-cultural diasporas, ethnic cleansing, or patriarchal religious fundamentalisms (Peterson 2010a).

The uneven and gendered effects of these trends are most visible in relation to production processes and working conditions. For the majority of families worldwide, one-third of which are female headed, restructuring has meant declining household income, reduced access to safe and secure employment, and decreased provision of publicly funded social services. These trends not only differentially affect women, men, and feminized 'others', but are also shaped by masculinist ways of thinking in regard to how 'work' is defined, who should do what kinds of work, and how different activities are *valued*. The effects are especially stark when we consider the reproductive economy.

The reproductive economy

Conventional – and continuing – neglect of the reproductive economy *exemplifies* masculinist and modernist bias and reflects habitual thinking that values the (masculinized) public sphere of power and formal (paid) work, at the expense of the marginalized (feminized) family/private sphere of emotional, domestic and caring (unpaid) labour. There are, however, important reasons for taking the RE seriously;

I note especially the politics of socialization, social reproduction, and informalization in GPE.

Socialization teaches us how to think and behave according to the codes of our particular culture; it is literally indispensable for the survival – social reproduction – of individuals and groups. Subject formation begins in the context of family life and the coding we learn early on is especially influential. This is where we first observe and internalize sex/gender differences, their respective identities, and divisions of labour. Moreover, gender acculturation is inextricable from beliefs about race/ethnicity, age, class, religion, nationality, and other axis of 'difference'.

Effective socialization matters *structurally* for economic relations. It produces individuals who are then able to 'work' and this unpaid reproductive labour (done primarily by women) saves capital the costs of producing key inputs. Socialization also instills attitudes, identities and belief systems that enable societies to function. Capitalism, for instance, requires not only that 'workers' accept and perform their role in 'production', but that individuals more generally accept hierarchical divisions of labour and their corollary: differential valorization of who does what kind of work. And most people internalize the ideology of masculinist states, religions, and heteropatriarchal families that insists 'real' men are self-confident successful breadwinners while 'real' women are devoted service providers, disproportionately responsible for the emotional and physical health of family members.

In spite of romanticized motherhood and a great deal of pro-family rhetoric, neoliberal globalization generates a 'crisis in social reproduction' (Bakker 2007) by depleting (Rai, Hoskyns and Thomas 2014) the emotional, cultural, and material resources necessary for the well-being of most women and families. Privatization reduces public spending; when social services are cut, women are disproportionately affected because they are more likely to depend on secure government jobs and on public resources in support of reproductive labour. When economic conditions deteriorate, women are culturally expected to fill the gap, in spite of fewer available resources, more demands on their time, and minimal increases in men's caring labour. Effects include more women working a 'triple shift', the feminization of poverty worldwide, and both short- and long-term deterioration in female health and human capital development. The effects are not limited to women because the increased burdens they bear are inevitably translated into costs to their families, and hence to societies more generally. As a survival strategy, women especially rely on informal work to ensure their own and their family's well-being (Sassen 2000).

Informal activities fall outside 'formal' (contractual, regulated) work arrangements; they vary from caring and domestic work in the household, to street vending, under-the-counter payments, and black market transactions on a global scale (Peterson 2013) (see Figure 15.3). They demand our attention because of their explosive growth worldwide (constituting perhaps one-half of all economic output), and how they blur licit–illicit, paid–unpaid, and public–private boundaries. In general, informal work is polarized between a small, highly skilled group able to take advantage of and prosper from deregulation and flexibilization, and the majority of the world's (feminized) workers who participate less out of choice than necessity.

Women, migrants, and the poor constitute the vast majority of informalized workers and they also do the informal work that is least valued and often the most

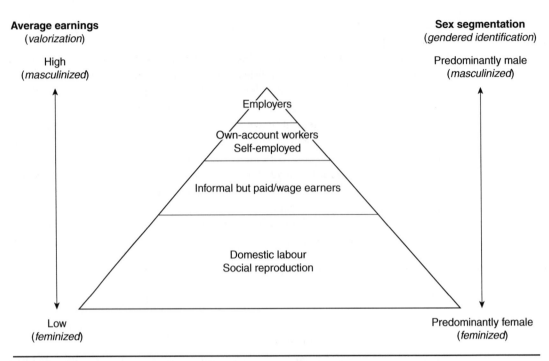

Figure 15.3 The gendered 'iceberg' of (licit) informal economic activities.
Source: Chen et al. (2005).

precarious. This is due in part to stereotypes of feminized work and the extent of informal activities that are situated in the home. There are also race/ethnicity, class, and national patterns in terms of which households engage in which forms of informal labour (e.g., childcare, domestic labour, food vending, petty trade). The salience of structural hierarchies is also due to patterns regarding what types of work are available (e.g., cleaning, caretaking, maintenance, food provisioning, personal services), where informalization is concentrated (e.g., poor and working class families worldwide; migrant labour in rural agriculture and global cities), and who is most likely to be available for and willing to undertake informal activities (i.e., women, migrants, and economically marginalized populations) (Chant and Pedwell 2008).

Interpreting informalization is controversial. Some individuals prosper in a less regulated environment. This is especially evident in micro-enterprises (favored by neoliberals) where innovation may breed success and multiplying effects; in tax evasion and international pricing schemes that favor larger operations; in developing countries in which informal activities are crucial for income generation; and in criminal activities that are 'big business' worldwide. Critics, however, argue that informalization favors capital over labour and that avoidance of regulations is directly and indirectly bad for wages, workers, the environment, and long-term prospects for societal and global well-being. Feminists expose both the role of informalization in devaluing women's labour and its increasing salience as a household survival strategy. Whether viewed positively or negatively, the scale and 'irregularity' of informal activities matter systemically and must be taken seriously.

The virtual economy

My reference to 'virtual' is not intended to *separate* the virtual from the material but to probe the *relationship* between materiality and the increasing dimension of non-materiality in the global economy: the exchange of symbolic money, the centrality of information and communication, and the role of signs and 'virtual reality' in aesthetics and consumption. I focus here on the virtual economy of global finance, which increasingly shapes winners and losers in GPE – as starkly demonstrated in economic crises.

Since the 1970s floating exchange rates, reduced capital controls, offshore transactions, new financial instruments, and the rise of institutional investors have interacted to amplify the speed, scale and complexity of *global financial transactions*. In general, the allure of financial trading exacerbates the devalorization of manufacturing and encourages short-term over long-term investments in industry,

Figure 15.4 Lurie's 'Foreign Affairs'.

Image: © Ranan Lurie. Reproduced with kind permission.

infrastructure, and human capital. The expansion, complexity, and non-transparency of global financial transactions make money laundering easier, which enhances opportunities for illicit financial trading as well as organized crime, and decreases tax contributions that underpin public welfare. Access to credit becomes decisive for individuals and states, and is deeply structured by familiar hierarchies. Increasing urgency in regard to 'managing money' and investment strategies shifts status and decision-making power within households, businesses, governments, and global institutions. These changes disrupt conventional identities, functions, and sites of authority, especially as pursuit of profits displaces provisioning needs, and governments compete for private capital at the expense of public welfare.

Moreover, the instability of financial markets increases *risks that are socialized* (hurting public welfare) and when crises ensue, the costs are gendered: loss of secure jobs and earning capacity due to women's concentration in precarious forms of employment; lengthened work hours for women as they 'cushion' the impact of reduced household income; decreased participation of girls in education and worsened health conditions for women; expanded child labour and women's licit and illicit informal activities; and even increased acts of violence against women.

And the effects are long term: girls and women are less able to participate as full members of society, have fewer skills required for safe and secure income generation, and the intensification of women's work with fewer resources imperils social reproduction more generally. Boys and men have fewer and less favorable 'formal' work opportunities, less likelihood of skilled, long-term employment, and the disruption of masculine breadwinner roles deepens personal insecurities, with often devastating effects. Finally, entire societies are affected as deteriorating conditions of social reproduction, health, and education have long-term consequences for collective well-being and national competitiveness in the new world economy (see Figure 15.4).

CONCLUSION

This chapter offered a wide-ranging survey of how gender matters in GPE. For reasons of space, it has neglected many important issues, not least the agency and resistance of women and other feminized groups (although certain of these are discussed in Chapter 27). While these certainly 'matter' for analyzing global politics, I have focused instead on an overview of global power relations as these structure the political economy of neoliberal globalization. A brief survey indicated how feminists deploy gender empirically and analytically to examine restructuring through a variety of theoretical orientations. The RPV analytics of three interacting 'economies' revealed how major trends tend toward a polarization of income and status between masculinized elites and feminized 'others'. This 'big picture' analysis also exposed how the *cultural code* of feminization naturalizes the *economic (material) devaluation* of feminized work, whether that work is done by women *or* men who are culturally, racially and/or economically marginalized. In this crucial sense, the chapter not only describes how 'gender matters'. It also argues that gender is not only about women and men, but about qualities, skills, ideas, identities, and practices that are devalued by being feminized. These are key points for understanding the political work that 'gender' does, how feminization links and 'naturalizes' multiple hierarchies, and how gender 'matters' for sustaining *and* obscuring global inequalities.

Questions for further debate

1. How is gender both an empirical and analytical category? How has the distinction shaped analyses of GPE? Which understanding of gender do you think is more important for understanding global politics, and why?
2. What is meant in this chapter by 'intersectionality'? How does understanding 'feminization as devalorization' advance intersectional analysis?
3. How are neoliberal policies of deregulation and privatization related to the major trends of the productive economy? Who are the winners and losers in today's global political economy?
4. What does 'crisis of social reproduction' refer to? Can you identify features of such crisis in your own family, community, and nation?
5. How are the three (productive, reproductive and virtual) economies interconnected (how do they influence each other)? How do hegemonic stereotypes of gender operate in all three economies?

Sources for further reading and research

Dickinson, T. D. and R. K. Schaeffer (2001) *Fast Forward: Work, Gender, and Protest in a Changing World,* Lanham, MD: Rowman & Littlefield.

Marchand, M. H. and A. Sisson Runyan (eds) (2011) *Gender and Global Restructuring: Sightings, Sites and Resistances,* 2nd edn, London: Routledge.

Peterson, V. S. (2003) *A Critical Rewriting of Global Political Economy: Integrating Reproductive, Productive, and Virtual Economies,* London: Routledge.

Peterson, V. S. and Anne Sisson Runyan (2010) *Global Gender Issues in the New Millennium,* Boulder, CO: Westview Press.

Rai, S. M. (2002) *Gender and the Political Economy of Development,* Cambridge: Polity Press.

Notes

1 For general feminist critiques, see Barker and Feiner 2004, Cook et al. 2000, Ferber and Nelson 2003, Marchand and Runyan 2010 and Peterson 2003.
2 For reasons of space, in the remainder of the chapter I cite only key references not already identified; for elaboration of argumentation and extensive citations, see Peterson 2003 and 2005.
3 For recent work on intersectionality, see Cho et al. 2013, May 2012, Peterson 2007, Phoenix and Pattynama 2006, Yuval-Davis 2006.

CHAPTER 16

Production, employment and consumption

Juanita Elias and Lucy Ferguson

LEARNING OUTCOMES

Upon completion, readers should be able to:

• Discuss the main ways in which global production is gendered.
• Understand what this means in two different sectors of global employment.
• Evaluate the gender dimensions of consumption practices.

INTRODUCTION

Global relations of production – how goods and services are produced, by whom and where – are the focus of much research in the social sciences, particularly in the discipline of international political economy (IPE). However, mainstream and 'critical' variants of IPE consistently fail to engage with the feminist analyses of production in any meaningful way (Waylen 2006). A focus on female workers has long been central to feminist approaches to international politics, and scholars have examined how processes associated with the globalization of production are embedded in global hierarchies of gender, class and ethnicity (Peterson and Runyan 1999; Pettman 1993). While the primary focus of this chapter is on women workers, we do not use gender as a straightforward synonym for women, and are also concerned with the construction of men and masculinities within global systems of production

(Elias 2008) as well as differences *between* women in terms of class, ethnicity and nationality.

International development organizations such as the World Bank have tended to have a specific concern with women's workforce participation, and present formal employment as the key route to empowerment for women (Bedford 2003). However, feminist analyses have exposed the gender biases inherent in the promotion of employment as a development tool, suggesting that 'the emancipatory prospects of female labour force participation are constrained by the prejudicial terms under which women enter the workforce' (Chant 2002: 550). That is, an increase in women's labour force participation does not necessarily lead to more equal gendered power relations. This chapter argues that the goal of incorporating women into the global workforce fails to account for how social and economic hierarchies permeate relations of production.

In order to explore the production of gendered hierarchies within the global political economy, we focus our analysis on two key areas of 'feminized' employment in the global economy – export manufacturing and the tourism industry – charting how gendered divisions and inequalities are produced and maintained within these sectors. The final part of the chapter looks at the issue of consumption – both in terms of the consumption practices of workers in the export manufacturing and tourism sectors and well as the role that so-called 'ethical' consumption practices could play in promoting greater equality in global workplaces.

WOMEN WORKERS IN GLOBAL PRODUCTION AND EMPLOYMENT

Women workers in the garment sector

Although overall women's share of industrial employment is fairly low compared to men, an important exception is in 'light' export-oriented manufacturing industries such as electronic component assembly and garments. From the late 1960s onwards, a number of states across some of the less developed regions of the world – particularly Taiwan and South Korea – undertook industrialization strategies that involved the establishment of export-processing zones that provided tax and other concessions to export sector firms. In 1975 there were 79 export-processing zones worldwide across 25 countries and by 2006 there were over 3,500 EPZs worldwide in 130 countries, employing a total estimated workforce of 66 million, of which 40 million are in China alone (Engman et al. 2007: 8).

Export sector firms are often part of complex global chains of industrial production that link them into the global market economy. The level of subcontracting that takes place within the garment industry is so high that most of the major retailers have little idea about where their products are made (and indeed the working conditions in the factories that made them). What makes these global commodity chains even more complex is how networks of home workers working from domestic residences often constitute an important, albeit invisible, part of labour-intensive manufacturing industries.

Gender matters in understanding these shifts in global production. Statistical surveys revealed the extent to which employment in export manufacturing is overwhelmingly feminized (Wood 1991). Standing (1999) has labelled these developments 'global feminization through flexible labour' – the emergence of 'feminized' jobs such as assembly line production in which there is little protection for the worker. Furthermore, Mehra and Gammage (1999) suggest that male-to-female wage differentials are greatest in countries where there has been an increase in female employment due to an expansion in export manufacturing.

Women workers in tourism

Since 2005, the agricultural sector (often associated with subsistence production and high levels of rural poverty) has been surpassed by services as the main sector of employment for women, employing 46.3 per cent of women and 41.2 per cent of men (ILO 2013). Tourism is one of the world's largest services industries, providing around 3 per cent of global employment – or 192 million jobs. As might be expected, gender matters in understanding the services industry as much as export industries. The ILO reports that women account for 90 per cent of workers in wage employment in the tourism, catering and accommodation sectors globally. Just like female export-manufacturing workers, women tend to be grouped in the lowest paying, lowest status forms of tourism employment and are most likely to lose their jobs during periods of labour retrenchment (ILO 2013). High levels of subcontracting, temporary and part-time employment among women workers again demonstrate how women are constructed as a 'flexible' low-paid workforce by the tourism industry and by employers.

While many service sector jobs (for example, domestic service or call centre work) also exhibit these gendered features there are dimensions of work in tourism that are specific to the industry. M. Thea Sinclair (1997b), for example, argues that work in tourism needs to be understood as a reflection of wider inequalities in the tourism industry. She points to the fact that the fun and escapism enjoyed by tourists depends on the labour provided by workers in the tourism industry (see Figure 16.1). However, these power relations need to be analysed carefully, as there are not only divisions between tourists and workers in terms of income and wealth, but also *between* workers, primarily along gender but also race lines.

In spite of assertions by United Nations World Tourism Organization and UN Women that employment in the tourism industry is a vehicle for gender equality and women's empowerment (UNWTO/UN Women 2011), there is little evidence to support this claim (Ferguson 2010). Work in tourism undoubtedly tends to broaden women's social horizons and often encourages confidence, self-esteem and international friendships, whilst an independent income for women can increase bargaining power in the household. However, it does little to redress inequalities of gender, class and ethnicity in the global economy. Rather, tourism production should be understood – like the garment sector – as an arena in which these global hierarchies are played out.

Figure 16.1 Women selling food in the tourist town of Copán, Honduras.

Photograph: Lucy Ferguson.

PRODUCING, PERFORMING AND RESISTING GENDER IN THE WORKPLACE

Understanding production as 'gendered' requires a focus on how both gender *relations* and gender *identities* are fashioned and refashioned through engagement with the productive economy (see also Chapter 15). For example, as was highlighted in the discussion of tourism, women entering formal paid work may experience greater levels of autonomy and power, but at the same time they may experience new forms of patriarchal power relations within the workplace. Thus Elson and Pearson employ the notion of a '*decomposition*', '*recomposition*' and '*intensification*' of gender relations as women enter formal employment, drawing our attention to the intersecting forms of gendered power relations in society that women workers are confronted with (Elson and Pearson 1981: 31; emphasis added).

Understanding the interconnections between gender relations and relations of production also requires a focus on social reproduction — those activities usually performed within the private sphere of the household that are essential to the functioning of the productive economy. These everyday caring activities (things such as childrearing, cooking etc.) are overwhelmingly devalued within capitalist economies (Hoskyns and Rai 2007). And yet, employers are often able to perpetuate ideas about women as mere 'secondary' income earners whose primary responsibilities lie with the household in order to justify lower rates of pay. For example, Lee's research into female factory workers in China notes the persistence of ideas held among managers concerning young female factory workers as 'girls who worked while waiting to be married off' and thus not deserving of training, promotion or better rates of pay (Lee, 1998: 128).

Salzinger (2003) notes in her research into factory employment in Mexico that managers' understandings of 'feminine' employment and female characteristics were integral to the perpetuation of powerful discourses concerning the 'docile' and 'dexterous' ('nimble fingered') female worker. These assumptions concerning women's secondary status as well as their supposed 'natural' suitability to monotonous work can also be understood as a powerful set of ideas that play a role in shaping workplace gender identities. It has been noted that these 'gendered discourses of work' have come to play an even more important part in gendering the workplaces of global factories than the ability to pay women workers low wages (Caraway 2006). As a study by Vilareal and Yu (2007) shows, women workers employed in multinational export-sector firms are often paid above average wages – women are not recruited into these industries simply because they are a source of low-cost labour. Rather, the evidence seems to suggest that it is the overwhelming influence of ideas concerning the natural suitability of women to assembly line production that accounts for the decision to recruit women. However, as Wright (2006) argues, the 'myth of disposability' operates as employers recruit women workers into assembly line jobs that inevitably have high labour turnover because of the repetitive, mundane and potentially debilitating nature of the work.

Such discourses of 'productive femininity' are a key mechanism for maintaining control and discipline over feminized groups of workers (Elias 2005). Thus we see in Pun's study of export sector employment in China that managers enforced workplace discipline by explicitly identifying female bodies as 'docile' labour (2005, 143–45). In addition to these discursive mechanisms, high levels of control and surveillance are also part of the everyday experience of women workers on assembly lines, striving to meet ambitious production targets and finding that their performance is subject to constant observation by supervisors. Another element of the gendered forms of labour control that characterize export production is the way in which these globalized discourses of productive femininity effectively combine with localized gender ideologies. Muñoz's (2008) study of a tortilla factory in Mexico reveals how single mothers with few employment options were subjected to forms of sexual harassment that ensured their subordinate workforce status. Interestingly however, Muñoz makes the important point that it is not just women who suffer oppressive workplace regimes. The same firm's US-based operations, benefitted from the employment of an almost entirely male immigrant workforce – a workforce who due to their often undocumented status were willing to accept below minimum wage and unlikely to get involved in industrial action. Indeed, this study provides important insights into how race and nationality are just as important as gender in terms of the structuring of factory workplace regimes.

Resistances to these forms of labour control are themselves often based on localized forms of gender identity. Work on Malaysian factory women, for example, has demonstrated how acts of labour resistance (often taking the form of so-called 'spirit possession' incidents) draw on localized ideas concerning the vulnerability of young women outside of the family home (Ong 1987). More organized forms of resistance in the form of trade union activism have been somewhat limited within export-sector industries. In part, this is because states keen to attract much needed foreign direct investment have often sought to limit labour rights. But there are studies that highlight women workers' collective struggles against the injustices that they face – especially in the garment industry (see for example Gunawardana 2007; Pangsapa 2007).

These themes of control and resistance can also be explored in the tourism industry. In general, research has found that an important distinction should be made in terms of whether women are employed in 'mass' tourism (for example, multinational hotel chains) or 'alternative' tourism (small-scale businesses located in rural communities). Women's work in mass tourism in developing countries has tended to follow similar patterns of control outlined earlier in relation to factory workers, where employment has tended to be segregated by traditional gender roles, and women overwhelmingly are employed in roles such as cooks, cleaners and waitresses (Chant 1997; Sinclair 1997a, 1997b) (see Figure 16.2). However, more nuanced research carried out with women tourism workers – particularly within the discipline of anthropology – has revealed patterns of contestation and resistance emerging.

Women in tourism communities in Belize, for example, have used stereotypes about 'women's work' to their advantage, enabling them to set up hotels and restaurants without appearing to threaten gendered power relations (McKenzie Gentry 2007: 491). In Turkey, women have crafted out their own spaces within tourism, which in the long term is contributing to the 'undoing of shame' (Tucker 2007: 101). Similarly, research into Mayan women working in Guatemala's informal tourism industry has demonstrated how women 'play around' with the expectations of tourists to construct different identities from their traditional gender roles (Cone 1995). Particularly interesting is Walter Little's concept of 'tourism as performance', through which he argues that Mayan women 'pattern their lives in ways that exploit tourists' perceptions of Maya women', allowing them to 'use performance and humor to make sales, protect themselves from police intimidation, and critique tourism development practices' (Little 2004: 532). This kind of research reminds us that despite the seemingly rigid structures of inequality in global production, many women find ways of using these opportunities to their advantage through their everyday interactions.

Figure 16.2 Women-owned businesses in the tourist town of Placencia, Belize.

Photograph: Lucy Ferguson.

GENDERING CONSUMPTION

Consumption as a socioeconomic phenomenon is being increasingly studied by political economists, particularly in relation to the growth of the 'trade justice' and fair trade movements. However, such research tends to focus on the consumption habits of consumers in post-industrial societies (Watson 2006) rather than exploring how transformations in global relations of production affect the consumption habits of those living in the less developed countries. In part, this reflects an overwhelming assumption that workers in these countries are 'excluded from the world of modern consumerism' (Weinstein 2006: 161). And yet, consumption practices are so central to the ways in which economies function. Clearly, gender matters in our analysis of consumption, and its role in global production. A focus on the social relations of consumption moves us away from the traditionally 'masculinized' sphere of production to the traditionally 'feminized' sphere of consumption, prompting us to explore a broader range of socioeconomic practices (Ferguson 2011). Consumption practices can also be a source of change in the global political economy, and this may or may not have positive benefits for women as workers. Here we discuss two key areas of research into consumption – first, women's consumption practices in developing countries and, second, the gender dynamics of initiatives aimed at promoting 'corporate social responsibility' (CSR).

Development and gendered consumption

As set out already, it is interesting to explore the ways in which gendered changes in production contribute to the rise of consumerism and materialism among local communities in developing countries. As Peterson (2003: 144) argues, 'while affluent consumption is the privilege of only a small percentage of the population, it shapes the choices (and valorization) of those without affluence'. Studies such as those undertaken by Freeman (2000) have incorporated an analysis of women's consumption practices into a wider analysis of the impact of working in the 'informatics' (data-entry) industry in Barbados. In particular, she highlights how workers' purchase of clothing and cosmetics acted to build a sense of self-esteem and identity as they were able to identify themselves as 'different' from factory workers. Wolf's research in Java (Indonesia) from the 1980s revealed similar forms of consumption practices among female factory workers (Wolf 1990). These case studies show how consumption can be understood as a performance of identity – an identity as an autonomous feminized consumer rather than a 'mere' worker. However, these gendered consumer identities may not be especially liberating. Women in Freeman's study could barely afford the clothes that they were pressured to buy in order to 'look the part' in the informatics firms.

Research from Asia reveals the ways in which the rise of consumer lifestyles have accompanied the region's ongoing economic transformation. What this literature highlights is how the rise of consumer cultures has contradictory impacts on women. For example, it is often tied to the promotion of middle-class ideals of feminine domesticity (Hooper 1998; Stivens 1998), or serves to trigger fears within socially conservative elements of the state and/or society concerning how more 'globalized' consumption practices may compromise supposedly 'traditional' gender values (Syed 2012; Jones 2010).

Thus, the implications of changes in consumption patterns for gender relations have been complex and uneven. The increasing individualization of economic and social life brought about by marketized consumption is often referred to as empowering for women, as family and community responsibilities are said to be lessened by the valorization of women as individual consumers. Indeed, many of the changes to cultures of consumption have offered greater freedom and choice to certain kinds of women. In some ways, women have gained a certain economic power through becoming consumers in their own right. In the words of Irene Tinker, such changes can be interpreted as 'empowerment just happened' – the suggestion that the socio-economic transformations of the last 20 years have led to shifts in gender relations that serve to cause 'cracks in the foundations of patriarchal control' (Tinker 2006: 270). However, any assessment of the ways in which consumption contributes to greater equality needs to be placed in a context of the accompanying pressures and stresses of consumer society. Arguably such changes in consumption habits have not contributed greatly to women's broader social empowerment. Moreover, they tend to exacerbate differences between women, and can reinforce inequalities of class, ethnicity and nationality.

Ethical consumption and gender

Over the last two decades there has been a growing awareness of the potentially unethical impacts of our consumption practices. These concerns have led to the establishment of 'fair trade' products that are designed to give producers a better share of the profits, and the establishment of corporate 'codes of conduct' – commitments by firms to ensure that minimum levels of employment standards and human rights are met. Codes of conduct are viewed as being particularly important in fragmented and complex production supply chains dominated by large buyers such as the big clothing brands and supermarket chains. Furthermore, the increased levels of competition between countries seeking to develop export manufacturing industries has been viewed as generating a 'race to the bottom' in labour standards in which the state can no longer be relied on to properly regulate labour abuses in these key sectors of the economy (see Figure 16.3).

Consumer campaigns for corporate social responsibility (CSR) have targeted export sector industries – in particular the garment and electronics sectors and commercial agricultural production. Because of the high levels of female employment in these sectors, a considerable amount of feminist research has sought to evaluate the impact of CSR and corporate codes of conduct for women workers. Frequently, codes of conduct fail to address the underlying problems that women workers experience in export sector work – problems that stem from their perceived 'secondary' status in the labour market. These include: low wages and wage inequality; a lack of protection and respect for pregnant workers or homeworkers; inadequate occupational health and safety; a lack of trade union rights; enforced overtime and

The latest tragedy to hit Bangladesh's ready-made garments industry has once again brought the power and influence of the industry into sharp focus. The collapse of Rana Plaza in April 2013 – an eight-storey building which housed five garment factories, many producing clothing for Western brands – led to the death of over 1000 people. This is not the first such incident. In 2005, a similar building collapsed leaving 64 garments workers dead. Since then, there have been fires, stampedes and other incidents at various garment factories, causing hundreds of deaths.

Senior government official Mainuddin Khondker, who headed a task force to inspect garments factories following last November's fire at Tazreen Fashions, in which over 100 people perished, admitted that 50 per cent of garment factories are located on premises which are not safe. However, he also admitted no action had ever been taken against a factory for violation of safety rules, inadequate fire safety or, indeed, against landlords for violation of building codes. The garments industry appears to be wrapped in a culture of impunity.

Since the 1980s, the industry has grown into a $20bn business that accounts for nearly 80 per cent of the country's export earnings. But more importantly perhaps for this poor, conservative Muslim nation, the industry has created jobs for four million workers, four-fifths of whom are women. Millions of young girls from poor families have found jobs in this industry, helping them to break out of a life of dependency and grinding poverty. But the country is paying a high price for this.

In order to capture the lower end of the global market, successive governments have promoted Bangladesh as the source of cheap clothing. Cheap labour, fiscal support such as duty-free import of fabrics and accessories, and new infrastructure to help smoother, quicker exports have helped the industry grow rapidly. But the lure of quick dollars has attracted a whole range of cowboy operators who cut corners to drive costs further down (BBC News 2013a).

Note: While there have clearly been regulatory failures on the part of the Bangladeshi state, it is also important to consider the role that international trade rules, garment retailers and consumers of cheap 'fast fashion' play in creating the conditions within which such tragedies occur.

Figure 16.3 The human cost of fast fashion.

over-long working days; and the intensity of work. Furthermore, workers may not even be aware that codes exist or the codes may not be adequately enforced and monitored (Pearson and Seyfang 2002). The *Women's Empowerment Principles* – a recent initiative by UN Women and the UN Global Compact – attempt to address some of these issues from a gender perspective.

Pearson (2007) suggests that one of the major problems with notions of CSR is that it is based on too narrow a definition of corporate responsibility, one that does not take account of workers' roles *outside* the workplace. Pearson argues that because firms directly benefit from those social relations of reproduction that sustain and maintain their workforces, they have responsibilities to workers that extend beyond the factory or plantation walls. To illustrate this claim, she points to the example of the *maquiladora* factories of the Mexican border town of Ciudad Juarez, a town in which there has been both a massive influx of migrants and exceptionally high levels of female murders. Most of these women were employees of the *maquiladoras*, but more significant is the fact that almost all were part of the population cohort from which the *maquiladoras* have drawn their labour force since the 1970s. As the *maquiladora* industry has expanded, the city's infrastructure has continued to deteriorate and many of the workers live in poor areas without police services or adequate public transport. Nevertheless, the factory owners absolved themselves of responsibility. The question needs to be raised, therefore, whether a more holistic definition of corporate social responsibility might better serve the needs of this group of female workers.

In spite of these criticisms, CSR is often also seen as having the potential to bring about change for women workers. Banana plantation workers in Nicaragua were able to push employers to improve working conditions once they became aware that the country's only buyer of bananas (Chiquita) has adopted CSR principles (Prieto-Carrón 2006). In this sense, despite the flaws of many codes of conduct, they are frequently recognized as a starting point from which workers and labour activists can seek to push corporations to improve working conditions. The UN Global Compact/UN Women Women's Empowerment Principles potentially offer an additional tool for holding companies to account for their role in perpetuating gender inequality.

CONCLUSION

When we look at everyday practices of employment and consumption and how these processes are deeply gendered, we are able to see how gender matters fundamentally in globalization of production. Thus, by developing an analysis of women's work experiences (including a discussion of agency and empowerment) within both the export manufacturing and tourism sectors, we have sought to provide the kind of fine-grained detail that shows how wider processes associated with globalization touchdown and impact on the lives of ordinary people around the world. Women's work, their experiences, the opportunities that work brings and also the problems that women workers encounter are mediated by numerous different factors. In this chapter, we have highlighted just some of them. These have included the tensions between work and empowerment, the complex relationship between resistance and women's agency and the issues involved in analysing consumption practices and corporate social responsibility.

What the extensive literature on women and employment in the global economy (of which we have overviewed just a small fraction) demonstrates is the complex and contradictory processes that occur when women enter the market economy. Employment does offer women opportunities, brings a level of independence and autonomy not previously available, and may break down traditional gender relations within families and households. But, at the same time, one of the major themes explored in this chapter was how women – especially women in the global south – are constructed as a source of exploitable labour. Indeed, ideas of 'productive' and 'flexible' femininity were shown to underpin the practices of globalized business. Thus we need to understand the relationships between these everyday patterns of work, production, reproduction and consumption to those broader structures of economic governance that foster such gendered systems of exploitation.

Questions for further debate

1. In the chapter, we use Elson and Pearson's analysis of *decomposition, recomposition* and *intensification* of gender relations as women enter employment. How does this relate this to your own understandings of women's work in the global economy?
2. Is women's employment the best way of promoting gender equality and women's empowerment?
3. Are gender inequalities in global production more significant than inequalities related to class, ethnicity and nationality?
4. What could be changed in order to make global production and consumption more likely to promote greater gender equality?

Sources for further reading and research

Freeman, C. (2000) *High Tech and High Heels in the Global Economy: Women, Work and Pink Collar Identities in the Caribbean*, Durham, NJ: Duke University Press.

Hale, A. and Willis, J. (2005) *Threads of Labour: Garment Industry Supply Chains from a Workers' Perspective*, Oxford: Wiley Blackwell.

Muñoz, C. B. (2008) *Transnational Tortillas: Race, Gender, and Shop-Floor Politics in Mexico and the United States*, Ithaca, NY: Cornell University Press.

Scott, L. M. (2005) *Fresh Lipstick: Redressing Fashion and Feminism*, Basingstoke: Palgrave Macmillan.

Wright, M. W. (2006) *Disposable Women and Other Myths of Global Capitalism*, London and New York: Routledge.

CHAPTER 17

Land, water and food

Monika Barthwal-Datta and Soumita Basu

LEARNING OUTCOMES

Upon completion, readers should be able to:

- Recognise gendered dimensions of resource politics, including the ways in which gender identities are constituted through everyday availability of resources such as land and water.
- Comprehend key gender issues relating to agriculture, especially as it relates to access to land and water as well as food production.
- Understand a range of policy and activist responses to the gendered machinations of resource politics.

INTRODUCTION

Gender is linked to, and fundamentally shapes, resource politics in a number of complex ways. Feminist activists have long pointed to ideological linkages between gender, particularly women, on the one hand, and nature, on the other, through the concept of 'ecofeminism' (see Chapter 6). More recently, others have emphasised the need to understand the relationships men and women share with the environment as 'rooted in their material reality, in their specific forms of interaction with the environment' (Agarwal 1992: 126). Indeed, as Michelle Leach points out, 'women's apparently timeless "special relationship with the environment" is actually shaped by specific social and economic processes; and changes in the character of their work and responsibilities may have important consequences for their management and use of natural resources' (1992: 15).

At the same time, the ways in which historical material developments at the global and local levels (e.g., capitalism, globalisation, industrialisation and urban development) may determine and shape these interactions, with different social, political and economic consequences for different groups, is also highlighted. Feminist perspectives therefore not only help illuminate, among other things, how ideational structures such as patriarchy have helped construct women and nature as organically subordinate to men, but also how our gendered experiences of and relationships with the environment – depending on our specific position in different socioeconomic and political hierarchies (e.g., class, caste, ethnicity and religion) – influence and shape our responses to environmental exploitation and degradation (Agarwal 1992). Feminists also use gender as an analytical category 'to study how masculinity and femininity – gender understood as a meaning system – produce, and are produced by, political economy [and indeed other spheres]' (Peterson 2005: 499).

Writing on 'gender, property rights, and natural resources', Meinzen-Dick et al. (1997) note: 'given the enormous diversity in property regimes, gender relations, cultural and environmental conditions, it may be heroic – or indeed foolhardy – to assume that we can identify patterns of resource use that apply beyond a specific case' (1304). Faced with a similar dilemma in writing this chapter, we follow the strategy of Meinzen-Dick et al. (1997): we first identify the conceptual linkages between gender and natural resources from a political economy perspective, and highlight common trends across resources and regions (such as the impact of development projects, globalisation and corporate capital) that help demonstrate these linkages. We then provide an overview of the 'gender gap' in assets (mainly land and water) that exists in agriculture in countries in the Global South, its consequences and the factors facilitating the former. The concluding section examines a range of policy and activist responses that seek to respond to some of the issues identified in the chapter.

GENDER AND NATURAL RESOURCES: CONCEPTUAL INSIGHTS

Land, food and water form the very basis of all our lives. In light of this, questions regarding ownership of and access to land and water, and availability of affordable and nutritious food, are pertinent. Along with factors such as class and geographical location, the gender identity of a person, whether they are women, men or identify with a third gender, lends meaning to these questions. Women, for instance, did not traditionally inherit land in most societies, an issue that continues to be on the contemporary feminist agenda (see Agarwal 1994; Deere and Leon 2003).

A gender analysis of resource politics does much more than shed light on gender-based inequalities. It highlights the ways in which the interplay of masculinities and femininities – embodied by individuals and institutions – is integral to the prevalent economic system, and the impact of these on the access to and management of resources. The growing trend of privatisation of water, for example, not only adversely affects rural women, who are traditionally responsible for collection of water for domestic consumption in rural households, but also reproduces the masculinity of water management which, as Juana Vera Delgado and Margreet Zwarteveen discuss in the context of Peru, 'was not just something that only men did, but also something that culturally belonged to the male domain and that was associated with perceptions of masculinity' (2007: 504). The latter arguably reinforces women's unpaid labour in the collection of water.

Gendering resource politics

In *The Death of Nature*, by Carolyn Merchant (1980), the dominant masculinity of industrial capitalism – led by scientific revolution and European Enlightenment ethics, and characterised by 'mechanistic, rationalized, [and] competitive' values (Sturgeon 2005: 806) – is drawn up as pitted against the environment, a feminine construct. Directed towards controlling nature, especially its propensity to exploit natural resources, capitalist economy is tied together with the environment in a masculine–feminine binary relationship. This relationship, explored also by other scholars besides Merchant (for instance, Meis and Shiva 1993), has been an important component of gender analysis of resources. It provides the leitmotif for feminist explorations into the significance of colonialism, the 'development' discourse, globalisation and corporatisation vis-à-vis the global political economy of resources.

Vandana Shiva, for instance, argues that the 'scientific management' of forests – or 'reductionist masculinist forestry' – introduced in India during the British colonial period had a different economic perspective to that of the indigenous 'alternative feminine forestry science':

> In a shift from ecological forestry to reductionist forestry all scientific terms are changed from ecosystem-dependent to ecosystem-independent ones. Thus while for women, tribals and other forest communities a complex ecosystem is productive in terms of water, herbs … fuel, fibre and as a genepool, for the forester, these components are useless, unproductive waste and dispensable. Two economic perspectives lead to two notions of 'productivity' and 'value' … [I]n reductionist commercial forestry, overall productivity is subordinated to industrial use, and large biomass to species that can be profitably marketed.
>
> (Shiva 1988: 61)

Contributions to the women in development (WID) literature (see Chapter 15) have also highlighted these and other ways (such as granting ownership of land to men) through which women – and their productive role – were sidelined in colonial governance (see Boserup 1970).

In the postcolonial period, the 'development' discourse also privileged, and came to be dominated by, the notion of 'productivity' emerging from the reductionist economic perspective, as described by Shiva in the citation above (see Shiva 1988: 3).

While the role of women as protectors of environment eventually began to be reiterated at this time, it is worth noting that policy documents such as *Our Common Future*, the report from the World Commission on Environment and Development (1987), which proposed the influential concept of 'sustainable development',[1] also presented 'women as problem' (Bretherton 2003). Specifically, women's reproductive capacity was seen to put pressure on environmental resources through population growth. This was a 'problem' that had to be controlled or managed through targeted policies such as women's education and reproductive healthcare.

In the twentieth century, natural resources were increasingly drawn into global market economies. The trend of delocalisation of natural resources gathered pace, with trade liberalisation being a crucial factor. The structural adjustment programmes (SAPs) of the 1980s, initiated by the World Bank and the International Monetary Fund (IMF), forced farmers in a large number of countries in the developing world to change their production patterns and focus on cash crops for world markets. This globalised and market-oriented production took multiple forms: 'extractive activities of various kinds, the expansion of large-scale commercial production of industrial crops such as oil palm, or the incorporation of smallholder producers into global markets through the production of cash crops such as coffee or cocoa' (Elmhirst and Resurreccion 2008: 9).

More recently, there has been large-scale corporatisation of farmlands, forestlands, rivers and other natural resources worldwide. As with international trade liberalisation, states have largely bowed down to capitalist logic with erstwhile commons being handed over to transnational corporations (TNCs). The physical distance between corporate managers and the resource, and the formers' ideological distancing from the latter, have led to widespread overexploitation of natural resources, often destroying the fine balance of sustenance and protection that had traditionally existed between communities and their local environment. Echoing Shiva, Nandita Ghosh notes, 'environmentally, global capital is predatory in its enclosure of commons such as privatizing water supply from a river, thus depleting its resources, degrading the livelihoods of inhabitants along the banks and possibly jeopardizing an entire eco-system' (2007: 447).

In the remaining part of this section, we introduce some key elements of contemporary resource politics relevant for underprivileged rural women in the developing world. This partly reflects a major empirical concern demonstrated in the feminist literature on the subject, but also serves to provide background to the next section that undertakes a broad feminist analysis of the political economy of agriculture – especially, the 'gender gap' in access to and control of land and water resources in countries in the Global South.

Women and natural resources in rural areas

Empirical observations from across the world point to the important role that women play in both productive and reproductive components of rural economies, contributing to activities such as subsistence production, income generation as well as domestic tasks like cooking, childrearing and caregiving (see, for instance, Agarwal 1994; Croll 1981; Sachs 1996). Here, while it is important to acknowledge the severely undervalued reproductive work done by women, it is also worth noting that 'the separation between productive and reproductive activities is often artificial, symbolised, perhaps, by a woman carrying a baby on her back while working in the fields' (Benería and Sen 1981: 292; see also Storeng et al. 2013). In order to carry out all these responsibilities, women have a direct stake in the availability of and access to natural resources (Leach 1992: 13). The more recent 'feminisation of agriculture' (see, for instance, Vepa 2005) has added to this burden. It involves the mass migration of (working age) men to urban centres in search of work, leaving behind women as heads of rural households and often bearing the sole responsibility of tending to the family farm or engaging in commercial farming. However, despite taking up roles that have tied women closely to nature, their access and rights relating to natural resources remain fragile.

For example, in many countries in South and Southeast Asia, Africa and South America, women – irrespective of their social status, unlike men – continue to face relatively limited access to land. This is usually due to factors such as discriminatory inheritance laws and deeply entrenched patriarchal social norms, and serves to severely undermine the livelihood and welfare opportunities for women. In the widespread absence of private ownership of resources, the rural poor – a large proportion of whom are women – have traditionally relied on common property resources for their subsistence and livelihood. As Bina Agarwal points out, however:

> [T]he availability of the country's natural resources to the poor is being severely eroded by two parallel, and interrelated trends – first, their growing degradation both in quantity and quality; second, their increasing statization (appropriation by the state) and privatization (appropriation by a minority of individuals), with an associated decline in what was earlier communal.
>
> (Agarwal 1992: 129)

While the nationalisation (or 'statisation') of natural resources may have weakened access to communal resources for the poor, large-scale privatisation of resources in recent decades has perhaps posed a more serious threat. The commodification of natural resources has highly restricted access among the rural poor, and negatively affected the lives of rural women in particular (see Meinzen-Dick et al. 1997: 1308–1309). For instance, as mentioned earlier, the privatisation of water tends to affect women adversely. It does so by increasing their unpaid labour involved in the collection of water – 'for example, Water Policy International has estimated that South African women collectively walk the equivalent of going to the moon and back 16 times daily in their search for fresh water' (Roberts 2008: 549).

These negative trends in resource politics have been resisted both at the local and transnational levels by women's and gender advocacy groups, among others. The activist and policy responses, along with the range of alternatives to the prevalent system of resource management proposed by them, are discussed in the concluding section.

AGRICULTURE IN THE GLOBAL SOUTH: GENDER CONCERNS

In a majority of developing countries around the world, agriculture remains the single most important source of livelihoods and a key driver of economic growth. In parts of Asia and Africa, for example, up to 70 per cent of domestic populations continue to live in rural areas, and agricultural activities such as farming, fishing, livestock rearing and forestry not only form the main source of income and food security, but also constitute their traditional way of life. In this respect, it becomes important to consider the multifunctionality of agriculture whereby it is not only the site of economic activity, but also one that is the source of a variety of social, cultural and ecological benefits and services (IAASTD 2008).

This discussion on agriculture, however, has to be placed within the context of the current global food economy, which has emerged against the backdrop of accelerated and uneven agricultural trade liberalisation (Clapp 2012). As indicated earlier, the latter was facilitated by the SAPs of the World Bank and the IMF in the late twentieth century, and further accelerated by the World Trade Organisation (WTO) with the 1994 Agreement on Agriculture (McMichael 2009; McMichael and Schneider 2011). As a result of these and other relevant policy developments (e.g., the deregulation of the financial sector in the United States at the turn of the century), poor small food producers in developing agricultural economies have found themselves seriously disadvantaged in competing with the domestic influx of cheap and heavily subsidised food from developed countries (Pritchard 2009: 97). Indeed, a large number have been forced to abandon agriculture as it is no longer a viable means of living for them.

The growing presence of TNCs in agriculture and land consolidation for the monocropping of export crops has also served to undermine small farmer access to agricultural land (McMichael and Schneider 2011). Farming practices such as multicropping and crop rotation that are more environment friendly have been marginalised, and women and men who demonstrate a more symbiotic relationship with natural resources, are subjugated within contemporary capitalist economies. Further, the participation of TNCs in agriculture is strongly characterised by dominant masculinities associated with farming, such as 'control over the land and environment', use of machines, display of physical strength and, more recently, 'managerial and entrepreneurial activity' (Little 2002: 667).

The above discussion illustrates how policies and practices related to the ownership, use and management of natural resources are gendered in nature and impact. Given the scale and extent of discrimination that women in agriculture continue to be subjected to in many countries in the Global South, it is also useful to examine gender as a variable – thus focusing on different experiences of women and men – in the study of resource politics. Women have traditionally played a central role in agriculture in developing countries, where, on average, they form over 40 per cent of the agricultural labour force. In many parts of Asia and Africa, this proportion is as high as 50 per cent (FAO 2011).

Yet, despite their significant and in many cases growing presence in agriculture, women continue to face serious inequalities and constraints in their ability to access agricultural resources, e.g., land, freshwater and forestlands. Compared to their male counterparts, female rural agricultural producers also lack sufficient access to other important resources such as markets, technology, financial support (such as credit and insurance services), education and skills training, and extension support. This 'gender gap' in agriculture means that in general, women lack sufficient means to maintain or boost their incomes by way of raising agricultural productivity (see, for instance, Pande 2000). This has welfare implications for female agricultural producers and their families, including food insecurity, as well as wider socio-economic fallouts given the importance of agriculture to economic growth in developing countries.

Access to agricultural land

Among all agricultural resources, land is the most highly valued. As the FAO points out, 'Access to land is a basic requirement for farming and control over land is synonymous with wealth, status and power in many areas' (2011: 23). In many developing countries, inadequate access to land and tenure insecurity remain serious issues affecting the agricultural productivity, livelihoods and food security of small farming households, who comprise the majority of rural populations in such places. In parts of South Asia (e.g., Bangladesh, Nepal and India) and Southeast Asia (e.g., Cambodia and the Philippines), landlessness is widespread, and large numbers of agricultural households lack titles to land they have lived and worked on for long periods of time.

Without land titles, rural households are highly vulnerable to unfair or forced land evictions, often facilitated by state agencies in favour of private investment interests. At the same time, when agricultural households lack security of tenure, they tend to invest less in agricultural practices that may help boost productivity, and involve the sustainable use and management of natural resources. This is because they are uncertain of their ability to reap the benefits of such investment in the medium to long term.

Both male and female agricultural producers are affected by inadequate access to land and tenure insecurity in developing countries. There are, however, deep inequalities with respect to the extent to which each group experiences these challenges. Moreover, as indicated previously, intersections between gender, on the one hand, and factors such as class, caste, ethnicity and religion, on the other, also have a bearing on access to land and tenure security among both men and women in developing societies. Nonetheless, the glaring gap in access to land between men and women in general in a large number of developing countries has led analysts to point to a number of wider issues to help understand this gender gap.

Factors underlying the gender gap in access to land

A number of social, economic and political factors have been cited as driving the gender gap that exists in developing countries in terms of access to land. In South America, for example, historically the gender gap relating to access to land is attributed to social norms such as the preference of males as the inheritors of private property, and males being privileged over females in marriages (Deere and Leon 2003). At the same time, gender bias at the community and state level against women in programmes of land distribution also plays a role, as does the fact that land markets in the region remain largely biased against women (ibid.). In the case of South Asia, Agarwal points out that in the majority of countries in the region, laws around the inheritance of private property acknowledged independent property rights for women as early as in the 1950s. Nonetheless:

> [I]n development policy governing the distribution of public land, the issue of women's land rights was not discussed ... till the 1980s. Hence the redistributive land reform programmes of the 1950s and 1960s in India, Pakistan and Sri Lanka, and of the 1970s in Bangladesh, continued to be modelled on the notion of a unitary male-headed household, with titles being granted only to men, except in households without adult men where women (typically widows) are clearly the heads. This bias was replicated in resettlement schemes, even in Sri Lanka where customary inheritance systems have been bilateral or matrilineal.
>
> (Agarwal 1994: 8–9)

Even today, in countries such as Bangladesh, national policies continue to discriminate against women as heads of households unless they are divorced or widowed (Chakma 2012). This means that despite state guarantees of benefits to rural agricultural workers such as credit facilities, subsidies and loans for farm inputs such as fertilisers, these benefits do not always reach female agricultural workers. This has real implications for the financial status of female agricultural producers as well as the socioeconomic welfare of households where females are engaged in agricultural production while male members may be employed in other sectors.

Where land titles exist, the omission of names of female members of rural farming households from these documents often remains a serious problem. It not only severely undermines the ability of female agricultural producers to access credit facilities and take out loans, but also jeopardises their ability to protect their interests in the face of forced or unfair land acquisitions. In countries such as the Philippines, India, and China, for example, land documentation generally remains incomplete, and in many areas the names of women also continue to be largely excluded from land-use certificates, despite their having the same land rights as men (Barthwal-Datta 2013).

Access to water for irrigation

Lack of access to agricultural land is often the reason behind a lack of access to water resources for irrigation. It is therefore not surprising that women in many countries in the Global South also experience the latter disproportionately. In most of South America, for example, access to water is premised on land ownership (UN-Water 2006: 4). As discussed earlier, there is a significant gender gap in land ownership. Often the same factors underlying this gap may be responsible for lack of access to water for irrigation. Despite women being water users and managers for both domestic and productive purposes, it is rural men who are seen to 'best represent the water related interests and needs of the household at the level of the community, and complete congruence of interests between men and women is assumed' (Goetz, cited in Meinzen-Dick and Zwarteveen 1998: 339). This understanding reflects the arbitrary separation of the public and the private, a matter of persistent concern for feminists, wherein 'the paradigmatic subject of the public and economic arena is male, where that of the domestic arena is female' (ibid.).

As with national land-related policies, irrigation management schemes often do not consider women as legitimate heads of households unless they are widowed or divorced. Consequently, they are not sufficiently (if at all) consulted or included in decision-making processes and implementation programmes related to these schemes (Ray 2007). Similarly, the monetisation of water for irrigation, to give another example, not only discriminates against the rural poor (the majority of whom are women)[2] who are unable to pay for it, it also does not take into account the benefits of irrigation for the purposes of poverty reduction and the environment (Zwarteveen 1998: 303).

The literature on gender and access to water for irrigation highlights three main concerns (Ray 2007: 431–33): First, women's access to irrigation water is often indirect (i.e., mediated by male members of household), and affects their overall income level – although formal allocation of irrigation rights is neither sufficient nor necessary to bring about a positive change in this respect. Second, irrigation management policies that are participatory in nature (i.e., directly include women) may not have a beneficial impact on women's access to water unless they take note of the different roles played in agriculture by men and women.

As Zwarteveen (1997: 1337) points out, preferences of men and women with respect to irrigation (e.g., quantity and timing) may be influenced by specific on-farm tasks being performed by them (e.g., men and women share the job of

Figure 17.1 River markets at Tonle Sap River in Kampong Chhnang, Kampong Chhnang Province, Cambodia.

Photograph: Chris Baker. Reproduced with kind permission.

transplanting rice in farms in Nepal, but women are responsible for weeding that is affected by the level of water in the paddy field) and 'gender-specific crop choices'; yet, gender differences in actual use of water are not a good guide for determining gender-differentiated water needs. This is because 'where women use water differently than men this is more likely to be caused by the fact that women have less access and rights to water, than by women having different water needs' (Zwarteveen 1997: 338). It therefore becomes more important to focus on the unequal power relations that constrain access to and control of water in the first place, rather than designing policies solely around existing patterns of use.

Finally, while access to water for irrigation may enhance the welfare of women by boosting household incomes, this may involve an increase in their overall workload without an accompanying increase in their ability to control the additional income generated (Ray 2007: 433).

Although agricultural policies in the last few decades have become far more cognisant of the links between gender and access to natural resources such as land and water, the design, implementation and evaluation of such policies in many developing countries continue to be gender biased. Societal norms around land ownership and inheritance, for example, remain deeply entrenched, and 'base inequalities in power that include sexism, patriarchy, racism, and class' continue to prevail and undermine access to agricultural resources (Patel 2010, cited in Wittman 2011: 96). At the same time, corporate acquisition of agricultural land continues to be widely and often indiscriminately endorsed by policymakers despite the serious environmental and welfare costs to local communities. This, as has been discussed earlier, serves to reinforce dominant masculine values that celebrate the subjugation of nature for the sake of progress and development. It results in a gendered form of violence against all – nature, men and women.

POLICY AND ACTIVIST RESPONSES

In the last 50 years, women and gender advocacy groups have galvanised around concerns regarding sustainability of natural resources against the backdrop of the environmental fallouts of industrial development, population growth and urbanisation. Beginning in the 1970s, there was a groundswell of local women's movements across the world including the Chipko movement in India, the Women's Greenbelt Movement in Kenya and women's activism in response to the Three Mile Island accident in the United States (Johnson 1999: 222). While the impact of these and other movements has varied over time and geographical location, the relevance of women's environmental activism, including towards the protection of natural resources, is widely recognised (see Chapter 6).

International policymaking has also taken account of gender and resource politics. The influential Report of the World Commission on Environment and Development, *Our Common Future*, recognised barriers to women's access to land and water in spite of their role in food production, and called on policymakers to factor in women's needs and interests and to increase their participation in management of resources (1987). *Agenda 21*, the declaration of the 1992

UN Conference on Environment and Development held in Rio de Janeiro, built on these linkages in the quest for sustainable development. It advocated, for instance, 'strengthening/developing legal frameworks for land management, access to land resources and land ownership – in particular, for women – and for the protection of tenants' (UN 1992). The Beijing Declaration (1995) of the Fourth World Women's Conference also recognises the importance of ensuring women's access to resources such as land and water. However, the scope of such international policies, both in terms of provisions and implementation, has been stymied by the parallel growth of the more powerful and insidious force of neo-liberal capitalism that privileges the interests of corporate capital above all. As Roberts (2008: 548) points out with regard to the privatisation of water, TNC representatives work actively to secure their interests in global water organisations such as Global Water Partnership, the World Water Council, and the World Commission on Water.

Partly in light of the inherent limitations of these global policy mechanisms, pitched against the growing corporatisation of resources, and supported by the increasing role of non-state actors in global politics, new transnational movements also emerged connecting local initiatives for resource management. The transnational peasant movement *La Via Campesina*, for instance, has led the way in developing the concept of 'food sovereignty' since the 1990s as an alternative to the prevailing, trade-based approach to food security, driven mainly by liberalised agricultural trade and industrial agriculture (Windfuhr and Jonsen 2005: 24).

Although there is no single agreed definition of food sovereignty, its core principles are widely agreed on (see Figure 17.2). In essence, food sovereignty refers to 'the rights of peoples to healthy and culturally appropriate food produced through ecologically sound and sustainable methods, and their right to define their own food and agriculture system' (Via Campesina 2007; Windfuhr and Jonsen 2005). It focuses on power relations within food systems that disadvantage or marginalise small farming households or peasants, fisherfolk, indigenous peoples, pastoralists among others. Other approaches to food that share concerns with food sovereignty include food justice movements (for example, see Alkon and Agyeman 2011; Gottlieb and Joshi 2010) and the Right to Food movement (for example, see Patel 2012; Ziegler et al. 2011)

Gender was not immediately foregrounded in the food sovereignty movement, but the interests of women farmers and the need to have gender-sensitive agricultural policies have been increasingly recognised within the movement (Desmarais 2003). Food sovereignty critiques those masculine values seen as undermining food systems – such as an overwhelming emphasis on industrial agriculture, a neoliberal international agricultural trade regime, rampant privatisation of natural resources and their (over)exploitation, etc. – in favour of approaches that are associated with more feminine values such as environmental sustainability, communal use and management of natural resources and agroecological farming practices. Further, it has come to recognise the ways in which 'women and girls are disproportionately disempowered through current processes and politics of food's production, consumption, and distribution' (Patel 2012).

Food – a basic human right. Everyone must have access to safe, nutritious and culturally appropriate food in sufficient quantity and quality to sustain a healthy life with full human dignity. Access to food must be declared a constitutional right and governments must guarantee the development of the primary sector to ensure the concrete realisation of this fundamental right.

Agrarian reform. Genuine agrarian reform giving landless and farming people – especially women – ownership and control of the land they work and returning territories to indigenous peoples without discrimination. The right to land must be free of discrimination on the basis of gender, religion, race, social class or ideology; land belongs to those who work it.

Protecting natural resources. The sustainable care and use of natural resources especially land, water and seeds. Those working the land must have the right to practise sustainable management of natural resources and to preserve biological diversity. This requires security of tenure, healthy soils and reduced use of agro-chemicals.

Reorganising food trade. Food is first a source of nutrition and only secondarily an item of trade. National agricultural policies must prioritise production for domestic consumption and food self-sufficiency. Food imports must not displace local production or depress prices, and export dumping or subsidised export must cease. Peasant farmers have the right to produce essential food staples for their countries and to control the marketing of their products.

Ending the globalisation of hunger. Food sovereignty is undermined by multilateral institutions and by speculative capital. The growing control of multinational corporations over agricultural policies has been facilitated by the economic policies of multilateral organisations, and the regulation and taxation of speculative capital and a strictly enforced code of conduct for transnational corporations is needed.

Social peace. Everyone has the right to be free from violence. Food must not be used as a weapon. Increasing levels of poverty and marginalisation in the countryside, along with the growing oppression of ethnic minorities and indigenous populations aggravate situations of injustice and hopelessness. The ongoing displacement, forced urbanisation and repression of peasants cannot be tolerated.

Democratic control. Small farmers must have direct input into formulating agricultural policies at all levels, including the current FAO World Food Summit. This requires the United Nations and related organisations to undergo a process of democratisation. Everyone has the right to honest, accurate information and open and democratic decision making. Rural women, in particular, must be granted direct and active decision making on food and rural issues.

(Via Campesina 2007)

Figure 17.2 Core principles of food sovereignty.

Thus, the gendered nature of resource politics, especially the specific concerns of women relating to access to and management of natural resources, has been recognised at the global level by intergovernmental as well as non-governmental organisations. However, the dominance of neoliberal capitalism is such that it constrains the range of possibilities available for addressing issues such as the 'gender gap' in access to agricultural land. For instance, legal mechanisms may be used to guarantee land rights to women, but better prices offered by TNCs make the lease or purchase of land by individuals and communities more expensive, potentially eroding local ownership and leading to negative consequences – such as overexploitation of land – for both the resource and the community. In light of this, it is imperative that gender concerns vis-à-vis land, water and food are understood within a complex web of social and environment justice issues (e.g., peasants' rights) that have emerged from the overwhelming capitalist hold over natural resources today.

Questions for further debate

1. In what ways does the concept of gender help explain contemporary resource politics?
2. Is it helpful to focus on 'women' in discussions relating to the political economy of land, water and food? If so, why? If not, why not?
3. What do you understand by the term 'gender gap' as it relates to access to agricultural land and water? To what extent is it prevalent in the Global South, and why?
4. How is food sovereignty a gendered approach to tackling food insecurity?
5. Critically review feminist responses to contemporary concerns about access to and use of natural resources, and propose a roadmap for activists and policy-makers.

Sources for further reading and research

Agarwal, B. (1994) *A Field of One's Own: Gender and Land Rights in South Asia*, Cambridge: Cambridge University Press.

Clapp, J. (2013) *Food*, Cambridge: Polity Press.

Cruz-Torres, M. L. and P. McElwee (eds) (2012) *Gender and Sustainability: Lessons from Asia and Latin America*, Tuscon, AZ: University of Arizona Press.

Jackson, C. (2003) 'Gender Analysis of Land: Beyond Land Rights for Women?', *Journal of Agrarian Change*, 3(4): 453–80.

Ray, I. (2007) 'Women, Water and Development', *Annual Review of Environment and Resources*, 32: 421–49.

Notes

1 'Sustainable development' is described as the 'process of change in which the exploitation of resources, the direction of investments, the orientation of technological development, and institutional change are made consistent with future as well as present needs' (WCED 1987: 17).

2 Although, as Zwarteveen (1998: 303) points out, 'access to water in public irrigation systems may be heavily dependent on access to male dominated and politically influenced social networks and administrative structures ... money may be a more neutral and accessible way for women to access water'.

CHAPTER 18

Development institutions and neoliberal globalisation

Penny Griffin

▌ LEARNING OUTCOMES

Upon completion, readers should be able to:

- Describe how development institutions reproduce development strategy that can be identified and described as 'neoliberal'.
- Explain how development institutions define the relationship between 'globalisation' and development and how this might impact on human bodies and behaviours.
- Discuss how, by understanding neoliberal rationality as gendered, we might begin to unravel and contest the hierarchies, exclusions and negative effects reproduced by neoliberal development strategy today.

▌ INTRODUCTION

The international movement of bodies, business and the global spread of consumer culture extend beyond popular culture performance spaces or postindustrial production sites and reach into people's daily lives, interpersonal relationships and their images of themselves and Others. As globalisation links populations in denser, faster and more complex ways, the political economy of desire will continue to complement and complicate the constantly unfolding global order.

(Nagel 2006: 546–547)

The question of who and what is considered real and true is apparently a question of knowledge. But it is also, as Foucault makes plain, a question of power. Having or bearing 'truth' and 'reality' is an enormously powerful prerogative within the social world [...]. Knowledge and power are not finally separable but work together to establish a set of subtle and explicit criteria for thinking the world.

(Butler 2004a: 215)

Today, we still have slave traders. They no longer find it necessary to march into the forests of Africa looking for prime specimens who will bring top dollar on the auction blocks in Charleston, Cartagena, and Havana. They simply recruit desperate people and build a factory to produce the jackets, blue jeans, tennis shoes, automobile parts, computer components, and thousands of other items they can sell in the markets of their choosing ... [assuring themselves] that the desperate people are better off earning one dollar a day than no dollars at all, and that they are receiving the opportunity to become integrated into the larger world community.

(Perkins 2005: 180–181)

This chapter examines the gendered underpinnings of neoliberal development strategy as embodied in development institutions, a key modus operandi of which is the 'neoliberal globalisation' thesis. By 'development institution', I am referring to those intergovernmental organisations that operate explicitly in reference to the so-called 'developing world' (see Figure 18.1). Development institutions are prominent (but by no means uncomplicated) examples of global governance, which takes shape in a variety of forms. They are worth examining in some detail, however, not least for an association with the developing world riddled with narratives of imperialism and inequality, but also the possibility of resistance and future change.

Although conventional (mainstream) approaches to International Relations (IR), International Political Economy (IPE) and Development Studies tend to avoid

---

- United Nations: in particular, the Economic and Social Council (ECOSOC), General Assembly Committees, the United Nations Development Programme (UNDP), the Millennium Project, the World Health Organisation (WHO) and the World Food Programme.

- 'Development banks': the World Bank Group; the Asian Development Bank (ADB); the African Development Bank; the Inter-American Development Bank (IDB); the Islamic Development Bank; the European Bank of Reconstruction and Development (EBRD). (NB There are other development banks, including the Islamic Development Bank, the East African Development Bank, the Development Bank of Singapore, the Central American Bank for Economic Integration (CABEI), the Brazilian Development Bank, the Korea Development Bank, the Council of Europe Development Bank and the Eastern and Southern African Trade and Development Bank, to name but a few).

- International Labour Organization (ILO)

- International Monetary Fund (IMF)

- Organisation for Economic Co-operation and Development (OECD)

- World Trade Organisation (WTO)

Figure 18.1 Key development institutions.

thinking about bodies, gender matters in and to the politics of neoliberal development precisely because the global political economy is peopled by bodies (bodies that are, contrary to conventional wisdom, important, diverse and everywhere). Gender matters because its study concerns the analysis of norms and standards in the global political economy that many hold to be true, essential and universal but a committed critique of which reveals to be power laden, regulatory and highly restrictive. Exposing the sexism and racism of dominant disciplines, discourses and practices is an immensely destabilising enterprise and also a highly emotive one, liable to incite bafflement, defensiveness and, sometimes, outright hostility. Bodies are meant, in IR and IPE, to be fixed, given and congruent to being taken for granted. To posit the 'international' as gendered is to threaten many of the apparently stable foundations that have allowed conventional analysis to simplify, model and explain the actions of the global political economy's key actors.[1]

NEOLIBERALISM, GLOBALISATION AND DEVELOPMENT

Neoliberal development strategy

The neoliberal orthodoxy that emerged during the late 1970s (often referred to as the 'Washington Consensus' and predominant internationally until the early 1990s) was primarily focused on market liberalism, the primacy of foreign direct investment (FDI), the outward orientation of economies and the contraction of the state and its machinery (see Figure 18.2). Development policymaking has, since the early 1990s, undergone some significant changes and is now far less reliant on crude, hastily assembled and short-term structural adjustment programmes (SAPs). It would be a mistake, however, to assume that this orthodoxy has failed or disappeared.

Although Washington Consensus development policymaking was heavily criticised for failing to integrate the social and economic dimensions of development

---

As espoused by the leading development institutions, neoliberal development strategy is based on four central tenets:

- A confidence in the market (**marketisation**) as the mechanism by which societies should be made to distribute their resources (although market imperfections may hamper distributive patterns, remove these and the 'allocative efficiency' of the market is restored).

- The use of private finance (in place of public spending) in public projects (**privatisation**).

- **Deregulation**, such that the removal of tariff barriers and subsidies ensures that the market is freed from the potential tyranny of nation state intervention and capital is granted optimal mobility.

- A commitment to **flexibilisation**, which refers to the ways in which production is organised in mass consumption society (that is, dynamically and flexibly).

Figure 18.2 Four central tenets of neoliberal development strategy.

and, in many cases, exacerbating social inequalities, its successor, the 'Post-Washington Consensus', is, in methodology and formulation, less of a radical departure than some have claimed (see, for example, Stiglitz 2003; World Health Organisation [WHO] 2009). The 'second-generation' policy reforms of Post-Washington Consensus development institutions are no less market centred than their predecessors. They are, however, more concerned to acknowledge and remedy 'market imperfections' (see, for example, Fine 2001).

Neoliberal globalisation and globalism

It is arguably now the case that 'globalisation', once *the* explanatory term for contemporary forms of economic restructuring, has been usurped. Or, at least, it has been usurped by a slightly more specific term, *neoliberal* globalisation (Larner 2003: 509). A global regime of 'free' trade has its roots in ancient civilizations, but it is the peculiarly twentieth-century processes of interchange that capture the contemporary imagination, led in large part by Western popular culture references to technological wizardry and cyberculture. The neoliberal globalisation thesis, applicable to a cultural form of late capitalism whereby 'every society is now industrialized or embarked on industrialization' (Gray 2002: 55), advocates the process of 'opening up' national economies to increased monetary flows and global actors. Less a consequence of 'a conscious decision of political leadership', globalisation is perhaps more fruitfully read as the result of 'structural changes in capitalism' and 'in the actions of many people, corporate bodies, and states, that cumulatively produce new relationships and patterns of behaviour' (Cox 1992: 26).

Involving very little agreement on definition and process, 'globalisation' is approached in various ways by those engaged in its study. Beyond academia (particularly within the policymaking community) the globalisation debate remains polarised between two (nominally 'economic') choices: economic 'globalisation' as the key means of reducing world poverty, or as an uneven process of capital transfer, exacerbating and entrenching the division between rich and poor. According to pro-globalisation ideology (globalism), globalisation represents a progressive and modernising increase in global connectivity, reproducing the 'intensification of world-wide social relations which link distinct localities' (Giddens 1990: 64). Humanity is modernised, integrated and advanced through a 'borderless world', within which the world market is advocated over structures of local production and emphasis placed on the prevalence of Western-type consumerism (see, for example, Friedman 1999; Ohmae 2002). For its critics, globalisation signifies human sacrifice, suffering, inequality and segregation, remaining the rather vague and figurative 'force' behind the liberal capitalist agenda and certain capitalist processes (see Bøås and McNeill 2003: 139). In either case, whether the consequences of globalisation are seen as 'catastrophic' or as 'the ultimate unification of the world', globalisation itself is often used in a rather loose and ideological sense (see, for example, Hettne *et al.* 1999; Kay 1997).

The point that I want to emphasise here is that, in simply debating globalisation's consequences according to this either/or division of attention, we make of globalisation an abstract liberal capitalist projection devoid of political intent. Thus we also (unfortunately) avoid questioning the ways in which this 'thing' called globalisation exists and what, therefore, globalisation means, discursively and practically. Unnuanced and 'bulldozer' readings of globalisation elide globalisation with trade liberalisation, modernisation and Westernisation (see, for example, Friedman 1999; Lapeyre 2004), such that it becomes inexorable and inevitable: a conceptual substitute for the internationalisation of the Western 'free market', measurable in terms of the intensity and velocity of worldwide economic exchange.

The etymological roots of 'free trade' are to be found in the expression 'trade freed from imperial preferences', the result of a period in history when European 'empires' dominated and reconfigured (for their own purposes) large parts of the non-European world. Whereas any benign and passive view (as often proffered by leading international institutions, particularly the IMF, the World Bank, other development banks and the WTO) loses the relationship between imperialism and the market economy, it is crucial that a more attentive reading holds onto the heavily sexualised and racialised genealogy of contemporary globalisation.

As a singular and monolithic term, then, globalisation tells us very little about the world, its political discourses and relations of power. We might assume, for example, that globalisation is the 'natural' successor of the post-Berlin Wall 'Cold War system', with the world 'an increasingly interwoven place' (Friedman 1999: 7). This tells us little about the complex social and economic systems that structure our relationships, and the products, practices, institutions and norms (and their effects) that these reproduce. Such a statement, and its recourse to natural determinism and structural inevitability, does, however, reproduce the 'myth' of globalisation, a myth that replaces the messy, contradictory and disjointed processes of global interaction with a simplified, clean and seductive agenda.

Centred on the achievability of economic 'development' through the social embedding of the market, neoliberal discourses have rather effectively communicated certain culturally constructed facts and knowledges on a global scale as simple 'common sense', dominating both globalisation discourse and contemporary development policymaking (see, for example, Griffin 2007). Deploying vivid images, clever metaphors and persuasive but highly manipulative narratives, the dominant rhetoric of globalisation, neoliberal globalism, distorts our understanding of the globalisation 'syndrome' in order to sell Western global finance (Veseth 2005: 3). The neoliberal globalisation thesis fails to tell us how, for example, globalisation might not constitute an unstoppable universal force but a fragile and socially contingent political project, or how one dimensional 'big pictures' of global capitalism distort and misrepresent the gendered and racist underpinnings of global restructuring projects, with all their unevenness and developmental disjunctures.

Descendant of a tradition of Western classical and neoclassical economic discourses,[2] neoliberalism displays the racist and sexist underpinnings of a highly culturally specific discourse predicated on the expansion of Western capitalism through a colonising imperative (see Figure 18.3). Yet, although there is a lot of talk about globalisation, for globalism's advocates, race, sex and gender do not feature much

- **Neoliberalism**: a pervasive discourse in development economics and policymaking, based on the assumed centrality of marketisation, privatisation, deregulation and flexibilisation.

- **Neoliberal globalisation**: a type of globalisation discourse and also a way of seeing the world based on the assumed centrality of the 'opening up' (through marketisation, liberalisation and industrialisation) of national economies to world monetary flows.

- **Neoliberal globalism**: the dominant ideology of neoliberal globalisation discourse, invariably presenting globalisation's 'triumphs' (the liberalisation and integration of world markets) as 'natural' and progressive phenomena.

Figure 18.3 Understanding neoliberalism.

at all. Pro-neoliberal globalisation's loudest voices (particularly the World Bank, the OECD, the WTO, the IMF and the UN under Kofi Annan) have steadily saturated the agenda with the 'inevitability' and 'fact' of neoliberal globalisation, presenting the 'liberalisation and integration of global markets as "natural" phenomena that advance individual liberty and material progress in the world' (Steger 2004: 5). In particular, the liberalisation of trade and the opening of development economies to global finance have been advocated as emancipatory, particularly with regards to the opportunities presented for poor women.

Developing countries, the primary recipients of Western policymaking, tend to feature in the neoliberal globalisation thesis as 'cultures of shortage or scarcity', ripe for transformation into 'markets of overabundance' (Wichterich 2000: vii–viii). Defining the relationship between 'globalisation' and development as progressive and essentially of benefit to developing countries, development institutions cite the 'impressive technological progress' that has 'spurred productivity gains around the world' as resulting in an increasing number of countries 'contributing today to world growth', which 'makes for a much more deeply integrated and vibrant world' (IMF Director of European Offices, Saleh Nsouli 2007). Likewise, former UN Secretary-General (and key UN reformer) Kofi Annan has argued that the relationship between development, security and human rights 'has only been strengthened in our era of rapid technological advances, increasing economic interdependence, globalization and dramatic geopolitical change' (2005: 5).

Globalisation, claims the World Bank, 'has helped reduce poverty in a large number of developing countries' but must be harnessed to 'better to help the world's poorest, most marginalised countries improve the lives of their citizens' (2000). Although, as former Bank Chief Economist Nicholas Stern argues, some 'anxieties' about globalisation are well founded, 'reversing globalisation' could only come at 'an intolerably high price' for poor people, destroying the 'prospects of prosperity' for many millions (Stern 2001).

Such statements, of course, do not challenge the basic neoliberal assumption that integration into a global, liberal market is the key determinant of a country's 'development'. The 'triumph of the market' has already been built into the neoliberal globalisation story (Cameron and Palan 2004: 77), so effectively in fact that it is made to seem the 'natural' result of efficient economic practice.

THE DEVELOPMENT INSTITUTION IN GENDERED PERSPECTIVE

Gender and the Post-Washington Consensus

A Post-Washington Consensus concern to acknowledge and remedy 'market imperfections' has taken form in broad policy incursions into the social constitution of economic inequalities. According to the World Bank's Social Development Sector, the Bank works to make 'policies and programs in developing and transitioning economies more equitable and sustainable' (World Bank 2008a), since 'social development' is 'a natural complement to economic development' with 'both intrinsic and instrumental value' (World Bank 2008b). Official development policy remains resoundingly centred on embedding the market, private capital and a deregulated economy in developing countries, and although country governments now play a more visible role in drafting policy documents (the World Bank and IMF's 'poverty reduction strategy papers', or PRSPs, are 'country led'), the macro- and micro-economic criteria they must meet are strict and orthodox (based on, for example, removing import quotas, improving export incentives, reforming the fiscal system, improving the financial performance of public enterprises, revising agricultural pricing, shifting public investment, revising industrial incentives, increasing public enterprise efficiency, and so on).

Of particular concern, at least since the late 1990s, has been the concept of making globalisation 'work' for all, particularly the poor, with special attention paid to the social and economic costs and benefits of global integration. Development institutions sit at a particularly crucial juncture between interstate and global networks of economic, political and cultural relations, since they are at once composed of but different to the nation-states that constitute them (not least since larger institutions now work directly with the non-governmental and civil society sectors). Although not always decisive in the politics of development, they are certainly pervasive. Despite gender, sex and sexuality having been widely acknowledged to play a not inconsiderable role in the practices, processes and structures of development (see, *inter alia*, Bedford 2005; Benería 2003a, 2003b; Elson 1996; Kabeer 2001), descriptions of 'development institutions' as themselves gendered (and therefore gender specific in their policy articulations) are rare. If everyone has a theory of gender (see Chapter 3), then, by extension, development institutions have a (or multiple) theory(ies) of gender. Such theories are neither overt nor avowed, but development institutions can, and do, distinguish between 'types of people' and bodies, and these distinctions impact significantly on the formation, implementation and effects of policy.

Neoliberal development strategy is, I argue, gendered in two ways, both of which are connected but (for the sake of analytical clarity) worth distinguishing:

- Neoliberal development is gendered in terms of *input*, which comes from the foundational economic rationality from which neoliberal strategy is formed.
- Neoliberal development is gendered in terms of *outcome*: in the practical experiences of the poor people these strategies target, and in terms of the future continuance of the neoliberal policies in question.

As Parpart argues, a (Post-Washington Consensus) concern for 'good governance' in international development has largely ignored both gender and power (2007: 207). Although the quality of governance is certainly an issue for development institutions, and good governance increasingly proffered and imposed as a conditionality for the granting or renewal of multilateral loans, assessment of the specific 'quality' of good governance assumes that it is good where it is 'clean' and therefore value neutral.[3]

Based on the assumption that an efficient market society is inherently more equitable, neoliberal globalisation's advocates rarely comment on the profound changes in human behaviour that economic restructuring has instigated. Although social concerns that might impact on market efficiency have aroused the interest of development institutions (which operate social departments much larger and broader in scope than 20 years ago), social concerns nevertheless remain policy relevant only as long as they can be quantified as tools for promoting market efficiency.

Correspondingly, 'gender equity' relates entirely to women's empowerment as measured according to their level of market access to 'assets' and 'opportunities'. This is a restrictive categorisation that excludes not only any labour supplied by those not identifiable as women, but also the 'informal' labour that women contribute to keep the 'formal' economy sustainable. As Hoskyns and Rai argue, the neglect of women's unpaid work in official statistics (such as the UN System of National Accounts) only contributes to 'a widespread and growing depletion of the capacities and resources for social reproduction', that is, 'the glue that keeps households and societies together and active' (2007: 298). This is an issue that demands the urgent attention of statisticians, economists and policymakers, since '[w]ithout unpaid services and their depletion being measured and valued, predictions are likely to be faulty, models inaccurate and development policies flawed' (ibid.).

Many development institutions (such as the ADB, the AfDB, the IDB and the World Bank) do operate 'gender policies' designed to streamline gender analysis into the lending, analytical and advisory 'products' that they offer. Operationally, however, 'gender' in official development discourse remains an analytical 'variable' that can be added to or removed from the fundamentals of economic growth and market access at will, and which therefore exists as an externality to 'good governance' conditionality. As such, it remains easy for these institutions to overlook how the very basic elements of global governance today (the processes, practices, structures and value-laden assumptions on which global economic and development policymaking are based) might not be 'value neutral'. Bound by the strictures of the macroeconomic frameworks of the institutions they work in to formulate 'effective' policy, many development staff struggle to combine advanced theoretical conceptualisations of gender and sex with the restrictive and binary definitions that operate in institutional practice. Thus the idea that, regardless of situation, there is only one 'normal' way to be a woman or a man and that heterosexuality alone is 'normal' (despite modern science's 'discovery' of numerous types of body, mixing together conventionally 'male' or 'female' anatomical components) proliferates.

Examining the 'facts' of neoliberal development

To take the neoliberal globalisation thesis at face value means ignoring how the transcendental liberal 'market', based on 'the social stereotype of the manufacturer of goods as an entrepreneurial inventor trying to create a new world', has not always been so, but was created in the late nineteenth century to displace traditional modes of manufacture and production, usurping the social stereotype 'of the maker of goods as an artisan practicing an ancient craft in the received ways' (Rosenberg and Birdzell 1986: 183). The recourse to 'natural' evolution and techno-determinism in neoliberal discourse conceals the many multifaceted processes of social engineering that have led to the creation of 'market society'. As Wichterich makes plain, the tendencies of neoliberal globalisation discourses are to 'take hold of and change social systems', eroding and revolutionising forms of work, strategies of social protection, lifestyles and value orientations everywhere, North and South (2000: vii). Importantly, where neoliberal development policymaking interacts with external social systems, it apportions value to those parts with which it can work, and devalorises, marginalises and excludes that which it conceives of as backward, inappropriate or unworkable (in practice, anything alien to the assumptions and modelling techniques of mainstream Western economics).

Instead of 'something' (or a sequence of 'things', like global trade, communications or foreign direct investment) in the world, and/or a rather unambiguous process grinding on seemingly in spite of us, neoliberal globalisation might more fruitfully be read in terms of historical, social and cultural relations of *power*. As much as anything, globalisation can be considered a selection of knowledges relating, as Kofman and Youngs argue, 'as much to a way of thinking about the world as it does to a description of the dynamics of political and economic relations within it' (1996: 1).

We do not simply 'know' that globalisation is real and true: careful examination of the 'facts' should lead us to question how we know what we know and what effects this production of knowledge has. The kinds of 'truths' and 'realities' that have been produced about and for the neoliberal globalisation thesis have resulted in a variety of outcomes. Above all, a tremendous amount of power goes into knowing what 'globalisation' is: selectively deployed information; ideologically driven decision making; *a priori* assumption about the world and its truths; the availability and accessibility of these truths. By rejecting any understanding of neoliberalism that posits it as the natural and inevitable unleashing of (value-neutral) market forces, we might instead give priority to analysis of neoliberal globalisation as a political project, generating new forms of domination while interacting with old ones. Thus might we better understand the processes and practices of global governance more broadly. Some examples are the following.

Fact 1: Neoliberal economics is value neutral

'Economic man', the market-able individual, fundamental to neoliberalism's economic assumptions and models is the result of a highly specific Western economic agenda. Like orthodox economic theory more generally, neoliberalism depends on and upholds as universal a view of a culturally specific but 'universal' self that, as descendant of the historical association between white, middle class and 'entrepreneurial' (once read as colonial) men's bodies, is masculinised and highly ethnocentric (see, for example, Griffin 2007: 220–25).

As feminists have frequently noted, the neoliberal thesis fails utterly to recognise the prevalence of 'economic man' in the policy prescriptions it promotes (see, for example, Benería 2003a: 117). Maximising 'economic man' is intended in economic discourse as a good approximation, or model, of humankind across time and space. For economic theory, the point of models is that they are meant to be used as a standard against which the real world is measured, rather than as the real world itself. In practice, however, the application of economic theory (the assumption, for example, that individuals behave as autonomous and individuated atoms maximising their utility in the market economy) has sought to distort reality to fit the model (see Figure 18.4).

'Rational economic woman' is a relatively recent concept in development policy-making, deployed to 'include' women in policies designed to achieve economic growth and efficiency, but also political freedom and 'social justice' (Rankin 2001: 19). In poor agrarian economies reliant on smallholder production and petty trade, women have, as Rankin articulates, increasingly been targeted as the desired beneficiaries and agents of micro-credit based progress (ibid.). 'Rational economic woman' is not, however, designed to challenge the (tacitly held) naturalised and dehistoricised associations between white men's bodies and their (superior) market capacity. No matter how market productive microcredit makes women in developing countries, the specific targeting of women in microcredit schemes is troubling: since the hours of 'informal economy' work that women do to sustain households are unrecognised in official measurements of domestic product (GDP) and economic growth, women's microcredit activities take place in addition to their average daily burden, while being the only means by which these women are measured effective or successful.

Consequently, rural women are targeted in these schemes not because they are considered universally capable market actors as per *homo economicus* (economic man), but because they are considered 'essentially' reproductive, caregiving and

---

- **Value neutrality**: the assumption that theories (such as those of economic action) are objective in their freedom from assumptions of value and/or human worth and that interests and desires do not, therefore, influence theoretical outcomes.

- **Economic man**: or *homo economicus*, the de facto approximation and model of the human individual in economic theory.

- **Gender mainstreaming policies**: designed to operationalise the inclusion of gender in *all* policies of the institution in question. Mainstreaming a gender perspective is, according to the United Nations Economic and Social Council (ECOSOC 2004), 'the process of assessing the implications for women and men of any planned action'.

Figure 18.4 Key concepts in economic theory.

domestically situated and, therefore, more responsible, reliable and trustworthy, since, as nurturers and carers of the household, women are considered less likely to display men's 'risk-taking' behaviour (see, for example, World Bank 2001). In no way does any of this challenge the fundamental predication of neoliberalism on a signifying economy of manliness.

Fact 2: Globalisation is reducing poverty

One neoliberal globalist claim of recent years has been that the distribution of income between the world's people has become more equal over the past two decades, with the number of people living in extreme poverty continuing to fall. IMF Director of European Offices, Saleh Nsouli, claims, for example, that, in the last five years, 'the world has experienced a strong and stable average real per capita growth', in the range of between 4 to 5 per cent annually, 'accompanied by low inflation' (Nsouli 2007). Such progressive trends, neoliberal globalism suggests, are due in large part to the rising density of economic integration between countries (Wade 2004: 567).

What this truth conceals is the enormously subjective quality of the statistics used by those measuring global poverty, particularly the World Bank, which has become the principal decider of international poverty levels. Other evidence might suggest that world inequality is probably rising, not least if China and India's preternaturally fast economic growth rates are removed from the equation. The point is, as Wade describes, that 'there is no single best measure of world income inequality' (2004: 8). Yet the argument that world poverty has dropped, while world inequality has lessened, continues unabashed: the World Bank claims progress in reducing extreme income poverty 'in many countries'; the United Nations continues to assert that they are on target for a reduction of global poverty levels, by half, by 2015.

Fact 3: Gender equality is essential to reducing poverty

Intuitively a sound argument, this thesis derives from a variety of sources, particularly from the earliest days of the women in development (WID) movement (which was particularly focused on achieving social justice and equity for women in international development). The neoliberal argument is that 'gender equality' leads to improved living standards, sustainable economic growth, and effective and accountable governance (see, *inter alia*, ADB 2003). This is because women's improved educational and employment opportunities, equality in political and social participation and increased health and welfare services allows women to be both more productive in the formal economy, while more able to nurture effectively in the informal.

The mathematics of development institutions' claims is, however, misleading. If, as Wade claims, falling income inequality 'is not a general feature of the world economy, even using the most favourable measures' (2004: 10), but the rates of women's participation in economies across the world continue to rise, the link between gender equality, women's presence in the 'formal' economy and poverty reduction is nothing more than conjectural. The World Bank, for example, proposes that Vietnam (with 'one of the highest rates of economic participation of women in the world') is 'one of the more advanced countries with respect to gender equality' (World Bank 2006b). Assuming a causal connection between women's economic participation and their gender equality, the Bank's Vietnam assessment fails, however, to provide any evidence to show how exactly this is so, or how this conclusion has been reached. We might reasonably surmise, given the Bank's reluctance to share its sources, that no such evidence exists.

In reference to 'gender equality', then, the issue is not one of debating whether gender equality is *per se* a good or bad thing, since the absurdity of arguing against equality is self-evident. A more useful approach might be to question whether women's equality can be measured at all in reference to their contribution only to the formal, productive economy (thereby imposing an arbitrary but heavily value-laden distinction between 'formal' and 'informal' economy contributions). How practically and theoretically viable it is to use 'gender' as a synonym for 'women' (and 'gender inequalities' as tantamount to women's exclusion from development) certainly, then, remains questionable, not least since a woman-centred description of 'gender' fails to inform us of the gender inequalities experienced by all those who are not women: not only men, but also children, adolescents and those who are unable or unwilling to define themselves as easily belonging to one of two sexes.

It would also be worth considering the imposed distinction, evident in a number of development institutions, between the so-called 'economic' and 'social' sectors. The World Bank, for example, has (it claims) 'made significant progress in mainstreaming gender issues in the social sectors of health and education', but has generally failed to integrate gender 'in the non-social sectors', such as 'the energy, finance, transport and agriculture sectors' (World Bank 2007b). This is a worrying sign that the formation of economic policymaking in developing countries (predicated on an understanding of 'development' symbolised by 'economic growth' alone) remains almost entirely devoid of social considerations.

THE IMPORTANCE OF CONTESTING NEOLIBERAL 'DEVELOPMENT'

Neoliberal assumptions in contemporary world politics constitute such powerful models for human interaction and behaviour because they are based on the assumption that people everywhere adhere to the rule of the market. To do this, and to therefore hope and dream of success, wealth and 'development', people must universally embrace the rules of an economic modus operandi dictated largely by Anglo-American neoliberal capitalism. They must identify themselves with certain cultural models of humanity and internalise the key principles of neoliberal economic doctrine. In so doing, they reproduce centuries of liberal ideology and rhetoric that have naturalised the essentiality of trade, the accumulation of capital and the centrality of economic growth through the liberal 'free market'. Thus people tailor their identities, their sense of self and their ambitions to fit with the global mantra of more trade equals more capital equals good for everyone.

The potential for Western models of economic activity to interact with, affect and reconfigure existing social hierarchies and distributions of power and resources is enormous, yet official discourse continues to describe globalisation primarily in positive and progressive terms. Whether viewed as the saviour of modernity or the nemesis of social development, a misleading and superficial portrait of globalisation has dominated, depicting a subject 'North' (bearer of capitalist doctrine) and an object 'South' (a permanently malleable resource responsive to and dependent on the workings of the North). The assumption that the market is and should be the key distributor of precious and fragile social resources remains, however (at least in globalist narration), uncontested.

It is important to consider at all times the positive and negative effects of certain policies and developmental interactions. Concerns about the loci, mechanisms and processes of delivery of developmental action and power may well make international development a more participatory and inclusive process, but understanding the contradictory and complex effects of global restructuring and assessing the contradictions of neoliberal rationality itself require challenging more than just cause and effect as conventionally conceived of. An abiding contradiction of Post-Washington Consensus international development policymaking is the shift to an official discourse of empowerment within an international institutional context clearly hierarchical in form and effect. The World Bank takes pains to advertise itself as an 'agency' of development, not a commander, but how much room poor people have within the dictates of Bank-approved but state-led economic management programmes is certainly not clear. Empowering the poor, women included, such that they have control over their own life strategies, is certainly worth struggling for: a time when the 'poor' are so 'empowered' that they might reject the governance dictates of Western institutions will be a fascinating one to live through, not least for the responses of the institutions they reject.

Questions for further debate

1. What can consideration of gender tell us in relation to neoliberal globalisation and development policymaking?
2. How might consideration of gendered relations of power and dominance lead us to rethink global governance?
3. Is neoliberal globalisation more 'myth' than reality? How and where in the politics of development do the myth and reality of neoliberal globalisation collide?
4. Is gender a synonym for women? Why has the inclusion of gender considerations in official development policymaking remained only minimal?
5. What are gender inequalities? Are they being reduced by neoliberal globalisation?

Sources for further reading and research

Benería, L. (2003) 'Economic Rationality and Globalization: A Feminist Perspective', in M. A. Ferber and J. A. Nelson (eds), *Feminist Economics Today: Beyond Economic Man*, Chicago and London: University of Chicago Press, 115–133.

Bergeron, S. (2003) 'The Post-Washington Consensus and Economic Representations of Women in Development at the World Bank', *International Feminist Journal of Politics*, 5(3): 397–419.

Elson, D. (1996), 'Gender-Aware Analysis and Development Economics', in K. P. Jameson and C. K. Wilber (eds), *The Political Economy of Development and Underdevelopment*, 6th edition, New York: McGraw-Hill, 70–80.

Jolly, S. (2000) '"Queering" Development: Exploring the Links Between Same-Sex Sexualities, Gender, and Development', *Gender and Development*, 8(1): 78–88.

World Bank (2006) *Gender Equality as Smart Economics: A World Bank Group Gender Action Plan (Fiscal years 2007–10)*, Washington, DC: World Bank.

Notes

1 I am, of course, rather deliberately overlooking important governmental and non-governmental organisations that operate in the global development space that are not included in the above (the UK's Department for International Development, the United States Agency for International Development, Swedish International Development Cooperation Agency, and so on). Mechanisms of *national* government do have a role to play in and effects on global governance, as do NGOs and other not-for-profit organisations. I use the 'development institution' here to refer essentially to the inter-governmental type of organisation that arose out of, or in response to, the United Nations Bretton Woods meeting (1942), and the subsequent rise both of the 'United Nations System' (which includes not only the UN and its associated institutions, but also the World Bank, the International Monetary Fund and the World Trade Organisation). I only refer to these because, unlike NGOs and national governments, they are multi-member and multilateral organisational structures of legitimate and feasible governance over their members' affairs. This is *not* to say that these organisations actually have or embody any legitimate case for intervening directly in the politics of their members (the Articles of the World Bank and IMF, for example, clearly prohibit intrusive practices), but that they have established for themselves a space in development where they are considered to be sources of development expertise and management excellence.

2 I appreciate that 'Western' is not a particular enlightening way of capturing the ethnocentricity of mainstream economic science and discourse. I employ 'Western' in as broad a sense as possible here, encompassing Anglo-American and Australasian economism, plus aspects of Northern European and Japanese economic theorising.

3 As an example of the often automatic association between 'clean' and 'good' governance, World Bank lead economist Kazi Matin states (in a commentary published in the *Bangkok Post*) that 'a clean government and the rule of law must increasingly become the norm, with corruption and the rule of personalities, increasingly the exception'. He goes on to say that 'recent experience also suggests that without such improvements, growth can also stall' (World Bank 2007a).

PART 5 INTERNATIONAL INSTITUTIONS

CHAPTER 19

Mainstreaming gender in international institutions

Jacqui True

LEARNING OUTCOMES

Upon completion, readers should be able to:

- Explain what is meant by 'gender mainstreaming' in theory and in practice.
- Analyse whether gender mainstreaming policies have been effective in reducing gendered inequalities.
- Account for some shortcomings of a 'gender mainstreaming' approach to gendering global governance.

■ INTRODUCTION

Gender mainstreaming is increasingly the dominant language through which policymakers worldwide understand women and men. It is one of the contemporary logics through which international organisations, governments and non-government organisations engage with the politics of the global – be it global security, development, poverty, or trade. Assessing and understanding mainstreaming is thus the task of feminist scholars, especially in the field of International Relations, where global power is the core subject of analysis. Feminist International Relations scholars use a critical lens to analyse gender mainstreaming and its effects. It is not our role to be proponents or critics of mainstreaming per se. Rather, the point is to examine institutional practices and how they augur with theoretical expectations and official policies at the international level. What are the implications of gender mainstreaming in international organisations for feminist understandings of power and global governance? Further, what are the implications of mainstreaming policies for the strategies of women's movements worldwide (see True and Parisi 2013)?

There are different ways to study gender mainstreaming in international organisations. Some feminist scholars approach mainstreaming from an *institutional* perspective asking how mainstreaming policies were adopted and implemented in particular organisational contexts. They explore the gendered national politics and their intersection with global norms purported by international organisations such as the United Nations. Alternatively they examine the relationship between feminist movements and gender-mainstreamed bureaucracies at the global level. Other feminist scholars approach mainstreaming from a *discursive* perspective asking how mainstreaming produces new forms of power through the diffusion of strategic language and framing processes that change the meaning of women, men and gender equality in myriad contexts. These approaches – institutional and discursive – are complementary (Cohn 2008: 194). They can be seen as part of a collective feminist effort to critically scrutinise the political transformations that gender mainstreaming enacts or intends to enact.

This chapter is in three parts. The first part discusses the origins of gender mainstreaming as an institutional gender equality strategy and its contested definitions across states, international organisations and advocacy networks. The second part explores gendered power in policy and bureaucratic structures and how feminist International Relations scholars interpret the meaning of mainstreaming politics within particular organisations. The third part considers the voice of women, women's movements and feminist advocates in gender mainstreaming. How far and in what ways have mainstreaming processes opened up opportunities for greater political participation and visibility of women or feminist actors on the international stage? Has the mainstreaming of gender equality objectives silenced or made issues of gendered power and domination more or less salient in international relations?

WHAT IS GENDER MAINSTREAMING?

The United Nations, the international institution with the broadest global scope, defines mainstreaming as applying 'a gender perspective in all policies and programmes so that, before decisions are taken, an analysis is made of the effects on women and men, respectively' (United Nations 1995: 116). The implication of this definition is that gender equality cannot be achieved without considering the gendered consequences of all policies, global and local. The Beijing Platform for Action ratified by all members states at the 1995 Fourth UN World Conference on Women advocated a new policymaking approach that involves working to 'promote a gender perspective in all legislation and policies' (Beijing Platform for Action [BPfA], para. 207(d), aided by the generation and dissemination of gender-disaggregated statistics, in order to 'eliminate obstacles to the exercise of women's rights and eradicate all forms of discrimination against women' (para. 207(c)).

Consequently during the 1990s the remit of many existing international and national agencies was expanded to include gender mainstreaming, replacing or supplementing their earlier focus on women's issues and gender equality policy (Squires 2005; True 2003).

Mainstreaming emerged as a concept first in the politics of global development in the 1980s. Feminist advocates challenged the women in international development (WID) paradigm developed in the 1970s during the UN Decade for Women and subsequent UN world conferences on women. The main policy documents of the period, such as the country reports of the International Labour Organisation (ILO), did not consider the role or impact of women's productive labour in paid and unpaid economies on mainstream development projects (Razavi and Miller 1995a: 6–8). Instead international donor support was given for small-scale income-generating women-only projects. These projects often reinforced women's economic marginalisation and relegated them to secondary roles. Critics argued that the WID approach focused on what development could get from women rather than on women's needs or how development policies should be altered to advance gender equality (Goetz 1995a; see also Moser 1993). They argued that integrating social justice and equity for women with mainstream development concerns privileged economic efficiency arguments and existing male-centred agendas focused on the formal market economy, neglecting underlying gendered social relations (Palmer 1992). However, the WID approach did bring analysis of women's unequal situation into the realm of macro-economic and international policymaking (Razavi and Miller 1995a: 18).

Through the critical analysis of feminist scholars and activists especially from the South, a new gender and development (GAD) paradigm was forged that analysed the impact of gender relations on policies. Drawing from socialist feminist theories of women's subordination, GAD advocates argued that no amount of formal, public power would help to eliminate the gender imbalance of power in the family household or informal economy. They sought 'to develop a theory of gender which was ... informed by gender analysis of the world economy' and that took into account women's unpaid reproductive labour (Razavi and Miller 1995a: 15). Rather than the efficiency gains to be had from utilising women's labour for economic development, GAD analysis focused on gender power relations and bottom-up development involving women's NGOs and participatory planning. As Razavi and Miller stated, 'the policy implications of social relations analysis ... involve[s] the political project of women's self-empowerment' (1995a: 32; see also Kabeer 1994).

The concept of 'gender mainstreaming' represented a further development – and more institutionally palatable version – of the GAD paradigm that emerged in the late 1980s. Gender mainstreaming in international organisations such as United Nations agencies, the World Bank, the International Labour Organisation, the International Criminal Court, the European Union and Asia Pacific Economic Cooperation marked the spread of gender analysis beyond development policy and Southern, developing countries to developed regions and a wider range of policy domains. The diffusion of mainstreaming policies reflected the global consensus about the limitations of women's policy agencies and gender equality objectives viewed in isolation from relationships to men and the gendered structures of the macro economy. The Beijing Platform for Action consolidated the shift to gender mainstreaming as a global gender equality strategy (Geisler et al. 1999; Krook and True 2012; True and Mintrom 2001).

Gender mainstreaming conceptualises change in processes as a critical step towards changes in outcomes. For instance, changes in the activities of an organisation – its projects, programmes and policies – should ultimately lead to improvements in women's material lives. Many international organisations and development agencies, however, adopted gender mainstreaming or the term 'gender' without changing their previous 'add women and stir' focus. Razavi and Miller (1995a) discuss the common confusion over the meaning of gender and the policy implications of the discursive shift from 'women' to 'gender' among state and global institutions (see also Baden and Goetz 1997). Depending on their institutional mandates, gender has been deployed in various ways by different international organisations (Staudt 2003): as a synonym for women in the UN human rights commission (Radmani 2005); as a policy focus on equity and justice in the private and public spheres in the Rome Statute of the International Criminal Court (Chappell 2008); as an acknowledgement of the labour market policy implications of differences between women and men in the European Union (True 2009), and as a business case for minimising these differences and their impacts in the World Bank and in Asia Pacific Economic Cooperation (Bedford 2008; Bergeron 2003; True 2008b).

Approaches to gender mainstreaming reflect different feminist theories or the synthesis of theories (see Dietz 2003). In particular, mainstreaming invokes *liberal feminism* and its demands for the inclusion or representation of women and perspectives on women's – as well as men's – lived realities in policymaking. It is informed by *difference feminism* and its stress on the significance of material and culturally sanctioned differences between women and men and the importance of taking these differences into account in the design, implementation and evaluation of policies to empower women in particular. Moreover, *poststructuralist feminism* can be seen in some approaches to gender mainstreaming that understand the subjects of policy as diverse and incorporate this diversity in the policymaking process by addressing gender difference but displacing it as the sole axis of difference (Squires 2005; Verloo 2005).

Theories of gender mainstreaming suggest that as a policy strategy it has both status quo oriented and transformative implications. Roanaq Jahan (1995) sees mainstreaming as both an integrationist, liberal feminist strategy and an agenda-setting approach that has the potential to radically alter organisational goals and outcomes. In their study for the Beijing Prepcoms, Razavi and Miller (1995b) argue that a liberal, integrationist approach to gender mainstreaming was adopted by UNDP, the World Bank and the ILO. This approach involved two main components: (1) integrating gender issues into all of the activities funded and executed by an organisation, and (2) diffusing responsibility for gender mainstreaming beyond the WID/gender units – through mechanisms such as gender training and guidelines – thus making it a routine concern of every bureaucratic unit (1995b: ii).

Beveridge and Nott (2002) also disaggregate gender mainstreaming into two types of approach, technocratic and participatory. Compared with Jahan's distinction, they focus on the actors involved in mainstreaming rather than the intention of the policy approach but the technocratic approach is akin to a liberal feminist, integrationist strategy modified by difference feminisms' attention to gender. Technocratic gender mainstreaming relies on gender specialists or line bureaucrats within international organisations to drive the process of gendering policies and programmes (True 2008c). For example, the globally influential Council of Europe definition of gender mainstreaming was conceived by a group of specialists with no input from grassroots feminist activists or women's movements. From its very inception in international organisations therefore, mainstreaming was seen as a part of the normal policymaking process with little room anticipated for dialogue with civil society (Verloo 2005). In the United Nations, the role of gender specialists is intended to be catalytic and to shift responsibility for gender mainstreaming to management and operation units within its agencies (Hannan-Andersson 1995). Yet evidence suggests that this technocratic approach has not been able to deliver on the promises of mainstreaming. Progress reports on gender mainstreaming in UN peacekeeping operations (2005: 3), for example, state: 'the notions that gender advisors are catalysts in gender mainstreaming efforts and that gender mainstreaming is the responsibility of all staff have [also] failed to be universally accepted' (see also UN Secretary-General 2012: para. 58 for the continued failure to mainstream gender across UN peace operations).

By contrast to the technocratic approach, reflecting liberal and difference feminisms, feminist scholars advocate a participatory approach to mainstreaming gender issues in global policies. The participatory approach to gender mainstreaming takes seriously difference feminism's attention to salient gender differences and poststructuralist feminism's concern with displacing gender – especially as it is treated as a synonym for women – and fixed meanings of gender equality. Feminists stress the substantive representation of women's interests in policy discussion or require experts to consult with, and be accountable to, women's movements. Involving women's movements in the policymaking process is expected to decrease the chances that women will be instrumentalised by policies – as objects or means to organisational ends – or treated as a homogenous group (Ackerly 2009; Lombardo and Maier 2006). It is hard to see how gender mainstreaming could work as a policy strategy inside organisations without the support and scrutiny of diverse social movements outside. Indeed mainstreaming gender issues in the Rome Statute of the International Criminal Court (see Chapter 20) and the eight United Nations Security Council Resolutions on women, peace and security has involved persistent lobbying by transnational feminist networks inside international organisations and outside them in the nascent realm of global civil society (Pratt and Devroe 2013).

Since the Beijing Conference and the launch of gender mainstreaming onto the global stage, mainstreaming has taken on a life of its own in the organisations in which it has been implemented. The next section analyses the politics of implementing gender mainstreaming in international organisations.

■ HOW DOES GENDER MAINSTREAMING WORK?

Feminist IR scholars analyse the discursive and the institutional politics of main-streaming gender in international organisations. *Institutional politics* refers to the political and material relationships, the bureaucratic and organisational dynamics that have shaped mainstreaming as policy strategy. *Discursive politics* refers to the language and meaning of gender equality and difference reflected in cultural norms, policy procedures, organisational identities and material structures. Let us consider each type of politics and how feminist scholars analyse them.

From an institutional perspective, we are interested in how gender mainstream-ing is adopted and implemented in international organisations and whether it becomes co-opted by existing norms and bureaucratic politics or brings about political transformation. Feminist research to date suggests that the impact of mainstreaming depends greatly on: 1) the characteristics of the policy issue or regime area; 2) the nature of governance in the international institution; and 3) the networks among gender specialists or officials (insiders) and women's movements or advocates (outsiders).

That these three criteria are important to the successful mainstreaming of gender can be illustrated by the case of gender mainstreaming in the International Criminal Court discussed in Figure 19.1. First, the criminal justice policy area concerned issues of direct violence and bodily harm in which gender specificity of the issues (e.g., rape and sexual violence) is clearly apparent. Second, the nature of governance in the International Criminal Court involves (hard) law and legal precedent and reasoning rather than (soft) bureaucratic procedures or strategic bargaining making the implementation of mainstreaming more transparent and amenable to monitor-ing. Third, the Women's Caucus for Gender Justice built significant relationships between judges, lawyers and officials with gender expertise inside the ICC and women advocates in the broader global civil society outside the institution. These advocates were able to mobilise local publics to participate in the global policy debate about international justice.

Gender mainstreaming in European Union development policy also discussed in Figure 19.1 presents a less transformative case. Here the non-urgent character of the issue area, the complex bureaucratic governance regime, and relatively weak transnational networks all contrive to marginalise gender issues even though main-streaming is official policy and supported by a variety of institutional mechanisms and technical tools. First, development policy raises issues of structural rather than direct violence, and responds to enduring poverty and inequality in foreign coun-tries as opposed to pivotal crises that typically mobilise publics and institutional actors. Second, the European institutions tasked with development policymaking are complex and multiple at national and regional levels and involve the financing of development aid as well as the designing of development policy and projects, and gender experts have mainly been employed as temporary consultants rather than permanent officials. In this context, gender mainstreaming presents itself as a radi-cal and a conservative strategy in the interests of activist bureaucrats who want to transform policy outcomes and career bureaucrats who want to address a gap with-out altering existing norms and standard operating procedures practices. But the

Gender mainstreaming was intended to rectify the slow pace of progress in women's status in developing countries and at the global level. It was proposed as an alternative to the marginalisation of women-specific projects and agencies in international development. Acknowledging the potential for marginalisation in all initiatives that seek to redress gender inequality and injustice, the Beijing Platform for Action states that: 'Women/gender units are important for effective mainstreaming, but strategies must be further developed to prevent inadvertent marginalisation as opposed to mainstreaming of the gender dimension throughout all operations' (para. 308).

The alliance between insiders (gender-sensitive lawyers and government officials) and outsiders (women's movements and human rights advocacy groups) in the Women's Caucus for Gender Justice (WCGJ) facilitated the mainstreaming as opposed to the marginalisation of gender justice concerns in the Rome Statute of the International Criminal Court (ICC). The Statute covers administration of the ICC, including the gender-balanced recruitment of judges and other personnel, and gender-sensitive court procedures, especially for the protection of victims and witnesses, as well as substantive legal provisions that make crimes of sexual violence, war crimes, crimes against humanity and acts of genocide gender specific. In addition, the Rome Statute provides mandates for the Court appointment of gender experts and legal expertise on violence against women and children (Article 36 [8] b and Article 44 [2]) (Spees 2003). Senior prosecutors and judges in the ICTY and ICTR have taken up demands for gender justice in their arguments and decisions. Gender experts holding new specialist positions within the ICC encourage the input of women's organisations in their ongoing work to make the Statute an effective human rights instrument.

However, despite the high-level attention given to mainstreaming policies, issues of gendered power, inequality and injustice continue to be marginalised in some international organisations. For example, in the EU, gender mainstreaming has become a form of rationalisation in disguise, an argument for getting rid of budget lines devoted to gender expertise and budgets for women's or gender-specific projects (Stratigaki 2005). This rationalisation of resources undermines the EU's priority on meaningfully addressing gender inequalities and injustices in international development. In their report on 'gender equality and women's empowerment in EU development cooperation', the European Parliament (2008) observed, that despite the 1995 Communication on integrating gender in all development cooperation and the 2007 gender equality strategy, gender issues are now largely absent in the plans for the 17 billion euros in development assistance to countries in Asia, the Middle East, Latin America and South Africa.

Figure 19.1 Mainstreaming or marginalisation?

organisational conflict among these divergent interests has sidelined the focus on gender inequalities. Third, although European development institutions encourage some participation from civil society the transnational pro-gender-equal development network is still relatively weak. The network is at an early stage of building solidarity among European and developing country NGOs and civil societies, and translating gender and development issues to political leaders and global publics.

An understanding of bureaucratic pathologies but, even more importantly, of gendered power in bureaucracies, however, is crucial to interpreting and explaining the resistance to gender mainstreaming and its failure to change practices in many international organisations (see Barnett and Finnemore 2005; True and Parisi 2013). Goetz and Sandler in Figure 19.2 reflect on the international political and bureaucratic contexts of gender mainstreaming and how these contexts have led to unintended and often perverse consequences that diverge greatly from the original intentions of mainstreaming.

Some feminists argue that making gender mainstreaming everyone's job effectively means that it becomes no one's job (Painter and Ulmer 2002; Tiessen 2007). UN gender specialists Anne-Marie Goetz and Joanne Sandler put it bluntly: 'gender mainstreaming is everywhere – there are 1,300 gender focal points in the United Nations system – and yet nowhere.' Everyone does it or is expected to, so no one needs to be employed to specifically focus on gender issues. Since 11 September 2001 the focus on security politics and UN reform has diminished the political urgency and space for promoting women's rights that existed in the 1990s (Sen 2005).

In this global context, the strength of gender mainstreaming in extending a gender perspective across all policy areas and jurisdictions is also precisely its weakness. It may serve to dissipate the expertise on women and divert resources away from specialist knowledge to training non-gender specialist staff and producing bureaucratic tools such as checklists, action plans, scorecards, implications statements and so on that can be used by anyone. These tools facilitate gender analysis but they are not dedicated gender specialists or fully accountable for the outcomes of gender mainstreaming. The creation of the UN Entity for Gender Equality and Women's Empowerment from four small agencies is tasked with marshalling the unified expertise and the resources needed to make significant progress in achieving gender equality globally. It is accountable for the progress of the world's women at the same time as other UN agencies are still expected to mainstream gender issues and analysis.

Figure 19.2 Gender mainstreaming vs. a global bureaucracy for women?

There are significant gender biases in the way international organisations operate on the ground despite their political commitments to gender mainstreaming on the international stage. Why, for instance, did the UN encourage the mainstreaming of a gender perspectives in post-conflict contexts at the global level in Security Council Resolution 1325 yet simultaneously contradict this stance on the ground in the stonewalling of gender quotas in Timor by the Electoral Affairs Division (Hall and True 2009; see the discussion in Figure 19.3)? International organisations, including the UN, often promote the inclusion of gender perspectives but see gender equality strategies primarily as a problem-solving device; as a way of increasing the legitimacy of international norms such as liberal democracy, humanitarian intervention, free trade, regional integration and so on (Whitworth 2004). Implementing gender mainstreaming has rarely led to serious questioning of liberal institutionalist norms and how they may privilege masculine agency and reinforce gendered inequalities in power and resources in the market, state and civil society.

Institutional politics and analysis are important for understanding why gender mainstreaming takes the forms it does in particular institutional settings and why it is often resisted and its potential to transform power relations compromised. But institutional analysis does not tell us how gender mainstreaming makes meaning in organisational processes and policies. Discursive analysis informed by poststructuralist feminism, however, reveals the changes and continuities in gendered norms in international organisations. It judges the success of mainstreaming as a policy strategy for integrating awareness of gender by whether or not languages and foundational concepts change (Cohn 2008: 194; Woodward 2003). From a discursive perspective, gender inequalities are located in systems of signification and meaning that produce power, not merely in material structures such as the international gendered division of labour. Gender hegemonies are controlled not by

- The United Nations Transitional Administration Mission in East Timor (UNTAET) governed the new independent state between 2000 and 2002. UNTAET followed the United Nations Security Council Resolution 1325 on Women, Peace and Security mandating women's rights to equally participate in all peacebuilding processes. In 2000 the East Timorese Women's Congress' Platform For Action, influenced by the 1995 Beijing Women's Conference, set a goal of at least 30 per cent women in all decision-making bodies to ensure women's representation in the new state. *Rede Feto*, the women's umbrella organisation, made the campaign for gender quotas its first priority for the constitutional assembly elections in 2001.

- However, the UN was internally divided over quotas. The quota debate became 'very fiery' and international in scope. Quotas were supported by CEDAW, UNSC 1325 and the UN special advisor to the Secretary-General on gender, and within UNIFEM and UNDP missions. But senior UN officials in the Electoral Affairs Division (EAD) charged with administering Timor's national elections were strongly opposed to quotas. The EAD outlawed gender quotas as not constituting 'free and fair elections' and threatened to pull out of running Timor-Leste's first elections if they had quotas. This use of coercion influenced the Timorese political elite, who changed their minds, and supported the UNTAET's opposition to gender quotas.

- The decision to oppose quotas illustrates the complex politics of the UN bureaucracy in its efforts to mainstream gender issues. Gender equality strategies may be championed at the top of the bureaucracy and at the grassroots but resisted on the ground by the officials tasked with implementing them. But Timor's quota campaign was not completely lost. Local women advocates convinced senior UN officials that affirmative actions to support and train women candidates were necessary. Without a quota, women candidates were successful in winning 25 per cent of seats in the new parliament (Hall and True 2009).

Figure 19.3 Mainstreaming in UN peacebuilding: championed at the top, resisted on the ground.

specific actors but by socially produced meanings that affect actors' self-understanding and perceived interests (Barnett and Duvall 2005: 20).

International organisations are deeply implicated in the construction and reproduction of hegemonic gender identities and differences through their practices. By making analysis of gender differences a core part of policymaking, gender mainstreaming potentially destabilises existing gendered meanings and masculine hegemonies (Lombardo 2005; Lombardo and Meier 2006; True 2003). For example, mainstreaming in the World Bank has forced a focus in development policy and programming on men's role in the family and their equal responsibility with women for unpaid social reproduction activities (see Chapters 15 and 18). Such a policy shift undermines masculine hegemony in public and private spheres. But at the same time, the treatment of gender equality as means to reducing poverty and expanding markets in developing countries produces new heterosexist norms of gender and family (Bedford 2013; Bergeron 2003). The differential gendered impacts of economic restructuring are addressed not through institutional or structural changes but by individualising the problem as one of appropriate gender relations in the private sphere. The underlying gendered structure of the global market and its dependence on informal household economies – and women's work – goes unquestioned.

Like all discourses, gender mainstreaming challenges some power relations and reproduces others. For example, gender mainstreaming in Asia Pacific Economic Cooperation, a regional trade organisation, empowers agents such as (potential) women entrepreneurs, women exporters, and women leaders but does not address the situation of many working women in an increasingly precarious and feminised labour force in the region. Similarly, in the European Union, gender mainstreaming normalises women's and men's identities as economic subjects. Mainstreaming policies are discursively framed primarily in terms of their benefits for economic growth, employment and development and women and men are viewed in terms of their 'productive potential', or as 'human resources' to be maximised (True 2008a). Gender equality is treated as a policy input rather than a normative ideal and ironically, because budgets have already been 'gender mainstreamed', there is meagre financial support to implement and monitor the strategy (Debusscher and True 2008)! Gender mainstreaming is not so much an advance on previous global and state strategies for achieving gender equality; it merely deploys different forms of power.

Mainstreaming has made small achievements toward breaking down masculine hegemonies and their organisational and policy norms. But the focus on institutional policies and technical procedures for mainstreaming gender equality, that is, official gender training, the focal points, checklists, toolkits, numerical gender-balanced decision making and the like, has often missed much of the big picture of how gendered power operates discursively to reinforce gender injustices.

HAVE WOMEN AND FEMINISM BEEN MAINSTREAMED?

Gender mainstreaming raises the issue of voice – whose voice is present and which agents are silent in the policymaking process? Both discursive and institutionalist feminist approaches are concerned with the voice and participation of women, women's and feminist movements in gender mainstreaming. Women have taken advantage of the new opportunities for visibility and voice that have been created by globalisation and changes in governance structures of states and international organisations (Caglar et al. 2013; Waylen 2006: 569–70).

Women's movements and transnational networks of feminist advocates have actively and visibly sought to mainstream gender issues in international organisations. In the cases of the United Nations Security Council (UNSC) and Asia Pacific Economic Cooperation (APEC), high-level gender mainstreaming mandates were adopted as a result of pressure from women's movements: the UNSC's Women, Peace and Security (WPS) agenda and the APEC Framework for the Integration of Women giving women the right to participate in peace/conflict and economic decision making respectively. The WPS agenda is unique, Carol Cohn (2004: 8) argues, because it was 'both the product of and the armature for a massive mobilisation of women's political energies'. 'Feminist insiders and outsiders at the UN have put tremendous, creative thought and energy into making [Resolution 1325] a living document – an ongoing commitment for the Security Council rather than a one-time rhetorical gesture' (Cohn 2004: 8). Collaboration between feminist advocates and UN officials helped to widely disseminate and raise awareness about that and subsequent SC resolutions' mandate making them meaningful on the ground, in local and international decision making.

From an institutionalist perspective, feminist engagement is a crucial factor in the success of the gender mainstreaming strategy. Where the impetus for mainstreaming comes from women's movements as opposed to institutional diffusion and isomorphism, the implementation process is more likely to be closely monitored and the international organisation held accountable for its commitments. Both the UNSC and APEC have benefited from transnational advocacy networks established to monitor policy implementation. The APEC Framework stresses the need for gender analysis of trade policy at global and national levels. The APEC Women Leaders Network, for instance, advocated formal, measurable accountability mechanisms in APEC such as the use of gender criteria[1] in the selection and approval for funding of APEC projects, adopted by APEC in 2002 (True 2008d). Thus, mainstreaming mandates can provide an ongoing political opportunity structure for making international organisations accountable for upholding women's rights and for building alliances inside and outside institutional power.

From a discursive perspective, the construction of gendered identities and subjects through mainstreaming processes is most important (Cohn 2008: 194). Carol Cohn (2008) and Laura Shepherd (2008a) both analyse the framing of gender mainstreaming in United Nations Security Resolution 1325. Cohn and Shepherd both argue that the conceptual framing of the Resolution both contests and conforms to the conventional rules and discursive practices of the UN Security Council. On the one hand, the mainstreaming of gender analysis in 1325 is a radical departure making women central to national and international security. As Shepherd (2008: 389) states: 'the significance of asking that the "actions and operations" of the UNSC be undertaken with gendered sensitivity is great' given the historic male dominance of international peace and security policy. On the other hand, however, gender mainstreaming is represented as the mere inclusion of women's issues: 'women's role in peacebuilding', 'the protection of women', 'women and girls affected by armed conflict' (Shepherd 2008: 390; see also Radmani 2005 for similar analysis of gender mainstreaming in the UN human rights regime). Women are never perpetrators of violence but 'objects of protective action' occupying civilian space. Moreover, men are explicitly the power holders in the UNSC rules of procedure (Shepherd 2008: 395). This gendered construction denies women the agency extended by the WPS agenda while perpetuating the feminisation of peace, and pacification of women, that is detrimental to both. As well as treating women as objects rather than subjects of decision making, the WPS agenda is silent about 'the gender constructs that underwrite war-making' (Cohn 2008: 198) and the political–economic structures of gendered inequality that make women especially vulnerable to violence in war and post-conflict (True 2012).

CONCLUSION

This chapter began with the question as to whether the mainstreaming of gender equality objectives has silenced or made issues of gendered power and domination more or less salient in international relations? I can now answer that question. Gender mainstreaming has not brought the revolution in gender relations or global governance that feminists hoped for. Yet it is naïve to expect bureaucratic structures with all their pathologies and power relationships to deliver anything more than incremental change that precipitates an ongoing process of reform and contestation. Institutionalist and discursive perspectives on gender mainstreaming agree on this point.

Feminist analyses give us crucial insights into the limitations of mainstreaming and its potential as a strategy for political transformation when harnessed by feminist advocates and deployed in specific institutions and local contexts. In some international organisations, such as the European Union and the World Bank, gender mainstreaming has conformed to a technocratic model where bureaucrats are the main actors relatively disconnected from women's activism in civil society (Daly 2005: 447). But gender mainstreaming at the international level has also involved significant feminist engagement as in the cases of the UNSC Women, Peace and Security agenda and APEC's Framework for the Integration of Women. Women and men's participation and advocacy is critical to the success of gender mainstreaming at the global level. International organisations are often places of masculine dominance and bureaucratic myopia with limited democratic accountability to broader publics. Ultimately therefore, the capacity of these institutions to progress awareness of gender inequalities and differences in their work and contribute to transformation in gender relations rests on the political knowledge and pressure of movements for global gender justice.

Questions for further debate

1. Does gender mainstreaming mean more than adding women to existing policies and programmes?
2. How does change in organisational processes [toward recognition of gender differences] lead to change in policy outcomes [toward greater gender equality]?
3. What does it mean to be successful in mainstreaming gender? What criteria or indicators would you use to measure the impact (positive or negative) of gender mainstreaming in an international institution or issue area such as security or trade?
4. Consider one case of an international organisation that has adopted gender mainstreaming. What has been the impact of working for gender mainstreaming inside the organisation on the social movements or advocacy networks outside, who initiated it?
5. Which is more likely to bring about transformation in global gender inequality – gender mainstreaming or an equal rights approach? Why?

Sources for further reading and research

Bedford, K. (2013) 'Economic Governance and the Regulation of Intimacy in Gender and Development: Lessons from the World Bank's Programming', in E. Caglar, E. Prügl and S. Zwingel (eds), *Feminist Strategies in International Governance*, London and New York: Routledge, 233–248.

Krook, M.-L. and J. True (2012) 'Rethinking the Life Cycles of International Norms: The United Nations and the Global Promotion of Gender Equality', *European Journal of International Relations*, 18(1): 103–27.

Lombardo, E. and P. Meier (2006) 'Gender Mainstreaming in the EU: Incorporating a Feminist Reading?', *European Journal of Women's Studies*, 13(2): 151–66.

Prügl, E. (2009) 'Does Gender Mainstreaming Work? Feminist Engagements with the German Agricultural State', *International Feminist Journal of Politics*, 11(2): 174–95.

True, J. and M. Mintrom (2001) 'Transnational Networks and Policy Diffusion: The Case of Gender Mainstreaming', *International Studies Quarterly*, 45: 27–57.

Note

1 These criteria include whether or not a project will have an impact on gender equality, and whether or not it includes women and men as project participants.

CHAPTER 20

International criminal law

Rosemary Grey

LEARNING OUTCOMES

Upon completion, readers should be able to:

- Understand what international criminal law is and where it is applied.
- Understand how sexual and gender-based crimes can constitute crimes under international criminal law.
- Engage in debates about the strengths and limitations of international criminal law as a response to sexual and gender-based violence.

INTRODUCTION

International criminal law (ICL) is the subset of international law under which individual people can be prosecuted for certain crimes, such as genocide, war crimes, crimes against humanity (see Figure 20.1). By curbing impunity for these crimes, ICL seeks to contribute to international peace and security, deter future atrocities, and provide justice and redress to the 'victims'.[1] The first prosecutions under ICL took place in the wake of World War II (WWII), and after a hiatus during the Cold War, prosecutions have continued in a number of international institutions, most notably United Nations' (UN's) *ad hoc* tribunals for Yugoslavia and Rwanda, and the International Criminal Court (ICC).

While it is not possible to present a detailed legal analysis of these crimes here, it is useful to highlight the key features of each:

– 'Genocide' refers to certain acts enumerated in the 1948 Genocide Convention, when committed with the intent to destroy a national, ethnic, racial or religious group.

– 'War crimes' means violations of war, as defined in the 1949 Geneva Conventions and elsewhere.

– 'Crimes against humanity' refers to certain crimes when committed as part of widespread or systematic attacks against a civilian population. The ICTY requires that the crimes must be committed in an armed conflict in order to constitute crimes against humanity, however, there is no such requirement in the ICTR, ICC or SCSL (Cryer et al. 2010: 235).

Figure 20.1 Genocide, war crimes and crimes against humanity.

The situations in which ICL applies include armed conflicts, widespread or systematic attacks on the civilian population, and genocides. As the feminist literature on ICL emphasizes, these situations typically involve very high levels of sexual and gender-based violence. Yet sexual and gender-based violence was largely overlooked in the early years of ICL. It was not until the 1990s that ICL emerged as a key site for the prosecution of sexual and gender-based violence, and trial records began to reflect the many ways in which wars are waged on gendered bodies. These changes have been the subject of much discussion, and often celebration, in the feminist literature on ICL. However, feminist scholars generally recognize that ICL is an incomplete response to sexual and gender-based violence, and acknowledge the necessity of further legal and non-legal interventions.[2]

This chapter summarizes and builds on the feminist literature on ICL, by critically examining the prosecution of sexual and gender-based violence under ICL from WWII onwards. As with any historical account it is necessarily selective, focusing on key trials and triumphs. However, consistent with a feminist approach to research, it also pays close attention to the gaps and silences around sex, sexuality, and gender. The chapter is divided into three sections. Section one maps the increasing visibility of sexual and gender-based violence under ICL from Nuremberg to today. Section two highlights some relevant themes and questions from recent cases in the ICC. Section three critically reflects on ICL as a response to sexual and gender-based violence, in light of the historical and contemporary issues discussed in the previous two sections.

SEXUAL AND GENDER-BASED VIOLENCE UNDER ICL

Sexual violence is closely connected with conflict and genocide, and is therefore an important issue for ICL. Sexual violence is used as a tool of dominance, destruction, humiliation and retaliation, and has been widely regarded as one of the spoils of war (MacKinnon 2009; see also Chapters 13 and 14). Rape, in particular, is often the weapon of choice, as 'even machetes are expensive compared to one implement that's totally free: the human body' (Axe and Hamilton 2013: ix). Gender-based violence, meaning violence that targets a particular gender, is also common in conflict situations. For example in the 1995 Srebrenica massacre, in Bosnia Herzegovina, more than 7,000 civilian Bosnian men of combatant age were killed in the context of ethnic cleansing. These men were targeted because of their gender, intersecting of course with their age and ethnicity (Brammertz and Jarvis 2010: 97; Chinkin 2009: 75). Gender-based violence often overlaps with sexual violence, such an in the 1991–1999 civil war in Sierra Leone during which thousands of women and girls were abducted by rebel forces and made into 'bush wives', who were required to provide sexual and domestic services for their 'husbands' (Oosterveld 2011: 65). These are just two examples of sexual and gender-based violence that have been addressed under ICL in recent years. ICL has not, however, always paid as much attention to sexual and gender-based violence as is warranted.

While the idea of ICL predates WWII, the military tribunals established by the allied victors after WWII were the earliest examples of ICL in practice. The first, the 1945 International Military Tribunal ('Nuremberg Tribunal'), had jurisdiction over the major war criminals of Germany, while the second, the 1946 International Military Tribunal for the Far East ('Tokyo Tribunal') tried the major war criminals of Japan. To their supporters, these tribunals represented a just alternative to summary executions, and were a sign that impunity for mass crimes would no longer be tolerated. To their detractors, however, the tribunals represented an example of 'victor's justice' (Cryer et al. 2010: 113–14, 118–19). The tribunals have also been criticized by feminist scholars, on the grounds that they overlooked some very serious sexual and gender-based violence crimes.

The charter of the Nuremberg Tribunal, which set out the crimes in that Tribunal's jurisdiction, did not list any sexual or gender-based crimes. This silence was replicated in the Tribunal's judgment, which made no reference to sexual or gender-based crimes, although prosecutors had presented evidence of mass rape at trial (Kirk McDonald 2000: 10). The judgment also made no reference to the persecution of homosexuals under Nazi rule, although between 10,000 and 15,000 homosexual men were reportedly sent to concentration camps and subjected to murder, forced labor, and medical experiments aimed at altering their sexuality (IMT Judgment, cf. Bureleigh and Wipperman 1991: 182–96; Heger 1972). Following the Nuremberg Tribunal, lower level German nationals were prosecuted in occupied Germany, under Control Council Law No 10. This Law recognized rape as a crime against humanity, however no individuals were prosecuted under this provision (Kirk MacDonald 2010: 10).

The charter of the Tokyo Tribunal, like that of the Nuremberg Tribunal, made no mention of sexual or gender-based crimes. However, this Tribunal used its general war crimes provisions to prosecute sexual violence, namely the rape and murder of 20,000 civilian women by Japanese forces in Nanking. In its description of these events, which it referred to as the 'Rape of Nanking', the Tribunal noted that these murders commonly involved the insertion of bayonets and other weapons into the vagina, types of violence that could readily be characterized as sexual violence (IMTFE Judgment 49, 604–49, 613). The Tribunal also noted that 20,000 men of military age were 'bound with their hands behind their backs, and marched outside the walls of the city where they were killed in groups by machine gun fire and with bayonets' (IMTFE Judgment 49, 606), an example of gender-based violence that echoes the facts, although exceeds the scale, of the Srebrenica massacre.

While the recognition of these crimes represented a positive step towards accountability for sexual and-gender based crimes, the Tokyo Tribunal's coverage of sexual and gender-based violence was far from complete. In particular, the Tribunal has been criticized for ignoring the Japanese military's abduction of 200,000 civilian women from occupied territories, for use as sexual slaves. The Tribunal's failure to address this violence is damning not just because of the numbers of victims, but because the allies were apparently aware of this practice, yet did not raise the issue before the Tribunal (Copelon 2000: 221–23; Kirk McDonald 2000: 10). Reflecting on this silence, Rhonda Copelon suggests that 'the notion of women as the "booty" of war and the entitlement of fighting men was never in question' (2000: 223).

In 1948 the UN General Assembly directed the International Law Commission to assess the possibility of establishing a permanent international criminal court. There would be little progress on this front for 50 years, due to the deterioration of relationships between UN member states during the Cold War. However, the post-war period also prompted the adoption of several instruments that helped define the 'core' international crimes, most notably the 1948 Genocide Convention, which defined the crime of genocide, and 1949 Geneva Conventions (subsequently extended by the 1977 Additional Protocols), which define many of the war crimes under ICL.

The positioning of sexual and gender-based violence in these post-WWII Conventions is viewed as problematic by many feminist scholars. The Genocide Convention, which entered force in 1951, makes no reference to sexual or gender-based violence. The Geneva Conventions refer to some forms of sexual and gender-based violence, however the terminology presents concerns. Rather than being enumerated as a 'grave breach', a designation that attracts individual criminal liability, Article 26 of Geneva Convention IV (on the protection of civilians) states that 'women shall be especially protected against any attack on their honor, in particular against rape, enforced prostitution, or any form of indecent assault'. This language of protection, honour and indecency is largely replicated in the 1977 Additional Protocols. Feminist scholars have criticized these provisions as they re-inscribe ideas about women's passivity, vulnerability, and need for protection. Moreover, the references to honour and indecency are seen to focus on the shame the attack brings to the woman's family and community, rather the violation of the woman's own sexual and bodily autonomy (Chappell 2003: 6–7; Charlesworth and Chinkin 2000: 314; Copelon 2000: 221). The provisions also render male victims invisible, a practice that persists, to some extent, in peace and security discourses today (Grey and Shepherd 2012).

The 1990s was a key decade in the history of ICL. With the Cold War at an end, and spurred into action by the crises in the former Yugoslavia and Rwanda, the UN Security Council created two *ad hoc* criminal tribunals under Chapter VII of the UN Charter: the International Criminal Tribunal for the former Yugoslavia (ICTY) in 1993 and the International Criminal Tribunal for Rwanda (ICTR) in 1994.

While many saw these tribunals as a sign that ICL could work in practice, others criticized the UN for failing to prevent or contain the violence in the first place (e.g. Schiff 2008: 42–44). In any case, it was clear that these *ad hoc* tribunals would not serve the deterrent purpose of a permanent institution, and that there jurisdiction was limited to a specific time and place. Thus, efforts to create a permanent international criminal court continued, culminating in the adoption of the Rome Statute of the International Criminal Court in 1998 ('the ICC Statute'). The Statute entered force on July 1, 2002, after being ratified by 60 States Parties, and the number of States Parties has doubled since then.

While the ICTY, ICTR and ICC share many common features, there are some key structural differences between these institutions (see Figure 20.2). In addition, these institutions differ in their treatment of sexual and gender-based violence. The ICTY and ICTR Statutes recognize a very restricted range of sexual or gender-based crimes: both Statutes list rape as a crime against humanity, and the ICTR Statute lists rape, enforced prostitution, and indecent assault as war crimes as well. However, prosecutors and judges in these tribunals, often encouraged by women's rights activists, have addressed a broad range of sexual and gender-based crimes by highlighting the sexualized or gendered dimensions of other crimes in those Statutes such as genocide, torture and enslavement (Askin 2003: 317–46; Brady 2012; Brammertz and Jarvis 2010: 101). Importantly, these tribunals have addressed sexual violence against men as well as women (Grey and Shepherd 2012: 126), although they have arguably been more effective at the latter than the former (Sivakumaran 2010: 271–75).

By contrast, the ICC Statute codifies a wide range of sexual and gender-based crimes. It lists rape, sexual slavery, enforced prostitution, forced pregnancy, enforced sterilization, and 'any other form of sexual violence' as war crimes and crimes against humanity, and recognizes persecution on the grounds of gender as a crime against humanity, for the first time in ICL (Articles 7(1)(g); 7(1)(h); 8(2)(b)(xxii); 8(2)(e)(vi)). These newly recognized crimes are important symbolically as well as practically, as they enhance the visibility of sexual and gender-based violence under ICL, while enabling the prosecution of a broader spectrum of crimes. The implementation of these crimes has presented some teething problems, but has also yielded results, as the case studies that follow illustrate.

International crimes are also increasingly being prosecuted under domestic courts, in accordance with the principle of complementarity (see Figure 20.2). The UN has also supported the creation of several 'quasi-international' courts, such as the Special Court for Sierra Leone in 2002. While these institutions are important sites for the prosecution of sexual and gender-based violence, there is unfortunately not enough space to discuss them in this chapter.

CASE STUDIES FROM THE ICC

Since commencing operations in 2002, the ICC has opened investigations in Uganda, the Democratic Republic of Congo, Sudan, the Central African Republic, Kenya, Libya, Ivory Coast and Mali, and the Prosecutor's Office has commenced

---

Relationship to the UN

The ITCY and ICTR are UN courts, while the ICC is not. Indeed, only two of the five permanent veto powers on the UN Security Council (France and the United Kingdom) are parties to the ICC Statute. That said, the ICC is not insulated from UN politics, as the Security Council has the power to refer situations to the ICC, order the deferral of proceedings, and encourage states to cooperate with the ICC by executing arrest warrants, facilitating investigations, etc. Aside from Security Council referrals, the ICC's jurisdiction can be triggered by a referral from a State Party to the ICC Statute, or by ICC Prosecutor.

Relationship to national courts

A second key difference is that while the ICTY and ICTR have primacy over national jurisdictions, the ICC is a court of last resort. It can only try a case if the state has not initiated proceedings or is unwilling or unable to conduct those proceedings genuinely. This principle, known as the principle of complementarity, is intended to respect state sovereignty while ensuring that international crimes do not go unpunished.

Role of victims

In the ICTY and ICTR, victims are external to the proceedings, except when called as witnesses for the prosecution or the defence. By contrast, the ICC Statute allows victims (or their legal representatives) to participate in the proceedings in their own right, and sets up a scheme though which victims may receive reparations following a conviction.

See UNSC Resolution 827 (1993); UNSC Resolution 955 (1994); ICC Statute, Preamble; Articles 12–17, 68, 75

Figure 20.2 Key differences between the ICTY, ICTR and ICC.

---

preliminary examinations in other situations both on, and outside, the African continent. While space precludes a systematic analysis of all of the cases arising out of these situations, it is useful to pull out a few key themes from cases involving sexual and gender-based violence, and consider what these cases signal for the continuing development of ICL.

New crimes, new challenges

As noted earlier, the ICC Statute codifies, for the first time under ICL, the crimes of 'other forms of sexual violence' and persecution on the grounds of 'gender'. These novel crimes have been the subject of discussion in some recent cases before the Court. In 2008, the Prosecutor put forward a charge of 'any other form of sexual violence', as a crime against humanity in the *Bemba* case, from the Central African Republic. The charge was based on evidence that members of the accused's armed group had ordered people to undress in public, in order to humiliate them (Arrest Warrant Decision at [39]). One might have expected the pre-trial judges to confirm the charge, given that the ICTR had previously defined forced nudity as an example of sexual violence (*Akayesu* Trial Judgment at [10A]). However, the judges found that the forced nudity was not sufficiently grave to constitute 'other forms of sexual violence' as a crime against humanity under the ICC Statute, because the Statute requires that the violence be 'of comparable gravity' to the other enumerated crimes, namely rape, sexual slavery, enforced prostitution, forced pregnancy and enforced sterilization. In the judge's view, the alleged acts of forced nudity did not satisfy that gravity threshold (Arrest Warrant Decision at [40]; [63]).

The crime of 'other forms of sexual violence' was discussed again in 2012 in the *Kenyatta* case, where the Prosecutor put forward a charge of 'other forms of sexual violence' as a crime against humanity. This time, the charge was based on the forced circumcisions and penile amputations of Luo (ethnic group) men during the 2007–2008 post-election violence in Kenya. The Prosecutor submitted that these acts 'weren't just attacks on men's sexual organs as such but were intended as attacks on men's identities as men within their society and were designed to destroy their masculinity' (Confirmation of Charges Decision at [264]). The pre-trial judges refused to confirm the charge, finding these acts did not constitute 'sexual violence' for the purposes of the ICC Statute (at [265]).

In reaching this conclusion, the judges explained that 'not every act of violence which targets parts of the body commonly associated with sexuality should be considered an act of sexual violence', a comment which echoed the ICTR's earlier statement that '[s]exual violence is not limited to physical invasion of the human body and may include acts which do not involve penetration or even physical contact' (*Akayesu* Trial Judgment at [688]). This non-physiological approach to defining 'sexual violence' has some clear advantages: it is flexible, and it leaves space for a consideration of the sociology and psychology of sexual violence. However, it also leaves the meaning of the term somewhat ambiguous, which is challenging in a legal context where consistency is important and where crimes must be clearly defined.

After finding that the forced circumcisions and penile amputations did not amount to 'sexual violence', the judges concluded 'instead, it appears from the evidence that the acts were motivated by ethnic prejudice', and suggested the allegations be incorporated into the more generic charge of 'other inhumane acts' (at [266] and [270]). In characterizing the acts in terms of ethnic prejudice 'instead' of sexual violence, the judges suggested that these two forms of violence are mutually exclusive concepts. Such a view, if indeed that was the judges' view, sits uncomfortably with an intersectional approach to gender analysis. It also sits uncomfortably with previous cases where sexual violence has been linked to ethnic politics, such as the *Bashir* case, where the ICC found that rape was committed with the intent of destroying the Fur, Masalit and Zaghawa ethnic groups (Second Arrest Warrant Decision at [30]) or the *Akayesu* case, where the ICTR found that sexual violence was committed as part of the Tutsi genocide (*Akayesu* Trial Judgment at [731–734]). The relationship between sexual and ethnic violence is likely to be considered further in upcoming cases, many of which involve allegations of both kinds of violence.

The crime of 'gender' persecution was applied for the first time in the *Mbarushimana* case, which related to the conflict in the Democratic Republic of Congo. In his arrest warrant application, the prosecutor referred to the commission of persecutory acts by the FDLR (an armed group) against women and men affiliated with the national armed forces, 'on the basis of their gender' (Arrest Warrant Application, Count 11). These acts included torture and rape, and other inhumane acts. This first attempt to apply the crime of 'gender' persecution led to some interesting analysis about the links between culturally constructed gender identity and violence, with the prosecution arguing:

> The rape of women and girls is carried out because they, as females, are easily targeted and can be put forth as objects of FDLR domination vis-à-vis the men in their families. Men and boys, who for example are forced to rape, suffer from persecution on the basis of gender, targeted to show FDLR dominance through violating their manhood in this manner.
>
> (at [97])

The pre-trial judges issued the arrest warrant, with the charge of 'gender' persecution on it (Arrest Warrant Decision at [27]). However, there was no further analysis of this crime, as the prosecutor subsequently changed the charge to one of persecution on the basis of 'political affiliation' (Document Containing the Charges, Count 13). The case was terminated soon after, because the pre-trial judges were not satisfied that the suspect provided the necessary contribution to the crimes (Confirmation of Charges Decision at [292]).

A further question around the crime of 'gender' persecution, which the Court is yet to rule on, is whether the crime covers persecution on the grounds of sexual orientation. 'Gender' is defined in the ICC Statute as 'the two sexes, male and female, within the context of society' (Article 7(3)). Some scholars argue that persecution on the grounds of 'gender', as so defined, would necessarily include persecution on the grounds of sexual orientation (Bedont 1999: 187–88; Copelon 2000: 237). Others regard the matter as more uncertain (Oosterveld 2005: 76–79). An affirmative answer to this question would enhance ICL's capacity to protect people from persecution, and promote the rights of LGBTI people more generally, and satisfy the Court's statutory requirement to interpret the Statute in accordance with 'internationally recognized human rights' (Article 21(3)). There is no guarantee, however, that the Court will adopt this progressive interpretation of 'gender,' or consider LGBTI rights to be 'internationally recognized human rights'.

Sexual exploitation of child soldiers

In 2012, the ICC handed down its first judgment, in the case of *Lubanga*. This case, along with some recent cases from the Special Court for Sierra Leone, was the first case under ICL to consider the issue of child soldiers. The accused, the leader of an armed group in the Democratic Republic of Congo, had been charged with the war crimes of 'conscripting or enlisting children under the age of fifteen years into armed forces or groups or using them to participate actively in hostilities'.

When these charges were first made public in March 2006, communities in the affected region reacted with disappointment. This disappointment was not directed to the child soldier crimes, per se. Rather, the problem was that Lubanga's group had allegedly committed other serious crimes, including sexual violence crimes, which were not reflected in the charges. Several NGOS had pressed the Prosecutor to expand the charges to reflect the fuller picture of criminality, but the Prosecutor declined to do so at the pre-trial stage (Avocats Sans Frontières et al. 2006; Human Rights Watch 2008a: 62; WIGJ 2007: 33). Instead, the prosecution highlighted evidence of sexual violence at trial, arguing that rape was a factor in the conscription of the female child soldiers, and part of their use in hostilities. The victims' representatives sought a recharacterization of the charges to reflect these emerging allegations of sexual violence, however the Court found this was not possible under the rules of procedure.

After a three-year trial the accused was convicted, but not in relation to sexual violence. While the Majority acknowledged the evidence of sexual violence against the girl soldiers, it declined to hold the accused liable for this violence. In Majority's view, the sexual violence fell outside the scope of the charges, as presented by the Prosecutor at the pre-trial stage (Trial Judgment at [629]–[630]). Judge Benito disagreed with the Majority on this point. She found that the combatant's use of the children's bodies was 'encoded in the charges' (Separate Opinion at [21]), and argued that:

> By failing to deliberately include within the legal concept of 'use to participate actively in the hostilities' the sexual violence and other ill-treatment suffered by girls and boys, the Majority of the Chamber is making this critical aspect of the crime invisible.
>
> (at [16])

While Judge Benito's separate opinion did not change the outcome of the case, it lent support to the argument that sexual violence can play a part in the war crimes of conscripting, enlistment and using child soldiers. Such support can be useful in a legal context, where arguments are judged on their source as well as their content. The Prosecutor's Office may decide to avail itself of this argument in future cases where the accused is charged with conscripting, enlisting or using child soldiers.

Sexual violence against men

In official UN documents on sexual violence, and in peace and security discourses more generally, it is often implied that sexual violence affects women and girls only (Sivakumaran 2007, 2010). This discursive practice re-inscribes ideas about women's passivity and vulnerability, while denying male victims' access to justice and to treatment (Grey and Shepherd 2012). For those reasons, it is important that ICL addresses male as well as female experiences of sexual and gender-based violence. This is not suggest that charges of sexual violence should *always* achieve gender parity; the allegations must follow the evidence. However, a commitment to investigating both male and female experiences of sexual violence, and incorporating both experiences into the charges where the evidence permits, is an important part of gender justice.

To that end, it is positive to see that the ICC has considered sexual violence against men in several recent cases. For example in *Mbarushima*, the prosecution referred to women being raped, as well as men being forced to commit rape. In *Bemba,* both male and female witnesses have testified about their experiences of rape, and the allegations of forced nudity involved victims of both sexes as well. However, violence against men and boys that could conceivably be regarded sexual violence is not always regarded as such. The *Kenyatta* case, where it was found that forced circumcision and penile amputation did not constitute sexual violence, is a case in point.

The *Lubanga* case is also relevant in this regard. There was some discussion of sexual violence against boy soldiers at trial, namely, that boy soldiers were forced to commit rape in the context of hostilities. For instance, in his opening statements, Prosecutor Moreno Ocampo told the Court that 'young boys were instructed to rape' (Transcript, January 26, 2009, p11) and Prosecution Witness 8, an ex-child soldier, testified that he had been instructed to commit rape and had done so once (Transcript February 25, 2009, p38). The prosecution cited Witness 8's testimony in its closing brief, but not as an example of sexual violence. Rather, the prosecution argued that the witness's willingness to admit to rape in open court was a sign of his credibility (Prosecution's Closing Brief at [427]). In their final judgment, the trial judges deemed Witness 8 an unreliable witness, and did not make any reference to sexual violence against boy soldiers (Trial Judgment at [479]). It remains to be seen whether similar evidence will come forward in future cases, and whether it will be characterized as sexual violence.

PROSECUTING SEXUAL AND GENDER-BASED VIOLENCE UNDER ICL: CRITICAL REFLECTIONS

Sexual and gender-based violence has moved from the peripheries to the centre of ICL in the last two decades. Sexual and gender-based violence have become more visible in legal instruments, and trial records are beginning to reflect the strategic as well as the opportunistic motivations for sexual and gender-based violence. The prosecution of these crimes under ICL evinces the international community's welcome, albeit long overdue, commitment to ending impunity for sexual and gender-based violence.

However, this progress is by no means linear, and significant impunity gaps remain. Prosecutors have at times declined to bring charges of sexual and gender-based violence. Evidence can be difficult to obtain, as victims of sexual violence may be reluctant to come forward due to fear of social stigmatization. Judges have sometimes resisted reading sexual and gender-based violence into the definitions of crimes where there is scope to do so, and even the most gender-sensitive judges will sometimes come up against the limits of the law. In addition, political dynamics outside the courtroom can thwart the best efforts to prosecute all crimes, including sexual and gender-based crimes. In particular, a lack of cooperation from states can obstruct prosecutions under ICL, as the international courts and tribunals rely on states to execute arrest warrants, facilitate investigations, etc. In the face of these challenges, the successful investigation and prosecution of sexual and gender-based violence across a range of institutions in recent years is a remarkable achievement.

Feminist actors have not only welcomed the increasing accountability for sexual and gender-based violence under ICL, they have been active agents of this progress. For example feminist activists and scholars, acting as the Women's Caucus for Gender Justice, participated in the negotiations over the ICC Statute (Stearns 1999), and feminist lawyers have served as Gender Advisors to Prosecutors in the in the ICTY, ICTR and ICC (MacKinnon 2009; Sellers 2009). However, feminist scholars, including many of those who have engaged most actively with ICL, have also offered some thoughtful critiques of ICL as a response to sexual and gender-based violence.

Kiran Grewal has argued 'there is an urgent need for women's rights advocates to rethink their endorsement of ICL's approach to sexual violence' (Grewal 2010: 78). Building on Copelon's earlier critique of ICL, she argues that the increasing visibility of conflict and genocide-related sexual violence in ICL may have negative consequences for the portrayal of sexual violence in the private sphere (Copelon 1995; Grewal 2010). In particular, ICL reinforces a binary between sexual violence in conflict or genocide, on the one hand, and sexual violence in everyday life, on the other, while obscuring the commonalities between these equally egregious phenomena. By treating sexual violence in situations of genocide and conflict as exceptional, ICL marginalizes the gender politics that inform sexual violence in 'peacetime' as well as in war.

A second line of critique relates to way that victims of sexual violence are treated in criminal proceedings, when they appear as witnesses for the prosecution. Relating one's history of sexual violence in a courtroom can be a very difficult experience, due to the nature of the crime, PTSD and other disorders, and social taboos around sexual violence. Victims may struggle to present a consistent account, particularly under cross-examination. As a result, victims of sexual violence may feel re-traumatised rather than empowered by their day in court (Franke 2006; Mertus 2004).

Personnel in international courts are generally aware of these issues, and make a concerted effort to interact sensitively with victims of sexual violence. In addition, there are rules in place to protect victims from unnecessary trauma. For example, Article 68(2) of the ICC Statute allows for victims to testify *in camera* (as opposed to in open court), and Article 68(3) allows victims to participate in the proceedings without being called by the prosecution or defense, a measure intended to give victims an independent voice in the proceedings. However, these provisions do not remove all the obstacles that may contribute to a victim's sense of disenfranchisement. Victims testifying for the prosecution or defense have little control over their own story, as they will be directed to speak about those issues most relevant to the case. As Julie Mertus observes, 'the legal process does not permit witnesses to tell their own coherent narrative; it chops their stories into digestible parts, selects a handful of parts and sorts and refines them to create a new narrative' (2004: 113).

A third line of critique relates to ICL's limited capacity to address the underlying causes of sexual and gender-based violence. As feminist scholars have cautioned, that legal responses to sexual and gender-based violence will have little effect, if the economic, political and cultural structures that cause and compound that violence remain intact. As Copelon observes:

> We cannot lay the ground for peace and security and exclude from consideration either global policies that breed economic insecurity or insecurity about identity, or the role of patriarchal and misogynist culture in everyday life.
>
> (Copelon 2000: 240)

Acknowledging these limitations on the utility of ICL does not mean that international criminal law is completely redundant, however, it reaffirms the importance of promoting gender justice outside of international courts and tribunals, as well as within them.

Questions for further debate and research

1. What are the costs and benefits of moving away from a conception of sexual and gender-based violence as 'violence against women'?
2. Should the ICC recognize persecution of people on the grounds of sexual orientation as a form of gender persecution? Is this an appropriate characterization of that type of persecution, and how might the recognition of this crime affect international support for the ICC?
3. What are the advantages and disadvantages of prosecuting sexual violence in international as opposed to national courts?
4. What are the advantages and disadvantages of prosecuting sexual violence rather than addressing this violence through other public institutions such as truth commissions?
5. The ICC Statute requires states to select a 'fair representation of male and female judges'. Does gender parity matter for judicial appointments in international courts?

Sources for further reading and research

Chappell, L. (2003) 'Women, Gender and International Institutions: Exploring New Opportunities at the International Criminal Court', *Policy Organisation and Society*, 22(1): 3–25.

Charlesworth, H. and C. Chinkin (2000) *The Boundaries of International Law*, Manchester: Manchester University Press.

Copelon, R. (2000) 'Gender Crimes as War Crimes: Integrating Crimes against Women into International Criminal Law', *McGill Law Journal*, 46: 217–40.

Engle, S. (2006) *Human Rights and Gender Violence: Translating International Law in Local Justice*, Chicago, IL: University of Chicago Press.

Oosterveld, V. (2011) 'The Gender Jurisprudence of the Special Court for Sierra Leone: Progress in the Revolutionary United Front Judgments', *Cornell International Law Journal*, 44: 49–74.

Notes

1 The term 'victim' is arguably problematic because it conflicts with some people's self-identification as 'survivors' and because it presupposes the existence of the crime before the charges have been proved beyond reasonable doubt, contrary to the presumption of innocence. However, the term is used throughout this chapter, consistent with the language used in the institutions being discussed.

2 See, for example, Bedont and Hall Martinez (1999), Chappell (2003), Charlesworth and Chinkin (2000), Copelon (1995, 2000) and Grewal (2010).

CHAPTER 21

Peacekeeping

Nadine Puechguirbal[1]

LEARNING OUTCOMES

Upon completion, readers should be able to:

- Understand the consequences of a lack of gender perspective in peacekeeping operations (the cost of ignoring gender).
- Understand the broader picture of peacekeeping operations within the women, peace, and security agenda.
- Suggest innovative ways to redress a lack of gender perspective in peacekeeping operations.

INTRODUCTION

The first UN peacekeeping operations deployed during the Cold War area were mainly composed of military personnel in charge of observing compliance with ceasefires agreed between former warring states. In the 1990s, the concept of peacekeeping evolved to encompass larger missions, including a civilian component, with a mandate to implement peace accords between intra-state stakeholders. Today's multidimensional peacekeeping operations in post-conflict situations are involved in a wide range of activities: restoring peace in a volatile security environment; organizing elections; disarming and reintegrating former combatants; monitoring human rights; consolidating the rule of law; working on good governance and so on.

Although conflict is a profoundly gendered experience, gender issues have not been part of mandates of peacekeeping missions throughout the world until recently. Actually, the situation started to change only after Resolution 1325 on 'Women, Peace and Security' was adopted by the UN Security Council on October 31, 2000; among other very important points, the resolution acknowledges the contribution of women in peace and security, reaffirms their roles in conflict prevention and resolution and calls for the inclusion of a gender entity in peacekeeping operations. However, in spite of progress achieved towards the inclusion of a gender perspective in peacekeeping operations, structural obstacles remain within the UN system that prevents a gender-informed approach on peace and security issues. 'Although the existence of SCR 1325 and gender mainstreaming guidelines for post-conflict contexts provide useful frameworks, it is not clear that anything other than tokenism results, and the central problem of bridging security and development with a gender-sensitive understanding of security is not addressed' (Barnes 2006: 24). In the UN language of most official documents and instruments, women are mainly portrayed as victims in need of protection and always associated with children, which prevents them from playing a more active role in political processes in post-conflict situations. Despite its groundbreaking approach, Resolution 1325 uses this langue of victimization too, thus limiting the scope of its implementation. As a result, peace and security issues are defined within the framework of a hypermasculine environment that participates in the remilitarization of the post-conflict society and prevents the development of a sustainable peace. Furthermore, a conflation between scarce resources, pressure to streamline the cost of peacekeeping missions, and an hyper-masculine environment that never really gave gender advisers space to deliver, has led to a major backlash in mainstreaming gender into peacekeeping operations.

GENDER, PEACE AND SECURITY ISSUES

In 2000, former Secretary General Kofi Annan tasked former Foreign Minister from Algeria Lakhdar Brahimi to chair a panel that would review how the UN was conducting operations linked to peace and security. The high-level panel was composed of nine people, including only two women. Although the report from the panel, known as the Brahimi Report was hailed as remarkable for its innovative views on peacekeeping, it was silent on gender-related issues in the field of peace and security. It only mentioned gender as a question of 'fair gender distribution' in UN field missions, thus coming short of an in-depth gender analytical perspective about peace and security: 'After the omission of gender in the Brahimi Report, the time was ripe to push a Security Council resolution on mainstreaming women in peace and security issues that would become binding international law' (Hill et al. 2001: 31).

Resolution 1325 was born partly because of the gender blindness of the Brahimi Report and the limitations of the language it used throughout its lengthy chapters:

> The lack of an integrated gender perspective in this review [the Brahimi Report] fueled NGOs to unite and strategize for greater inclusion and participation of women.

> The coalition of women's organizations contributed recommendations for engendering the Brahimi Report to concerned actors. These include: posting gender advisers at all levels and gender units in peacekeeping operations; requiring gender sensitivity training for all participants in peacekeeping operations; creating a code of conduct for peacekeepers that includes gender issues.
>
> (Hill and Poehlman-Doumbouya 2001: 31)

We must pay attention to language in UN documents, resolutions and peace agreements. Language sets the framework that defines how women are seen and treated in post-conflict environments; it explains why stereotypes – about what men and women are expected to do, what space they should occupy, who legitimately can claim access to and control over resources, who should hold power – are so easily perpetuated and replicated from decision making to grassroots' levels within peacekeeping missions. Most of the resolutions that the UN Security Council and the General Assembly have adopted on different subjects related to peace and security mainly define women as helpless individuals who bear the brunt of war. As victims, women are part of the vulnerable groups, together with the children, the handicapped and the elderly. As the French anthropologist Françoise Héritier explains, we should stop considering that women belong to a minority sociological category like those categories based on age, color, religion, handicap and ethnicity. She writes, 'to consider sex as a sociological variable similar to the other categories means that we tacitly acknowledge the masculine norm of reference' (Héritier 2002: 191).

Furthermore, women are always associated with children in need of protection. This approach clearly removes the agency of women who are not seen as actors in charge of their own lives, but are apprehended through their vulnerabilities, defined as victims, as 'women-and-children' disempowered and dependent on the male members of the community that will provide for them.

As Paula Donovan from the Office of the UN Special Envoy for AIDS in Africa, explains:

> Unlike children and the frail elderly, women aren't naturally in need of protection. But like subjugated groups throughout history, women have been overpowered. Women need protection from the *un*natural order imposed on our universe – the manmade laws, customs, practices and indulgences that rule modern 'civilization.' They have the aptitude, but are denied the wherewithal to devise and construct their own protections.
>
> (Donovan 2006: 4)

As a result, the victimization of women is reinforced through the rhetoric of the 'protected' versus the 'protectors', which is clearly understood by peacekeepers as being part of their mission of bringing back security and stability in the host country. They were briefed about all the atrocities that had been committed by armed groups against the civilian population, especially against the most vulnerable persons in need of protection, namely the 'women-and-children'. The hypermasculine environment of a peacekeeping operation fosters this kind of definition of security that prevents women from being seen as key stakeholders in peace processes, raising their voice at the negotiation table and fully participating in the reconstruction of their post-conflict society:

> For the protectors to wield this public superiority, there must be a certain constructed 'protected.' The protected is the person who is not at ease in the public sphere. The protected's natural habitat is the domestic sphere – that is, the sphere of life where caring matters more than strategizing. Consequently, the protected is feminized insofar as the protected needs somebody who can think strategically and act in her (the protected's) best interests.
>
> (Enloe 2007: 61)

Thus, the first difficulty in integrating a gender perspective into peacekeeping operations lies in overcoming the language barrier for a better understanding of peace and security issues that would not victimize women but would consider them as actors and citizens with rights. Security has always been defined according to the masculine norm of reference that makes women's interests, needs and expectations irrelevant. As Cynthia Enloe observes, 'Militarized masculinity is a model of masculinity that is especially likely to be imagined as requiring a feminine complement that excludes women from full and assertive participation in postwar public life' (Enloe 2002: 23). Indeed, the concept of militarized masculinity is embedded in peacekeeping insofar as uniformed personnel are mainly composed of men who are visible and bound by the manly culture of the organization with its own norms, codes and preconceived ideas about local men and women; they feel powerful as well as rightfully involved in a mission to establish a precarious peace in a country that is recovering from warfare (see Figures 21.1 and 21.2, both of which arose from group work with students at the UN University for Peace; in Figure 21.1, the man is saying 'My wife … a child with big feet' – this is adapted from the Somali saying, 'A woman is a child with big feet').

In male-dominated peacekeeping operations, security revolves around the cessation of hostilities between warring factions, arrest of (male) gang leaders or disarmament of the main rebel groups who are mainly men. There is a belief among peacekeepers that once men with weapons have been overpowered, a general atmosphere of security will prevail for the whole population, including women. There is little understanding of the differential impact of conflict on women and men, boys and girls and the long-term consequences of sexual violence against women that continues to prevail long after war is over because of gender roles entrenched in culture and tradition. As Ann Tickner emphasizes, '[t]he achievement of peace, economic justice, and ecological sustainability is inseparable from overcoming social relations of domination and subordination; genuine security requires not only the absence of war but also the elimination of unjust social relations, including unequal gender relations' (Tickner 1992: 128). Militarized organizations tend to define security as a halt to the fighting whereas ordinary women tend to define it as being safe in their own house or in a refugee camp, feeling safe enough to walk in the streets without fearing of being sexually assaulted. Again according to Ann Tickner, 'women have defined security as the absence of violence, whether it be military, economic or sexual' (Tickner 1992: 66).

Figure 21.1 Gender roles in peacetime: what do women, men, boys and girls do? Group work with students at the UN University for Peace. 'My wife … a child with big feet' is adapted from the Somali saying, 'A woman is a child with big feet'. *Image:* Author.

Figure 21.2 Gender roles in a post-conflict environment: what is the situation for women, men, boys and girls? Group work with students at the UN University for Peace. *Image:* Author.

In the same vein, women's needs are overlooked in the UN Disarmament, Demobilization and Reintegration programs (DDR) because they are seen as not representing an immediate threat to security. Actually, even when women have fought as combatants, there is no room for them in DDR programs that are defined according to the simple motto, 'One man, one weapon.' Vanessa Farr, specialist in gender and DDR issues, confirms that: 'If women do not feel safe or welcomed in a DDR process, they are likely to "self-demobilize" – in other words, to disappear from view without taking advantage of any of the opportunities of demobilization, such as job re-training, healthcare and the like' (Farr 2003: 32). Women ex-combatants will be compelled to demobilize rapidly to reintegrate into the civilian society after a war that has been apprehended as a temporary upheaval, an exceptional moment that allowed women to take up non-traditional roles and use violence. There is pressure from the post-conflict society to come back to a so-called pre-war order, synonymous of peace and order, with narrowly defined gender roles. If the participation of women in war is seen as an incongruity, then little attention will be paid to them in DDR and they will not benefit from all DDR programs that mainly target male ex-combatants. The same situation happens for women who were not soldiers but who played multiples roles in conflict, either as supplier, spy, cook, or sexual slave and had very often to take care of children and the elderly during the fighting. They are not seen as a relevant 'caseload' that could be targeted for assistance in DDR processes because they were not directly associated with guns, although they were victims of the violence produced by those guns.

Interestingly enough, it seems that former male combatants are given priority in reintegration programs because the perception is that they represent a threat to peace and security. In Haiti, male gang members were disarmed after a big military operation in the main slums orchestrated by the peacekeeping mission on the ground. Later on, the mission designed a community violence reduction program that targeted idle young men from the slums, with the aim of empowering them through work. The rationale behind this decision was that if they were employed, they would not be tempted to join gangs and commit acts of violence. Who needed a job at the community level? No assessment was conducted, and more jobs were given to men than to women based only on the assumption that men were more dangerous to the stability of society than women: 'Insecurity that is male on male (for instance, armed militias fighting each other) is more detrimental to political stability and stable governments than male on female violence is' (Enloe and Puechguirbal 2004: 8).

GENDER MAINSTREAMING IN PEACEKEEPING OPERATIONS

As we have seen previously, the wide mobilization of NGOs and other key actors led to the adoption of what has been called the 'historic' Resolution 1325 on 'Women, Peace and Security' on October 31, 2000. Although the resolution mainly stresses the vulnerabilities of women and girls as victims of war instead of emphasizing their agency, it makes visible the key role that women play in conflict resolution as well as in the promotion of peace and security. This visibility would give some leverage to women's organizations in their battle to have their voices heard in peace processes. At the same time, the resolution requests the inclusion of a gender component in peacekeeping missions. Since the adoption of Resolution 1325, the UN Department of Peacekeeping Operations (DPKO) has taken a few initiatives to integrate a gender perspective into its policies, programs and activities, both at the headquarters in New York and in field missions. In addition, whereas a gendered language has been non-existent in the past, there is today a systematic reference to Resolution 1325 in the mandates of peacekeeping missions. For instance, the mandate of the UN Stabilization Mission in Haiti (MINUSTAH) states: '[The Security Council], reaffirming the importance of appropriate expertise on issues relating to gender in peacekeeping operations and post-conflict peacebuilding in accordance with resolution 1325 (2000)' (Security Council Resolution 1702, MINUSTAH 2006).

Following a request by the Security Council that all UN entities develop a strategy for the implementation of Resolution 1325 (2000), DPKO designed a Global Action Plan on Resolution 1325 in 2006:

> The Global Action Plan incorporates the individual work plans of each Office/ Division and is framed around three broad goals: policy guidance for peacekeeping missions to ensure that post-conflict transitions advance gender equality; operational support to guide gender mainstreaming in peacekeeping missions; and increasing the numbers of women serving in peacekeeping missions.
>
> (DPKO 2006)

This strategy raises one key question: how can DPKO make senior managers accountable on gender issues in a system that does not take into account gendered indicators to measure the work of each staff member? Without the commitment of senior officials to take gender mainstreaming seriously, it is questionable whether the integration of a gender perspective into peacekeeping operations will make a difference (see Figures 21.3 and 21.4).

In the wake of the adoption of Resolution 1325, however, gender units were established in peacekeeping missions headed by a senior gender adviser (SGA). A gender unit's mandate can be sum up as follows: a) to ensure the mainstreaming of a gender perspective throughout the work of all the peacekeeping mission's

---

The term '**gender mainstreaming**' was endorsed by the Beijing Platform of Action in 1995 as the strategy that would allow the achievement of the goals under each of the Platform 12 critical areas, such as: 'governments and other actors should promote an active and visible policy of mainstreaming a gender perspective in all policies and programmes, so that, before decisions are taken, an analysis is made of the effects on women and men, respectively' (Platform for Action, Fourth World Conference on Women, Beijing 1995, paras 57, 79, 105, 123, 141, 164, 189, 202, 229, 238, 252, 273).

The Agreed Conclusions of the UN Economic and Social Council of September 17, 1997 defines gender mainstreaming as follows: 'Mainstreaming a gender perspective is the process of assessing the implications for women and men of any planned action, including legislation, policies or programmes, in all areas and at all levels. It is a strategy for making women's as well as men's concerns and experiences an integral dimension of the design, implementation, monitoring and evaluation of policies and programmes in all political, economic and societal spheres so that women and men benefit equally and inequality is not perpetuated. The ultimate goal is to achieve gender equality' (E.1997.L.O. para.4. Adopted by ECOSOC 17/7/97).

Figure 21.3 Gender mainstreaming.

In multidimensional peacekeeping operations, DPKO has a twofold responsibility for gender mainstreaming: '(a) incorporating gender perspectives into its own work in all phases of peacekeeping operations; and (b) assisting the efforts of the affected population in post-conflict situations to incorporate gender perspectives into work on reconstructing administrative structures, institution-building, combating organized crime, enforcing the rule of law and implementing other post-conflict activities, including nation-building'.

With the aim of better targeting the peacekeeping mission's policies, programs and activities, it is highly important to understand the issues at stake in a post-conflict environment based on a shift in gender roles during war. Peacekeepers have to understand the differential impact of war on women, men, boys and girls, such as:

- **impact linked to gender roles:** during conflict, pre-existing social inequalities are magnified, making women and girls more vulnerable to certain forms of violence such as sexual violence (rape used as a weapon of war)
- **sources of vulnerability for women and girls:** besides its obvious psychological impact, sexual violence against women and girls during conflict has important health and social ramifications
- **women and girls as active agents and participants in conflict:** women and girls are not only victims in armed conflict; they are also active agents. In many conflict and post-conflict situations, they have been instrumental in promoting peace. However, women continue to be largely absent from formal peace processes.

Therefore, before developing a program to mainstream gender issues, it is necessary to understand the situation in the host country and to identify areas of possible intervention that are in line with the mission mandate. This is done through a gender analysis that looks at the different roles and activities that women, men, girls and boys have in a particular society and the societal relationships between them. It means asking 'Who does what?'; 'Who makes decisions?'; 'Who derives the benefits?'; 'Who uses resources such as land or credit?'; 'Who controls these resources?' and 'What other factors influence relationships?' (such as laws about property rights and inheritance). Examining these aspects of a society reveals the differences in the experiences of women, men, girls and boys and the differences in their needs (DPKO 2004).

Figure 21.4 Gender mainstreaming in the DPKO.

components and b) to provide technical support/advice to government institutions and civil society organizations, including women's organizations, in compliance with relevant UNSC resolutions (1325, 1820, 1888, 1889, 1960, 2106 and 2122). One related problem is the location of the gender unit within the peacekeeping operation; very often relegated to the humanitarian pillar of an integrated peacekeeping mission, the gender unit has no leverage to ensure a proper gender mainstreaming into the mission's components. This setting participates in the marginalization of gender issues that are treated separately from peace and security issues defined according to a male perspective. In 2013 still, gender is understood as mainly relevant to humanitarian and development issues, thus creating a deep schism in the way peacekeeping operations are conducted in the field (masculinized security-related issues versus feminized humanitarian-related issues).

If the responsibility of a senior gender adviser is to advise senior leadership on gender mainstreaming, it would make sense to have that person and the unit that s/he leads at the highest level of the mission, i.e., in the Office of the Special Representative of the Secretary General (SRSG). Indeed, although the ultimate responsibilities for gender mainstreaming lie with the SRSG, the burden of delivering falls on the shoulders of the senior gender adviser.

Sandra Whitworth writes: '[a] separate gender unit tends to result in local women's NGOs liaising with the unit, while other local political actors – the majority of whom will likely be men – deal with UN officials in mainline departments and offices, the majority of whom are also men who often enjoy more direct access to the chief of mission' (Whitworth 2004: 131). There is in fact a common belief in peacekeeping missions that gender issues are the sole responsibility of the senior gender adviser and that s/he will take care of all gender-related matters in the mission area, thus preventing senior management getting involved in promoting a gender mainstreaming approach that would concern all sections and units, irrespective of their activities. It is interesting to observe, for instance, that mission staff members working for the Political Affairs Division will organize meetings with representatives of male-dominated political parties but will omit to invite women. The perception is that the senior gender adviser will convene separate meetings with women only. The same situation prevails with the Electoral Division that will promote a generic participation of all citizens in the post-conflict electoral process, but will not make special efforts to trigger the participation of women as voters and candidates. In countries where women won't be able to enjoy their rights as citizens if some mechanisms are not put in place to encourage their participation in electoral and political processes, this lack of gender perspective may further marginalize them. Sandra Whitworth also explains that:

> One of the reasons gender has become a safe idea is that the manner in which it has been used within UN understandings of peace and security issues has transformed it from a critical to a problem-solving tool, which does not challenge prevailing practices in response to armed conflict, peace and security.
>
> (Whitworth 2004: 139)

Turning gender into a problem-solving instrument prevents the UN from adopting a critical view of how peacekeeping operations are conducted and from even questioning the whole concept of operation as well as important issues like militarized masculinities and the long-term impact of peacekeeping on local women and men, boys and girls. Integrating a gender perspective into peacekeeping makes the goals of the mission look more acceptable because it helps to 'repackage' its militaristic approach.

A lot of effort has been made in designing and implementing gender training for peacekeepers, military, police and civilian staff. Although gender training could certainly improve the way security sector personnel conduct their mission in the host country and help to build their own capacity in their daily work, very often training falls short of what is expected in terms of behavioral change. Gender training is compulsory in peacekeeping missions for all newcomers but it is only part of an induction course that includes all other activities of the mission. Lack of time and resources prevent gender units in mission from providing a more in-depth training that could make a difference in the behavior of peacekeepers. In April 2007, the UN International Research and Training Institute for the Advancement

of Women (INSTRAW) launched an online discussion among experts from different fields linked to the security sector, NGOs, international organizations and civil
society on good and bad practices of gender training for security sector personnel
(2007). One can highlight the following four main recommendations that resulted
from this discussion:

1. Addressing traditional male roles and norms in the gender training (to discuss
   issues of masculinities in an overwhelmingly male-dominated security sector).
2. Engaging men as trainers (to improve the impact of gender training on other
   men).
3. Prioritizing training for senior managers and officials (gender responsiveness
   among top managers is key for an efficient gender mainstreaming process in
   mission).
4. Organizing pre-deployment gender training for peacekeeping personnel (to
   better prepare peacekeepers in understanding their country of assignment).

Since 2007 however, little progress has been achieved in improving the way training
is conducted for peacekeepers: 1) issues of masculinities are never discussed and
addressed; 2) although more men work as trainers today, it is difficult to assess if
they make a difference while addressing an audience of men; 3) most senior managers and officials still dismiss gender as irrelevant and never find the time to receive
proper training; and 4) some troop contributing countries have integrated gender
into the curriculum of their own training, with UN support, but again it is difficult
to assess if it makes a difference once their peacekeepers are deployed.

BACKLASH ON GENDER AND PEACEKEEPING

A lack of gender perspective in peacekeeping operations will reinforce the visibility
and legitimacy of men as the main stakeholders in peacebuilding processes and, at
the same time, will contribute to the invisibility of women who will remain
confined to the traditional roles of caretakers and caregivers. Since most of the
peacemakers or special peace envoys appointed by the UN and the international
community at large are men, they will fail to take into consideration the needs,
perspectives and expectations of women. Donald Steinberg, formerly a member of
the Luanda-based Joint Commission charged with implementing the peace accords
in Angola, explains:

> Addressing an audience of African scholars on the Lusaka Protocol in late 1994, I was
> asked about the role of women in its negotiating and implementation. I responded
> that there was not a single provision in the agreement that discriminated against
> women. 'The agreement is gender-neutral,' I proclaimed, somewhat proudly.
> (Steinberg 2007)

He later realized that the exclusion of women in the Lusaka peace process
contributed to the inability of the international community to successfully develop

and maintain a sustainable peace. As he writes: 'It took me only a few weeks after my arrival in Luanda to realize that a peace agreement that is "gender-neutral" is, by definition, discriminatory against women and thus far less likely to be successful' (Steinberg 2007). Only men were sitting around the negotiation table from the UN, the Angolan government, the main supporting countries and the rebel UNITA movement. The consequences were clearly stated: 'Not only did this silence women's voices on the hard issues of war and peace, but it also meant that issues such as internal displacement, sexual violence, abuses by government and rebel security forces, and the rebuilding of social services such as maternal health care and girls' education were given short shrift – or no shrift at all' (Steinberg 2007).

On May 5, 2006, the Darfur Peace Agreement (DPA) was signed between the Government of Sudan and a breakaway faction of the Sudan Liberation Army (SLA). Darfur women were invited to participate only at the seventh round of discussion thanks to the support of the international community. The participation of women from the beginning could have facilitated the promotion of a more inclusive peace process: 'Women were able to achieve some progress at least in the wording of the agreement on specifically gender-related issues in the mere three weeks that they were permitted to take part in the negotiations. Had they been included from the beginning, they might well have been able to do much more, including on the core security and political issues' (International Crisis Group 2006: 7). However, one might wonder whether the inclusion of gender-sensitive language in the peace accord that would take into consideration women's needs would be enough to advance women's rights in post-conflict. As we have seen in previous peace negotiation processes in Burundi, Democratic Republic of the Congo or Côte d'Ivoire, the participation of women has hardly been sustained in the different stages of the rehabilitation of their society:

> Beyond bringing more women to the peace negotiation table, the difficulty is to ensure that they will stay involved in the political life of their country once the peace process has been launched and that they will not be shunted aside by male actors. Women have to remain mobilized after the negotiations and take an active part in the political life of their society.
>
> (Puechguirbal 2004: 61)

Once they have left the peace process, women would experience difficulties in returning to the different stages of the reconstruction of their own society because all responsibilities would have already been shared among the male stakeholders.

The Gender Unit of the African Union/United Nations in Darfur (UNAMID) has been supporting the participation of women in the peace process and promoting the implementation of Resolution 1325 at the national and local level. Indeed, women have been consulted and shared achievements, challenges and recommendations on the promotion and implementation of the resolution, with special focus on the thematic areas of protection of women's human rights in particular sexual violence prevention and response; women's active participation through effective women's engagement in peacebuilding, conflict resolution, decision making, and post-conflict reconstruction process. These activities of UNAMID Gender Unit have been well documented but unfortunately not widely disseminated as good practices because they gained no visibility beyond the mission's level.

For the past few years, a backlash has been observed in peacekeeping that prevent an all-inclusive transition to peacebuilding. Recent peacekeeping operations have been through a process of rethinking the use of resources and posts to ensure a more streamlined mission that would help with current budget constraints. Gender units and child protections units were the first to be considered for cut or merge or disappearance and attempts were made to ensure that those functions would slowly be handed over to humanitarian and developments agencies. This move would seriously prevent the peacekeeping mission from delivering on its women, peace and security mandate. We are slowly sliding back to the pre-1325 era, when gender was a concept mainly associated with development issues that had nothing to do with peace and security. The pattern of recurrent questioning of the use of gender units keeps emerging in all discussions. Furthermore, intense discussions and debates often take place at DPKO about the number of posts needed to ensure proper gender mainstreaming and the gains made over the years are slowly but subtly eroded.

The existence of a gender unit needs to be fully justified at each budget exercise or creation of a new mission and preparation of a staffing table. Whereas the components of political affairs, civil affairs, human rights, or the police always get the majority of posts, sometime more than 50 people in one component in big peacekeeping operations, the gender unit can only rely on three or four approved positions, international and national included. Interestingly enough, even since the 'Brahimi report', the mentality towards – and value accorded – the work of political affairs, civil affairs, human rights, rule of law, the police and the military has not changed, which has an impact on resources provided to those components. Among all these posts, not a single one is tasked with ensuring a gender perspective in the political, police or rule of law work, although such a move would greatly facilitate gender mainstreaming. As a result, a small gender unit, often located in the humanitarian pillar, will have the impossible task of mainstreaming gender into all programs and activities of the mission and will be pressurized to deliver.

NEW INITIATIVES ON GENDER AND PEACEKEEPING: COUNTERING THE BACKLASH

In July 2013, the DPKO Senior Gender Adviser alerted the leadership of the department about the backlash that gender advisers were experiencing in peacekeeping operations. In the UN Peacekeeping Mission of Stabilization in Haiti (MINUSTAH) for example, there were discussions about merging the gender unit with human rights or civil affairs, thus cutting on posts and unit. As we have seen previously, a lack of understanding about the political work of the gender unit, as well as a lack of support by top management, made it difficult to sustain gains and achievements in gender mainstreaming.

With the support of the DPKO Under-Secretary General, it was decided to try a pilot project in MINUSTAH, the peacekeeping mission in Haiti, by proceeding with a reconfiguration of its gender unit. The rationale behind the reconfiguration process was that the senior gender adviser should be in a more strategic position to advise the top leadership of the mission. Indeed, to implement the mandate of the mission towards transition, the senior gender adviser should be located at the level of the SRSG's office for the following two reasons: a) Since the ultimate responsibility of gender mainstreaming lies with the SRSG, the SGA would be in a better position to advise and support the SRSG in the implementation of her/his mandate and: b) being positioned within the SRSG's office, the SGA would have a better overview of all mission's components and be strategically placed with enough authority to reach out to the head of sections.

This process should take into account the fact that strong political support is generally required at the highest level in the mission to facilitate the work of the SGA, given the common reality of limited understanding and awareness and sometimes passive resistance on the part of peacekeeping personnel to the implementation of the gender mandate. As the mission in Haiti is entering a phase of transition, the gender capacity should focus, as a priority, on strengthening the work of the mission's components in integrating gender in the priority areas of women's participation (democratic governance) and women's security (security sector reform).

Peacekeeping missions that have transitioned in recent years have adhered to the principle of retaining a SGA until the transition from peacekeeping to peacebuilding missions is complete – Timor Leste and Burundi are good examples. It is therefore important that DPKO does not deviate from this established good practice (that still needs to be documented and widely shared). The work of the SGA during the transitional period is critical for facilitating interaction with the UN country team (UNCT) composed of the main UN agencies, negotiating transfer of responsibilities as necessary and ensuring that the mission components do not abrogate their responsibilities of gender mainstreaming (in spite of the UN country team presence) but continue to be engaged in addressing gender concerns in their respective areas of responsibility.

This requires the presence of a strong senior gender adviser in the mission who is placed in the OSRSG, thereby facilitating both internal and external engagement processes. Transitioning the gender-related aspects of MINUSTAH's tasks to the UNCT needs to be informed by four important factors, namely: a) the availability of robust capacity within UN agencies (particularly UN Women and UNDP) to support and complement the mission's work; b) a realistic assessment of the workload of the gender unit in relation to MINUSTAH's gender mainstreaming mandate; c) the extent of coherence and integration between the work of the mission and the UNCT partners; and d) the established global practice for the transitioning of gender components in UN peacekeeping missions. As a result, the retention of a gender capacity at the highest level of the mission is necessary to ensure that the mission will be fully equipped to implement its mandate towards transition. Maybe this pilot project is the future of gender in peacekeeping operations to prevent the absorption of gender-related issues in development and humanitarian agencies, thus ensuring that peacekeeping missions continue to implement the Women, Peace and Security mandate.

CONCLUSION

The multidimensional nature of today's peacekeeping operations puts peacekeepers directly in contact with the lives of the population in the host country. As a result, it is extremely important that peacekeepers deployed in a post-conflict society understand the differential impact of war on women and men, boys and girls so as to not further marginalize the most vulnerable groups of the population. As it is written in the Gender Resource Package for Peacekeeping Operations developed by DPKO in 2004 to provide guidance on gender issues to mission staff: 'Having an in-depth understanding of the different needs, priorities and potentials of women and men, and girls and boys, in a particular country should ultimately lead to better-informed decisions and more effective implementation of the mission mandate' (DPKO 2004). Peacekeepers should not only avoid reinforcing the vulnerabilities of the local people, but also should use the capacities of local men and women to empower them and not undermine their peacebuilding efforts.

However, the very composition of a peacekeeping operation poses a problem insofar as it is still structured around male-dominated military and police contingents with their hypermasculine culture and norms. Their conception of peace and security issues revolves around the cessation of hostilities and disarmament of men with guns, whereas members of the local civil society, women in particular, promote a broader approach on security. One can observe the following:

> Interestingly enough, there is a widely shared view that after we have tackled the main issue of insecurity, e.g. disarming male gang leaders, militia, rebels, military groups, we will at the same time solve women's problems of insecurity. That is why, with the support of the international community, men allow themselves the right to represent women at the official peace negotiations because they are the voices of the mainstream.
>
> (Puechguirbal 2005: 9)

A gender-sensitive approach in peacekeeping would enable its members to better understand the context of mission, slightly change their own perceptions about the host community and consider women as active agents of change for peace, instead of hopeless victims in need of protection. But there is a trap. Using gender as a problem-solving mechanism to make the work of peacekeepers more effective and more inclusive prevents us from questioning the very definition, goal and mandate of a peacekeeping operation. Is the peacekeeping model the best solution to today's theater of operations where uniformed personnel interact with local men, women, boys and girls on a daily basis?

Finally, the militaristic approach of peacekeeping frequently excludes women from the transition to peacebuilding and reconstruction efforts. Women are not consulted in peace processes based on the rational that they were not exposed to direct fighting in war, although they were in charge of keeping together whole communities and extended families. Armed conflicts are being apprehended as a temporary breakdown of law and order that will soon return to the *status quo ante bellum* as defined by the men in power; in this context, it seems extremely difficult to challenge traditional gender roles and build up a new society on the remnants of the patriarchal order shattered by the war.

Today, we observe a real backlash in the integration of a gender perspective in peacekeeping operations mainly due to the perpetuation of bias and perceptions driven by the patriarchal culture of the UN. If the feminists of the UN and the gender advisers working in peacekeeping and political missions are not vigilant about the threat to gender mainstreaming, it is feared that the gains and progresses will be slowly reversed and will disappear off the political agenda.

Questions for future debate

1. What are the limitations of Resolution 1325 (2000) in empowering women in post-conflict situations?
2. What could be an all-inclusive definition of security in a post-conflict environment?
3. Why would the concept of 'militarized masculinity' be a hindrance to the integration of a gender perspective into a peacekeeping mission?
4. What are the critical elements of a successful gender mainstreaming approach in peacekeeping operations?
5. What are the elements that could explain why women's gains cannot be sustained in a post-conflict society?

Sources for further reading and research

Enloe, C. (2013) *Seriously!: Investigating Crashes and Crises as If Women Mattered*, London and Berkeley, CA: University of California Press.

Higate, P. (2004) 'Gender and Peacekeeping, Case Studies: the DRC and Sierra Leone', *Institute for Security Studies*, Monograph no. 91, Pretoria: Institute for Securities Studies.

Lessons Learnt Unit, Department of Peacekeeping Operations (2000) *Mainstreaming a Gender Perspective in Multidimensional Peace Operations*, New York: United Nations.

Olsson L. and Tryggestad L. Torunn (eds) (2001) *Women and International Peacekeeping*, London and Portland, OR: Frank Cass.

Puechguirbal N. (2010) 'Discourses on Gender, Patriarchy and Resolution 1325: a Textual Analysis of UN Documents', *International Peacekeeping, Women, Peace and Conflict: A Decade after Resolution*, 17(2):1325.

Note

1 The views expressed in this chapter are those of the author and do not represent the official position of the United Nations.

CHAPTER 22

Peacebuilding[1]

Laura J. Shepherd

LEARNING OUTCOMES

Upon completion, readers should be able to:

- Demonstrate that they are familiar with the most significant feminist scholarship on peacebuilding.
- Demonstrate understanding of the core feminist critiques of mainstreaming scholarship on peacebuilding.
- Explain the main international institutions engaged in peacebuilding and how they try to implement gender-responsive peacebuilding practices.

INTRODUCTION

In his 1992 *Agenda for Peace*, then-Secretary-General of the United Nations Boutros Boutros-Ghali insisted that, having overcome the 'immense ideological barrier' that characterised the era of 'Cold War', the organisation must:

> [S]tand ready to assist in peacebuilding in its different contexts; rebuilding the institutions and infrastructures of nations torn by civil war and strife; and building bonds of peaceful mutual benefit among nations formerly at war.
>
> (United Nations 1992)

- '[A]ctivities undertaken on the far side of conflict **to reassemble the foundations of peace** and provide the tools for building on those foundations something that is more than just the absence of war'.

- 'Peacebuilding involves a range of measures targeted to reduce the risk of lapsing or relapsing into conflict by **strengthening national capacities at all levels for conflict management**, and to **lay the foundations for sustainable peace and development**. Peacebuilding strategies must be coherent and tailored to specific needs of the country concerned, based on national ownership, and should comprise a carefully prioritized, sequenced, and therefore relatively narrow set of activities aimed at achieving the above objectives' (http://www.un.org/en/peacebuilding/pbso/pbun.shtml).

Figure 22.1 What is peacebuilding?

From its origins in the works of Johan Galtung (1975; see also Galtung 1969) the concept and practices of peacebuilding have been distinguished from peacemaking and peacekeeping, both operationally (see Brahmini et al. 2000; Panyarachun et al. 2004; United Nations 1996) and in scholarly literature (see Denskus 2007; Doyle and Sambanis 2000; Gawerc 2006). Although clearly and inextricably related to both peacemaking and peacekeeping, peacebuilding activities have come to represent 'the front line of preventative action' (Doyle and Sambanis 2000: 779) through the production of stable political, social and economic institutions in the aftermath of war (see Figure 22.1).

This chapter begins by outlining feminist contributions to and critiques of scholarship on peacebuilding. In the second section, I provide an overview of the policy framework supporting gender-sensitive peacebuilding and explain how that framework is being operationalised. The third section of the chapter looks at the core peacebuilding institutions that operate in the international system and evaluates key challenges facing peacebuilding enterprise in the coming years.

FEMINIST SCHOLARSHIP ON PEACEBUILDING

Just as conventional literature on International Relations has historically tended to ignore gender as a salient category of analysis, relational power dynamic or socio-political identity marker, conventional literature on peacebuilding reproduces this blindness to 'the question of gender' (Moran 2010: 262). Despite the recognition among peacebuilding agencies of the need to integrate a gender perspective into their operations, some scholars in the field of peace research and research on peace-building still tend to assume that peacebuilding activities are experienced similarly by all irrespective of gender identity and performance. Mary Moran notes, for example, that '[Roland] Paris's influential book *At War's End: Building Peace After Conflict* (2004) … contains no index entries for "women", "men", or "gender"' (2010: 262); a survey I conducted of the contents of *International Peacekeeping*, the premier journal that 'reflects debates about peacebuilding and monitoring of agreements', reveals that only 4 per cent of articles published in the journal since its inception in 1994 contain 'gender' in the title or abstract. (I have high hopes for *Peacebuilding*, a new journal launched in 2013, but at the time of writing it has only published two issues so it does not seem fair to critique its lack of feminist credentials just yet ...)

A significant literature has developed, however, that specifically engages with gendered logics and practices of peacebuilding. In much the same way as scholarship on gender and conflict more broadly insists that to seek to understand the socio-political dynamics of war and peace without paying attention to gender is to construct a partial and thin account of such dynamics (see Chapters 9, 10, 11 and 12), a number of highly influential collections that address peacebuilding from a variety of feminist perspectives contribute to a more holistic understanding of peacemaking, peacebuilding and post-conflict reconstruction than that allowed within conventionally gender-blind academic literature (see the sources for further reading and research provided at the end of the chapter).

Weaving together insights from a range of disciplinary perspectives (including peace studies, development studies, international relations, anthropology and economics), these scholars remind us not only that the individuals involved in peace processes are embodied agential subjects, whether male or female, but also that the concepts deployed in policies aiming to facilitate peacebuilding, including 'peace' itself, are inherently gendered.

Key insights

Feminist analyses of peacebuilding have both challenged and developed academic and policy debates about peacebuilding in many ways; here I focus on three particular thematic contributions made by this body of literature.

Equality of access

First, we can identify in some feminist works on peacebuilding an emphasis on equality of formal and informal institutional access. Caroline Sweetman, for example, argues that '[i]ntegrating a gender perspective into peacebuilding and reconstruction is an essential step in the process of ensuring democratic decision making at all levels of society' (2005: 6–7). Similarly, based on their study of gendered peacebuilding, Cheryl de la Rey and Susan McKay insist that '[a]dvancing women's global status demands that they be co-architects with men of re-emerging post-conflict societies' (2006: 150). In this literature, scholars make explicit the links between formal gender equality in governance institutions, resource allocation and decision-making fora and the formation of a society that values the voice and activities of all its members equally.

This research agenda also incorporates scholarship that emphasises intersectionality, work on peacebuilding that emphasises the 'dialogue necessary for recognising and moving beyond historical differences that have so violently excluded different ethnic groups in the past' (Baines 2005: 221). In short, feminist scholars of peacebuilding recognise the salience not only of gender difference but also of other markers of identity that humans use to distinguish themselves from others (race, able-bodiedness, sexuality, ethnicity, class and so on) and insist that true equality must negotiate these differences and mediate the multiple ways in which these markers can be mobilised to silence or marginalise individuals or social collectives.

Conceptualising peace

Second, feminist scholarship has focused on the conceptual architecture of peace agreements and policy documents. In her analysis of Angolan peace processes, Zoë Wilson concludes 'that peacemaking and peace-building efforts have reiterated rather than addressed distinctive vulnerabilities Angolan women experience today because such efforts are undergirded by gender-biased assumptions' (2005: 242). From engagements with United Nations Security Council (UNSC) Resolution 1325 (frequently represented as the first international policy document directly addressing gender in conflict prevention and conflict resolution, as I discuss further later) to discussions of gender and security sector reform (on the former, see Cohn, Kinsella and Gibbings 2004; Shepherd 2008c; Willett 2010; on the latter, see Mobekk 2010; Shepherd 2010b), feminist scholars have sought to understand the ways in which the language used to write policy has implications beyond textual representation and can be seen as constitutive of the reality of which it purports to speak (see Otto 2009; Puechguirbal 2010). These works on gender and representation in peacebuilding examine not only the assumptions about the inherent or biologically determined capacity of women to facilitate peace (see Cohn 2004; Cohn and Ruddick 2004; Pankhurst 2004) but also the ways in which writing gendered bodies into policy documents can pre- and proscribe engagement with the political agenda enshrined within the document itself.

Emphasising women's agency

Third, the gendered politics and practices of peacebuilding have been analysed in meticulous detail by feminist scholarship that seeks to examine agency, particularly women's agency in post-conflict societies. Setting aside for a moment the question of how exactly one determines a 'post-conflict' society, given that '[a] time of post-war reconstruction, later, may be re-designated as an *inter bellum* – a mere pause between wars' (Zarkov and Cockburn 2002: 9; emphasis in original), this body of work provides rich empirical insights into the specifics of peace processes in a range of contexts. Derived from situated, contextual and sympathetic research conducted all over the world, feminist accounts of peacebuilding from Afghanistan (Kandiyoti 2005) to Zimbabwe (Meintjes 2001) remind us of the importance of paying attention to differences in gender-differentiated experiences of peacebuilding as well as highlighting the commonalities of some experiences (see Afshar 2004). Such comparative analysis could not occur without the nuanced field accounts of the minutiae of peace negotiations, socio-political reconstruction and community rebuilding provided by feminist activists, academics and advocates that take gender as a primary analytical focus.

▊ THE POLICY ARCHITECTURE OF PEACEBUILDING

Before we look at the actors and agencies involved in peacebuilding practices, it is useful to explore the policies and frameworks that support those practices. There are a number of important documents, produced by United Nations entities and other organisations, that have an impact on how peacebuilding is managed and whether it is sensitive to gender or not.

Disarmament, demobilisation and reintegration (DDR) and security sector reform (SSR)

Initial engagement with conflict resolution and post-conflict reconstruction was governed by 'DDR' programmes: processes aimed at the **d**isarmament of individuals or combatant collectives, the **d**emobilisation of combatants and their **r**eintegration into society. 'First-generation' or traditional DDR programmes tended to focus on dismantling formal military structures and building sustainable socio-political institutions to facilitate peace processes, whereas 'second-generation' DDR programmes have extended their remit to include communities affected by armed conflict (United Nations 2010). In both cases, however, the commitments upheld by practitioners in DDR programmes, often but not exclusively under the auspices of the United Nations, relate explicitly to the strategic aims of DDR more broadly: 'to support the peace process, create political space and contribute to a secure environment' (United Nations 2010: 3).

Despite the fact that 'the policies and programmes of international funding agencies typically concentrate on reconstruction of physical, political, educational, and economic infrastructures, not people's lives' and that, as a consequence, gender has historically been represented as of secondary importance in DDR programmes (McKay 2004: 20), the publication by the United Nations of the *International Disarmament, Demobilisation and Reintegration Standards*, for example, indicates something of a shift in orientation by the key institutions involved in DDR practices, containing as it does an entire chapter devoted to 'Women, gender and DDR'. The United Nations Secretary-General, alongside other actors, represents DDR as foundational to effective peacebuilding; in one report, the Secretary-General noted the central importance of DDR to 'basic safety and security', a precondition of peacebuilding activities (United Nations 2009b: 6). The *IDDRS* explicitly engage 'stereotypical beliefs' about gender and articulate a willingness to institutionalise the 'gender-aware interventions and female-specific actions that should be carried out in order to make sure that DDR programmes are sustainable and equitable' (United Nations 2006: 5.10). Only if DDR programmes are 'gender responsive' will post-conflict communities be able to create durable peace.

In addition to DDR programmes, other policy initiatives facilitating the creation of gender-sensitive peacebuilding include security sector reform (SSR). SSR intersects with DDR and also engages questions of legitimacy and authority in the security sector of post-conflict societies, in an effort to ensure that 'forces do not regroup ...; bribery and corruption are eliminated; and the sector (including

These are all freely available online, accessible using your search engine of choice:

– Center for International Peace Operations (ZIF) & Deutsche Gesellschaft für Internationale Zusammenarbeit (GIZ), 'Trainer Manual: Mainstreaming Gender into Peacebuilding Training'
– 'Gender in Peacebuilding Design, Monitoring and Evaluation'
– 'Accord Insight: Women Building Peace'
– International Alert, 'Gender in Peacebuilding: Taking Stock'
– 'Gender Equity and Peacebuilding: From Rhetoric to Reality'
– 'Gender, peace-building and transitional justice in African contexts'.

In addition, the websites listed on the companion website have training resources and background papers.

Figure 22.2 Resources for gender-sensitive peacebuilding.

leadership structures) is fully transformed so as to gain credibility, legitimacy and trust in the public eye' (Anderlini and Conaway 2004: 31). Peacebuilding efforts are often grounded in both DDR and SSR programmes, and multiple policy platforms and toolkits exist to enshrine the centrality of gender awareness in these practices (see Figure 22.2). Scholarly work on SSR, however, suggests that '[t]he gap between policy and practice persists and gender issues are still treated as an afterthought' (Mobekk 2010: 288), which may be an obstacle to the creation of sustainable peace.

UNSCR 1325 and the 'Women, Peace and Security' agenda

United Nations Security Council Resolution (UNSCR) 1325 (2000) is widely acknowledged as the foundation of gender-sensitive policy formulation in the sphere of peace and security (see Moran 2010: 262), and this is also the case in the realm of peacebuilding. The resolution itself owes a debt to a number of previous UNSC Resolutions as well as other UN Declarations and Reports including 'the Windhoek Declaration and the Namibia Plan of Action' (United Nations Security Council 2000: Preamble). UNSCR 1325 'called for, *inter alia*, the increased participation of women in decision-making related to the prevention, management and resolution of conflict' (Otto 2006–7: 116; emphasis in original). At the time of writing, UNSCR 1325 has been translated into over 100 different languages, from Albanian to Zulu, and 42 countries have adopted National Action Plans to facilitate the implementation of UNSCR 1325 in peace operations and conflict prevention.

Although UNSCR 1325 has received significant challenges from academics and policymakers alike, it remains a profoundly influential document that continues to shape gender-sensitive policy on peace and security. Since 2000, when UNSCR 1325 was adopted, there have been a further six resolutions adopted, all of which together form what is known as the 'women, peace and security' (WPS) agenda at the United Nations. These resolutions are UNSCR 1820 (2008),

UNSCR 1888 (2009), UNSCR 1889 (2009), UNSCR 1960 (2010), UNSCR 2106 (2013), and UNSCR 2122 (2013). The WPS agenda intersects with peace-building in two main ways. First, the WPS agenda is usually describing as having three 'pillars' that need to be in place to support meaningful and lasting peace and security: protection (from gender-based and sexualised violence or discrimination); prevention (of gender-based and sexualised violence and the derogation of rights); and participation (of women and girls in all peace and security governance processes, from peacemaking to post-conflict reconstruction). As you can see, this last pillar directly relates to peacebuilding activities, with the other two pillars relating indirectly, through activities undertaken in periods of post-conflict recovery to reform political, judicial and security institutions that inhibit gender-based violence in the first instance and then properly punish perpetrators when it does occur.

Second, in addition to the conceptual affinities between WPS and peacebuilding, a number of the key WPS resolutions explicitly mention peacebuilding, specifically women's leadership in peacebuilding activities. All the WPS resolutions highlight women's agency in peace and security governance, but UNSCR 1889 and UNSCR 2212 in particular focus on women's full and equal participation in all phases of peacebuilding. The Preamble of UNSCR 1889 states explicitly that the Security Council is:

> [D]eeply concerned about the persistent obstacles to women's full involvement in the prevention and resolution of conflicts and participation in postconflict public life, as a result of violence and intimidation, lack of security and lack of rule of law, cultural discrimination and stigmatization, including the rise of extremist or fanatical views on women, and socioeconomic factors including the lack of access to education, and in this respect, [recognises] that the marginalization of women can delay or undermine the achievement of durable peace, security and reconciliation.
>
> (United Nations Security Council 2009: Preamble)

From this, we can see that the UN Security Council, the only UN entity whose resolution have the automatic status of universally binding international law, acknowledges the necessity of including women and girls in all peacebuilding activities in order to achieve lasting peace and security. UNSCR 1889 also calls on the Secretary-General to submit a report to the Council addressing women's participation and inclusion in peacebuilding activities, which remains an important document in the pursuit of gender-sensitive peacebuilding.

The Secretary-General's seven-point plan

The most recent development in gender-sensitive peacebuilding was the publication in 2010 of the United Nations Secretary-General's Report 'Women in Peacebuilding'. In UNSCR 1889 (2009), which is one of the 'women, peace and security' resolutions mentioned earlier, 'the Report lays out a seven-point action plan to enhance women's participation in peacebuilding, with commitments across a range of issue areas (United Nations Secretary-General, 2010: 3, *passim*). Specifically, the seven-point plan commits the UN to:

- 'promoting women's greater engagement in peace processes' (United Nations Secretary-General 2010: para. 26)
- taking action to 'ensure women's participation in, and the availability of gender expertise to, peace processes' (United Nations Secretary-General 2010: para. 28)
- providing 'financing for gender equality and women's empowerment' (United Nations Secretary-General 2010: para. 34)
- 'increasing the proportion of women civilians deployed to post-conflict environments' (United Nations Secretary-General 2010: para. 37)
- 'increasing the proportion of women decision makers in post-conflict governance institutions' (United Nations Secretary-General 2010: para. 40)
- supporting 'the rule of law, which is of paramount importance in post-conflict countries' (United Nations Secretary-General 2010: para. 45)
- and to 'correct for the pervasive biases that direct post-conflict resources overwhelmingly towards men' (United Nations Secretary-General 2010: para. 49).

The UN Peacebuilding Support Office is working closely with another UN entity, UN Women, to operationalise and implement the seven-point plan. These offices have developed a set of measures to track the implementation of the Plan (see Figure 23.3), and the Peacebuilding Commission is cited in the original Report as having an important role to play in supporting women's engagement with peacebuilding. The Report concludes that the security of women, and women's agency in peace and security governance processes, act as 'force multipliers' for lasting peace (United Nations Secretary General 2010: para. 53).

PEACEBUILDING INSTITUTIONS

We have focused so far on peacebuilding activities undertaken by or with United Nations entities and we will discuss these organisations again later. It is important to recognise, however, that many state and non-state actors are involved in direct peacebuilding activities with post-conflict states. State actors tend to direct financial resources through development programmes (such as AusAID in Australia, or the Department of International Development in the UK) and support multilateral efforts either through regional organisations (such as the provision of US$3 million to Darfur by the African Union in 2013) or through donations to international governmental organisations such as the World Bank and the United Nations. The United Nations Peacebuilding Fund, the financial arm of the United Nations Peacebuilding Commission (see later), disburses funds donated by UN member states. Since it was set up in 2006, the Fund has received deposits of over US$455 million, nearly 92 per cent of which has been committed by member states. As of 2013, the UK's Department of International Development is by far the largest contributor to the Fund, depositing over US$81 million, followed by Sweden, the Netherlands, Norway, Canada, Japan and Germany.

There are also influential non-state actors that undertake a range of peacebuilding activities such as ACCORD (African Centre for the Constructive Resolution of Disputes) and USIP (the United States Institute for Peace). Often, during conflict, humanitarian actors such as Oxfam, Save the Children and the Red Cross organisation are 'in country', on the ground helping people already, so they are well placed to play an active role in reconstruction once peace has been established.

The United Nations Peacebuilding Commission

Recognising that efforts toward peacebuilding needed to be integrated to maximise efficiency, the United Nations Peacebuilding Committee (UNPBC) was inaugurated as an intergovernmental advisory body in 2005 following the adoption of Resolutions by both the UN Security Council and the UN General Assembly (1645 and 60/180 respectively). In UNSCR 1645, the Security Council tasked the Commission with developing outlines of best practice in post-conflict reconstruction, and securing political and material resources to assist states in transition from conflict to peacetime. As explained in an addendum to the 2005 report *In Larger Freedom: Towards Development, Security and Human Rights for All*, then-Secretary-General Kofi Annan suggested that the Commission should:

> [P]rovide a central node for helping to create and promote comprehensive strategies for peacebuilding both in general terms and in country situations. It should encourage coherent decision-making on peacebuilding by Member States and by the United Nations Secretariat, agencies and programmes ... It must also provide a forum in which representatives of the United Nations system, major bilateral donors, troop contributors, relevant regional actors and organizations, the international financial institutions and the national or transitional authorities of the country concerned can share information about their respective post-conflict recovery activities, particularly as pertains to achieving coherence between the security/political and development/economic issues, in the interests of greater effectiveness.
>
> (United Nations General Assembly 2005)

Organisationally, the UNPBC defers to the UN Security Council, as it is the Council that mediates requests for assistance from governing authorities. Under normal circumstances, 'client' countries, or countries that seek to include their peacebuilding activities on the agenda of the Commission, must submit a request first to the Security Council and the General Assembly, the former of which then refers the case to the UNPBC. (The Commission does allow for recommendations directly from the Economic and Social Council, the General Assembly, concerned member states of the United Nations and/or the Secretary-General 'in exceptional circumstances' although in all cases the consent of the client country must be secured prior to its inclusion on the agenda.) Since it was founded, the UNPBC has provided advice and support on peacebuilding activities in six countries, all of which are still on the agenda: Burundi and Sierra Leone (placed on the agenda in 2006); Guinea-Bissau (2007); Central African Republic (2008); Liberia (2010); and Guinea (2011).

The UNPBC through a gendered lens

As noted in the founding Resolution, and building on the institutional architecture outlined earlier, the UNPBC is called on 'to integrate a gender perspective into all its work' (United Nations Security Council 2005: OP 20). Evidence of this commitment can be found in some of the annual reports submitted by the Commission; in 2007, for example, the UNPBC noted that '[g]ender equality was identified as a critical cross-cutting issue for peace consolidation in both Burundi and Sierra Leone' (UNPBC 2007a: 6). The Commission also held a workshop titled 'Gender and Peacebuilding: Enhancing Women's Participation' in January 2008 under the auspices of its Working Group on Lessons Learned, which aims to consolidate information and experience from previous activities relevant to the agenda of the Commission.

The Background Note provided to delegates at the workshop was authored by Jennifer Klot, a senior policy advisor at the Social Science Research Council responsible for its programmes on HIV/AIDS, gender and security. In her report, Klot notes that '[a]lthough women's participation and gender equality is a "predictable" peacebuilding gap, it is striking how far this core issue is lacking in institutional capacity, policy and operational guidance, programme implementation, data, monitoring and evaluation, knowledge and resources' (UNPBC 2008a: 9). Klot makes five specific recommendations to the Commission to ameliorate the situation (UNPBC 2008a: 11):

1. Increase women's participation in peacebuilding
2. Strengthen institutional capacity for gender equality and peacebuilding
3. Respond to gaps in knowledge and information on gender and peacebuilding
4. Increase coherence of UN actions in support of gender equality and peacebuilding
5. Ensure adequate resources to mainstream gender equality into peacebuilding.

These recommendations, alongside a need to monitor gender mainstreaming mechanisms and mechanisms through which women can gain access to justice and participate fully in public life, including formal political activities, were also highlighted in the Summary Notes of the Chair (UNPBC 2008b: 4). '[I]ntegrating a gender perspective' in peacebuilding must mean more than recognising that 'men and women are affected differently by conflict' (UNPBC 2010: 17) if it is to facilitate the transformation of gendered logics and structures of power; and, second, that gender-sensitive peacebuilding is often assumed to rely on the inclusion of (notably women-centred) civil society organisations, but that it is problematic to adopt such an approach uncritically.

The inclusion of quotas mandating gender equality in peace agreements can go some way towards ameliorating a representative imbalance, although this strategy is not without costs and it is premised on a conflation of descriptive and substantive political representation that is widely recognised as problematic (see Celis et al. 2008; Childs and Krook 2006). While acknowledging its shortcomings, which include the fact that a 'focus on female representatives ignores important differences among women, at the same time that it overlooks men as potential actors on behalf of women as a group' (Celis et al. 2008: 99), quotas have been used to good effect to begin a transition in governance in post-conflict countries. In Burundi, for example, after the 2010 elections women occupied 32.1 per cent of seats in the lower House and 46.3 per cent of seats in the Senate (Inter-Parliamentary Union 2011). This represents a significant increase in the proportion of women in formal political institutions; in 1993 the percentage overall was 14.4 per cent (Inter-Parliamentary Union 2000).

Echoing the Commission's concerns about the legitimacy of peacebuilding operations, which manifests in part as fidelity to the model of modern (sovereign) statehood, all of the frameworks comment on the need for an inclusive approach to peacebuilding to support – and perhaps supplement – this state-centric vision of political authority. Crucially, 'stakeholders … including civil society [and] women's organisations' are seen to play 'key roles in peacebuilding' (UNPBC 2009: 2) in the strategic frameworks in place for Burundi, the Central African Republic and Guinea-Bissau. Again, as with the issue of institutional access discussed earlier, this is representative of efforts at democratisation in peacebuilding, on the understanding that debates about governance should not be limited to elite groups or formal institutions. The Peacebuilding Commission has specific guidance in place for engagement with civil society organisations (CSOs) and 'recognizes the important contribution of civil society, including non-governmental organizations and the private sector, to all stages of peacebuilding efforts' (UNPBC 2007b: Art. 1).

Targeting funds for gender-sensitive peacebuilding

In the 2010 Secretary-General's Report that we discussed earlier, he committed 'to ensure that at least 15 per cent of United Nations-managed funds in support of peacebuilding are dedicated to projects who principle objective … is to address women's specific needs, advance gender equality, or empower women' (United Nations Secretary General 2010: para. 36). In order to achieve this, the UN Peacebuilding Fund adopted what is known as a 'gender marker' in 2009. This is a way of tracking how much money is spent on enhancing gender equality. Projects are categorised on a scale of zero to three (see Figure 22.3).

- **Score 3** for projects that are targeted 100 per cent to women beneficiaries and/or address specific hardships faced by women and girls in post-conflict situations.

- **Score 2** for projects with specific component, activities and budget allocated to women.

- **Score 1** for projects with women mentioned explicitly in their objectives, but no specific activities are formulated or a budget reserved.

- **Score 0** for projects that do not specifically mention women.

Figure 22.3 UN Peacebuilding Fund's 'gender marker' scale.

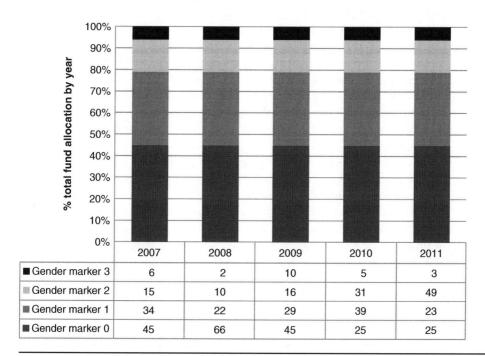

Figure 22.4 UN PBF percentage allocation to gender-sensitive projects over time.
Source: Data from the United Nations Peacebuilding Fund (2011).

As you can see from the scale in Figure 22.3, although this is a mode of categorisation described as a 'gender marker' it is actually concerned with women's
participation in peacebuilding activities. Although this might be problematic
(because 'gender is not a synonym for women'; see Carver 1996), the adoption
of the 'gender marker' has enabled the Peacebuilding Fund to track allocated
funding over time (see Figure 22.4), and analysing these data shows that there
has been an overall proportional increase in funding allocated to GM2 projects,
with a concomitant decrease to funding allocated to GM0 projects since 2008.
This hopefully translates to more gender-responsive peacebuilding activities 'on
the ground'.

In addition to the 'gender marker', the Fund announced a 'gender promotion
initiative' in 2011. This was a separate pot of money (US$5 million) dedicated to
special projects that specifically enhance women's participation in peacebuilding.
The initiative aims to:

- Help implement the commitments of the Secretary-General's seven-point
  action Plan on Women's Participation in Peacebuilding.
- Address gender-equality concerns and strengthen women's empowerment
  within the PBF portfolio.
- Stimulate UN system learning in programming of gender-responsive peacebuilding projects, including the collection and dissemination of good practices
  (United Nations Peacebuilding Fund 2011).

Seven new projects were developed under this initiative, of a pool of 22 proposals submitted by 15 of the 16 countries declared eligible by the UN Secretary-General. These projects are aimed at all aspects of women's empowerment, from economic empowerment (in Guinea Bissau), to participation in decision making (in Sierra Leone) and surviving gender-based and conflict-related sexual violence (in Guatemala and Guinea). There are three more general projects (in Nepal, North Sudan and South Sudan) that address capacity building and gender-responsive recovery.

This kind of targeted funding plays an invaluable role, not only in showing demonstrable evidence of the political will in the United Nations peacebuilding entities to implement the recommendations from the UN Secretary-General's 2010 Report but also in ensuring that the structural conditions for lasting peace are configured in such a way as to include women from the outset. 'Gender mainstreaming' in peacebuilding (see Chapter 19) means making sure that women are present and their concerns, issues and experiences are fully integrated into peace processes from the very beginning. The 'gender marker' and the PBF's 'gender promotion initiative' go some way towards making this happen, but there is still a long way to go.

It is important to remember, for example, that even – perhaps especially – projects that are categorised as GM0 projects, which do not specifically mention women, require oversight from the Peacebuilding Support Office's gender advisor. Often, projects will be developed that are 'GM0' projects but that have profoundly gendered effects on the local communities. One example I was given was that of a well-building project. As it was considered solely to be an infrastructural project, aimed at improving a resettled community's access to clean drinking water, it did not attract the attention of any gender specialists, until it was realised that in that community, water collection was predominantly undertaken by women and girls. The placement of and route to and from the proposed well was therefore going to have a disproportionate impact on the community's women and girls. This project therefore needed a gender analysis to be undertaken to understand the gendered impacts of well building in that specific community.

CONCLUSION

This chapter has outlined some feminist scholarship on peacebuilding, and shown how the core insights from this literature can help us understand peacebuilding more holistically, through a 'gendered lens'. We also discussed the main policy documents relating to gender-sensitive peacebuilding at the international level and investigated some of the institutions engaged in peacebuilding in contemporary global politics. The final focus was on the United Nations peacebuilding institutions: the Peacebuilding Commission, the Peacebuilding Support Office and the Peacebuilding Fund. Through examining the ways in which the Fund targets resources at projects designed to enhance gender equality through women's empowerment, and also examining the ways in which the Commission attempts to integrate gender as a cross-cutting thematic concern in all areas of its activity, we can see the steps that these important institutions are taking to implement the UN Secretary-General's seven-point plan (2010) and to fully achieve gender-sensitive peacebuilding.

Questions for further debate

1. Why is it important to consider peacebuilding 'through a gendered lens'?
2. How effective have the various United Nations peacebuilding institutions been at operationalising gender-sensitive peacebuilding?
3. How do UN initiatives compare with other unilateral, bilateral or multilateral peacebuilding activities currently ongoing?
4. How can we make sure that women get a 'seat at the table' during peace negotiations and in peacebuilding post-conflict?
5. What are the most important things to keep in mind when providing a gender analysis of peacebuilding projects?

Sources for further reading and research

de la Rey, C. and S. McKay (2006) 'Peacebuilding as a Gendered Process', *Journal of Social Issues*, 62(1): 141–53.

Meintjes, S., A. Pillay and M. Turshen (eds) (2001) *The Aftermath: Women in Post-Conflict Transformation*, London: Zed Books.

Moran, M. H. (2010) 'Gender, Militarism and Peace-Building: Projects of the Post-conflict Moment', *Annual Review of Anthropology*, 39, 261–74.

Pankhurst, D. (2004) 'The "Sex War" and Other Wars: Towards a Feminist Approach to Peacebuilding', in H. Afshar and Deborah Eade (eds), *Development, Women and War: Feminist Perspectives*, Oxford: Oxfam GB, 8–42.

Sweetman, C. (ed.) (2005) *Gender, Peacebuilding and Reconstruction*, Oxford: Oxfam GB.

Note

1 This chapter is a heavily modified version of 'Gender and Peacebuilding', in J. Mathers (ed.) (forthcoming 2015) *Handbook on Gender and War*, Cheltenham: Edward Elgar.

PART 6 IDENTITIES, ORDERS, BORDERS

CHAPTER 23

Migration

Jindy Pettman with Lucy Hall

LEARNING OUTCOMES

Upon completion, readers should be able to:

- Understand the ways in which migration creates both opportunities and constraints that are also gendered.
- Identify the connections between the global political economy of migration and gender.
- Explain the 'paradox' of globalization in relation to the nation-state, migration and citizenship.

INTRODUCTION

Gender matters in migration, and in the study of migration. Migration studies have largely assumed the migrant to be a man, with the woman left behind, or following after (Kelson and De Laet 1999). Women experience migration – the decision to go, the process of moving, the consequences of displacement or resettlement – differently from men. This is partly because women are positioned differently in relation to many of the aspects or sites of migration, from family politics, through the mix of opportunities and constraints experienced at the border or in the new state, to wars that trigger large-scale displacement, and the global political economy with its increasingly globalized division of labour.

This chapter asks how and why gender matters in international migration. It begins by asking how IR has treated migration, and then traces a brief history of migration, with particular attention to its connections with international politics and globalization processes. Gendering migration provides a deeper interrogation of the kinds of migration flow and their particular patterns, and of the different stages in migration. It raises questions regarding how different kinds of boundaries function, and why 'immigration' is so often racialized. Along the way, the chapter asks why some (migrant, female) bodies are more visible, and more troublesome, than others.

Gender travels along with bodies. Gender meanings are renegotiated, resisted and reclaimed along the way, including through transnational women's organising around migration and identity rights and wrongs. New and emerging post-migration and transnational gendered identities and affiliations further unsettle the presumed nation-state, territory–people nexus.

GENDER, MIGRATION AND IR

IR has not shown much interest in gender, including its own. It has shown even less interest in migration, even though crossing state borders *is* international (Pettman 1996). People frequently cross borders in response to events in international politics, especially during or after wars. Most people cross state borders in flows that reflect global or regional structural relations of power and wealth, mainly from poorer to richer states. All these macro-level aspects of migration are the stuff of International Relations and the global political economy (see Chapters 15, 16 and 17). So too is that central player in IR, the nation-state, with its territorially based membership and sovereignty. States determine (more or less effectively) who may leave their territory, and who may enter, reside, work, and possibly become citizens of the state. While states are changing, and giving up on some kinds of sovereign power, especially in relation to corporate capital and neoliberal restructuring, they retain and exercise their power to secure their own borders.[1] This is especially the case in the post-9/11 world, where the 'securitization of immigration' (Tastsoglou and Dobrowolsky 2006: 3) and 'homeland defence' are shorthands to indicate the ways in which migration is seen to challenge the state and its national community. In the process, migration can become a foreign policy issue, a security issue and a national political issue touching on identity politics, citizenship, labour and human rights.

Migration is also an international agenda item, as evidenced by the entry into force of the International Convention on the Protection of All Migrant Workers and Members of Their Families (hereafter the Convention) in 2003. States that have ratified the Convention are obliged to report on the progress towards full implementation of the Convention within one year of its entry into force and every five years thereafter. However a mere 17 per cent of states have signed this Convention and very few states have signed other relevant international conventions that extend citizenship and labour rights to migrant workers (True 2012: 58). Furthermore, the countries that have ratified this Convention collectively host about 7 per cent of the global migrant population (UNDESA 2011: xxii). These statistics indicate that although migration is on the international agenda, steps taken to 'govern' migration through international conventions have had minimal impact on states. Gender infuses these migration politics, even when not specifically articulated or utilised as an analytical framework in academic studies or policy documents (World Survey 2006).

A (his)story of migration

The controversial and highly regulated nature of migration currently is of relatively recent origin. Huge numbers of people have migrated over the centuries, and many of us occupy our residence and citizenship (not necessarily in the same state) because of our own, our parents' or our ancestors' migration. People often flow along tracks laid down in conquest and colonization. Settler states such as the US, Australia and Israel are built on a history of colonization and migration (Stasiulis and Yuval-Davis 1995). For example, the 2011 Census shows that 26 per cent of Australians were born overseas, the largest source countries being the UK (20.8 per cent), New Zealand (9.1 per cent), China (6.0 per cent), India (5.6 per cent), Italy (3.5 per cent) and Vietnam (3.5 per cent) (Australian Bureau of Statistics 2013). Today, many move along former colonial webs, between the ex-British Caribbean to the UK and to Canada, for example.

Other aspects of geopolitical power affect migration flows. Tracking refugee flows provides a way of mapping violent political conflicts. The Office of UN High Commissioner for Refugees (UNHCR) notes that 'refugee movements and other forms of forced displacement provide a useful (if imprecise) barometer of human security and insecurity' (UNHCR, in Edwards 2009: 800). There are large numbers of refugees who flee from violence and live on the other side of their state border. The profile of displacement across the Middle East is undergoing dramatic change with ongoing armed conflict in Syria. In 2013, there were 1.8 million Syrian refugees across Iraq, Jordan, the Lebanon, Turkey and Egypt and North Africa and a further 4.25 million who were internally displaced (US Department of State 2013).

Despite the global financial crisis trends indicate that the total number of migrants has not fallen in recent years (IOM 2011: 49). In 2010, the total number of international migrants in the world was estimated at 214 million people – up from 191 million in 2005 (UNDESA 2011). Currently, the US is the largest recipient of international migrants, with 42.8 million in 2010, followed by the Russian Federation, with 12.2 million (many of whom would have been classified as internal migrants before the breakup of the Soviet Union), and Germany with 10.7 million (UNDESA 2011: 2). The countries with the highest proportion of international migrants in their population are Qatar (87 per cent), the United Arab Emirates (70 per cent), Kuwait (69 per cent), Jordan (46 per cent), the Occupied Palestinian Territory (44 per cent), Singapore (41 per cent) and Israel (40 per cent), each telling a very different story of migration flows (UNDESA 2011: 3).

Some states make it hard for their citizens to leave; others (or sometimes the same ones) make it hard to get in. Nowadays, states do not welcome immigrants with open arms. Immigration regulations and state borders have hardened. There is increasing political resistance to migration, usually meaning migration from particular states or regions. We need then to look at individual state immigration policies, and practices, including at the numbers and sources of illegal or undocumented migrants within the state, and their rights, or more likely vulnerabilities, as people are increasingly 'prisoners of territory' (Moses 2006: 12) or seen as out of place.

The hardening of state borders and migration restrictions in turn encourages illegal migration and fuels smuggling and trafficking practices (Milly 2007; see also Chapter 8). The border functions as both barrier and transit zone. The border functions to create different categories and statuses, including refugee, alien, undocumented worker, even terrorist. These ways of naming travelling experiences homogenise very mixed categories and freeze the dynamics and mobility between categories, as well as between states. Migrants may enter a country legally and then overstay their visa, or enter illegally and then take advantage of a state-offered amnesty. Refugees may flee across the border, and stay near it, hoping to return soon, or be reunited with others left behind; these camps often become permanent townships and home for generations. Some make it out, merging into the local population, while a few more may be 'processed' and resettled half a world away. Some may embrace their new home and be reluctant to return even when it becomes safe to do so.

'Migration' may call up pictures of a unidirectional move from State A to State B, with resettlement and new citizenship to follow. This classic picture is now a minority view, although some who thought they were temporary migrants got stuck or decided to stay. Others move back and forward along circuits of migration or engage in multiple migrations. It makes a difference which bodies we imagine when we call up people moving. For example, if we see 'migrant women', do we see professional women or domestic workers? Other categories include marriage migration (usually female, although in very different circumstances), sex trafficking (why, again, largely women, and girls?), international students (some of whom will marry or find employment and/or citizenship in the new state); and international adoptions.[2] While international tourists also queue at migration counters and negotiate borders, we do not usually include them in migration stories, although some of their travels may lead to migration or transnational relationships.

In any particular state or region, some migrants are more welcome than others. Who is not welcome, or not allowed? Who are suspect even when they are citizens or were born there? Some migrants are more migrant than others. Migrant bodies are racialized as well as classed and gendered, which renders some for ever migrant, even after generations. Here are associations of (some) migrant bodies with flood, contamination, danger; or with disloyalty, incompatibility, criminality or worse. These representations of migrantness contrast with mobilizations around the right of free movement (Moses 2006), of human rights for migrants (Brysk and Shafir 2004), of multiculturalism (Ong 2004); and the politics of identity and belonging that imagine very different affiliations and entitlements.

We must ask which bodies move and why? Where do they move to and how do they experience the move, and its consequences? And why do some bodies, and some forms of migration, become especially visible, and subject to debate within the media or politics of any particular state? There is a danger here, too: if we focus on poorer, racialized women's bodies, and on more vulnerable or sexualized work, do we contribute to the exoticizing, or stigmatizing, that makes some women especially vulnerable when they are seen to be 'out of place' (Pettman 2008)? Do we compound gender stereotyping by implying that women are only unskilled or deskilled migrants, when many women move as knowledge workers or move to nursing or welfare positions in the new state? (Kofman 2004).

Her story/ies of migration

The 2004 World Survey on the Role of Women in Development focused on Women and International Migration (2006). It argued, 'As a fundamental organizing principle of society, gender is central in any discussion of the causes of international migration – the decision-making involved and the mechanisms associated with enacting migrating decisions – as well as the consequences of migration' (2006: 11). It deplored the 'dearth of data' on women and migration (2006: 11), noting that statistics for international migration are very uneven and unreliable, and are rarely disaggregated in terms of age or gender (note that the statistics in Figure 23.1 are 'estimated'). However, feminists have been curious about women on the move for some time, especially since Mirjana Morokvasic's ground breaking intervention 'Birds of Passage Are Also Women' (1984). Feminists have since generated excellent theoretical and specific site studies. As well, many migrant women have written their stories or given testimony to researchers or NGOs and, of course, many migrant women are feminist scholars too.

Between 2005 and 2010 the UN Department of Economic and Social Affairs (UNDESA) reported that the total number of people migrating internationally grew from 195 million people to 214 million, a total increase of 19 million (UNDESA 2011: 6). Of the 19 million, approximately 47 per cent were women (UNDESA 2011: 6). Of the 214 million international migrants approximately 66 million women were in 'more developed' countries, 39 million in the 'less developed' countries and 5.5 million in the 'least developed' countries (UNDESA 2011: 58–61). In 2010, female migrants outnumbered male migrants in Europe, followed by Oceania, Northern America and Latin America and the Caribbean; however,

Development group	Percentage female				
	1990	1995	2000	2005	2010
World...	49.1	49.3	49.4	49.2	49.0
More developed regions............................	52.0	51.7	51.8	51.6	51.5
Less developed regions.............................	45.9	46.1	46.1	45.6	45.3
Least developed countries......................	46.7	47.6	47.4	47.4	47.4

Figure 23.1 Female migrants as a percentage of the international migrant stock by development group, 1990–2010.

male migrants continued to outnumber female migrants in Africa and Asia (UNDESA 2011: xx). However, some poorer or 'least developed' countries have large numbers of refugees, who may or may not be counted in the migration figures. North America and Western Europe continue to have the largest numbers of women migrants; although Europe had the highest proportion of women migrants and Western Asia and Southern Africa had the lowest. In 2010, 49.8 per cent of legal migrants to the US and 51.6 per cent of legal migrants to Australia and New Zealand were women.

The proportion of women migrants in emigrating countries varies widely, with many more men than women migrating from Mexico, while more women than men migrated from the Philippines. In Thailand, many male Burmese migrants are in the construction industry, while Burmese women and girls are directed into various kinds of hospitality work, including sex work, and some are subject to further migration, including through trafficking (see Chapter 8). Fiji exports citizens for work in gendered flows, with (male) soldiers, and (female) nurses going to very different destinations.

Whether men or women leave (and the decision to leave may or may not be their own), the whole process is already gendered, in terms of different roles and relationships in the home, the kinds of work available locally or through migration in a gendered labour force, and the ways mobility and the borders are experienced. Forms of exploitation, violence or discrimination facing migrants in the new state are also gendered, and mediated through other body differences, including race, class and nationality. It is not only 'the migrant' that is affected by migration; those who stay behind may as a consequence take on new kinds of work and responsibility. Women who remain often take up work traditionally done by men, and may be unwilling or find it difficult to revert back to work or domestic roles typically associated with women if the men return.

Given the extraordinary diversity, and dynamism, of migration, and the ways it affects home and new state, and those touched by the moving, it is very difficult to generalise. Wenona Giles reminds us that the terms used to differentiate between various categories of forced migrants; asylum seekers, refugees, internally displaced persons (IDPs) and trafficked persons do not refer to inherent characteristics of people (2013: 83). These categories are legal descriptors that have a tremendous impact on the types of assistance and human rights protection persons forced to flee might be able to access (Giles 2013: 83). These legal descriptors, however, do overshadow the gendered complexities that compel people to flee. Someone may identify or be identified with more than one of these categories. For example, a refugee may be further displaced within their country of asylum due a natural disaster. An asylum seeker may also be trafficked or smuggled across a border in order to seek refugee status. So while legal descriptors are important they also obscure the very complex situations which force people to flee.

UNHCR reported that, at the end of 2012, 45.2 million people were forcibly displaced worldwide as a result of persecution, conflict, generalized violence and human rights violations. Of this 15.4 million people are refugees, nearly one million (937,000) asylum seekers and 28.8 million are IDPs;[3] between 70–75 per cent of forcibly displaced people are identified as 'women and children' (UNHCR 2012: 3).

This assertion constructs bodies: woman refugee as victim, fearful, passive – and bundles 'women' in with 'children' in ways that deny agency and resilience that may be present, even in the most dire circumstances. It obscures bodies: do we see boy or girl children? It disguises family configurations: do we see households headed by men, women, boys or girls? It disguises the very different, gendered experiences of political violence that drive refugees: girl children's experiences of violence and flight are often different from boys of the same state (Brocklehurst 2006), as are refugee women's experiences (Forbes Martin and Tirman 2009; Giles 2013; Indra 1999; Nolin 2006). Gender-related persecution has, however, been recognized as grounds to grant refugee status. Currently 14 states have implemented or amended refugee legislation to instruct adjudicators to recognize gender-based persecution as a potential ground for refugee protection. The recognition of gender-related persecution 'stands out as a rare counter trend, thanks in large measure to feminist advocacy, scholarly research and networking inside and outside governmental institutions' (Macklin 2008: 32).

THE GLOBAL POLITICAL ECONOMY OF MIGRATION

There is a global political economy of migration, which reflects the changing hierarchy of states and regions, the increasingly globalized division of labour, and shifting gender relations. Almost one in every 10 persons in developed countries is a migrant, while only one in every 70 persons in developing countries is a migrant. These flows are likely to intensify under the threat of climate change.

Gender matters at all levels and stages of labour migration. Gender structures the wider labour market, too (Peterson 2003). Migrant workers contribute to economic development in the new state, and to the state they left. Remittances are one aspect of this latter contribution. Women are especially significant in remittance flows, for men often remit to their wives at home, and women remit to female relatives especially those caring for their children (see also Kunz 2011). In this way, women are expected to contribute to family, community and national development (INSTRAW 2007b).[4]

The global labour market is increasingly bipolarised (Chang and Ling 2000). Professionals, market managers, and techno-skilled workers may be in demand, and move relatively freely. Those who are unskilled, deskilled and casualized are also increasingly feminized – more likely to be women, and/or in conditions of work traditionally associated with women. These workers are not a residual or incidental effect of globalization; rather they are intrinsic, underpinning and servicing global capital and its elites. Sassen remarks on the 'feminization of survival, because it is increasingly on the backs of women' that family support, business profits and government revenue are secured (2000: 506). These service workers are increasingly likely to be migrant workers, whose conditional or illegal status compounds the vulnerabilities they already experience as poorer, less protected workers, and often as women.

Millions of women are now on the move across state borders and often over vast distances (Pettman 2008). Many move to various forms of care work. This increasingly transnational labour market is compounded by other operations of gender, including through global restructuring (Marchand and Runyan 2000). In richer countries, more women are going 'out' to work even as the welfare state and public provision is wound back. In poorer states, neoliberal reforms and increasing health and education costs in particular increase the need to find new forms of work and pay, even while reducing employment in those same areas, in which women predominated. Richer states and families are importing women workers from poorer states and communities in a new transnational division of reproductive labour (Parrenas 2001). Thanh-Dam Truong describes such transnational care as a 'massive transfer of reproductive labour from one class, ethnic group, nation or region to another' (1996: 33). Pettman has described this form of labour as 'international sex and service' (2008), referring especially to the kinds of women's work – domestic work, care of children, the sick and elderly, and sex work – that is increasingly transnationalized.

Transnational reproductive labour

Women moving internationally for care work are, like women everywhere, caught between the public and private, and between productive and reproductive work, where the latter is seen as women's work, or as not really work at all. This makes for a triple burden of vulnerability, as women, as migrants, and in forms and places of work that are largely unregulated or hard to monitor, or organise. Often this work takes place in households, complicating relations among women, between employer and worker, who are usually from different classes, ethnicities and increasingly national backgrounds. Human Rights Watch has documented the abuse of domestic workers predominantly from the Philippines, Sri Lanka and Indonesia in Saudi Arabia, observing that while many domestic workers benefit from decent working conditions others experience a range of abuses including non-payment of salaries, forced confinement, food deprivation, excessive workload and instances of severe psychological, physical and sexual abuse (HRW 2008b: 2).

Transnational care sustains different forms of employment and consumption in more developed countries or richer families, enabling women more public participation and independence, even as it deprives families in poorer states of labour and emotional care. There may be a roll-on effect, so that the migrating woman's family may be cared for by female kin or pay for a poorer woman to do her work (see Figure 23.2). So while the international division of labour changes, the gendered division of labour does not. 'Rather than challenging the gendered division of labor or making demands upon the government to take more responsibility for developing comprehensive child care and elderly care programs, the hiring of foreign domestic workers has tended to maintain the tradition of domestic labour as women's work – simply shifting the burden from one set of women to another' (Maher 2004: 135). Which leads us to ask: Why is it everywhere women who are overwhelmingly responsible for 'domestic' work?

Transnational care work is gendered. It is also (as gender always is) racialized and culturalized. In Singapore for example, there are some 100,000 international

'When women migrate internationally for social reproductive jobs, they enhance the quality of care in the receiving states at the same time as their own families and children suffer the loss of their attention ... the children of female migrants and those who care for them indirectly absorb some of the cost of first-world social reproduction. The transfer of female labor from less developed to more developed states initiates a transnational "chain of care" that exacerbates international inequalities' (Maher 2004: 132).

An example:

'A professional woman in Los Angeles who earns a salary of $4000 a month in the formal market hires a migrant woman from Guanajuato, Mexico for $800 a month to care for her children and elderly father and to perform some housekeeping. The migrant woman hires a woman living in Guanajuato to care for her own children remaining there, paying her $100 per month. This Mexican woman might then depend upon the unpaid labor of a female relative to care for her elderly parents' (Maher 2004: 146).

Figure 23.2 Transnational social reproduction.

domestic workers (IDWs), mostly from the Philippines, some from Indonesia, and from Sri Lanka. A racialization and nationalization hierarchy of IDWs is reflected in recruitment agencies' advertisements and in media stereotyping of particular nationalities (Yeoh and Huang 2000). While Filipinas are more in demand and better paid, and valued as good English speakers, they are also seen as more worldly and political. Indonesians are seen as hardworking and obedient, while Sri Lankans are infantilised (Pettman 2008). These images, in turn, affect the reception of women in their new states and workplaces, making them vulnerable to further sexualization and stigmatization.

This is not to say that all migrant women in transnational care chains are exploited, although many are, and some are subject to abuse and violence. Neither is it to say that all are passive or reactive, responding only to family pressures or structural demands. Many women move to sustain their households, some move to escape abusive or dangerous homes and others move for adventure and independence. All make their way in circumstances that demand constant negotiation. Some women are politicized before they move or through the move, and join local groups and NGOs to struggle for their rights as women, migrants, or workers (Law 2002).

Gender is performative. Gender identities are constantly being reproduced and recreated along the migration pathways. Many women tell stories of their travels that are rewarding, even heroic, giving meaning to the challenges, losses and gains along the way. These stories may not accord with academic studies of migration, especially those that either do not see women or see them primarily as victims or dependents. Feminist scholars who take women's experiences seriously and regard them as knowledge makers, theorising complex personal, social, cultural and international relations along migration chains, generate better, more inclusive records of these exchanges (Aguilar 1999; Hilsdon 1998; Kunz, 2012). These, in turn, deepen our understanding of gendered dynamics of globalization and the links between migration, development and gender; Sassen remarks that global care chains are 'a strategic site where the gender dynamics of the current processes of globalization can be detected, studied, and theorised' (quoted in INSTRAW 2007a: 1).

GENDER/POST-MIGRATION

The previous section focused on transnational care workers, who may move as strictly controlled temporary workers, or as workers who settle in the new state and may be able to sponsor family reunion there. Women move along different tracks, and into very diverse situations. Much will depend on whether they expect to resettle or return, whether the choices are theirs, whether they were escaping or forced to leave, whether they move alone or have family or community with them, and whether they find such attachments supportive or constraining, exploitative or violent. And what is their reception in the new state? What are their rights, as women, as workers, as migrants – and how accessible are those rights? Are there women's organizations and movements to support them as women? Or do they identify primarily with 'the community' or religion, rather than as women? Is there a possibility of acquiring citizenship?

The first chapter invited us to think carefully 'about how the body manifests in our understandings of IR' (see Chapter 3). In this case, in terms of migration, we need to ask which bodies? These are never only sexed bodies – bodies are raced, classed, 'read' for age, ability and sexuality or sexualized. Some migrant women's bodies can merge into the dominant or local community, while others become visible in ways that may endanger them, or attract unwanted attention. Gender relations and gender scripts indicate what might be seen as right, or wrong, or 'punish those who fail to do their gender right' (see Chapter 3). When we look at bodies out of place, the possibility for transgression and offence are multiplied. Some performances of femininity may be beyond the limits of intelligibility because of the new cultural context. Forms of dress, mobility and exchange from home may not be welcome in the new place. But gender performance also changes over time and place; for example, in France and in Malaysia, more Muslim daughters than their mothers might wear the veil, not as tradition but as part of a modern identity politics. Women are especially visible, not only as bearers of sex, but as bearers of culture and identity. They may find themselves subject to intense border patrols, from the inside or outside of their supposed identity group. In the face of migration or besieged minority status, women themselves can become the territory (Bloul 1993), expected to honour their gendered role, as symbols and reproducers of the community (Yuval-Davis 1997).

Gender/migration/belonging

Migration produces difference. The visible presence of 'others' can trigger debates about who 'we' are, who belongs here, and who cannot belong. That strange word 'naturalization', meaning to acquire citizenship, hints that there is something alien about the stranger, the guest worker, the migrant. The pre-eminent nation-state that IR favours assumes a coincidence of authority, territory and identity, such that it is possible to call up 'the national interest' or 'national identity', despite the obvious fact that no state is culturally homogenous and states' boundaries, of territory and belonging, shift (Steans 2006). Here again is the paradox of an age of globalization in which state surveillance and political panics about people moving have hardened the borders, producing images such as 'fortress Europe' and the fence between Mexico and the US. As Jacqueline Berman identifies, in the so-called 'West' this paradox of globalization has 'generated a sense of anxiety, especially around the modern nation-state, in what might be called a crisis over boundaries' (Berman 2003: 39). In this sense, boundaries need not be read as a reference to territorial or geographic boundaries, but imagined boundaries between 'citizen' and 'alien', 'us' and 'them'. In the context of globalization, what does belonging mean, now, with so many people on the move, resident outside their countries of birth, and with transnational families and links even for those who stay at home?

State sovereignty is under attack from above through the market and new technologies; from below, with the resurgence of religious and cultural identities; and from without, through more sustained attention to and international action for human rights (Falk 2004: 178). The state has given up some of its welfare and other provisions that were designed to underpin the lives and livelihoods of their citizens. Crucial decisions about our economy or wellbeing are made in board rooms or international financial institutions far beyond state and citizen reach, causing 'deflated citizenship' (Seidmann 2004). Sassen argues that market globalization amounts to 'a savage attack on the principles of citizenship' (2004: 195). She points to the emergence of new political subjects and new transnational affiliations and claims. Why then should citizenship remain a territorially based, often exclusive, identity and status (see Chapter 26)?

Chandra Mohanty reflects on becoming a US citizen at a time of intense militarization and masculinization of US foreign policy and empire building, seeking 'to examine this "new" status, to ask what it means for an immigrant woman of color turned US citizen to engage in transnational feminist politics at a time when some of "my" peoples are seen as non-citizens and threats to the US nation' (2006: 8). She argues:

> If the racialized, gendered, heterosexual figure of the citizen patriot, the risky immigrant, the sexualized and de-masculinized, external enemy and potential domestic terrorist are all narratives and state practices mobilized in the service of [US] empire, an appropriate question to ask is whether and how the academy, and academic disciplines ... are involved in contesting or buttressing these practices.
>
> (Mohanty 2006: 14)

This remains a critical question for feminist citizenship and migration studies more broadly.

Travelling gender

'It's not just tangible things and people, but also ideas and images such as democracy, modernity and gender relations, that travel' (Davids and van Driel 2005: 10). So too does feminism, in its various and increasingly transnational forms. Feminisms migrate, along with and independent of women moving across state borders. Feminist language and perspectives are picked up and adapted, modified and developed by women theorizing and organizing at local and national levels, often using internationally generated or validated claims for their own purposes (Ackerly 2001; Antrobus 2004; Davis 2005). So notions of women's rights as human rights, or reproductive rights, are picked up and reworked; campaigns are mobilized, solidarities are built using new technologies and travelling connections (see Chapter 28).

Questions for further debate

1. Why, in an age of globalization, with reputedly free movement of goods, services, technology and finance, are proposals for the free movement of people usually met with such alarm and resistance?
2. Are you a migrant? Is anyone in your family a migrant? If so, where from, why did they leave, why did they come here? (How) does gender matter in these experiences?
3. Where is home? Can we have more than one home?
4. When does a migrant cease to be a migrant? Or can it be an inheritable condition?
5. What might a study of gender and migration tell us about how borders function in global politics today?

Sources for further reading and research

Forbes Martin, S. and J. Tirman (eds) (2009) *Women Migration and Conflict: Breaking a Deadly Cycle*, Dordrecht, Heidelberg, London and New York: Springer.
International Migration Review (2006) Special Issue 'Gender and Migration Revisited', 40(1).
Oishi, N. (2005) *Women in Motion: Globalization, State Policies and Labour Migration in Asia*, Stanford, CA: Stanford University Press.
Piper, N. (2007) *New Perspectives on Gender and Migration: Livelihood, Rights and Entitlements*, New York: Routledge.
Tastsoglou, E. and A. Dobrowolsky (eds) (2006) *Women, Migration and Citizenship: Making Local, National and Transnational Connections*, Aldershot and Burlington, VT: Ashgate.

Notes

1 Some states are tightening citizenship provisions including a 'citizenship test' in terms of language, political knowledge and 'values'. See, for example, Kymlicka (2003) comparing North American and UK reception to such citizenship tests.
2 The only form of migration that almost always carries with it the right of citizenship in the new state (Brysk 2004).

3 These figures too are unreliable. Far more people are displaced within their own state by armed conflict and human rights violations. Many of those labelled as 'economic migrants' might also be fleeing from violence, discrimination or for survival (see also Sara Davies, 'FactCheck: Are Asylum Seekers really Economic Migrants?', The Conversation, 2013. Available at http://theconversation.com/factcheck-are-asylum-seekers-really-economic-migrants-15601 (accessed 7 August 2013)).

4 The current focus on remittances as a link between migration and development constructs migrant women workers in an instrumental way, familiar in the 'efficiency' approach to 'women in development'.

CHAPTER 24

Religion

Katherine E. Brown

LEARNING OUTCOMES

Upon completion, readers should be able to:

- Recognize the significance of gender for understanding the role of religion in global politics and the importance of religion in shaping gender in global politics.
- Identify ways in which religion and gender intersect at the level of the individual, the state and transnationally.
- Evaluate how religion and gender are transformed through global politics.

INTRODUCTION

Engaging in critical gender analysis of religion proves challenging as there is often a double blindness at work. On the one hand, most contemporary gender studies, whether in the social sciences, humanities or natural sciences, are 'religion blind', while, on the other, many studies in religion continue to be 'gender blind' (King and Beattie 2004: 1). As international relations and the discipline of IR grapple with the 'war on terror' such blindness becomes untenable. It has been understood both in policy circles and in academia, as a war driven by 'religious fanatics', with no respect for women, who attack the rights and freedoms of secular, liberal, Western states that uphold gender equality (Razack 2008; see also Chapter 12).

Specifically, the military intervention in Afghanistan has been framed in terms of 'saving Muslim women' from the Taliban, and while not the only justification for it, a gendered and racialized narrative can certainly be observed. Although such narratives were challenged both within Afghanistan and outside it (Abu-Lughod 2002) the Khazai administration has placed great emphasis on women's participation in politics and education as a way to distinguish itself from its 'fanatical religious' predecessors and to acquire international aid funding. Despite setting up this narrative, a recent report from the UK House of Commons reveals it is the said same gains in women's rights in Afghanistan that are most at risk from NATO withdrawal. It is alleged that the promises, reforms and programmes were shallow at best. Women's groups in Afghanistan, especially those that embraced the new 'liberation' narrative, feel abandoned as 'the West' is increasingly unwilling to sacrifice 'blood and treasure' in the country. Their concerns are sometimes dismissed as 'women's issues', as peripheral to the war and IR, but a closer examination shows how integral gender is to the operation of war, politics, and religion.

Furthermore failure to analyze the gendered and religious discourses of the War on Terror means that latent 'fear of Islam' born of Orientalism, is often overlooked. Such Islamophobia and Orientalism casts Muslims and Islam as timeless, backward, and homogenous, exiled into an irretrievable state of otherness (Kabbani 1994). Muslims are forced into a position of 'forever' at risk and permanently suspect of 'being terrorists' (Pantazis and Pemberton 2009). In practical terms, this has meant an increase in violence against Muslims living in the West (for example, see statistics from the UK Home Affairs Committee 2005: 20). Often this violence is targeted at Muslim women wearing a *hijab* because they are visibly identifiable as religiously 'different' subjects. Yet Muslim men are also, of course, gendered; they become cast as 'folk devils': violent, criminal, backward, and bearded, subject to increasing state surveillance and public suspicions. The Islamophobia that drives violence and interventions is often tied to fears for the 'secular state' and nationalist agendas. Ironically, this same 'War on Terror' that seeks to save Muslim women from danger, therefore operates as a protection racket that also disempowers them (Sjoberg and Peet 2011). It is clear that gendered bodies become sites of ideological battlegrounds and are used to justify specific political agendas.

However, 'gender' is not something that 'happens' to war, politics or religion as a fixed category. Considering religious practices, institutions, traditions, narratives of redemption, creation stories, eschatological utopias, and iconic images reveals how religions have created and legitimated gender, enforced, oppressed, and warped it, but also subverted, transgressed, transformed, and liberated it. Recognizing this dual impact is important because unacknowledged biases within our studies render us partially sighted. Those who consider religious affiliation as a sign of false consciousness, for example, often fail to recognize how religious faith and practice have served as a source of encouragement and empowerment for women. They do not consider the agency of women as religious subjects. Conversely, those who experience religion positively tend to ignore the dark side of religious institutions and practices. This is something to consider when reading through the debates here and how to approach the topics acknowledging your own position and those of the authors presented.

GENDER, WOMEN, AND RELIGIONS

Cultural images, ideas, norms and stereotypes about women permeate religious traditions and inform wider cultural practices. In the Christian faith, the complex figures of the Virgin Mary, Eve, and Mary Magdalene have led to certain social norms regarding motherhood, chastity, and marriage for women worldwide. This has had significant implications for those women who have children outside of wedlock, as the Magdalene Laundries in Ireland show. Until late into the twentieth century 'difficult' girls (because they were sexually active, or sexually abused, or simply poor) were sent to 'laundries' by their families or the state. The asylums/ laundries were operated by holy orders of nuns that sought to protect society from the contagion of 'wayward' women while simultaneously attempting to reform them through a harsh regimen of laundry work and devotional rituals (Titley 2006). Sometimes known as Penitents, they had committed no crimes, but they could not easily leave, they were forced to work without pay under extremely harsh conditions. It is estimated some 10,000 women passed through the laundries between 1922 and 1996. Yet the four religious orders behind them are refusing to contribute financially to the compensation scheme set up for the 600 survivors who 'worked' under them (although they are willing to help in other ways). Here we see the complex interactions between religious institutions, the state and religious ideals of womanhood that permeate Irish society. While this story could simply be understood in terms of economic exploitation of vulnerable women by four institutions and the state, this narrative would ignore the fact that the gendered religious ideals of the mainstream Catholicism enabled Irish society to justify, ignore, and accept the treatment of these women.

Furthermore, when widely accepted religious ideals about motherhood, womanhood, and sexuality are challenged women can be met with condemnation and punishment. This was the case of Tunisian protester Amina Tyler, who at 19 years old, posted a topless picture of herself on the internet with the writing scrawled on her: 'my body belongs to me and is not the source of anyone's honour' (see Figure 24.1). Subsequently in a Skype interview she reported that her family subjected her to physical abuse and an imam told her she was bewitched. She also said she was subjected to a 'virginity test'. She also posted a picture of herself stood against a wall with her graffiti in Arabic 'a woman's body is not a sin'. A few months later she attempted to graffiti a mosque and was arrested.

Her Arabic text can be read as a rejection of religious groups utilizing cultural norms of family honour in order to discipline women's bodies. As Tyler said in an interview: 'At the beginning I did not even know what they [Femen] were, but I really liked what they were doing to promote women's freedom' (Tyler, quoted in Tourn 2013). She also noted in the interview 'that women have reached the height of self-determination: we no longer obey any authority, neither family nor religious. We know what we want and we make our own decisions'. Her protests coincide with other Tunisian feminist activists who are also worried by the rise to power of the Islamist En-Nahda party in the wake of the 2012 democratic election. While En-Nahda leaders have tried hard to convince the public that they will not curb personal freedom laws, many Tunisian women remain concerned.

Figure 24.1 Tunisian protester Amina Tyler.

The Islamist conservative response to her action was predictable: '[H]er act could bring about an epidemic. It could be contagious and give idea [sic] to other women', said Adel Almi, head of Tunisia's Commission for the Protection of Virtue and Prevention of Vice (quoted in Salek 2013). However, liberal commentators in the West were outraged as well, labeling Femen racist, classist, imperialist, colonialist, Eurocentric, Islamophobic, and sexist for excluding women who don't have vaginas (they do not accept non-cis women as members). A number of Muslim women responded that they did not need saving and that the Femen's subsequent 'topless *jihad*' in solidarity was offensive (see Figure 24.2). Muslim women and others challenge the notion that feminist struggles must be associated with the right to uncover themselves; rights must include the right to cover, and specifically to wear a *hijab*.

Amina has also now left the Femen group because she says it is Islamophobic. Femen is clear that it is anti-religions, and has carried out similar acts in Catholic churches. The merging of race, religion, and gender in this particular protest made Femen worldwide news in a way their protests in Europe had not.

Feminism's relationship with religion has been complex. Many feminists, such as those who align themselves with Femen, argue that all organized religion is inherently patriarchal and must be fought against. This leaves little space in feminist discourses for women who find meaning and agency within their religion. Similarly, religious fundamentalists demand they abandon the quest for women's rights in order to remain 'true' believers. It seems religious women can have rights or religion.

Women have also been able to use religious imagery and themes to their benefit. For example, in Argentina women used their roles as mothers, embodied in the Catholic construction of Marianismo (valuing the reproductive ability of women and moral strength of women) to claim political justice. As mothers of 'the

Figure 24.2 Anti-Femen protester.

disappeared', the *Asociación Madres de Plaza de Mayo* could claim justice from the ruling regime (as discussed in Chapter 3). This also reveals the blurring of the 'private' or 'domestic' sphere and the public sphere as they used the traditional understanding of women's roles in the home as the linchpin of their public protests. Other examples include the weekly vigils of Jewish 'Women in Black' (referring to their clothing), which called attention to their opposition to war (critics called them 'black widows'). Similarly women of Machsom Watch (an Israeli military check point) document human rights abuses at Israeli checkpoints and use their moral authority as mothers and grandmothers embedded in Judaism to challenge Israeli soldiers (Sharoni 2012).

Fighting, and being an active member of a state's armed forces is often presented as the ultimate male sacrifice and sign of citizenship. However, a number of religious movements prohibit participation in war and violence. In the United Kingdom, the Quaker religious movement became strongly associated with conscientious objection in the two World Wars. They sought to offer a different masculine ideal, of courage for one's convictions and self-improvement. This alternative narrative of masculinity and citizenship was not widely accepted by society and pacifists and conscientious objectors faced considerable hostility, harassment, and imprisonment at times of war. In the United States, COs were referred to as 'sissies' and 'parlor pinks', implying a lack of masculinity and association with homosexuality, which at the time was considered deviant (Gullace 2002). In Canada, Mennonite male conscientious objectors also had the difficult task of reconciling Mennonite ideals of non-resistant pacifism with religious gender roles of the ideal man in the Second World War. Mennonites, as protestant fundamentalists, promoted a hyper-masculinity in attempts to counter cultural perceptions of them as emasculated by their religious zeal and repressed sexuality. A religious machismo dominated their religious discourses around masculinity. To realize this outside their community they likened their 'alternative service' to the military as much as possible, and sought to take on dangerous tasks in order to demonstrate they were not weak 'soft' men (Epp 1999; Stewart-Winter 2007).

These examples demonstrate a number of points. First, women's agency and power (or lack of) within States is shaped in part by underlying or overt religious norms about the role of women in society and the family. Thus religious symbolism and norms intersect with issues of race and gender to produce culturally intelligible subjects. Consequently, challenging those ideas about womanhood can be perilous. This leads to the second point, while challenges may be perilous they do occur, and reveal that gender and religious understandings of gender are not static. Indeed, religious institutions and organizations constantly have to re-affirm what womanhood is within their traditions and how it applies to society. The third point is that such discussions about gender and religion are not only about women. They are also about how religions help define key ideas of masculinity and male privilege.

SECULARISM, NATIONALISM, AND PUBLIC–PRIVATE DIVIDE

The previous examples also point to the connections between state power and religious institutions. Central to the myth of the foundation of the modern state is the separation of 'Church and State', namely secularism. Secularism is the association of the worldly, the temporal, and the process of secularization is frequently seen as the 'natural' evolution of international relations (Asad 2003; Juergensmeyer 1993). Secularism places religion within the 'domestic' sphere (beyond politics) in order to preserve the smooth running of the state. Laicism (the need to privatize religion) underpins much political and IR theory and practice. Experienced mostly overtly in France and Turkey, the aim is to protect the liberties of 'free thinking' individuals and preserve the stability of the state from religion. Indeed for realist, liberal and Marxist thinkers in International Relations, religion is an 'opiate' for the masses and obscures the fundamental material, structural or psychological motives of states and their peoples (Hurd 2004). Second, the refusal to act in a secular manner in international relations is seen as dangerous, extremist, and backward by many IR thinkers and practitioners. Concerns with theocratic states, such as Iran or Saudi Arabia, and the former Taliban-ruled Afghanistan, are that they insist on behaving outside of the 'secular norm', and the reasoning behind their policies it is assumed cannot be fully understood or predicted. Fears of Shari'a law (Islamic jurisprudence) emerging in the Western world, and the demonization of Shari'a serve as a good example of this. Third, it is assumed that with globalization, comes the universalizing of human rights and the generation of some form of global morality (Held 1995; Fukuyama 1989). Here the argument is that over time religion is not necessary in the public sphere as a universal morality takes on a global structure. Thus the secular is a cultural formation with 'its own practices, its own sensorium, its own hierarchy of faculties, its own habits of being' (Asad 2003; Warner 2008).

However, to understand the relationship between secularism and religion in these terms ignores a range of secular positions, and ignores the reality that religion has refused to stay in the place allocated to it by *laïcité*. Furthermore it ignores the gendering at work in these constructions. The private sphere is typically associated with the domestic, the emotional, spirituality, the corporeal, and the weak to be protected, although paradoxically it is also dangerous and threatening. It is also usually associated with the female–feminine. In contrast the public sphere is the space of men, for rationality, reason, secularity. These binaries are not only gendered; they are hierarchical. The language used to deny women suffrage is similar to the justifications given for the exclusion of religion from the public sphere. Secularism becomes more than an inevitable consequence of international relations but a process to create gendered subjects. This can be seen typically by controlling the visibility and mobility of female bodies. As Banu Gökarıksel and Katharyne Mitchell (2005: 150) write in their comparison of the veil debates in Turkey and France, 'secularism is one of the many technologies of control that state actors wield to discipline the wayward bodies of those defined as existing outside the cultural boundaries of the nation, particularly women and migrants'.

By banning religious symbols in public places, secularists seek to purge the body politic of 'particularist' influences and 'personal sentiments' (Gökarıksel and Mitchell 2005: 149–50). In other words, they aim to purify the public sphere and thus clear the way for the 'free and unhindered interaction of rational individuals.' Indeed when veiled women do enter into the public space, commentary assumes ontological priority is accorded to their religious identity and observances. In particular, you may know a Muslim woman when you see her because she wears a *hijab*. Paradoxically, while her religious practice makes her visible and defines her presence in the public sphere, the religious motivations behind her veil are often ignored, subsumed under assumptions about rebellious politics of living in the West, coercion by patriarchs no matter where they live, or protection from the male gaze.

From the debates over religious symbols in the public sphere, the extensive debates on the *hijab*, one might assume that there is a negative reaction when political leaders publicly perform their religious faith. The juxtaposition between religion and reason in 'secular states' means reference to religious faith can be seen to undermine decisions about war, or health policies, for example, despite these having strong moral and ethical undercurrents. For example when Tony Blair's religious observances became more public during the Iraq War, popular press blamed his wife's Catholicism and her 'undue' influence over him. It was not until after he left political office that he was able to set up the 'Faith Foundation' and convert to Catholicism. In the United States, secularism functions differently, religious devotion and conviction is expected of political leaders. Obama's religious convictions came under intense scrutiny during recent elections, with numerous conspiracy theories abound doubting it: 12 percent of Americans in 2008 (Pew 2008) believed he was Muslim, while, paradoxically, he also faced criticism of his controversial former Christian pastor, the Reverend Jeremiah Wright of Chicago.

Similarly, the Republican presidential candidate Mitt Romney's Mormon faith also caused much public debate, while Sarah Palin's Pentecostalism was downplayed by Republicans even though she was selected partly because she appealed to the

'New Christian Right' and the 'Tea Party' movements. The concerns are not that the candidates and Obama were religious, or that religiosity *per se* is a negative thing, but that voters expected to know about, understand, and evaluate their faith as a factor in weighing up their suitability to be president (or vice president). For the previous American President, George W. Bush, his protestant faith appeared to have an influence on policies regarding health care and international development. In his first month in office as President he issued an executive order that forbade any non-governmental organization that receives funds from the US agency for development to either provide safe abortion or to advocate it. In October 2002 American funding to the World Health Organization was frozen pending an investigation into its policies on human reproduction and contraception. This could be interpreted as a simple appeal to a neoconservative support base or the consequence of his religious convictions, but the decisions were produced by, and reproduce, particular assumptions about gender, religion and global politics.

While women often find their bodies subject to gendered violence and their rights curtailed by nationalist struggles (often with the approval of the state) they are not only 'victims'. Swati Parashar's work (2010) on India and Pakistan, and Caron Gentry and Laura Sjoberg's (2007) writings on women and violence point to how women become agents for nationalist–religious causes, and how their agency is then understood by others. Parashar discusses Asiya Andrabi, a prominent devout Muslim activist in Kashmir who leads the *Dukhtaran-e-Millat* (Daughters of Faith), an all-women's group often referred to as a 'soft terror outfit' (2010: 439). Her group is explicitly and overtly religious in its nature, believes that *jihad* is the only way Islamic values can be imposed in Kashmir and rejects the Indian state. The Daughters of Faith have targeted unveiled women by throwing paint on them, vandalized cinemas and beauty parlors, arguing that they promote corruption and decadence that are dangerous to women and Kashmir (2010: 439). She is not the only female figure active in militant politics in the region, further south in 2008, 30-year-old Pragya Singh Thakur was arrested on terrorism charges in connection with Hinduvata right-wing militancy (Parashar 2010: 442). She is linked to the 2006 bombing in Maelagon on the eve of the Muslim festival of Eid, killing 37. Hers was part of an anti-Muslim Hindu 'reprisal terrorism', that connects to the issue of Indian secularism, religious settlement, Kashmir and Indian–Pakistani relations. Parashar concludes that women's participation in religio-nationalist movements is an articulation of both their political and their religious identities.

These discussions show how religion can provide the 'common ground' a cultural marker of identity and belonging as well as a sign of difference. Yet it also shows how constructions of religious identity in the public sphere are often feminized and delegitimized in global politics as irrational and not belonging.

TRANSNATIONAL RELIGIOUS MOVEMENTS AND ROLE OF WOMEN

Religions are often global in their morality and reach, their influence extending beyond state borders. Fear of Catholics in many places is linked to their fidelity not to their country but to the Pope. Thus while Stalin quipped 'how many divisions does the Pope have?', the power of the Roman Catholic Church to guide and influence the faithful should not be underestimated. The Church's views on contraception, on HIV/AIDs, on poverty and other religions influences the behaviors and political opinions of Catholics all over the world. This was recognized by Muslims in Turkey, Gaza and Pakistan when they protested following a lecture by Pope Benedict on Islam at Regensburg University in 2006, in which he explored the historical and philosophical differences between Islam and Christianity, and the relationship between violence and faith. During his address, Pope Benedict quoted a fourteenth-century Christian emperor: 'Show me just what Muhammad brought that was new and there you will find things only evil and inhuman, such as his command to spread by the sword the faith he preached'. He then went on to say that violence was 'incompatible with the nature of God and the nature of the soul'.

In his 2008 end-of-year message, Pope Benedict said that the Church considered the distinction between men and women as central to human nature. Deviating from these traditional gender roles was 'a violation of the natural order.' During his time in office, while his stance softened on the use of condoms (saying that in 'some circumstances' it might be permitted), the Catholic Church's views on gay marriage remain firmly in opposition. To highlight this position the transgender-lesbian and queer movement Sisters of Perpetual Indulgence protest in exaggerated and sexualized religious garb. This is a transnational movement, that while not religious in its nature, expresses itself through religious imagery and symbolism. Like many Catholic nuns, Sisters of Perpetual Indulgence go through a period of aspirancy, a postulant stage and a novitiate before becoming fully professed; the entire process to become a 'Sister' takes a year or more (Wilcox 2012). The group has expanded from San Francisco where it was founded in 1979, and now includes women, men, and transgender people of all sexualities, although the group is still predominantly made up of gay men, in chapters or abbeys across the world. They are identifiable in most countries by their white faces and glamorous makeup, as well as their creative headdresses. Some orders wear uniforms that closely resemble traditional Catholic nuns' habits; others wear dresses or skirts below their coronets and veils (Wilcox 2012). Sisters claim to be 'nuns for the twenty-first century' and nuns who serve communities not served by traditional nuns of any religion (Wilcox 2012). For many of the sisters, the charity work they do, and the street protests they participate in, are linked to their sense of spirituality, which is frequently formed of a bricolage of religious traditions and linked to their subject life experiences.

While this movement might seem to mock those of faith, they tap into an important mode of understanding about spirituality. Meredith McGuire has long argued that many women's forms of spirituality in the U.S. fail to register on traditional measures of religiosity. In the European context, Linda Woodhead and Evea Sointu (2008) note how women are drawn to 'subject-life' or spiritual forms of religious expression. Ong (1990) reminds us how Islam in Malaysia is not lived solely according to a text-based understanding of Islam that would deny a more fluid notion of worship. Indeed, spiritualist and vernacular understandings of Islam are more common than stereotypes of Islam would suggest, although an Arabization process does appear to occurring (Bernal 1994; Ong 1990). Bernal (1994) argues, in relation to Sudan, that this is not a return to traditional practices or more 'authentic' ways of being Muslim, but expresses a rupture in social and cultural order. These new ways of being Muslim tend to deny the importance and spaces for women's worship, such as at shrines. These new scripturalist understandings of Islam represent their incorporation in the world system.

Adopting new positions, such as new veiling and *purdah* practices, are not simply rejections of the West, they are following a course of action with its own inherent meaning. For many third world Muslims, Saudi Arabia has come to represent 'the' authentic expression of Islam. Many pilgrims on *hajj* are predisposed to absorb the practices, symbols and ideas prevalent in Saudi Arabia, and Saudi oil wealth has enabled it to promote particular understandings of faith across the Muslim world through schools, textbooks, charities, Islamic financing and banks. Importantly, to adopt such new practices were also signs of wealth and 'sophistication' for many women and households; only wealthy families could afford for their women not to work. The adoption of fundamentalist Islam also helped shift practice (to a degree) away from pharonic female circumcision (labiaotomy) to the less injurious sunna form (clitroidechtomy). As Bernal concludes: 'It is particularly because Islam can be constructed from local understandings as well as from transnational sources, that it offers ideological resources that can be mobilized to various ends, including the legitimation of new gender roles' (1994: 62).

CONCLUSION

In this chapter, I have discussed how religion impacts on global politics in gendered ways, but also how gender is transformed by religious institutions and practices too. It also reveals how religion itself is framed through understandings of global politics. How the spiritual impacts on the secular and vice versa is shown to be more complex than can be captured in a simple linear, unidirectional, conceptualization.

Questions for further debate

1. Should the *burqua* (full face veil) be banned in public spaces?
2. Should Muslims living as minorities within a state be allowed to use Shari'a law as the basis for their legal settlements to family disputes (non-criminal law)? Should other religious minorities be afforded the same?
3. In what ways do religious narratives on gender impact on women's rights worldwide?
4. How might incorporating religion into your analysis complement or add to other topics in this textbook?
5. Is Islamophobia different to 'racism' or 'anti-semitism'?

Sources for further reading and research

Abu-Lughod, L. (2002) 'Do Muslim Women Really Need Saving? Anthropological Reflections on Cultural Relativism and its Others', *American Anthropologist*, 104(3): 783–90.

Afshar, H., R. Aitken and M. Franks (2005) 'Feminisms, Islamophobia and Identities', *Political Studies*, 53(2): 262–83.

Bracke, S. (2003) 'Author(iz)ing Agency: Feminist Scholars Making Sense of Women's Involvement in Religious "Fundamentalist" Movements', *European Journal of Women's Studies*, 10(3): 335–46.

Habermas, J. (2008) 'Secularism's Crisis of Faith: Notes on Post-secular Society', *NPQ*, Fall: 16–29.

Parashar, S. (2010) 'The Sacred and the Sacrilegious: Exploring Women's "Politics" and "Agency" in Radical Religious Movements in South Asia', *Totalitarian Movements and Political Religions*, 11: 3–4, 435–55.

CHAPTER 25

Nationalism

Dibyesh Anand

Upon completion, readers should be able to:

- Explain what is meant by 'primordialism' and nationalism as 'social construction'.
- Analyse the relationship between nation, culture, and gender.
- Evaluate the role that gender has played in nationalist conflict.

INTRODUCTION

Who are you? Who am I? The answers to such questions will depend on the context as well as on the person being questioned. But individuals have only limited say in shaping the collective to which they are deemed to belong. For example, you may think of yourself as a non-believer in national boundaries, but the state will remind you again and again about your nationality. Our rights and access to resources will often depend on our nationality in a particular country. You may not agree with ethnic classification, but during civil strife who you are seen as may determine whether you live or die. For more than a century national identity has been the primary form in which collective aspirations have been expressed throughout the world. Religion, ethnicity, gender, sexuality, class, race – all these have usually taken a backseat to the dominance of national identity. One has only to look at the willingness of millions to sacrifice their lives and many more to take the lives of others in the name of their nation.

If one studies the twentieth century closely, it is clear that the most pervasive ideology was neither communism nor capitalism but nationalism. Wars took place, murders were celebrated and mourned, people were encouraged to look beyond their immediate family and identify with a collective and at the same time the locus of empathy was particularised – all in the name of nationalism. A careful analysis of the nationalised lives people have lived in contemporary times shows that, though the ideal norm is of a nation with its own state, in reality, states are mostly multi-national and it is states that often seek to create a sense of nationhood among their people to ensure stability. Nationalism is the primary ideology through which the state seeks to gain internal sovereignty. The exact form of dominant nationalism within a state depends on many factors. The State may be successful in fostering an inclusive nationalism or it may come up with a majoritarian nationalism that excludes minorities within. The latter then may lead to minority nationalisms and sometimes violent resistance to the existing state and demand for a new state. What I have said so far about nationalism as an ideology captures many events of the last century – inter-state wars as well as civil wars. There is no doubt that nationalism matters in global politics.

But how does gender matter in/to nationalism? The literature on the subject has largely ignored gender as an analytical category. In recent years when gender and nationalism has been studied, mostly by feminist scholars, it highlights the central role of women in nationalism and nationalist movements and debates whether nationalism as an ideology domesticates or emancipates women. 'Understanding nationalism as gendered means recognizing its varied impact on women and men of different social groupings' (Puri 2004: 110). A more sophisticated approach does not focus on women but on ways in which the discourse of nationalism intersects with those of masculinity and femininity. We can investigate not how pre-given women or men act but how their identity as men or women gets shaped through a nationalist discourse and that in turn (re)produces a national identity. In this chapter, I will outline the main debates around nationalism and then analyse the different ways in which gender is central to, but does not exhaust, nationalism.

THEORISING NATIONALISM

Primordialists argue that nations have an essence that is historical, natural and almost unchanging. Most proponents of nationalism claim that their nation has ancient historical roots. For instance, Zionists claim all Jews for more than 2,500 years to be part of a single nation, while Palestinian nationalism also traces itself back to more than 1,000 years of continuity. Contrary to the claims of primordialists, I argue that national identity is not an essence, but a performance, a construction, an articulation, a discourse (see Chapter 1 on 'performativity'). It is as much a process as it is a product – it is a productive process. The performance of a national identity does not take place in a vacuum, but in a power-laden international political and cultural context. This international context, in turn, is marked by asymmetries of structural and representational power in which the West (more as a source of ideas and less as a political actor) remains dominant. The rhetoric of nationalism often ignores that the need to present one's own community as a nation is a modern phenomenon.

As Mayall (1990) points out, nationalism has become structurally embedded as the basis of the modern state everywhere only in recent times. Nationalism is, on the one hand, an ideological movement toward the construction of a nation. On the other hand, it is a product of heightened consciousness of national identity among a people:

> [T]he appeals to nationalism are always politically important—nationalism is still regarded as a (if not 'the') prime driver of and legitimator for political, government and state policy and action, both internal and external. Moreover, in that the distribution of power within political, social and economic structures, including global structures, tends to ensure that these structures are reproduced, political legitimacy and loyalty (i.e. nationalism) has a fundamental role in this process.
>
> (Tooze 1996: xvii)

Let us explore different ways in which nationalism and national identity has been perceived. Please note the difference between nation, nationalism, national identity and national culture. The term 'nation' implies shared commonality that is recognisable and can be mobilised politically – culture, common language, history, heritage, ethnicity, religion, race, etc. A sense of 'shared history' is crucial to the concept of nation. Nationalism is the ideology that a nation should have a state of its own or at the very least have a right to self-determination. National identity refers to those aspects of culture that are seen as central to what brings people together as a nation.

Similarly, national culture indicates a strong overlap between a nation and a culture. A multicultural nation or a multinational culture (the United States can be seen as a good example of the former while China can be seen as an example of the latter) tend to complicate the simplistic notion of national culture. This discussion still leaves out states or nation-states, although the political entity that claims to represent the nation or that nations seek to achieve is the state. In fact, international relations is, in practice, interstate relations. States are the predominant political actors in contemporary international relations while nationalism remains a powerful ideology, often used to bolster the legitimacy of the state (if the state claims to represent a nation, it is seen as legitimate) or to challenge the legitimacy of the state (separatist nationalism would claim that the existing state does not represent their will). If international relations were only about abstract states, we would be talking about culture here. Culture becomes significant because of the central role played by nationalism and national identity in propping up states or shaping the states.

The concept of culture has become crucial to the formulation of distinctive identities especially, but not exclusively, in relation to the issue of who belongs and who does not belong in or to specific political communities (see Figure 25.1). This is where the culture concept and the idea of 'nation' intersect, for the latter is often defined not simply as a political community characterised by a particular culture, but as a political community by virtue of its possession of a particular culture ... To the extent that nations are assumed to be cultural units encompassing 'a people' it

The dominant understanding of culture is that it is something that a social group shares, that defines the 'we' and 'us', and allows for recognising the boundaries between us and them, Self and the Other. A definition of culture in terms of shared sense of belonging has an important impact. It can be mobilised differently by different actors. Nationalism is one such ideology that claims to speak on behalf of an existing national culture while at the same time shaping one. For instance, right-wing nationalists may insist that any dissent from their version of national culture is unpatriotic and a treason, while critical dissidents may argue that their national culture is accommodative and allows for plurality of views.

Culture is as much about contestation within it about what are the main features of it. The view of an Iranian feminist or a Revolutionary Guard about what is the core of Iranian–Islamic culture would be very different. In this sense, cultures are always in process. They are not an end product that can be easily identified.

Figure 25.1 Culture.

follows that each nation is entitled, via a democratic principle of self-determination, that is, a sovereign state that is co-equal with all other such entities in an international system of states (Lawson 2006: 4).

Primordialists argue that there is an ethnic/nationalist 'essence' underlying many contemporary nationalisms. Primordialism is an umbrella term to describe scholars who hold that nationality is a 'natural' part of human beings and that nations have existed since time immemorial (perennialist). Most primordialists would acknowledge that the concept of nationalism is a new phenomenon (arising in the eighteenth and nineteenth centuries) but would claim that the nation and the national culture have ancient roots. They would talk of a 'golden age' in the distant past, the decline since and then a will to resurgence. Can you think of possible problems with a primordialist view of nationalism? The main criticism is that the assumption that primordial attachments and the cultural sources that generate them are 'given' does not square with facts – they are evidently invented/constructed. National cultures have evolved and are often 'invented traditions' (see Hobsbawm and Ranger 1983).

The instrumentalist/modernist position in contrast has a belief in the modernity of nations and nationalism. For them, political elites play an important part in shaping national identities. It argues that nationalism appears in a crisis period of transition between tradition and modernity when old ties are no longer relevant. It thus provides identity in a time of rapid change. This crisis could be due to economic or political or cultural transformation. It could be seen in terms of massive movement of people from rural to urban areas (thus lessening the disciplining of people through church or community) due to industrial revolution (with its new demands for workers) and then need for an ideology to ensure workers devote themselves to their work/do not get distracted by radical ideas. Nationalism, which asserted that the interest of a British worker lies with her/his capitalist master and not with a German or a French worker, was a useful tool of social order and discipline.

A nation therefore is constructed as a coherent and bounded political collective that has supremacy over itself and people believe in this construction. Therefore, the role of the state is crucial here. The modern state does not follow from nation but precedes it.

There are then ethnosymbolist positions taken by scholars such as Anthony Smith (1991) which claim to occupy a middle-way position in the instrumentalist–primordialist debate. They criticise that in their determination to reveal the invented character of nationalism, modernists systematically overlooked the persistence of earlier myths, symbols, values and memories in many parts of the world and their continuing significance for large numbers of people. These scholars aim to uncover the symbolic legacy of pre-modern ethnic ties for today's nations. But, in my view, these positions do not work. They are conceptually confused, they underestimate the differences between modern nations and earlier ethnic communities, and they underestimate the fluidity and malleability of ethnic identities. The relationship between modern national identities and the cultural material of the past is at best problematic.

Where does this leave us? You can decide for yourself whether nations are ancient or modern or a product of both. My view leans toward seeing nations as modern construction but not merely a product of modern socioeconomic forces but also a discourse in itself: a discourse that is also connected to (and product and productive of) gender and race. And importantly, there are different types of nationalism and theory that might fit in one region of the world (say Europe) but should not be seen as the model on the basis of which nations in other regions ought to be judged.

WOMEN AND NATIONALISM

Nationalism has at its core notions of camaraderie and sacrifice. Both are gendered. It is often a homosocial bonding between men that strengthens the nation; nationalist myths are replete with stories of such men. The sacrifices involve both men and women – in a typical nationalist drama, the men prove their loyalty by their willingness to give up life to protect their nation, the women do so by ensuring that they perform their primary duty of taking care of the home front as well as supporting their menfolk. Most of the literature on nationalism tends to ignore the gendered aspect of the phenomenon. One can read Gellner (1983), Anderson (1991) (see Figure 25.2), Smith (1991) and other doyens of the theory of nationalism without even realising that women exist as actors in political societies. Men act, but their masculinity is left unremarked. This lack of awareness of gender as a crucial dynamic in nationalism is telling of the gender-blind (masculinist writing passing off as ungendered) character of mainstream theorising of nationalism. They underestimate the role of women in nationalism movements and ignore the gendered nature of nationalist discourses. As Nira Yuval-Davis points out, the Oxford University Press reader on nationalism introduces the only extract on national and gender relations in the last section on 'Beyond nationalism' (1997: 3). Feminist writers in recent times have highlighted the role of women and gender in the phenomenon under discussion here. Note that I mention women and gender both.

> The most famous thesis within the instrumentalist position is of nation as imagined community provided by Benedict Anderson. His argument is that the nation is a modern social construction, it is an 'imagined political community – and imagined as both limited and sovereign' (1991: 5–7) that emerged significantly due to 'print capitalism' and the spread of vernacular language and literacy. The nation is 'imagined' because its members neither meet nor interact with each other yet in the minds of each lives the image of their communion.
>
> Nations are imagined as a community because regardless of the actual inequality, the nation is conceived as a fraternity.

Figure 25.2 The work of Benedict Anderson.

Gender is central to understanding how nationalisms operate. Despite nationalism's ideological investment in the idea of popular unity, nations have historically amounted to the sanctioned institutionalisation of gender difference. 'No nation in the world gives women and men the same access to the rights and resources of the nation-state' (McClintock 1993: 61).

Nationalism projects a sense of community demanding occasional sacrifices of individuality in the greater service of the collective, but it is a community with clearly distinct expectations of men and women. It is not so much that women are absent in nationalist thinking, but that while symbolically very important, their role as agents is at best supportive of men as primary actors. The nation is often represented in terms of a family and 'women are the symbol of the nation, men its agents, regardless of the role women actually play in the nation' (*Feminist Review* 1993: 1). Anthias and Yuval-Davis (1992) point out that there are five major ways in which women have participated in ethnic and national process:

- as biological reproducers of members of ethnic collectivities
- as reproducers of the boundaries of ethnic/national groups
- as participating centrally in the ideological reproduction of the collectivity and as transmitters of its culture
- as signifiers of ethnic/national differences
- as active participants in national struggles.

The primary role of women in all nationalist movements is one of mother. Nations get produced and reproduced through their biological ability to bear children, the future carriers of national identity. This biological 'ability' may give a certain respect and dignity to women as mothers, but it also domesticates their body. Nationalism often reduces women to their womb. But the nationalist expectation of women as mother is dependent on the context. In China, it is the national duty of most women (except some minority nationality women) to restrict themselves to having one child. In Singapore and some European countries, the government may encourage at the very least one child from its majority ethnic women (the unstated fear being that minority women have more children and may thus overtake the local population). In societies facing severe stress, having more children could be the greatest duty toward the nation. For some Palestinians in Israel, as the following poem reminds, having more children is seen as a resistance to the might of the Israeli state:

> 'Write down, I am an Arab!
> Fifty thousand is my [ID] number
> Eight children, the ninth will come next summer
> Angry? Write down, I am an Arab!'
>
> (from Lustick, in Kanaaneh 2002: 65)

A child is supposed to inherit a lot of his values and beliefs from his upbringing within his family (the use of 'his' is deliberate for in the discourse of nationalism the child as a future citizen of the nation is mostly male). It is the private realm of the family that will train him to be a good citizen in the public and hence it is the responsibility of the mother to ensure that her child is aware and proud of his nation. A good mother performs her duty by instilling a sense of national pride, an awareness of national and ethnic difference within a child ('make friends with him but not him'). Women are also seen as prime representations of their culture and nation, as vessels of their national culture. How they dress, how they behave, what their aspirations are: all these questions are markers of difference between national cultures and women are seen as having the primary responsibility in ensuring the perpetuation of their culture. The debate over the veiling of Muslim women is an excellent example of this (see Chapter 24).

Are women victims or actors when it comes to nationalism? Does nationalism domesticate them by valorising their roles as mothers? Or does it liberate them by offering opportunities to participate publicly in struggles? Palestinian and Israeli women crying and wailing over their dead husbands and sons; pregnant Palestinian women suffering humiliating delays at the checkpoints; women as protestors, soldiers, suicide bombers, and politicians; women as symbols of national honour and shame – these are some of the contradictory and diverse images that come to my mind. Thus, in nationalist movements women are victims, active agents, soldiers, mothers, perpetrators of violence, resistance against violence, and so on. McClintock argues that:

> A feminist theory of nationalism might be strategically fourfold: investigating the gendered formation of sanctioned male theories; bringing into historical visibility women's active cultural and political participation in national formations; bringing nationalist institutions into critical relation with other social structures and institutions, while at the same time paying scrupulous attention to the structures of racial, ethnic and class power that continue to bedevil privileged forms of feminism.
>
> (McClintock 1993: 63)

To rectify the gender-blind discussions on nationalism, feminist writers initially highlighted women as actors in nationalist movements. Almost all nationalist movements, most conspicuously anti-colonial ones (Jayawardena 1986), had a significant number of women participating in nationalist struggles. Anti-colonial nationalists used the private–public divide, with its strong gendered connotation, in the European thinking (state having little jurisdiction over the private) to assert a national difference (by reforming and buttressing the private and then using this to gain confidence to launch a wider political movement; Chatterjee 1993) but at the same time in a more advanced stage of the movement, allowed/encouraged women as public actors. It was often the case that women had more freedom during advanced stages of nationalist struggle than in the immediate aftermath of a period of initial national consolidation of the new postcolonial state. Algeria is a good example where women were very active in the struggle against French colonialists but after independence, the expectation was for them to go back to their 'natural' role in the private sphere. In this sense, nationalism affords freedom and agency to women but essentially as a strategic move. The normative picture remains one of man as actor and protector, woman as supportive and protected.

GENDER, NATIONALISM AND THE NON-NATIONALIST OTHER

A feminist investigation that focuses only on identifying and highlighting the contribution and the role of women in nationalism and nationalist movements has its own limitations, for it adopts a simplistic notion of male and female bodies. A more sophisticated feminist take on gender matters in nationalism will also recognise that one needs to investigate politics of gender within nationalism. Is the normative nationalist actor any male? Or are they males of a certain kind (the attitude toward queer people in most nationalisms is a case in point)? Does the biological identity of a being a male automatically make him an agent of nationalism or does he have to prove his credentials as a man and as a nationalist man? Clearly, nationalism (and wars and militarisation around it) offers a good opportunity to nationalised men to prove their masculinity and their nationalism.

'Nationalism has typically sprung from masculinized memory, masculinized humiliation and masculinized hope' (Enloe 1989: 44). Enloe's insight on nationalism challenges a simplistic equation of the gender question in nationalism with the role of women. Elsewhere (Anand 2008, 2007a), I have argued that a close study of contemporary nationalisms (especially, but not exclusively, those that are associated with identification of the enemies of the nation and violence against them) shows that nationalism should be conceptualised as a political move to create, awaken, and strengthen a masculinist–nationalist body that is always already vulnerable to the exposure of the masculine as non-masculine. As expressions of collective politics, the international and the national cannot function without individual corporeal bodies that perform. The body is crucial to the nationalist project, and performing bodies in the nation-politics are predominantly, although not exclusively, male-identified bodies, especially when conjured up as active agents. A focus on masculine bodies does not imply that feminine bodies are secondary for no conception of masculine can exist without a constitutive mirror opposite feminine. Peterson is right when she argues that 'it is women's bodies, activities, and knowing that must be included if we are to accurately understand human life and social relations' (1992: 11). But it is equally important that we reconceptualise political movements of dominance (such as nationalism) for what they first and foremost are – construction/ expression of masculinised bodies. We cannot understand nationalism unless we see it as constituted primarily through, to modify Peterson, men's bodies, activities and knowing even while recognising that the categories men and women are not biologically but socially constructed. In an excellent article on nationalism, sexuality and masculinity, Nagel says:

> My point here is that the 'microculture' of masculinity in everyday life articulates very well with the demands of nationalism, particularly its militaristic side. When, over the years I have asked my undergraduate students to write down on a piece of paper their answer to the question: 'What is the worst name you can be called?' the gender difference in their responses is striking. The vast majority of women respond: 'slut' (or its equivalent, with 'bitch' a rather distant second); the vaster majority of men respond: 'wimp' or 'coward' or 'pussy'. Only cowards shirk the call to duty; real men are not cowards. Patriotism is a siren call that few men can resist, particularly in the midst of a political 'crisis'; and if they do, they risk the disdain or worse of their communities and families, sometimes including their mothers.
>
> (Nagel 1998: 252)

Gender and sexuality are not epiphenomenal (of secondary importance) but rather constitutive of national identity and conflicts based on these identities. For instance, masculinity, war and American national identity were intimately linked, during the wars in the Philippines in the 1890s, Vietnam in the 1960s and the War on Terror from 2001 onwards. The interventionists often portrayed wars as a trial by fire for American masculinity and opportunity to consolidate American national identity. In the eyes of the interventionists, there was a worry that 'the United States had become too soft in its battle against a supposedly determined and single-minded foe … the nation was hamstrung by too "civilized" a code of conduct and by a volatile democratic public opinion, a "disadvantage" that totalitarian countries did not have to contend with' (Hilfrich 2003: 65). An example of a crude display of sexuality was in the not-much-reported action of Lyndon B. Johnson as narrated by a reporter:

> 'Soon LBJ was waving his arms and fulminating about his war. Who the hell was Ho Chi Minh, anyway, that he thought he could push America around? Then the President did an astonishing thing: he unzipped his trousers, dangled a given appendage, and asked his shocked associates: "Has Ho Chi Minh got anything like that?"'
>
> (Darby 1987, cited in Hilfrich 2003: 60)

This hierarchisation of the Self and the Other where the Self's national identity is better can be seen especially during times of stress and conflict. For example, freedom-loving, god-fearing, family-oriented consumerist American national identity versus repressive, godless, ruthlessly egalitarian communist Soviet Union (from the American perspective) was a familiar theme during the Cold War. Gender played an interesting role in Cold War propaganda. Belmonte (2003) analyses documents and articles disseminated by the US Information Agency between 1945 and 1960 and shows how Soviet gender equality was presented as going against family values, which in turn defined American female identity (primarily as a homemaker). An interesting cartoon with the caption 'Even if we are superwomen, I still wish we had fun like Americans' reflects a criticism of the Soviet notion of gender equality in favour of American femininity (Belmonte 2003). Of course, the Soviets had their own ways of constructing a superior social national identity: egalitarian, socialist, patriotic Soviet identity against fascistic, capitalist, unequal American society. Images changed rapidly in the post-Cold War. In the so-called War on Terror, the image of Islam as bad for women and the West as defender of women's rights is one of the defining motifs (see Chapters 12 and 24). Of course, gender and sexuality are not the only or main dynamic in the creation of national identity. Race and/or religion may play an equal or more important role. But, without doubt, nationalism relies on inclusion and exclusion, remembering and forgetting, identity and difference.

CONCLUSION

You will have noticed how the language of the so-called 'War on Terror' was based on an 'Us–Them' distinction: 'Us' is strong, brave, democratic, just, humane and pitted against 'Them' who are cowardly, weak, illegal, authoritarian, extremist, radical, dangerous and inhumane (see also Chapter 13). Therefore those who fight against terrorism (as categorised by the USA) are on the side of the good; the terrorists and their 'rogue state' backers are, of course, evil, and those who refuse to participate are weaklings (such as the French during the Iraq invasion). National identity gets more rigid and acutely defined especially in situations of war and conflict. We witness that in the USA in the aftermath of the terrorist attack on the World Trade Centre.

Thus, we see how national identity, nationalism, and hence national culture gets constructed and renewed every day through the activities and lives of its supposed subjects/carriers. Gender plays an important role in this process and so do other markers of identity we have not looked at (such as class, religion, race, sexuality and so on).

What you need to take away from this chapter is that national identity, and hence national culture, is always in the process of flux and change. It is not fixed. It is constructed. It is therefore always contested. For instance, Israeli Jewish women protesting against Israeli occupation of Palestinian territories through activist organisations such as 'Women in Black' have a different notion of what a good Israeli Jewish national culture ought to be in comparison to those who deny the very existence of Palestinians as a people. Similarly, those Palestinians who recognise Israel and want to live with it peacefully either as part of one single secular democratic state or two separate states side by side and those Palestinians who see not only Israel but all Jews as the enemy would have very different notions of what a Palestinian national culture should be. Nationalism, therefore, is an internal contestation over what the features and boundaries of the nation are. It is also about creating/asserting the identity of the nation by distinguishing itself from the Others of the nation. Gender plays a central role in this process of national identification, bodies that matter in nationalism are gendered bodies, the demarcation of the national Self from the non-national Other is achieved through specific representations of masculinity and femininity, and nationalist violence is legitimised in gendered terms (defending the honour of 'our' women against the enemy men). The durability of the concept of nation makes it an important subject of investigation for international relations. The fact of the constructedness of nationalism is less interesting than the gendered and racialised process of construction. It is not enough to say that a nation is a fabricated entity, but how is it fabricated, why does the fabrication successfully sell itself as natural, how does it scavenge on already existing gender relations while at the same time reinscribing and maybe even challenging it?

Questions for further debate

1. If nationalism is a social construction, why does it have an almost universal appeal?
2. How would you analyse the relationship between nation, culture and gender?
3. How do representations of the Other play an important part in the constitution of the national Self?
4. Choose two examples of nationalism – one European and one non-European – and compare and contrast the role of women in it.
5. How is masculinity relevant for understanding discourses of nationalism?

Sources for further reading and research

Elshtain, J. B. (1992) 'Sovereignty, Identity, Sacrifice', in V. Spike Peterson (ed.) *Gendered States: Feminist (Re)Visions of International Relations*, Boulder, CO: Lynne Rienner.

Feminist Review (1993) Special Issue 'Nationalisms and National Identities' (44).

Nagel, J. (1998) 'Masculinity and Nationalism: Gender and Sexuality in the Making of Nations', *Ethnic and Racial Studies*, 21(2): 242–69.

Parker, A., M. Russo, D. Sommer and P. Yaeger (eds) (1992) *Nationalism and Sexualities*, London and New York: Routledge.

Ranchod-Nilsson, S. and M. A. Tetreault (eds) (2000) *Women, States, and Nationalism*, London and New York: Routledge.

CHAPTER 26

Citizenship, nationality and gender

Denise M. Horn

LEARNING OUTCOMES

Upon completion, readers should be able to:

- Discuss the historical concept of 'citizenship' and changing global values.
- Discuss the gendered implications of nationality and citizenship laws, explaining how citizenship includes and excludes people, and what that implies for both men and women.
- Discuss citizenship as a form of protection, a matter of rights, and as a global concept.

INTRODUCTION

Why should we care about 'citizenship' in IR? Like democratization, a focus on nationality and citizenship illustrates inclusions and exclusions within society that become replicated on the international level. Although matters of nationality and citizenship laws are left to sovereign states, in our globalized world, where people are highly mobile, domestic citizenship laws have international implications, particularly where rights are concerned. Both men and women are affected by unequal citizenship and nationality laws, and feminists have interrogated the problem of unequal citizenship in a variety of ways. Here, we discuss feminist interrogations of the concept of citizenship, nationality and citizenship, gender and international law, and the 'myth' of protection and the state.

FEMINIST RETHINKING OF TRADITIONAL VIEWS OF THE STATE AND CITIZENSHIP

Feminists utilize the lens of gender to investigate the unequal power relations within states and globally; as Spike Peterson and Anne Sisson Runyan note, gender is a 'meta-lens that produces particular ways of seeing, thinking, and acting in the world. [...] As long as the power of a gender as a meta-lens continues to operate, it will produce and reproduce inequalities, injustices, and crises of global proportions' (2010: 37). Further, feminists contend that the very concepts that form the basis of International Relations theory are gendered: 'If the anarchic conception of the relations among states reflects androcentric notions, so too do conceptions of the state itself, as a structure of coercion within a particular territory, or as a voluntary association constructed by contract among consenting individuals' (Horn 2003: 882). Jackie Stevens (1999) defines the state as a membership organization with rules for inclusions and exclusions that make possible certain familial forms of inequality. In contrast to liberal accounts of the state premised on the notion that individuals, families, races, and ethnicities pre-exist the state and, as pre-political existents, deserve protection from the state by incorporation in the 'private sphere', Stevens (1999) argues that the state shapes the contours of individual identity and nationality by conventions, marriage rules, immigration law, and citizenship rules about property and territory. Rather than accept the received view of the nation-state, which presumes the priority of nation to the formation of the modern state, Stevens demonstrates that the nation is a political convention, a creation of the state, which produces and sustains these ties (Horn 2003: 882; Stevens 1999). Citizenship and nationality provides a view of the gendered nature of state and international structures.

Citizenship has been conceptualized in many ways, but there are generally three theoretical views: The liberal-individualist viewpoint, where citizenship is predicated on economic rights and the ownership of property; enlightened citizens, pursuing their own self-interest have duties to the state in return for protection of their property and bodily selves. Politically, however, they are essentially passive. The civic republican view of citizenship focuses on the political nature of man, where politics occurs within the political space of civil society, a site of discourse and demands on the state; however, this type of democratic engagement requires a great deal of time and energy that very few have the luxury of contributing. Finally, participatory democrats place high value on political activity, but extend the site of this activity to include the community and the workplace (Jaggar 2005: 92fn). These representations have been investigated and questioned by feminist philosophers and IR theorists, who focus on the 'lived realities' of people's lives and the consequences of consigning citizenship to these categories.

Citizenship and political life

The 'social contract' as envisioned by liberal theorists such as John Locke and Jean-Jacques Rousseau serves as the basis of the liberal-individualist approach. In the age of Enlightenment, Locke and Rousseau (and others) imagined a state that was responsive to its people, where individuals had evolved from subjects of a monarch to citizens of a community. The notion of citizenship, however, has an older pedigree, following from the ancient and classical philosophers who theorized the relationship between the individual and the community, arguing that those who chose to belong to a community would subject themselves to the rules of that community, but were also free to leave if those rules did not suit them (Plato, *Crito*). The classical philosopher Epicurus (*Principal Doctrines, number 31*), situated citizenship on an ethical foundation, arguing that citizenship arises from the need to ensure the physical security of each individual: 'Natural justice is a pledge of reciprocal benefit, to prevent one man from harming or being harmed by another'. In a sense, citizens of a community implicitly (and often, explicitly) agree not to harm each other in order to maintain their own safety.

In the seventeenth century, Hugo Grotius (1625) introduced the revolutionary idea that persons are *sui juris* (under their own jurisdiction); that is, persons are sovereign as *individuals* who possess 'natural rights' not given by the state, but each person bears the responsibility to protect the rights of others. Thomas Hobbes argued in *The Leviathan* (1651) that individuals gave up their rights to the absolute rule of the government in order to secure personal safety and property. If that government proved to be ineffective or weak, however, citizens had the right (and duty) to overthrow that government and begin anew. John Locke (1689), by way of contrast, centred his concept of rights within the individual, placing those rights within the concept of God – in effect, arguing that the rights of man are inalienable because of their humanity as granted by a creator, superseding the reach of government. For Jean-Jacques Rousseau (1762), the government is the direct result of the general will – that is, sovereignty lies in the democratic decision-making ability of the populace. Each individual has his or her own egoistic rights, but should those rights run counter to the individual will, they should be 'forced to be free', for the general will is the representation of the best intentions within society: 'Each of us puts his person and all his power in common under the supreme direction of the general will; and in a body we receive each member as an indivisible part of the whole' (Rousseau [1762] 1982: 159).

These differences gave rise to the continuing tension between natural rights (theorized by modern philosophers as 'human rights', which are theoretically inviolate, subjective, and universal) and *civil* rights, which are granted by the state and can thus be retracted should the 'social contract' be abrogated. These approaches to the relationship of the state and citizen, however, are based on pre-conceived notions of what kind of person was *suited* for the responsibilities of citizenship, because, despite the Enlightenment ideal of innate human rights or dignity (as proposed by Immanuel Kant in his conception of the categorical imperative), those ideals were predicated on a *male* identity of the citizen.[1] But even male identity did not mean automatic inclusion. For the classical philosophers, 'humanity' was not automatically extended to all people, but rather to freeborn male property owners who were fully fledged citizens of the state. This included neither women nor slaves; in Roman citizenship laws, freeborn women's rights were limited, while male and female slaves enjoyed none of the rights given to citizens; as property they lacked 'legal personhood'.[2]

Feminist critiques of traditional approaches to citizenship

Carole Pateman (1988) challenges the presumptions of the 'social contract', arguing that women were never included in the original contract, and thus were never part of the state-building project. The liberal definitions of citizens appear 'unsexed' but in reality, were built on a Western male model, where (some) men, as property owners, formed the basis of the public sphere – the privileged space of politics. Women, however, were:

> [I]ncorporated into the private sphere through the marriage contract as wives subservient to their husbands, rather than as individuals. The private sphere, a site of subjection, is part of civil society, but separate from the 'civil' sphere; each gains meaning from the other and each is mutually dependent on the other.
>
> (Tickner 2001: 105)

The public sphere is where 'citizenship is performed': Historically, this has included 'fighting, governing, buying and selling property and eventually working for wages', traditionally masculine endeavors (Jaggar 2005: 92). Martha Nussbaum (2007) argues that the classical tradition of the social contract assumes that all citizens enjoy some sort of mutual benefit from the arrangement, which ignores the power asymmetries that exist in all societies.

The 'public/private' divide and its relationship to citizenship has also given rise to a number of feminist critiques, which point to gendered power relationships but also offer alternative visions of politics and citizenship. For early feminists of the nineteenth century, challenges to the *status quo* were couched in traditional gender roles: Men were still considered the natural 'protectors' of the family and the state, but women could bring a purity and morality to politics that had long been dominated by the low vices of men. In the twentieth century, feminist theorists focused on 'the symbolic power of the maternal to develop practices of citizenship that are widely viewed as feminine [...] Arguments that the culturally feminine values of purity, care, and responsibility should infuse public as well as private life suggest that political and domestic realms are continuous rather than separate' (Jaggar 2005: 93; Ruddick 1989; Tronto 1994). Blurring the lines between the public and the private spheres, feminists proclaimed that the 'personal is political', pointing to the need for an approach to politics based on individual identities and the realities of lived experiences, rather than taking the family unit (and the patriarchal implications of such) as the basic unit of society.

Another critique focuses on women's exclusion from the public sphere, particularly women's representation in government, policymaking and the military. Gender roles play a part in this in both the liberal model of citizenship and the civic republican approach: In the former, citizenship 'relies on an implicitly masculine understanding of the citizen as soldier and worker' while in the latter, citizenship rights and responsibilities are 'so demanding that citizen responsibilities can be met only by people who belong to a relatively leisured elite – an elite that, on the prevailing gender division of labor, is likely to be disproportionately male' (Fraser and Gordon 1997; Jaggar 2005: 93; Kittay 1999). 'Full citizenship' in a state is often contingent upon one's ability to contribute in multiple public spheres, creating a situation of 'classes' of citizenship, where those consigned to the private sphere are 'second class'. By emphasizing the importance of the workplace as a site of political engagement, as participatory democrats do, the public sphere is widened, but this may not take into account women's (unpaid) labour in the home (Jaggar 2005).

An alternative to this focus on the traditional public/private split emphasizes the impact of women's activism, particularly as a rebuke to liberal individualism. Martha Ackelsberg, for instance, argues that women's activism represents a form of 'subaltern counterpublics', illustrating the reality that individuals act not just as 'citizens' but as members of a variety of different communities with differing needs, including class, race, ethnic and cultural communities (Ackelsberg 1988, 2005). Third World feminists have argued that the organization around particular needs, issues of welfare, and contesting the abuses wrought by globalization has given rise to a more open and democratic political space (Jaggar 2005; Kabeer 1994; Moser 1991). Further, by drawing attention to the importance of politics in everyday life, feminists challenge 'older conceptions of citizenship by suggesting not only that citizens may be female but also that women and men often *do* citizenship differently from each other and do it in different locations' (Jaggar 2005: 95; Kaplan 1997).

The successes of the transnational women's movements of the twentieth and twenty-first centuries, for instance, have been notable in that women's organizing transcended state politics, reaching beyond borders to redefine 'women's rights as human rights' (Bunch 1990). The violation of 'human rights' had long been perceived as those rights violated by the state within the public sphere, which ignores those abuses committed within the private sphere, typically one's home or community. The transnational women's movement brought 'women's issues' to the international agenda, demanding that states recognize that abuses against women in the private sphere – abuses such as rape, domestic violence, dowry deaths, and female infanticide – were, in fact, human rights abuses (see Chapters 7 and 27). This approach resulted in a variety of international conventions, among them the Convention on the Elimination of all Forms of Discrimination Against Women (CEDAW), adopted by the UN General Assembly in 1979 (Keck and Sikkink 1998).

WHERE DO YOU BELONG? NATIONALITY AND CITIZENSHIP

'Nationality' and 'citizenship' are often used interchangeably (and in some states, they are legally equated) but the terms are different: Nationality refers to the legal relationship between an individual and his or her state, while citizenship has a broader meaning. It can imply membership in a state, the right to demand rights, the expectation that those rights will be fulfilled, or that the state will provide particular goods based on those rights, such as security, infrastructure, and sometimes welfare. Citizenship also implies duty: In return for the provision of goods, the state expects something in return, usually in the form of service, obedience and taxes (that is, the social contract). Nationality, by the same token, refers to a legal

- *Jus sanguinis*: **Parents are citizens**. The Latin phrase *jus sanguinis* means 'right of blood'. In this approach, citizenship is granted based on ancestry or ethnicity, and is related to the concept of a nation state, common in Europe. States normally limit the right to citizenship by descent to a certain number of generations born outside the state and, in some cases, it is limited to the patrilineal or matrilineal line. This form of citizenship is common in civil law countries.

- *Jus soli*: **Born within a country**. 'The right of soil' grants citizenship to those born within a state, regardless of the citizenship of the parents. This form of citizenship is common in common law countries; it originated in England, where those who were born within the realm were subjects of the king.

- *Jure matrimonii*: **Marriage to a citizen**. These laws vary widely, extending the right to some forms of marriage but not to others.

- **Naturalization**. States often grant citizenship to people who have immigrated to that state and have resided there for a given number of years. Perspective citizens may have to pass a test, swear allegiance to their new state and, in some cases, renounce their prior citizenship.

Figure 26.1 How citizenship is granted.

association with a state, which may or may not indicate the granting of full citizenship rights. Under international law, each state is responsible for deciding the basis on which one is granted nationality, although international law generally requires that states bear responsibility for protecting their nationals and must allow their own nationals to reside within their borders. Nationality can be conferred through birth, descent, naturalization, or marriage. Citizenship, however, can be limited or expanded in a variety of ways, as we have noted (see Figure 26.1). Race and gender have played key roles in how citizens are perceived, their duties and obligations, and how they are treated by the state, and reflect divisions of power (Peterson and Runyan 2010: 87). For instance, a woman may share the same nationality as a man, but they may have different rights and duties as citizens (e.g., military service); likewise, in the history of many states, such as the US or South Africa, multiple races were considered nationals, but full citizenship rights (such as access to employment, education, and mobility) have been limited to particular racial categories.

Women's exclusion from the rights of full citizenship has historically been expressed through domestic laws regarding nationality. Virginia Woolf, in her essay *Three Guineas* (1938), famously argued: 'As a woman, I have no country. As a woman I want no country. As a woman my country is the whole world'. While this could be read as a call for women's superiority or the global triumph of maternal ethics, her argument, in fact, addresses the longstanding tradition of women's *dependent nationality*, meaning that her nationality (and thus, her citizenship) was not her own, but rather dependent on that of her father and her husband. She could not claim innate citizenship based on an individual right through birth or descent, but rather, must think of her citizenship only in relational terms.

Woolf's critiques remain relevant. Nationality laws have been based on patriarchal expectations of gender roles. The nationality of married women has historically been tied to her relationship to a man: first her father, then her husband. At the beginning of the twentieth century, the widely accepted principle of *dependent nationality* was based on two assumptions: Families should share the same nationality to protect the unity of the family, and that important decisions regarding the family would be made by the husband. Thus, a woman who married a foreigner would take on his nationality, and, in many cases, lose her own (and her own nationality had been conferred on her because of her *father's* citizenship). The rationality behind dependent nationality assumes a conflict of loyalties to one's state and to one's family should nationalities differ; in many states, 'the assumption that a married woman's primary location is in the private sphere, within the home, and under the protection of her husband, has prevailed. Accordingly, her need for a separate public identity and legal relationship with a state is not taken into account' (United Nations 2003: 5). Dependent nationality assumed that a woman's husband would decide where the family would reside – and further assumed that that place of residency would be his country of origin. Even if the family were to reside in the wife's country of origin, she would become an alien national in her own country, without access to the rights of a citizen; thus, as Woolf argued, women have no country at all.

What this implies is that women's roles within the state are considered dispensable or unimportant – that her worth as a citizen is only as useful to the state as she is useful in the family. If her husband were to change his own nationality, so too would the wife, whether she chooses to or not; if her husband should die or the couple divorce, in states where citizenship is tied to marriage, the woman risks becoming stateless unless her country of birth allows her to revert to her former nationality. Thus married women are disempowered because they are deprived of making choices regarding nationality and citizenship.

Nationality, gender, and the evolution of international law

In addition to women's suffrage, the issue of citizenship and nationality became a rallying point for early feminists and emerging transnational movements. In 1930, Chrystal MacMillan led a deputation to the Hague Codification Conference to demonstrate on behalf of married women's rights to nationality – when those efforts were ineffective, women's rights activists mounted a massive international campaign with the League of Nations to secure equal citizenship and nationality rights for women and men, but the campaign did not result in a treaty on women's nationality. However, the efforts of the Inter-American Commission on Women, created in 1928, brought forth the 1933 Montevideo Convention on the Nationality of Women, which provides that 'there shall be no distinction based on sex as regards nationality'. Further, the 1933 Montevideo Convention on Nationality establishes the principle that 'neither matrimony nor its dissolution affects the nationality of the husband or wife or of their children' (Knop and Chinkin 2001: 525; United Nations 2003: 6).

The 1948 United Nations Universal Declaration of Human Rights includes the principle of non-discrimination and includes the right to a nationality. These principles were elaborated on in the 1957 Convention on the Nationality of Married Women, which establishes the independent nationality of married women and permits the alien wife to acquire her husband's nationality through 'privileged naturalization procedures'. Despite the Convention, not all states changed their dependent nationality laws, particularly those newly independent states, which had based their laws on common law or civil law systems. These states resisted implementing nationality laws, often reflecting the deep-seated cultural and social subordination of women. Several states maintain unequal nationality laws, precluding a married woman from holding a nationality other than that of her husband (United Nations 2003: 7).[3]

Protection: citizenship as inclusion and exclusion

Feminist theorists have also interrogated assumptions that outline the relationship between citizen and the state, where the security of the state is equated with the security of the individual. The realist tradition in International Relations, for example, assumes that the pursuit of national security promotes the security of members of the nation-state.

'There is an ingrained assumption that security for the individual is adequately understood purely in terms of his or her membership in a given national community' (Steans 1998: 105). Feminist scholars are less sanguine about this assumption. Echoing Virginia Woolf's insight that the state has been markedly unsuccessful in protecting the bodily integrity and physical security of women, feminist IR scholars suggest that the security of individuals varies according to their economic, political, social, and personal circumstances. Individual security is structured by gender, race, class, and sexual orientation (Horn 2003: 882).

Citizenship, then, is both a principle of inclusion and exclusion. In terms of protection, what the state provides may vary according to implicit or explicit categories of citizenship. This, according to Woolf, implied that a woman would always be an outsider to the state, as she could make no claim to citizenship in her own right. Thus any claims by the state that it served to 'protect' her would be false, for it only served to protect those who could actually derive benefits from the state – that is, men:

> 'Our country,' she will say, 'throughout the greater part of its history has treated me as a slave; it has denied me education or any share of its possessions. "Our" country still ceases to be mine if I marry a foreigner. "Our" country denies me the means of protecting myself, forces me to pay others a very large sum annually to protect me, and is so little able, even so, to protect me that Air Raid precautions are written on the wall. Therefore if you insist upon fighting to protect me, or "our" country, let it be understood, soberly and rationally between us, that you are fighting to gratify a sex instinct which I cannot share; to procure benefits which I have not shared and probably will not share; but not to gratify my instincts, or to protect myself or my country.
>
> (Woolf 1938: 108)

Protection, as Woolf notes, is often couched in dependency on the state, which, in many states, is also related to patriarchal ideals of family. Thus, the 'man' of the house protects the women, and in return they serve him and are loyal members of the household. Similarly, in states where citizenship requires military service, women's exclusion from military roles represents exclusion from full citizenship (Hooper 2001; Stiehm 1982).

Iris Marion Young (2005) has extended this approach to explore feminist theoretical approaches to the 'State as protector' logic, particularly the work of feminists such as Catherine MacKinnon (1987), who argue that inequality is present in society because of hierarchies of power that privilege men over women. Thus, the protector role can be perceived as a form of sexual patriarchal domination, where men have created 'comradely male settings that gain them specific benefits from which they exclude women, and they harass women in order to enforce this exclusion and maintain their superiority' (Young 2005: 17). However, the protector role may also reflect a 'more benign image of masculinity, more associated with chivalry' – the image of the man as the protector of his family from the aggressive 'other' who wishes to invade and destroy the home/homeland. On this view, the feminine woman is happy to defer to the valiant man's protection, and in doing so, 'female subordination [...] derives from this position of begin protected' (Stiehm 1982; Young 2005: 19). Young equates this type of masculinist protection to Foucault's notion of 'pastoral power', where those who express care for individuals also exert power over them, even when that power appears benevolent (Foucault 1988, 1994; Young 2005: 19).

Protection can thus be read as either self-interested domination or as a form of care. In either situation, however, democratic citizenship loses its meaning. Young argues that, in a 'security State' (such as the US in the post-9/11 period), 'the state demotes members of a democracy to dependents', where 'state officials adopt the stance of masculine protector, telling us to entrust our lives to them, not to question their decisions about what will keep us safe'. Once citizens accept that the state will play the role of protector, dissent becomes more difficult or impossible – indeed, dissent would disrupt the very notion of 'good citizenship', which 'consists of cooperative obedience for the sake and the safety of all' (Young 2005: 21). This is yet another critique of the liberal social contract approach, and a call for a more inclusive meaning of citizenship.

▌ CONCLUSION: CITIZENSHIP AND GENDER

The possession of citizenship, as we have seen, infers that one also possesses certain rights. Feminists have explored this connection and questioned the equality of citizenship(s), the gendered nature of nationality, and the logic of protection within a state. These issues have important consequences for both domestic and international politics, as we have seen in the development of international law surrounding nationalities. Gender matters because citizenship and nationality laws reveal that one's gender dictates how a state will treat you: Are you a 'full' citizen or are you a 'dependent' citizen? Do you have the right to your own nationality? Property? The right of free movement? The chance to work or live in the same country as your spouse?

Further, considering how gender roles are reflected on meta-levels, we have seen that patriarchal social norms are reflected in the conception of the state as 'protector', whether through oppression or through a sense of benevolent duty. In either situation, citizens (both women and men) become dependents (or, to use a more traditional term, 'subjects') of the state, rather than fully realized citizens who may make demands on the state. This is a troubling outcome for democratic states that have become 'securitized', as well as for those states struggling to emerge as democratic states from a legacy of authoritarian rule, such as those states of the former Soviet Union, or emerging democracies in Southeast Asia. For states that maintain laws restricting full citizenship rights to men (particularly those who are 'native born'), the state itself may suffer as the potential for women to contribute to economic, social and political spheres is ignored. As we have seen, however, globalization continues to encourage a larger notion of citizenship, in which different forms of political activism, based on people's lived realities, may contribute to a further evolution of 'citizenship' itself.

Questions for further debate

1. In what ways are both men and women harmed or disadvantaged by unequal citizenship or nationality laws? How do distinctions based solely on gender affect other rights?
2. Should nationality and citizenship laws take into consideration the different experiences of men and women, and address them with different – but equal – laws?
3. Does the concept of 'global citizen' compete with state sovereignty?
4. Can an individual maintain 'loyalty' to more than one state? Do the rights and responsibilities of citizenship of one state imply a conflict of interests in another?
5. Should culture and tradition be reflected in nationality laws, or should there be universal agreement?

Sources for further reading and research

Jaggar, A. (2005) 'Arenas of Citizenship: Civil Society, the State, and the Global Order', in M. Friedman (ed.), *Women and Citizenship*, Oxford: Oxford University Press.

Kaplan, T. (1997) *Crazy for Democracy: Women in Grassroots Movements*, New York: Routledge.

Stiehm, J. (1982) 'The Protected, the Protector, the Defender', *Women's Studies International Forum*, 5: 367–76.

Woolf, V. (1938) *Three Guineas*, New York: Harcourt Brace.

Young, I. M. (2005) 'The Logic of Masculinist Protection: Reflections on the Current Security State', in M. Friedman (ed.), *Women and Citizenship*, Oxford: Oxford University Press.

Notes

1 Rousseau, however, in his description of the 'sovereign', or the 'general will', did, in fact, include women.

2 Some argue that Plato's *Republic* was the precursor to modern feminism, because Socrates gives a place to women in the good society. Others, however, argue that this is a misreading: women can never be a 'Philosopher–King' but rather remain at the 'abdomen' of society: the workers, producers, guardians. This thus negates any notion of women's rationality or ability to reach a state of wisdom and leadership. See, for example, Nancy Tuana (1994) *Feminist Interpretations of Plato*.

3 Nationality laws affect men as well women. Immigration policies that allow married foreign women speedy access to permanent residency often do not extend to foreign men. Because the focus is often on traditional family roles, these laws assume that men are more likely to seek employment outside the home, thus 'threatening' the livelihood of male nationals. Foreign male nationals may also be perceived as a threat to the cultural or social fabric of a nation. Women provide no such threat in this conception – they are neither potential providers nor potential competition for jobs, and they may provide more children for the nation (see Anne McClintock 1995). For example, citizenship laws within the United Arab Emirates permit citizenship for a foreign woman married to a national of the UAE, provided she renounce her former citizenship. However, foreign husbands of female nationals are not eligible for citizenship.

CHAPTER 27

Transnational activism

Valentine M. Moghadam

LEARNING OUTCOMES

Upon completion, readers should be able to:

- Provide a clear definition of transnational activism, especially by women's rights groups, and the factors and forces that have generated it.
- Understand the relationship between globalization and transnational feminist activism.
- Identify a number of key transnational feminist networks.

INTRODUCTION

Transnational activism has been the focus of a growing body of literature since the 1990s. It is defined as cross-border collective action, involving people from two or more countries around specific campaigns or longer term movements. Transnational activism takes different forms, from lobbying and advocacy to protests and direct action. It is carried out by small groups, networks, organizations or mass movements. This chapter examines the growth of such activism and references some of the scholarship that it has generated.

The 1990s saw the emergence of many studies analysing the growth of what was variously called non-governmental organizations (NGOs) and international non-governmental organizations (INGOs), global civil society, transnational advocacy networks (TANs), global social movements (GSMs) and transnational social movement organizations (TSMOs) (see Mohanty 2003b; Smith et al. 1997). Little attention, however, was paid to the women's movement or to women's transnational organizing and activism. Exceptions included the pioneering volume by Keck and Sikkink (1998), which examined TANs organized around human rights, the environment, and violence against women. O'Brien, Goetz, Scholte and Williams (2000) studied the ways in which global unions, women's movements, and environmental organizations engaged with multilateral economic institutions such as the World Bank, the International Monetary Fund, and the World Trade Organization. Finally, a collection by Cohen and Rai (2000) on global social movements included essays on feminist networking for conflict resolution and to advance women's human rights. With the growth of Islamist movements, a parallel body of work examined various forms of Islamist activism. Studies initially focused on Islamist movements within single societies; later, especially after September 11, 2001, the focus shifted to transnational linkages (Moghadam 2009; Wiktorowicz 2004).

The 'Battle of Seattle' in late 1999 gave rise to yet another body of literature, or rather, a new direction for research on INGOs, TANs, and GSMs. With the dramatic appearance of a seemingly international movement of activists opposed to the new global economic order – and especially its trade agenda as controlled by the World Trade Organization – it became clear to analysts that a new global movement was in the making (Broad 2002; Smith and Johnston 2002). This came to be called the Global Justice Movement (GJM), and the new movement focused its transnational activist energies against neoliberal capitalism, institutions of global governance, and the powerful capitalist countries, banks and corporations behind the new world order. For several years after the Seattle protests, a wave of protests engulfed most of the world, and especially European countries, as highly organized networks of activists launched protests in their own countries or travelled abroad to take part in others (della Porta 2007). In Brazil, the growing influence of the left-wing Workers Party and the election of one of its leading member, Lula, to the presidency in 2002 gave the GJM a new institutional base – the annual World Social Forum (WSF), first held in Porto Alegre in 2001. Launched as an alternative to the World Economic Forum – an annual gathering in Davos, Switzerland, of the world's leading politicians and businessmen – the WSF brings together national and transnational activists.

Feminist scholars studying these new global developments noticed a paucity of attention to the gender dynamics of the new transnational activism, including the role of women in movement leadership, the place of feminist issues on movement or network agendas, and the impact of the less salutary forms of transnational organizing (such as religious fundamentalism) on women's rights. One group of feminist scholars had begun studying Islamist movements in the 1980s. Notable among them were Iranian feminists, who had experienced the adverse effects of Islamization in Iran following the revolution of 1979. Another group of scholar–activists went on to form an international solidarity network called Women Living under Muslim Laws (WLUML), and they carried out their own studies of Islamist movements. As early as 1990, WLUML warned of an 'Islamist international' that would do more harm than good (Moghadam 2005).

Transnational feminist organizing and advocacy had appeared in the 1980s but it was not until the mid-1990s that it came to the attention of feminist scholars. Preparations for the UN's Fourth World Conference on Women, to take place in Beijing in September 1995, gave resources to existing women's groups and provided the impetus for the formation of new ones. Studies appeared that examined feminist transnational organizing and activism (Berkovitch 1999; Sperling et al. 2001; Naples and Desai 2002; Steinstra 2000). They connected women's movements and organizations to international or global processes such as the role of international organizations or the United Nations Decade on Women, and they examined the ways in which women's organizations engaged with the world of public policy. Moghadam (2005, 2013) explained the worldwide social movement of women in terms of globalization processes such as the feminization of labour, growing social inequalities, and increased access to the new information and computer technologies (ICTs) by educated and politically active women (see Chapter 31 for further discussion of ICTs).

GLOBAL FEMINISM?

While not all feminists agree on the matter, many assert that 'the women's movement' is a global phenomenon, and that despite cultural differences, country specificities, and organizational priorities, there are observed similarities in the ways in which women's rights activists frame their grievances and demands, form networks and organizations, and engage with state and intergovernmental institutions. Some of these similarities include adoption of discourses of women's human rights and gender equality; references to international agreements such as the Convention on the Elimination of All Forms of Discrimination Against Women (CEDAW) and the Beijing Platform for Action; campaigns for legal and policy reforms to ensure women's civil, political, and social rights; solidarity and networking across borders; and coalitions with other civil society groups. Another observation is that women's rights activists – whether in South Asia, Latin America, the Middle East, or North Africa – are opposed to 'fundamentalist' discourses and agendas and espouse feminist discourses and goals, whether explicitly or implicitly. Sperling, Ferree and Risman (2001) have rightly asserted that *feminist action* is an appropriate term to define that in which the participants explicitly place value on challenging gender hierarchy and changing women's social status, whether or not they adopt the feminist label.

Like other transnational social movements, the global women's movement is heterogeneous and internally differentiated. This was especially evident during the Fourth World Conference on Women, which took place in Beijing, China, in September 1995. For three weeks, women's groups from across the world came to China to take part in the massive non-governmental forum that preceded but also overlapped with the official, intergovernmental conference. At the latter, those women's groups with UN accreditation were able to enter conference halls, lobby delegates, disseminate their literature, and hold rallies. This was hardly a movement with a centre or a bureaucracy or a hierarchy. It was a *movement of movements*, albeit highly networked. And, although the women's groups at Beijing had something to say about an array of issues, with different priorities emphasized, they also had common grievances concerning war, peace, fundamentalisms and the new economic order.

In previous work (Moghadam 2005), I have defined transnational feminist activism as entailing the mobilization of women from three or more countries around a specific set of grievances and goals. In this chapter, I discuss two types of contemporary transnational feminist activism. The first type is organized and sustained mobilization, and takes the form of what I have called the *transnational feminist network*. In the previous work, I examined three types of transnational feminist network (TFNs) that emerged in the 1980s and continue to be active to this day: networks that target the neoliberal economic policy agenda; those that focus on the danger of fundamentalisms and insist on women's human rights, especially in the Muslim world; and women's peace groups that target conflict, war, and empire. In this chapter, I elaborate on the transnational feminist peace and anti-imperialist groups.

The second type of transnational activism to be described in this chapter is what I call *feminist humanitarianism and international solidarity*. Here, groups of women come together in new or established networks to engage in humanitarian and soli-daristic work across borders. This second type includes episodic campaigns in which diverse groups mobilize to support a women's rights cause in one or another country. An example is the international solidarity campaign after 2006 to support feminist activism in the Islamic Republic of Iran.

Transnational feminist activism is deeply connected to globalization processes. I have defined globalization as a multidimensional process – entailing economic, political, cultural, and geographic aspects – in which capital, goods, peoples, organizations, and discourses take on an increasingly transnational or global character within the capitalist world system (Moghadam 2005: 35). In this connection, transnational activism is both a response to the downside of globalization ('globalization-from-above', including neoliberal capitalism, the increasing power of institutions of global governance, growing inequalities, and persistent poverty) and a contributor to a more people-oriented globalization ('globalization-from-below', including the institutionalization of economic justice, peace, and human rights). Transnational feminist activism has arisen in the same structural context, uniting women across the globe around common grievances and goals. But because the world system is unequal and hierarchical, and because globalization's impacts are differentiated across regions and social groups, there are also points of contention among transnational feminist activists (see, e.g., Dufour and Giraud 2007).

THE ROAD TO TRANSNATIONAL FEMINISM

Women have worked together across borders for women's rights since at least the era of first-wave feminism. Struggle for political and social rights and for peace and anti-militarism united women in the early decades of the 20th century. In mid-century the women's movement began to diverge, grouping itself within national boundaries or economic zones, emphasizing different priorities, and aligning with divergent ideological currents.

Feminist groups encompassed liberal, radical, Marxist and socialist ideologies, and these political differences constituted one form of division within feminism. The Cold War cast a shadow on feminist solidarity, in the form of the East–West divide. Another division took the form of North–South, or First World–Third World differences in terms of priority feminist issues; many First World feminists saw legal equality and reproductive rights as key feminist demands and goals, while many Third World feminists emphasized underdevelopment, colonialism, and imperialism as obstacles to women's advancement. Disagreements came to the fore at the beginning of the United Nations' Decade for Women, and especially at its first and second world conferences on women, which took place in Mexico City in 1975 and in Copenhagen in 1980, respectively.

A shift in the nature and orientation of international feminism began to take place in the mid-1980s, during preparations for the third UN world conference on women, which was held in Nairobi, Kenya, in 1985. The shift took the form of bridge building and consensus making across regional and ideological divides, and the emergence of a women's organization of a new type, the TFN. What enabled this were three critical economic and political developments within states and regions, and at the level of the world system:

- The transition from Keynesian economics (with its emphasis on government intervention for full employment and citizen welfare) to neoliberal economics (with its emphasis on free markets, privatization, and trade and financial liberalization), along with a new international division of labour that relied heavily on (cheap) female labour.
- The decline of the welfare state in the core countries and the developmental state in the Third World, which placed a heavy burden on women's reproductive or domestic roles.
- The emergence of various forms of fundamentalist and right-wing religious movements, which threatened women's autonomy and human rights.

These global changes led to new ways of thinking and forms of organizing. The new economic and political realities led to a convergence of feminist perspectives: for many First World feminists, economic issues and development policy became increasingly important, and for many Third World feminists, increased attention was now directed to women's legal status, autonomy, and rights. This was accompanied by the formation of a number of transnational feminist networks that brought together women from both developed and developing countries to respond to economic pressures and patriarchal movements. They engaged in policy-oriented research, advocacy, and lobbying around issues pertaining to women and development, and women's human rights. Many of the women who formed or joined the TFNs were scholar–activists who had been, and continued to be, involved in the women and development research community (see Figure 27.1)

What should be noted is the impact of the computer revolution, for feminist advocacy and solidarity campaigns in the 1990s were spearheaded in part by the

Critique of economic policy

Transnational feminist network	Website	Location
Development Alternatives with Women for a New Era (DAWN)	http://www.dawn.org.fj/	Fiji
Network Women in Development Europe (WIDE)	http://www.eurosur.org/wide/home.htm	Brussels
Women's Environment and Development Organization (WEDO)	http://www.wedo.org/	New York
International Women's Tribune Center (IWTC)	http://www.iwtc.org/	United States

Peace, anti-militarism, conflict resolution

Transnational feminist network	Website	Location
Women for Women International (WWI)	http://www.womenforwomen.org/	United States
Women in Black	http://www.womeninblack.org/	Various countries
Women's International League for Peace and Freedom (WILPF)	http://www.wilpf.org/	Switzerland, United States
Code Pink	http://www.codepink4peace.org/	United States
MADRE	www.madre.org	United States
Medica Mondiale	http://www.medicamondiale.org/?L=1	Germany

Advocacy for women's human rights and anti-fundamentalism

Transnational feminist network	Website	Location
Association for Women's Rights in Development (AWID)	http://www.awid.org/	Canada
Center for Women's Global Leadership (CWGL)	http://www.cwgl.rutgers.edu/	United States
Collectif 95 Maghreb Egalité	http://www.euromedrights.org/eng/category/countries/regional-members/collectif-95-maghreb-egalite/	Algiers, Rabat, Tunis
Equality Now	http://www.equalitynow.org/	United States, Kenya
MADRE	http://www.madre.org/index.html	United States
Women Living Under Muslim Laws (WLUML)	http://www.wluml.org/	Nigeria, Pakistan, United Kingdom
Women's Caucus for Gender Justice	http://www.iccwomen.org/	United States
Women's Learning Partnership (WLP)	http://www.learningpartnership.org	United States
Women for Women International	www.womenforwomen.org	United States

Figure 27.1 Types of transnational feminist network.

new information and computer technologies. These helped women connect and share information, plan and coordinate activities more rapidly, and mobilize more extensively. As TFNs proliferated in the 1990s, the new technologies helped bridge the North–South divide among women activists; TFNs were now able to transcend the earlier political and ideological differences through the adoption of a broader feminist agenda that included a critique of neoliberalism and structural adjustment policies as well as an insistence on women's full citizenship, reproductive rights, bodily integrity, and autonomy no matter what the cultural context. Eventually, that common agenda took the form of the 1995 Beijing Declaration and Platform for Action.

Along the way to Beijing, however, there were other venues in which the world's women agreed on issues pertaining to gender justice, notably the UN world conferences of the 1990s – the United Nations Conference on the Environment and Development (UNCED) in Rio de Janeiro in 1992, the Human Rights Conference in Vienna in 1993, the International Conference on Population and Development (ICPD) in Cairo in 1994, and the World Summit for Social Development (the Social Summit) in Copenhagen in 1995. At these conferences, women declared that environmental issues were women's issues, that women's rights were human rights, that governments were expected to guarantee women's reproductive health and rights, and that women's access to productive employment and social protection needed to be expanded. Slowly, new frames emerged that resonated globally and have come to be adopted by women's groups throughout the world: *women's human rights; gender justice; gender equality; ending the feminization of poverty; ending violence against women.*

Policy successes followed in the 1990s. TFN lobbying led to the insertion of important items in the final Vienna Declaration of the 1993 Conference on Human Rights, such as the assertion that violence against women was an abuse of human rights, and attention to the harmful effects of certain traditional or customary practices, cultural prejudice, and religious extremisms. The Declaration also stated that human rights abuses of women in situations of armed conflict – including systematic rape, sexual slavery and forced pregnancy – were violations of the fundamental principles of international human rights and humanitarian law.

Some scholars have distinguished between professionalized women's lobbying groups (NGOs or INGOs) and 'grassroots' women's groups. The former are said to be elitist while the latter are more movement oriented. This may be an arbitrary distinction, however, because many of the professionalized TFNs are led and staffed by feminist activists with strong commitments to gender equality, women's empowerment, and social transformation. Moreover, the global women's movement is diffuse and diverse, with different types of mobilizing structure, discourse, and action repertoire. The overarching frame is that of achieving gender equality and human rights for women and girls. How that is achieved varies – through direct action, grassroots organizing, research and analysis, lobbying efforts, coalition building, humanitarian action. All these strategies are, in my view, movement oriented (see Figure 27.2).

What are some of the strategies that transnational feminist networks deploy to achieve their goals? Like other transnational social movements, they create, activate

	DAWN	WIDE	WLUML	Marche Mondiale	MADRE	Women for Women International	Code Pink
Grassroots organizing		X		X			X
Research and analysis	X	X	X	X	X	X	X
Lobbying	X	X				X	
Public advocacy and education		X	X	X	X	X	X
Coalition building	X	X	X	X	X		X
Humanitarian action					X	X	X
International solidarity	X	X	X	X	X	X	X
Public protest				X			X

Figure 27.2 Strategies deployed by transnational feminist networks.

or join global networks to mobilize pressure outside states. In the 1990s and into the new century, TFNs built or took part in coalitions, such as Jubilee 2000; the Coalition to End the Third World Debt; Women's International Coalition for Economic Justice; the Women and Trade Network; 50 Years is Enough; Women's Eyes on the Bank; United for Peace and Justice. After the Battle of Seattle, they become active players in the global justice movement, taking part in the World Social Forum, where the Feminist Dialogues became a regular feature (Eschle and Maiguashca 2010). And while women's groups long have been identified with peace movements, the new conflicts associated with globalization and American milita-rism led to the creation of new transnational feminist peace networks. Working alone or in coalitions, transnational feminist networks mobilize pressure outside states via e-petitions, action alerts, and appeals; acts of civil disobedience; other forms of public protest; and sometimes direct action.

Second, TFNs participate in multilateral and inter-governmental political arenas. They observe and address UN departments such as ECOSOC and bodies such as the Commission on the Status of Women (CSW); and they consult UN agencies and regional commissions. By taking part in and submitting documents to IGO meetings, and by preparing background papers, briefing papers and reports, they increase expertise on issues. By lobbying delegates they raise awareness and cultivate supporters. The purpose of such interaction with IGOs is to raise new issues – such as gender and trade, women's human rights, and violence against women in war zones – with a view toward influencing policy.

Third, TFNs act and agitate within borders and vis-à-vis states to enhance public awareness and participation. They work with labour and progressive religious groups, the media, and human rights groups on social policy, humanitarian, development and militarization issues. They link with local partners, take part in local coalitions, and provoke or take part in public protests. And, fourth, they network with each other, in a sustained process of *inter-networking* and *Internet-working*. In all these ways, their activism spans local, national, regional and transnational terrains. The 'gift' of the Internet has allowed them to transcend borders, boundaries and barriers in their collective action against neoliberalism, militarism, and fundamentalisms.

FEMINISM AGAINST WAR AND EMPIRE

Feminists and women's groups have been long involved in peace work, with analyses of the causes and consequences of conflict, methods of conflict resolution and peace building, and conditions necessary for human security. One of the oldest transnational feminist networks, and indeed, one of the world's oldest peace organizations, is the Women's International League for Peace and Freedom (WILPF), founded in 1915 by 1,300 women activists from Europe and North America opposed to what became known as World War I (Enloe 2007: 14). The activities of anti-militarist and human rights groups such as WILPF, Women Strike for Peace (USA), the Women of Greenham Common (UK), and the Mothers and Grandmothers of the Plaza de Mayo (Argentina) are well known, and their legacy lies in ongoing efforts to 'feminize' or 'engender' peace, nuclear disarmament and human rights.

The era of globalization and the end of the Cold War were accompanied by a new wave of conflicts – including those in Afghanistan, Bosnia and Central Africa – along with serious violations of women's human rights. Women's groups responded by underscoring the specific vulnerability of women and girls during wartime, the pervasive nature of sexual abuse, and the need to include women's groups in peace negotiations. New women-led peace, human rights, and humanitarian organizations were formed, as were more professionalized networks; these included Women in Black, Medica Mondiale, Women Waging Peace, and Women for Women International. Advocacy networks and scholar–activists produced research to show that women's groups had been effective in peacebuilding in Northern Ireland as well as in Bosnia and Central Africa.

In response to such research, lobbying, and advocacy initiatives, the United Nations Security Council issued a resolution that was embraced by women's groups, if not governments themselves. In March 2000 the UN Security Council, in its Proclamation on International Women's Day, recognized that gender equality is an integral component of peace, and in October convened a special session to consider the situation of women in armed conflict. On 31 October it passed Resolution 1325, calling on governments – and the Security Council itself – to include women in negotiations and settlements with respect to conflict resolution and peacebuilding.

However, while Security Council Resolution 1325 was widely hailed as a historic achievement in a domain usually considered off-limits to women and the preserve of men, its import was undermined not long afterwards, when new conflicts erupted that would sideline the Resolution in the name of the 'global war on terror'.

The aftermath of September 11, 2001 and the invasion of Iraq in 2003 galvanized women across the globe, who rallied to existing peace organizations or built new ones. Women participated in huge numbers in anti-war activities, in India, Pakistan, Turkey, Tunisia, South Africa. In the USA, a new peace group was formed, the now-famous Code Pink: Women for Peace, aptly dubbed by one sympathetic analyst 'the new Mothers of Invention'.

Code Pink was formed in November 2002 by a group of women who had worked with each other as well as in other networks. Medea Benjamin co-founded Global Exchange in 1988 with Kevin Danaher; Jodie Evans had worked for former California governor Jerry Brown; and Gael Murphy was a long-time public health advisor in Africa and the Caribbean. The group's name is a play on the national security colour codes established by the Bush Administration in the aftermath of September 11. As they explain on their website: 'While Bush's color-coded alerts are based on fear, the Code Pink alert is based on compassion and is a feisty call for women and men to "wage peace"'.

Activists have shown their creativity and innovative style of protest in various ways. One innovation is the issuance of 'pink slips' to political culprits. Activities have included a four-month vigil at the White House to oppose the war in 2003; a march of about 10,000 women on 8 March 2003 in Washington, DC, on the occasion of International Women's Day; several protests around the time of George Bush's second presidential inauguration in January 2004; and a steady stream of protests on Capitol Hill and cities across the United States. Wearing pink costumes and engaging in daring acts of public protest, Code Pink activists have become known for infiltrating Congressional meetings, unfurling anti-war banners, shouting anti-war slogans and badgering members of Congress on their stand on the war, military spending, healthcare for veterans, and support for Iraqi civilians. In one bold act that received much national and international coverage, a Code Pink activist, her hands painted red, approached then Secretary of State Condoleeza Rice on Capitol Hill and accused her of having the blood of the Iraqi people on her hands.[1]

In addition to its strategy of direct action, Code Pink's action repertoire includes feminist humanitarianism and international solidarity, as evidenced by visits to Baghdad to demonstrate opposition to war and solidarity with the Iraqi people. Founders Medea Benjamin and Jodie Evans, along with Sand Brim, travelled to Iraq in February 2003, and another trip was organized in December 2003. In December 2004 Code Pink coordinated the historic 'Families for Peace Delegation' to Amman, Jordan, involving the three Code Pink founders and a member of the anti-war group United for Peace and Justice (UFPJ), along with several relatives of fallen American soldiers and families of 9/11 victims. According to one report:

> In an inspiring act of humanity and generosity, they brought with them $650,000 in medical supplies and other aid for the Fallujah refugees who were forced from their homes when the Americans destroyed their city. Although the American press failed to cover this unprecedented visit, the mission garnered enormous attention from Al-Jazeera, Al-Arabiyya, and Dubai and Iranian television, who witnessed first hand the depths of American compassion.
>
> (Milazzo 2005: 103)

Code Pink's mission statement identifies itself as 'a women-initiated grassroots peace and social justice movement working to end the war in Iraq, stop new wars, and redirect our resources into healthcare, education and other life-affirming activities'. Toward this end, it works with other feminist and social justice networks, including the National Organization for Women and United for Peace and Justice. Along with MADRE, Women in Black, and Women for Women International, Code Pink engages in operational activities, information exchange and solidarity work, as well as direct action to protest government policies or inaction. It has also been active in CARA, the Council for Assisting [Iraqi] Refugee Academics. More recently, in the 10th year of its existence, Code Pink has called for the closure of the Guantanamo prison complex and the release of its prisoners; the end of drone strikes over Afghanistan, Pakistan, and Yemen; support for whistleblowers such as Edward Snowden; and – as always – the conversion of the military budget to one devoted to social and infrastructural projects.

In addition to Code Pink, networks such as the Women's Initiatives for Gender Justice, Women in Conflict Zones Network, PeaceWomen, and Women Waging Peace engage in research, lobbying, and advocacy to ensure that war criminals are brought to justice and that local women's peace groups are recognized. They also advocate for the International Criminal Court (established in 1999 as the first international war crimes court; see Chapter 20) and for continued progress of the UN's 'Women, Peace and Security' agenda at the Security Council. In 2007, the Nobel Women's Initiative was formed by six women Nobel Peace Prize winners – Shirin Ebadi of Iran, Jodie Williams of the USA, Betty Williams and Mairead Corrigan of Northern Ireland, Wangari Matthei of Kenya and Rigoberto Menchu of Guatemala. Its first international conference, focusing on women, conflict, peace, and security in the Middle East, took place in Galway, Ireland, in May 2007, and was attended by about 75 women from across the globe. In 2011 the initiative organized another conference on ending sexual violence in armed conflict; demanded an end to impunity in connection with the murders of women in Mexico; and called for an inquiry into rape as a weapon of war in Burma. The Laureates also created programmes for young women's leadership in peacebuilding.

FEMINIST HUMANITARIANISM AND INTERNATIONAL SOLIDARITY

While almost all transnational feminist networks may be regarded as internationalist and solidaristic – inasmuch as they are concerned about the plight of 'sisters' across borders and boundaries of nationality, religion, and class – not all engage in humanitarian work. I define feminist humanitarianism as operational work, informed by the strategic goal of achieving women's human rights and gender equality, which is carried by women's groups to alleviate suffering or to meet basic needs. (This understanding is very different from the 'humanitarian intervention' that was conceptualized in the 1990s to justify bombing Serbia and later invading Iraq.) Feminist networks that engage in this type of humanitarianism include MADRE, Medica Mondiale Kosovo, and Women for Women International.

	Year established	Core goals and activities	Country projects	$ disbursed
MADRE	1983	Gender, economic and environmental justice; programs in peacebuilding; women's health and freedom from violence; mobilizing resources for partner organizations to meet immediate needs of women and their families and develop long-term solutions to the crises they face	Colombia, Cuba, Guatemala, Haiti, Iraq, Kenya, Nicaragua, Palestine, Panama, Peru, Sudan	$22 million since 1983
Women for Women International	1993	Addressing women's needs in conflict and post-conflict environments; helping to effect transition from victims to active citizens; provision of microcredits and business services	Afghanistan, Bosnia, Colombia, DR Congo, Iraq, Kosovo, Nigeria, Rwanda, Sudan	$33 million as of 2006
Medica Mondiale	1999	Women's human rights and security: 'We support traumatized women and girls in war and crisis zones'; medical assistance and counselling; safe houses	Aceh, Afghanistan, Albania, Bosnia, Cambodia, DR Congo, Iraq, Kosovo, Liberia, Sudan, Uganda	n.a.
Code Pink	2003	Against war, militarism; U.S. out of Iraq; support U.S. troops by bringing them home; provision of medical supplies for Iraqis; no war with Syria; call to direct military budget for social expenditures; end drone strikes	Iraq, Pakistan, Palestine, Syria, Yemen	n.a.

Figure 27.3 Feminist humanitarian networks: key features.

Given space limitations, I elaborate only on MADRE in this chapter (see Figure 27.3 for comparative data on four humanitarian feminist networks).

MADRE began its work during the US-sponsored Contra war in Nicaragua in 1983 and initially devoted itself to that issue. As a progressive women's organization, MADRE invariably champions causes and pursues feminist humanitarianism and internationalism in contexts that are challenged by US hegemony. In all countries, MADRE partners with sister organizations. It has worked in Cuba, Nicaragua, El Salvador, Palestine and Haiti, providing aid for women and children through women's groups in the countries. Starting in 2004, MADRE has worked with its Sudanese partner Zeinab for Women in Development to provide emergency aid for displaced women and families in Darfur. In 2005 MADRE sent $500,000 worth of clothing and bedding to small refugee camps.

MADRE's work in Iraq dates back to the 1991 Gulf War, when it began collecting an assortment of needed supplies for Iraqi families, including milk and medicine. It continued this work throughout the 1990s, and frequently decried the detrimental effects on women and children of the sanctions regime. After the 2003 invasion and occupation of Iraq, MADRE partnered with UNICEF/Iraq and provided 25,000 citizens with supplies and emergency aid, including essential drugs and medical supplies to those in need. Working with its local feminist partner, the Organization of Women's Freedom in Iraq (OWFI), MADRE helped to address the problem of 'honour killings' – which spiked after the invasion – and to support the creation of women's shelters for victims of domestic and community violence in Baghdad, Kirkuk, Erbil and Nasariyeh. As Yanar Mohammad, an OWFI founder and leader, explained to me in a meeting in Amsterdam in May 2005, the campaign has given rise to a web of shelters and an escape route for Iraqi women, which is known as the Underground Railroad for Iraqi Women and is largely run by OWFI volunteers.

We end by turning to an ongoing example of feminist internationalism: the extension of solidarity to 'sisters' across borders. This is the international campaign to support Iranian women's rights activists. Feminism in Iran has a long and complex history, including activism at the height of the 1979 revolution followed by a long period of post-revolutionary quietism. At the start of the new millennium, however, small networks began meeting to strategize for change in the country's legal and policy frameworks, notably the family law, which places women in a subordinate position within the family. The first public protests took place in June 2005, at the end of the presidency of Mohammad Khatami and just before the new and very conservative president Mahmoud Ahmadinejad took office. Subsequent protests and rallies were broken up by police and a number of feminist activists arrested. The result of the state's repression was a decision to change the strategy, and the One Million Signatures Campaign was launched in September 2006. The campaign was adopted from the highly successful campaign of Moroccan feminists, initiated in the early 1990s. (This is an example of how feminist ideas and strategies 'travel', in this case from South to South.)

The Campaign was a grassroots, door-to-door initiative to obtain signatures for a change in family laws and other legal instruments unfavourable to women. Activities included collecting signatures on the metro or in parks, participating in rights workshops, and writing articles in support of women's rights for the Campaign's website, Change for Equality. Despite its peaceful nature, however, the Campaign was subject not only to harassment but prosecution. Campaign activists were charged with security crimes, including acting against the state and spreading propaganda against the state. By 2009, more than 50 Campaign activists – the majority of whom were in their twenties, women and men alike, living in Tehran and in the provinces – were arrested, threatened or called into court. In January 2008, the authorities closed down a longstanding women's magazine, *Zanan*, which was an early exponent of 'Islamic feminism'. The office of lawyer Shirin Ebadi, the Nobel Peace Prize winner and human rights advocate, was raided and closed down by police in December 2009. Still, cyberactivism continued in the form of the 'Feminist School', the online campaign platform.

Women's rights activists in Iran requested international solidarity to support the campaign for law reform toward gender equality; and to bring pressure to bear on the government for the release of feminist protestors. Expatriate Iranian feminists played an important role in helping to mobilize support from TFNs and women's groups everywhere, such as DAWN, WLUML, WLP, Equality Now, and the Nobel Women's Initiative, as well as Amnesty International. Feminist international solidarity with Iranian women's rights activists was an example of 'cyberactivism': this included the global circulation via the Internet of action alerts and petitions, and the launching of a multilingual website – formed in Tehran – that provided extensive information on the campaign. The crackdown that followed the outbreak of the green protests in July 2009, when Iranians protested the outcome of the presidential election that gave Ahmadinejad a second term, also spelled an end to the campaign. More arrests ensued, including that of the women's rights lawyer Nasrine Sotoudeh, the mother of two small children. Her plight became the focus of considerable transnational feminist activism. Sotoudeh remained in prison until October 2013, when incoming president Rowhani ordered the release of a number of political prisoners. Many other feminist activists, including Shirin Ebadi, left Iran for exile in Europe or North America.

CONCLUSION

Transnational feminism is characterized by a critique of social and gender inequalities and a set of strategies to enhance women's rights within the family and society; by networks that engage in research, lobbying, and advocacy for women's human rights and gender equality; by bold acts of direct action; and by acts of cross-border humanitarianism and solidarity. Transnational feminist networks are one of the principal organizational forms of global feminism; many of them target discriminatory or oppressive laws, policies, and norms; and they take part in global campaigns to alleviate suffering or show solidarity with nationally based feminism action.

By definition, transnational feminist action occurs across borders and thus entails the recognition of different contexts and priorities. While transnational feminist action exhibits similarities in critiques, goals, strategies, and mobilizing structures, some differences and disagreements are identifiable. One pertains to abortion and gay/Lesbian rights, where, in some cases, the decision not to raise the matter results from strategic priority setting within a movement, network, or coalition. Another difference pertains to the use of the term *feminist*. In some regions or countries where the term is either associated with the North or strategically inadvisable, advocates talk of *women's rights* or of *law reform*.[2] And in some of these same countries, women's rights groups frame their struggle as one for *civil society*, or for *democracy*, or for *national development* as well as for women's rights.

A significant number of South-based feminist groups – notably in Latin America and in North Africa – network with each other. Still, many transnational feminist networks, along with other global social movements and networks, are based largely in the North or are resourced, staffed, and funded largely from the North. This is a reflection of the inequalities of the contemporary capitalist world system, with its asymmetric economic zones of core, periphery, and semi-periphery. While such a discrepancy is unavoidable at present, it should not diminish the intent and results of transnational feminist humanitarianism and international solidarity that emanate from the core. These are, after all, a way of reversing the logic of the world system and of neoliberal globalization.

Questions for further debate

1. How do the local and the global intersect in transnational activism?
2. How do locally based feminists adopt the global women's rights agenda and transnational discourses to local contexts?
3. In what ways does transnational feminism matter in global politics?
4. Why might some feminists be resistant to the idea of a *global feminism*?
5. Does transnational/global feminism attenuate North–South differences among women?

Sources for further reading and research

Antrobus, P. (2004) *The Global Women's Movement: Origins, Issues and Strategies*, London: Zed Books.

Basu, A. (ed.) (1995) *The Challenge of Local Feminisms: Women's Movements in Global Perspective*, Boulder, CO: Westview Press.

Ferree, M. M. and A. M. Tripp (eds) (2006) *Global Feminism: Transnational Women's Activism*, New York: New York University Press.

Moghadam, V. M. (2013) *Globalization and Social Movements: Islamism, Feminism, and the Global Justice Movement*, 2nd edn, Lanham, MD: Rowman & Littlefield.

Mohanty, C. T. (2003) *Feminism without Borders: Decolonizing Theory, Practicing Solidarity*, Durham, NC: Duke University Press.

Notes

1 This occurred on 24 October 2007 and was widely reported. Rice had been on Capitol Hill to testify before the House Foreign Relations Committee.
2 This is the case in many African countries. In the Middle East, Iranian women's rights activists defiantly call themselves feminists, and *secular* feminists; this is also true of the *Association Tunisienne des femmes democrates* and of several Algerian women's groups. But the term feminist is generally eschewed in both Jordan and Egypt.

PART 7 INFORMATION, COMMUNICATION, TECHNOLOGY

CHAPTER 28

Art, aesthetics and emotionality

Emma Hutchison and Roland Bleiker[1]

■ **LEARNING OUTCOMES**

Upon completion, readers should be able to:

- Understand how prevailing images of humanitarian politics are both deeply emotional and deeply gendered.
- Appreciate the broader implications of such stereotypical visual patterns for the theory and practice of International Relations.
- Articulate how a feminist aesthetic holds potential to transform established conceptions of global politics.

■ **INTRODUCTION**

The realm of art and of aesthetics may seem a world away from that of global politics. The study of aesthetics is the study of taste and beauty and how together they awaken in us a certain affective sensibility. In short: a rather effeminate realm. Global politics, by contrast, is dominated by hard power and masculine military might. The men in charge wage 'dispassionate debates' and speak in a rational strategic language that banishes emotion to the realm of weakness and irrationality (Cohn 1987: 688).

Or is it really so? In the past two decades there have been conscious efforts to challenge these assumptions and approach the study of global politics with an aesthetic sensibility (see Figure 28.1). How can insights derived from art help us rethink the realities of global politics? How can they reveal the emotional dimensions of seemingly rational decisions? And what do such engagements tell us about the gendered dimensions of the international and its various political manifestations?

The purpose of this chapter is to expose and explore these links between art, emotions and gender. We begin with a specific example that highlights one art form and one political realm: photographic representations of humanitarian crises. We examine their deeply gendered nature. Whether they relate to war, famines or natural disasters, images of suffering often replicate gender stereotypes in a highly emotional manner. Almost all disaster media coverage prominently features images of women and children in deep distress. They are depicted as emotional and passive, as if they had no agency and were only waiting for rational men to rescue them. We then discuss the broader implications of these aesthetic patterns by drawing on some pioneering feminist scholars, such as Jean Bethke Elshtain and Cynthia Enloe. Their contributions show how such gender stereotypes feed into and perpetuate deeply entrenched gendered narratives of global politics. In a final step, we show how women – and men – have challenged these problematic narratives through various artistic endeavours.

- Art may appear a fanciful place to inquire about the links between gender and politics. But look around you. Our everyday life is replete with aesthetic patterns that are highly political and highly gendered. Advertisements for perfumes or cars, for instance, regularly depict gender stereotypes in a way that are both obvious and, at the same time, highly effective. Significant here is that aesthetics is not simply about art. Aesthetics is about perception, taste, emotion and meaning – phenomena that animate, distinguish and give colour to our lives. Aesthetics is about who we are and what we do.

- In the past two decades International Relations scholars have begun to look to aesthetics for alternative political insights, so much so that we can now speak of an 'aesthetic turn' (Bleiker 2001, 2009). Two issues are key:

   — First is the recognition that all knowledge of global politics is based on representations that are inevitably subjective, and thus enmeshed in power relations that are both gendered and emotional. Artists intuitively know that. Their aesthetic contribution emerges not from authentically depicting the world, but from engaging the process of representation. Picasso's painting *Guernica*, for instance, became such a powerful symbol of the horrors of war because it brought out a kind of truth that goes beyond external appearances. This is why some of the most significant insights into world politics emerge not from endeavours that ignore representation, but from those that explore how representative practices themselves have come to constitute and shape political events.

   — Second is that aesthetic sources can offer us alternative insights into international relations: a type of reflective understanding that emerges not from systematically applying the technical skills of analysis that prevail in the social sciences, but from cultivating a more open-ended level of sensibility about the political. We might then be able to appreciate what we otherwise cannot even see: the gendered foundations of power or the emotional nature and consequences of political events (Moore and Shepherd 2010: 301, 305–308).

- Aesthetics, in this sense, is about the ability to step back, reflect and see political conflict and dilemmas in new ways. This is why aesthetics refers not only to practices of art – from painting to music, poetry, photography and film – but also, and above all, to the type of insights and understandings they engender.

Figure 28.1 Aesthetic politics.

Figure 28.2 Picasso painting *Guernica* (Paris, 1937).

Image: Wikimedia Commons.

The resulting feminist aesthetic encourages us, quite literally, to view the world differently. Seeing, in this sense, is a form of agency, an active engagement with politics, for established models of international relations can ultimately only change when we and our aesthetic sensibilities do.

GENDERED IMAGES OF HUMANITARIAN CRISES

We cannot possibly survey all art forms and all political realms. This is why we start with a very specific example: photographs of humanitarian crises. Featured on newspaper front pages and through the internet, these images of suffering and crises are common. They provide a poignant place from which to examine the intersections between art, emotions and gender in global politics.

Crisis imagery is imbued with a specific representational aesthetic: it is designed to pull a viewer in, tug on our heartstrings and, through an often sublime horror, entice a viewer to look again. Unlike most other social and political phenomena, where women's roles are often under-represented, crisis imagery is one realm in which representations of women tend to outnumber those of men. Indeed, through dominant crisis imagery women are brought into focus in a highly visible and emotive manner.

The visual focus on women in disaster settings has much to do with their perceived ability to communicate human tragedy and need. Pictured often up close and in distress, women are thought to provide a humanizing face for what is often large-scale, distant and de-humanizing disaster. So recognizable are women in times of crisis that some contend they have come to be seen as the 'ideal' or 'universal disaster victim' (Dogra 2011; Enarson and Meyreles 2004: 49). As such, images of women enduring hardship are said to have become a 'standardized' (Briggs 2003: 179) or 'conventionalized' (Malkki 1996: 388) representation of catastrophe. As Kate Manzo (2008) puts it, women have become 'humanitarian icons': globally identifiable symbols capable of raising humanitarian awareness and sympathy.

But what kind of gendered – and emotional – political dynamics are at play in depictions of humanitarian crises? How do these dynamics shape the political and ethical issues at stake? Dominant crisis images resonate with and replicate instantly recognizable gender stereotypes. Women are presented not only in a range of customarily female social roles – such as that of a caregiver – but also and all too often as 'tearful, beleaguered, and overwhelmed', as 'struck down' and paralysed by catastrophe (Enarson and Meyreles 2004: 49). Frequently women are used to depict processes of mourning, distress, hardship and suffering: their eyes will be downcast or searching religiously for the sky; their hands will be on their head, they will kneel or crouch or look somehow physically diminished; they will stare up into the camera, visibly distressed. At best, they will seek other's help or be trying to care for or feed children (see, for example, Briggs 2003; Childs 2006; Dogra 2011; Enarson 2006; Fordham 1998: 128; Strüver 2007). Characteristic here as well is that crisis imagery tends to place women in a domestic (private rather than public) home-life setting (Childs 2006: 205).

Arguably the most classic – as well as stereotypical and readily identifiable – gendered humanitarian symbol is the image of the mother and child. Indeed, so commonplace and powerful are images of women together with children in disaster/humanitarian aid discourses that some scholars contend that the mother-and-child image has come to be understood as an international 'symbol of distress', as a marker of charity and humanitarianism (Manzo 2008: 649–51).

Much of the emotional and cultural symbolism of the mother-and-child image emerges from the customary notion of motherhood, specifically that motherhood is a female role (see Åhäll 2012; Briggs 2003: 183–4). As Lisa Malkki (1996: 388) explains, the image of mother and child presents something that goes to the heart of humanity and is essential to all cultures, a 'sentimentalized, composite figure – at once feminine and maternal, childlike and innocent'. But there is more to this visual pattern, as Malkki (1996: 388) knows: there is also a lack of power and a cry for help to those who have the ability to deliver (see Figures 28.3 and 28.4).

The gendered dimensions of such crisis imagery are readily apparent. Women are represented in a manner that taps into conventional gender stereotypes. Significant here is that women are portrayed as passive – powerless and prone to the circumstances surrounding them. Women are shown not as active agents but as vulnerable and needy victims, devoid of the capacity and agency to help themselves. Women and women's social roles after disaster are thus typecast; women are presented in a singular light that highlights and links a traditional familial domesticity with a sense of fragility and vulnerability. Implicated here as well are conventional notions of women as incapacitated and powerless in times of turmoil and grief, which prompts further established perceptions of women as dependent on others for rescue and survival.

Figure 28.3 US Navy Lieutenant Commander Loring Isaac Perry comforting an Indonesian woman and her child who lost everything during the tsunami in the city of Meulaboh, on Sumatra, Indonesia.
Image: Wikimedia Commons.

At the same time, however, it is arguably through these gendered stereotypes – i.e., through the implied sense of female passivity, dependence and ever present emotionality – that such imagery so readily mobilizes humanitarian compassions. It has been said that through such frames disaster is in effect 'feminized': the excessive use of feminine gender stereotypes shape how viewers come to consider the respective humanitarian situation more generally (Kelleher 1997; Sassen 2002a). Distant disaster is consequently perceived through a gendered lens: women come to represent all disaster victims, who then too become perceived of with a corresponding sense of stricken powerlessness. The apparent fragility and helplessness of women prompts viewers to bring into play a host of preconceived ideas about how all

- Figure 28.3 is from the 2004 Asian tsunami, which was one of the most devastating natural catastrophes of recent times. It claimed more than 275,000 lives and one left one billion people homeless. The photograph represents a visual theme that was very common in the worldwide media coverage of the disaster: it depicts a woman and child as victims and a Western rescue/aid worker providing assistance. In many instances, victims were portrayed in a more desperate, emotional and needy state than is visible in this photograph. That said, the visual patterns are clear.

- Such and other, more dramatic, images played a key role in mobilizing support for the relief and reconstruction effort. They demonstrated the need and positive impact of aid. In fact, the humanitarian response to the tsunami was as unprecedented as its scale of destruction.

- But these images also entrenched gender stereotypes. They presented women as fragile, powerless, submissive. A benevolent male Western rescue worker provides both assistance and solace. He is in charge and has the ability to deliver. Note too, that in the official description of the photograph the US Lieutenant Commander has a name, whereas the women/child victims remain nameless. One has to visually assume that they are reliant on the distribution of foreign aid. Although this was indeed the case at that dramatic moment, one could have presented them in different ways too, as pursuing a reconstruction activity or as helping Western aid workers to distribute aid among themselves (see Hutchison 2014).

Figure 28.4 The 'woman and child' metaphor.

disaster victims would think, feel and act – the dominant interpretation of which would be to assume both the inability of survivors to cope and consequently the necessity of outside assistance.

Dominant crisis imagery thus presents a significant paradox – one that highlights how gender constructions are subsumed, complicit in and reproduced through discourses of humanitarian disaster. On one hand, it may be precisely because such imagery is inherently gendered that it can mobilize compassion, political will and necessary aid (Braumann 1993). Research has also found that employing stereotypical feminine frames is often rationalized through the idea that some representation for women, even if stereotypical, is better than none at all (for a summary of this position, see Carpenter 2005). But, on the other hand, such imagery relies on and replicates a reductionist, one-dimensional perspective of women's social roles and agency. Indeed, through such singular, excessively feminine stereotyping female agency is essentialized and limited, whittled down to an established and simplistic gender cliché: women are typecast as emotionally fragile, vulnerable and at the same time helpless, powerless and perpetually needy.

TOWARDS A FEMINIST POLITICAL AESTHETIC

There are two ways in which feminist politics can break – and, indeed, has broken – through these gender stereotypes. First is the need to recognize and problematize deeply entrenched gender patterns. Second is the effort to provide alternative aesthetic options. We briefly touch on both of these strategies.

For decades feminist scholars have fought hard to expose and interrogate the types of gender construction we highlighted in the previous section. Feminist International Relations scholarship began by challenging the assumption that global politics is gender neutral. The respective scholars situated gender front and centre in the reproduction of global politics as a practice and discipline. They sought to show that 'gender makes the world go round' (Enloe 2000a: 1), that not merely is the personal political but moreover that 'the personal is international' (Enloe 2000a: 195). Significant for feminist scholars is therefore that the gendered dynamics of prevailing political aesthetics – such as the crisis imagery we examined – are not merely marginalizing and subjugating women but are also part of larger gendered patterns and mindsets that shape and constrain how we think about global politics.

Feminist International Relations scholars demonstrate the effects of gendered imagery by drawing out how such accounts reproduce constructed notions of ideal male and female identities and roles. In her pioneering book *Women and War*, Jean Bethke Elshtain (1987: 3) drew a picture of opposing yet mutually reinforcing gender images. She labelled these gender ideals the 'just warrior and beautiful soul'. For Elshtain (1994: 109), the 'just warrior' metaphor captures male identity as it has been inscribed through discourses of 'armed civil virtue'. The just warrior is 'a figure central to the story of war and politics in the West': a figure bound by honour and implicated in violence. The 'beautiful soul' is, likewise, a time-honoured and established metaphor for female identity: the woman who waits at home and often exhorts men to war by honouring them for their deeds. The cleavages here are clear: women are keepers of the home and family; men, the defenders of the public realm, the people, the power, the state (Elshtain 1994: 114).

Male/female binaries are for feminists a chief vehicle through which the global political life has been constituted. Foremost is that sovereign statehood is founded on and sustained by ideas and images of masculinized power and dignity versus feminized sacrifice (Enloe 2000a: 197). Elshtain (1987), for instance, writes that the just warrior/beautiful soul dichotomy has shaped men's and women's self-under-standings and actions in relation to war and peace. Moreover since 'just warriors' are the protectors of the state, the state itself is seen as 'manly' (Hooper 2001): it is 'male-defined and male-dominated' (Youngs 2004: 81). Women are in this light cast merely as bystanders in the international political order. As the very opposite of traditional masculine power and subjectivity, women are situated outside global politics.

Aesthetics matter to feminist inquiry because artistic representations are a power-ful mechanism through which traditional gender roles and ideals have been (and continue to be) constructed. Consider again our examination of crisis imagery. We demonstrated how an overwhelming focus on feminized representational frames depicts women through a singular and stereotypical lens that ultimately renders them passive – as helpless caregivers and victims. We then drew out that this is significant for women and how we think about women's roles and potentials in so far that ensuing meanings continue in a long history of essentializing and limiting female political agency. Powerful and 'seductive' gender ideals that confine and regulate how both men and women consider their possible political actions are thus mobilized through aesthetic frames. Cynthia Enloe explains that feminized imagery recreates the myth that 'only men, not women or children, have been imagined as capable of the sort of public decisiveness international politics is presumed to require' (Enloe 2000a: 4). Feminized political imagery therefore not only produces reductionist understandings of female political capacity but also, and in doing so, reinforces the mindset that global politics is a realm where conventional 'hard' male forms of power must prevail (Cohn 1987).

These gendered dynamics are, of course, part of larger trends of imaging women. Prevailing historic imagery of women in both war and peacetime typically stereo-types women in ways that marginalize and often depoliticize their social involve-ment (see MacDonald, Holden and Ardener 1987). Historically, the world of art too has revolved around a masculine ideal, leading to the proliferation of a mascu-line gaze (Korsmeyer 2004: 6). Women became the subjects of men's watchful eyes and tastes. Rey Chow (1992: 105) has suggested that the appropriation of female bodies through the predominant masculine mindset and framing is one way through which women are rendered especially vulnerable and helpless. They are 'consigned to visuality', reduced to the stereotypes that have become so entrenched that they are naturalized.

The naturalization of gender norms – both in terms of actions and emotionality – is one way through which aesthetics yields considerable power (see Figures 28.5, 28.6 and 28.7). Images of masculine power and action versus feminine passivity and inac-tion have over time come to be considered as truths rather than the 'deeply encoded ... symbolic constructions' that they are (Elshtain 1994: 110). Feminist scholars have

Emotions are central to both the aesthetic and the gendered dimensions of politics. They have long been seen to embody all that is feminine. Historically perceived to encapsulate women's 'dangerous desires', emotions were thought to be feelings or bodily sensations that overtook individuals, distorting thought and the ability to make calculated 'rational' and ethical judgement. Political decisions were meant to be free of passion, for giving in to impulsive urges would inevitably lead to irrational acts of violence and harm. Such views are part of a deeply entrenched Western cultural and scholarly tradition, which has sought to decouple emotions and rationality, at the expense of women (see Elster 1999; Jaggar 1989: 145–47). Women were in particular viewed to possess 'unwieldy', 'irrational' emotions. Female emotionality was perceived as perpetual and ever present, and as such it was historically held that politics was the place of men.

Feminists have recognized that these very attitudes to reason and emotion lie at the root of the problematic gendered links between sovereignty and conflict (Elshtain 1987; Peterson 1992b). They have challenged prevailing gendered emotional dynamics, showing how historical attempts to establish so-called rational and objective political decisions are often based on subtle, easily overlooked gendered systems of exclusion (Bergeron 2001: 984). The very idea of 'epistemological objectivism' – rational knowledge independent of a subject – is often intrinsically linked with a particular and often masculine worldview (Jaggar 1989).

There is a new but rapidly growing body of literature that recognizes how emotions have long played an implicit but important role in both the theory and practice of international relations (for a summary, see Bleiker and Hutchison 2008). In fact, few realms are more infused with emotion than politics: war and terrorism, for instance, are highly emotional phenomena.

Fear and anger play a key role in political realism, from Thucydides to Hobbes and from Morgenthau to Waltz. Trust has, likewise, been central to liberal visions of a more cooperative international order. Emotions, then, are a central part of our lives. They matter to men as much as they do to women. They are an intrinsic part of rational decision making, for numerous neuroscientific studies meanwhile show that emotion and cognition are intrinsically linked.

Figure 28.5 Naturalization of gender norms.

All gender stereotypes are based on deeply entrenched aesthetic patterns. They are often so old and so entrenched that we no longer recognize their subjective and problematic nature. Consider dress codes for men and women. We all – mostly – adhere to them. Few men would, for instance, dress up in a skirt when they go to work in a bank. Doing so would violate social codes that are widely accepted. But there is nothing objective about the respective dress codes. They have emerged at a particular time in history and then have been around so long that they have become accepted as normal, even natural.

The same is the case with the mother–child metaphor we introduced in the context of representations of humanitarian crises. It is a stereotype that goes back to the very beginnings of historical narratives. One of many examples is the visual prominence in Christian art of the pieta: the Madonna mourning the loss of her child. It is so widely depicted and recognized that this visual metaphor has become an icon of compassion and grief (Cohen 2001: 178–81; Dogra 2011: 336; Zarzycka 2012). And this metaphor is, of course, linked to perhaps the most iconic image of Christian art, that of the Madonna and Child. But, of course, like any metaphor, this one too is based on very particular religious, cultural and, not least, *gendered* assumptions about the world.

Figure 28.6 Madonna and Child.

sought therefore to uncover the gendered assumptions and social dynamics that are proliferated in the realm of the everyday, from TV programmes to newspaper ads and internet sites (see Shepherd 2013; Zalewski 2013).

For some, traditional ideas of masculinity and femininity may seem no longer so present, so powerful, or even so normal. Perhaps some consider that gender ideals have been done away with altogether and that women in particular are now free to be as they like. After all, women today don military fatigues; women too can go to war and fight. But such an apparent reversal or 'solution' to the construction of gender identities and roles is not always viewed as evidence of women's emancipation. That both sexes now engage in battle can rather be seen as illustrative of just how powerful and seductive masculinized narratives of power and war have become (Elshtain 1987: 8; Elshtain 1994: 111; Enloe 1983). Simply put, the symbolism of war – what it means culturally and politically to possess superior military might – has meant that war has become interesting, thrilling even, to the extent that women seek to incorporate some of the so-called 'just warrior' into their 'beautiful soul'. But even here the reality is far more complex. The 'shocking' images of Lynndie England, for instance, as well as the heroic rescue of Private Jessica Lynch, both demonstrate the continuing influence of the age old fear that women and female sexuality can be used as a threatening interrogation tool or weapon (Oliver 2007: 5).

All is not doomed, however. Since aesthetics have helped to make global politics, even as gendered a political realm as it may now be, aesthetics can also help to break

Figure 28.7 Madonna and Child with Saints Bernardino of Siena and Jerome, behind them two angels (Matteo di Giovanni, 1435–1495).

Image: Wikimedia Commons.

down gendered patterns and mindsets. There are numerous feminist activists who have embarked on innovative and influential aesthetic engagements with gender stereotypes. Consider the famous Guerrilla Girls, an anonymous group of female art activists operating since the early 1980s. They seek to reveal and challenge gender-based exclusions in numerous locations, for instance in museums (see Figure 28.8). The facts are clear, they point out: 'Do women have to be naked to get into the Met. Museum? … Less than 5% of the artists in the Modern Art sections are women, but 85% of nudes are female' (Guerrilla Girls 2012). One of their most well-known campaigns thus prompts us to wonder about the consequences of such gendered aesthetic practices.

Consider a second example, this time from the recent Arab spring uprising in Egypt. One of the most remarkable episodes occurred when a young woman blogger called Aliaa Elmahdy posted a nude photograph of herself on her blog. She did so to protest gender discrimination in Egypt and called for more personal freedom, including sexual autonomy. Her private-cum-public act of defiance caused extensive public protests and unsettled the country's gender assumptions (see Figure 28.9). In an insightful study of this episode, Xzarina Nicholson (2013) shows how Elmahdy's visual act of dissent challenges numerous religious, ideological and political norms. Paradoxically, and as illustrated by the activism of the Guerilla Girls, the naked female body can be both an expression of domination and act of dissent.

Figure 28.8 Someone dressed as a Guerilla Girl.

Image: Wikimedia Commons.

Figure 28.9 Graffiti comparing media attention to Aliaa Elmahdy with a lack of attention paid to Samira Ibrahim, who protested against virginity checks on female protestors by the Egyptian Army.

Image: Wikimedia Commons.

CONCLUSION

We have demonstrated what an engagement with aesthetics and emotions can contribute to a gendered analysis of global politics. Two key insights stand out.

First is the recognition that aesthetic practices are a powerful mechanism through which men and women have come to understand their political capacity, agency and actions. These aesthetic representations touch on all aspects of our lives, from TV shows to dress codes, from advertising campaigns for perfumes to the organization of national celebrations and military parades. We illustrated the issues at stake with regard to one realm: media images of humanitarian crises. Taking the mother–child metaphor as an example, we highlighted both the effective and the highly problematic nature of deeply entrenched gender stereotypes. Women and children are 'good' victims. They generate empathy in viewers and thus enable humanitarian action. But the very same depictions also entrench highly problematic gender stereotypes. Women are seen as highly emotional, passive, unable to help themselves and thus reliant on the rescue and support of rational men.

While deeply entrenched, such stereotypes have, of course, not remained unchallenged. Feminist International Relations scholarship has not only exposed and critiqued these and related gender assumptions, but also revealed how they lie at the very heart of international power relations. Likewise, feminist activists have embarked on numerous campaigns to raise awareness of gender stereotypes and break through them. It is in this sense that aesthetics is paradoxically both an essential part of gender discrimination and an equally essential part of overcoming them.

Questions for further debate

1. How do aesthetic practices entrench global gender relations?
2. How do aesthetic practices challenge global gender relations?
3. To what extent is the woman/child metaphor a reflection of either natural attributes or socially assigned roles?
4. How are emotions linked to gender stereotypes?
5. What can an aesthetic approach to world politics help us explain that traditional approaches in IR cannot apprehend?

Sources for further reading and research

Bleiker, R. ([2009] 2012) *Aesthetics and World Politics*, New York: Palgrave.

Danchev, A. and D. Lisle (2009) 'Introduction: Art, Politics, Purpose', *Review of International Studies*, 35(4): 775–9.

Elshtain, J. B. (1987) *Women and War*, New York: Basic Books.

Shepherd, L. J. (2013) *Gender, Violence and Popular Culture: Telling Stories*, New York: Routledge.

Zalewski, M. (2013) *Feminist International Relations: Exquisite Corpse*, New York: Routledge.

Note

1 We would like to thank Constance Duncombe for valuable insight and assistance in preparing this chapter.

CHAPTER 29

Popular culture and the politics of the visual

Christina Rowley

LEARNING OUTCOMES

Upon completion, readers should be able to:

- Recognise the importance of popular and visual culture – and the gendered dynamics thereof – for the study of world politics.
- Understand some of the ways in which (gendered) popular cultural texts, images and practices can be analysed.
- Develop critiques of gendered representations of world politics in popular media.

INTRODUCTION

In the context of a textbook discussing life and death issues – war, genocide, poverty, sexualised violence – a chapter on popular culture sounds trivial. Popular culture is ostensibly everything that world politics *is not*: fiction, entertainment, amusement. It is not that popular culture has no value as an object of academic study – there are scholars and disciplines of cultural studies, film studies, media and communication studies – but the division of academia into discrete disciplines permits IR scholars to ignore popular culture and claim that it is not important to the study of world politics. The (gendered) distinctions that IR scholars make, explicitly or implicitly, between 'fact' and 'fiction', between domestic and international (spheres), 'hard' and 'soft' (power), 'high' and 'low' (politics), underpin and permit the view of popular culture as irrelevant to IR or, worse, a frivolous distraction. Crucially, it is the understanding of popular culture as irrelevant that implicates the terrain as particularly important and the discourses therein as immensely powerful in terms of their constitutive function (their ability to construct realities) in contemporary society (Rowley 2011).

In contrast, Cynthia Enloe (1996) asks us to devote more of our analytical attention to the 'margins, silences and bottom rungs' of world politics, in order to reveal the quantity and variety of power that must be exerted, in multiple sites, to keep the world functioning as it does. Popular culture comprises one such set of sites (see later for a brief discussion of definitions of popular culture). People make sense of world politics via the knowledge, understandings and attitudes that are created through interactions in the realm of the popular, the mundane, the everyday (Rowley and Weldes 2012): workplaces and holidays, TV shows, advertisements. Popular cultural representations often resonate, or share structural similarities, with 'factual' (e.g., academic, media, government) discourses of world politics; indeed, they are mutually constitutive. As Jutta Weldes demonstrates, popular cultural texts such as magazines, novels, films and television shows are important because they are implicated in the production of common sense and therefore in the 'manufacture of consent' for states' foreign policies (1999: 119; 2003a). Popular cultural artefacts not only make use of the same background meanings (cultural resources) as do policymakers, in order to construct a compelling vision of the world; they also create cultural resources on which other cultural and state actors – and people more generally – draw.

The mutual constitution of popular cultural and other discourses and representations can be understood as their *intertextuality*. One of the key logics through which intertextuality operates is gender (see, for example, Hooper 2001; Rowley 2011; Weber 2005b). Moreover, as what frequently 'goes without saying' (Barthes 1973: 11) in both popular culture and world politics, gender is not only a logic of intertextuality, but at the same time is also what enables this intertextuality to be obscured from view. Finally, since gender (and specifically gender as difference) often manifests itself in and through visual representations, and since so much of contemporary popular culture is played out through visual media, the politics of the visual is particularly important.

In this chapter, I explore some of the ways in which we can investigate the diverse interconnections between gender, world politics and popular culture, including the gendered intertextuality of popular culture and world politics. I have chosen to focus almost exclusively on mass media cultural texts, produced in and for Anglo-American audiences. I do not discuss the (gendered) politics of modelling, music (Franklin 2005) or Bollywood (e.g., Dudrah 2006; Mishra 2002). I barely mention sports, foodways, graffiti, knitting or gardening. This may seem natural to some readers. After all, should we not concentrate on those cultural artefacts that are made in and by the dominant states within the world system, and that are financially and culturally the most influential? However, Enloe (1996) reminds us of the dangers of disregarding large parts of the world's population and their activities when we are trying to account for how world politics 'works'. I mention these absences and omissions so that, as you are reading, you can reflect on the sheer magnitude of what has not been said in this chapter – on the silences, margins and exclusions constructed in and by this discussion.

GENDER AND THE POLITICS OF POPULAR AND VISUAL CULTURE

Popular culture

Popular culture is a vague notion (Cruz and Guins 2005: 4; Williams 1981), but most people can give examples of popular culture, and 'know it when they see it'. It includes texts and practices produced for, about and engaged in by 'the masses', such as film, TV, music, fashion, sport, tourism, clubbing, foodways, news media, hobbies, the internet. Popular culture is often defined in specific contrast to 'high' culture: cinema vs. theatre, graffiti/comics vs. fine art, pop music vs. opera, trash fiction vs. classical literature. However, this dichotomy is problematic, and should make us stop and think about where else we have seen binaries function to exclude important issues from the agenda. One example worth noting is that those media forms, genres and texts that are most denigrated as mass-produced culture are typically those most feminised and/or associated with women consumers, e.g., soap operas, romance novels and boybands.

The study of popular culture requires the study not only of culture as commercial commodities but, crucially, also how these products are actively interpreted and used by people: consumption is not passive. People make their own culture/cultural meanings out of resources and commodities provided by dominant cultural systems (Fiske 1989: 15) through, for example, graffiti-ing buildings or creating YouTube videos for pop songs. Production is not always explicitly/intentionally supportive or critical of mass-produced popular culture but, because texts and discourses always express both domination and subversion, power and resistance, they are never exclusively one or the other. Jeans (denim trousers), for example, do not have one defined meaning: they have been associated with (at least) two identity 'strands': (1) physical labour, ruggedness and the outdoors; and (2) youth, freedom, and rebellion. Jeans are sold as the quintessential sign of non-conformity but are, paradoxically, one of the most conformist items of clothing available. Unusually, perhaps, jeans can also function to represent certain types of masculinity *and* femininity as well as having a particular 'unisex' status in Western society. Such semiotic richness[1] – the resource bank of potential meanings that can be generated – is only activated in lived experiences (e.g., by people buying and wearing jeans, photographing them, or cutting them up and making new items) and via the specific discursive practices in and through which identities are performatively produced. Popular culture is a terrain, a site of struggles over meaning, which involves taking account of both texts (representations) and practices (their active consumption and interpretation).

The politics of the visual

We live in a world highly dependent on communication through visual images, and we often prioritise the visual over our other senses, yet we are rarely *explicitly* taught how to read visual images (Howells 2003: 2). Reading images may appear instinctive but interpreting visual information relies on shared cultural understandings just as much as does understanding written texts, which themselves have an indispensable visual component. So, 'looking is not as straightforward an activity as might be supposed' (Mirzoeff 1999: 21–2; see also Sturken and Cartwright 2001: 10). Something as apparently natural as understanding two-dimensional images to represent three dimensions is a culturally specific *learned* practice[2] and looking is an active process of meaning making. With visual images, we often assume we have gleaned their meaning immediately and without any reflection (because of their apparent resemblance/correspondence to 'reality' and to 'real' referent objects), thus obscuring the interpretive labour that has been performed in our reading. Visual images are, in this sense, perhaps more powerful than textual representations. Although we may remain unaware that we are doing so, we learn to read images for complex gendered, racialised and class-based (among other) codes from an early age, and images resonate on many different levels, going 'beyond the purely rational level of awareness' (Hall 1999: 311).

For feminists, the politics of visual representation is particularly important because gender inequality has historically been justified through claims about visible physical differences between men and women. Gender and racial differences 'are made to seem "real" and therefore "true"… because the differences we can "see"… appear to ground their "truth" beyond history, in what is naturally so' (Hall 1999: 314). Furthermore, there are important (gendered) power relations to be considered between the 'looker' and the 'looked at'. Historically, man has been the subject, the agent 'doing the looking', while woman has been the object of his gaze, the spectacle (think, for example, of the nude female model prevalent in classical art and sculpture, and the ways in which the female body is depicted in much the same ways in music videos and British 'page 3' images today). The gendered politics of visual meaning extends far beyond popular culture alone.

For people in the minority world (the West/global North), electronic (and) visual media[3] now play an unpredecentedly influential role in the ways in which people receive, consume and interpret information about the world and, because of their visual components, people are often unaware of this *mediation* at work. For many 'eyewitnesses' of 9/11 (those in downtown Manhattan who saw the planes crash into the World Trade Center), visual cultural codes were integral to their experiences, as many 'used the metaphor of cinema to try and verbalise the enormity of what had happened' (Dalby 2008: 443; Mirzoeff 2002: 8). For the majority of US citizens, as for many others, the mediated, mediatised event *is* 9/11 – that is, people's experience of 9/11 is primarily a filmic/televisual one. This example highlights the centrality of popular, visual, (and) media culture in our daily lives and experiences – cultural spaces, practices and representations which are always already gendered. In the next section, I explore different approaches to the study of popular culture, paying particular attention to methods developed and deployed by feminists and gender theorists.

APPROACHING THE ANALYSIS OF POPULAR AND VISUAL CULTURE

Here, I delineate ways in which the gendered analysis of popular cultural texts and practices can be approached with regard to three key themes: *production*,

- '[T]he Women's Movement has assumed without question the importance of film in the women's struggle ... The reason for this interest in the media is not difficult to locate: it has been at the level of the image that the violence of sexism and capitalism has been experienced' (Johnston 1973, quoted in Thornham 1999: 11).

- '[W]ith the exception of some resistant forms, music, theatre, TV weather forecasts, and even cereal box scripts tend to endorse prevailing power structures by helping to reproduce the beliefs and allegiances necessary for their uncontested functioning' (Shapiro 1992: 1).

- '[S]tate action is made commonsensical through popular culture ... Popular culture ... to the extent that it reproduces the content and structure of the dominant foreign policy discourse, helps to produce consent for foreign policy and state action' (Weldes 1999: 119).

- '[B]y failing to analyse popular visual language as integral to global communications, disciplinary IR risks misunderstanding contemporary subjectivity, spatiality, and temporality. By failing to grasp who we are, where we are, and when we are, IR cannot possibly comprehend what we say and do, much less what we hear, feel and see' (Weber 2008: 138).

- 'There is talk that many Vietnam films are antiwar, that the message is war is inhumane and look what happens when you train young American men to fight and kill, they turn their fighting and killing everywhere, they ignore their targets and desecrate the entire country, shooting fully automatic, forgetting they were trained to aim. But actually, Vietnam War films are all pro-war, no matter what the supposed message, what Kubrick or Coppola or Stone intended. Mr. and Mrs. Johnson in Omaha or San Francisco or Manhattan will watch the films and weep and decide once and for all that war is inhumane and terrible, and they will tell their friends at church and their family this, but ... [military servicemen] are excited by them, because the magic brutality of the films celebrates the terrible and despicable beauty of their fighting skills. Fight, rape, war, pillage, burn. Filmic images of death and carnage are pornography for the military man; with film you are stroking his cock, tickling his balls with the pink feather of history, getting him ready for his real First Fuck. It doesn't matter how many Mr. and Mrs. Johnsons are antiwar – the actual killers who know how to use the weapons are not' (Swofford 2003: 6–7).

Figure 29.1 Gender and popular culture: key insights.

representation and *consumption*. The relative importance of these concepts has been the subject of intense academic debate and disagreement. Whatever methodological approach we favour, we must remain aware that we cannot account for the complex ways in which gender and popular culture matter in global politics without considering all three (see Figure 29.1).

Production

To paraphrase Cynthia Enloe: where are the women film directors? Women have become gradually more numerous as executives and decision makers in the big studios (Hass 2005), but how many world-famous female directors can you name? Leni Riefenstahl or Sofia Coppola may come to mind; but, in 2007, just 6 per cent of the top 250 grossing Hollywood films were directed by women – down from 9 per cent in 1998 (Goldstein 2008).[4] Unless we believe that women are somehow by their very nature just bad at making popular films, this should prompt us to ask questions about how the film industry is gendered. How do people gain access to places on film studies courses and to jobs thereafter? Who is able to take up an unpaid or low-paid internship? Do women get as much support from their families to go into directing? Who makes the decisions about which films will get made and by whom, and on what criteria are these decisions based? What industry support is there for women who want to direct (Friedman 2007)? Crucially, however, we must also ask about the ways in which directing is constructed as a gendered skill as well as (not just about) directors' sex. In an *LA Times* article, Patrick Goldstein (2008) quoted production designer Polly Platt as speculating that women find some aspects of directing terrifying, while men enjoy the power. An anonymous female executive in the *New York Times* suspected that women do not have the ruthless streak required for success (Hass 2005). Directing is constructed as a masculine skill but articulated as being derived from 'biological' sex differences in order to naturalise this construction.

There are other questions we can ask about the gendered production of popular culture – for example, about the intersection of gender and race in global fashion and cosmetics industries. Think about 'skin tone' makeup: what images are conjured? Similarly, what colour is a pair of 'neutral' or 'natural' tights (pantyhose)? Most major US and UK cosmetics producers do not make products specifically targeted at Arabic, African(-American/-Caribbean) or Asian women, or their ranges are very limited in comparison with the choice available for Caucasian women. We should also consider the ways in which production might be gendered in less immediately obvious ways. Enloe (2007) has traced the production of the 'humble sneaker', its intimate connections with global processes of militarisation and the creation of export-processing zones in which labour is cheap and feminised.

David Robb (2004) has examined the relationship between Hollywood and the US military, finding that, in return for assistance to make films and television programmes, often by providing resources such as military bases for filming, equipment such as planes and helicopters, and even troops as extras, the Pentagon often 'requests' script changes. If changes are not made, the US military can prevent films being screened at US and overseas bases, which can have a very negative effect on films' success. The Pentagon's primary requirement in return for assistance is that the films 'aid in the recruiting and retention of personnel' (US Army quoted in Robb 2004: 26). Robb has documented the ways in which scripts for blockbusters, such as *Black Hawk Down*, *Pearl Harbor* and *Top Gun*, have been altered, sometimes substantially, at the behest of the Pentagon's film liaison office. That the Pentagon has so much influence over the production of popular culture is of particular importance for feminist scholars of world politics, given the links between militarisation and masculinisation that feminist scholars have been concerned to expose and theorise.[5]

Representation I: Textual analysis

The above discussion about the militarisation and alteration of texts to suit the US military directly feeds into this section's focus on representations. In cultural analysis, *text* includes written documents (newspaper articles, books and scripts), visual artefacts (photographs, paintings), audio material (e.g., songs, music, podcasts) and other media (sculpture, adverts, films, websites, music videos). Additionally, the ways in which discourses are conceptualised – as systems of meaning production – implies that pretty much anything can potentially be 'read' as a text. Dances, shopping malls, militarised rituals at border crossing points and the ways in which supermarkets are laid out, all can be analysed through the concept of the text.

We might be tempted to analyse popular cultural representations primarily for their 'truth value' (historical accuracy) – i.e., what a film from a particular period can tell us about that era, or making judgements about whether individual films present a 'balanced' ('true') or 'biased' ('propaganda') view of the world. However, representations should not be viewed as simple reflections of either 'true' or 'distorted' 'reality'. Maps are a particularly apposite example of this: maps are neither true nor false: they are representations of the world. As with *all* representations, maps represent a simplified account of the world in order to highlight the information that is particularly important in a specific context.[6] Simplifications, generalisations, abstractions: all are inherently *political* processes (Rowley and Weldes 2008: 193). Representations such as maps, photographs or films are 'complex structures of linguistic and visual codes organised to produce specific meanings. They are not merely collections of images or stereotypes' (Thornham 1999: 12). A focus on stereotypes, whether good or bad, positive or negative, leads to simplistic readings that constrain our analysis to characters and bodies (Wiegman 2000: 161) and neglects the ways in which these come together to produce meaning that goes beyond the sum of a text's constituent elements.

Analysing cultural and media representations for their gendered dynamics has been an important aspect of both feminist scholarship and feminist activism since the 'second wave' in the 1960s and 1970s (see Johnston's quote in Figure 29.1). There is now a massive body of literature on gender and popular culture, analysing, for example, 'femmes fatales' (Doane 1991), 'working girls' (Tasker 1998), 'action chicks' and action cinema (Inness 2004; Tasker 1993) in film and television, as well as on the construction of feminisms, femininities and masculinities in a variety of contexts (e.g., Cohan and Hark 1993; Hollows 2000; Hollows and Moseley 2006). *The West Wing* (TWW) is a particularly fruitful site for analysing (gendered) representations of world politics (see, *inter alia*, Beavers 2002; Gans-Boriskin and Tisinger 2005; Philpott and Mutimer 2005) (see Figure 29.2). The gendered representations and feminist potential of the science fiction genre are discussed in Figure 29.3.

Representation II: Visual analysis

Often, when we analyse the representations in films, novels or television shows, as in Figures 29.2 and 29.3, we are interested in the plot or storyline and therefore focus on the script, on what particular characters say and do. Less frequently do we pay attention to the specifically visual elements that code characters in different ways, or in the visual clues that we may not consciously pick up on but that remain central to the practice of representation. However, we must be aware of the limitations inherent in applying analytical methods designed for written texts to visual images (Evans and Hall 1999: 7). We can learn a lot about the meaning and function of shots by analysing how they are framed and cut together (Monaco 2000).

The West Wing (TWW) (1999–2006) offered a behind-the-scenes portrayal of fictional US Democratic President Josiah Bartlet and his team of White House advisors. At its peak, TWW attracted weekly US audiences of around 17–18 million (Philpott and Mutimer 2005: 337). TWW has been praised for its portrayals of independent, powerful women. For the most part, female political actors are presented as 'the same' as their male counterparts, equally able to do their jobs, irrespective (rather than because) of their gender. In this sense, women are equal 'precisely because they do not think like women, but like politicians. They make no demands on the part of women' (2005: 350; Ringelberg 2005: 91–92).

Insofar as overtly gendered issues such as abortion, gay rights and gay marriage, forced prostitution and sex trafficking are debated and given coverage, and conceptual links are made between, for example, violence against women and the global arms trade ('The women of Qumar'), TWW clearly demonstrates a commitment to feminism (Rowley 2006). However, women are also often shown in peripheral roles, used as foils and supports for the male characters' storylines, objectified or otherwise deployed to create sexual tension (Garrett 2005: 189). Furthermore, emotion is usually feminized and typically negatively portrayed as a basis for decision making, while a sense of fairness and justice is portrayed as a rational rather than emotional attribute and is therefore positively valued.

During the seventh-season presidential election between Republican Arnold Vinick (based on John McCain) and Matthew Santos (based on Barack Obama), Santos's campaign manager, Josh, deploys gender binaries quite explicitly in his explanation of how US presidential elections 'work': 'People think the campaign's about two competing answers to the same question. They're not. They're a fight over the question itself.' Republicans win by focusing on security; Democrats win on domestic issues. This is the 'mommy problem': 'When voters want a national daddy, someone to be tough and strong and defend the country, they vote Republican. When they want a mommy, someone to give them jobs, health care – the policy equivalent of matzo ball soup – they vote Democratic' ('The Mommy Problem').

What becomes clear in an interrogation of TWW through gender(ed) lenses is the variety of ways in which gender 'goes without saying' (Barthes 1973: 11). It is not only overtly 'feminist' issues that are presented as gendered; gender is always and everywhere present as a narrative function in the storylines and episodes.

Figure 29.2 Gender and *The West Wing*.

How a shot is composed and framed is its *mise-en-scène*. How the shot is cut together into a sequence or scene is known as *montage* (more commonly called editing).[7] Point-of-view (POV) shots encourage the spectator to identify with the character. Alternating over-the-shoulder shots during a conversation encourages the audience to assume an omniscient (all-knowing) position in relation to the two talking characters. These aspects of a film are important because of the dominance of male protagonists in films and because the omniscient spectatorial position encourages the notion that 'the whole truth' can be (is being) represented from an external and objective standpoint, rather than drawing attention to the partial perspective of the camera (i.e., what is not in the frame/scene).

We can also look at the ways in which props, costumes, and other symbols are visually represented within shots and scenes to create layers of meaning: they provide us with a lot of information about, for example, genre and generic expectations, and the qualities and attributes of characters (e.g., race, gender, class, sexuality), often without our being consciously aware of these meaning-making processes at work. Anneke Smelik reminds us that 'codes in dressing, certain gestures, stylistic décor, or extended looks can at a glance invoke the homosexuality of a character' (2000: 135). Monaco (2000: 161–77) discusses a number of

Despite its ostensible focus on radically 'other' worlds, SF self-consciously reflects on familiar political themes and offers us resources with which to critique our own worlds (Rowley 2005; Rowley and Weldes 2012). Through utopias and dystopias, SF also extrapolates the consequences of current social, cultural, political, economic and technological trends and explores 'what we might become if and when the present restrictions on our lives vanish, or show[s] us new problems and restrictions that might arise' (Pamela Sargent in Cranny-Francis 1990: 221).

SF provides us with new ways of, and spaces for, thinking about gender. Displacing narratives onto other times and/or places strips contemporary patriarchal society of its naturalising discourses (Cranny-Francis 1990: 222). Writing more than 20 years ago, Vivien Sobchack (1990) found that both women/femaleness and human sexuality more generally were repressed and/or neglected in many popular SF film narratives. In more recent times, mainstream SF cinema has explicitly engaged with women, feminism and notions of gender equality. For example, director Paul Verhoeven has claimed that the portrayal of sexual equality was an important aim in making *Starship Troopers* (Hansen 2001: 275) and it has become almost commonplace for futuristic SF films and TV shows to present women soldiers without comment (see, inter alia, *Firefly, Serenity, Battlestar Galactica* and various *Star Trek* series).

In *Firefly* and *Serenity*, the depiction of some planet-worlds as dominated by patriarchal values, while others have established liberal feminist egalitarian systems, represents feminism 'as an ongoing political project that is neither inevitable nor passé' (Rowley 2007: 322). However, representations of gender relations focus on changes in/to women's rights and femininities while leaving masculine identities largely unchallenged and unproblematised. Despite the inclusion of a female warrior, soldiering practices – indeed, all traditionally male roles – do not appear to be gendered significantly differently from their twenty-first century equivalents (324). With specific reference to the short-lived *Space: Above and Beyond*, Nickianne Moody (2002: 51) makes a point that has broader resonance in terms of the feminist potential of much contemporary mainstream SF. Insofar as films and TV shows portray gender equality as taken-for-granted, although their portrayals of women's expanded military roles might be seen as 'positive' shifts, at the same time, these texts deny the *exploration* of struggle and the space for us (the audience) to consider how these feminist aims might come to be achieved in our worlds.

Figure 29.3 Gender and feminism in science fiction (SF).

(overlapping) ways in which images function. *Icons* resemble what they represent: an image of a phonebox represents a phonebox. (However, this should not be implied to mean that all visual images can be read straightforwardly or that they are more 'obvious', 'true' or 'accurate' than text-based representations). Representational strategies that we interpret also include *symbols*, whereby an abstract image stands in for another concept, e.g., red roses commonly reference love; doves symbolise peace; gold medals = victory. Some symbols can be connected in some way with the thing they represent. So, a thermometer climbing indicates rising temperature, while muscles may signal physical strength, and an image of the White House (or the use of the term 'White House') can signify the office of the US president or, more broadly, 'the government'.

Representations function differently depending on context (including montage and *mise-en-scène*): if an image of a cork popping out of a champagne bottle follows a shot of two lovers in a hotel room, it may symbolise male ejaculation, or male potency. If, however, the popping champagne cork comes immediately after the end of a sporting event, it will more likely be taken to connote victory.[8] In a scene about a merger or financial takeover, it might imply the settlement of the business deal.

Figure 29.4 Untitled mural, Temple Meads Enterprise Zone, Bristol (UK).
Photograph: Author.

Figures 29.4 and 29.5 illustrate visual analysis through a discussion of a mural created for the 'See No Evil' urban art exhibition in Bristol.

Spray-painted by graffiti artists FLX One and Dones in a prominent location outside Bristol's main railway station, this mural offers a searing critique of power in contemporary British society. Twelve different animals, each representing a different social institution, are gathered around the devil at a table, in a direct reference to Da Vinci's depiction of Jesus and the 12 disciples eating the Last Supper. However, instead of eating a sacred meal, the table is littered with stacks of chips; in front of the devil, a mushroom cloud explodes. The characters are playing poker and the stakes couldn't be higher: they are gambling with people's lives.

In what ways is gender deployed in this image? First, through clothing or comportment, each animal is coded male and associated with a traditionally masculine occupation/institution. On the far left stand two religious figures: a Church of England bishop/archbishop, and a Roman Catholic cardinal (neither of whom may be a woman), represented as locust and praying mantis, respectively. Next to them, so dark that he almost disappears into the background, sits a gorilla lighting a large cigar. The weaponry on which he leans suggests he is an arms dealer. The three characters closer to the devil are, collectively, the dogs of war: a pitbull represents enlisted men (pitbulls are associated with the working class in Britain), while a huge grey mastiff and a British bulldog are dressed as officers.

On the right-hand side of the mural, the snake's tie and fat cat's suit identify them as bankers/ businessmen, while the crow's wig implies a barrister/judge. The final cluster comprises a pig wearing a police helmet and two rodents holding notebooks, representing the media. Some of these last characters – the crow, the 'paparazzi mice' (Wikipedia 2013) – are potentially more ambiguously gendered, but their body language and facial expressions appear masculine (one of the mice wears a trilby).

Second, the variety of masculinities displayed in this image highlights the complexity of gender (and class) relations: each institution is overwhelmingly male dominated, but each animal's masculinity is different. The devil is covered with taut and rippling muscles, and the gorilla also appears overpowering, but both are calm, while the pitbull (smaller but similarly physically strong) is baring his teeth, eager to be let loose, having to be restrained. The power of the other animals comes not from their physical strength but is implied by their socioeconomic and cultural status.

Figure 29.5 Analysis of street art.

Consumption

From textually derived spectators to actual audiences (Gripsrud 2000: 206): 'spectators bring diverse identities, histories, cultural competences, and responses – both conscious and unconscious – to the movies' (White 2000: 121) and other popular cultural texts and practices. Consequently, theorising the interpretations that audiences make of popular culture is one of the most important and the most complex issues facing scholars today. It goes to the heart of our understandings of how popular culture *functions* in contemporary society. We cannot assume that all readers everywhere and for all time read texts or images in the same unified way, nor that they necessarily read artefacts in the way that 'authors' intend, be these 'authors' singers, film studios, directors, PR consultants, spin doctors or advertising executives. Furthermore, we also need to take account of the affective and emotional dimensions of interpretation that are integral to processes of meaning making. Anthony Swofford (2003: 6–7) highlights some of these issues particularly forcefully.

Over the last 25 years, feminist cultural studies scholars have explored a number of aspects of women's consumption, and the interpretation of feminism and femininities, in a variety of local and global contexts.[9] There is also a burgeoning literature on fan studies, an important focus of which has been on 'slash' fiction and the popular cultural texts that fans produce.[10] In the discipline of IR, however, very little research has been conducted on audience interpretations. Mainstream IR has eschewed the local and individual levels of analysis in favour of large *n* quantitative data sets and analyses conducted at the state/supra-state level, but even critical IR scholars have tended to focus more on textual analysis than on consumption.

In part, this may be because (in comparison with discursive/visual analysis) the methodological obstacles to accessing audiences' interpretations are not insignificant. It is not physically possible to invite every one of the several million regular viewers of *24* to a focus group. The design of the research project also has a huge impact on the data and research outcomes themselves, whether we use questionnaires, focus groups, in-depth interviews, participant observation or some combination of these. Social media spaces such as blogs, YouTube, Facebook, Twitter, Tumblr and Pinterest pose new challenges to existing methods – the vast amounts of data created require combinations of qualitative and quantitative (computer-aided) analysis – and demand that we consider carefully the validity of our current conceptualisations for how people consume and interpret popular culture. Digital games (also known as computer games or video games) provide an interesting perspective on consumption in this regard, because they are participatory and interactive in a more comprehensive way than films and television shows. They also offer new ways to think about some of the issues raised by visual analysis, such as identification and affect, in that they both offer and require a more obviously (inter)active and invested role on the part of the player, in terms of identifying with the gamer's avatar (protagonist/main character) and the emotional responses engendered during gameplay.

Machin and Suleiman have used interviews and material from web forums to ask gamers about their experiences of first-person-shooter games such as *Delta Force* and concluded that gamers offered contradictory views, on the one hand, seeing 'the representation of war in these games as realistic, as corresponding to the facts. On the

other hand, they distance themselves from games-as-political-representations'
(2006: 19). However, we cannot assume that all people play games in the same ways.
When Mary Flanagan investigated what teenage girls do when they play *Grand Theft
Auto*, one girl reported that 'she pays no attention to the mission structures in the
game, but rather, prefers to "just drive"'. Another 'noted that she "wanted to just help
people"' (2006: 500). Little research has engaged in a sustained way with the *gendered*
meanings that people make out of the games they play. In a study of young male
gamers, Kathy Sanford and Leanna Madill did not see evidence that learners were
thinking consciously and reflectively about cultural models of the world, or that:

> [T]hey were consciously reflecting on the values that make up their real or videogame
> worlds … Resistance to hegemonic hypermasculinity in game play does not necessar-
> ily lead the players to challenge gender stereotypes … it does not cause them to be
> more aware of their privileged positions of power.
>
> (Sanford and Madill 2006: 300)

Even this very short discussion of one or two aspects of audience consumption demonstrates that it is essential that we investigate how meaning is made through engagement with popular cultural texts and practices in concrete situations. In terms of our
feminist curiosity, we must explore not only how sex/gender differences affect the
ways in which people consume, but also how people interpret the images they see
and the actions they engage in as gendered – in short, how representations are interpreted as gendered, as well as how gendered beings interpret. (See Feminist Frequency
(www.feministfrequency.com) for gendered analyses of digital games and gamers.)

CONCLUSION

In this chapter, I have provided a brief overview of some of the key concepts and
methods in the analysis of contemporary popular culture, with a specific focus on
the ways in which gender functions in (some) popular cultural representations of
world politics. The final point I wish to make is to emphasise the importance of
analysing how representations are interpreted by people in particular contexts,
which allows us to move beyond an understanding of gender as defined by 'innate',
'natural' or 'biological' sexual differences between men and women. We are then
able to investigate gender as complex matrices of meanings about sex, sexuality,
gendered identities, including emotional responses and desires, meanings that are
constantly being performed in those particular texts and contexts. IR scholars need
to do more to investigate these texts, sites and performances of meaning, and need
to examine them with gendered lenses in order to gain deeper and more complex
understandings of how our worlds 'work'.

Questions for further debate

1. Think about the popular cultural images, texts and practices you most enjoy
   engaging in or with. In what ways are these preferences connected with your

identity? How are these cultural artefacts and practices connected with processes of global politics? How are they gendered?

2. Are male and female celebrities treated differently in national and/or international media? How do other aspects of identity – e.g., race, sexual orientation, dis/ability – intersect with the ways in which celebrities are portrayed and discussed?

3. What kinds of masculinities (and femininities) are hegemonic (prevalent) in war films from different decades? How do war films' gendered representations and narratives change over time? Do war films made in different countries and cultures 'do' gender differently?

4. How can our understandings of the gendered politics of the visual/the visual politics of gender go beyond an analysis of gender as simply about 'bodies'? What do we need to think about if we are interested in analysing cultural practices, as opposed to media representations?

5. How does popular culture appear throughout this textbook? Who is using it, and to make what types of argument? What popular cultural narratives, texts and practices are missing/silenced and what are the implications of this for our study of global political issues and dynamics?

Sources for further reading and research

Hooper, H. (2001) *Manly States: Masculinities, International Relations and Gender Politics*, New York: Columbia University Press.

Lisle, D. (1999) 'Gender at a Distance: Identity, Performance and Contemporary Travel Writing', *International Feminist Journal of Politics*, 1(1): 66–88.

Rowley, C. and J. Weldes (2012) 'The Evolution of International Security Studies and the Everyday: Suggestions from the Buffyverse', *Security Dialogue*, 43(6): 513–30.

Weber, C. (2006) *Imagining America at War: Morality, Politics, and Film*, London and New York: Routledge.

Weldes, J. (1999) 'Going Cultural: *Star Trek*, State Action and Popular Culture', *Millennium*, 28(1): 117–34.

Notes

1 Semiotics is the study of texts and practices for the cultural signs and codes they contain. See Barthes (1973) for some short and accessible examples of early semiotic analysis.

2 See the discussion accompanying the set of images and optical illusions in Monaco (2000: 152–55, 194).

3 In common usage, 'the media' is usually employed as a singular noun, referring to an amorphous collection of texts and institutions such as newspapers, magazines, radio and television, the internet and social media. It is sometimes intended more specifically to imply *news* media or *electronic* media and at other times as a broader concept incorporating film, computer games and other forms of popular culture, invoking a more general notion of communication.

4 See White (2000: 123–27) for a brief overview of women filmmakers.

5 For a variety of ways to conceptualise the intersection of militarism and masculinities, see Cooke and Woollacott (1993), Elshtain (1995), Enloe (2007), Higate and Hopton (2004), Jeffords (1989), Parpart and Zalewski (2008), Whitworth (2008), Young (2003) and Zalewski and Parpart (1998).

6 In addition to differences of scale (e.g., road atlas versus walking map), see, for example, the differences between Mercator and Peters projections, or between a political map and a relief map of the same area.

7 Montage and *mise-en-scène* can also be more directly interconnected – for example, using a split screen to show two people in different locations having a telephone conversation.

8 It is important to note that, although the same image may have different meanings in different contexts, the traces of 'other' meanings remain present in any reading of that image. That is to say, the 'ejaculatory' reading is present in the 'victory' interpretation and vice versa (as are other possible interpretations).

9 See, *inter alia*, Ang (1985, 1996), Brunsdon and Spigel (2008: Part II), Hermes (2005), Newcomb (2006: Part 4), Radway (1984) and Stacey (1994).

10 For example, Clerc (2000), Hellekson and Busse (2006), Jenkins (1992, 2006), Lewis (1992), Penley (1992, 1997) and Thomas (2002).

CHAPTER 30

Sex, gender and cyberspace

M. I. Franklin

LEARNING OUTCOMES

Upon completion, readers should be able to:

- Explain historical and analytical distinctions when talking about the internet, the web, Web 2.0 and cyberspace and explain how these overlapping terms differ.
- Undertake new avenues of gender-sensitive theory and research that explore the practice of everyday life online in a global and digital age.
- Navigate a diverse literature across the humanities and social sciences at the intersection of online and offline gender power relations and explain how these ongoing debates over the relationship between internet technologies and society contribute to rethinking gendered bodies and world order.

INTRODUCTION

As Cynthia Enloe has pointed out, the personal is not only political but also international (1989). This century, in an increasingly web-dependent yet unevenly distributed world in terms of internet access, know-how and want-to, this nexus has taken on not only global but also digitised and *cyberspatial* dimensions. In the Global North at least, everyday life on the ground ('offline') and in cyberspace ('online') have become inseparable, to the point that many of today's youth regard internet access as a right (BBC News 2010). And recent statistics show that increasing numbers of people, especially in the Global South, are accessing the internet more and more via mobile phones (Internet World Stats 2012; Millward 2012). In schools and universities in the internet's heartlands learning and teaching have gone online as well while corporations and intergovernmental organisations are putting computer literacy and internet access high on their business, international cooperation and development agendas.

Yet despite these empirical indications of its increasing embedding in social, cultural, and political life around the world, academic and public debates still rage about whether the internet, however defined (see Figure 30.1), is a force for good or, conversely, a force for ill (Madden et al. 2012; Turkle 2011). These debates can be divided roughly into two camps: the pessimistic and the optimistic schools of thought. Both sides have in common a tendency to regard internet design, access and use in ahistorical and technologically determinist ways (Franklin 2013a: 39, *passim*). Scholars investigating the interrelationship between technological developments, like the internet, and socio-political transformations also tend to follow this pattern. The same is often true for feminist approaches, as they concentrate on the darker side of the internet, e.g., in perpetuating sex-gender stereotypes, the 'sexploitation' of women and children online, in entrenching forms of socioeconomic disenfranchisement by the emergence of a global 'digital divide' between the 'information rich' and the 'information poor' (Gurumurthy and Singh 2012).

- **Internet/world wide web; Web 2.0/social media.** These two pairs of terms are often used interchangeably. They designate successive, albeit overlapping generations of the internet's short history in three respects: 1) the internet is the term for the infrastructure that allows computer-mediated communications and information exchange based on a transborder transmission architecture (e.g., for financial transactions, or email); 2) the pioneering set of software applications that made the internet accessible to ordinary people to find things online in a relatively user-friendly way by hyperlinking (e.g., using web browsers such as Explorer or Firefox); and 3) since the early 2000s combining all these activities onto one, integrated platform to allow emailing, web searching, news and entertainment, blogging or sharing photos and videos in one space. Web 2.0 is the technical term for the shift in design, access, and use that drive these converged internet services. Social media is a popular term for today's global brands in internet service provisions, social networking services such as Facebook, Tumblr and LinkedIn, and microblogging services such as Twitter or Weibo, multimedia news and entertainment based on 'peer-to-peer' exchange such as Wikipedia or YouTube and mobile phone apps including Whatsapp and Foursquare.

- **Cyberspace; virtuality.** These terms cover, in a variety of ways across the disciplines, issues arising from the sociocultural implications and effects of the above, more technical terms. To talk of cyberspace is to acknowledge the phenomenological as well as the physical and psycho-emotional dimensions to how internet technologies (a term that we can use to cover all of the above specifications) co-constitute society, culture and politics at the individual and community level: 'Cyberspace can be called the virtual lands, with virtual lives and virtual societies [that] ... do not exist with the same physical reality that "real" societies do ... The physical exists in cyberspace but it is reinvented' (Jordan 1999: 1). Embodiments are being (re)invented as organic and machine interactions that emerge through the intersection of physical and computer-mediated or virtual realities (Franklin 2012; Hayles 1999: 12–14; Jordan 1999).

Figure 30.1 Conceptual delineations.

This polarisation tends to overlook the other side of the story, one in which the internet provides opportunities for personal and community empowerment, education, extended familial and affective relationships across timezones and lifeworlds. These sorts of positive computer-mediated, that is web-based interactions have been as unforeseen as they have been nurtured since the early days of the web (Franklin 2004; Jordan 1999; Karim 2003). As internet access and its web-based goods and services become increasingly ubiquitous either/or mindsets can overlook that, like other human-made inventions that have changed the way people live and interact – from the railways to labour-saving devices, from recording technologies to satellite TV and mobile telephones – the internet has a history. True, this is a relatively short and fast-paced history, dating from the late 1980s, but it is also a multiplex and contested one (Abbate 2001; van Dijck 2013; Spiller 2002). Moreover this is a history, and with this a constellation of overlapping and converging computer codes, media systems, information and communication technologies, that is still being written (Mattelart 2003). Debates about the gendered dimensions of internet design, access, and use are also characterised by the above dynamics which, in turn, colour theory and research into the gender power relations of how people use, or do not use internet technologies around the world intersect with their race, class, and religion dimensions (Harcourt 1999; Kolko et al. 2000; Wyatt et al. 2002).

This chapter's first claim is that the different ways in which people use the internet (Barkai 2012; Franklin 2013b) at the personal and societal level is analytically distinct from yet also intertwined with its skewed geographies of access, ownership and control. As the internet becomes increasingly embedded in everyday life, international development, social and political institutions, and gender-sensitive analyses need to take account of the intermingling and delinking of online and offline domains at all points of this compass. Even after over a quarter of a century, the online–offline/local–global nexus of today's internet continues to challenge traditional levels of analysis, andro- and state-centric conceptions of political life.

A second claim is that a lot of work still needs doing to unpack how internet-worked computer systems collide and collude with geopolitical power shifts of our time, engender new global markets and economic powers, create new sorts of lifeworlds, social conventions and political movements (e.g. Anonymous, Wikileaks). These dynamics present specific challenges for reconceptualising the body within feminist approaches to world politics. This is because nowadays it is difficult to ignore that computer-mediated geographies also constitute those 'power relations and practices which impact so directly … on actual bodies' (Pettman, cited in Chapter 3). Women's groups, community activists and international NGOs know this as they work to harness the web and nowadays social media for their work, e.g., against online bullying, child pornography, online violence against women and other forms of sexual abuse, on the one hand or, on the other, enlist the web for educational and awareness raising projects, support networks, and community. So this chapter is not proposing that there is a straightforward split between the gender–power relations of 'fleshy' or digital embodiments. The gender politics of everyday life in what some call 'meatspace' (conventional lifeworlds) and 'cyberspace' (virtual worlds online) are analytically distinct yet also co-constituted in theory and practice (Deuber-Mankowsky 2008: 993–94; Franklin 2013a: 51–55).

But before considering how these claims relate to theory and research by looking at four illustrative scenarios, we first need to counter some stubborn misconceptions about the interrelationship between gender and technology, on the one hand and, on the other, between technology (in this case, internet technologies), society and politics.

Of technosceptics and technophiles

Opposing views on how, or indeed why the internet has made such a difference (Franklin 2013b) often share two common misconceptions about the interrelationship between techno-economic and socio-political transformations. The first is the assumption that all technologies are neutral, value free. In other words, technologies neither do good nor cause harm unless used to do so (e.g., the 'guns don't kill, people do' argument). In contrast to these more instrumental views of how technology and society interact, social constructivist approaches argue that technologies are historical and inseparable from the sociocultural, political and economic context in which they emerge. Moreover they need to be regarded as more than singular objects, large or small. The (gender) politics of technological design and use are also imbued with social and cultural practices and power relations of knowledge and domination (Mansell and Silverstone 1996; Quintas 1996; Shields 1996; Wacjman 1991). For instance, while people kill by using guns, these weapons are designed (by people) to kill.

The second assumption is perhaps even more difficult to counter because it contains a grain of truth and appears to follow logically from these instrumentalist or utilitarian views of technology. This assumption is that because advanced technological artefacts and systems, like personal computers or the internet, emerged in the richer, literate parts of the Global North they are irrelevant for disadvantaged parts of the world. Projects to provide computer skills or internet access to poor communities or disenfranchised groups according to this view need to take second place to more pressing needs such as shelter, food and water or adequate health care. However, even when we consider a particular technology as socially constructed, by knowledge or social conventions for instance, this does not mean to say that it remains impervious to change, or reducible to its point of origin. Social uses, and non-uses can in turn affect how a technology develops or not as the case may be, sometimes by accident and sometimes by design (e.g., the use of social media in the Middle East and North African region in recent times, or advocacy around women's and human rights online – see later). There is a tension here, for scholars, activists, and policymakers alike. While richer nations 'dump' their obsolete gadgets, software, and e-waste onto poorer nations, or global corporations such as Apple and Microsoft take advantage of cheaper labour and laxer labour laws in poorer parts of the world to produce high-end consumer electronics, populations in said 'information-poor' regions have been using the internet, social media and mobile phones for their own needs (Adam and Green 1998; Holderness 1998; Jensen 2006: 239–40). The popularity of mobile phone-based financial transactions in sub-Saharan Africa and long-distance love and romance across the Australian outback are two cases in point.

These two assumptions affect theory and research in three ways. First, they limit where scholars look when examining the way gender power relations, world politics and the rise of the internet are interconnected. In the second instance, they limit awareness of understandings that conceptualise technology as practices as well as artefacts, as complex social and value systems as well as commodities. Seeing a technology as just a thing, that is as value free and therefore impermeable to the world until someone uses it, leads to reductionist and binary thinking. The age-old habit of dichotomising between human minds and bodies is mirrored in this case by a dichotomisation between humans and their human-made technological forms on the other side of the coin. These assumptions underpin a tradition of unease in scholarly and popular commentaries on the internet's effect on society to date despite increasing evidence that the ways in which people live and experience the world through their bodies are intertwined with computer use and media consumption of a different order than has been the case in previous generations (Haraway 1997b; Hayles 1999; Madden et al. 2012). In the Western academic tradition, there is a longstanding, normative preference for the study of an observable physical world and thereby 'tangible' sorts of organic embodiment. Setting up a value hierarchy such as this (i.e., flesh-and-blood and face-to-face interactions are ontologically primary) then limits critical work into the variety of ways that we make use of the internet, and the internet as the media of today 'uses' us, frames our world. This reciprocity, albeit unevenly distributed, has been reconfiguring if not transforming the rules of the game in the practice, and thereby study of world politics; from the level of analysis problem, to the relationship between states and markets, future of national sovereignty and role of non-state actors.

An *a priori* preference for all things 'of the flesh' or 'face to face' also limits how scholars might want to consider the way that the real-life virtual realities and mediated intimacies that people engage when online, on the move, are both liberating and porous to big power or big money. Online helplines and support networks and the recent outcry over widespread US-sanctioned online surveillance are two examples. The third effect is related to how we consider the temporal element when analysing internet phenomena. This is a tendency to (over-)emphasise the 'now' at the expense of even short-term historical perspective. Even a couple of years is a long time in internet business terms, yet all technologies, no matter how new or fast changing, have genealogies. They are the sum of longer or shorter histories. These longer timelines need tuning into because they can temper the marketisation and advertising effects of increasingly shorter product cycles in the global business of internet products and service provision. This is a global market in which the historical concentration of market power, political leverage and infrastructural development lies in the Global North, the US to be precise.

Feminist technological visions

Along with more pessimistic analyses, feminist scholars of science and technology have been exploring the more positive flipside to technological innovations such as the internet to counter forces of domination or socioeconomic disenfranchisement. With gaps in the historical record still palpable around women's contribution to the internet itself (Spiller 2002; Wacjman 1995) these studies look to temper ethnocentric and androcentric empirical and analytical frameworks as they uncover the historical record and contemporary practices of women inventing, encountering and so socially shaping technology (Creedon 1993; Halbert 2004; Haraway 1997b; Wyatt 2008a). Gender-sensitive and feminist-inspired treatments have pivoted on questions around the 'interactive and immersive modes of engagement' (Kennedy 2002: 5/6), virtual performativities included, that emerge from computer-induced and enhanced embodiments. These bring with them a range of new terms, with their respective political and cultural iconographies, e.g., 'cyber-feminist' or 'post-human' theorisations of the body, solidarity and intersubjectivity (see González 2000; Hayles 1999: 4–5; Kennedy 2002: 5–6; Leung 2001; Sofia 1999). The four illustrative scenarios that follow can help anchor some of these claims in research terms.

FOUR RESEARCH SCENARIOS

Human–machine embodiments that matter

> [S]cience and technology are possible means of great human satisfaction, as well as a matrix of complex dominations. Cyborg imagery can suggest a way out of the maze of dualisms in which we have explained our bodies and our tools to ourselves ... It means both building and destroying machines, identities, categories, relationship, spaces, stories.
>
> (Haraway 1990: 223)

This quotation is from Donna Haraway's *A Manifesto for Cyborgs* ([1985] 1990), a landmark essay from the early years of electronic communications. Haraway aims to jettison binary thinking from the feminist lexicon (see Figure 30.2). To do so she introduces the *cyborg*, an abbreviation of 'cybernetic organism' and popularised in popular science fiction such as the television series and film franchise *Star Trek*. She turns these popular characterisations of cybernetic organisms as malevolent beings into a feminist futurist metaphor for real-life liberation in a digitalised world. In this reading, the cyborg is not a scary hi-tech monster. Rather, she argues for an imagining of cyborg embodiments as a *post-gender* trope for agency and empowerment in hi-tech settings that are dominated by commercial and military interests. Her 'blasphemous' declaration, 'I'd rather be a cyborg than a goddess' (Haraway 1990: 223) recalls feminist political debates around the perils of biological essentialism in Second Wave feminism (Halbert 2006; Wyatt 2008a). But it is also a call grounded in her argument that post-gendered or post-human embodiments formed by real life human–machine intimacies are not flights of fancy. The cyborg is already scientific 'fact' and social reality. Let's see why.

Advances in biotechnology and computing have been steadily challenging and blurring binary categories that privilege an *a priori* hierarchy of mind over body, human actions or consciousness over forms of automation or artificial intelligence; material objects over their representation or (physical) presence over (computer) mediated forms; real-life relationships over those encountered in fantasy and

Like Judith Butler, Donna Haraway is interested in challenging forms of gender essentialism that overlook the ways in which social relations as embodied experiences emerge through longstanding human–machine co-dependencies. During the course of the twentieth century, commentators have debated the sociocultural, political and economic implications of the increasing intertwining of everyday life and technology; in the home, the workplace, and public institutions. Since the late 1980s at least this interdependence has taken on an electronic, that is a computer-mediated dimension.

The gendered dimensions that govern technological design, access and use (e.g., family dynamics of television viewing to who controls access to the game console, dishwasher or satnav in the car) have exercised feminist scholars at all levels of analysis. Haraway's 'ironic myth' of the cyborg as a feminist liberationist ideal goes hand in hand with her scathing critique of 1980s' neoliberal orthodoxy (1990: 203, passim). Her argument is that human–machine interactions, those acted out and on in online environments included, are part of the contemporary world. We all live with these relationships, many of which do and can provide opportunities to resist what are 'often virulent forms of oppression, nostalgically naturalised in the face of current violation' (Haraway 1990: 214–15). As with her previous work and since, the Cyborg Manifesto challenges feminists to take on board a more 'subtle understanding of [the] emerging pleasures, experiences, and powers with serious potential for changing the rules of the game' in worlds comprised of offline and online realities (Haraway 1990: 214–15).

Figure 30.2 Cyborg Manifesto.

computer simulations or on-the-ground social realities over online ones. First, biotechnology, as scientific R&D and commercial enterprise, has been reconstructing, enhancing, and synthesising organic bodies for some time now. From the deepest, microscopic reaches of human DNA up to body parts (internal organs and external limbs), bioengineering and biogenetics can manufacture and replace, improve and extend the human organism accordingly.

Second, advances in robotics, computer programming, and their applications in biotechnological forms have developed digital hearing aids and other implants to malfunctioning eyes and ears. Both are involved in the design of sophisticated, digitally controlled prostheses, the monitors and life-support machines that populate hospitals and medical surgeries, emergency services and backup systems. Both are central to the development of performance-enhancing drugs used in the (legal) treatment of heart, kidney and other chronic diseases and (criminalised) uses of performance-enhancing drugs in top-level sport. From the now cheesy characters in old TV shows[1] to real-life existing bionic men and women athletes,[2] from robotic and android prototypes in the lab and science fiction to biogenetically engineered 'monsters' such as the *Oncomouse*™ (see Haraway 1997b; Hayles 1999: 222 *passim*), these life forms are no longer fantasy. The organic and the inorganic, and the way in which both are ICT dependent are a fact of everyday social realities, and life-enhancing dreams. These include CCTV, mobile telephony with web access, GPS navigational tools, 'smart homes', biometric passports, fingerprinting, iris and body scans at national borders, complex surveillance and security systems on earth and in outer space, surgical (laser and virtual) techniques to heal and make over physical deficiencies. Given the high R&D investment and economic stakes, biotechnologies are a global business, dominated by transnational conglomerations spanning the pharmaceutical, agroindustrial, 'Big Science' and IT sectors, military–industrial complexes and national R&D priorities.

Cyber-babes, action heroines and virtual icons

By the same token, these state-funded and commercial applications cross-pollinate with popular science fiction imagery. They also play a role in the multi-million dollar, global entertainment and media industry of computer and video games and ordinary practices of everyday life online. These too have been challenging, as well as exploiting and refashioning sex-gender roles, and communicative cultures. Their uptake has been impacting on where people hang out, in the way web-savvy generations communicate, from New York to Tokyo, London to Beijing, Bombay to Honolulu. These are the computer-constituted and web-based spaces of virtual worlds, computer and video games, and on-the-ground embedded online discussion forums. The characters, *avatars*, and user–practitioners who populate these cyberspatial worlds are encountered and activated by people going online in partially or totally immersed modes of computer or internet use. Longstanding debates about sexual and racial stereotyping in so-called real life ('RL') have been shifting in light of how being online can provide release as well as confinement to the biological body. Computer-generated morphologies take on a life of their own as applications such as Photoshop (see Figure 30.3 for a comic view) allow ordinary people relatively easy to use tools to manipulate their own likeness, make film clips and create their own avatars, ideal selves according to the software available. Here, debates about the global cultural economy and gender politics of ICT consumption in hyper-commercialised arcades of online shopping, violence, sex and other sorts of online 'mayhem' fold into concerns about individual and social well-being for today's 'digital natives'. Others focus on the gender politics of racialised, militarised, and eroticised representations of computer-encoded masculinity and femininity that contradict claims that anything goes, and you can be anyone online; a debate that focuses on both the troubling and the liberationist ethos of gaming and virtual worlds (Kennedy 2002; Leung 2001; Sampaio and Aragon 1998).

So, exit Haraway's 'heretical' cyborg vision and enter computer games and virtual realities, where bodies are pixelated, animated, and hyper-real. A case in point is the commercial, virtual compatriot of Haraway's cyborg, 'Lara Croft' (see Figure 30.4). Lara Croft is the main actor–character, whose actions are steered and manipulated

Figure 30.3 'Checkers Online'.

Cartoon: Nina Paley (http://www.ninapaley.com/). Reproduced with kind permission.

Computer and video games are a major segment of the global software market, overtaking sales in DVD, music and video in the UK and worldwide in 2008 to the tune of US$32 billion (see Lancaster 2008). All major IT and media corporations (e.g., Sony, Microsoft, Nintendo) have major business stakes in ensuring the continuation of the industry's explosive growth this century as gaming is no longer the preserve of (male) computer geeks (see O'Brien 2006). From high-level programmers down to assemblage and distribution, the industry plays a significant role as a source of employment as well (Sinclair 2009). The Chinese and Indian markets show similar trends. Japan's historical lead in internet penetration, the development of hi-tech commodities and culture industries aside, computer game players and ICT consumers are increasingly made up of populations in mainland China, South Korea, south-east Asia, and the Indian subcontinent. According to the Entertainment Software Association, in the USA alone 51 per cent of American households have a computer game console if not two in the home. The average game player is around 30 years old, with 45 per cent female (ESA 2013: 2–4). Not only do the sorts (genres) of video/computer game on the market vary but so too do the ways in which people access games for free or as a purchase; from traditional computer consoles such as the Xbox to 'multi-player universes' such as World of Warcraft via the web, or increasingly via handheld devices such as mobile phones and tablet computers (ESA 2013: 4, 8–9). Most attention, in academic and public debates has been paid to the harmful or addictive effects of computer gaming for younger users. Here concerns focus on war games where explicit violence, hyper-real simulations of combat action and, for many critics, sex–gender, racial, and class stereotypes drive the action and engage the player not only emotionally but also physically through a mixture of software simulation and direct input from the military. The *Call of Duty* franchise is a case in point, still the number 1 in video games in the US in 2013 (ESA 2013: 9).

Non-combative genres however are also a sizeable share of the market and go back to the early years (e.g., Pong, Dungeons and Dragons), including still popular games such as The Sims, and sports. There is also a burgeoning market alternative, 'indie' and feminist, video/computer games (O'Brien 2006).

Tomb Raider, along with *Grand Theft Auto*, is a computer game developed in the UK. The former was launched in 1996 with its latest version launched in early 2013 shifting millions of copies within weeks (Markuch 2013; Votta 2013) and so becoming a sales chart-topper in the UK and globally the month of its release. *Tomb Raider* centres on the adventures of its main character ('impersonated' by you, the player), Lara Croft. With her transgender desirability, 'supernatural agility' and 'preternaturally large breasts whose origins and alteration have their own narrative in the Lara Croft universe' (Deuber-Mankowsky 2008: 992) she was then transfigured into real-life Hollywood icon, Angelina Jolie, in the 2001 film of the same name. Lara Croft's role as the well-endowed, gun-toting, turbocharged, no-nonsense 'super-fem' protagonist in this game has sparked debates about whether she caters to sexist stereotypes or, on the contrary, operates as a computer-age example of '"active" or "strong" female characters [that can also] "signify a potential threat to the masculine order"' (Kennedy 2002).

Figure 30.4 Computer and video games.

by the player – in 'first-shooter' mode – to a greater or lesser degree of success, points scored in surmounting obstacles of ever increasing difficulty, of the immensely successful video game *Tomb Raider*.

Unknown cyber-pleasures and big business

Feminist debates on the gender politics and physical attributes of successive generations of female cultural icons (real and fictional) are not new – Marilyn Monroe, Barbie, Twiggy and Madonna are precursors. Lady Gaga, Angelina Jolie and the Lara Croft character are contemporary versions. Lara Croft, however, is a computer-generated, *virtual* heroine with a transnational reach: a global, cyber-based brand. As such, she embodies a different order of gender performativities, socio-political and techno-economic challenges to existing 'masculinist' frameworks. She also intersects with longstanding political demarcation lines in feminist praxis. For what do Barbie dolls, the female cast of *Baywatch*, Seven of Nine (from *Star Trek Voyager*) and Lara Croft have in common? Synthetically enhanced physiology, cross-gender admirers and a reach into bedrooms the world over. And what do Jane Fonda, Madonna, Pamela Anderson, Posh Spice (aka Victoria Beckham) and Angelina Jolie have in common? They are global (white, Western) celebrities who perform – for better or worse – 'offline' variations of certain, highly time-sensitive idealised embodiments.[3] Like Lara Croft or Barbie, these are bodies that have been designed – nurtured, groomed, physically and visually enhanced; in 'natural' ways such as power yoga or dieting or by cosmetic or pre-emptive medical surgery, as in the case of Angelina Jolie. And when none of these suffices, through the re-visualising techniques of global advertising. These real-life and virtual-world (re-)embodiments exemplify the 'leaky separations' that figure in Haraway's cyborg imagery. Their political implications, or moral virtues for that matter, are hotly contested and celebrated. Precisely because the knife cuts both ways these 'politics of representation ... racist, homophobic as well as sexist modes – [are] a vital issue which the games industry [and scholars] should not ignore' (Kennedy 2002: 5–6).

To sum up these first three scenarios; fleshy and pixelated bodies are already being refashioned – enhanced or 'corrected' – in computer-mediated communications, mediatised settings and real-life situations. The gender troubles of classical dimorphism (see Chapter 3) are being superimposed by gender troubles of another order as encoded or digitised simulacra that in a web-based age travel between offline and online realms alongside physical and social lives that also unfold on the ground and in cyberspace. The main point is less whether Lara Croft, along with other computer simulations and digital identities are 'real' or not. For Lara Croft players and those of us attached to the avatars that perform our online selves, they are, or can be authentic, too. In economic and material terms moreover, Lara Croft is a cyber-babe of the first order. The point to note is that her actions, the globally inflected online/offline worlds she interfaces with (of both designers and players) are not strictly a male, masculinist, or exclusively online preserve. Like cybernetic organisms, computer-generated worlds and their actors are a feminist issue. The way they can take leave of the classical confines of private – domestic and intimate – spaces as they operate on and through internet domains makes them also a global one.

Internet rights are women's rights

There is another scenario mentioned already that is worth exploring and need not require the skills or desire to become a computer game enthusiast. Here, everyday cyberspace is entered, navigated and then co-created by ordinary people from all racial and ethnic backgrounds the world over. Here the way people use the internet links up on-the-ground domains and offline lives with cyberspatial ones in a traditionally embodied sense; physical actors connecting up across variable distances and timezones. The internet and the web – taken here to mean interconnected physical and digital transmission pathways, access points and variously moderated meeting places – operate in several ways simultaneously; as (inter)connective space, personal–political platform, information resource, research field, and means for organising and mobilising. Individuals, and groups or communities enter and exit as they wish, conforming to formal and informal rules for online behaviour. While traversing the web, these practitioners are reconfigured as nicknames, email addresses, camera images, or 'tweets'. As such, they are analytically and empirically distinct from total immersion virtual realities or digitalia of virtual embodiments examined earlier. Co-existing alongside the latter from the earliest days, these sorts of 'internet communities', 'news-groups' and 'discussion forums' are as old as the internet itself. The social networking sites, microblogs and mobile apps that characterise this generation of internet access and use exploit as well as dovetail with earlier formats, many of which are still in use.[4]

As individuals, communities, and on-the-ground locales get connected across borders and then online, all sorts of things start to happen. This is a computer-mediated domain for 'cyberspatial practices of everyday life' (Franklin 2004, 2013b), which entail translocal, transnational connections between diasporic generations and those in their countries of origin (Karim 2003), identity formation along unexpected lines and of social and political contestation, in which women feature strongly. One example of how these cultures of use link to other sorts of work on the ground is in the area of gender and ICT advocacy in international settings where internet-related policy agendas are put in place. The UN has been a prominent broker of these events.

Women's and feminist groups in what is now called 'global civil society' are no strangers to UN summits; the 1995 Beijing Conference on the Status of Women and its successive summits is one case in point. The World Summit on the Information Society is another (APC 2012; Franklin 2005; Gurumurthy 2003; WSIS 2003). They have been active in these arenas since the 1960s at least (Harcourt 1999; Jørgensen 2013). Thanks to the networking faculties of internet technologies, from email to social networking, women's activism in the form of transnational advocacy networks (Jensen 2006) around specific gender-based issues and broadranging programmes promoting women's rights and the internet is an integral feature to UN 'ICT for Development' initiatives as well as intergovernmental summits such as the UN Internet Governance Forum (see suggested reading and web resources for some examples). One example that investigates where and how women can use the internet for empowering and educational ways yet do so often under difficult conditions on the ground and increasing surveillance online is the EROTICS (Exploratory Research on Sexuality and the Internet) project. This research project undertaken under the auspices of the Association for Progressive Communications (APC) Women's Rights Programme takes a comparative and international perspective on the conditions under which women use the internet in different locales.

In this case, the focus is on how policy decisions affecting the terms of access and use of online content (e.g., taboo topics such as sexuality, medical information about breast cancer, online support for victims of sexual abuse, human rights advocacy) has a direct effect on women's ability to make choices in many parts of the world where freedom of expression, sexuality and the right to education are not a given. Censorship, online surveillance and gender-based access restrictions (e.g., public internet access) all point to how 'the growing practice of online content regulation can either impede or facilitate the different ways women use the internet and the impact on their sexual expression, sexualities and sexual health practices and the assertion of their sexual rights' (Kee 2011). To recall Cynthia Enloe's iconic observation cited at the start of this chapter, if women's rights are human rights (Bunch 1990) then internet rights are also women's rights (Liddicoat 2011).

These longstanding advocacy platforms that work to keep the need for gender-inclusive and human-centred decisions high on national and international policy agendas dovetail with increasing calls for a human rights-based approach to internet governance agenda setting at the multilateral level (Franklin 2013a; Internet Rights and Principles Coalition 2013). These calls have been gathering pace in the wake of the Arab Uprisings in 2010–11, the Wikileaks affair in the same period and more recently revelations of US-led state surveillance of our online communications at a global level. This is a long, uphill battle, however, given that at time of writing corporatised, androcentric, and instrumentalist mindsets still predominate in national legislatures and global venues where the future of the internet is being decided.

CONCLUSION

> Whether we are located in positions that enable direct access to digital communications technology or not, the impact of ICTs [information and communication technologies] in shaping our sense of spatial, temporal, and social relations with each other is undeniable.
>
> (Kee 2005: 3)

A core premise of this volume is that global politics are practised, 'co-constituted' by gendered bodies and that 'interrogating the political practices through which bodies come to matter at all in global politics' (see Chapter 3) is intrinsic to the practice and study of the contemporary world. Internet technologies connect the micro with the macro quite literally, the domestic/private to the public, the local to the would-be global, intimate, face-to-face communications with distant, non-proximate intimacies. In so doing, they also reconfigure our sense of embodiment, indeed, ideas about the mind–body relationship and 'social-ness'. For some people, this means being able to leave cages of flesh and blood, disability or sex-gender stereotyping 'in-real-life'. Second, the relationship between women, gender and technology has been a feminist and a global issue from the get-go.

While there is a lot of thought and research on how to think 'in more sophisticated ways about virtual technologies' (Hayles 1999: 290) and in ways that do not do violence to, or erase physical embodiment altogether, a particular vision of the future internet is now being marketed as the next silver bullet for the world's structural inequalities. Here too gender hierarchies are embedded at the online–offline nexus. To this end, twenty-first-century multilateral institutions have headlined 'ICTs for development' as the vanguard narrative of how these new technologies can 'save' the world from itself (UN 2000). But the question remains, whose and which internet, what sorts of ICT for development exactly and on whose terms of access and use? These high-level initiatives that place the internet at the hub of development narratives trace all too familiar lines of colonial power and privilege and hierarchies of gender, class and ethnicity. Where poorly paid young women and men work on corporate ICT production lines, in credit card call centres, on 'click farms' to drive online traffic to web businesses, in computer-programming departments in offshore affiliates of IT giants or on temporary visas in the Silicon Valley, their absence from decision making further up the political 'food chain' is in reverse proportion to the contribution their physical and intellectual labour makes to sustaining the internet as we know it. In this respect, both the internet and the web are more than the sum of their parts. Web 2.0 media and communications now and in the future cannot be adequately analysed in neutralised technical terms. The power relations of internet design, access and use co-constitute gender matters in global politics. Critical scholars need to treat ICT as more than a footnote to 'real' concerns around gender politics at the international level. What is at stake is the survival of alternative, inclusive visions of internet futures – and pasts as our memories go digital. To borrow from Sandra Whitworth (2000), inquiries into sex, gender and cyberspace at the heart of twenty-first-century society and politics amount to more than a call to 'add the internet and stir'.

Questions for further debate

1. In the scholarly and popular literature that has accompanied the rise of the web and social media 'virtual reality' and 'real life' tend to be seen as either diametrically opposed or in a hierarchical relationship (e.g., offline relationships are assumed to be more valuable, more socially acceptable than online ones). Do you agree? If so, why? If not, why not?
2. Would you rather be a goddess or a cyborg (see Haraway 1990)?
3. If the physical body, virtual lives, and machines are so interdependent why then do we still consider performance-enhancing technologies in sport (e.g., clothing and equipment, prostheses, chemical or hormonal supplements) as cheating yet comparable technologies in medical and health care (pacemakers, prostheses, chemical or hormonal supplements) as life enhancing?
4. Do you think that online forms of verbal abuse or simulated violence, e.g., cases of 'cyber-rape' (see Kolko et al. 2000) or cyberbullying, should be punishable in the same way as comparable acts are in offline situations?
5. Do you think that people should be able to remain anonymous online, e.g., in order to be able access information about sexual health or sexuality in private, and without fear of reprisal? If so, do you think there are limits to anonymity (see Question 4)?

Sources for further reading and research

Association of Progressive Communications (2012) *Going Visible: Women's Rights On The Internet*, Report to Addressing Inequalities: The Heart of the Post-2015 Development Agenda and the Future We Want for All, Global Thematic Consultation, UN Women/UNICEF, October 2012; http://www.worldwewant2015.org/file/287493/ download/311684 (accessed 18 August 2013).

Franklin, M. I. (2002) 'Reading Walter Benjamin and Donna Haraway in the Age of Digital Reproduction', *Information, Communication and Society*, 5(4): 591–624.

Haraway, D. J. (1992) *Primate Visions: Gender, Race, and Nature in the World of Modern Science*, London and New York: Verso.

Haraway, D. J. (1997) 'Gender for a Marxist Dictionary: the Sexual Politics of a Word', in L. McDowell and J. Sharp (eds), *Space, Gender, Knowledge: Feminist Readings*, London, New York, Sydney and Auckland: Arnold: 53–72.

Shah, N. (2008) 'Material Cyborgs; Asserted Boundaries: Formulating the Cyborg as a Translator', *European Journal of English Studies*, 12(2): 211–225.

Notes

1 The *Six Million Dollar Man* and *Bionic Woman*, American television series from the 1970s and 1980s, for example.

2 For instance, the 'bionic' legs developed for Oscar Pistorius, the South African disabled track athlete who achieved global sporting fame at the 2008 and 2012 Para-Olympics in Beijing and London. Biotechnological implants have provided disabled athletes with new, superpower legs that underscore just how 'leaky' the boundary between bodies and technological enhancements have become in real life (Haraway 1990).

3 We could include (debates about) James Dean, GI Joe, Michael Jackson, David Beckham, Daniel Craig and, in political mediatised terms, Barack Obama and Vladimir Putin as male cultural icons, object of desire.

4 For instance, German-based Turkish communities (e.g., *Vaybee!*), internet portals for the Kurdish diaspora (e.g. *Viva Kurdistan!*), Pacific Island communities based in the islands, USA, New Zealand and Australia (e.g. *Planet Tonga*) and other postcolonial media diasporas that would not exist or persist were it not for the internet (Franklin 2004; Karim 2003).

CHAPTER 31

New social media and global resistance

Suzanne Levi-Sanchez and Sophie Toupin[1]

LEARNING OUTCOMES

Upon completion, readers should be able to:

- Describe some of the key debates and approaches surrounding the relationship between feminisim, activism and new media.
- Outline how feminist activism has changed new media, technology and communication practices.
- Evaluate the impact of the hacker movement on society in general and social movements specifically.

INTRODUCTION

The proliferation of new media, including practices, applications and tools, currently structures not only how people interact, but also how collective actions influence ideas and messages both globally and locally. Technology now has the capability of inciting and shaping social movements, but also, and maybe more importantly, being shaped by them. The diverse sets of practices within new media circles inspire many questions about their significance. We discuss and deconstruct these issues in order to understand their significance. In particular, we investigate the ways in which new media have been both a source and a consequence of reconfiguring gender relations within society as well as in shaping social movements (for a timeline of 'new media' see Figure 31.1).

- **1965:** First email system named MAILBOX developed at MIT. This system only could exchange mail between users of the same computer

- **1969:** The birth of the internet. The Advanced Research Projects Agency Network (ARPANET), initially funded by the US department of Defense, was set up as a project for use by universities and research labs in the US

- **1972:** Ray Tomlinson created the @ symbol and system allowing computer users to designate other computers for messaging. Internet pioneer Jon Postel, who we will hear more of later, was one of the first users of the new system, and is credited with describing it as a 'nice hack'

- **1983:** Richard Stallman launches the GNU project, the first open-source software collaborative, a precursor to FLOSS

- **1986:** LISTSERV, the first email management system, was invented by Eric Thomas, which eventually allowed for the formation of numerous online listserves, usergroups and other affinity groups collaborating on projects, protests, and other forms of social activism

- **1991:** The world wide web (WWW) is released

- **1994:** Mosaic, the first browser for the WWW was invented, allowing people to navigate different sites and search for sites within one platform

- **1999:** Indymedia, a global network of media activists aimed at reporting on political and social issues mostly during protest, emerges out of the Battle in Seattle during the World Trade Organization (WTO) meeting in 1999. The Independent Media Centers (IMC) established open online publishing platforms from which citizen journalists and media activists could report back from the street

- **2000:** Riseup.net, a tech collective that provides online communication tools for activists working on social justice issues, is created. The collective provides activist and activist groups with access to secure email, mailing lists and comprehensive information regarding all kinds of online security measures. Other such tech collectives are: Nadir.org in Germany, Autistici.org in Italy, Resist.ca in Canada, etc.

- **2001:** The Creative Commons license is created. It is also known as copy left licensing and is seen by many hackers as a hack of the copyright model as it makes it mandatory under different modalities to share and render ones work accessible. Wikipedia begins

- **2003:** Wordpress, an open-source software that allows for publishing and hosting blogs, is launched. Anonymous, a loosely connected group of online activists, forms. Although the term 'hacktivist' spawned from the Cult of the Dead Cow in 1996, it took on a new and much more organized meaning in 2003

- **2004:** Facebook connects Harvard with other universities. In one year, Facebook realizes 1 million users

- **2005:** YouTube goes live. Reddit, a social news and entertainment website, is launched. Reddit is widely used by hackers

- **2006:** Twitter and Wikileaks begins

- **2007:** Tumblr is created

- **2008:** Lulz, a group with a name denoting laughter based on the victim of their pranks, started with Operation (or Project) Chantology, a denial of service protest against Scientology in 2008 and led to offshoots LulzSec and Operation AntiSec

- **2009:** Kickstarter, the crowdfunding platform, makes its debut

- **2010:** Diaspora, an alternative to Facebook, is created by four NYU students. Other alternatives include: Social Swarm, Lorea, Briar, Sukey, etc. Instagram is launched

- **2011:** Lorea, a free self-managed social network, is created in a squatted social center in Amsterdam, which later launches a social networking platform called N-1.cc in 2012. The Unlike Us Network, a research network of artists, designers, scholars, activists and programmers who work on alternatives in social media, is created. Global Revolution TV is set up and allows activists from the Occupy Movement to live stream demonstrations with computers and smart phones, transforming how protests are covered. Its motto: The Revolution will be Live-Streamed!

- **2012–ongoing:** LEAP Encryption Access Project is developed by and for activists, dedicated to adapting encryption technology to make it easy to use and widely available (leap.se).

Figure 31.1 New media timeline.

In this chapter, we examine the intersection of gender, social resistance, and technology. Particularly, we look at the ways in which gender relations within social movements have changed communication practices and helped shape and design technologies to embrace these practices. The use of new media and other emerging tools by social movements has led to an abundance of scholarly work (Bennett 2012; Carpentier 2007; Castells 2008, 2012; Downing 2001; Jenkings 2006b). Specific practices and responses developed by feminists or from feminist perspectives have also been highlighted in the work of scholars (Braidotti 1996; Dunbar-Hester 2010; Eubanks 2011; Gajjala and Ju Oh 2012; Haraway 1991; Plant 1997; Sassen 2002b). From community radio, to the production of videos, zines, blogs and comix reportage for social change, feminists and feminist affinity groups within social movements have been able to amplify their voices and practices while at the same time foregrounding their own values and principles.

The questions we address in this chapter include: What roles do feminists play in (re)shaping new media practices? What is the relationship between online and offline activism, particularly feminist activism? How is technology, including new media, both a source and a consequence of gender relations? How are feminists helping to shape technologies and communication practices that embrace social justice for all? And, how are these specific feminist practices shaping and being shaped by social movements?

TECHNOLOGY: MESSAGES OR MEANINGS – DETERMINISM, CONSTRUCTIVISM, INTERPRETIVISM AND MORE

There are many theoretical frameworks relating to technology (see Figure 31.2). Feminists have highlighted shortcomings in recent scholarship on technology and social resistance, in turn helping to craft unique feminist stances on technology and social movements. The different theories provide a rich starting point for understanding the intersection between gender, technology, and social resistance. Technofeminist scholarship (Wajcman 1991, 2004), while bridging and borrowing from this literature, has developed a framework unique to the community and relevant to understanding gender relations, technology, and social movements.

Technological determinism

New media specifically, and technology in general, have often been presented as either positive or negative for women and LGBTQ (Lesbian, gay, bi-sexual, transgendered, and queer) lives. Technological determinism is a stance that argues technology is neutral, and it is the ways in which we use it that are good or bad. Proponents of this approach also believe that it is technological improvement and development that drives social change. The idea that it is thanks to Facebook (the 'Facebook Revolution') that authoritarian regimes were toppled in Tunisia and Egypt, among others, during the Arab Spring, stems largely from this perspective.

THEORIES	SUMMARY OF THE MAIN TENETS
Technological determinism	Technological determinism asserts that technology is neutral. As opposed to being good or bad, this theory argues that it depends on how technology is used for social change rather than there being a dynamic relationship between technology and social change.
Constructivism/Interpretivism	Constructivism argues that the historical, cultural, political and economic context behind technology is socially constructed. Therefore, it is crucial to understand technology through a critical perspective.
Technological affordances	Technological affordances is somewhat of a middle ground between constructivism and technological determinism. It recognizes the effectiveness of certain media over others, while recognizing some of the ways these media are socially constructed.
Intersectionality	Intersectionality emerged from a critic of 'Western' and 'white' feminism. Intersectionality recognizes that oppressive social inequalities are linked to other social processes with which they coexist such as class, (dis)ability, ethnicity, social status, sexual orientation, etc. This theory builds on constructivist and interpretivist approaches.

Figure 31.2 Different theories of technology.

These claims can be highlighted in communication philosopher Marshall McLuhan's famous stance: The medium is the message. This stance highlights that it is the medium that is being used (Facebook, Twitter, etc.) that shapes and controls 'the scale and form of human association and action' (McLuhan 1964). Over the years, McLuhan's work has been so influential that most media and communications theories stem or are derived from this perspective.

Constructivism

Feminist scholars (Douglas 1987; Wajcman 1991, 2005) tend to criticize technological determinism. For them, a deterministic approach excludes how individuals and institutions shape the design of technology (e.g., proprietary vs. free/libre/open source software, the 'femininity' of typewriters vs. the 'masculinity' of computers) and the extent to which technology is being used to legitimatize certain practices over others (Douglas 1987). Constructivism also helps explain men's historical hold on technology and the continuing under-representation of women in this field (Wajcman 1991, 2004). Judy Wajcman, the present head of the Sociology Department at London School of Economics, (LSE), pioneered technofeminism. The core of her argument stems from recognizing technology is a key source of men's power and a defining feature of masculinity. As part of her technofeminist framework, Wajcman fully recognizes that gender is not the only axis of social hierarchy and identity as there is variability in gendering by place, nationality, class, race ethnicity, sexuality, and generation.

The social constructivist approach highlights how certain ideas and belief systems have become dominant over the years and how the use and practices of certain technology have been abandoned over others (Douglas 1987). Currently, the majority of feminist scholars on technology ally theoretically with some form of constructivism/interpretivism.

Technological affordances

The critique of technological determinism was a pivotal moment for shaping the discipline of Science, Technology and Society (STS). Along the development of social constructivist approaches to technology, an approach known as 'technological affordances' (Gibson 1977; Norman 1988; Salomon 1993) was developed. This approach recognizes the uniqueness and effectiveness of certain media over others, not completely dismissing the 'medium is the message' principle, while recognizing some of the social construction associated with technology (Douglas 1987) and also the intended and unintended consequences of the design and use of a technology (see Figure 31.3).

Intersectionality

Feminist scholars and practitioners now realize that oppressive social inequalities are linked to other social processes with which they coexist. Intersectional feminists argue that feminism cannot be studied, understood, or practiced, from a single, immediate, standpoint as understanding requires engaging with the culture, class, sexuality, nationality, race, and other power structures that create various forms of inequality. Given that socialization is an inherently social phenomenon, and that society is inherently complex, intersectional feminists argue that feminists ought to approach the world through an acknowledgement of this complexity and plural axes of exclusion.

In the *Tyranny of Structurelessness* (1972), for example, Jo Freeman argues that equitable participation in what appear as open processes (i.e., meetings, demonstrations or online communities organized by social movements) are generally dominated by those with class, race, and gender privilege, including access to free time, feeling empowered to speak online or off, and by increased access to digital

---

The technological affordances associated with new media have helped amplify the reach of the Occupy Movement (OM). They also helped reveal the dubious and sometimes violent tactics of the police towards peaceful demonstrators. The corporate media and public attention given to OM took a different turn when two white girls were peppered spray in the face having already been arrested by the New York Police Department (NYPD). The video of the incident was caught on a smartphone and quickly uploaded onto YouTube. The attention the movement received resulted in more people witnessing principles of autonomy, self-management, and direct democracy (https://www.youtube.com/watch?v=TZ05rWx1pig).

Figure 31.3 The Occupy Movement and new media technological affordances.

The gender-based violence that has happened during the Arab Spring, particularly in Egypt, was widely reported on social media. As a response to violence against women, feminists generated a strong rebuttal that brought many women and men together against such violence both online and off.

The international campaign entitled Global Protest against Sexual Terrorism Practiced on Egyptian Female Protesters was launched both online and offline. This was crucial in exposing not only the violence against women during the massive protest happening at Tahrir Square, but also to highlight the epidemic of sexual and gender-based violence in Egypt. The international campaign aimed at tapping into transnational feminist and social justice networks using popular social media such as Facebook and Twitter. Under this campaign lay the principle that empowerment through social resistance will only emerge when respect and social justice are established, violence is rejected, and minority voices are heard.

Figure 31.4 Global Protest against Sexual Terrorism Practiced on Egyptian Female Protesters.

literacies, information, and communication technologies (ICTs), and programming expertise (Costanza-Chock, 2012). This is one situation in which it is necessary to pay attention to multiple, intersectional, forms of privilege and exclusion.

Techno-institutionalism?

Douglass C. North defined an institution as 'any constraint on human action' (1981: 4). In many ways, albeit informally, that is exactly what technology does, particularly as it pertains to social resistance and social movements. Protest can be seen as a form of informal institution, especially when enhanced by usage of new technology, which provides a virtual structure in which to operate. The informal institution, ironically, becomes more institutionalized by the very fact that it is moderated through the constraints technology imposes coupled with regulatory bodies such as the United States Federal Communication Commission (FCC.gov), the Canadian Radio-Television and Telecommunications Commission (CRTC), and so on.

The constraints of technology on women's agency (and other forms of agency) are particularly relevant as they pertain to those with historically limited access to power, money, and education. The institution of technology only amplifies already existing structures of power. As we have seen with the constructivist approach, the engagement of social movements with technology does not preclude the existence of inequalities of class, gender, ethnicity, ability, etc. among its participants. Conversely, agency and individual identities are seen as being less important in the virtual sphere, while constructivists, intersectionality, and most feminist theories would argue otherwise.

▍ THE RISE OF TECHNO-RESISTANCE

Social resistance and the idea of political change through internet activism have created new spaces for social movements (see Figure 31.4 for an example). To have a balanced understanding of technology and its possibilities, one needs to understand that its empowering dimension goes hand in hand with its disempowering dimension. Addressing both the empowering and disempowering aspects of technology is a question of responsibility for activists. Among the disempowering dimensions are the privacy and surveillance issues, in addition to the predicament of participation.

The aspects of the internet that empower, as we have seen with the technological affordances and technological deterministic approaches, have created beliefs that acting on the internet is sufficient to bring about change. Such approaches are reminiscent of colonialist and post-colonialist stances on modernity in that technology will save the world from dictatorships and bring about democracy. The 'social media revolution' stance that was conveyed by the media and at times in scholarship has largely eclipsed the actual grassroots work being undertaken on the ground to bring about changes. It has also removed 'politics' from technology.

The apparently equal participatory aspect of technology often hides the basis on which most online corporate platform runs. Facebook, Twitter, Instagram, and Tumblr, among others, base their corporate (financial) model on the level of popularity and 'use' of their products by prosumers (a portmanteau term to capture the individual as both producer and consumer). The paradox that emerges from the creation of these platforms is that while social movements use these seemingly 'free' corporate platforms to reach a wider public, at the same time, they enable those they are fighting against to make profits and collect information on them. Hackers who are crafting free software technologies urge activists to let go of corporate and insecure online platforms for both individual and collective use and rather opt for the free (as in freedom rather than free as being available without paying for a service) technology that they are designing for them.

To fund their projects, activists have begun to use crowd-sourced funding opportunities in a time of scarce resources. Crowd source funding can also be a way to redistribute wealth to people such as those in need of medical care. In countries in which limited health care is provided by the state (such as in the United States) such practice might be a way to resist the present system that favors a minority while plaguing a majority. Rolling Jubilee is a good illustration of the potential of crowd sourcing for the greater good. The project started in 2012 in the USA aimed at collecting donations through crowd-sourced funding online as a way to buy off medical debts incurred by individuals, freeing them from heavy indebtedness due to necessary health care.

HACKTIVISM

Hacktivism is the marriage of hacking and activism. The term was created by a member of the Cult of the Dead Cow in 1996 but, because of its ambiguity, has been somewhat contested. Gabriella Coleman (2013) prefers to talk about the hacker community in general, as she argues hackers are so named due to the nature of their efforts: Defending the right to freedom of expression and understanding the internet as a human right. Hacktivism is a practice led by hackers who aim at seeking positive social change through hacking and disseminating information to the public.

Hackers attempt to maintain their privacy and the privacy of other activists by building independent and encrypted networks to counter data gathering by governments and corporations. Some also provide free access to free networks and services such as email and mailing lists (example of tech collectives providing such services are Riseup.net in the USA, Resist.ca in Canada, Nadir.org in Germany, etc.) using free (as in 'freedom', not as in 'without cost') software for achieving technological, and ultimately political autonomy.

A version of technological determinism has been at the core of creating the mythology around a hacker identity, an identity that was largely born in the 1960s. The hacker identity is grounded in utopian ideas and based on the belief that by mastering technology a group of people could be free from the restrictions and norms imposed by the states and the economy (Söderberg 2013; Wyatt 2008b). For instance, part of the hackers' claim is that the industrial society has been surpassed with a post-industrial, information society where the outcomes (e.g., social change) are determined by the inner trajectory of technological development (Söderberg 2013). Such mythology has been a driving force within the hacker community helping to create meaning through what social movement theorists call a collective action frame (Benford and Snow 2000). The collective imagination where the internet is a 'free' space, not mediated by states or by the economy, would help, it is argued, shape the basis for a free society.

While rallying many behind utopian ideas and helping to create new mental possibilities (where online activism is possible), feminist scholars, practitioners, and hacktivists, sensitive to constructivist approaches, identified important limitations with technological determinism. Nonetheless, the hackers' utopia despite its limitations has been a driving force for the hacker movement enabling the development of projects that have changed the way we understand technology. Also, and more recently, some scholars have been trying to demonstrate that technological deterministic statements and grassroots activism are not necessarily mutually exclusive (see Proulx 2009; Söderberg 2013).

Hacktivism is 'not strictly the importation of activist techniques into the digital realm. Rather it is the expression of hacker skills in the form of electronic direct action' (see metac0m 2003). The tactics used by hacktivists have, over the years, included electronic civil disobedience, virtual sit-ins, distributed denial of service (DDoS) attacks, among others. One of the first participatory collective hacktivist actions occurred in the late 1990s when the collective called the Electronic Disturbance Theatre (EDT), composed of artists and hackers, designed a computer program called FloodNet. This program enabled massive and easy-to-use electronic civil disobedience. EDT sought to replicate the 'disturbances' happening in the streets in to the virtual realm and called for civil disobedience online. Their aim was to show solidarity with the Zapatista movement (Meikle 2003; Taylor and Jordan 2004) largely by slowing down traffic to certain websites, such as those associated with the Mexican government. Shortly thereafter an online demonstration was organized in Germany in 2001 against the airline company Lufthansa, which was being accused of doing business for migrant-deportation purposes.

Despite the many hacktivist-led projects, women and LGBTQ people have been drastically under-represented in the technical disciplines related to hacktivism, such as programming, network development, system administration, or hardware development and tinkering. There are quite a few reasons that explain the lack of women, and to some extent, LQBTQ people in the hacker community. On the one hand, technology has been associated for close to a century with masculinity. On the other hand, the feminist movement of the 1980s associated technology with patriarchy and largely discarded the use of technology (Cockburn 1985). These negative takes on technology have remained dominant at the societal level, despite later utopian visions of the internet by such feminists as Sady Plant (1997) that imagined online spaces as free of offline discrimination and violence. Such understanding of the internet has, however, been countered by more critical accounts both about how hierarchies of identity play out in online representations and discourses (Daniels 2009; Nakamura 2002, 2007) and about the gendered dimensions of digital access (Eubanks 2010; Sassen 2002b).

More recently, groups such as Anonymous have used their power as an anonymous network and pool of people with high-end computer skills to attempt to bring attention to victims of sexual assaults. A recent case led to the suicide of a young woman in response to online bullying triggered by her sexual assault. Such examples of Anonymous taking on gender-based violence are indicative of a stream of hacktivists who are saying no to violence against women. It also solidifies the potential for socially crowd sourced 'justice' as Anonymous provided evidence and empowered a local social movement in support of the victim.

The dominant association of men and technology, however, has been a cultural and social creation (see Wacjman 1991, 2004). A notable exception of women and technology is with the case of Malaysia, where a high percentage of women are studying and evolving in the world of computer science (Lagesen 2008). In Malaysia, computer science is not perceived as masculine, but rather perfectly suitable for women's work as it is work that is done inside a house rather than outside in an office. Despite the fact that the Malaysian case is different from the generalized and Western perspective that technology is associated with men, it is nonetheless highly gendered.

FEMINIST HACKTIVISM

Feminist hacktivism is emerging as a new practice. Scholarship, however, is still evolving and largely based on small sets of case studies. One potential starting point for understanding one stream of feminist hacktivism is to envisage 'opening up' the concepts of hacking and hacktivism. This might result in making the concepts more acceptable to people who do not necessarily identify as hackers, but nonetheless practice or are interested in hacking. Feminist hacktivists are thus starting to challenge the narrow notion of hacking as a term strictly associated with computers and security.

The key questions are: How will feminist hacktivists reconcile both their hacker and feminist identities? How can feminist hacktivism not lose its politically engaged tone, while at the same time trying to reach out to more people who might not identify as hackers, but maybe more as makers? The involvement of more hackers with an intersectional feminist perspective might help create a distinct subculture of feminist hacktivism. This might crystalize progressive hacktivist practices that help by proliferating differences rather than destroying them. As a case in point, the transition that happened in the past few years from hackers to makers has helped create a movement with the effect of democratizing the 'making' practices. However, these practices, conducted in makerspaces rather than hacklabs or hackerspaces (Maxigas 2012), have had conflicting results. On the one hand, makerspaces have been rendered socially welcoming, helping to create a professional credible image, while rendering the practice politically neutral by for instance accepting large sums of funding by the U.S. Defense Advanced Research Projects Agency (DARPA) (see Altman 2012). One of the main challenges for feminist hacktivists will be the ways in which they can bring politics back into feminism and hacking, while avoiding the neutral stance taken by the makers' movement.

PRIVACY

The hacker community has been advocating for autonomy and freedom on the internet for many decades now. The recent leaks about the USA National Security Agency's PRISM program somewhat exonerates the hacker community's suspicions about the extent of the violation of privacy rights. Their project to create autonomy and freedom on the internet is resonating more and more in the imaginary of the general public, a public that is trying to make sense of such complex privacy and surveillance issues. Individuals are realizing the extent to which their participation in online (corporate) platforms such as Facebook, Instagram, and Tumblr, among others, are, in fact, eroding individual and collective rights of privacy.

Conversely, information gathering through social media is commonplace and its information byproducts are available through search mechanisms by an individual, automated system or groups of individuals and systems that are available to everyone and can be abused by someone seeking to locate and harm another individual. Social movements share these vulnerabilities and as they appear to become more and more dependent on social media and crowd sourcing, they will also find that their loss of privacy will affect the movement and force new strategies to emerge.

The understanding that the information collected can be mapped geographically and conceptually develops the understanding of how an individual's privacy dissolves as they become more involved with technology and public forums. Unfortunately, the awareness of this loss of privacy and information permanence may affect an individual's behavior related to self-expression and may inhibit their actions intended to strengthen a social movement or exercise their right to freedom of speech if they do not know which tools to use to protect their privacy.

At the present time, few women are involved in the creation of free/libre/open-source software, perhaps better known as FLOSS, leaving the field badly represented by women. In her seminal book *Coding Freedom* (2013), Gabriella Coleman defines free, libre and open-source software (FLOSS) as 'nonpropri-etary but licensed software, much of which is produced by technologists located around the globe who coordinate development through Internet- based projects.'

A study conducted by Ghosh et al. (2002) suggested that 1 per cent of women are involved in the development of FLOSS; although in recent years more women are getting involved, thanks in part to groups of women programmers such as Linux Chicks, and Feminist Hackerspaces, their contributions remain small. This lack of participation impinges on the overall development of FLOSS. Examples of FLOSS include Open Office, Lorea, Diaspora and Social Swarm rather than Facebook and Twitter, Gimp as opposed to Photoshop, and Linux in place of other operating systems such as Mac OS or Windows.

Figure 31.5 Women (or lack of) in the free, libre and open-source movement.

An individual's willingness to support a social movement can be disrupted by a loss of privacy, since anonymity can allow people to participate without the fear of repercussions. Therefore, we should consider how our sense of privacy is dramati-cally affected by the availability and use of technology such as social media inte-grated with video from smartphones or other sensing systems. The privacy violations that we are willing to accept are growing in exchange for the conveniences of centralized and integrated systems (such as with Google products: Gmail, Google Hang-Out, Google Chrome, Google as search engine) and the acceptance of the internet as a 'service' to 'clients/users'.

The free, libre and open-source movement (FLOSS), in conjunction with the hacker community, is constantly improving free and open source software that are non-corporate and help develop better cryptography to secure one's communication online (see Figure 31.5). Examples include OpenPGP, which enables you to encrypt emails, and Off the Record (OTR) plug-ins to engage in instant messaging with your friends securely through clients such as Pidgin (PC) and Adium (Mac), among others. These tools help you encrypt your communications and end your reliance on proprietary software (for more tech tools for activists visit www.prism-break. org). Eventually – it is to be hoped – a balance will be found between privacy, con-venience, and the value of our information. But, for this to happen, more and more people need to recognize the importance of having such a battle at the social, legal, and political levels.

CONCLUSION

In this chapter, we have looked at the intersection of gender, social resistance, and technology. We gave an overview of the theoretical frameworks that have informed the ways in which we understand technology in relation to other phenomena. We demonstrated that social movements and the perception of gender issues in society are often influenced by evolving technologies, which, in turn, are shaped by both social movements and gendered ideas and ideals. The most striking example is the hacker community, which has tried for more than a decade now to develop tools for social movements as a way to ensure their autonomy and freedom from both the state and corporations. Through the examples laid out in this chapter, we have also seen that the use of technology by and for social movements is producing new ways of bringing people together, posing new questions, and organizing alternative opportunities for change.

Gender issues are important to keep in mind when understanding technology in relation to social movements as it is both a source and consequence of gender relations. Collectively, we can see the improvements in speed and effectiveness of how social movements and feminists activists can form and react to a social problem enabled by technology such as new media. However, the use of new media, particularly corporate media, poses new challenges for social movements and feminist activists. Feminist activists are also trying to push the boundaries of technology with their usage and their development. What is pending is the ways in which feminists will develop practices at the crossroads of hacktivism and intersectional identity issues. What will be the impact on feminism as both theory and practice? We have yet to know how these processes will play out and influence – and be influenced by – both feminist and hacker communities.

Questions for further debate

1. Why is it important for social movements to use alternative online tools and platforms?
2. How can gender be performed online in such a way that social transformation occurs?
3. How can one fight against gender-based violence and discrimination online and offline? Can you come up with examples of such practices? Are they effective? If so, why? If not, why not?
4. According to you are there tensions between a hacker identity and a feminist/queer identity? Can both identities co-exist, and if so how? If you believe they cannot co-exist, explain why.
5. How do online and offline social movement practices coalesce?

Sources for further reading and research

Castells, M. (2008) 'The New Public Sphere: Global Civil Society, Communication Networks, and Global Governance', *Annals of the American Academy of Political and Social Science*, 616(1): 78–93.

Castells, M. (2012) *Networks of Outrage and Hope: Social Movements in the Internet Age*, Cambridge: Polity Press.

Costanza-Chock, S. (2012) 'Mic Check! Media cultures and the Occupy movement', *Social Movement Studies*, 11(3–4): 375–85.

Eubanks, V. (2011) *Digital Dead End: Fighting for Social Justice in the Information Age*, Cambridge, MA: MIT Press.

Fenton, N. and V. Barassi (2011) 'Alternative Media and Social Networking: The Politics of Individuation and Political Participation', *Communication Review*, 14(3), 179–96.

Note

1 The authors are grateful to Ryan Integlia for his technical assistance.

Afterword

Terrell Carver

ENGENDERING THE ACADEMY: BRINGIN' IT ALL BACK HOME . . .

But after taking this particular journey through a feminist introduction to International Relations, where exactly is 'home'? Given the ways in which feminist curiosity has been deployed in the chapters of this book to 'make sense' of global politics, what exactly could 'home' mean?

In answering these questions, I am tempted to say 'where the heart is' and observe that in all chapters, the heart is with the disempowered, excluded, marginalised and – as we learn – *feminised* 'others' of this world. Home is therefore a metaphor, a signal for transferred meaning: maybe we wouldn't like to invite them *all* in, but we'd view them with respect and acknowledge them as 'like the home folks' in at least some minimal but significant ways. Feminist curiosity – if I have it right – says that it's ok to be curious about people, wherever they are, but not to impose, presume or rush into anything. But it doesn't tell us in advance who or what is important, or even what the 'problem' is – following one's curiosity is about working these things out as you go. Thus these chapters have ranged widely over global politics, freely politicising where curiosity takes the contributors and presenting someone's 'sense' to the reader.

However, given the status of this book as an introductory text, we need to reflect on how it fits with and functions in an academic setting, where institutions matter. Perhaps we had better acknowledge here that 'home' in this context is 'IR', the discipline that assigns the academic study of global politics to itself. What, then, is IR when it is at home and where it is most 'homely'?

The answer, of course, is IR's home base in 'realism', the point of departure from which the discipline sets out, the point of origin for this twentieth-century social science, the first chapter of standard textbooks (or at least right up front), and lecture one of the 'Introduction to IR' course. Stories are journeys, too, and voyages of discovery, expeditions into the unknown. And realism is where IR says it all began. Naturally this is located for us in another galaxy, long, long ago and far away, otherwise known as the Peloponnesian War, and in particular in an abstract from Thucydides' remarkable near-contemporary and often eye-witness history, an abstract otherwise known as 'the Melian debate'.

Once upon a time IR textbooks started from the distant security of this homeland and sallied forth in time and space, hitting the high spots of *Realpolitik*, such as Machiavelli, the formation of rival nation-states with the Peace of Westphalia in 1648, Hobbes's hard-minded *Leviathan*, and the workings of the international system ever since, with further watersheds, waves of debating, centrifugal schools and centripetal professionalisms. By the 1990s it was taking quite a few chapters to guide students through all this material in ascending chronological order and descending order of importance. When feminist IR entered on the scene, it was, in some textbooks, about Chapter 28, give or take a few positions, and down there in the dimness it jostled for position with post-structuralists, green politics, perhaps Marxists, or anyway other small and distant worlds, not quite cold and lifeless, but certainly not hot items, pole position, top seeds or anything else proclaiming visibility and priority. Feminists and allied scholars have worked hard to move this 'approach' up the ladder of success.

This has been hard work, risking not life but certainly career prospects, and perseverance appears to be winning out. After all, in the academic world, where rigorous evaluation and peer review are harnessed to publication, whether of articles or books, and, of course, to hiring and promotion, then it will take time for any new approach to prove itself against what is already tried and tested, done and dusted, hosed and home. Feminism might be the latest thing and feminists full of themselves, but they will have to get their 'stuff' into the journals, on the bookshelves, approved as courses, licensed as higher degrees. They will need to get recognition at the conferences and congresses, obtain critical mass and professional visibility, found journals and establish book series, become external examiners and get appointed to PhD committees, win prizes and become association presidents. Then they can expect … exactly what?

Well, this has all happened, and here we are. We have set out with feminist curiosity, used the gender lens, incorporated intersectionality and interdisciplinarity: race/ethnicity, religion, language, communicative codes, nationality, identity, subjectivity, bio-power, sexuality, sex, intersex, (dis)ability, culture ('pop' and otherwise), semiotics, visual media, bodies, gender (on several definitions), methodology (whether arguably feminist or allegedly 'non'), post-coloniality, rights, performativity, masculinity, virtual reality, and those perennial IR favourites: war, violence, conflict resolution and peace. We have reached the 'afterword'. Whose home is this?

I suggest we try the homeland security of IR realism, where – so we have been told – we really started from. We'll see how homely it is now, and whether we really want to go back there, or indeed if we can ever go home again. This conclusion, then, is 'the chapter on IR'. Well, what is it and how does it look, here in the after-word, all cold and lonely? Surely we should be happy to light the hearth and make a home? The terms of debate and tenets of the discipline are very well known – and here we should begin to wonder why. The answer to this is obvious: all those text-books, all those great figures of the discipline, all those landmark articles, all that laying on of hands. Despite their differences, they all have something in common to be different about: the nation-state as the defining unit or level of analysis, the anarchy of states in their inter-relationality, the international system, order or soci-ety as non-sovereign regulator, war as the consequential, ineradicable and ever pre-sent political 'given', geopolitics as the sum of national interests, and diplomacy as strategy thinly disguised.

Why use this 'lens'? What does it help us see? What gets excluded? Who's look-ing? And where? I am tempted to say, 'at you, kid', but then it isn't that easy to see how humans are visible at all here. They are simply assumed as some generality, or perhaps level of generality, existing in some way(s), beneath these 'analytical' abstractions. Would it help us to turn back to Hobbes or Machiavelli or Thucydides and consider what they say, or at least seem to presuppose, about 'human nature'? Would it help us to go instead to some 'first principles', whether of the body or the mind, specify how these categories arose and why they are good ones? Perhaps these realist terms are the categories that humans use when they 'do' international rela-tions as world leaders, diplomats and policy advisors – but in that case IR would not be academic or scientific, and would have no purchase on what happens, and add no value.

Perhaps it's a mistake here to look for humans, and IR is right to look at systems, mechanisms and regularities. After all, these are 'hardwired' items, they operate predictably, and they help us make 'sense' of things. 'Boys and toys' is neither an inaccurate description of IR realists, nor completely off-base as a description of who runs the world and how. But can IR realism sustain itself as a discourse of mecha-nisms, a science of regularities, an analytical practice of prediction? Does it result in useful technologies of inter-governmental control, or strategic fine-tuning in diplo-macy, or efficiency savings in national expenditure, or even health and safety at the coalface of global political work? Textbooks will tell you that it might, must or should. But I wonder how many 'international actors' are out there (by which I mean humans) who would swear that their realist training represents their opera-tional bible, or even that they'd like it to? If there were such satisfied customers, we could find their blurbs on the back cover, and in the chapter headings. I have yet to see one. Isn't that something to be curious about?

Perhaps this discussion is caricatured and overblown, and essentially missing the point. The point is that realism is just that: a starting point. IR is a much larger academic subject, and a much broader church. Successive waves of migrating ideas have been 'brought back in': history, culture, class, possibly even race, religion, lit-erature, art and women! So it's not so mechanistic and coldly inhuman after all. But adding these things in doesn't stir the mix much. They are welcomed into the IR home, provided, of course, that they represent persons and activities that meet the 'international' test. Otherwise, they belong somewhere else, most probably sociol-ogy or cultural studies, where the disciplinary framing is often, quite conveniently, 'national'. Now we have an eclectic discipline, open to new conceptualisations and problems, but still with a clear boundary line of demarcation, an 'international' border to tell us what international borders really are, an international home exclusively for those people and things that qualify for 'diplomatic' privileges and places, and a clear candidate for peaceable incorporation into the academic system of degrees, majors and departments.

Rather unfortunately, however, this doesn't satisfy my curiosity. Why, if we had to add all this 'back in', did we have to start from such a cold and lifeless little planet in the first place? If Planet IR now looks that way – after 31 chapters of human (all too human) life and death, suffering and destruction, violence and dislocation, instability and transgression – then do we want to go back there? Would all this feminist sense find it a cosy home? It looks like it needs a woman's touch, but what kind of touch would that be? Perhaps it needs some feminist touchpaper instead.

Feminists of my acquaintance disagree about this, and I invite readers to join in. At one of the workshops from which this volume derives – having travelled a long road of authorial and editorial hard work to reach your eyes – just exactly this issue came up. Several speakers expressed their dissatisfaction with IR realism, and the practice of starting there in 'Week 1' of the courses they did, the ones they teach, the core course that their students are required to take. Surely the week on feminism should move up the weekly roster in 'Intro' courses, right up near the front. Perhaps, the discussion continued, 'we' should just start there! Oh, um, well … other voices said, you really need to learn 'the basics' first, and then you can criticise them, but otherwise feminism – presumed to be a critique – would not really make sense. No one would know precisely what it was about. Or in any case, students really need a 'good grounding' in the discipline, otherwise they won't get jobs, and there isn't much we can do about that.

The woman next to me intervened. 'I think that's really dangerous!' she said. By Week 2, the collective thinking continued, it's all over, and the damage has been done. Doing IR realism in Week 1 makes it the origin, the centre, the homeland of security for anyone joining 'the discipline', the natural home we're all (even if unfortunately or restively) comfortable in, because we grew up there. And in that way feminist IR will be doomed to marginality, and feminists in IR to a Sisyphean process of self-exclusion from the 'mainstream'. How to solve this problem?

Cynthia Enloe's new Foreword – women talking together over green tea and *sake* – doesn't sound very incendiary, and rather unlikely to disturb the civil peace (or gender 'peace') in Japan, never mind anywhere else. But then politics works in mysterious ways, and there's no doubt that Cynthia has disturbed the academic world of IR, at least somewhat. Asking 'Where are the women?' is asking the rest of the question, 'Where are the people?' when 'people' is taken to mean 'men' as such, males and masculine-identified 'very important' persons. IR, of course, has trouble asking about 'people' in the first place, given that the focus on the 'international' has evoked a discourse of 'state actors', *below which* mere personalities are said – when methodological purity is at risk – to have less explanatory power, and hardly count as a 'variable' at all.

On the one hand, the gendered and feminist position is both a critique and a wake-up call for those interested in politics to think through the 'international' framing (i.e., 'away from home') in order to get to the human terms out of which politics surfaces, most usually (for some of us, anyway) in the global media as killings that matter, and grieveable bodies. My hope lies with good ol' feminist fearlessness, challenging those who say – in a tepid and tentative way – 'I don't really "do" gender', and responding, as a feminist colleague of mine did in a very loud voice, 'LIAR'.

Well, readers, I hope that I have aroused your curiosity, and I hope you realise that you are looking at the answer – don't go home! Take your start from this book, or do the best with your students or friends, so together you traverse the 31 chapters' worth of raging curiosity, puzzling material and thoughtful judgements that follow from feminist curiosity about global politics. You may have to start over to do it, but that's no bad thing. Then have a look at IR realism, if you like – or if you must – and see what you think about it. I think it's a cold and lonely place claiming that 'Boys and Toys Я Us' whether we like it or not. But you decide, weigh the costs and make the choices. And feel free to disagree!

BIBLIOGRAPHY

Abbate, J. (2001) *Inventing the Internet*, Boston, MA: MIT Press.

Abu-Lughod, L. (2002) 'Do Muslim Women Really Need Saving? Anthropological Reflections on Cultural Relativism and its Others', *American Anthropologist*, 104(3) 783–90.

Ackelsberg, M. (1988) 'Communities, Resistance, and Women's Activism: Some Implications for a Democratic Polity', in A. Bookman and S. Morgen (eds), *Women and the Politics of Empowerment*, Philadelphia, PA: Temple University Press.

Ackelsberg, M. (2005) 'Women's Community Activism and the Rejection of "Politics": Some Dilemmas of Popular Democratic Movements,' in M. Friedman (ed.), *Women and Citizenship*, Oxford: Oxford University Press.

Ackerly, B. A. (2001) 'Women's Human Rights Activists as Cross-Cultural Theorists', *International Feminist Journal of Politics*, 3(3): 311–46.

Ackerly, B. A. (2008) *Universal Human Rights in a World of Difference,* Cambridge: Cambridge University Press.

Ackerly, B. A. (2009) 'Women's Organizations and Global Governance: The Need for Diversity in Global Civil Society', in L. Cabrera (ed.), *Global Governance/Global Government*, Albany, NY: SUNY Press.

Ackerly, B. A., Stern, M. and True, J. (eds) (2006) *Feminist Methodologies for International Relations*, Cambridge: Cambridge University Press.

Action (BPFA) Available at http://www.un.org/womenwatch/daw/Ibeijing/pdf IBDPfA%2OE. pdf.

Adam, A. and Green, E. (1998) 'Gender, Agency, Location and the New Information Society' in B. Loader (ed.), *Cyberspace Divide: Equality, Agency and Policy in the Information Society*, London and New York: Routledge.

Addis, E., Russo, V. E. and Sebesta, L. (eds) (1994) *Women Soldiers: Images and Reality*, New York: St. Martin's Press.

African Rights (1995) *Rwanda: Death, Despair and Defiance* (rev. ed.), London: African Rights.

Afshar, H. (2004) 'Women and Wars: Some Trajectories Towards a Feminist Peace', in H. Afshar and D. Eade (eds), *Development, Women and War: Feminist Perspectives*, Oxford: Oxfam GB.

Afshar, H. and Eade, D. (eds) (2004) *Development, Women and War: Feminist Perspectives*, Oxford: Oxfam GB.

Afshar, H. and Maynard, M. (eds) (1994) *The Dynamics of 'Race' and Gender: Some Feminist Interventions*, London: Taylor & Francis.

Agarwal, B. (1992) 'The Gender and Environment Debate: Lessons from India', *Feminist Studies*, 18(1): 119–58.

Agarwal, B. (1994) *A Field of One's Own: Gender and Land Rights in South Asia*, Cambridge: Cambridge University Press.

Agathangelou, A. M. (1997) *The Cypriot 'Ethnic' Conflict in the Production of Global Power*. PhD Dissertation, Department of Political Science, Maxwell School of Citizenship and Public Affairs, Syracuse University.

Agathangelou, A. M. (2000) 'Nationalist Narratives and (Dis)appearing Women: State-sanctioned Sexual Violence', *Canadian Woman Studies*, 19: 12–21.

Agathangelou, A. M. (2004) *The Global Political Economy of Sex: Desire, Violence, and Insecurity in Mediterranean Nation States*, New York: Palgrave Macmillan.

Agathangelou, A. M. (2006) 'Colonising Desire: Bodies for Sale, Exploitation and (In)Security in Desire Industries', *Cyprus Review*, 18: 37–73.

Agathangelou, A. M. (2008) 'Seductions of Imperialism: Incapacitating Life, Fetishizing Death and Catastrophizing Ecologies', in J. R. Pruce (ed.), *Human Rights And Human Welfare*, Boulder, CO: University of Denver Press.

Agathangelou, A. M. (2010) 'Economies of Blackness and Sacrifice of (Homo)Virilities: Accumulation, Disasters and Slaughterhouses', in S. Nair and S. Biswas (eds), *International Relations and States of Exception: Margins, Peripheries and Excluded Bodies*, London and New York: Routledge.

Agathangelou, A. M. (2012) 'The Living and Being of the Streets: Fanon and the Arab Uprisings', *Globalizations*, 9(3): 451–66.

Agathangelou, A. M. (2013) 'Making Anew an Arab Regional Order? On Poetry, Sex, and Revolution', in A. M. Agathangelou and N. Soguk (eds), *Arab Revolutions and World Transformations*, London: Routledge.

Agathangelou, A. M., Kim, A., Kumar, A., Lai, N., Maisonville, D., Rosser, E. and White, M. (2007) *Technologies of Empire and (In)Secure Possibilities*, Toronto: York University Centre for International and Security Studies.

Agathangelou, A. M. and Ling, L. H. M. (2002) 'An Unten(ur)able Position: The Politics of Teaching for Women of Color in the U.S.', *International Feminist Journal of Politics*, 4: 368–98.

Agathangelou, A. M. and Ling, L. H. M. (2003) 'Desire Industries: Sex Trafficking, UN Peacekeeping, and the Neo-Liberal World Order', *Brown Journal of World Affairs*, 10(1): 133–49.

Agathangelou, A. M. and Ling, L. H. M. (2009) *Transforming World Politics: From Empire To Multiple Worlds*, London: Routledge.

Agathangelou, A. M. and Spira, T. (2007) 'Sacrifice, Abandonment, and Interventions for Sustainable Feminism(s): The Non-Profit Organization Industry and Transbordered Substantive Democracy', in S. Sarker (ed.), *Sustainable Feminism(s)*, Amsterdam: Jai Press/Elsevier.

Aguilar, D. D. and Lacsamana, A. (eds) (2004) *Women and Globalization*, New York: Humanity Books.

Aguilar, F. (1999) 'Ritual Passage and the Reconstruction of Self-Hood in International Labour Migration', *Sojourn*, 4(1): 98–139.

Agustín, L. (2005) 'Migrants in the Mistress's House: Other Voices in the "Trafficking" Debate', *Social Politics*, 12(1): 96–117.

Åhäll, L. (2012) 'Motherhood, Myth and Gendered Agency in Political Violence', *International Feminist Journal of Politics*, 14(1): 103–20.

Åhäll, L. and Shepherd, L. J. (eds) (2012) *Gender, Agency and Political Violence (Rethinking Political Violence)*, London: Palgrave Macmillan.

Ahmed, S. (2004) *The Cultural Politics of Emotion*, London: Routledge.

Ahmed, S. (2010) *The Promise of Happiness*, Durham, NC: Duke University Press.

Akpinar, A. (2003) 'The Honour/Shame Complex Re-visited: Violence Against Women in the Migration Context', *Women's Studies International Forum*, 26(5): 425–42.

Akram, S. M. (2000) 'Orientalism Revisited in Asylum and Refugee Cases', *International Journal of Refugee Law*, 12(1): 7–40.

Alberts, D. S. and Hayes R. E. (2003) *Power to the Edge: Command and Control in the Information Age*, US Department of Defense Command and Control Research Program, June 2003. Available at http://www.dodccrp.org/files/ Alberts_Power.pdf (accessed 15 April 2009).

Alexander, M. J. (1994) 'Not Just (Any)Body Can Be a Citizen: The Politics of Law, Sexuality and Postcoloniality in Trinidad and Tobago and the Bahamas', *Feminist Review*, Autumn: 5–23.

Alexander, M. J. (2005) *Pedagogies of Crossing: Meditations on Feminism, Sexual Politics, Memory, and the Sacred*, Durham, NC: Duke University Press.

Alexander, M. J. and Mohanty, C. T. (eds) (1997) *Feminist Genealogies, Colonial Legacies, Democratic Futures*, New York: Routledge.

Alison, M. (2004) 'Women as Agents of Political Violence: Gendering Security', *Security Dialogue*, 35(4): 447–63.

Alison, M. (2008) *Women and Political Violence: Female Combatants in Ethno-National Conflict*, London: Routledge.

Alkon, A. H. and Agyeman, J. (eds) (2011) *Cultivating Food Justice: Race, Class, and Sustainability.*, Cambridge, MA: MIT Press.

Altinay, A. G. (2004) *The Myth of the Military-Nation: Militarism, Gender, and Education in Turkey*, New York and London: Palgrave Macmillan.

Altman, M. (2012) 'Hacking at the Crossroad: US Military Funding of Hackerspaces', *Journal of Peer Production* 2. Available at http://peerproduction.net/issues/issue-2/invited-comments/hacking-at-the-crossroad/ (accessed 2 August 2 2013).

Alvarez, E. S. (1990) *Engendering Democracy in Brazil: Women's Movements in Transition Politics*, Princeton, NJ: Princeton University Press.

Alvarez, E. S. (2000) 'Translating the Global: Effects of Transnational Organizing on Local Feminist Discourses and Practices in Latin America', *Meridians*, 1: 29–67.

Amnesty International (2011)*Annual Report, 2011.* Available at http://www.amnesty.org/en/region/iraq/report-2011#section-65-10 (accessed 4 August 2013).

Amnesty International USA (2005) Rape as a Tool of War: A Fact Sheet. Available at http://www.amnestyusa.org/women/rapeinwartime.html (accessed on 7 January 2009).

Anand, D. (2007a) 'Gendered Anxieties: Representing Muslim Masculinity as a Danger', *British Journal of Politics and International Relations*, 9(2): 257–69.

Anand, D. (2007b) *Geopolitical Exotica: Tibet in Western Imagination*, Minneapolis, MN: University of Minnesota Press.

Anand, D. (2008) 'Porno-Nationalism and the Male Subject: An Ethnography of Hindu Nationalist Imagination in India', in J. Parpart and M. Zalewski (eds), *Rethinking the 'Man' Question in International Politics*, London: Zed Books.

Anderlini, S. (2000) *Women at the Peace Table: Making a Difference*, New York: UNIFEM.

Anderlini, S. N. and Pampell Conaway, C. (2004) 'Security Sector Reform'. Available at http://www.international-alert.org/sites/default/files/library/TKSecuritySectorReform.pdf (accessed 9 June 2011).

Anderson, B. (1991) *Imagined Communities: Reflections on the Origins and Spread of Nationalism*, rev. edn, London: Verso.

Andrijasevic, R. (2007) 'Beautiful Dead Bodies: Gender, Migration and Representation in Anti-Trafficking Campaigns', *Feminist Review*, 86: 24–44.

Ang, I. (1985) *Watching Dallas: Soap Opera and the Melodramatic Imagination*; trans. Della Couling, London: Methuen.

Ang, I. (1996) *Living Room Wars: Rethinking Media Audiences for a Postmodern World*, London: Routledge.

Annan, K. (2005) 'In Larger Freedom: Towards Development, Security and Human Rights for All', Report of the United Nations Secretary-General to the General Assembly, 59th Session. Available at http://www.un.org/ largerfreedom/ (accessed 15 April 2009).

Anonymous (2002) *A Woman in Berlin*, London: Virago.

Anthias, F. and Yuval-Davis, N. (1992) *Racialized Boundaries: Race, Nation, Gender, Colour and Class and the Anti-Racist Struggle*, London: Routledge.

Antrobus, P. (2004) *The Global Women's Movement: Origins, Issues and Strategies*, Dhaka: University Press Limited; London and New York: Zed Books.

Anzaldúa, G. E. (1987) *Borderlands = La Frontera: The New Mestiza*, San Francisco: Aunt Lute.

Appadurai, A. (1996) *Modernity at Large: Cultural Dimensions of Globalization*, Minneapolis, MN: University of Minnesota Press.

Appadurai, A. (1998) 'Dead Certainty: Ethnic Violence in the Era of Globalization', *Development and Change*, 29: 905–25.

Aradau, C. (2004) 'The Perverse Politics of Four-Letter Words: Risk and Pity in the Securitisation of Human Trafficking', *Millennium: Journal of International Studies*, 33(2): 251–77.

Aradau, C. (2008) *Rethinking Trafficking in Women: Politics out of Security*, Houndsmills: Palgrave Macmillan.

Arat-Koç, S. (2007) '(Some) Turkish Transnationalism(s) in an Age of Capitalist Globalization and Empire: "White Turk" Discourse, the New Geopolitics, and Implications for Feminist Transnationalism', *Journal of Middle East Women's Studies*, 3: 35–57.

Arditti, R. (1999) *Searching for Life: The Grandmothers of the Plaza de Mayo and the Disappeared Children of Argentina*, London and Berkeley, CA: University of California Press.

Arendt, H. (1970) *On Violence,* San Diego, CA: Harvester.

Arruzza, C. (2012) 'The Gender of Occupy Wall Street', *International View Point*, 12 March 2012. Available at http://www.internationalviewpoint.org/ spip.php?article2610 (accessed 15 August 2013).

Asad, T. (2003) *Formations of the Secular: Christianity, Islam, Modernity*, Stanford, CA: Ashgate.

Asian Development Bank (2003) *Policy on Gender and Development*, Manila: Asian Development Bank.

Askin, K. D. (2003) 'Prosecuting Wartime Rape and Other Gender Related Crimes: Extraordinary Advances, Enduring Obstacles', *Berkeley Journal of International Law*, 21(2): 288–349.

Association of Progressive Communications (2012) *Going Visible: Women's Rights On The Internet*, APC-Women's Rights Programme Report to Addressing Inequalities: The Heart of the Post-2015 Development Agenda and the Future We Want for All, Global Thematic Consultation, UN Women/Unicef, October. Available at http://www.worldwewant2015. org/file/287493/download/311684

Australian Bureau of Statistics (2013) *Cultural Diversity in Australia, Reflecting a Nation: Stories from the 2011 Census,* Canberra: ABS. Available at http://www.abs.gov.au/ausstats/ abs@.nsf/Lookup/2071.0main+features902012-2013 (accessed 4 May 2014).

Auerbach S. (2007) 'Nationalism: Jewish Conscription and Russian Repatriation in London's East End, 1916–1918', *Journal of British Studies*, 46(3): 594–620.

Avocats Sans Frontières, Center for Justice and Reconciliation, Coalition Nationale pour la Cour Pénale Internationale RCD, Fédération Internationale des Ligues des Droits de l'Homme, Human Rights Watch, International Center for Transitional Justice, Redress, Women's Initiatives for Gender Justice (2006) Joint letter to the Chief Prosecutor of the International Criminal Court, 1 August 2006. Available at http://www.hrw.org/ news/2006/07/31/dr-congo-icc-charges-raise-concern (accessed 16 July 2013).

Axe, D. and Hamilton, T. (2013) *Army of God: Joseph Kony's War in Central Africa*, New York: PublicAffairs.

Bacchetta, P. (2004) *Gender in the Hindu Nation: RSS Women as Ideologues*, New Delhi: Women Unlimited.

Bacevich, A. J. and Prodromou, E. H. (2003/4) 'God is not Neutral: Religion and US Foreign Policy after 9/11', *Orbis*, 48(1): 43–54.

Baden, Sally and Goetz, Anne-Marie (1997) 'Who Needs (Sex) When You Can Have (Gender)', *Feminist Review*, 56(Summer), 3–25.

Bagchi, J. (1990) 'Representing Nationalism: Ideology of Motherhood in Colonial Bengal', *Economic and Political Weekly*, 20–27 October: 65–70.

Baines, E. (2005) 'Les Femmes aux Milles Bras: Building Peace in Rwanda', in D. Mazurana, A. Raven-Roberts and J. Parpart (eds), *Gender, Conflict and Peacekeeping*, Lanham, MD, and Oxford: Rowman & Littlefield.

Bakker, I. (ed.) (1994) *The Strategic Silence: Gender and Economic Policy*, London: Zed Books.

Bakker, I. and Gill, S. (eds) (2003) *Power, Production and Social Reproduction: Human In/security in the Global Political Economy*, Houndsmills: Palgrave Macmillan.

Balasingham, A. A. (1993), *Women Fighters of Liberation Tigers*, Jaffna, Sri Lanka: Thasan.

Banksy (2006) *Wall and Piece*, London: Century.

Barkai, Moran (2012) *Revolution: Share! The Role of Social Media in Pro-Democratic Movements,* ed. Wilfried Rütten. European Journalism Centre. Available at http://www.ejc.net/revolution_share/

Barkawi, T. and Laffey, M. (2001) *Democracy, Liberalism and War: Rethinking the Democratic Peace Debate*, Boulder, CO: Lynne Rienner.

Barker, D. and Feiner, S. (2004) *Liberating Economics: Feminist Perspectives on Families, Work, and Globalization*, Ann Arbor, MI: University of Michigan Press.

Barnes, K. (2006) 'Reform or More of the Same? Gender Mainstreaming and the Changing Nature of UN Peace Operations', YCISS Working Paper Number 41, October 2006. Available at http://www.yorku.ca/yciss/whatsnew/documents/WP41-Barnes.pdf (accessed 15 April 2009).

Barnett, M. and Duvall, R. (2005) 'Power in Global Governance', in M. Barnett and Duvall, R. (eds), *Power in Global Governance*, Cambridge: Cambridge University Press.

Barnett, M. and Finnemore, M. (2004) *Rules for the World: International Organizations in Global Politics*, Ithaca, NY: Cornell University Press.

Barry, K. (1979) *The Prostitution of Sexuality. The Global Exploitation of Women*, New York: New York University Press.

Barthes, R. (1973) *Mythologies*, trans. A. Lavers, St Albans: Paladin.

Barthwal-Datta, M. (2013) *Food Security in Asia*, London: International Press.

Bastick, M. and Valasek, K. (eds) (2008) *Gender and Security Sector Reform Toolkit*, Geneva, CH: DCAF, OSCE/ODIHR and UN-INSTRAW.

Basu, A. (1995) 'When Local Riots are not Simply Local: Collective Violence and the State of Bijnor, India, 1988–93', *Theory and Society*, 24(1): 35–78.

Basu, K. (2006) 'Globalization, Poverty and Inequality: What is the Relationship? What Can Be Done?', *World Development*, 34(8): 1361–73.

Bauman, Z. (1991) *Modernity and the Holocaust*, Cambridge: Polity Press.

BBC News (2008) '1968 – Myth or Reality? The Archive Hour – The My Lai Tapes', *Radio Four BBC*, 15 March 2008. Available at http://www.bbc.co.uk/radio4/1968/mylai.shtml (accessed 15 April 2009).

BBC News (2010) 'Internet Access is "a Fundamental Right"', 8 March 2010. Available at http://news.bbc.co.uk/2/hi/technology/8548190.stm (accessed 3 January 2013).

BBC News (2013a) 'Dhaka Factory Collapse: Can Clothes Industry Change?'. Available at http://www.bbc.co.uk/news/world-asia-22302595.

BBC News (2013b) 'Shot Pakistan Schoolgirl Malala Yousafzai addresses UN', BBC News, 12 July 2013. Available at http://www.bbc.co.uk/news/world-asia-23282662 (accessed 17 October 2013).

Beal, C. (2000) 'Brave New World', *Jane's Defense Weekly*, 9 February: 22–26.

Beaumont, P. (2006) 'Hidden Victims of a Brutal Conflict: Iraq's Women', *The Guardian*, 8 October 2006.

Beavers, S. (2002) 'The West Wing as a Pedagogical Tool', *PS: Political Science and Politics*, 35: 213–16.

Bedford, K. (2003) 'How Employment Became Emancipation: Tracing the World Bank's Effort to Get Women into Work', in D. S. Cobble, A. B. Chaloupka and B. Hutchison (eds), *Reconfiguring Class and Gender*, New Brunswick, NJ: Institute for Research on Women/Institute for Women's Leadership.

Bedford, K. (2005) 'Loving to Straighten out Development: Sexuality and "Ethnodevelopment" in the World Bank's Ecuadorian Lending', *Feminist Legal Studies*, 13(3): 295–322.

Bedford, Kate (2008) 'Governing Intimacy in the World Bank', in Shirin M. Rai and Georgina Waylen (eds), *Global Governance: Feminist Perspectives,* Basingstoke: Macmillan Palgrave, pp. 84–106.

Bedford, Kate (2013) 'Economic Governance and the Regulation of Intimacy in Gender and Development: Lessons from the World Bank's Programming', in Guelay Caglar, Susanne Zwingel and Elisabeth Prugl (eds), *Feminist Strategies in International Governance,* New York: Routedge, p. 233–48.

Bedont, B. (1999) 'Gender-Specific Provisions in the Statute of the International Criminal Court', in F. Lattanzi and W. Schabas (eds), *Essays on the Rome Statute*, Ripa di Fagnano Alto: il Sirente.

Bedont, B. and Hall Martinez, K. (1999) 'Ending Impunity for Gender Crimes Under the International Criminal Court', *Brown Journal of World Affairs*, 6(1): 65–85.

Beitz, C. (1979) *Political Theory and International Relations*, Princeton, NJ: Princeton University Press.

Bellamy, A. J. (2008) *Fighting Terrorism: Ethical Dilemmas*, London: Zed Books.

Belmonte, L. A. (2003) 'A Family Affair? Gender, the U.S. Information Agency, and Cold War Ideology, 1945–1960', in J. C. E. Gienow-Hecht and F. Schumacher (eds), *Culture and International History*, New York: Berghahn Books.

Benería, L. (2003a) 'Economic Rationality and Globalization: A Feminist Perspective', in M. A. Ferber and J. A. Nelson (eds), *Feminist Economics Today: Beyond Economic Man*, Chicago, IL, and London: University of Chicago Press.

Benería, L. (2003b) *Gender, Development and Globalization: Economics as if All People Mattered*, New York and London: Routledge.

Benería, L. and Sen, G. (1981) 'Accumulation, Reproduction, and "Women's Role in Economic Development": Boserup Revisited', *Signs*, 7(2): 279–98.

Benford, R. D. and Snow, D. A. (2000) 'Framing Processes and Social Movements: An Overview and Assessment', *Annual Review of Sociology*, 26: 611–39.

Benhabib, S. (1992) 'The Debate over Women and Moral Theory Revisited', in S. Benhabib (ed.), *Situating the Self: Gender, Community and Postmodernism in Contemporary Ethics*, New York: Routledge.

Benhabib, S. (ed.) (1992) *Situating the Self: Gender, Community and Postmodernism in Contemporary Ethics*, London: Routledge.

Benhabib, S. (2002) *The Claims of Culture: Equality and Diversity in a Global Era*, Princeton, NJ: Princeton University Press.

Benhabib, S. (2004) *The Rights of Others*, Cambridge: Cambridge University Press.

Bennett, W. L. (2012) 'The Personalization of Politics: Political Identity, Social Media, and Changing Patterns of Participation', *ANNALS of the American Academy of Political and Social Science*, 644(1): 20–39.

Bennholdt-Thomsen, V., Faraclas, N. and Werlhof, C. V. (eds) (2001) *There Is an Alternative: Subsistence and Worldwide Resistance to Corporate Globalization*, London: Zed Books.

Berger, M., Wallis, B. and Watson, S. (eds) (1995) *Constructing Masculinity*, London and New York: Routledge.

Bergeron, S. (2001) 'Political Economy Discourses of Globalization and Feminist Politics', *Signs*, 26(4): 983–1006.

Bergeron, S. (2003) 'The Post-Washington Consensus and Economic Representations of Women in Development at the World Bank', *International Feminist Journal of Politics*, 5(3): 397–419.

Bergeron, S. (2004) *Fragments of Development: Nation, Gender and the Space of Modernity*, Ann Arbor, MI: University of Michigan Press.

Bergeron, S. (2009) 'An Interpretive Analytics to Move Caring Labor Off the Straight Path', *Frontiers,* 30(1): 55–64.

Berkovitch, N. (1999) *From Motherhood to Citizenship: Women's Rights and International Organizations*, Baltimore, MD: Johns Hopkins University Press.

Berman, J. (2003) '(Un)Popular Strangers and Crises (Un)Bounded: Discourses of Sex-trafficking, the European Political Community and the Panicked State of the Modern State', *European Journal of International Relations*, 9: 37–86.

Bernal, V. (1994) 'Gender, Culture, and Capitalism: Women and the Remaking of Islamic "Tradition" in a Sudanese Village', *Comparative Studies in Society and History*, 36(1): 36–67.

Beveridge, F. and Nott, S. (2002) 'Mainstreaming: A Case for Optimism and Cynicism', *Feminist Legal Studies*, 10(3): 299–311.

Bharucha, R. (2000) 'Thinking Through Culture: A Perspective for the Millennium', in R. Thapar (ed.), *India: Another Millennium*, London: Penguin.

Biswas, S. (2002) 'The "New Cold War": Secularism, Orientalism and Postcoloniality', in G. Chowdhry and S. Nair (eds), *Power, Postcolonialism and International Relations*, London: Routledge.

Blackless, M., Charuvastra, A., Derryck, A., Fausto-Sterling, A., Lauzanne, K. and Lee, E. (2000) 'How Sexually Dimorphic Are We? Review and Synthesis', *American Journal of Human Biology*, 12(1): 151–66.

Blaydes, L and Lizner, D. (2007) 'The Political Economy of Women's Support for Fundamentalist Islam', Paper presented at the American Political Studies Association Annual Conference. Available at http://blaydes.bol.ucla.edu/Women.pdf.

Bleiker, R. (2001) 'The Aesthetic Turn in International Political Theory', *Millennium: Journal of International Studies*, 30(3): 509–33.

Bleiker, R. ([2009] 2012) *Aesthetics and World Politics*, New York: Palgrave.

Bleiker, R. and Hutchison, E. (2008) 'Fear No More: Emotions and World Politics', *Review of International Studies*, 34(1): 115–35.

Bloom, M. (2011) *Bombshell*, New York: Viking Press.

Bloul, R. (1993) 'Engendering Muslim Identities: De-Territorialization and Ethnicization Processes in France', *Gender Relations Project*, Canberra: Australian National University Press.

Blunt, A. and Rose, G. (1994) *Writing Women and Space: Colonial and Postcolonial Geographies*, New York: Guilford Press.

Bøås, M. and McNeill, D. (2003) *Multilateral Institutions: A Critical Introduction*, London: Pluto Press.

Boesten, J. (2007) 'Marrying Your Rapist: Domesticated War Crimes in Peru', in D. Pankhurst (ed.), *Gendered Peace. Women's Struggles for Post-War Justice and Reconciliation*, New York: Routledge.

Bordo, S. (2003) *Unbearable Weight: Feminism, Western Culture and the Body*, rev. edn, London and Berkeley, CA: University of California Press.

Borum, R. (2011) 'Radicalization into Violent Extremism II: A Review of Conceptual Models and Empirical Research', *Journal of Strategic Security*, 4(4): 37–62.

Boserup, E. (1970) *Women's Role in Economic Development*, New York: St. Martin's Press.

Bouvard, M. G. (1994) *Revolutionising Motherhood: The Mothers of the Plaza de Mayo*, Lanham, MD: Rowman & Littlefield.

Bracewell, W. (1996) 'Women, Motherhood, and Contemporary Serbian Nationalism', *Women's Studies International Forum*, 19(1–2): 25–33.

Brady, H. (2012) 'The Power of Precedents', *Australian Journal of Human Rights*, 18(2): 75–108.

Brah, A. and Phoenix, A. (2004) 'Ain't I A Woman? Revisiting Intersectionality', *Journal of International Women's Studies*, 5(3): 75–86.

Brahmini, L. et al. (2000), 'Report of the Panel on United Nations Peace Operations'. Available at http://www.un.org/peace/reports/peace_operations/ (accessed 9 February 2013).

Braidotti, R. (1996) 'Cyberfeminism With a Difference'. Available at http://www.let.uu.nl/womens_studies/rosi/cyberfem.htm (accessed 2 August 2013).

Braidotti, R., Charkiewicz, E., Hausler, S. and Wieringa, S. (1994) *Women, the Environment and Sustainable Development: Towards a Theoretical Synthesis*, London: Zed Books.

Brammertz, S. and Jarvis, J. (2010) 'Lessons Learned in Prosecuting Gender Crimes Under International Law: Experiences from the ICTY', in C. Eboe-Osuji (ed.), *Protecting Humanity: Essays in International Law and Policy in Honour of Navanethem Pillay*, Leiden and Boston, MA: Martinus Nijhoff Publishers.

Brassett, J. (2009) 'British Irony, Global Justice: A Pragmatic Reading of Chris Brown, Banksy and Ricky Gervais', *Review of International Studies*, 35: 219–45.

Braumann, R. (1993) 'When Suffering Makes a Good Story', in J. Francois (ed.), *Life, Death and Aid: The Medicines Sans Frontieres Report on World Crisis Intervention*, London: Routledge.

Bretherton, C. (1998) 'Global Environmental Politics: Putting Gender on the Agenda?', *Review of International Studies*, 24(1): 85–100.

Bretherton, C. (2003) 'Movements, Networks, Hierarchies: A Gender Perspective on Global Environmental Governance', *Global Environmental Politics*, 3(2): 103–19.

Briggs, L. (2003) 'Mother, Child, Race, Nation: The Visual Iconography of Rescue and the Politics of Transnational and Transracial Adoption', *Gender and History*, 15(2): 179–200.

Brittain, M. (2006) 'Benevolent Invaders, Heroic Victims and Depraved Villains: White Femininity in Media Coverage of the Invasion of Iraq', in K. Hunt and K. Rygiel (eds), *Engendering the War on Terror: War Stories and Camouflaged Politics*, London: Ashgate.

Broad, R. (ed.) (2002) *Global Backlash: Citizen Initiatives for a Just World Economy*, Lanham, MD: Rowman & Littlefield.

Brocklehurst, H. (2006) *Who's Afraid of the Children? Children, Conflict and International Relations*, Aldershot: Ashgate.

Brogan, B. (2002) 'Theresa Given Her Own Range of Shoes', *Daily Telegraph*, 22 November 2002. Available http://www.telegraph.co.uk/news/uknews/ 1413965/Theresa-given-her-own-range-of-shoes.html (accessed 15 April 2009).

Brown, C. (1992) *International Relations Theory: New Normative Approaches*, Hemel Hempstead: Harvester Wheatsheaf.

Brown, C. (1994) 'The Rights and Interests of Women in the People's Republic of China: Implementation of a New Law', in K. Dhirendra (ed.), *Modernizing China*, Leiden: Brill Academic Publishers.

Brown, C. (2002) *Sovereignty, Rights and Justice: International Political Theory Today*, Cambridge: Polity Press.

Brown, K. (2013) 'Gender and Global Counter-radicalization Efforts: Women and Emerging Counter-Terror Measures', in M. Satterthwaite and J. Huckerby (eds), *Gender, National Security, and Counter-Terrorism: Human Rights Perspectives*, Abingdon: Routledge.

Brown, W. (2001) *Politics out of History*, Princeton, NJ: Princeton University Press.

Brown, W. (2005) *Edgework: Critical Essays on Knowledge and Politics*, Princeton, NJ: Princeton University Press.

Browning, C. (1998) *Ordinary Men: Reserve Police Battalion 101 and the Final Solution in Poland*, New York: HarperPerennial.

Browning-Cole, E. and Coultrap-McQuin, S. (eds) (1992) *Explorations of Feminist Ethics: Theory and Practice*, Bloomington and Indianapolis, IN: Indiana University Press.

Brownmiller, S. (1975) *Against Our Will: Men, Women and Rape*, New York: Simon & Schuster.

Brunsdon, C. and Spigel, L. (eds) (2008) *Feminist Television Criticism A Reader*, 2nd edn, Maidenhead: Open University Press.

Brysk, A. (2004) 'Children Across Borders: Patrimony, Property, or Persons?', in A. Brysk and G. Shafir (eds), *People Out of Place: Globalization, Human Rights, and the Citizenship Gap*, New York and London: Routledge.

Brysk, A. and Shafir, G. (eds) (2004) *People Out of Place: Globalization, Human Rights, and the Citizenship Gap*, New York and London: Routledge.

Buckingham, S. (2004) 'Ecofeminism in the Twenty-First Century', *Geographical Journal*, 2: 146–54.

Bunch, C. (1990) 'Women's Rights as Human Rights: Towards a Re-Vision of Human Rights', *Human Rights Quarterly*, 12(4): 486–98.

Bunch, C. (1995) 'Transforming Human Rights from a Feminist Perspective', in J. Peters and A. Wolper (eds), *Women's Rights, Human Rights: International Feminist Perspectives*, London: Routledge.

Bureleigh, M. and Wipperman. W. (1991) *The Racial State: Germany 1933–1945*, Cambridge: Cambridge University Press.

Bush, G. W. (2001a) 'Remarks by the President Upon Arrival'. Available at http://georgewbush-whitehouse.archives.gov/news/releases/ 2001/09/20010916-2.html.

Bush, G. W. (2001b) 'President Discusses Economic Recovery in New York City'. Available at http://georgewbush-whitehouse.archives.gov/news/ (accessed 15 April 2009).

Bush, G. W. (2001c) 'President Rallies Troops at Travis Air Force Base'. Available at http://georgewbush-whitehouse.archives.gov/news/releases/2001/10/20011017-20.html (accessed 15 April 2009).

Bush, G. W. (2001d) 'President Signs Afghan Women and Children Relief Act', *Feminist Daily News Wire*, 12 December 2001. Available at http://feminist.org/news/newsbyte/uswirestory.asp?id=6016 (accessed 17 April 2009).

Bush, G. W. (2006) 'Press Conference by the President'. Available at http://www.whitehouse.gov/search/?keywords=Bush,%20G.W.%20(2006)%20%E2%80%98Press%20conference%20by%20the%20President (accessed 10 July 2008).

Bush, G. W., Powell C. and Ashcroft J. (2001) 'President Urges Readiness and Patience', *White House*, 15 September 2001. Available at http://georgewbush-whitehouse.archives.gov/news/releases/2001/ 09/20010915-4.html (accessed 7 December 2008).

Bush, L. (2001) 'Radio Address by Laura Bush to the Nation', Office of Mrs. Bush, 17 November 2001. Available at http://avalon.law.yale.edu/sept11/ fl_001.asp (accessed 17 April 2009).

Busia, A. (1993) 'Performance, Transcription and the Languages of the Self: Interrogating Identity as a "Post-Colonial" Poet', in S. M. James and A. Busia (eds), *Theorizing Black Feminisms: The Visionary Pragmatism of Black Women*, New York, Routledge.

Buss, D. and Herman, D. (2003) *Globalizing Family Values: The Christian Right in International Politics*, London, Minneapolis, MN: University of Minnesota Press.

Butalia, U. (1993) 'Community, State and Gender: On Women's Agency during Partition', *Economic and Political Weekly*, 24 April, 17:12–20.

Butalia, U. (2000) *The Other Side of Violence: Voices from the Partition of India*, Durham, NC: Duke University Press.

Butler, J. (1990) *Gender Trouble: Feminism and the Subversion of Identity*, London: Routledge.

Butler, J. (1993) *Bodies That Matter: On the Discursive Limits of 'Sex'*, London: Routledge.

Butler, J. (1999) *Gender Trouble: Feminism and the Subversion of Identity*, rev. edn, New York: Routledge.

Butler, J. (2004a) *Undoing Gender*, London and New York: Routledge.

Butler, J. (2004b) *Precarious Life: The Powers of Mourning and Violence*, London: Verso.

Byrne, B. (1996) 'Towards a Gendered Understanding of Conflict', *IDS Bulletin*, 27(3): 31–40.

Cagatay, N., Elson, D. and Grown, C. (eds) (1995) 'Gender, Adjustment and Macroeconomics', *World Development*, 23(11), 1827–36.

Caglar, G., Prügl, E. and Zwingel, S. (eds) (2013) *Feminist Strategies in International Governance*, London and New York: Routledge.

Caiazza, A. (2001) 'Why Gender Matters in Understanding 9/11: Women, Militarism and Violence', Briefing Paper, Institute for Women's Policy Research.

Cameron, A. and Palan, R. (2004) *The Imagined Economies of Globalization*, London: SAGE.

Campbell, D. (1992) *Writing Security: United States Foreign Policy and the Politics of Identity*, Manchester: Manchester University Press.

Caprioli, M. (2000) 'Gendered Conflict', *Journal of Peace Research*, 37: 53–68.

Caprioli, M. (2004a) 'Feminist IR Theory and Quantitative Methodology', *International Studies Review*, 6: 253–69.

Caprioli, M. (2004b) 'Democracy and Human Rights versus Women's Security: A Contradiction?', *Security Dialogue*, 35: 411–28.

Caprioli, M. and Boyer, M. A. (2001) 'Gender, Violence, and International Crisis', *Journal of Conflict Resolution*, 45: 503–18.

Caraway, T. (2006) 'The Political Economy of Feminization: From "Cheap Labor" to Gendered Discourses of Work', *Politics and Gender*, 1(3): 399–429.

Card, C. (ed.) (1991) *Feminist Ethics*, Lawrence, KS: University Press of Kansas.

Carney, G. (2003) 'Communicating or Just Talking: Gender Mainstreaming and the Communication of Global Feminism', *Women and Language*, 26: 52–60.

Carpenter, R. C. (2003) '"Women and Children First": Gender, Norms, and Humanitarian Evacuation in the Balkans 1991–95', *International Organization*, Fall, 57: 661–94.

Carpenter, R. C. (2005) 'Women, Children and Other Vulnerable Groups: Gender, Strategic Frames and the Protection of Civilians as a Transnational Issue', *International Studies Quarterly*, 49: 295–334.

Carpenter, R. C. (2006) *'Innocent Women and Children': Gender, Norms and the Protection of Civilians*, London: Ashgate.

Carpentier, N. (2007) 'Theoretical Frameworks for Participatory Media', in N. Carpentier, P. Pruulmann-Vengerfeldt, K. Nordenstreng, M. Hartmann, P. Vihalemm, B. Cammaerts and H. Nieminen (eds), *Media Technologies and Democracy in an Enlarged Europe*, Tartu, Estonia: Tartu University Press.

Carreiras, H. (2006) *Gender and the Military: Women in the Armed Forces of Western Democracies*, Abingdon and New York: Routledge.

Carson, R. (1962) *Silent Spring*, Boston, MA: Houghton-Mifflin.

Carter, C., Branston, G. and Allan, S. (eds) (1998) *News, Gender and Power*, London: Routledge.

Carver, T. (1996) *Gender is not a Synonym for Women*, London and Boulder, CO: Lynne Rienner.

Carver, T. (2007) 'GI Jane: What are the "Manners" that "Maketh a Man"?', *British Journal of Politics and International Relations*, 9(2): 313–17.

Castells, M. (1996) *The Rise of the Network Society: The Information Age: Economy, Society and Culture, Volume 1*, Oxford: Blackwell.

Castells, M. (2008) 'The New Public Sphere: Global Civil Society, Communication Networks, and Global Governance', *Annals of the American Academy of Political and Social Science*, 616(1): 78–93.

Castells, M. (2012) *Networks of Outrage and Hope: Social Movements in the Internet Age*, Cambridge: Polity Press.

Celis, K., Childs, S., Kantola, J. and Krook, M. L. (2008) 'Rethinking Women's Substantive Representation', *Representation*, 44(2), 99–110.

Chakma, M. (2012) 'Female Agri Workers Deprived of Statutory Benefits', *New Age*, 3 November. Available at http://www.newagebd.com/detail.php?date=2012-11-03&nid=28843#.UJiY8WllfiN.

Chamberlain, G. (2008) 'India is Split as Gandhi Daughter Shuns the Sari', *The Observer*, 17 August 2008. Available at http://www.guardian.co.uk/world/ 2008/aug/17/india.fashion/print (accessed 15 April 2009).

Chan, Stephen (2011) 'On the Uselessness of New Wars Theory: Lessons from Africa', in C. Sylvester (ed.), *Experiencing War*, London: Routledge.

Chang, G. (2000) *Disposable Domestics: Immigrant Women Workers in the Global Economy*, Cambridge: South End Press.

Chang K. and Ling, L. H. L. (2000) 'Globalization and Its Intimate Other: Filipina Domestic Workers in Hong Kong', in M. Marchand and A. Sisson Runyan (eds), *Gender and Global Restructuring*, London: Routledge.

Chant, S. (1997) 'Gender and Tourism Employment in Mexico and the Philippines', in M. T. Sinclair (ed.), *Gender, Work and Tourism*, London: Routledge.

Chant, S. (2002) 'Researching Gender, Families and Households in Latin America: From the 20th into the 21st Century', *Bulletin of Latin American Research*, 21(4): 545–75.

Chant, S. and Pedwell, C. (2008) *Women, Gender and the Informal Economy: An Assessment of ILO Research and Suggested Ways Forward*, Geneva: ILO.

Chappell, L. (2003) 'Women, Gender and International Institutions: Exploring New Opportunities at the International Criminal Court', *Policy Organisation and Society*, 22(1): 3–25.

Chappell, L. (2008) 'The International Criminal Court: A New Arena for Transforming Gender Justice', in Shirin M. Rai and Georgina Waylen (eds.), *Global Governance: Feminist Perspectives,* Basingstoke: Palgrave, pp. 160–184.

Charlesworth, H. and Chinkin, C. (2000) *The Boundaries of International Law*, Manchester: Manchester University Press.

Chatterjee, P. (1989) 'The Nationalist Resolution of the Women's Question', in K. Sangari and S. Vaid (eds), *Recasting Women: Essays in Colonial History*, New Delhi: Kali for Women.

Chatterjee, P. (1993) *Nationalist Thought and the Colonial World*, rev. edn, Minneapolis, MN: University of Minnesota Press.

Chen, M., Vanek, J. and Carr, M. (2004) *Mainstreaming Informal Employment and Gender in Poverty Reduction*, Ottawa: Commonwealth Secretariat/IDRC.

Chen, M., Vanek, J., Lund, F., Heintz, J. with Jhabvala, R. and Bonner, C. (2005) *Progress of the World's Women: Women, Work and Poverty*, New York: United Nations.

Chenoy, A. M. (2002) *Militarism and Women in South Asia*, New Delhi: Kali for Women.

Childs, M. (2006) 'Not Through Women's Eyes: Photo-Essays and the Construction of A Gendered Tsunami Disaster', *Disaster Prevention and Management*, 15(1): 202–12.

Childs, S. and Krook, M. L. (2006) 'Gender and Politics: The State of the Art', *Politics*, 26(1): 18–28.

Chinkin, C. (1999) 'Gender Inequality and International Human Rights Law', in A. Hurrell and N. Woods (eds), *Inequality, Globalisation, and World Politics*, Oxford: Oxford University Press.

Chinkin, C. (2004) 'Gender, International Legal Framework and Peace-Building', in K. Karamé (ed.), *Gender and Peace-building in Africa*, Oslo: NUPI.

Chinkin, C. (2009) 'Gender-Related Violence and International Criminal Law and Justice', in A. Cassese (ed.), *The Oxford Companion to International Criminal Justice*, Oxford: Oxford University Press.

Cho, S., Crenshaw, K. W. and McCall, L. (eds) (2013) 'Intersectionality: Theorizing Power, Empowering Theory', *Signs*, 38(4).

Chow, R. (1992) 'Postmodern Automatons', in J. Butler and J. W. Scott (eds), *Feminists Theorize the Political*, New York: Routledge.

Chowdhry, G. and Nair, S. (2002) 'Introduction: Power in a Postcolonial World: Race, Gender and Class in International Relations', in G. Chowdhry and S. Nair (eds), *Postcolonialism and International Relations: Reading Race, Gender and Class*, London and New York: Routledge.

Chowdhry, G. and Nair, S. (eds) (2002) *Power, Postcolonialism and International Relations: Reading Race, Gender And Class*, London and New York: Routledge.

Christiansen, F. and Rai, S. (1996) *Chinese Politics and Society: An Introduction*, London: Harvester Wheatsheaf.

Chukukere, G. C. (1995) *Gender Voices and Choices: Redefining Women in Contemporary African Fiction*, Enugu: Fourth Dimension Publications.

Ciscel, D. and Heath, J. (2001) 'To Market, to Market: Imperial Capitalism's Destruction of Social Capital and the Family', *Review of Radical Political Economics*, 33: 401–14.

Clapp, J. (2012) *Food*, Cambridge: Polity Press.

Clerc, S. (2000) 'Estrogen Brigades and "Big Tits" Threads: Media Fandom On-Line and Off', in D. Bell and B. Kennedy (eds), *The Cybercultures Reader*, London: Routledge.

Cochrane, K. (2007) 'Bush's War on Women', *New Statesman*, 29 January 2007. Available at http://www.newstatesman.com/print/200701290031 (accessed 15 April 2009).

Cockburn, C. (1985) *Machinery of Dominance: Women, Men and Technical Know-How*, London: Pluto Press.

Cockburn, C. (1998) *The Space Between Us: Negotiating Gender and National Identities in Conflict*, London: Zed Books.

Cockburn, C. (1999) 'Gender, Armed Conflict and Political Violence', Washington: World Bank. Available at http://www.genderandpeacekeeping.org/resources/3_Gender_Armed_Conflict_and_Political_Violence.pdf (accessed 15 April 2009).

Cockburn, C. (2001) 'The Gendered Dynamics of Armed Conflict and Political Violence', in C. Moser and F. C. Clark (eds), *Victims, Perpetrators Or Actors? Gender, Armed Conflict and Political Violence*, London: Zed Books.

Cockburn, C. (2004) 'The Continuum of Violence: A Gender Perspective on War and Peace', in W. Giles and J. Hyndman (eds), *Sites of Violence: Gender and Conflict Zones*, Berkeley, CA, Los Angeles and London: University of California Press.

Cockburn, C. (2007) *From Where We Stand: War, Women's Activism and Feminist Analysis*, London and New York: Zed Books.

Cockburn, C. (2010) 'Gender Relations as Causal in Militarization and War: A Feminist Standpoint', *International Feminist Journal of Politics*, 12(2): 139–57.

CODEPINK (2009) 'About Us'. Available at http://www.codepink4peace.org/article.php?list=type&type=3 (accessed 15 April 2009).

Coghlan, T. (2008) 'First British Woman and Three Special Forces Soldiers Killed in Afghanistan' *Daily Telegraph*, 18 June 2008. Available at http://www.telegraph.co.uk/news/newstopics/onthefrontline/2150869/First-British-woman-and-three-special-forces-soldiers-killed-in-Afghanistan.html (accessed 15 April 2009).

Cohan, S. and Hark, I. R. (eds) (1993) *Screening the Male: Exploring Masculinities in Hollywood Cinema*, London: Routledge.

Cohen, R. and Rai, S. M. (eds) (2000) *Global Social Movements*, London: Athlone Press.

Cohen, S. (2001) *States of Denial: Knowing about Atrocities and Suffering*, Cambridge: Polity Press.

Cohn, C. (1987) 'Sex and Death in the Rational World of Defense Intellectuals', *Signs: Journal of Women in Culture and Society*, 12(4): 687–718.

Cohn, C. (1990) '"Clean Bombs" and Clean Language', in J. B. Elshtain and S. Tobias (eds), *Women, Militarism and War: Essays in History, Politics and Social Theory*, Lanham, MD: Rowman & Littlefield.

Cohn, C. (1994) 'Wars, Wimps, and Women: Talking Gender and Thinking War', in M. Cooke and A. Wollacott (eds), *Gendering War Talk*, Princeton, NJ: Princeton University Press.

Cohn, C. (1998) 'Gays in the Military', in M. Zalewski and J. Parpart (eds), *The 'Man' Question in International Relations*, Boulder, CO: Westview Press.

Cohn, C. (2004) 'Feminist Peacemaking', *Women's Review of Books*, 21(5): 8–9.

Cohn, C. (2006) 'Motives and Methods: Using Multi-Sited Ethnography to Study US National Security Discourses', in B. A. Ackerly, M. Stern and Jacqui True (eds), *Feminist Methodologies for International Relations*, Cambridge: Cambridge University Press.

Cohn, C. (2008) 'Mainstreaming Gender in UN Security Policy: A Path to Political Transformation?', in S. M. Rai and G. Waylen (eds), *Global Governance: Feminist Perspectives*, Basingstoke and New York: Macmillan Palgrave.

Cohn, C., Kinsella, H. and Gibbings, S. (2004) 'Women, Peace and Security: Resolution 1325', *International Feminist Journal of Politics*, 6(1), 130–40.

Cohn, C. and Ruddick, S. (2004) 'A Feminist Ethical Perspective on Weapons of Mass Destruction', in Sohail H. Hashmi and Steven P. Lee (eds), *Ethics and Weapons of Mass Destruction: Religious and Secular Perspectives*, Cambridge, UK: Cambridge University Press, pp. 405–435.

Coleman, G. (2013) *Coding Freedom: The Ethics and Aesthetics of Hacking*, Princeton, NJ: Princeton University Press.

Collard, A. and Contrucci, J. (1988) *Rape of the Wild*, London: Women's Press.

Commonwealth of Australia (2007) 'Becoming an Australian Citizen' Barton ACT 2600: Attorney General's Department. Available at http://www.citizenship.gov.au/test/resource-booklet/citz-booklet-full-ver.pdf (accessed 15 April 2009).

Communalism Combat (2002) 'Inferno' *Communalism Combat*. Available at http://www.sabrang.com/cc/archive/comapril2002.pdf (accessed 15 April 2009).

Cone, C. A. (1995) 'Crafting Selves: The Lives of Two Mayan Women', *Annals of Tourism Research*, 22(2): 314–27.

Connell, R. W. (1987) *Gender and Power*, Cambridge: Polity Press.

Connell, R. W. (1995) *Masculinities*, Oxford: Polity Press.

Connell, R. W. (2002a) 'Masculinities, the Reduction of Violence and the Pursuit of Peace', in C. Cockburn and D. Zarkov (eds), *The Postwar Moment: Militaries, Masculinities and International Peacekeeping*, London: Lawrence & Wishart.

Connell, R. W. (2002b) *Gender*, Cambridge: Polity Press.

Connolly, C. (1991) 'Washing Our Linen: One Year of Women Against Fundamentalism', *Feminist Review*, 37: 65–72.

Connolly, W. E. (1991) *Identity/Difference: Democratic Negotiations of Political Paradox*, Ithaca, NY, and London: Cornell University Press.

Conquest, R. (1968) *The Great Terror: Stalin's Purge of the Thirties*, New York: Macmillan.

Conway, J. (2008) 'Geographies of Transnational Feminisms: The Politics of Place and Scale in the World March of Women's Social Politics', *International Studies in Gender, State and Society*, 15: 207–31.

Cook, J., Roberts, J. and Waylen, G. (eds) (2000) *Towards a Gendered Political Economy*, London: Macmillan.

Cooke, M. (1996) *Women and the War Story*, Berkeley, CA: University of California Press.

Cooke, M. and Woollacott, A. (eds) (1993) *Gendering War Talk*, Princeton, NJ: Princeton University Press.

Copelon, R. (1995) 'Gendered War Crimes: Reconceptualizing Rape in Time of War', in J. Peters and A. Wolper (eds), *Women's Rights, Human Rights*, London and New York: Routledge.

Copelon, R. (1998) 'Surfacing Gender: Reconceptualizing Crimes Against Women in Time of War', in L. A. Lorentzen and J. Turpin (eds), *The Women and War Reader*, London: New York University Press.

Copelon, R. (2000) 'Gender Crimes as War Crimes: Integrating Crimes against Women into International Criminal Law', *McGill Law Journal*, 46: 217–40.

Cortright, D. and Lopez, G. A. (eds) (2007) *Uniting Against Terror*, London: MIT Press.

Costanza-Chock, S. (2012) 'Mic Check! Media Cultures and the Occupy Movement', *Social Movement Studies*, 11(3–4): 375–85.

Cowburn, M. (2005) 'Hegemony and Discourse: Reconstructing the Male Sex Offender and Sexual Coercion by Men', *Sexualities, Evolution and Gender*, 7(3): 215–31.

Cox, R. (1992) 'Global Perestroika', in R. Miliband and L. Panitch (eds), *Social Register 1992, New World Order?* Available at http://socialistregister.com/node/33 (accessed 15 April 2009).

Cranny-Francis, A. (1990) 'Feminist Futures: A Generic Study', in A. Kuhn (ed.), *Alien Zone: Cultural Theory and Contemporary Science Fiction Cinema*, London: Verso.

Crawford, N. (2003) 'Feminist Futures: Science Fiction, Utopia, and the Art of Possibilities in World Politics', in J. Weldes (ed.), *To Seek Out New Worlds: Exploring Links Between Science Fiction and World Politics*, New York: Palgrave Macmillan.

Crawley, M. (2006) *Mr Sorkin Goes to Washington: Shaping the President on Television's The West Wing*, Jefferson, NC: McFarland.

Creed, B. (2000) 'Film and Psychoanalysis', in J. Hill and P. C. Gibson (eds), *Film Studies: Critical Approaches*, Oxford: Oxford University Press.

Creedon, P. J. (1993) *Women in Mass Communication*, London, Thousand Oaks, CA, and New Delhi: SAGE.

Crenshaw, K. (1995) 'Mapping the Margins: Intersectionality, Identity Politics, and Violence Against Women of Color', in K. Crenshaw, N. Gotanda, G. Peller and K. Thomas (eds), *Critical Race Theory: The Key Writing That Formed The Movement*, New York: New Press.

Cresswell, T. (1994) 'Putting Women in their Place: The Carnival at Greenham Common', *Antipode*, 26(1): 35–58.

Croll, E. J. (1981) 'Women in Rural Production and Reproduction in the Soviet Union, China, Cuba, and Tanzania: Socialist Development Experiences', *Signs*, 7(2): 361–74.

Crow, B. (ed.) (2000) *Radical Feminism: A Documentary Reader*, New York: New York University Press.

Cruz, O. and Guins, R. (2005) 'Entangling the Popular: An Introduction to Popular Culture: A Reader', in R. Guins and O. Z. Cruz (eds), *Popular Culture: A Reader*, London: SAGE.

Cryer, R., Friman, H., Robinson, D. and Wilmshurst, E. (2010) *An Introduction to International Criminal Law and Procedure*, Cambridge: Cambridge University Press.

Dahlberg L. and Siapiera E. (eds) (2007) *The Internet and Radical Democracy: Exploring Theory and Practice*, New York and London: Palgrave Macmillan.

Dal Secco, A. (2007) 'Truth and Reconciliation Commissions and Gender Justice', in D. Pankhurst (ed.), *Gendered Peace. Women's Struggles for Post-War Reconciliation and Justice*, New York: Routledge.

Dalby, S. (2008) 'Warrior Geopolitics: Gladiator, Black Hawk Down and The Kingdom of Heaven', *Political Geography*, 27: 439–55.

Daly, M. (1990) *Gyn/Ecology: The Metaethics of Radical Feminism*, reissued edn, Boston, MA: Beacon Press.

Daly, M. (2005) 'Gender Mainstreaming in Theory and Practice', *Social Politics: International Studies in Gender, State and Society*, 12(1): 447–59.

Danchev, A. and Lisle, D. (2009) 'Introduction: Art, Politics, Purpose', *Review of International Studies*, 35(4): 775–79.

Daniels, J. (2009). *Cyber Racism: White Supremacy Online and the New Attack on Civil Rights*. Lanham, MD: Rowman & Littlefield.

Darby, P. and Paolini, A. J. (1994) 'Bridging International Relations and International Relations', *Alternatives*, 19: 371–97.

Das, V. (1998) 'Official Narratives, Rumour and the Social Production of Hate', *Social Identities*, 1(1): 109–25.

Davids, T. and van Driel, F. (2005) 'Changing Perspectives', in T. Davids and F. van Driel (eds), *The Gender Question in Globalization: Changing Perspectives and Practices*, Aldershot and Burlington, VT: Ashgate.

Davies, G. (2006) 'How Many Have Died in Iraq?', *The Guardian*, 19 October 2006.

Davis, K. (2005) 'The Global Localization of Feminist Knowledge: Translating Our Bodies, Ourselves', in T. Davids and F. van Driel (eds), *The Gender Question in Globalization: Changing Perspectives and Practices*, Aldershot and Burlington, VT: Ashgate.

D'Costa, B. (2011) *Nationbuilding, Gender and War Crimes in South Asia*, New York: Taylor & Francis.

de Abreu, A. A. (1998) 'Mozambican Women Experiencing Violence', in M. Turshen and C. Twagiramariya (eds), *What Women Do in Wartime. Gender and Conflict in Africa*, London: Zed Books.

de Bary, T. and Weiming, T. (eds) (1980) *Confucianism and Human Rights*, New York: Columbia University Press.

de la Rey, C. and McKay, S. (2006) 'Peacebuilding as a Gendered Process', *Journal of Social Issues*, 62(1), 141–53.

de Mel, N. (2007), *Militarising Sri Lanka: Popular Culture, Memory and Narrative in the Armed Conflict*, New Delhi: SAGE.

de Sousa Santos, B. (2006) *The Rise of the Global Left: The World Social Forum and Beyond*, London and New York: Zed Books.

de Soyza, N. (2011) *Tamil Tigress*, Sydney: Allen & Unwin.

Dean, R. D. (2001) *Imperial Brotherhood: Gender and the Making of Cold War Foreign Policy*, Amherst, MA: University of Massachusetts Press.

Debusscher, P. and True, J. (2008) 'Lobbying the EU for Gender-Equal Development', in J. Orbie and L. Tortell (eds), *The European Union and the Social Dimension of Globalisation*, New York: Routledge.

Deere, C. D. and Leon, M. (2003) 'The Gender Asset Gap: Land in Latin America', *World Development*, 31(6): 925–47.

Defense and Advanced Research Projects Agency (DARPA). Available at http://www.darpa. mil/ (accessed 15 April 2009).

Defrancisco, V. P., Laware, M. R. and Palczewski, C. H. (2003) 'The Home Side of Global Feminism: Why Hasn't the Global Found a Home in the U.S.?', *Women and Language*, 26: 100–109.

Deibert, R. (2000) 'International Plug 'n' Play? Citizen Activism, the Internet, and Global Public Policy', *International Studies Perspectives*, 1(3): 255–72.

Delgado, J. V. and Zwarteveen, M. (2007) 'The Public and Private Domain of the Everyday Politics of Water: The Constructions of Gender and Water Power in the Andes of Peru', *International Feminist Journal of Politics*, 9(4): 503–11.

della Porta, D. (ed.) (2007) *The Global Justice Movement: Cross-National and Transnational Perspectives*, Boulder, CO, and London: Paradigm Publishers.

Democracy Now! (2008) 'Sarah Palin and the Wasilla Church of God', *Democracy Now! The War and Peace Report*, 9 September 2008. Available at http://www.democracynow. org/2008/9/9/sarah_palin_and_the_wasila_church (accessed 15 April 2009).

Denskus, T. (2007) 'Peacebuilding Does Not Build Peace', *Development in Practice*, 17(4): 6546–662.

Der Derian, J. (1997) 'Virtual Security: Technical Oversight, Simulated Foresight, and Political Blindspots in the Infosphere', in J. M. Beier and S. Mataija (eds), *Cyberspace and Outerspace: Transitional Challenges for Multilateral Verification in the 21st Century*, Toronto: York Centre for International and Security Studies.

Der Derian, J. (2003) 'War as Game', *Brown Journal of International Affairs*: 37–48.

Der Derian, J. (2009) *Virtuous War: Mapping the Military-Industrial-Media-Entertainment-Network*, 2nd edn, New York: Routledge.

Dershowitz, A. M. (2008) '24 and the Use of Torture to Obtain Preventive Intelligence', in Minter, R. (ed.), *Jack Bauer for President: Terrorism and Politics in 24*, Dallas, TX: Benbella Books.

Desmarais, A. A. (2003) 'The Via Campesina: Peasant Women on the Frontiers of Food Sovereignty', *Canadian Woman Studies*, 23(1): 140–45.

Deuber-Mankowsky, A. (2008) 'The Phenomenon of Lara Croft', in M. Ryan (ed.), *Cultural Studies: An Anthology*, Malden, MA, and Oxford: Wiley Blackwell.

Di Nicola, A. (2007) 'Researching into Human Trafficking: Issues and Problems', in M. Lee (ed.), *Human Trafficking*, Cullompton: Willan Publishing.

Diamond, I. and Quinby, L. (1988) *Feminism and Foucault: Reflections on Resistance*, Boston, MA: Northeastern University Press.

Dicken, P. (1992) *Global Shift: Industrial Change in a Turbulent World*, London: Harper & Row.

Dickinson, T. D. and Schaeffer, R. K. (2001) *Fast Forward: Work, Gender, and Protest in a Changing World*, Lanham: Rowman and Littlefield.

Dietz, M. G. (2003) 'Current Controversies in Feminist Theory', *Annual Review of Political Science*, 6: 399–431.

Dimond, J. P. (2010). *Feminist HCI for Real: Designing Technology in Support of Social Movement*, PhD Dissertation. Available at http://jilldimond.com/wp-content/uploads/2012/08/dimond-dissertation.pdf (accessed 2 August 2013).

Division for the Advancement of Women (DAW) (2007) 'Convention on the Elimination of All Forms of Discrimination Against Women'. Available at http://www.un.org/womenwatch/daw/cedaw/ (accessed 15 April 2009).

Doane, M. A. (1991) *Femmes Fatales: Feminism, Film Theory, and Psychoanalysis*, New York: Routledge.

Dobash, R. P. and Dobash, R. E. (2004) 'Women's Violence to Men in Intimate Relationships: Working on a Puzzle', *British Journal of Criminology*, 44(3): 324–49.

Doezema, Jo (2002) 'Who Gets to Choose? Coercion, Consent and the UN Trafficking Protocol', *Gender and Development*, 10(1): 20–27.

Dogra, N. (2011) 'The Mixed Metaphor of "Third World Women": Gendered Representations by International Development NGOs', *Third World Quarterly*, 32(2): 333–48.

Dolan, C. (2002) 'Collapsing Masculinities and Weak States – A Case Study of Northern Uganda', in F. Cleaver (ed.), *Masculinities Matter! Men, Gender and Development*, London: Zed Books.

Donato, K., Gabaccia, D., Holdaway, J., Manalansan IV, M. and Pessar, P. (2006) 'A Glass Half Full? Gender in Migration Studies', *International Migration Review*, 40(1): 3–26.

Donnelly, J. (1993) *International Human Rights*, Boulder, CO: Westview Press.

Donovan, P. (2006) 'Gender Equality, Now or Never: A New UN Agency for Women', Office of the UN Special Envoy for AIDS in Africa, June 2006. Available at http://www.icn.ch/waa_wom_agency_pp.pdf (accessed 11 April 2009).

Doty, R. L. (1996) *Imperial Encounters: The Politics of Representation in North-South Relations*, Minneapolis, MN: University of Minnesota Press.

Douglas, N. (1981) *Structure and Change in Economic History*, New York: Norton.

Douglas, S. J. (1987) *Inventing American Broadcasting: 1899–1922*. Baltimore, MD: Johns Hopkins University Press.

Douglass, M. (2006) 'Global Householding in Pacific Asia', *International Development Planning Review*, 28(4): 421–45.

Dower, N. (2007) *World Ethics: The New Agenda*, 2nd edn, Edinburgh: Edinburgh University Press.

Downing, J. (2001) *Radical Media: Rebellious Communication and Social Movements*, Thousand Oaks, CA: SAGE.

Doyle, M. W. and Sambanis, N. (2000) 'International Peacebuilding: A Theoretical and Quantitative Analysis', *American Political Science Review*, 94(4): 779–801.

Dudink, S. and Hagemann, K. (2004) 'Masculinity in Politics and War in the Age of Democratic Revolutions 1750–1850', in S. Dudink, K. Hagemann and J. Tosh (eds), *Masculinities in Politics and War: Gender in Modern History*, Manchester and New York: Manchester University Press.

Dudrah, R. K. (2006) *Bollywood: Sociology Goes to the Movies*, New Delhi: SAGE.

Dufour, P. and Giraud. I. (2007) 'The Continuity of Transnational Solidarities in the World March of Women, 2000 and 2005: A Collective Identity-Building Approach', *Mobilization*, 12(3): 307–28.

Duijzings, G. (2000) *Religion and the Politics of Identity in Kosovo*, London: C. Hurst.

Dunbar-Hester, C. (2010) 'Beyond "Dudecore"? Challenging Gendered and "Raced" Technologies Through Media Activism', *Journal of Broadcasting & Electronic Media*, 54(1): 121–35.

Dyrkton, J. (1996) 'Cool Runnings: The Coming of Cyberreality in Jamaica', in R. Shields (ed.), *Cultures of Internet: Virtual Spaces, Real Histories, Living Bodies*, London, Thousand Oaks, CA, New Delhi: SAGE.

Dyvik, S. L. (2010) 'Gendered War and Reconstruction: The Politics of Representation and the 'Liberation' of Afghan Women', unpublished paper presented on the panel 'Gender and War: Transnational Perspectives' at the SGIR Conference, Stockholm, September 2010.

Easlea, B. (1983) *Fathering the Unthinkable: Masculinity, Scientists and the Nuclear Arms Race*, London: Pluto Press.

Edwards, A. (2009) 'Human Security and the Rights of Refugees: Transcending Territorial and Disciplinary Borders', *Michigan Journal of International Law* 3: 763–807.

Ehrlich, P. and Ehrlich, A. (1990) *The Population Explosion*, London: Hutchinson.

Eichenberg, R. C. (2003) 'Gender Differences in Public Attitudes toward the Use of Force by the United States, 1990–2003', *International Security*, 28: 110–1.

Eisenstein, Z. (2004) *Against Empire: Feminisms, Racism and the West*, London: Zed Books.

Eisenstein, Z. (2007) *Sexual Decoys: Gender, Race and War in Imperial Democracy*, London: Zed Books.

El Bushra, J. (2000) 'Transforming Conflict: Some Thoughts on a Gendered Understanding of Conflict Processes', in S. Jacobs, R. Jacobson and J. Marchbank (eds), *States of Conflict. Gender, Violence and Resistance*, London: Zed Books.

Elam, D. (1994) *Feminism and Deconstruction: Ms. En Abyme*, New York: Routledge.

Elias, J. (2005) 'The Gendered Political Economy of Control and Resistance on the Shop-floor of the Multinational Firm: A Case Study from Malaysia', *New Political Economy*, 10(2): 203–22.

Elias, J. (2008) 'Hegemonic Masculinities, the Multinational Corporation, and the Developmental State: Constructing Gender in "Progressive" Firms', *Men and Masculinities*, 10(4): 405–21.

Elmhirst, R. and Resurreccion, B. P. (2008) *Gender, Environment and Natural Resource Management: New Dimensions, New Debates*, London: Earthscan.

Elshtain, J. B. (1987) *Women and War*, Chicago, IL: University of Chicago Press.

Elshtain, J. B. (1994) 'Thinking about Women and International Violence', in P. R. Beckman and F. D'Amico (eds), *Women, Gender and World Politics: Perspectives, Policies and Prospects*, Westport, CT: Bergin and Garvey.

Elshtain, J. B. (1995) *Women and War*, 2nd edn, London and Chicago, IL: University of Chicago Press.

Elshtain, J. B. (2003) *Just War Against Terror: The Burden of American Power in a Violent World*, New York: Basic Books.

Elson, D. (ed.) (1991) *Male Bias in the Development Process*, Manchester: Manchester University Press.

Elson, D. (1996) 'Gender-Aware Analysis and Development Economics', in K. P. Jameson and C. K. Wilber (eds), *The Political Economy of Development and Underdevelopment*, 6th edn, New York: McGraw-Hill.

Elson, D. and Pearson, R. (1981) 'The Subordination of Women and the Internationalization of Factory Production', in K. Young, C. Wolkowitz and R. McCullagh (eds), *Of Marriage and the Market*, London: CSE Books.

Elster, J. (1999) *Alchemies of the Mind: Rationality and the Emotions*, Cambridge: Cambridge University Press.

Empower Foundation (2012) *Hit and Run. Sex Workers Research on Anti Trafficking in Thailand*. Available at: http://www.empowerfoundation.org/sexy_file/Hit%20and%20Run%20%20RATSW%20Eng%20online.pdf

Enarson, E. (2006) 'Women and Girls Last? Averting the Second Post-Katrina Disaster', in *Understanding Katrina: Perspectives from the Social Sciences*, Social Science Research Council. Available at http://understandingkatrina.ssrc.org/Enarson/ (accessed 20 June 2013).

Enarson, E. and Meyreles, L. (2004) 'International Perspectives on Gender and Disaster', *International Journal of Sociology and Social Policy*, 24(10/11): 49–93.

Engle, S. (2006) *Human Rights and Gender Violence: Translating International Law in Local Justice*, Chicago, IL: University of Chicago Press.

English, R. (2009) *Terrorism: How to Respond*, Oxford: Oxford University Press.

Engman, M., Onodera, O. and Pinali, E. (2007) *Export Processing Zones: Past and Future Role in Trade and Development*, OECD Trade Policy Working paper No. 53. Available at http://www.olis.oecd.org/olis/2006doc.nsf/ LinkTo/NT0000922E/$FILE/JT03227583. PDF (accessed 15 April 2009).

Enloe, C. (1983) *Does Khaki Become You?: The Militarization of Women's Lives*, London: Pandora.

Enloe, C. (1989) *Banana, Beaches and Bases: Making Feminist Sense of International Politics*, Berkeley, CA: University of California Press.

Enloe, C. (1990) 'Womenandchildren: Making Feminist Sense of the Persian Gulf Crisis', *The Village Voice*, 25 September.

Enloe, C. (1993) *The Morning After. Sexual Politics at the End of the Cold War*, Berkeley, CA: University of California Press.

Enloe, C. (1996) 'Margins, Silences and Bottom Rungs: How to Overcome the Underestimation of Power in the Study of International Relations', in S. Smith, K. Booth and M. Zalewski (eds), *International Theory: Positivism and Beyond*, Cambridge: Cambridge University Press.

Enloe, C. (1998) *Does Khaki Become You? The Militarization of Women's Lives*, 2nd edn, London: Pandora.

Enloe, C. (2000a) *Bananas, Beaches and Bases: Making Feminist Sense of International Politics*, 2nd edn, Berkeley, CA: University of California Press.

Enloe, C. (2000b) *Maneuvers. The International Politics of Militarizing Women's Lives*, London: University of California Press.

Enloe, C. (2002) 'Demilitarization – Or More of the Same? Feminist Questions to Ask in the Postwar Moment', in C. Cockburn and D. Zarkov (eds), *The PostWar Moment, Militaries, Masculinities and International Peacekeeping*, London: Lawrence & Wishart.

Enloe, C. (2004a) *The Curious Feminist*, Berkeley, CA: University of California Press.

Enloe, C. (2004b) 'Wielding Masculinity Inside Abu Ghraib: Making Feminist Sense of an American Military Scandal', *Asian Journal of Women's Studies*, 10: 89–102.

Enloe, C. (2007) *Globalization and Militarism: Feminists Make the Link*, Plymouth and Lanham, MD: Rowman & Littlefield.

Enloe, C. and Puechguirbal, N. (2004) 'Failing to Secure the Peace: Practical Gendered Lessons from Haiti & Iraq', paper presented at the Boston Consortium on Gender, Security and Human Rights, Fletcher School of Law and Diplomacy, Tufts University, 26 Oct.

Epicurus (1964) *Letters, Principal Doctrines and Vatican Sayings*, New York: Pearson.

Epp, M. (1999) 'Heroes or Yellow-bellies: Masculinity and the Conscientious Objector', *Journal of Mennonite Studies*, 17: 107–17.

ESA (Entertainment Software Association) (2013) 2013 Sales, Demographic and Usage Data: Essential Facts About the Computer and Video Game Industry. Available at www.theesa.com/facts/pdfs/ESA_EF_2013.pdf (accessed 30 August 2013).

Eschle, C. and Bice, M. (2010) *Making Feminist Sense of the Global Justice Movement*, Lanham, MD: Rowman & Littlefield.

Eubanks, V. (2011) *Digital Dead End: Fighting for Social Justice in the Information Age*. Cambridge, MA: MIT Press.

European Parliament (2008) *Gender Equality and Women's Empowerment in Development Cooperation*. Available at http://www.oecd.org/dataoecd/ 56/46/28313843.pdf (accessed 15 April 2009).

Europol (2009) 'TE-SAT: EU Terrorism Situation and Trend Report', The Hague: European Police Office.

Evans, J. and Hall, S. (1999) 'What is Visual Culture?', in J. Evans and S. Hall (eds), *Visual Culture: The Reader*, London: SAGE.

Fahy, T. (ed.) (2005) *Considering Aaron Sorkin: Essays on the Politics, Poetics and Sleight of Hand in the Films and Television Series*, Jefferson, NC: McFarland.

Falk, R. (2004) 'Citizenship and Globalism: Markets, Empire and Terrorism', in A. Brysk and G. Shafir (eds), *People Out of Place: Globalization, Human Rights, and the Citizenship Gap*, New York: Routledge.

Faludi, S. (2007) *The Terror Dream: What 9/11 Revealed about America*, London: Atlantic Press.

Farr, V. (2003) 'The Importance of a Gender Perspective to Successful Disarmament, Demobilization and Reintegration Processes', *Disarmament Forum*, Geneva: UNIDIR. Available at http://www.unidir.ch/pdf/articles/pdf-art1995.pdf (accessed 15 April 2009).

Feinberg, L. (1993) *Stone Butch Blues*, Ann Arbor, MI: Firebrand Books.

Feminist Majority Foundation (n.d.) 'The Women's Treaty: CEDAW', Feminist Majority Foundation. Available at http://www.feminist.org/global/ issue.asp?issue=cedaw (accessed 15 April 2009).

Fenton, N. and Barassi V. (2011) 'Alternative Media and Social Networking Sites: The Politics of Individuation and Political Participation', *Communication Review*, 14(3): 179–96.

Ferber, M. and Nelson, J. (eds) (2003) *Feminist Economics Today: Beyond Economic Man*, Chicago, IL: University of Chicago Press.

Ferguson, K. (2002) 'This Species Which is Not One: Identity Practices in Star Trek: Deep Space Nine', *Strategies: Journal of Theory, Culture and Politics*, 15: 181–95.

Ferguson, L. (2007) 'Production, Consumption and Reproduction in Global Political Economy: The Case of Tourism Development in Central America', unpublished PhD thesis, University of Manchester.

Ferguson, L. (2008) 'Reproductive Provisioning and "Everyday Life" in Global Political Economy', Institute for Political and Economic Governance (IPEG) Working Paper No. 32. Available at http://www.bisa-ipeg.org/papers/ 32%20Ferguson.pdf (accessed 10 April 2009).

Ferguson, L. (2010) 'Interrogating "Gender" in Development Policy and Practice: The World Bank, Tourism and Microenterprise in Honduras', *International Feminist Journal of Politics,* 12(1): 3–24.

Ferguson, L. (2011) 'Tourism, Consumption and Inequality in Central America', *New Political Economy,* 16(3): 347–371.

Fine, B. (2001) 'Neither the Washington Nor the Post-Washington Consensus: An Introduction', in B. Fine, C. Lapavitsas and J. Pincus (eds), *Neither Washington Nor Post-Washington Consensus: Challenging Development Policy in the Twenty-First Century*, London and New York: Routledge.

Finnane, A. (2000) 'Dead Daughters, Dissident Sons, and Human Rights in China', in A. M. Hilsdon, M. Macintyre, V. Mackie and M. Stivens (eds), *Human Rights and Gender Politics: Asia Pacific Perspectives*, London: Routledge.

Finnemore, M. and Sikkink, K. (1998) 'International Norm Dynamics and Political Change', *International Organization*, 52: 887–917.

Fisher, J. (1998) 'Renee Epelbaum: Standing up to Terror', *The Guardian*, 13 February 1998.

Fiske, J. (1989) *Understanding Popular Culture*, London: Routledge.

Flanagan, M. (2006) 'Making Games for Social Change', *AI and Society*, 20: 493–505.

Floro, M. and Dymski, G. (2000) 'Financial Crisis, Gender, and Power: An Analytical Framework', *World Development*, 28(7): 1269–83.

Fogarty, B. E. (2000) *War, Peace and the Social Order*, Boulder, CO, and Oxford: Westview Press.

Food and Agricultural Organization (United Nations) (2011) *The State of Food and Agriculture 2010–11: Women in Agriculture: Closing the Gender Gap*. Rome: FAO. Available at http://www.fao.org/docrep/013/i2050e/i2050e.pdf.

Food and Agricultural Organization (United Nations) (2012) *The State of Food Insecurity in the World 2012*. Rome: FAO. Available at http://www.fao.org/docrep/016/i3027e/i3027e.pdf.

Foot, R. (2000) *Rights Beyond Borders: The Global Community and the Struggle over Human Rights in China*, Oxford: Oxford University Press.

Forbes Martin, S. and Tirman, J. (eds) (2009) *Women, Migration and Conflict: Breaking a Deadly Cycle*, Dordrecht, Heidelberg, London and New York: Springer.

Fordham, M. H. (1998) 'Making Women Visible in Disasters: Problematizing the Private Domain', *Disasters*, 22(2): 126–43.

Forsythe, D. (2002) *Human Rights in International Relations*, Cambridge: Cambridge University Press.

Foster, E. A. (2011) 'Sustainable Development: Problematising Normative Constructions of Gender within Global Environmental Governmentality', *Globalisations*, 8(2): 135–49.

Foucault, M. (1977) *Discipline and Punish*, trans. A. Sheridan, New York: Vintage.

Foucault, M. (1988) 'Technologies of the Self', in L. Martin, H. Guttman and P. Hutton (eds), *Technologies of the Self: A Seminar with Michel Foucault*, Amherst, MA: University of Massachusetts Press.

Foucault, M. (1994) '*Omnes et Singulatim:* Toward a Critique of Political Reason', in J. D. Faubion (ed.), *The Essential Works of Foucault*, New York: New Press.

Francis, B. (2002) 'Relativism, Realism and Feminism: An Analysis of Some Theoretical Tensions in Research on Gender Identity', *Journal of Gender Studies*, 11(1): 39–54.

Franke, K. M. (2006) 'Gendered Subjects of Transitional Justice', *Columbia Journal of Gender and Law*, 15(3): 813–27.

Franklin, M. I. (2001) 'InsideOut: Postcolonial Subjectivities and Everyday Life Online', *International Feminist Journal of Politics*, 3(3): 387–422.

Franklin, M. I. (2002) 'Reading Walter Benjamin and Donna Haraway in the Age of Digital Reproduction', *Information, Communication and Society*, 5(4): 591–624.

Franklin, M. I. (2004) *Postcolonial Politics, the Internet, and Everyday Life: Pacific Traversals Online*, London and New York: Routledge.

Franklin, M. I. (2005) *Gender Advocacy at the World Summit on the Information Society: Preliminary Observations*, Research Report for the Ford Foundation, Media, Arts, and Culture Portfolio. Available at http://www.genderit.org/upload/ad6d215b74e2a8613f-0cf5416c9f3865/Consultancy_1_.FF.WSIS.Report.Final.pdf (accessed 15 April 2009).

Franklin, M. I. (2007a) 'NGOs and the "Information Society": Grassroots Advocacy at the UN – a cautionary tale', *Review of Policy Research*, 24(4): 309–30.

Franklin, M. I. (2007b) 'Democracy, Postcolonialism, and Everyday Life: Contesting the 'Royal We' Online', in L. Dahlberg and E. Siapera (eds), *The Internet and Radical Democracy: Exploring Theory and Practice*, New York and London: Palgrave Macmillan.

Franklin, M. I. (2012) 'Being Human and the Internet; Against Dichotomies', *Journal of Information Technology: Organization, Management, Information and Systems,* 27(4), 315–318.

Franklin, M. I. (2013a) *Digital Dilemmas: Power, Resistance and the Internet*. New York: Oxford University Press.

Franklin, M. I. (2013b) 'How Does the Way We Use the Internet Make a Difference?', in M. Zehfuss and J. Edkins (eds), *Global Politics: A New Introduction*, 2nd edn, New York: Routledge.

Fraser, N. and Gordon, L. (1997) 'A Genealogy of "Dependency": Tracing a Keyword of the Welfare State', in *Justice Interruptus: Critical Reflections on the 'Postsocialist' Condition*, New York: Routledge.

Freeman, C. (2000) *High Tech and High Heels in the Global Economy: Women, Work, and Pink Collar Identities in the Caribbean*, Durham, NC: Duke University Press.

Freeman, J. (1972) 'The Tyranny of Structurelessness', *The Second Wave*, 2(1): 20. Available at http://struggle.ws/hist_texts/structurelessness.html (accessed 15 August 2013).

Friedman, J. (2005) *China's Urban Transition*, Minneapolis, MN: University of Minnesota Press.

Friedman, J. (2007) 'Directing Gender Buzz', *Los Angeles Times*. Available at http://articles.latimes.com/2007/feb/19/business/fi-women19 (accessed 16 July 2008).

Friedman, T. (1999) *The Lexus and the Olive Tree*, London: HarperCollins.

Fukuyama, F. (1989) 'The End of History', *National Interest*. Available at http://ps321.community.uaf.edu/files/2012/10/Fukuyama-End-of-history-article.pdf.

Fuller, C. (1996) *Caste Today*, Delhi: Oxford University Press.

Furedi, F. (1997) *Population and Development: A Critical Introduction*, New York: St. Martin's Press.

Fuss, D. (1989) *Essentially Speaking: Feminism, Nature and Difference*, London: Routledge.

G. I. Jane (1997) Caravan Pictures, directed by Ridley Scott.

GAATW (Global Alliance Against Trafficking in Women) (2010) *Beyond Borders: Exploring Trafficking's Links to Gender, Migration, Labour, Globalisation and Security*, GAATW Working Paper Series. Available at http://www.gaatw.org/publications/WP_on_Globalisation.pdf

Gabriel, R. and Neal, L. A. (2002) 'Post-Traumatic Stress Disorder Following Military Combat or Peace Keeping', *British Medical Journal*, 324: 340–41.

Gajjala, R. and Ju Oh, Y. (2012) *Cyberfeminism 2.0*, New York: Peter Lang.

Galtung, J. (1969) 'Violence, Peace and Peace Research', *Journal of Peace Research*, 6(3): 167–91.

Galtung, J. (1975) *Essays in Peace Research, Volume 1*, Copenhagen: Eljers.

Galtung, J. (1990) 'Cultural Violence', *Journal of Peace Research*, 27(3): 291–305.

Galtung, J. (1996) *Peace by Peaceful Means: Peace and Conflict, Development and Civilization*, Oslo: International Peace Research Institute.

Gans-Boriskin, R. and Tisinger, R. (2005) 'The Bushlet Administration: Terrorism and War on The West Wing', *Journal of American Culture*, 28: 100–13.

Gardiner, J. K. (ed.) (2002) *Masculinity Studies and Feminist Theory*, New York: Columbia University Press.

Garrett, L. (2005) 'Women of the West Wing: Gender Stereotypes in the Political Fiction', in T. Fahy (ed.), *Considering Aaron Sorkin: Essays on the Politics, Poetics and Sleight of Hand in the Films and Television Series*, Jefferson, NC: McFarland.

Gavey, N. (2005) *Just Sex? The Cultural Scaffolding of Rape*, New York and Hove: Routledge.

Gawerc, M. I. (2006) 'Peace-Building: Theoretical and Concrete Perspectives', *Peace & Change*, 31(4): 435–78.

Geisler, G., Keller, B. and Norman, A-L. (1999) 'WID/Gender Units and the Experience of Gender Mainstreaming in Multilateral Organisations: Knights on White Horses?', Report Submitted to the Norwegian Ministry of Foreign Affairs by Chr. Michelsen Institute.

Gellner, E. (1983) *Nations and Nationalism*, Oxford: Blackwell.

Gellner, E. (1998) *Nationalism*, London: Phoenix.

Gendercide Watch (2000) Case study: The European Witch-hunts, c. 1450–1750, and Witch-hunts Today. Available at http://www.gendercide.org/case_witchhunts.html (accessed 12 December 2013).

Gentry, C. E. (2013) 'Patriarchal Terrorism', *International Feminist Journal of Politics* Annual Conference, Brighton.

George, A. and Bennett, A. (2005) *Case Studies and Theory Development in the Social Sciences*, Cambridge, MA: Belfer Centre for Science and International Affairs.

Gerbner, G., Mowlana, H. and Nordenstreng, K. (eds) (1993) *The Global Media Debate: Its Rise, Fall, and Renewal*, Norwood, NJ: Ablex Publishing Corporation.

Ghosh, N. (2007) 'Women and the Politics of Water: An Introduction', *International Feminist Journal of Politics*, 9(4): 443–54.

Ghosh, R. A., Glott, R., Krieger, B. and G. Robles (2002) *Free/Libre and Open Source Software: Survey and Study. Deliverable D18: Final Report. Part IV: Survey of Developers,* International Institute of Infonomics, University of Maastricht and Berlecon Research GmbH.

Giacomello, G. and Ericksson J. (eds) (2009) 'The Forum: Who Controls the Internet? Beyond the Obstinacy or Obsoleteness of the State', *International Studies Review*, 11(1): 205–30.

Gibson, J. J. (1977) 'The Theory of Affordances', in R. Shaw and J. Bransford (eds), *Perceiving, Acting and Knowing*, Hillsdale, NJ: Erlbaum.

Gibson, J. W. (1994) *Warrior Dreams: Paramilitary Culture in Post-Vietnam America*, New York: Hill & Wang.

Gibson-Graham, J. K. (1996) *The End Of Capitalism (As We Knew It): A Feminist Critique Of Political Economy*, Oxford: Blackwell.

Giddens, A. (1990) *The Consequences of Modernity*, Cambridge: Polity Press.

Giles, W. (2013). 'Women Forced to Flee' in C. Cohn (ed.), *Women and Wars,* Cambridge: Polity Press.

Giles, W. and Hyndman, J. (2004) 'Introduction. Gender and Conflict in a Global Context', in W. Giles and J. Hyndman (eds), *Sites of Violence. Gender and Conflict Zones*, London: University of California Press.

Gilligan, C. (1982) *In a Different Voice: Psychological Theory and Women's Development*, Cambridge: Cambridge University Press.

Githens-Mazer, J. and Lambert, R. (2010) 'Why Conventional Wisdom on Radicalization Fails', *International Affairs*, 86(4): 889–901.

Givhan, R. (2005) 'Condoleezza Rice's Commanding Clothes', *Washington Post*, 25 February 2005. Available at http://www.washingtonpost.com/wp-dyn/articles/A51640-2005 Feb24.html (accessed 15 April 2009).

Global Alliance Against Trafficking in Women (GAATW) (2007) *Collateral Damage. The Impact of Anti-Trafficking Measures on Human Rights Around the World*, Bangkok: GAATW. Available at http://www.soros.org/ initiatives/health/focus/sharp/articles_publications/publications/collateraldamage_20070927/GAATW%20Collateral%20Damage.pdf (accessed 15 April 2009).

Goetz, A.-M. (ed.) (1995a) 'Getting Institutions Right for Women', *IDS Bulletin*, 26(3): 33–53.

Goetz, A.-M. (1995b) 'The Politics of Integrating Gender to State Development Processes: Trends, Opportunities and Constraints in Bangladesh, Chile, Jamaica, Mali, Morocco, and Uganda', Occasional Paper No. 2. Geneva, Switzerland: UNRISD.

Goetz, A.-M. and Sandler, J. (2006) 'Should We Swap Gender?', paper presented at the Annual Convention of the International Studies Association, March, San Diego.

Gökarıksel, B. and Mitchell, K. (2005) 'Veiling, Secularism and the Neoliberal Subject: National Narratives and Supranational Desires in Turkey and France', *Global Networks*, 5(2): 147–65.

Goldhagen, D. (1997) *Hitler's Willing Executioners: Ordinary Germans and the Holocaust*, New York: Vintage.

Goldstein, J. S. (2001) *War and Gender: How Gender Shapes the War System and Vice Versa*, Cambridge: Cambridge University Press.

Goldstein, P. (2008) 'Film Directing is Still a Man's World', *Los Angeles Times*. Available at http://articles.latimes.com/2008/may/20/entertainment/et-goldstein20 (accessed 15 April 2009).

González, J. (2000) 'The Appended Subject: Race and Identity as Digital Assemblage', in B. E. Kolko, L. Nakamura and G. B. Rodman (eds), *Race in Cyberspace*, New York and London: Routledge.

Gottlieb, R. and Joshi, A. (2010) *Food Justice*, Cambridge: MIT Press.

Gray, C. H. (1997) *Postmodern War: The New Politics of Conflict*, New York: Guilford Press.

Gray, J. (2002) *False Dawn: The Delusions of Global Capitalism*, London: Granta.

Grewal, G. (2001) 'Dislocating Cultures: Identities, Traditions and Third-World Feminism', *Hypatia: A Journal of Feminist Philosophy*, 16: 102–106.

Grewal, I. (2005) *Transnational America: Feminisms, Diasporas, Neoliberalisms*, Durham, NC: Duke University Press.

Grewal, I. and Kaplan, C. (eds) (1994) *Scattered Hegemonies: Postmodernity and Transnational Feminist Practices*, Minneapolis, MN: University of Minnesota Press.

Grewal, K. (2010) 'Rape in Conflict; Rape in Peace: Questioning the Revolutionary Potential of International Criminal Justice for Women's Human Rights', *Australian Feminist Law Journal*, 33: 57–79.

Grey, R. and Chappell, L. (2012) 'Prosecuting Sex Crimes in the ICC's First Trial: One Step Forwards and One Step Backwards', *Human Rights Defender*, 20(3): 5–8.

Grey, R. and Shepherd, L. (2012) 'Stop Rape Now? Masculinity, Responsibility and Conflict-Related Sexual Violence', *Men & Masculinities*, 16(1): 115–35.

Griffin, P. (2007) 'Sexing the Economy in a Neoliberal World Order', *British Journal of Politics and International Relations*, 9(2): 220–38.

Griffin, S. (1978) *Woman and Nature: The Roaring Inside Her*, San Francisco: Sierra Club Books.

Gripsrud, J. (2000) 'Film Audiences', in J. Hill and P. C. Gibson (eds), *Film Studies: Critical Approaches*, Oxford: Oxford University Press.

Grosz, E. (1994) *Volatile Bodies: Towards a Corporeal Feminism*, Bloomington, IN: Indiana University Press.

Grotius, H. [1625] (2001) *The Rights of War and Peace*, New York: Cosimo Classics.

Grovogui, S. (2002) 'Postcolonial Criticism: International Reality and Modes of Inquiry', in G. Chowdhry and S. Nair (eds), *Power, Postcolonialism and International Relations: Reading Race, Gender and Class*, London and New York: Routledge.

Grown, C., Elson, D. and Çagatay, N. (eds) (2000) 'Growth, Trade, Finance, and Gender Inequality', *World Development*, 28(7): 1211–30.

Guardian, The (2013) 9 July.

Guerrilla Girls. (2012) 'Posters/Actions: Do Women STILL Have to be Naked to Get Into the Museum?' Available at http://www.guerrillagirls.com/posters/ nakedthroughtheages.shtml (accessed 26 June 2013).

Guha, R. (2004) 'Past and Present: The Spread of the Salwar', *The Hindu*, 24 October. Available at http://www.hindu.com/mag/2004/10/24/stories/2004102400380300.htm (accessed 15 April 2009).

Gullace, N. F. (2002) *The Blood of Our Sons: Men, Women, and the Renegotiation of British Citizenship During the Great War*, New York: Palgrave Macmillan.

Gunawardana, Samanthi (2007) 'Perseverance, Struggle and Organization in Sri Lanka's Export Processing Zones: 1978–2003', in Kate Bronfenbrenner (ed.), *Global Unions: Challenging Transnational Capital Through Cross-Border Campaigns*, Ithaca, NY: Cornell University Press.

Gurumurthy, A. (2003) 'A Gender Perspective to ICTs and Development: Reflections towards Tunis'. Available at http://www.worldsummit2003.de/ en/web/701.htm (accessed 15 April 2009).

Gurumurthy, A. and Singh, P. J. (2012) 'Reclaiming Development in the Information Society', in C. Wichterich (ed.), *In Search of Economic Alternatives for Gender and Social Justice: Voices from India,* Brussels: WIDE/ITforChange.

Gusterson, H. (1998) *Nuclear Rites: A Weapons Laboratory at the End of the Cold War,* Berkeley, CA: University of California Press.

Gutierrez, M. (ed.) (2003) *Macro-Economics: Making Gender Matter–Concepts, Policies and Institutional Change in Developing Countries,* London: Zed Books.

Hague, E. (1997) 'Rape, Power and Masculinity: The Construction of Gender and National Identities in the War in Bosnia-Herzegovina', in R. Lentin (ed.), *Gender and Catastrophe,* London: Zed Books.

Halbert, D. (2004) 'Shulamith Firestone: Radical Feminism and Visions of the Information Society', *Information, Communication and Society,* 7(1): 115–35.

Halbert, D. J. (2006) 'Shulamith Firestone: Radical Feminism and Visions of the Information Society', *Information, Communication & Society,* 7(1): 115–35.

Hale, S. (2001) 'Liberated, But Not Free, Women in Post-War Eritrea', in S. Meintjes, A. Pillay and M. Turshen (eds), *The Aftermath: Women in Post-Conflict Transformation,* London and New York: Zed Books.

Hall, S. (1999) 'Part III: Introduction', in J. Evans and S. Hall (eds), *Visual Culture: The Reader,* London: SAGE.

Halley, J. (2006) *Split Decisions: How and Why to Take a Break from Feminism,* Princeton, NJ: Princeton University Press.

Hamber, B. (2003) *Flying Flags of Fear: The Role of Fear in the Process of Political Transition,* paper presented at the Risk, Complex Crises and Social Futures conference, Amman, Jordan, 11–13 October 2003.

Hamber, B., Nageng, D. and O'Malley, G. (2000) 'Telling it Like it is: Understanding the Truth and Reconciliation Commission from the Perspective of Survivors', *Psychology in Society,* 26: 18–42.

Hannan-Andersson, C. (1995) 'Moving Positions Forward: Strategies for Gender and Development Cooperation', in E. Friedlander (ed.), *Look at the World Through Women's Eyes: Plenary Speeches from the NGO Forum, Beijing '95,* NGO Forum on Women, Beijing '95, New York: Women Ink.

Hansen, L. (2000) 'The Little Mermaid's Silent Security Dilemma and the Absence of Gender in the Copenhagen School', *Millennium: Journal of International Studies,* 29(2): 285–306.

Hansen, L. (2001) 'Feminism in the Fascist Utopia', *International Feminist Journal of Politics,* 3: 275–83.

Hansen, L. (2006) *Security as Practice: Discourse Analysis and the Bosnian War,* Abingdon: Routledge.

Haq, F. (2007) 'Militarism and Motherhood: Women of the Lashkar-e-Tayyaba', *Signs,* 32(4): 1023–46.

Haralanova, C. (2013) 'Hacktivism: The Art of Practicing Life and Computer Hacking for Feminist Activism', *Dpi Magazine* 27. Available at http://dpi.studioxx.org/en/hacktivism-art-practicing-life-and-computer-hacking-feminist-activism#sthash.bFN3zCUq.dpuf (accessed 2 August 2013).

Haraway, D. (1990) 'A Manifesto for Cyborgs: Science, Technology, and Socialist Feminism in the 1980s', in L. Nicholson (ed.), *Feminism/Postmodernism,* New York and London: Routledge.

Haraway, D. (1991) *Simians, Cyborgs, and Women,* New York: Routledge.

Haraway, D. (1992) *Primate Visions: Gender, Race, and Nature in the World of Modern Science,* New York and London: Verso.

Haraway, D. (1997a) 'Gender for a Marxist Dictionary: the Sexual Politics of a Word', in L. McDowell and J. Sharp (eds), *Space, Gender, Knowledge: Feminist Readings*, London, New York, Sydney and Auckland: Arnold.

Haraway, D. (1997b) *Modest_Witness@Second_Millennium.FemaleMan© Meets_Onco-Mouse™: Feminism and Technoscience*, New York and London: Routledge.

Harcourt, W. (ed.) (1999) *Women@Internet: Creating New Cultures in Cyberspace*, London: Zed Books.

Harcourt, W. (ed.) (1999) *Women@Internet: Creating New Cultures in Cyberspace*, London: Zed Books.

Hardt, M. and Negri, A. (2000) *Empire*, Cambridge, MA, and London: Harvard University Press.

Harris, J. (2003) 'Dreams of Global Hegemony and the Technology of War', *Race and Class*, 45(2): 54–67.

Harris, P. (1999) 'Hundreds Burnt to Death in Tanzanian Witch-hunt', *Sunday Telegraph*, 22 August 1999.

Harvey, D. (1989) *The Condition of Postmodernity: An Enquiry into the Origins of Cultural Change*, Cambridge, MA, and Oxford: Blackwell.

Hasan, Z. (1989) 'Minority Identity, Muslim Women Bill Campaign and the Political Process', *Economic and Political Weekly*, 7 January 1989, xxiv(1): 44–50.

Hass, N. (2005) 'Hollywood's New Old Girls' Network', *New York Times*. Available at http://www.nytimes.com/2005/04/24/movies/24hass.html (accessed 15 April 2009).

Hastings, A. (1997) *The Construction of Nationhood; Ethnicity, Religion and Nationalism*, Cambridge: Cambridge University Press.

Hattenstone, S. (2009) 'Myra, Margaret and Me' *The Guardian*, 21 February 2009. Available at http://www.guardian.co.uk/artanddesign/2009/feb/21/marcus-harvey-margaret-thatcher (accessed 15 April 2009).

Hawkesworth, M. (2004) 'The Semiotics of Premature Burial: Feminism in a Postfeminist Age', *Signs: Journal of Women in Culture and Society*, 29(4): 961–85.

Hawkesworth, Mary E. (2006) *Globalization and Feminist Activism,* Lanham: Rowman & Littlefield.

Hawthorne, S. and Winter, B. (eds) (2003) *After Shock: September 11, 201 Global Feminist Perspectives,* Vancouver: Raincoast Books.

Hayles, N. K. (1999) *How We Became Posthuman: Virtual Bodies in Cybernetics, Literature, and Informatics*, Chicago, IL, and London: University of Chicago Press.

Haynes, J. (2005) 'Religion and International Relations After "9/11"', *Democratization*, 12(3): 398–413.

Hayward, S. (2006) *Cinema Studies: The Key Concepts*, 3rd edn, Abingdon: Routledge.

Head, J. (2008) 'Thai School Offers Transsexual Toilet', BBC News. Available at http://news.bbc.co.uk/1/hi/world/asia-pacific/7529227.stm (accessed 15 April 2009).

Heger, H. (1972) *The Men with the Pink Triangle*, Hamburg: Merlin-Verlag.

Hekman, S. (1995) *Moral Voices, Moral Selves: Carol Gilligan and Feminist Moral Theory*, Cambridge: Polity Press.

Held, D. (1995) *Democracy and the Global Order*, London: Polity Press.

Held, V. (1993) *Feminist Morality: Transforming Culture, Society and Politics*, Chicago, IL: University of Chicago Press.

Held, V. (ed.) (1995) *Justice and Care: Essential Readings in Feminist Ethics*, Boulder, CO: Westview Press.

Held, V. (2006) *The Ethics of Care: Personal, Political, and Global*, Oxford: Oxford University Press.

Hellekson, K. and Busse, K. (eds) (2006) *Fan Fiction and Fan Communities in the Age of the Internet: New Essays*, Jefferson, NC: McFarland.

Heller, D. A. (2005) *The Selling of 9/11: How a National Tragedy Became a Commodity*, New York: Palgrave Macmillan.

Hemmings, C. (2005) 'Telling Feminist Stories', *Feminist Theory*, 6(2): 115–39.

Hemmings, C. (2011) *Why Stories Matter: The Political Grammar of Feminist Theory*, Durham, NC, and London: Duke University Press.

Henwood, F., Kennedy, H. and Miller, M. (eds) (2001) *Cyborg Lives? Women's Technobiographies*, York: Raw Nerve Books.

Héritier, F. (2002) *Masculin/Féminin II, Dissoudre la Hiérarchie*, Paris: Editions Odile Jacob.

Herman, E. S. and McChesney R. (1997) *The Global Media – The New Missionaries of Corporate Capitalism*, London and Washington, DC: Cassell.

Hermes, J. (2005) *Re-Reading Popular Culture*, Malden, MA: Blackwell.

Hesford, W. (2005) '*Kairos* and the Geopolitical Rhetorics of Global Sex Work and Video Advocacy', in W. E. Hesford and W. Kozol (eds), *Just Advocacy? Women's Human Rights, Transnational Feminisms and the Politics of Representation*, New Brunswick: Rutgers University Press.

Hettne, B., Inotai, A. and Sunkel, O. (eds) (1999) *Globalism and the New Regionalism*, New York: St. Martin's Press.

Higate, P. (2007) 'Peacekeepers, Masculinities, and Sexual Exploitation', *Men and Masculinities*, 10(1): 99–119.

Higate, P. and Henry, M. (2004) 'Engendering (In)security in Peace Support Operations', *Security Dialogue*, 35: 481–98.

Higate, P. and Hopton, J. (2004) 'War, Militarism and Masculinities', in R. W. Connell, J. Hearn and M. Kimmel (eds), *The Handbook of Studies on Men and Masculinities*, New York: SAGE.

Hilfrich, F. (2003) 'Manliness and "Realism": The Use of Gendered Tropes in the Debates on the Philippine-American and on the Vietnam War', in J. C. E. Gienow-Hecht and F. Schumacher (eds), *Culture and International History*, New York: Berghahn Books.

Hill, F. and Poelhman-Doumbouya, S. (2001) 'Women and Peace in the United Nations', *New Routes, A Journal of Peace Research and Action*, special issue, 6(3). Available at http://www.life-peace.org/sajt/filer/pdf/New_Routes/ nr200103.pdf (17 April 2009).

Hill, K. and Hughes, J. (1998) *Cyberpolitics: Citizen Activism in the Age of the Internet*, Oxford: Rowman & Littlefield.

Hilsdon, A.-M. (1998) 'The Good Life: Cultures of Migration and Transformation of Overseas Workers in the Philippines', *Pilipinas*, 29: 49–62.

Hintjens, M. H. (2001) 'When Identity becomes Knife: Reflecting on the genocide in Rwanda', *Ethnicities*, 1(1): 25–55.

Hirschmann, N. (1989) *The Subject of Liberty: Toward A Feminist Theory of Freedom*, Princeton, NJ: Princeton University Press.

Ho, P. and Edmonds, R. L. (eds) (2008) *China's Embedded Activism: Opportunities and Constraints of a Social Movement*, London: Routledge.

Hobbes, T. [1651](1994) *Leviathan*, Indianapolis, IN: Hackett.

Hobsbawm, E. and Ranger, T. (1983) *The Invention of Tradition*, Cambridge: Cambridge University Press.

Hochschild, A. (1998) *King Leopold's Ghost: A Story of Greed, Terror, and Heroism in Colonial Africa*, Boston, MA: Houghton-Mifflin.

Hoffman, B. (1999) 'Terrorism Trends and Prospects', in I. Lesser, J. Arquilla, B. Hoffman, D. F. Ronfeldt and M. Zanini, *Countering the New Terrorism*, Santa Monica, CA: Rand Corporation.

Hoffman, B. (2002) 'Rethinking Terrorism and Counterterrorism Since 9/11', *Studies in Conflict and Terrorism*, 25(5): 303–16.

Hoffman, B. (2006) *Inside Terrorism*, New York: Columbia University Press.

Holderness, M. (1998) 'Who are the World's Information Poor?', in B. Loader (ed.), *Cyberspace Divide: Equality, Agency and Policy in the Information Society*, London and New York: Routledge.

Hollows, J. (2000) *Feminism, Femininity and Popular Culture*, Manchester: Manchester University Press.

Hollows, J. and Moseley, R. (eds) (2006) *Feminism in Popular Culture*, Oxford: Berg.

Home Office (2009) *The United Kingdom's Strategy for Countering International Terrorism, 2009 (Prevent)*, London: HMSO.

Hoogland, R. C. (2002) 'Fact and Fantasy: The Body of Desire in the Age of Posthumanism', *Journal of Gender Studies*, 11(3): 213–31.

Hooper, B. (1998) '"Flower Vase and Housewife": Women and Consumerism in Post-Mao China', in K. Sen and M. Stivens (eds), *Gender and Power in Affluent Asia*, London: Routledge.

Hooper, C. (1999) 'Masculinities, IR and the "Gender Variable": A Cost-Benefit Analysis for (Sympathetic) Gender Skeptics', *Review of International Studies*, 25: 475–91.

Hooper, C. (2001) *Manly States: Masculinities, International Relations and Gender Politics*, New York: Columbia University Press.

Horn, D. M. (2003) 'Feminist Approaches to International Relations' in M. Hawkesworth and M. Kogan (eds), *Encyclopedia of Government and Politics*, 2nd edn, London: Routledge.

Horne, J. (2004) 'Masculinity in Politics and War in the Age of Nation-States and World Wars, 1850–1950', in D. Stefan, K. Hagemann and J. Tosh (eds), *Masculinities in Politics and War: Gender in Modern History*, Manchester and New York: Manchester University Press.

Hoskyns, C. and Rai, S. (2007) 'Recasting the Global Political Economy: Counting Women's Unpaid Work', *New Political Economy*, 12(3): 297–317.

House of Commons Home Affairs Committee (2005) 'Terrorism and Community Relations: Sixth Report of Session 2004–2005 vol. 1', HC165-I London: The Stationery Office Ltd. Available at http://www.publications.parliament.uk/pa/cm200405/cmselect/cmhaff/165/165.pdf

Howells, R. (2003) *Visual Culture*, Cambridge: Polity Press.

Hozic, A. (2001) *Hollyworld: Space, Power, and Fantasy in the American Economy*, Ithaca, NY: Cornell University Press.

Hudson, V. M. and den Boer, A. M. (2004) *Bare Branches: The Security Implications of Asia's Surplus Male Population*, Cambridge, MA: MIT Press.

Human Rights in China (HRIC) (1998) 'Report on the Implementation of CEDAW in the People's Republic of China'. Available at http://hrichina.org/fs/ downloadables/reports/cedaw_98.pdf?revision_id=14195 (accessed 15 April 2009).

Human Rights Watch (2008a) *Courting History: The Landmark International Criminal Court's First Years*. New York: Human Rights Watch. Available at http://www.hrw.org/sites/default/files/reports/icc0708webwcover.pdf (accessed 16 July 2013).

Human Rights Watch (2008b) *As If I'm Not Human: Abuses against Asian Domestic Workers in Saudi Arabia*. Human Rights Watch. Available at http://www.hrw.org/sites/default/files/reports/saudiarabia0708_1.pdf (accessed 11 August 2013).

Human Security Commission (HSC) (2005) *The Human Security Report 2005*, Oxford: Oxford University Press.

Hunt Alternatives Fund and International Alert (2004) *Inclusive Security, Sustainable Peace: A Toolkit for Advocacy and Action*. Available at http://www.huntalternatives.org/pages/87_inclusive_security_toolkit.cfm (accessed 9 February 2013).

Hunt, K. (2002) 'The Strategic Co-optation of Women's Rights: Discourse in the War on Terrorism', *International Feminist Journal of Politics*, 4(1): 116–21.

Hunt, K. (2005) 'Challenging and Reinforcing Dominant Myths: Transnational Feminists Use the Internet to Contest the War on Terrorism', in J. Leatherman and J. Webber (eds), *Charting Transnational Democracy: Beyond Global Arrogance*, New York: Palgrave Macmillan.

Hunt, K. (2006) 'Embedded Feminism and the War on Terror', in K. Hunt and K. Rygiel (eds), *Engendering the War on Terror: War Stories and Camouflaged Politics*, Aldershot: Ashgate.

Hunt, K. and Rygiel, K. (eds) (2006) *(En)gendering the War on Terror*, Aldershot: Ashgate.

Hurd, E. S. (2004) 'The Political Authority of Secularism in International Relations', *European Journal of International Relations*, 10(2): 235–62.

Hurtado, A. (1996) *The Color of Privilege: Three Blasphemies on Race and Feminism*, Ann Arbor, MI: University of Michigan Press.

Hussain, S. (2005) 'The War on Terror and the Issue of Muslim Women', in N. Lahoud and A. H. Anthony (eds), *Islam in World Politics*, London: Routledge.

Hutchings, K. (2000) 'Towards a Feminist International Ethics', *Review of International Studies*, Special Issue, 26(5): 111–30.

Hutchings, K. (2004) 'From Morality to Politics and Back Again: Feminist International Ethics and the Civil-Society Argument', *Alternatives*, 29: 239–64.

Hutchings, K. (2007a) 'Feminist Perspectives on a Planetary Ethic', in W. M. Sullivan and W. Kymlicka (eds), *The Globalization of Ethics*, Cambridge: Cambridge University Press.

Hutchings, K. (2007b) 'Feminist Ethics and Political Violence', *International Politics*, 44(3): 90–106.

Hutchings, Kimberly (2011) 'Gendered Humanitarianism: Reconsidering the Ethics of War', in Christine Sylvester (ed.) *Experiencing War*, New York, NY: Routledge.

Hutchison, E. (2014) 'A Global Politics of Pity? Disaster Imagery and the Emotional Construction of Solidarity after the 2004 Asian Tsunami', *International Political Sociology*, 8(1) : 1–9.

Hyndman, J. (2004) 'Mind the Gap: Bridging the Feminist and Political Geography', *Political Geography*, 23(3): 307–22.

Ignatieff, M. (1998) *The Warrior's Honor. Ethnic War and the Modern Conscience*, London: Chatto & Windus.

Ilaiah K. (2003) 'Why I am not a Hindu: A Sudra Critique of Hindutva Philosophy', in A. Rao (ed.), *Gender and Caste: Issues in Contemporary Indian Feminism*, Delhi: Kali for Women.

Imam, A. (1997) 'Engendering African Social Sciences: An Introductory Essay', in *Engendering African Social Sciences*, Dakar: CODESRIA.

Inayatullah, N. and Blaney, D. L. (2004) *International Relations and the Problem of Difference*, New York: Routledge.

Incite! Women of Color Against Violence (ed.) (2006) *Color of Violence: The Incite Anthology*, Cambridge: South End Press.

Indra, D. (1999) *Engendering Forced Migration: Theory and Practice*, New York and Oxford: Berghahn Books.

Inness, S. A. (ed.) (2004) *Action Chicks: New Images of Tough Women in Popular Culture*, New York: Palgrave Macmillan.

Inter-American Development Bank (IDB) (2006) 'Statement from the President of the IDB on International Women's Day', 8 March 2006. Available at http://www.iadb.org/news/articledetail.cfm?language=ENandartid=2872 (accessed 15 April 2009).

International Assessment of Agricultural Knowledge, Science and Technology for Development (IAASTD) (2008) *Agriculture at a Crossroads: Global Report*. Available at http://www.unep.org/dewa/agassessment/reports/IAASTD/EN/Agriculture%20at%20a%20Crossroads_Global%20Report%20(English).pdf.

International Commission on Intervention and State Sovereignty (ICISS) (2001) *The Responsibility to Protect*, Ottawa: International Development Research Centre. Available at http://www.iciss.ca/pdf/Commission-Report.pdf (accessed 15 April 2009).

International Criminal Court, *Bashir* (Second Arrest Warrant Decision). 12 July 2010, Pre-Trial Chamber I. ICC-02/05-01/09-94.

International Criminal Court, *Bemba* (Arrest Warrant Decision). 10 June 2008, Pre-Trial Chamber III. ICC-01/05-01/08-14-tENG.

International Criminal Court, *Kenyatta* (Confirmation of Charges Decision). 23 January 2012, Pre-Trial Chamber II. ICC-01/09-02/11-382-Red.

International Criminal Court, *Lubanga* (Separate Opinion of Judge Benito). 14 March 2012, Trial Chamber I. ICC-01/04-01/06-2842.

International Criminal Court, *Lubanga* (Trial Judgment). 14 March 2012, Trial Chamber I. ICC-01/04-01/06-2842.

International Criminal Court, *Mbarushimana* (Arrest Warrant Application). 20 August 2010. ICC-01/04-01/10-11-Red2.

International Criminal Court, *Mbarushimana* (Arrest Warrant Decision). 28 September 2010, Pre-Trial Chamber I. ICC-01/04-01/10-1.

International Criminal Court, *Mbarushimana* (Confirmation of Charges Decision). 16 December 2011, Pre-Trial Chamber I. ICC-01/04-01/10-465-Red.

International Criminal Court, *Mbarushimana* (Document Containing the Charges). 3 August 2011. ICC-01/04-01/10-330-AnxA-Red.

International Criminal Tribunal for Rwanda, *Akayesu* (Trial Judgment). 2 September 1998, Trial Chamber I. ICTR-96-4-T.

International Crisis Group (2006) 'Beyond Victimhood: Women's Peacebuilding in Sudan, Congo and Uganda', Africa Report No. 112, 28 June 2006. Available at http://www.peacewomen.org/resources/1325/PDF/beyond_victimhood_ PB.pdf (accessed 15 April 2009).

International Labour Organization (ILO) (2001) 'Human Resources Development, Employment and Globalization in the Hotel, Catering and Tourism Sector', Geneva: International Labour Office. Available at http://www.ilo.org/public/ english/dialogue/sector/techmeet/tmhct01/tmhct-r.pdf (accessed 10 April 2009).

International Labour Organization (ILO) (2005) *A Global Alliance Against Forced Labour*, Geneva: ILO.

International Labour Organization (ILO) (2007) 'Global Employment Trends for Women Brief', *ILO Working Paper*, March 2007, Geneva: International Labour Office.

International Labour Organisation (ILO) (2013) *International Perspectives on Women and Work in Hotels, Catering and Tourism*, Geneva: ILO.

International Migration Review (2006) 'Special Issue on "Gender and Migration Revisited"', *International Migration Review*, 40(1).

International Military Tribunal for the Far East, IMTFE Judgment, 12 November 1948, in Pritchard, J. and Zaide, S. M. (eds), *The Tokyo War Crimes Trial, Volume 22*, New York: Blackwell.

International Military Tribunal, IMT Judgment, 1 October 1946.

International Monetary Fund (IMF) (2007) 'IMF-World Bank Report Calls for Greater Attention to Gender Equality and Fragile States to Reach Global Targets by 2015', International Monetary Fund, 13 April 2007. Available at http://www.imf.org/external/np/sec/pr/2007/pr0773.htm (accessed 15 April 2009).

International Research and Training Institute for the Advancement of Women (INSTRAW) (2007a) 'Remittances', Gender, Remittances and Development Working Paper 4, United Nations INSTRAW. Available at http://www.un-instraw.org/en/publications/working-papers/index.php (accessed 15 April 2009).

International Research and Training Institute for the Advancement of Women (INSTRAW) (2007b) 'Global Care Chains', Gender, Remittances and Development Working Paper 2,

United Nations INSTRAW. Available at http://www.un-instraw.org/en/publications/working-papers/index.php (accessed 15 April 2009).

International Research and Training Institute for the Advancement of Women (INSTRAW) (2007c) Virtual Discussion on Gender Training for Security Sector Personnel. Available at http://www.un-instraw.org/en/ index.php?option.

International Telecommunication Union (ITU) (2006) 'WSIS: Promoting the Goals of the United Millennium Declaration', International Telecommunication Union. Available at http://www.itu.int/osg/spu/wsis-themes/UNMDG/ index.html (accessed 15 April 2009).

International Telecommunication Union (ITU) (2009) *WSIS Forum 2009*, Web Portal. Available at http://www.itu.int/wsis/implementation/2009/forum/geneva/index.html (accessed 15 April 2009).

Internet Rights and Principles Coalition (2013) The Charter of Human Rights and Principles for the Internet Booklet, IRP Coalition (UN Internet Governance Forum). Available at http://internetrightsandprinciples.org/site/wp-content/uploads/2014/02/IRP_booklet_2nd-Edition14Nov2013.pdf

Internet World Stats (2012) *Internet Usage Statistics—The Internet Big Picture*. Available at http://www.internetworldstats.com/stats.htm (accessed 13 May 2014).

Inter-Parliamentary Union (2000) 'Women in National Parliaments'. Available at http://www.ipu.org/wmn-e/arc/classif151200.htm (accessed 9 February 2013).

Inter-Parliamentary Union (2011) 'Women in National Parliaments'. Available at http://www.ipu.org/wmn-e/classif.htm (accessed 9 February 2013).

IOM (2011) World Migration Report: Communicating Effectively About Migration, Geneva: IOM. Available at http://www.iom.int/cms/en/sites/iom/home/what-we-do/migration-policy-and-research/migration-research-1/world-migration-report/world-migration-report-2011.html (accessed 4 May 2014).

Irwin, W. (ed.) (2001) *The Matrix and Philosophy: Welcome to the Desert of the Real*, Chicago and La Salle, IL: Open Court.

Isikoff, M. and Hosenball, M. (2008) 'Terror Watch – The New Face of Terror – Is Al Qaeda Recruiting Westerners to Get Past U.S. Security?', *Newsweek*, 30 March 2008. Available at http://www.newsweek.com/id/130155/page/1 (accessed 15 April 2009).

Jabri, V. (1999) 'Explorations of Difference in Normative International Relations', in V. Jabri and E. O'Gorman (eds), *Women, Culture and International Relations*, Boulder, CO: Lynne Rienner.

Jabri, V. (2006a) 'Shock and Awe: Power and the Resistance of Art', *Millennium: Journal of International Studies*, 34(3): 819–39.

Jabri, V. (2006b) 'War, Security and the Liberal State', *Security Dialogue*, 37(1): 47–64.

Jackson, C. (ed.) (2001) *Men at Work: Labour, Masculinities, Development*, London: Frank Cass.

Jackson, R. (2005) *Writing the War on Terrorism: Language, Politics, and Counter-Terrorism*, Manchester: Manchester University Press.

Jackson, R. Breen Smyth, M. and Gunning, J. (2009) *Critical Terrorism Studies: A New Research Agenda*, London: Routledge.

Jacobsen, M. and Bruun, O. (eds) (2000) *Human Rights and Asian Values: Contesting National Identities and Cultural Representations in Asia*, London: Routledge.

Jacobs, S., Jacobson, R. and Marchbank, J. (eds) (2000) *States of Conflict. Gender, Violence and Resistance*, London: Zed Books.

Jacoby, T. (2006) 'From the Trenches: Dilemmas of Feminist IR Fieldwork', in B. A. Ackerly, M. Stern and J. True (eds), *Feminist Methodologies for International Relations*, Cambridge: Cambridge University Press.

Jaffrelot, C. (2003) 'Communal Riots in Gujarat: The State at Risk?', *Heidelberg Papers in South Asian and Comparative Politic*s, South Asia Institute, University of Heidelberg, 17: 1–20.

Jaggar, A. M. (1983) *Feminist Politics and Human Nature*, London: Harvester Press.

Jaggar, A. M. (1989) 'Love and Knowledge: Emotion in Feminist Epistemology', in A. M. Jaggar and S. R. Bordo (eds), *Gender/Body/Knowledge: Feminist Reconstructions in Being and Knowing*, New Brunswick: Rutgers University Press.

Jaggar, A. M. (2005) 'Arenas of Citizenship: Civil Society, the State, and the Global Order', in M. Friedman (ed.), *Women and Citizenship*, Oxford: Oxford University Press.

Jahan, R. (1995) *The Elusive Agenda: Mainstreaming Women in Development*, London: Zed Books.

Jayawardena, K. (1986) *Feminism and Nationalism in the Third World*, London: Zed Books.

Jeffords, S. (1989) *The Remasculinization of America: Gender and the Vietnam War*, Bloomington, IN: Indiana University Press.

Jeffords, S. and Rabinovitz, L. (eds) (1994) *Seeing Through the Media: The Persian Gulf War*, New Brunswick: Rutgers University Press.

Jeffreys, S. (1997) *The Idea of Prostitution*, North Melbourne: Spinifex.

Jenkins, H. (1992) *Textual Poachers: Television Fans and Participatory Culture*, New York: Routledge.

Jenkins, H. (2006a) *Fans, Bloggers and Gamers: Exploring Participatory Culture*, New York: New York University Press.

Jenkins, H. (2006b) *Convergence Culture: Where Old and New Media Collide*, New York: University Press.

Jensen, H. (2006) 'Women's Human Rights in the Information Society', in R F. Jørgensen (ed.), *Human Rights in the Global Information Society*, Cambridge, MA, and London: MIT Press.

Joachim, J. (2003) 'Framing Issues and Seizing Opportunities: The UN, NGOs and Women's Rights', *International Studies Quarterly*, 47(2): 247–74.

Johnson, M. P. (1995) 'Patriarchal Terrorism and Common Couple Violence: Two Forms of Violence against Women', *Journal of Marriage and Therapy*, 57(2): 283–94.

Johnson, S. H. (1999) 'An Ecofeminist Critique of the International Economic Structure' in M. K. Meyer and E. Prügl (eds.), *Gender Politics in Global Governance*, Oxford: Rowman & Littlefield.

Jones, A. (1994) 'Gender and Ethnic Conflict in Ex-Yugoslavia', *Ethnic and Racial Studies*, 17(1): 115–34.

Jones, A. (1996) 'Does Gender Make the World Go Round? Feminist Critiques of International Relations', *Review of International Studies*, 22(4): 405–29.

Jones, A. (2000) 'Gendercide and Genocide', *Journal of Genocide Research*, 2(2): 185–214.

Jones, A. (2001) 'Genocide and Humanitarian Intervention: Incorporating the Gender Variable', *Journal of Humanitarian Assistance*. Available at http://www.jha.ac/articles/a080.htm (no date).

Jones, A. (ed.) (2003) *The Feminism and Visual Culture Reader*, Abingdon: Routledge.

Jones, A. (2004) 'Gender and Genocide in Rwanda', in A. Jones (ed.), *Gendercide and Genocide*, Nashville, TN: Vanderbilt University Press.

Jones, A. (2005) 'Gendercidal Institutions against Women and Girls', in L. Biason and M. Vlachová (eds), *Women in an Insecure World: Violence against Women – Facts, Figures and Analysis*, Geneva: Centre for the Democratic Control of Armed Forces.

Jones, A. (2008) *Crimes against Humanity: A Beginner's Guide*, Oxford: Oneworld.

Jones, C. (2010) 'Materializing Piety: Gendered Anxieties about Faithful Consumption in Contemporary Urban Indonesia', *American Ethnologist*, 37(4): 617–637.

Jones, E., Hodgins-Vermaas, R., McCartney, H., Everitt, B., Beech, C., Poynter, D. et al. (2002) 'Post-Combat Syndromes from the Boer War to the Gulf War: A Cluster Analysis of Their Nature and Attribution', *British Medical Journal*, 324: 321–29.

Jordan T. (1999) *Cyberpower*, London and New York: Routledge.

Jørgensen, R. F. (ed.) (2006) *Human Rights in the Global Information Society*, Cambridge, MA, and London: MIT Press.

Jørgensen, R. F. (2013) *Framing the Net: The Internet and Human Rights*, Cheltenham and Northampton, MA: Edward Elgar Publishing

Judd, E. R. (2002) *The Chinese Women's Movement: Between State and Market*, Stanford, CA: Stanford University Press.

Juergensmeyer, M. (ed.) (2003) *Global Religions: An Introduction*, New York: Oxford University Press.

Kabbani, R. (1994) *Imperial Fictions: Europe's Myths of the Orient*, London: Pandora.

Kabeer, N. (1994) 'Gender-Aware Policy and Planning: A Social-Relations Perspective', in M. Macdonald (ed.), *Gender Planning in Development Agencies*, Oxford: Oxfam GB.

Kabeer, N. (2001) *Reversed Realities: Gender Hierarchies in Development Thought*, London and New York: Verso.

Kaldor, M. (1999) *New and Old Wars: Organized Violence in a Global Era*, Cambridge: Polity Press.

Kanaaneh, R. A. (2002) *Birthing the Nation: Strategies of Palestinian Women in Israel*, Berkeley, CA: University of California Press.

Kandiyoti, D. (1988) 'Bargaining with Patriarchy', *Gender and Society*, 2(3): 274–90.

Kandiyoti, D. (2005) *The Politics of Gender and Reconstruction in Afghanistan*, Geneva: UNRISD.

Kandiyoti, D. (2007) 'The Politics of Gender and Reconstruction in Afghanistan', in D. Pankhurst (ed.), *Gendered Peace. Women's Struggles for Post-War Reconciliation and Justice*, New York: Routledge.

Kaplan, E. A. (ed.) (2000) *Feminism and Film*, Oxford: Oxford University Press.

Kaplan, T. (1997) *Crazy for Democracy: Women in Grassroots Movements*, New York: Routledge.

Karim, K. H. (2003) 'Mapping Diasporic Mediascapes', in K. H. Karim (ed.), *The Media of Diaspora*, London and New York: Routledge.

Katz, S. T. (1994) *The Holocaust in Historical Context, Volume 1: The Holocaust and Mass Death before the Modern Age*, Oxford: Oxford University Press.

Kay, C. (ed.) (1997) *Globalisation, Competitiveness and Human Security*, London and New York: Routledge.

Kaye, R. (2008) 'Pastor: GOP May Be Downplaying Palin's Religious Beliefs', CNN. Available at http://www.cnn.com/2008/POLITICS/09/08/palin.pastor/index.html (accessed 15 April 2009).

Keck, M. E. and Sikkink, K. (1998) *Activists Beyond Borders: Advocacy Networks in International Politics*, Ithaca, NY: Cornell University Press.

Kee, J. (2005) 'Women's Human Rights: Violence Against Women, Pornography and ICTs', paper presented at Women Claiming the Information Society (WOCTIS), Berlin, 11 September 2005. Available at http://www.genderit.org/resources/WOCTIS_paper_jk.pdf (accessed 15 April 2009).

Kee, J. (ed.) (2011) *EROTICS: Sex, Rights and the Internet – An Exploratory Research Study*, APC Women's Network Support Program. Available at http://www.genderit.org/resources/erotics-sex-rights-and-internet-research-study (accessed 8 September 2013).

Kegan Gardiner, J. (ed.) (2002) *Masculinity Studies and Feminist Theory*, New York: Columbia University Press.

Kelleher, M. (1997) *The Feminization of Famine: Expressions of the Inexpressible?*, Durham, NC: Duke University Press.

Kelson, G. and DeLeat, D. (eds) (1999) *Gender and Immigration*, London: Macmillan.

Kempadoo, K. (2005) 'Introduction. From Moral Panic to Global Justice: Changing Perspectives on Trafficking', in K. Kempadoo (ed.), *Trafficking and Prostitution Reconsidered: New Perspectives on Migration, Sex Work and Human Rights*, Boulder, CO: Paradigm Publishers.

Kennedy, H. W. (2002) 'Lara Croft: Feminist Icon or Cyberbimbo? On the Limits of Textual Analysis', *International Journal of Computer Game Research*. Available at http://www.gamestudies.org/ 0202/kennedy/ (accessed 15 April 2009).

Kent, A. (1995) *Between Freedom and Subsistence: China and Human Rights*, Oxford: Oxford University Press.

Kent, A. (1999) *China, the United Nations and Human Rights: The Limits of Compliance*, Philadelphia, PA: University of Pennsylvania Press.

Keohane, R. O. (1989) 'International Relations Theory: Contributions of a Feminist Standpoint', *Millennium: Journal of International Studies*, 18: 245–54.

Kessler, S. J. (1990) 'The Medical Construction of Gender: Case Management of Intersexed Infants', *Signs: Journal of Women in Culture and Society*, 16(1): 3–26.

Kincaid, J. (1988) *A Small Place*, New York: Plume.

King, U. and Beattie, T. (2004) *Gender, Religion and Diversity: Cross-Cultural Perspectives*, London: Continuum.

Kirk McDonald, G. (2000) 'Crimes of Sexual Violence: The Experience of the International Criminal Tribunal', *Columbia Journal of Transnational Law*, 39: 1–18.

Kirollos, M. (2013) 'Sexual Violence in Egypt: Myths and Realities', *Jadaliyya*, 16 July 2013. Available http://www.jadaliyya.com/pages/index/13007/sexual-violence-in-egypt_myths-and-realities (accessed 17 October 2013).

Kittay, E. F. (1999) *Love's Labor: Essays on Women, Equality and Dependency*, New York: Routledge.

Kizzia, T. (2006) 'Long, Strange Journey to Governor's Office Nears Its Conclusion', *Anchorage Daily News*, 2 November 2006. Available at http://religionclause.googlepages.com/ Palin-article.pdf (accessed 15 April 2009).

Knapp, G. (2005) 'Race, Class, Gender: Reclaiming Baggage in Fast Travelling Theories', *European Journal of Women's Studies*, 12: 249–65.

Knop, K. and Chinkin, C. (2001) 'Remembering Chrystal Macmillan: Women's Equality and Nationality in International Law,' *Michigan Journal of International Law*, 22 (4): 523–85.

Kofman, E. (2004) 'Gendered Global Migrations: Diversity and Stratification' *International Feminist Journal of Politics*, 6(4): 643–67.

Kofman, E. and Youngs, G. (eds) (1996) *Globalization: Theory and Practice*, London and New York: Continuum.

Kolko, B. E., Nakamura, L. and Rodman G. B. (2000) 'Race in Cyberspace: An Introduction', in B. E. Kolko, L. Nakamura and G. B. Rodman (eds), *Race in Cyberspace*, New York and London: Routledge.

Korsmeyer, C. (2004) *Gender and Aesthetics: An Introduction*, New York and London: Routledge.

Kramer, L. (2000) *After the Lovedeath: Sexual Violence and the Making of Culture*, Berkeley, CA, Los Angeles and London: University of California Press.

Krishna, S. (1993) 'The Importance of Being Ironic: A Postcolonial View on Critical International Relations Theory', *Alternatives*, 18(3): 385–417.

Krog, A. (2001) 'Locked into Loss and Silence: Testimonies of Gender and Violence at the South Africa Truth Commission', in C. Moser and F. C. Clark (eds), *Victims, Perpetrators Or Actors? Gender, Armed Conflict and Political Violence*, London: Zed Books.

Kronsell, A. (2006) 'Studying Silences on Gender in Institutions of Hegemonic Masculinity', in B. Ackerly, M. Stern and J. True (eds), *Feminist Methodologies for International Relations*, Cambridge: Cambridge University Press.

Krook, M.-L. and True, J. (2008) 'Global Strategies for Gender Equality: The United Nations After Beijing', paper presented at the Annual Convention of the International Studies Association, San Francisco, CA, 26–29 March 2008.

Kudva, N. and Beneria, L. (eds) (2005) *Rethinking Informalization: Poverty, Precarious Jobs and Social Protection*, Cornell University Open Access Repository. Available at http://ecommons.library.cornell.edu/bitstream/1813/3716/1/Rethinking%20Informalization.pdf (accessed 15 April 2009).

Kundnani, A. (2004) 'Wired for War: Military Technology and the Politics of Fear', *Race and Class*, 46(1): 116–25.

Kunz, Rahel (2011) *The Political Economy of Global Remittances: Gender, Governmentality and Neoliberalism*, New York: Routledge.

Kuokkanen, R. (2008) 'Globalization as Racialized, Sexualized Violence: The Case of Indigenous Women', *International Feminist Journal of Politics*, 10: 216–23.

Kurkiala, M. (2003) 'Interpreting Honour Killings: The Story of Fadime Sahindal in the Swedish Press (1975–2002)', *Anthropology Today*, 19(1): 6–7.

Kymlicka, W. (2003) 'Immigration, Citizenship, Multiculturalism: Exploring the Links', *Political Quarterly*, 74(1): 195–208.

Laenui, P. (1999) 'Is There an Indigenous Seat at the Modern Communications Luau?', in R. C. Vincent, K. Nordenstreng and M. Traber (eds), *Towards Equity in Global Communication: MacBride Update*, Cresskill, NJ: New Hampton Press.

Lagesen, V. A. (2008) 'A Cyberfeminist Utopia? Perceptions of Gender and Computer Science Among Malaysian Women Computer Science Students and Faculty', *Science, Technology and Human Values*, 33(1): 5–27.

Lancaster, J. (2008) 'Is it Art?', *London Review of Books*, 1 January 2009. Available at http://www.lrb.co.uk/v31/n01/lanc01_.html (accessed 15 April 2009).

Lane, C. (2003) 'The White House Culture of Gender and Race in *The West Wing*: Insights from the Margins', in P. Rollins and J. O'Connor (eds), *Hollywood's White House, the American Presidency in Film and History*, Lexington, KY: University Press of Kentucky.

Lapeyre, F. (2004) 'Globalization and Structural Adjustment as a Development Tool', International Labour Office Working Paper No. 31. Available at http://www.ilo.org/wcmsp5/groups/public/-dgreports/-integration/documents/publication/wcms_079123.pdf (accessed 15 April 2009).

Lapsley, R. and Westlake, M. (2006) *Film Theory: An Introduction*, 2nd edn, Manchester: Manchester University Press.

Laqueur, W. (1996) 'Postmodern Terrorism', *Foreign Affairs*, 75(5): 24–36.

Laqueur, W. (2000) *The New Terrorism: Fanaticism and the Arms of Mass Destruction*, London: Oxford University Press.

Larcombe, W. (2005) *Compelling Engagements: Feminism, Rape Law and Romance Fiction*, Sydney: Federation Press.

Larner, W. (2003) 'Neoliberalism?', *Environment and Planning D: Society and Space*, 21(5): 509–12.

Larrabee, M. J. (ed.) (1993) *An Ethic of Care*, New York: Routledge.

Larsen, A. (2004) 'Affective Technologies – Emotions and Mobile Phones', *Receiver: Connecting to the Future* 11. Available at http://www.academia.edu/ 472410/Affective_Technologies._Emotions_and_Mobile_Phones (accessed 15 August 2013).

Lavrin, A. (1998) 'International Feminisms: Latin American Alternatives', *Gender and History*, 10.

Law, L. (2002) 'Sites of Transnational Activism: Filipino Non-Government Organisations in Hong Kong', in B. Yeoh, P. Teo and S. Huang (eds), *Gender Politics in the Asia-Pacific Region*, London and New York: Routledge.

Lawson, S. (2006) *Culture and Context in World Politics*, Basingstoke: Palgrave Macmillan.

Leach, M. (1992) 'Gender and the Environment: Traps and Opportunities', *Development and Practice*, 2(1): 12–22.

Leach, M. (2007) 'Earth Mother Myths and Other Ecofeminist Fables: How a Strategic Notion Rose and Fell', *Development and Change*, 38(1): 67–85.

Lee, C. K. (1998) *Gender and the South China Miracle: Two Worlds of Factory Women*, Berkley, CA: University of California Press.

Lee, M. (2007) 'Introduction: Understanding Human Trafficking', in M. Lee (ed.), *Human Trafficking*, Cullompton: Willan Publishing.

Lemkin, R. (1944) *Axis Rule in Occupied Europe*, Washington, DC: Carnegie Endowment for International Peace.

Lerner, G. (1986) *The Creation of Patriarchy*, Oxford: Oxford University Press.

Leung, L. (2001) 'The Past Lives of a Cyborg: Encountering "Space Invaders" from the 1980s to the 1990s', in F. Henwood, H. Kennedy and N. Miller (eds), *Cyborg Lives: Women's Technobiographies*, York: Raw Nerve Books.

Levitt, P. and Jaworsky, N. (2007) 'Transnational Migration Studies: Past Developments and Future Trends', *Annual Review of Sociology*, 33: 129–56.

Lewis, L. A. (ed.) (1992) *The Adoring Audience: Fan Culture and Popular Media*, London: Routledge.

Lewis, R. and Mills, S. (2003) *Feminist Postcolonial Theory: A Reader*, London: Routledge.

Liddicoat, J. (2011) 'Internet Rights are Women's Rights!', *GenderIT.org*, 13 September 2011. Available at http://www.genderit.org/editorial/internet-rights-are-womens-rights (8 September 2011).

Liddington, J. (1989) *The Long Road to Greenham: Feminism and Anti-Militarism in Britain since 1820*, London: Virago.

Ling, L. H. M. (2002) *Postcolonial International Relations: Conquest and Desire Between Asia and the West*, Basingstoke and New York: Palgrave.

Lingis, A. (2006) 'Ethics in the Globalized War', *Eurozine*, 29 November. Available at http://www.eurozine.com/pdf/2006-11-29-lingis-en.pdf (accessed 15 April 2009).

Lister, R. (2003) *Citizenship: Feminist Perspectives*, 2nd edn, New York: New York University Press.

Lister, R. (2007) 'Inclusive Citizenship: Realizing the Potential', *Citizenship Studies*, 11(1): 49–61.

Little, J. (2002) 'Rural Geography: Rural Gender Identity and the Performance of Masculinity and Femininity in the Countryside', *Progress in Human Geography*, 26(5): 665–70.

Little, W. (2004) 'Performing Tourism: Maya Women's Strategies', *Signs*, 29(2): 528–33.

Lloyd, A. (1995) *Doubly Deviant, Doubly Damned*, London: Penguin Books.

Lloyd, I. (2013) 'Despite Legal Moves, PNG's Terrifying Witchcraft Killings Look Set to Continue', Time.com, 5 June. Available at http://world.time.com/ 2013/06/05/despite-legal-m oves-pngs-terrifying-witchcraft-killings-look-set-to-continue/(accessed 12 December 2013).

Lloyd, M. (2005) *Beyond Identity Politics: Feminism, Power and Politics*, London: SAGE.

Loader, B. (ed.) (1998) *Cyberspace Divide: Equality, Agency and Policy in the Information Society*, London and New York: Routledge.

Locher, B. and Prügl, E. (2001) 'Feminism and Constructivism: Worlds Apart or Sharing the Middle Ground?', *International Studies Quarterly*, 45(1): 111–29.

Locke, J. [1689](1980) *Second Treatise of Government*, Indianapolis, IN: Hackett.

Loh, C. (1995) 'The Vienna Process and the Importance of Universal Standards in Asia', in M. Davies (ed.), *Human Rights and Chinese Values; Legal, Philosophical and Political Perspectives*, Hong Kong: Oxford University Press.

Lombardo, E. (2005) 'Integrating or Setting the Agenda? Gender Mainstreaming in the European Constitution-Making Process', *Social Politics: International Studies in Gender, State and Society*, 12(3): 412–32.

Lombardo, E. and Meier, P. (2006) 'Gender Mainstreaming in the EU: Incorporating a Feminist Reading?', *European Journal of Women's Studies*, 13(2): 151–166.

Lorde, A. (2001) 'The Master's Tools Will Never Dismantle the Master's House', in C. L. Moraga and G. E. Anzaldúa (eds), *This Bridge Called My Back: Writings by Radical Women of Color*, Berkeley, CA: Third Woman Press.

Lorentzen, L. A. and Turpin, J. (eds) (1998) *The Women and War Reader*, London: New York University Press.

Lovelock, J. E. (1979) *Gaia: A New Look at Life on Earth*, New York: Oxford University Press.

Lovink, G. and Rasch, M. (eds) (2013) 'Unlike Us Reader: Social Media Monopolies and Their Alternatives', *Amsterdam: Institute of Network Cultures*. Available at http://network-cultures.org/wpmu/portal/publication/unlike-us-reader-social-media-monopolies-and-their-alternatives/ (accessed 15 August 2013).

Lyon, D. and Spini, D. (2004) 'Unveiling the Headscarf Debate', *Feminist Legal Studies*, 12(3): 333–45.

McAdam, D., McCarthy, J. D. and Zald, M. N. (eds) (1996) *Comparative Perspectives on Social Movements: Political Opportunities, Mobilizing Structures and Cultural Framings*, Cambridge: Cambridge University Press.

McBride, J. (1995) *War, Battering and Other Sports: The Gulf between American Men and Women*, New Jersey: Humanities Press.

MacBride, S. et al. (1980) *Many Voices, One World: Towards a new more just and more efficient world information and communication order*, report by the International Commission for the Study of Communication Problems, Paris, London and New York: Unesco, Kogan Page Ltd, Unipub.

McCall, L. (2005) 'The Complexity of Intersectionality', *Signs*, 30(3): 1771–800.

McChesney, R., Wood, E. and Foster, J. (eds) (1998) *Capitalism and the Information Age: The Political Economy of the Global Communication Revolution*, New York: Monthly Review Press.

McClintock, A. (1993) 'Family Feuds: Gender, Nationalism and the Family', *Feminist Review*, 44: 61–80.

McClintock, A. (1995) *Imperial Leather: Race, Gender, and Sexuality in the Colonial Contest*, New York: Routledge.

MacDonald, E. (1988) *Shoot the Women First*, London: Arrow Books.

MacDonald, S., Holden, P. and Ardener, S. (eds) (1987) *Images of Women in Peace and War: Cross-Cultural and Historical Perspectives*, Houndsmills: Macmillan with Oxford University Press.

McGuire, M. B. (2008) *Religion: The Social Context*, 5th edn, Long Grove, IL: Waveland Press.

Machin, D. and Suleiman, U. (2006) 'Arab and American Computer War Games: The Influence of a Global Technology on Discourse', *Critical Discourse Studies*, 3: 1–22.

McKay, S. (2004), 'Reconstructing Fragile Lives: Girls' Social Reintegration in Northern Uganda and Sierra Leone', in C. Sweetman (ed.), *Gender, Peacebuilding and Reconstruction*, Oxford: Oxfam GB.

MacKenzie Gentry, K. (2007) 'Belizean Women and Tourism Work: Opportunity or Impediment?', *Annals of Tourism Research*, 34(2): 477–96.

MacKenzie, M. (2012) *Female Soldiers in Sierra Leone: Sex, Security and Post-Conflict Development*, New York: New York University.

MacKinnon, C. (1987) *Feminism Unmodified: Discourses on Life and Law*, Cambridge: Harvard University Press.

MacKinnon, C. (1993) 'Crimes of War, Crimes of Peace', in S. Shute and S. Hurley (eds), *On Human Rights: the Oxford Amnesty Lectures 1993*, New York: Basic Books.

MacKinnon, C. (2009) 'The International Criminal Court and Gender Crimes', speech at Consultative Conference on International Criminal Justice, New York. Available at http://www.icc-cpi.int/NR/rdonlyres/2B344A20-EBDC-406C-8837-3973274F4501/280839/speech110909.pdf (accessed 16 July 2009).

MacKinnon, K. (2006) *Are Women Human? And Other International Dialogues*, Boston, MA: Harvard University Press.

McKittrick, K. (2006) *Demonic Grounds: Black Women and the Cartographies of Struggle*, Minneapolis, MN: Minnesota University Press.

Macklin, A. (2008) 'Legal Aspects of Conflict-Induced Migration by Women' in S. Forbes Martin and J. Tirman (eds), *Women, Migration and Conflict: Breaking a Deadly Cycle*, Dordrecht, Heidelberg, London and New York: Springer.

McLuhan, M. (1964) *Understanding Media: The Extensions of Man*, New York: McGraw-Hill.

McMichael, P. (2000) 'Globalisation: Trend or Project?, in R. Palan (ed.), *Global Political Economy: Contemporary Theories*, London and New York: Routledge.

McMichael, P. (2009) 'A Food Regime Analysis of the "World Food Crisis"', *Agriculture and Human Values*, 26(4): 281–95.

McMichael, P. and Schneider, M. (2011) 'Food Security Politics and the Millennium Development Goals,' *Third World Quarterly*, 32(1): 119–39.

McNay, L. (1992) *Foucault and Feminism*, Cambridge: Cambridge University Press.

Madden, M., Cortesi, S., Gasser, U., Lenhart, A. and Duggan, M. (2012) 'Parents, Teens, and Online Privacy', *Pew Internet and American Life Project*, 20 November. Available at http://www.pewinternet.org/Reports/2012/Teens-and-Privacy/Summary-of-Findings.aspx (accessed 9 September 2013).

Magubane, Z. (2001) 'Which Bodies Matter?: Feminism, Poststructuralism, Race and the Curious Theoretical Odyssey of the "Hottentot Venus"', *Gender and Society*, 15: 816–34.

Magubane, Z. (2004) 'Revolution Betrayed? Globalization, Imperialism and the Post Apartheid State', *South Atlantic Quarterly*, 103: 657–71.

Maher, K. H. (2004) 'Globalized Social Reproduction: Women Migrants and the Citizenship Gap', in A. Brysk and G. Shafir (eds), *People Out of Place: Globalization, Human Rights, and the Citizenship Gap*, New York and London: Routledge.

Majid, R. and Hanif, S. (2003) 'Language, Power and Honour: Using Murder to Demonise Muslims', *Islamic Human Rights Commission*. Available at http://www.ihrc.org.uk/show.php?id=803 (accessed 15 April 2009).

Majumdar, S. (1995) 'Women on the March: Right Wing Mobilisation in Contemporary India', *Feminist Review*, 49: 75–92.

Makuch, E. (2013) 'Tomb Raider Reboot Sells 4 Million Copies', *Gamespot*, 23 August. Available at http://www.gamespot.com/news/tomb-raider-reboot-sells-4-million-copies-6413588 (accessed 30 August 2013).

Maley, J. (2006) 'Sexual Harassment Rife in Armed Forces', *The Guardian*, 26 May. Available at http://www.guardian.co.uk/uk/2006/may/26/ gender.military (accessed 15 April 2009).

Malkki, L. (1996) 'Speechless Emissaries: Refugees, Humanitarianism, and Dehistoricization', *Cultural Anthropology*, 11(3): 377–404.

Mama, A. (1995) *Beyond the Masks: Race, Gender and Subjectivity*, London and New York: Routledge.

Mama, A. (1997) 'Heroes and Villains: Conceptualizing Colonial and Contemporary Violence', in M. J. Alexander and C. T. Mohanty (eds), *Feminist Genealogies, Colonial Legacies, Democratic Futures*, London and New York: Routledge.

Mama, A. (2007) 'Is It Ethical to Study Africa? Preliminary Thoughts on Scholarship and Freedom', *African Studies Review*, 50: 1–27.

Mamdani, M. (1996) *Citizen and Subject: Contemporary Africa and the Legacy of Late Colonialism*, Princeton, NJ: Princeton University Press.

Mansell, R. and Silverstone, R. (eds) (1996) *Communication by Design: The Politics of Information and Communication Technologies*, Oxford: Oxford University Press.

Mansell, R. and When, U. (1998) *Knowledge Societies: Information Technology for Sustainable Development*, Oxford: Oxford University Press.

Manzo, K. (2008) 'Imaging Humanitarianism: NGO Identity and the Iconography of Childhood', *Antipode*, 40(4): 632–57.

Marchand, M. and Runyan, A. S. (eds) (2000) *Gender and Global Restructuring: Sightings, Sites and Resistances*, London and New York: Routledge.

Marcus, S. (1992) 'Fighting Bodies, Fighting Words: A Theory and Politics of Rape Prevention', in J. Butler and J. Scott (eds), *Feminists Theorise the Political*, London: Routledge.

Meis, M. and Shiva, V. (1993) *Ecofeminism*. London: Zed Books.

Marshall, E. (2003) 'Factsheet: Bush's Other War', *International Women's Health Coalition*, 19 May. Available at http://www.iwhc.org/index.php? option=com_content&task=view &id=2406&Itemid=587 (accessed 15 April 2009).

Marshall, M. (1964) *Understanding Media: The Extensions of Man*, London and New York: Routledge.

Marshall, P. and Thatun, S. (2005) 'Miles Away. The Trouble With Prevention in the Greater Mekong Sub-Region', in K. Kempadoo (ed.), *Trafficking and Prostitution Reconsidered: New Perspectives on Migration, Sex Work and Human Rights*, Boulder, CO: Paradigm Publishers.

Martin, R. and Reidy, D. A. (eds) (2006) *Rawls's Law of the Peoples: A Realistic Utopia?*, Oxford: Blackwell Publishing.

Matin, K. (2007) 'Obstacles on the Road to Prosperity', *Bangkok Post*, 2 July. Available at http://www.readbangkokpost.com/business/2007_currency_crisis/avoiding_the_ middle_income_tra.php (accessed 15 April 2009).

Mattelart, A. (1994) *Mapping World Communication: War, Progress, Culture*, Minneapolis, MN: University of Minnesota Press.

Mattelart, A. (2003) *The Information Society*, Thousand Oaks, CA, London and New Delhi: SAGE.

Maxigas (2012) 'Hacklabs and Hackerspaces – Tracing Two Genealogies', *Journal of Peer Production*, 2: 1–10.

May, C. (2002) *The Information Society: A Sceptical View*, Cambridge and Oxford: Polity Press.

May, V. M. (2012) 'Intersectionality', in C. M. Orr, A. Braithwaite and D. Lichtenstein (eds), *Rethinking Women's and Gender Studies,* New York: Routledge.

Mayall, J. (1990) *Nationalism and International Society*, Cambridge: Cambridge University Press.

Mayer, C. (2008) 'Prince Harry's War' *Time Magazine*, 5 March. Available at http://www. time.com/time/magazine/article/0,9171,1719691,00.html (accessed 15 April 2009).

Mayer, T. (ed.) (2000) *Gender Ironies of Nationalism: Sexing the Nation*, New York: Routledge.

Mazurana, D., Raven-Roberts, A. and Parpart, J. (eds) (2005), *Gender, Conflict and Peacekeeping*, Lanham, MD, and Oxford: Rowman & Littlefield.

Mbembe, A. (2001) *On the Postcolony*, Berkeley, CA: University of California Press.

Mehra, R. and Gammage, S. (1999) 'Trends, Countertrends and Gaps in Women's Employment', *World Development*, 27(3): 533–50.

Meikle, G. (2003) *Future Activism: Media Activism and the Internet*, London: Routledge.

Meintjes, S. (2001) 'War and Post-War Shifts in Gender Relations', in S. Meintjes, A. Pillay and M. Turshen (eds), *The Aftermath: Women in Post-Conflict Transformation*, London: Zed Books.

Meintjes, S., Pillay, A. and Turshen, M. (2001a) 'There is No Aftermath for Women', in S. Meintjes, A. Pillay and M. Turshen (eds), *The Aftermath: Women in Post-Conflict Transformation*, London and New York: Zed Books.

Meintjes S., Pillay A. and Turshen M. (eds) (2001b) *The Aftermath. Women in Post-conflict Transformation*, London: Zed Books.

Meinzen-Dick, R. S., Brown, L. R., Feldstein, H. S. and Quisumbing, A. R. (1997) 'Gender, Property Rights, and Natural Resources', *World Development*, 25(8): 1303–15.

Meinzen-Dick, R.S. and Zwarteveen, M. (1998) 'Gendered Participation in Water Management: Issues and Illustrations from Water Users Associations in South Asia', *Agriculture and Human Values*, 15(4): 337–45.

Meis, M. and Shiva, V. (1993) *Ecofeminism*, London: Zed Books.

Menon, R. and Bhasin, K. (1998) *Borders and Boundaries: Women in India's Partition*, New Delhi: Kali for Women.

Menon, U. (2003) 'Do Women Participate in Riots? Exploring the Notion of "Militancy" Among Hindu Women', *Nationalism and Ethnic Politics*, 9(1): 20–51.

Merchant, C. (1980) *The Death of Nature: Women, Ecology, and the Scientific Revolution*, New York: HarperCollins.

Mernissi, F. (1991) *The Veil and the Male Elite: A Feminist Interpretation of Women's Rights in Islam*, London: Basic Books.

Mertus, J. (2004) 'Shouting from the Bottom of the Well', *International Feminist Journal of Politics*, 6(1): 110–28.

MetacOm (2003) *What Is Hacktivism? 2.0*. Available at www.edshare.soton.ac.uk/ 8762/2/ whatishacktivism.pdf (accessed 15 August 2013).

Metrics 2.0 – Business and Market Intelligence (2006) 'Global Entertainment and Media Industry Will Grow to $1.8 Trillion in 2010', *Metrics 2.0-Business and Market Intelligence* 19 September 2006. Available at http://www.metrics2.com/blog/2006/09/19/global_entertainment_media_industry_will_grow_to_1.html (accessed 15 April 2009).

Mies, M. and Shiva, V. (1993) *Ecofeminism*, London: Zed Books.

Milazzo, L. (2005) 'Code Pink: The 21st Century Mothers of Invention', *Development*, 48(2): 100–104.

Milgram, S. (1974) *Obedience to Authority*, New York: Harper & Row.

Miller, D. and Slater, D. (2000) *The Internet: An Ethnographic Approach*, Oxford: Berg.

Miller, T., Govil, N., McMurria, J., Maxwell, R. and Wang, T. (2004) *Global Hollywood*, London: BFI Publishing.

Millward, S. (2012) 'Now With Over 1 Billion Netizens, This is How Asia Is Social and Mobile in 2012', *TechinAsia*. Available at http://www.techinasia.com/ asia-social-mobile-infographic-2012/ (accessed 9 September 2013).

Milly, D. (2007) 'What Japanese Policymakers Should Know About How Government Contributes to Irregular Migration', *Japan Focus Newsletter*, 18 September.

Mirzoeff, N. (1999) *An Introduction to Visual Culture*, London: Routledge.

Mirzoeff, N. (ed.) (2002) *The Visual Culture Reader*, 2nd edn, London: Routledge.

Mishra, V. (2002) *Bollywood Cinema: Temples of Desire*, London: Routledge.

Mitchell, C. (2005) 'Behind the Ethnic Marker: Religion and Social Identification in Northern Ireland', *Sociology of Religion*, 66(1): 3–21.

Mitchell, W. J. T. (2002) 'Showing Seeing: A Critique of Visual Culture', in N. Mirzoeff (ed.), *The Visual Culture Reader*, 2nd edn, Abingdon: Routledge.

Mobekk, E. (2010), 'Gender, Women and Security Sector Reform', *International Peacekeeping*, 17(2): 278–91.

Modood, T. (2008) 'Multicultural Citizenship and the Anti-Sharia Storm', *Open Democracy*, 14 February. Available at http://www.opendemocracy.net/ article/faith_ideas/europe_ islam/anti_sharia_storm (accessed 15 April 2009).

Moghadam, V. M. (1994) *Identity Politics and Women: Cultural Assertions and Feminisms in International Perspectives*, Oxford: Westview Press.

Moghadam, V. M. (2005) *Globalizing Women: Transnational Feminist Networks*, Baltimore, MD: Johns Hopkins University Press.

Moghadam, V. M. (2009) *Globalization and Social Movements: Islamism, Feminism, and the Global Justice Movement*, Lanham, MD: Rowman & Littlefield.

Moghadam, V. M. (2013) *Globalization and Social Movements: Islamism, Feminism, and the Global Justice Movement*, 2nd edn, Lanham, MD: Rowman & Littlefield.

Mohanty, C. T. (1991a) 'Cartographies of Struggle: Third World Women and the Politics of Feminism', in C. T. Mohanty, A. Russo and L. Torres (eds), *Third World Women and the Politics of Feminism*, Bloomington, IN: Indiana University Press.

Mohanty, C. T. (1991b) 'Under Western Eyes: Feminist Scholarship and Colonial Discourses', in C. T. Mohanty, A. Russo and L. Torres (eds), *Third World Women And The Politics of Feminism*, Bloomington, IN: Indiana University Press.

Mohanty, C. T. (2003a) 'Under Western Eyes Revisited: Feminist Solidarity Through Anticapitalist Struggles', *Signs: Journal of Women in Culture and Society*, 28: 499–535.

Mohanty, C. T. (2003b) *Feminism Without Borders: Decolonizing Theory, Practicing Solidarity*, London and Durham, NC: Duke University Press.

Mohanty, C. T. (2006) 'US Empire and the Project of Women's Studies: Stories of Citizenship, Complicity and Dissent', *Gender, Place and Culture*, 13(1): 7–20.

Mohanty, C. T., Russo, A. and Torres, L. (eds) (1991) *Third World Women and the Politics of Feminism*, Bloomington and Indianapolis, IN: Indiana University Press.

Momsen, J. H. (2004) *Gender and Development*, London: Routledge.

Monaco, J. (2000) *How to Read a Film: The World of Movies, Media, Multimedia: Language, History, Theory*, 3rd edn, Oxford: Oxford University Press.

Montenegro, S. (1997) Interview: Nacla Report on the Americas. Available at http://www. hartford-hwp.com/archives/47/307.html (accessed 15 April 2009).

Moody, N. (2002) 'Displacements of Gender and Race in Space: Above and Beyond', in Z. Sardar and S. Cubitt (eds), *Aliens R Us: The Other in Science Fiction Cinema*, London: Pluto Press.

Moon, S. (2005) *Militarized Modernity and Gendered Citizenship in South Korea*, Durham, NC: Duke University Press.

Moore, C. and Shepherd, L. J. (2010) 'Aesthetics and International Relations: Towards a Global Politics', *Global Society: Interdisciplinary Journal of International Relations*, 24(3): 299–309.

Moraga, C. L. and Anzaldúa, G. E. (eds) (2001) *This Bridge Called My Back: Writings by Radical Women of Color*, Berkeley, CA: Third Woman Press.

Moran, M. H. (2010) 'Gender, Militarism and Peace-Building: Projects of the Postconflict Moment', *Annual Review of Anthropology*, 39: 261–74.

Morgenthau, H. (1952) 'Another "Great Debate": The National Interest of the United States', *American Political Science Review*, 46(4): 961–88.

Morgenthau, H. (1973) *Politics Among Nations*, 5th edn, New York: Knopf.

Morokvasic, M. (1984) 'Birds of Passage Are Also Women', *International Migration Review*, 18(4): 886–907.

Morrell, Robert (2005) 'Youth Fathers and Masculinity in South Africa Today', *Agenda*, 7–10.

Moser, C. (1991) 'Gender Planning in the Third World: Meeting Practical and Strategic Needs', in R. Grant and K. Newland (eds.), *Gender and International Relations*, Bloomington, IN: Indiana University Press.

Moser, C. (1993) *Gender Planning and Development: Theory, Practice and Training*, London: Routledge.

Moser C. and Clark F. C. (eds) (2001) *Victims, Perpetrators or Actors? Gender, Armed Conflict and Political Violence*, London: Zed Books.

Moser, C. and McIlwhaine, C. (2001), 'Gender and Social Capital in Contexts of Political Violence: Community Perspectives from Colombia and Guatemala', in C. Moser and F. Clark (eds), *Victims, Perpetrators or Actors? Gender, Armed Conflict and Political Violence*, London: Zed Books.

Moses, J. W. (2006) *International Migration: Globalization's Last Frontier*, London: Zed Books.

Mudimbe, V. Y. (1994) *The Idea of Africa*, Bloomington, IN: Indiana University Press.

Muggah, R., Maughan, P. and Bugnion, C. (2003), 'The Long Shadow of War: Prospects for Generation Disarmament, Demobilisation and Reintegration in the Republic of Congo'. Available at http://www.oecd.org/dataoecd/ 49/32/35113279.pdf (accessed 10 February 2013).

Mukhopadhyay, M. (1995) 'Gender Relations, Development Practice and "Culture"', *Gender and Development*, 3: 13–18.

Mukhopadhyay, M., Steehouwer G. and Wong, F. (1996) *Politics of the Possible: Gender Mainstreaming and Organizational Change: Experiences from the Field*, London: Oxfam.

Mukhta, P. (2000) 'Gender, Community, Nation: The Myth of Innocence', in S. Jacobs, R. Jacobson and J. Marchbank (eds), *States of Conflict. Gender, Violence and Resistance*, London: Zed Books.

Munn, J. (2008) 'The Hegemonic Male and Kosovar Nationalism, 2000–2005', *Men and Masculinities*, 10(4): 440–56.

Muñoz, C. B. (2008) *Transnational Tortillas: Race, Gender, and Shop-floor Politics in Mexico and the United States*, Ithaca, NY: Cornell University Press.

Muppidi, H. (2004) *The Politics of the Global*, Minneapolis, MN: University of Minnesota Press.

Murphy, E. and Ringheim, K. (2002) 'Interview with Jo Doezema of the Network of Sex Work Projects: Does Attention to Trafficking Adversely Affect Sex Workers' Rights', *Reproductive Health and Rights: Reaching the Hardly Reached*, Seattle: PATH Publications. Available at http://www.path.org/ files/RHR-Article-2.pdf (accessed 15 April 2009).

Nadelmann, E. A. (1990) 'Global Prohibition Regimes: The Evolution of Norms in International Society', *International Organization*, 44: 479–526.

Nader, L. (1989) 'Orientalism, Occidentalism, and the Control of Women', *Cultural Dynamics*, 2(3): 323–55.

Nagar, R. (2002) 'Women's Theater and the Redefinitions of Public, Private and Politics in North India', *Acme: An International E-Journal for Critical Geographers*, 1: 55–72.

Nagar, R. (2008) 'Languages of Collaboration', in P. Moss and K. Falconer Al-Hindi (eds), *Feminisms In Geography: Rethinking Space, Place and Knowledges*, Lanham, MD: Rowman & Littlefield.

Nagel, J. (1998) 'Masculinity and Nationalism: Gender and Sexuality in the Making of Nations', *Ethnic and Racial Studies*, 21(2): 242–61.

Nagel, J. (2006) 'Ethnicity, Sexuality and Globalization', *Theory, Culture and Society*, 23: 545–47.

Nakamura, L. (2002) *Cybertypes: Race, Ethnicity, and Identity on the Internet*, London: Routledge.

Nakamura, L. (2007) *Digitizing Race: Visual Cultures of the Internet*, Minneapolis, MN: University of Minnesota.

Naples, N. A. and Desai, M. (eds) (2002) *Women's Activism and Globalization: Linking Local Struggles and Transnational Politics*, London and New York: Routledge.

Narayan, R. K. (2006) *The Ramayana*, New Delhi: Penguin.

Narayan, U. (1997) *Dislocating Cultures: Identities, Traditions and Third-World Feminism*, London and New York: Routledge.

Narayan, U. and Harding, S. (2000) *Decentering the Center: Postcolonial and Feminist Challenges to Philosophy*, Indianapolis, IN: Indiana University Press.

Nathan, A. J. (1994) 'Human Rights in Chinese Foreign Policy', *China Quarterly*, 139: 622.

Nations Internet Governance Forum, Hyderabad, India, 3–6 December 2008. Available at www.intgovforum.org/cms/2008-igf-hyderabad (accessed 7 January 2013).

Nayak, M. (2006) 'Orientalism and "Saving" US State Identity After 9/11', *International Feminist Journal of Politics*, 8(1): 42–61.

Nelson, A. and Tu, T. L. N. (eds) (2001) *Technicolor: Race, Technology, and Everyday Life*, New York and London: New York University Press.

Nelson, L. and Seager, J. (eds) (2005) *A Companion to Feminist Geography*, Malden: Blackwell.

Ness, C. (ed.) (2008) *Female Terrorism and Militancy: Agency, Utility, and Organization*, Abingdon: Routledge.

Newcomb, H. (ed.) (2006) *Television: The Critical View*, 7th edn, Oxford: Oxford University Press.

Ng, E. and Toupin, S. (2013) 'Occupy and Feminist Practice: A Case Study of Online and Offline Activism at Occupy Wall Street', *Networking Knowledge: Journal of the MeCCSA-PGN, Special issue: Protest and the New Media Ecology*, 6(3): 90–114.

Nguyen, M. (2001) 'Tales of an Asiatic Geek Girl: *Slant* from Paper to Pixels', in A. Nelson and T. L. N. Tu (eds), *Technicolor: Race, Technology, and Everyday Life*, New York and London: New York University Press.

Nicholson, X. (2013) *Visual Dissent and the Arab Spring: The Role of Images in Contesting Gender Politics During the Arab Spring*, unpublished honours thesis, University of Queensland.

Nijeholt, G. L. À., Vargas V. and Wieringa S. (eds) (1998) *Women's Movements and Public Policy in Europe, Latin America, and the Caribbean*, New York: Garland Publishing.

Nnaemeka, O. (ed.) (1998) *Sisterhood, Feminisms and Power: From Africa to the Diaspora*, Trenton, NJ: Africa World Press, Inc.

Nnaemeka, O. (2005) 'African Women, Colonial Discourses, and Imperialist Interventions: Female Circumcision as Impetus', in O. Nnaemeka (ed.), *Female Circumcision and the Politics of Knowledge: African Women in Imperialist Discourses*, Westport, CT: Praeger.

Noddings, N. (1984) *Caring: A Feminine Approach to Ethics and Moral Education*, Berkeley, CA: University of California Press.

Nolin, C. (2006) *Transnational Ruptures: Gender and Forced Migration*, Aldershot and Burlington, VT: Ashgate.

Nordstrum, C. (1997) *A Different Kind of War Story*, Philadelphia, PA: University of Pennsylvania Press.

Nordstrum, C. (1998) 'Girls Behind the (Front) Lines', in L. A. Lorentzen and J. Turpin (eds), *The Women and War Reader*, London: New York University Press.

Norman, D. (1988) *The Design of Everyday Things*, New York: Basic Books.

North, D. C. (1981) *Structure and Change in Economic History*, New York: Norton.

Nowrojee, B. (2007) '"Your Justice is Too Slow": Will the International Criminal Tribunal for Rwanda Fail Rwanda's Rape Victims?', in D. Pankhurst (ed.), *Gendered Peace. Women's Struggles for Post-War Justice and Reconciliation*, New York: Routledge.

Nsouli, S. M. (2007) 'What is the IMF Doing to Help Countries Maximize the Benefits of Globalization?', Crans Monatana Forum, 18th Annual Session, Monaco, 29 June. Available at http://www.imf.org/external/np/speeches/2007/062907.htm (accessed 15 April 2009).

Nussbaum, M. (2000) *Women and Human Development*, Cambridge: Cambridge University Press.

Nussbaum, M. (2004) 'Body of the Nation: Why Women were Mutilated in Gujarat', *Boston Review – A Political and Literary Forum*. Available at http://bostonreview.net/BR29.3/nussbaum.html (accessed 15 April 2009).

Nussbaum, M. (2007) *Frontiers of Justice: Disability, Nationality, Species Membership*, Cambridge, MA: Harvard University Press.

O'Brien, L. (2006) 'Why There Are No Indie Video Games and Why That's Bad For Gamers', *Slate*. Available at http://www.slate.com/id/2142453 (accessed 15 April 2009).

O'Brien, Erin (2011) 'Fuelling Traffic: Abolitionist Claims of a Nexus between Legalised Prostitution and Trafficking', *Crime, Law and Social Change*, 56(5): 547–565.

O'Brien, R., Goetz, A. M., Scholte, J. A. and Williams, M. (2000) *Contesting Global Governance: Multilateral Economic Institutions and Global Social Movements*, Cambridge: Cambridge University Press.

Oakley, A. (1972) *Sex, Gender and Society*, London: Temple Smith.

Oberoi, H. (1994) *The Construction of Religious Boundaries: Culture, Identity and Diversity in the Sikh Tradition*, Oxford: Oxford University Press.

Office of the High Commissioner for Human Rights (2005) 'The International Convention on Migrant Workers and its Committee: Fact Sheet', UN New York and Geneva. Available at http://www.ohchr.org/Documents/Publications/FactSheet24rev.1en.pdf (accessed 7 August 2013).

Office to Monitor and Combat Trafficking in Persons (US Department of State). *Images of Human Trafficking*. Available at http://www.gtipphotos.state.gov/ photos.htm (accessed 20 February 2009).

Ohmae, K. (2002) *The Borderless World: Power and Strategy in the Global Marketplace*, London: Profile Books.

Oishi, N. (2005) *Women in Motion: Globalization, State Policies and Labour Migration in Asia*, Stanford, CA: Stanford University Press.

Okeke, P. (1996) 'Postmodern Feminism and Knowledge Production: The African Context', *Africa Today*, 43: 223–34.

Okin, S. M. (1989) *Justice, Gender and the Family*, New York: Basic Books.

Oliver, K. (2007) *Women and Weapons of War: Iraq, Sex and the Media*, New York: Columbia University Press.

Omang, J. (2006) 'Looking for Answers in Argentina', *Agence Global*, 24 March. Available at http://www.agenceglobal.com/article.asp?id=856 (accessed 15 April 2009).

Ong, A. (1987) *Spirits of Resistance and Capitalist Discipline: Factory Women in Malaysia*, Albany, NY: SUNY Press.

Ong, A. (1990) 'State Versus Islam: Malay Families, Women's Bodies, and the Body Politic in Malaysia', *American Ethnologist*, 17(2): 258–76.

Ong, A. (2004) 'Latitudes of Citizenship: Membership, Meaning, and Multiculturalism', in A. Brysk and G. Shafir (eds), *People Out of Place: Globalization, Human Rights, and the Citizenship Gap*, New York and London: Routledge.

Oosterveld, V. (2005) 'The Definition of Gender in the Rome Statute of the International Criminal Court: A Step Forward or Back for International Criminal Justice', *Harvard Human Rights Journal*, 18: 55–84.

Oosterveld, V. (2011) 'The Gender Jurisprudence of the Special Court for Sierra Leone: Progress in the Revolutionary United Front Judgments', *Cornell International Law Journal*, 44: 49–74.

Organisation for Economic Co-operation and Development (OECD) (2008) 'Gender and Sustainable Development: Maximising the Economic, Social and Environmental Role of Women', *Social and Welfare Issue*, OECD, 6 March. Available at http://www.oecd.org/LongAbstract/0,3425,en_2649_37419_40235085_119666_1_1_1,00.html (accessed 15 April 2009).

Organisation for Economic Co-operation and Development (OECD) (2011) *OECD Council Recommendation on Principles for Internet Policy Making*, 13 December, Paris: OECD. Available at www.oecd.org/internet/ieconomy/49258588.pdf (accessed March 28, 2013).

Ortiz, I. and Cummins, M. (2011) 'Global Inequality: Beyond the Bottom Billion – A Rapid Review of Income Distribution in 141 Countries', Working papers 1105, UNICEF, Division of Policy and Strategy. Available at http://www.unicef.org/socialpolicy/index_58230.html (accessed 6 June 2013).

Otis, E. (2008) 'Beyond the Industrial Paradigm: Market-Embedded Labour and the Gender Organization of Global Service Work in China', *American Sociological Review*, 73: 15–36.

Otto, D. (2006/7) 'A Sign of "Weakness"? Disrupting Gender Certainties in the Implementation of Security Council Resolution 1325', *Michigan Journal of Gender and Law*, 13: 113–75.

Otto, D. (2009) 'The Exile of Inclusion: Reflections on Gender Issues in International Law Over the Last Decade', *Melbourne Journal of International Law*, 11(10): 11–26.

Oyewùmi, O. (ed.) (2003) *African Women and Feminism: Reflecting on the Politics of Sisterhood*, Trenton, NJ: African World Press, Inc.

Oyewùmí, O. (ed.) (2005) *African Gender Studies: Theoretical Questions and Conceptual Issues*, New York: Palgrave Macmillan.

Pacific Review (2008) 'Global Accountability and Transnational Networks: The Women Leaders Network and the Asia Pacific Economic Forum', *Pacific Review*, 21(1): 1–26.

Painter, G. and Ulmer, K. (2002) *Everywhere and Nowhere: Assessing Gender Mainstreaming in European Community Development Cooperation*, APRODEV and One World Action 2002. Available at http://www.oneworldaction.org/Resources/One%20World%20Action/Documents/PDF/gendereverywhere.pdf (accessed 15 April 1009).

Palan, R. (2000) 'New Trends in Global Political Economy', in R. Palan (ed.), *Global Political Economy: Contemporary Theories*, London and New York: Routledge.

Palmer, I. (1992) 'Gender Equity and Economic Efficiency in Adjustment Programmes', in H. Afshar and C. Dennis (eds), *Women and Adjustment Policies in the Third World*, London: Macmillan.

Pande, R. (2000) 'Globalization and Women in the Agricultural Sector', *International Feminist Journal of Politics*, 2(3): 409–412.

Pandey, G. (1990) *The Construction of Communalism in Colonial North India*, New Delhi: Viking.

Pangsapa, P. (2007) *Textures of Struggle: The Emergence of Resistance among Garment Workers in Thailand*, Ithaca, NY: Cornell University Press.

Pankhurst, D. (2004) 'The "Sex War" and Other Wars: Towards a Feminist Approach to Peacebuilding', in H. Afshar and D. Eade (eds), *Development, Women and War: Feminist Perspectives*, Oxford: Oxfam GB.

Pankhurst, D. (ed.) (2007) *Gendered Peace. Women's Struggles for Post-War Justice and Reconciliation*, New York: Routledge.

Pantazis, C. and Pemberton, S. (2009) 'From the "Old" to the "New" Suspect Community Examining the Impacts of Recent UK Counter-Terrorist Legislation', *British Journal of Criminology*, 49(5): 646–66.

Panyarachun, A. et al. (2004) *A More Secure World: Our Shared Responsibility*, New York: United Nations.

Pape, R. (2005) *Dying to Win: The Strategic Logic of Suicide Terrorism*, Chicago, IL: University of Chicago Press.

Parashar, S. (2009) 'Feminist IR and Women Militants: Case Studies from South Asia', *Cambridge Review of International Affairs*, 22(3): 235–56.

Parashar, S. (2010) 'The Sacred and the Sacrilegious: Exploring Women's "Politics" and "Agency"', *Radical Religious Movements in South Asia, Totalitarian Movements and Political Religions*, 11(3–4): 435–55.

Parashar, S. (2011a) 'Gender, Jihad, and Jingoism: Women as Perpetrators, Planners, and Patrons of Militancy in Kashmir', *Studies in Conflict and Terrorism*, 34(4): 295–317.

Parashar, S. (2011b) 'Embodied "Otherness" and Negotiations of Difference: A Critical Self Reflection on the Politics of Emotions in Researching Militant Women', *International Studies Review*, 13(4): 687–708.

Parashar, S. (2014) *Women and Militant Wars: The Politics of Injury*, London: Routledge.

Parekh, B. (2000) *Rethinking Multiculturalism: Cultural Diversity and Political Theory*, London: Macmillan.

Parpart, J. (2007) 'Gender and Global Governance', in A. McGrew and N. K. Poku (eds), *Globalization, Development and Human Security*, Cambridge: Polity Press.

Parpart, J. and Zalewski, M. (eds) (2008) *Rethinking the Man Question; Sex, Gender and Violence in International Relations*, London: Zed Books.

Parrenas, R. (2000) 'Migrant Filipina Domestic Workers and the International Division of Reproductive Labor', *Gender and Society*, 14(4): 560–80.

Parrenas, R. (2001) *Servants of Globalization: Women, Migration and Domestic Work*, Stanford, CA: Stanford University Press.

Parrenas, R. (2005) *Children and Global Migration: Transnational Families and Gendered Woes*, Stanford, CA: Stanford University Press.

Parry-Giles, T. and Parry-Giles, S. (2006) *The Prime-Time Presidency:* The West Wing *and US Nationalism*, Urbana, IL: University of Illinois Press.

Patel, R. (2010) *The Value of Nothing: How to Reshape Market Society and Redefine Democracy*, New York: St. Martin's Press.

Patel, R. (2012) 'Food Sovereignty: Power, Gender, and the Right to Food', PLoS Med 9(6): e1001223. Available at http://www.plosmedicine.org/article/info%3Adoi%2F10.1371%2Fjournal.pmed.1001223.

Pateman, C. (1980) 'The Disorder of Women', *Ethics*, 91(1): 20–34.

Pateman, C. (1988) *The Sexual Contract*, Stanford, CA: Stanford University Press.

PeaceWomen (n.d.) 'Resolution Watch'. Available at http://www.peacewomen.org/security_council_monitor/resolution-watch (accessed 9 February 2013).

Peach, L. (1994) 'An Alternative to Pacifism? Feminism and Just War Theory', *Hypatia: Journal of Feminist Philosophy*, 9(2): 152–72.

Peacock, S. (ed.) (2007) *Reading 24*, London: I.B. Tauris.

Pearce, J. (2006) 'Bringing Violence "Back Home": Gender Socialisation and the Transmission of Violence Through Time and Space', in M. Glasius, M. Kaldor and H. Anheier (eds), *Global Civil Society*, London: SAGE.

Pearson, R. (2007) 'Beyond Women Workers: Gendering CSR', *Third World Quarterly*, 28(4): 731–49.

Pearson, R. and Seyfang, G. (2002) '"I'll Tell You What I Want . . .": Women Workers and Codes of Conduct', in R. Jenkins et al. (eds), *Corporate Responsibility and Labour Rights: Codes of Conduct in the Global Economy*, London: Earthscan.

Penley, C. (1992) 'Feminism, Psychoanalysis, and the Study of Popular Culture', in L. Grossberg, C. Nelson and P. Treichler (eds), *Cultural Studies*, New York: Routledge.

Penley, C. (1997) *NASA/Trek: Popular Science and Sex in America*, London: Verso.

Penttinen, E. (2008) *Globalization, Prostitution and Sex-Trafficking: Corporeal Politics*, London: Routledge.

Perkins, J. (2005) *Confessions of an Economic Hit Man*, London and New York: Penguin.

Peterson, D. and Wrangham, R. (1997) *Demonic Males: Apes and the Origins of Human Violence*, Boston, MA: Mariner Books.

Peterson, V. S. (1990) 'Whose Rights? A Critique of the "Givens" in Human Rights Discourse', *Alternatives*, 15(3): 303–44.

Peterson, V. S. (1992a) 'Introduction', in V. S. Peterson (ed.), *Gendered States: Feminist (Re)Visions of International Relations Theory*, Boulder, CO: Lynne Rienner.

Peterson, V. S. (ed.) (1992b) *Gendered States: Feminist (Re)Visions Of International Relations Theory*, Boulder, CO: Lynne Rienner.

Peterson, V. S. (1998) 'Gendered Nationalism', in L. Lorentzen, and J. Turpin (eds), *The Women and War Reader*, New York and London: New York University Press.

Peterson, V. S. (1999) 'Sexing Political Identities/Nationalism as Heterosexism', *International Feminist Journal of Politics*, 1(1): 34–65.

Peterson, V. S. (2003) *A Critical Rewriting of Global Political Economy: Integrating Reproductive, Productive, and Virtual Economies*, London: Routledge.

Peterson, V. S. (2005) 'How (the Meaning of) Gender Matters in Political Economy', *New Political Economy*, 10(4): 499–521.

Peterson, V. S. (2007) 'Thinking Through Intersectionality and War', *Race, Gender and Class*, 14(3–4): 10–27.

Peterson, V. S. (2010a) 'Informalization, Inequalities and Global Insecurities', *International Studies Review*, 12: 244–270.

Peterson, V. S. (2010b) 'A Long View of Globalization and Crisis', *Globalizations*, 7(1): 179–193.

Peterson, V. S. (2012) 'Rethinking Theory', *International Feminist Journal of Politics*, 14(1): 5–35.

Peterson, V. S. (2013) 'Informal Work', in D.M. Figart and T. Warnecke (eds), *Handbook of Research on Gender and Economic Life*, Cheltenham: Edward Elgar Publishing Ltd.

Peterson, V. S. and Sisson Runyan, A. (1993) *Global Gender Issues*, Boulder, CO: Westview Press.

Peterson, V. S. and Sisson Runyan, A. (1999) *Global Gender Issues*, 2nd edn, Boulder, CO: Westview Press.

Peterson, V. S. and Sisson Runyan, A. (2010) *Global Gender Issues in the New Millennium*, 3rd edn, Boulder, CO: Westview Press.

Peterson, V. S. and Sisson Runyan, A. (2013) *Global Gender Issues*, 4th edn, Boulder, CO: Westview Press.

Peterson, V. S. and True, J. (1998) 'New Times and New Conversations', in M. Zalewski and J. Parpart (eds), *The 'Man' Question in International Relations*, Oxford and Boulder, CO: Westview, pp. 14–27.

Petitt, A. (2006) 'Greenham: No Failure like Success', *Open Democracy*, 19 October. Available at http://www.opendemocracy.net/globalization-vision_reflections/greenham_4013.jsp (accessed 15 April 2009).

Pettman, J. (1996) *Worlding Women: A Feminist International Politics*, London and New York: Routledge.

Pettman, J. (1997) 'Body Politics: International Sex Tourism', *Third World Quarterly*, 18(1): 93–108.

Pettman, J. (1999) 'Globalisation and the Gendered Politics of Citizenship', in N. Yuval-Davis and P. Werbner (eds), *Women, Citizenship and Difference*, London and New York: Zed Books.

Pettman, J. (2003) 'Gendering Globalization in Asia through Miracle and Crisis', *Gender, Technology and Development*, 7(2): 171–87.

Pettman, J. (2004) 'Global Politics and Transnational Feminisms', in L. Ricciutelli, A. Miles and M. McFadden (eds), *Feminist Politics, Activism and Vision: Local and Global Challenges*, London and New York: Zed Books.

Pettman, J. (2008) 'International Sex and Service', in E. Kofman and G. Youngs (eds), *Globalization: Theory and Practice*, London: Pinter.

Pew Research Center for the People and the Press (2008) *Mid-October 2008 Political Survey*. Available at http://people-press.org/reports/questionnaires/462.pdf.

Philpott, S. and Mutimer, D. (2005) 'Inscribing the American Body Politic: Martin Sheen and Two American Decades', *Geopolitics*, 10: 335–55.

Phoenix, A. and Pattynama, P. (eds) (2006) 'Special Issue: Intersectionality', *European Journal of Women's Studies*, 13(3).

Pillay, A. (2001) 'Violence Against Women in the Aftermath', in S. Meintjes, A. Pillay and M. Turshen (eds), *The Aftermath. Women in Post-conflict Transformation*, London: Zed Books.

Pine, L. (2004) 'Gender and the Family', in D. Stone (ed.), *The Historiography of the Holocaust*, Basingstoke: Palgrave Macmillan.

Piper, N. (2007) *New Perspectives on Gender and Migration: Livelihood, Rights and Entitlements*, New York: Routledge.

Piper, N. and Roces, P. (eds) (2003) *Wife or Worker? Asian Women and Migration*, Boulder, CO: Lynne Reinner.

Planned Parenthood Federation of America (2003) *George W. Bush's War on Women: A Pernicious Web*, 14 January. Available at http://www.plannedparenthood.org/issues-action/other/bush-war-6069.htm (accessed 10 April 2008).

Planned Parenthood Federation of America (2006) 'The War on Women: A Pernicious Web – A Chronology of Attacks on Reproductive Rights', *Planned Parenthood*. Available at http://www.plannedparenthood.org/ files/PPFA/report_waronwomen-chronology.pdf (accessed 15 April 2009).

Plant, S. (1996) 'On the Matrix: Cyberfeminist Simulations', in R. Shields (ed.), *Cultures of Internet: Virtual Spaces, Real Histories, Living Bodies*, London, Thousand Oaks, CA, New Delhi: SAGE.

Plant, S. (1997) *Zeroes and Ones: Digital Women and the New Technoculture*, New York: Doubleday.

Plato (2002) *Five Dialogues*, Indianapolis, IN: Hackett.

Plümper, T. and Neumayer, E. (2003) 'The Unequal Burden of War: the Effect of Armed Conflict on the Gender Gap in Life Expectancy', *International Organization*, 60(3): 723–54.

Plunkett, M. C. B. and Southall, D. P. (1998) 'War and Children', *Archives of Disease in Childhood*, 78: 72–77.

Pollis, A. (1996) 'Cultural Relativism Re-visited: Through a State Prism', *Human Rights Quarterly*, 18(2): 320.

Polson, E. (2011) 'Belonging to the Network Society: Social Media and the Production of a New Global Middle Class', *Communication, Culture & Critique*, 4(1): 144–63.

Power, M. (2004) 'Social Provisioning as a Starting Point for Feminist Economics', *Feminist Economics*, 10(3): 3–20.

Prakash, G. (1995) 'Orientalism Now', *History and Theory*, 34: 199–212.

Pratt, N. C. and Devroe, S. R. (eds) (2013) *Gender, Governance and International Security*, New York: Routledge.

Prieto-Carrón, M. (2006) 'Corporate Social Responsibility in Latin America: Chiquita, Women Banana Workers and Structural Inequalities', *The Journal of Corporate Citizenship*, 21: 1–9.

Prieto-Carrón, M. and Bendell, J. (2002) *If You Want to Help Then Start Listening to Us! From Factories and Plantations in Central America, Women Speak Out About Corporate Responsibility*, Occasional Paper, Bath: New Academy of Business. Available at http://www.new-academy.ac.uk/research/gendercodesauditing/report.pdf (accessed 15 April 2009).

Principles for the Internet. Available at http://internetrightsandprinciples.org/wpcharter/ (accessed 8 September 2013).

Pritchard, B. (2009) 'The Long Hangover from the Second Food Regime: A World-Historical Interpretation of the Collapse of the WTO Doha Round', *Agriculture and Human Values*, 26(4): 297–307.

Proulx, S. (2009) 'Can the Use of Digital Media Favour Citizen Involvement?' *Global Media and Communications*, 5(3):1–15.

Prügl, E. (1999) *The Global Construction of Gender: Home-Based Work in the Political Economy of the 20th Century*, New York: Columbia University Press.

Prügl, E. and Lustgarten, A. (2006) 'The Institutional Road Towards Equality: Mainstreaming Gender in International Organisations', in J. Jaquette and G. Summerfield (eds), *Women and Gender Equity in Development Theory and Practice: Institutions, Resources, and Mobilization*, Chapel Hill, NC: Duke University Press.

Puar, J. K. and Rai. A. S. (2002) 'Monster, Terrorist, Fag: The War on Terrorism and the Production of Docile Patriots', *Social Text*, 20(3): 117–38.

Puechguirbal, N. (2003a) 'Gender Training for Peacekeepers: Lessons from the DRC', *International Peacekeeping*, 10(3): 113–28.

Puechguirbal, N. (2003b) 'Women and War in the Democratic Republic of the Congo', *Signs, Journal of Women in Culture and Society*, 28(4).

Puechguirbal, N. (2004) 'Involving Women in Peace Processes: Lessons from Four African Countries (Burundi, DRC, Liberia and Sierra Leone)', in K. Karamé (ed.), *Gender and Peace-building in Africa*, Oslo: NUPI.

Puechguirbal, N. (2005) 'Gender and Peace Building in Africa: Analysis of Some Structural Obstacles', in D. Rodriguez and E. Natukunda-Togboa (eds), *Gender and Peace Building in Africa*, San José, CA: University for Peace.

Puechguirbal, N. (2010) 'Discourses on Gender, Patriarchy and Resolution 1325: A Textual Analysis of UN Documents', *International Peacekeeping*, 17(2): 172–87.

Pun, N. (2005) *Made in China: Women Factory Workers in a Global Workplace*, Durham, NC: Duke University Press.

Puri, J. (2004) *Encountering Nationalism*, Oxford: Blackwell.

Pyle, J. (2006) 'Globalization, Transnational Migration, and Gendered Care Work: Introduction', *Globalizations*, 3(3): 283–96.

Quintas, P. (1996) 'Software by Design', in R. Mansell and R. Silverstone (eds), *Communication by Design: The Politics of Information and Communication Technologies*, Oxford: Oxford University Press.

Radcliffe, S. and Westwood, S. (1996) *Remaking the Nation: Identity and Politics in Latin America*, London: Routledge

Radmani, L. (2005) *Gender Mainstreaming in the United Nations Human Rights Treaty Bodies*, unpublished PhD dissertation, University of Sydney.

Radway, J. (1984) *Reading the Romance: Women, Patriarchy, and Popular Literature*, London: Verso.

Rafael, V. (1997) 'Your Grief is Our Gossip. Overseas Filipinos and Other Spectral Presences', *Public Culture*, 9(1): 267–91.

Rai, S. (2002) *Gender and the Political Economy of Development*, Cambridge: Polity Press.

Rai, S. (2007) *The Gender Politics of Development: Essays in Hope and Despair*, London and New York: Zed Books.

Rai, S. and Hoskyns, C. (2007) 'Recasting the Global Political Economy: Counting Women's Unpaid Work', *New Political Economy*, 12(3): 297–317.

Rai, S., Hoskyns, C. and Thomas, D. (2014) 'Depletion: The Cost of Social Reproduction', *International Feminist Journal of Politics*, 16(2).

Rankin, K. N. (2001) 'Governing Development: Neoliberalism, Microcredit and Rational Economic Woman', *Economy and Society*, 30(1): 18–37.

Ratha, D., Mohapatra, S., Vijayalakshmi, K. and Xu, Z. (2007) 'Remittance Trends 2007. Migration and Development Brief 3'. Available at http://siteresources.worldbank.org/EXTDECPROSPECTS/Resources/476882-1157133580628/BriefingNote3.pdf (accessed 15 April 2009),

Rawls, J. (1971) *A Theory of Justice*, Cambridge, MA: Harvard University Press.

Rawls, J. (1999) *The Law of the Peoples*, Cambridge, MA: Harvard University Press.

Ray, I. (2007) 'Women, Water and Development,' *Annual Review of Environment and Resources*, 32: 421–49.

Razack, H. S. (2008) *The Eviction of Muslims from Western Law and Politics*, Toronto: University of Toronto Press.

Razavi, S. and Miller, C. (1995a) 'From WID to GAD: Conceptual Shifts in the Women and Development Discourse', Occasional Paper 1, United Nations Research Institute for Social Development, February 1995. Available at http://www.unrisd.org/unrisd/website/document.nsf/0/d9c3fca78d3db32e80256b67005b6ab5/$FILE/opb1.pdf (accessed 15 April 2009).

Razavi, S. and Miller, C. (1995b) 'Gender Mainstreaming: A Study of Efforts by the UNDP, the World Bank and the ILO to Institutionalize Gender Issues', Occasional Paper 4, United Nations Research Institute for Social Development, August 1995. Available at http://www.unrisd.org/80256B3C005BCCF9/(httpAuxPages)/FC107B64C7577F9280256B67005B6B16/$file/opb4.pdf (accessed 15 April 2009).

Reardon, B. A. (1996) *Sexism and the War System*, New York: Syracuse University Press.

Regan, P. M. and Paskevicuite, A. (2003) 'Women's Access to Politics and Peaceful States', *Journal of Peace Research*, 40: 287–302.

Rehn, E. and Sirleaf, E. J. (2002) *Women, War and Peace, The Independent Experts' Assessment on the Impact of Armed Conflict on Women and Women's Role in Peace-building*, New York: UNIFEM.

Rheingold, H. (1994) 'A Slice of Life in My Virtual Community', in L. Harasim (ed.), *Global Networks: Computer Networks and International Communication*, Cambridge, MA: MIT Press.

Rice, X. and Sturcke, J. (2008) 'Call for Watchdog to Monitor Peacekeeper Child Abuse', *The Guardian*, 27 May.

Rich, B. (1994) *Mortgaging the Earth: The World Bank, Environmental Impoverishment and the Crisis of Development*, London: Earthscan.

Richards, A. (2011) 'The Problem with "Radicalization": The Remit of "Prevent" and the Need to Refocus on Terrorism in the UK', *International Affairs*, 87(1): 143–52.

Richards, P. (1995) 'Rebellion in Liberia and Sierra Leone. A Crisis of Youth?', in O. Furley (ed.), *Conflict in Africa*, London: I.B.Tauris.

Richardson, L. (2005). *What Terrorists Want: Understanding the Terrorist Threat*, London: John Murray.

Ringelberg, K. (2005) 'His Girl Friday (and Every Day): Brilliant Women Put to Poor Use', in T. Fahy (ed.), *Considering Aaron Sorkin: Essays on the Politics, Poetics and Sleight of Hand in the Films and Television Series*, Jefferson, NC: McFarland.

Robb, D. (2004) *Operation Hollywood: How the Pentagon Shapes and Censors the Movies*, Amherst, NY: Prometheus.

Roberts, A. (2008) 'Privatizing Social Reproduction: The Primitive Accumulation of Water in an Era of Neoliberalism', *Antipode*, 40(4): 535–560.

Roberts, D. (2007) *Human Insecurity: Global Structures of Violence*, London: Zed Books.

Robins, K. and Levidow, L. (1995) 'Socializing the Cyborg Self: The Gulf War and Beyond', in C. H. Gray (ed.), *The Cyborg Handbook*, New York: Routledge.

Robinson, F. (1999) *Globalizing Care: Ethics, Feminist Theory and International Relations*, Boulder, CO: Westview Press.

Robinson, F. (2003) 'Human Rights and the Global Politics of Resistance: Feminist Perspectives', *Review of International Studies*, Special Issue, 29(4): 161–80.

Robinson, F. (2006) 'Beyond Labour Rights: The Ethics of Care and Women's Work in the Global Economy', *International Feminist Journal of Politics*, 8(3): 321–42.

Robinson, F. (2011) *The Ethics of Care: A Feminist Approach to Human Security*, Philadelphia, PA: Temple University Press.

Rollins, P. and O'Connor, J. (eds) (2003) The West Wing: *The American Presidency as Television Drama*, Syracuse, NY: Syracuse University Press.

Romaniuk, P. (2010) 'Institutions as Sword and Shields: Multilateral Counter-Terrorism Since 9/11', *Review of International Studies*, 36(3): 591–613.

Rosenberg, N. and Birdzell, L. E. (1986) *How the West Grew Rich: The Economic Transformation of the Industrial World*, London: Basic Books.

Rouse, S. (1996) 'Gender, Nationalism and Cultural Identity: Discursive Strategies and Exclusivities', in K. Jayewardena and M. D. Alwis (eds), *Embodied Violence: Communalising Female Sexuality in South Asia*, London: Zed Books.

Rousseau, J. [1762] (1982) *The Basic Political Writings*, Indianapolis, IN: Hackett.

Rowbotham, S. (1972) *Women, Resistance and Revolution*, London: Penguin.

Rowbotham, S. (1995) 'Feminist Approaches to Technology: Women's Values or a Gender Lens', in S. Mitter and S. Rowbotham (eds), *Women Encounter Technology*, London and New York: Routledge.

Rowe, C. (2013) *The Politics of Protest and US Foreign Policy: Performative Construction of the War on Terror*, Hoboken, NJ: Taylor & Francis.

Rowley, C. (2005) 'The Politics of Science Fiction', *International Feminist Journal of Politics*, 5: 319–27.

Rowley, C. (2006) '"They're Beating the Women!" Gendered Representations of International Relations in *The West Wing*', unpublished conference paper, International Studies Association Annual Convention, San Diego, 27–31 March. Available at http://citation.allacademic.com/meta/p_mla_apa_research_citation/0/9/8/6/2/pages98629/p98629-1.php

Rowley, C. (2007) 'Firefly/Serenity: Gendered Space and Gendered Bodies', *British Journal of Politics and International Relations*, 9: 318–25.

Rowley, C. (2011) *An Intertextual Analysis of Vietnam War Films and US Presidential Speeches*, unpublished PhD thesis. Available at http://ethos.bl.uk/OrderDetails.do?uin=uk.bl.ethos.540884

Rowley, C. and Weldes, J. (2012) 'The Evolution of International Security Studies and the Everyday: Suggestions from the Buffyverse', *Security Dialogue* 43(6): 513–30.

Rowley, C. and Weldes, J. (2008) 'Identities and US Foreign Policy', in M. Cox and D. Stokes (eds), *US Foreign Policy*, Oxford: Oxford University Press.

Rowley, M. (2003) 'A Feminist's Oxymoron: Globally Gender-Conscious Development', in E. Barriteau (ed.), *Confronting Power, Theorizing Gender: Interdisciplinary Perspectives in the Caribbean*, Kingston: University of the West Indies Press.

Ruddick, S. (1989) *Maternal Thinking: Towards a Politics of Peace*, London: Women's Press.

Ruddick, S. (1993) 'Notes Towards a Feminist Peace Politics', in M. Cooke and A. Woollacott (eds), *Gendering War Talk*, Princeton, NJ: Princeton University Press.

Rupert, M. (1995) *Producing Hegemony: The Politics of Mass Production and American Global Power*, Cambridge: Cambridge University Press.

Rygiel, K. (2006) 'Protecting and Proving Identity: The Biopolitics of Waging War through Citizenship in the Post 9/11 Era', in K. Hunt and K. Rygiel (eds), *Engendering the War on Terror: War Stories and Camouflaged Politics*, London: Ashgate.

Sachs, C. (1996) *Gendered Fields: Rural Women, Agriculture, and Environment*, Boulder, CO: Westview Press.

Sachs, C. (ed.) (1997) *Women Working in the Environment*, Bristol: Taylor and Francis.

Saich, T. (1991) 'The Rise and Fall of the Beijing People's Movement', in J. Unger (ed.), *The Pro-Democracy Protests in China*, New York: M.E. Sharpe Inc.

Said, E. (1978) *Orientalism*, London: Vintage.

Said, E. (1985) 'Orientalism Reconsidered', *Cultural Critique*, 1: 89–107.

Said, E. (1997) *Covering Islam: How the Media and the Experts Determine how we see the Rest of the World*, New York: Vintage.

Salek, C. (2013) 'Amina Tyler: Tunisian Woman Receiving Death Threats For Trying to Start Feminist Group', *PolicyMic*, 24 March. Available at http://www.policymic.com/articles/30887/amina-tyler-tunisian-woman-receiving-death-threats-for-trying-to-start-feminist-group (accessed 7 December 2013).

Salman, R. (1991) *Imaginary Homelands*, London: Penguin.

Salomon, G. (1993) *Distributed Cognitions: Psychological and Educational Considerations*, Cambridge: Cambridge University Press.

Salter, L. (2003) 'Democracy, New Social Movements and the Internet: A Habermasian Analysis', in M. McCaughey and M. D. Ayers (eds), *Cyberactivism: Online Activism in Theory and Practice*, London: Routledge.

Salzinger, L. (2003) *Genders in Production: Making Workers in Mexico's Global Factories*, Berkeley, CA: University of California Press.

Sampaio, A. and Aragon, J. (1998) '"To Boldly Go (Where No Man Has Gone Before)": Women and Politics in Cyberspace', in T. W. Luke and C. Toulouse (eds), *The Politics of Cyberspace: A New Political Science Reader*, New York and London: Routledge.

Sandilands, C. (1997) 'Mother Earth, the Cyborg and the Queer: Ecofeminism and (More) Questions of Identity', *NWSA Journal*, 9(3): 18–40.

Sandilands, C. (2002) 'Lesbian Separatist Communities and the Experience of Nature: Toward a Queer Ecology', *Organisation and Environment*, 15(2): 131–63.

Sandilands, C. (2005) 'Unnatural Passions?: Notes Toward a Queer Ecology', *Invisible Culture: An Electronic Journal for Visual Culture*. Available at www.rochester.edu/in_visible_culture/issue9/sandilands.

Sandilands, C. (2008) 'Queering Ecocultural Studies', *Cultural Studies*, 22(3–4), 455–76.

Sands, P. (2008) *Torture Team: Deception, Cruelty and the Compromise of Law*, London: Allen Lane.

Sanford, K. and Madill, L. (2006) 'Resistance Through Video Game Play: It's a Boy Thing', *Canadian Journal of Education*, 29: 287–306.

Sarker, S. (ed.) (2007) *Sustainable Feminisms*, Amsterdam: Jai Press/Elsevier.

Sarkar, T. (1995) *Women and Right Wing Movements: Indian Experiences*, London: Zed Books.

Sarkar, T. (1996) 'Hindu Women: Politicization Through Communalism', in K. Rupesinghe and K. Mumtaz (eds), *Internal Conflicts in South Asia*, London: SAGE.

Sarkar, T. and Bhutalia, U. (eds) (1995) *Women and the Hindu Right*, New Delhi: Kali for Women.

Sassen, S. (1998) *Globalization and Its Discontents*, New York: New Press.

Sassen, S. (2000) 'Women's Burden: Counter-Geographies of Globalization and the Feminization of Survival', *Journal of International Affairs*, 53(2): 503–24.

Sassen, S. (2002a) 'Women's Burden: Counter Geographies of Globalization and the Feminization of Survival', *Nordic Journal of International Law*, 71(2): 255–74.

Sassen, S. (2002b) 'Towards a Sociology of Information Technology', *Current Sociology*, 50(3): 365–88.

Sassen, S. (2004) 'The Repositioning of Citizenship', in A. Brysk and G. Shafir (eds), *People Out of Place: Globalization, Human Rights, and the Citizenship Gap*, New York and London: Routledge.

Satrapi, M. (2003) 'Veiled Threat', *The Guardian*, 12 December. Available at http://www.guardian.co.uk/world/2003/dec/12/gender.uk/print (accessed 15 April 2009).

Saunders, P. (2005) 'Traffic Violations. Determining the Meaning of Violence in Sexual Trafficking Versus Sex Work', *Journal of Interpersonal Violence*, 20(3): 343–60.

Savarkar, V. D. (trans.) (1971) *Six Glorious Epochs of History*, Bombay: Bal Savarkar.

Scarlet Alliance (2008) 'International Migration of Sex Workers'. Available at http://www.scarletalliance.org.au/issues/migration/ (accessed 15 April 2009).

Schiff, B. (2008) *Building the International Criminal Court*, Cambridge and New York: Cambridge University Press.

Schiller, D. (1999) *Digital Capitalism: Networking the Global Market System*, Cambridge, MA: MIT Press.

Schmid, A. P. and Jongman, A. J. (2006) *Political Terrorism*, London: Transaction.

Schwarz, H. (1997) *Writing Cultural History in Colonial and Post-Colonial India*, Philadelphia, PA: University of Philadelphia Press.

Scott, J. W. (1992) '"Experience"', in J. Butler and J. Scott (eds), *Feminists Theorize the Political*, London: Routledge (a longer version was published in *Critical Inquiry*, 1991, 17: 773–97).

Sedgwick, M. (2010) 'The Concept of Radicalization as a Source of Confusion', *Terrorism and Political Violence*, 22(4): 479–94.

Segal, L. (1990) *Slow Motion. Changing Masculinities, Changing Men*, London: Virago.

Segal, L. (1997) 'Sexualities', in K. Woodward (ed.), *Identity and Difference*, London: SAGE.

Seidman, G. (2004) 'Deflated Citizenship: Labor Rights in a Global Era', in A. Brysk and G. Shafir (eds), *People Out of Place: Globalization, Human Rights, and the Citizenship Gap*, New York and London: Routledge.

Seifert, R. (1995) 'War and Rape: A Preliminary Analysis', in A. Stiglmayer (ed.), *Mass Rape: The War against Women in Bosnia-Herzegovina*, Lincoln and London: University of Nebraska Press.

Seifert, R. (1999) 'The Second Front: The Logic of Sexual Violence in Wars', in B. S. Manfred and S. L. Nancy (eds), *Violence and Its Alternatives*, London: Macmillan.

Sellers, P. V. (2009) 'Gender Strategy is Not Luxury for International Courts', *American University Journal of Gender, Social Policy & the Law*, 17(2): 301–26.

Sen, A. (2006) 'Reflecting on Resistance: Hindu Women "Soldiers" and the Birth of Female Militancy', *Indian Journal of Gender Studies*, 13(1): 1–35.

Sen, A. (2008) *Shiv Sena Women: Violence and Communalism in a Bombay Slum*, New Delhi: Zubaan.

Sen, G. (2005) 'Neolibers, Neocons and Gender Justice: Lessons from Global Negotiations', Occasional Paper 9, United Nations Research Institute for Social Development. Available at http://www.unrisd.org/ 80256B3C005BCCF9/(httpAuxPages)/15E6EA635E8A955B C12570B500357029/$file/OP9pdf.pdf (accessed 15 April 2009).

Sered, S. (1991) 'Rachel, Mary, and Fatima', *Cultural Anthropology*, 6: 131–46.

Shabot, S. C. (2006) 'Grotesque Bodies: A Response to Disembodied Cyborgs', *Journal of Gender Studies*, 15(3): 223–35.

Shapiro, M. J. (1992) *Reading the Postmodern Polity: Political Theory as Textual Practice*, Minneapolis, MN: University of Minnesota Press.

Sharlach, L. (1999) 'Gender and Genocide in Rwanda: Women as Agents and Objects of Genocide', *Journal of Genocide Research*, 1(3): 387–99.

Sharma, N. (2006) 'White Nationalism, Illegality and Imperialism: Border Controls as Ideology', in K. Hunt and K. Rygiel (eds), *Engendering the War on Terror: War Stories and Camouflaged Politics*, London: Ashgate.

Sharoni, S. (2012) 'Gender and Conflict Transformation in Israel/Palestine', *Journal of International Women's Studies*, 13(4): 113–28.

Shaw, M. (2007) *What is Genocide?*, Cambridge: Polity Press.

Shaw, V. S. and Walker, R. B. J. (2006) 'Situating Academic Practice: Pedagogy, Critique and Responsibility', *Millennium*, 35: 155–65.

Shepherd, L. J. (2006) 'Veiled References: Constructions of Gender in the Bush Administration Discourse on the Attacks in Afghanistan Post-9/11', *International Feminist Journal of Politics*, 8: 19–41.

Shepherd, L. J. (2008a) 'Power and Authority in the Production of United Nations Security Council Resolution 1325', *International Studies Quarterly*, 52(2): 383–404.

Shepherd, L. J. (2008b) 'Visualising Violence: Legitimacy and Authority in the "War on Terror"', *Critical Studies on Terrorism*, 1: 213–26.

Shepherd, L. J. (2008c) *Gender, Violence and Security: Discourse as Practice*, London: Zed Books.

Shepherd, L. J. (2010a) 'Feminist Security Studies', in R. A. Denemark (ed.), *International Studies Encyclopedia, Volume 4*, Malden, MA, and Oxford: Wiley Blackwell.

Shepherd, L. J. (2010b) 'Women, Armed Conflict and Language/Gender, Violence and Discourse', *International Review of the Red Cross*, 92(877): 143–59.

Shepherd, L. J. (2011) 'Gender and Global Social Justice: Peacebuilding and the Politics of Participation', in H. Widdows and N. Smith (eds), *Global Social Justice*, London and New York: Routledge.

Shepherd, L. J. (2013) *Gender, Violence and Popular Culture: Telling Stories*, New York: Routledge.

Shields, R. (ed.) (1996) *Cultures of Internet: Virtual Spaces, Real Histories, Living Bodies*, London, Thousand Oaks, CA, and New Delhi: SAGE.

Shiva, V. (1988) *Staying Alive: Women, Ecology and Development*. New Delhi: Kali for Women.

Shohat, E. (ed.) (1998) *Talking Visions: Multicultural Feminism in a Transnational Age*, Cambridge: MIT Press.

Shohat, E. (2002) 'Area Studies, Gender Studies and the Cartographies of Knowledge', *Social Text*, 20(3): 67–78.

Shumway, C. (2004) 'Pattern Emerges of Sexual Assault Against Women Held by US Forces', *The New Standard*, 16 June. Available at http://newstandardnews.net/content/?action=show_item&itemid=478 (accessed 15 April 2009).

Sideris, T. (2001a) 'Problems of Identity, Solidarity and Reconciliation', in S. Meintjes, A. Pillay and M. Turshen (eds), *The Aftermath. Women in Post-conflict Transformation*, London: Zed Books.

Sideris, T. (2001b) 'Rape in War and Peace: Social Context, Gender, Power and Identity', in S. Meintjes, A. Pillay and M. Turshen (eds), *The Aftermath. Women in Post-conflict Transformation*, London: Zed Books.

Sinclair, B. (2009) 'NPD: 2008 Game Sales Reach $21 Billion, Wii Play Sells 5.28M', *GameSpot*. Available at http://www.gamespot.com/news/6203257.html (accessed 15 April 2009).

Sinclair, M. T. (1997a) 'Gendered Work in Tourism: Comparative Perspectives', in M. T. Sinclair (ed.), *Gender, Work and Tourism*, London: Routledge.

Sinclair, M. T. (1997b) 'Issues and Theories of Gender and Work in Tourism', in M. T. Sinclair (ed.), *Gender, Work and Tourism*, London: Routledge.

Singh, J. G. (1996) *Colonial Narratives/Cultural Dialogues: Discoveries of India in the Language of Colonialism*, London: Routledge.

Singh, K. (2006) *Train to Pakistan*, New Delhi: Lotus Collection.

Sivakumaran, S. (2007) 'Sexual Violence Against Men in Armed Conflict', *European Journal of International Law*, 18(2): 253–76.

Sivakumaran, S. (2010) 'Lost in Translation: UN Responses to Sexual Violence Against Men and Boys in Situations of Armed Conflict', *International Review of the Red Cross*, 92(877): 259–77.

Sivanandan, A. (2006) 'Race, Terror and Civil Society', *Race and Class*, 47(3): 1–8.

Sjoberg, L. (2006) *Gender, Justice and the Wars in Iraq: A Feminist Reformulation of Just War Theory*, Lanham, MA: Rowman & Littlefield.

Sjoberg, L. (2009) 'Feminist Interrogations of Terrorism/Terrorism Studies', *International Relations*, 23(1): 69–74.

Sjoberg, L. (2011) 'Conclusion: The Study of Women, Gender, and Terrorism', in L. Sjoberg and C. E. Gentry, *Women, Gender, and Terrorism*, Athens, GA: University of Georgia Press.

Sjoberg, L. and Gentry, C. (2007) *Mothers, Monsters, Whores: Women's Violence in Global Politics*, London: Zed Books.

Sjoberg, L. and Gentry, C. (2008) 'Profiling Terror: Gendering the *Strategic Logic of Suicide Terror* and Other Narratives', *Austrian Journal of Political Science*, 37(2): 1–16.

Sjoberg, L. and Gentry, C. (eds) (2011) *Women, Gender, and Terrorism*, Athens, GA: University of Georgia Press.

Sjoberg L. and Peet J. (2011) 'A(nother) Dark Side of the Protection Racket', *International Feminist Journal of Politics*, 13(2): 163–82.

Slocum, J. D. (ed.) (2006) *Hollywood and War: The Film Reader*, New York: Routledge.

Smelik, A. (2000) 'Gay and Lesbian Criticism', in J. Hill and P. C. Gibson (eds), *Film Studies: Critical Approaches*, Oxford: Oxford University Press.

Smith, A. (2005) *Conquest: Sexual Violence and American Indian Genocide*, Cambridge: South End Press.

Smith, A. D. (1991) *National Identity*, London: Penguin.

Smith, J. (2008) 'British Women Are Already Suffering from Islamic Law', *The Independent*, 10 February, 38.

Smith, J., Chatfield, C. and Pagnucco R. (eds) (1997) *Transnational Social Movements and Global Politics*, New York: Syracuse University Press.

Smith, J. and Johnston H. (eds) (2002) *Globalization and Resistance: Transnational Dimensions of Social Movements*, Lanham, MD: Rowman & Littlefield.

Smith, M. (2006) 'Discourses on Development: Beyond the "African Tragedy"', in M. Smith (ed.), *Beyond the 'African Tragedy': Discourses on Development and the Global Economy*, Aldershot: Ashgate.

Smith, S. and Baylis, J. (2005) 'Introduction', in S. Smith and J. Baylis (eds), *The Globalization of World Politics: An Introduction to International Relations*, 3rd edn, Oxford: Oxford University Press.

Snyder, C. R. (1999) *Citizen-Soldiers and Manly Warriors: Military Service and Gender in the Civic Republican Tradition*, Lanham, MD: Rowman & Littlefield.

Sobchack, V. (1990) 'The Virginity of Astronauts: Sex and the Science Fiction Film', in A. Kuhn (ed.), *Alien Zone: Cultural Theory and Contemporary Science Fiction Cinema*, London: Verso.

Söderberg, J. (2013) 'Determining Social Change: The Role of Technological Determinism in the Collective Action Framing of Hackers', *New Media and Society*, 15(8): 1277–93.

Sofia, Z. (1999) 'Virtual Corporeality: A Feminist View', in J. Wolmark (ed.), *Cybersexualities: A Reader on Feminist Theory, Cyborgs and Cyberspace*, Edinburgh, Edinburgh University Press.

Sointu, E. and Woodhead, L. (2008). 'Spirituality, Gender, and Expressive Selfhood', *Journal for the Scientific Study of Religion*, 47(2): 259–76.

Spees, P. (2003) 'Women's Advocacy in the Creation of the International Criminal Court: Changing Landscapes of Justice and Power', *Signs: Journal of Women and Culture*, 28(4): 1233–56.

Sperling, V., Ferree, M. M. and Risman, B. (2001) 'Constructing Global Feminism: Transnational Advocacy Networks and Russian Women's Activism', *Signs*, 26(4): 1155–86.

Spiller, N. (2002) *Cyber_Reader: Critical Writings for the Digital Era*, London and New York: Phaidon Press Ltd.

Spivak, G. C. (1988) 'Can the Subaltern Speak?', in C. Nelson and L. Grossberg (eds), *Marxism and the Interpretation of Culture*, Urbana, IL: University of Illinois Press.

Spivak, G. C. (1999) *A Critique of Postcolonial Reason: Towards a History of the Vanishing Present*, Cambridge, MA: Harvard University Press.

Springer, C. (1998) 'The Pleasure of the Interface', in P. D. Hopkins (ed.), *Sex/Machine: Reading in Culture, Gender, and Technology*, Indiana, IN: Indiana University Press.

Squires, J. (2005) 'Is Mainstreaming Transformative? Theorizing Mainstreaming in the Context of Diversity and Deliberation', *Social Politics*, 12(3): 366–88.

Stabile, C. A. and Kumar, D. (2005) 'Unveiling Imperialism: Media, Gender and the War on Afghanistan', *Media, Culture and Society*, 27(5): 765–82.

Stacey, J. (1994) *Star Gazing: Hollywood Cinema and Female Spectatorship*, London: Routledge.

Staeheli, L. A., Kofman, E. and Peake, L. (eds) (2004) *Mapping Women, Making Politics: Feminist Perspectives on Political Geography*, New York: Routledge.

Stam, R., Burgoyne, R. and Flitterman-Lewis, S. (1992) *New Vocabularies in Film Semiotics: Structuralism, Post-structuralism and Beyond*, London: Routledge.

Standing, G. (1999) 'Global Feminization through Flexible Labour: A Theme Revisited', *World Development*, 27(3): 583–602.

Stasiulis, D. and Yuval-Davis, N. (eds) (1995) *Unsettling Settler Societies: Articulations of Gender, Race, Ethnicity and Class*, London: SAGE.

Staudt, K. (2003) 'Gender Mainstreaming: Conceptual Links to Institutional Machineries', in S. M. Rai (ed.), *Mainstreaming Gender, Democratizing the State? Institutional Mechanisms for the Advancement of Women*, Manchester: Manchester University Press.

Steans, J. (1998) *Gender and International Relations: An Introduction*, New Brunswick: Rutgers University Press.

Steans, J. (2003) 'Engaging from the Margins: Feminist Encounters with the 'Mainstream' of International Relations', *British Journal of Politics and International Relations*, 5(3): 428–54.

Steans, J. (2006) *Gender and International Relations: Issues, Debates and Future Directions*, 2nd edn, Cambridge: Polity Press.

Steans, J. (2007) 'Debating Women's Human Rights as a Universal Project; Defending Women's Human Rights as a Political Tool', *Review of International Studies*, January, 33: 11–27.

Steans, J. (2013) *Gender in International Relations*, Oxford: Polity Press.

Steans, J. and Ahmadi, V. (2005) 'Negotiating the Politics of Gender and Rights: Some Reflections on the Status of Women's Human Rights at Beijing Plus Ten', *Global Society*, 19(3): 227–45.

Stearns, C. (1999) 'Gender Issues', in R. S. Lee (ed), *The International Criminal Court: The Making of the Rome Statute*, The Hague: Kluwer Law International.

Stec, L. (1997) 'Female Sacrifice: Gender and Nostalgic Nationalism in Rebecca West's *Black Lamb and Grey Falcon*', in J. Pickering and S. Kehde (eds), *Narratives of Nostalgia, Gender and Nationalism*, London: Macmillan.

Stefan, D., Hagemann, K. and Tosh, J. (2004), in D. Stefan, K. Hagemann and J. Tosh (eds), *Masculinities in Politics and War: Gender in Modern History*, Manchester and New York: Manchester University Press.

Steger, M. B. (ed.) (2004) *Rethinking Globalism*, Lanham, MD: Rowman & Littlefield.

Steinberg, D. (2007) 'Failing to Empower Women in Peace Building: A Cautionary Tale from Angola', *PeaceWomen E-News*, 25 April. Available at http://www.peacewomen.org/news/1325News/Issue88.htm#analysis (accessed 15 April 2009).

Stern, M. (2006) '"We" the Subject: The Power and Failure of (In)security', *Security Dialogue*, 37(2): 187–205.

Stern, M. and Zalewski, M. (2009) 'Feminist Fatigue(s): Reflections on Feminist Fables off Militarization', *Review of International Studies*, 35(3): 611–30.

Stern, N. H. (2001) *Engendering Development: A Comment*, Washington, DC: World Bank.

Steven, E. P. (1973) 'Marianismo: The Other Face of Machismo', in A. Pescatello (ed.), *Female and Male in Latin America: Essays*, Pittsburg, PA: University of Pittsburg Press.

Stevens, J. (1999) *Reproducing the State*, Princeton, NJ: Princeton University Press.

Stewart, F., Huang, C. and Wang, M. (2001) 'Internal Wars: An Overview of the Economic and Social Consequences', in F. Stewart and V. Fitzgerald (eds), *War and Underdevelopment*, Oxford: Oxford University Press.

Stewart-Winter, T. (2007) 'Not a Soldier, Not a Slacker: Conscientious Objectors and Male Citizenship in the United States during the Second World War', *Gender & History*, 19(3): 519–42.

Stiegler, B. (2008) *Acting Out*, Stanford, CA: Stanford University Press.

Stiehm, J. (1982) 'The Protected, the Protector, the Defender', *Women's Studies International Forum*, 5: 367–76.

Stienstra, D. (2000) 'Dancing Resistance from Rio to Beijing: Transnational Women's Organizing and United Nations Conferences, 1992–6', in A. S. Runyan and M. Marchand (eds), *Gender and Global Restructuring: Sightings, Sites and Resistances*, London and New York: Routledge.

Stiglitz, J. (2003) 'Challenging the Washington Consensus', *Brown Journal of World Affairs*, IX(2): 33–40. Available at http://www.watsoninstitute.org/bjwa/archive/9.2/Feature/stiglitz.pdf (accessed 15 April 2009).

Stivens, M. (1998) 'Sex, Gender and the Making of the New Malay Middle Class', in K. Sen and M. Stivens (eds), *Gender and Power in Affluent Asia*, Routledge: London.

Stivens, M. (2000) 'Introduction: Gender Politics and the Re-Imagining of Human Rights in the Asia-Pacific', in A. M. Hilsdon, M. Macintyre, V. Mackie and M. Stivens (eds), *Human Rights and Gender Politics: Asia Pacific Perspectives*, London: Routledge.

Storeng, K. T., Akoum, M. S. and Murray S. F. (2013) '"This Year I Will Not Put Her to Work": The Production/Reproduction Nexus in Burkina Faso', *Anthropology & Medicine*, 20(1): 85–97.

Storey, J. (2006) *Cultural Theory and Popular Culture: An Introduction*, 4th edn, Harlow: Pearson.

Storr, W. (2011) 'The Rape of Men: The Darkest Secret of War', *The Guardian*, 17 July. Available at http://www.theguardian.com/society/2011/jul/17/the-rape-of-men (accessed 7 Dec 2013).

Stratigaki, M. (2005) 'Gender Mainstreaming vs Positive Action: An Ongoing Conflict in EU Gender Equality Policy', *European Journal of Women's Studies*, 12(2): 165–86.

Strüver, A. (2007) 'The Production of Geopolitical and Gendered Images through Global Aid Organisations', *Geopolitics*, 12(4): 680–703.

Sturgeon, N. (2005) 'Review of *The Death of Nature: Women, Ecology and the Scientific Revolution*', *Environmental History*, 10(4): 805–809.

Sturken, M. and Cartwright, L. (2001) *Practices of Looking: An Introduction to Visual Culture*, Oxford: Oxford University Press.

Swain, M. B. (1993) 'Women Producers of Ethnic Arts', *Annals of Tourism Research*, 20: 32–51.

Sweetman, C. (2005) 'Editorial', in C. Sweetman (ed.), *Gender, Peacebuilding and Reconstruction*, Oxford: Oxfam GB.

Sweetman, C. (ed.) (2005) *Gender, Peacebuilding and Reconstruction*, Oxford: Oxfam GB.

Swofford, A. (2003) *Jarhead: A Soldier's Story of Modern War*, London: Simon & Schuster.

Syed, Md Azalanshah Md (2012) 'Malay Women as Discerning Viewers: Asian Soap Operas, Consumer Culture and Negotiating Modernity', *Gender, Place and Culture: A Journal of Feminist Geography*, 20(5): 647–663.

Sylvester, C. (1994) *Feminist Theory and International Relations in a Postmodern Era*, Cambridge: Cambridge University Press.

Sylvester, C. (2005) 'The Art of War/The War Question in (Feminist) IR', *Millennium*, 33(3): 855–78.

Sylvester, C. (2007a) 'Anatomy of a Footnote', *Security Dialogue*, 38(4): 547–58.

Sylvester, C. (2007b) 'Whither the International at the End of IR', *Millennium*, 35(3): 551–73.

Sylvester, C. (2008) 'Roundtable Discussion: Reflections on the Past, Prospects for the Future in Gender and International Relations', *Millennium: Journal of International Studies*, 37(1): 153–79.

Sylvester, C. (2011a) *Experiencing War*, London: Routledge.

Sylvester, C. (ed.) (2011b) 'Forum: Emotion and the Feminist IR Researcher', *International Studies Review*, 40(4): 687–708.

Sylvester, C. (2012) *War as Experience: Contributions from International Relations and Feminist Analysis*, London: Routledge.

Tadiar, N. X. M (1998) 'Prostituted Filipinas and the Crisis of Philippine Culture', *Millennium*, 27(4): 927–54.

Talalay, M., Farrands, C. and Tooze, R. (eds) (1997) *Technology, Culture and Competitiveness: Change and the World Political Economy*, London and New York: Routledge.

Tasker, Y. (1993) *Spectacular Bodies: Gender, Genre, and the Action Cinema*, London: Routledge.

Tasker, Y. (1998) *Working Girls: Gender and Sexuality in Popular Cinema*, London: Routledge.

Tastsoglou, E. and Dobrowolsky, A. (eds) (2006) *Women, Migration and Citizenship: Making Local, National and Transnational Connections*, Aldershot and Burlington, VT: Ashgate.

Taylor, C. C. (1999) *Sacrifice as Terror: The Rwandan Genocide of 1994*, Oxford: Berg.

Taylor, P. and Jordan, T. (2004) *Hacktivism and Cyberwars – Rebel with a Cause*, Abingdon: Routledge.

Terranova, T. (2000) 'Free Labour: Producing Culture for the Digital Economy', *Social Text*, 18(2): 33–58.

Terranova, T. (2004) *Network Culture: Politics for the Information Age*, London: Pluto Press.

Tétreault, M. A. (ed.) (1994) *Women and Revolution in Africa, Asia, and the New World*, Columbia, SC: University of South Carolina Press.

Tétreault, M. A. and Lipschutz, R. D. (2005) *Global Politics as if People Mattered*, Lanham, MD: Rowman & Littlefield.

Theweleit, K. (1987a) *Male Fantasies, Vol. 1: Women, Floods, Bodies, History*, Minneapolis, MN: University of Minnesota Press.

Theweleit, K. (1987b) *Male Fantasies, Vol. 2: Male Bodies: Psychoanalyzing the White Terror*, Minneapolis, MN: University of Minnesota Press.

Thobani, S. (2001) 'Sunera Thobani's Speech', *Independent Media Centre*, 1 October. Available at http://print.indymedia.org/news/2001/10/923_ comment.php (accessed 15 April 2009).

Thobani, S. (2003) 'War and the Politics of Truth-Making in Canada', *International Journal of Qualitative Studies in Education*, 16(3): 399–414.

Thomas, L. (2002) *Fans, Feminisms and 'Quality' Media*, London: Routledge.

Thompson, J. B. (1995) *The Media and Modernity: A Social Theory of the Media*, Cambridge and Oxford: Polity Press.

Thornham, S. (ed.) (1999) *Feminist Film Theory: A Reader*, Edinburgh: Edinburgh University Press.

Tickner, J. A. (1992) *Gender in International Relations: Feminist Perspectives on Achieving Global Security*, New York: Columbia University Press.

Tickner, J. A. (1997) 'You Just Don't Understand: Troubled Engagements Between Feminists and IR Theorists', *International Studies Quarterly*, 41: 611–32.

Tickner, J. A. (2001) *Gendering World Politics: Issues and Approaches in the Post-Cold War Era*, New York: Columbia University Press.

Tickner, J. A. (2005) 'What is Your Research Program? Some Feminist Answers to International Relations Methodological Questions', *International Studies Quarterly*, 49: 1–22.

Tickner, J. A. (2006) 'Feminism Meets International Relations: Some Methodological Issues', in B. Ackerly, M. Stern and J. True (eds), *Feminist Methodologies for International Relations*, Cambridge: Cambridge University Press.

Tickner J. A. and Sjoberg, L. (eds) (2011) *Feminism and International Relations: Conversations about the Past, Present and Future*, London and New York: Routledge.

Tiessen, R. (2007) *Everywhere But Nowhere: Gender Mainstreaming in Development Institutions*, Bloomfield, CT: Kumarian Press.

Tinker, I. (2006) 'Empowerment Just Happened: The Unexpected Expansion of Women's Organizations', in J. S. Jaquette and G. Summerfield (eds), *Women and Gender Equity in Development Theory and Practice: Institutions, Resources and Mobilization*, Durham, NC: Duke University Press.

Titley, B. (2006) 'Heil Mary: Magdalen Asylums and Moral Regulation in Ireland', *History of Education Review*, 35(2): 45–69.

Togeby, L. (1994) 'The Gender Gap in Foreign Policy Attitudes', *Journal of Peace Research*, 31: 375–92.

Tohidi, N. (1991) 'Gender and Islamic Fundamentalism, Feminist Politics in Iran', in C. Mohanty, A. Russo and L. Torres (eds), *Third World Women and Politics of Feminism*, Indianapolis, IN: Indiana University Press.

Tooze, R. (1996) 'Prologue: States, Nationalism and Identities – Thinking in IR Theory', in J. Krause and N. Renwick (eds), *Identities in International Relations*, London: Macmillan.

Topping, A. (2013) '"Malala is my Idol": UN Speech brings British Pupils to Tears', *The Guardian*, 13 July. Available at http://www.theguardian.com/world/2013/jul/12/malala-idol-un-speech-pupils (accessed 17 October 2013).

Toupin, S. (2013) 'An Open-Air Self-Managed Social Center Called Occupy', *Contention: The Multidisciplinary Journal of Social Protest*, 1(1):13–30.

Tourn, F. (2013) 'Amina Tyler, Topless Tunisian Femen Protester, Tells Of Fear Of Being "Raped And Beaten" By Police', *Huffington Post UK*, 28 March. Available at http://www.huffingtonpost.co.uk/2013/03/28/amina-topless-tunisian-femen-protester-interview_n_2972559.html (accessed 7 December 2013).

Tronto, J. (1994) *Moral Boundaries: A Political Argument for an Ethic of Care*, New York: Routledge.

True, J. (2003) 'Mainstreaming Gender in Global Public Policy', *International Feminist Journal of Politics*, 5(3): 368–96.

True, J. (2008a) 'Trading-in Gender Equality: Gendered Meanings in EU Trade Policies', in E. Lombardo, P. Meier and M. Verloo (eds), *The Discursive Politics of Gender Equality: Stretching, Bending and Policy-Making*, New York: Routledge.

True, J. (2008b) 'Global Accountability and Transnational Networks: The Women Leaders Network and the Asia Pacific Economic Forum', *Pacific Review*, 21(1): 1–26.

True, J. (2008c) 'Gender Specialists and Global Governance Organizations', in M. Sawer and S. Grey (eds) *Women's Movements: In Abeyance or Flourishing in New Ways?*, New York: Routledge.

True, J. (2008d) 'Gender Mainstreaming and Trade Governance in the Asia-Pacific Economic Cooperation Forum (APEC)', in G. Waylen and S. Rai (eds) *Global Governance: Feminist Perspectives*, New York: Palgrave.

True, J. (2009) 'Trading-off Gender Equality for Global Europe: The European Union and Free Trade Agreements', *European Foreign Affairs Review*, 20(4): 723–42.

True, J. (2012) *The Political Economy of Violence Against Women*, New York. Oxford University Press.

True, J. and Hall, N. (2009) 'Gender Mainstreaming in a Post-Conflict State: Toward Democratic Peace in Timor Leste', in K. Lee Koo and B. Da Costa (eds), *Gender and Global Politics in Asia-Pacific*, Basingstoke: Palgrave Macmillan.

True, J. and Mintrom, M. (2001) 'Transnational Networks and Policy Diffusion: The Case of Gender Mainstreaming', *International Studies Quarterly*, 45(1): 27–57.

True, J. and Parisi, L. (2013) 'Gender Mainstreaming in Global Governance', in Guelay Caglar, Susanne Zwingel and Elisabeth Prugl (eds), *Feminist Strategies in International Governance*, New York: Routledge, pp. 37–56.

Truong, T. D. (1996) 'Gender, International Migration and Social Reproduction: Implications for Theory, Policy, Research and Networking', *Asian and Pacific Migration Journal*, 5(1): 27–52.

Truong, T. D. (1999) 'The Underbelly of the Tiger: Gender and the Demystification of the Asian Miracle', *Review of International Political Economy*, 6(2): 133–65.

Tuana, N. (1994) *Feminist Interpretations of Plato*, Philadelphia, PA: Pennsylvania State University Press.

Tuastad, D. (2003) 'Neo-Orientalism and the New Barbarism Thesis: Aspects of Symbolic Violence in the Middle East Conflict(s)', *Third World Quarterly*, 24(4): 591–99.

Tucker, H. (2007) 'Undoing Shame: Tourism and Women's Work in Turkey', *Journal of Tourism and Cultural Change*, 5(2), 87–105.

Turcotte, H. (2008) 'Contending the Limits of Political Space', *International Studies Review*, 10(3): 662–64.

Turcotte, H. (2011) 'Contextualizing Petro-Sexual Violence', *Alternatives: Global, Local, Political*, 36(3): 200–20.

Turkle, S. (1996) *Life on the Screen: Identity on the Age of the Internet*, New York: Simon & Schuster.

Turkle, S. (2011) *Alone Together: Why We Expect More from Technology and Less From Each Other*, New York: Basic Books.

Turley, H. (2004) 'Protestant Evangelism, British Imperialism and Crusonian Identity', in K. Wilson (ed.), *A New Imperial History: Culture, Identity and Modernity in Britain and the Empire, 1660–1840*, Cambridge: Cambridge University Press.

Turshen, M. (1998) 'Women's War Stories', in M. Turshen and C. Twagiramariya (eds), *What Women Do In Wartime. Gender and Conflict in Africa*, London: Zed Books.

Turshen, M. (2001a) 'The Political Economy of Rape: An Analysis of Systematic Rape and Sexual Abuse of Women During Armed Conflict in Africa', in C. Moser and F. C. Clark (eds), *Victims, Perpetrators or Actors? Gender, Armed Conflict and Political Violence*, London: Zed Books.

Turshen, M. (2001b) 'Engendering Relations of State to Society in the Aftermath', in M. Meintjes, A. Pillay and M. Turshen (eds), *The Aftermath. Women in Post-conflict Transformation*, London: Zed Books.

Turshen, M. and Twagiramariya, C. (eds) (1998) *What Women Do In Wartime. Gender and Conflict in Africa*, London: Zed Books.

U.S. Department of Defense (2003) 'Public Affairs Guidance (PAG) On Embedding Media', *Defense LINK*, 28 February 2003. Available at http://www.defenselink.mil/news/Feb2003/d20030228pag.pdf (accessed 15 April 2009).

U.S. Department of State (2008) 'Trafficking in Persons Report 2008', *Diplomacy in Action*, U.S. Department of State. Available at http://www.state.gov/g/ tip/rls/tiprpt/2008/ (accessed 15 April 2009).

Uberoi, M. (2005) *The Mahabharata*, New Delhi: Penguin.

Ullman, H. K. and James, P. W. (1996) *Shock and Awe: Achieving Rapid Dominance*, Washington, DC: National Defense University Press.

UNICEF (2002) 'Afghanistan is Among Worst Places on Globe for Women's Health, Say UNICEF and CDC', 6 November 2002. Available at http://www.unicef.org/newsline/02pr59afghanmm.htm (accessed 15 April 2009).

UN Women/UNWTO (2011) *Global Report on Women in Tourism*, Madrid: UNWTO.

United Nations – Water (2006) 'Gender, Water and Sanitation: A Policy Brief', UN-Water and the Interagency Network on Women and Gender Equality. Available at http://www.unwater.org/downloads/unwpolbrief230606.pdf.

United Nations (1945) *Charter of the United Nations*. Available at http://www.un.org/en/documents/charter/index.shtml (accessed 9 February 2013).

United Nations (1992) 'Agenda for Peace: Preventative Diplomacy, Peacemaking and Peacekeeping'. Available at http://www.un-documents.net/a47r120a.htm (accessed 9 June 2011).

United Nations (1995) *Beijing Declaration and Platform for Action*, New York: United Nations.

United Nations (1996) 'An Inventory of Post-Conflict Peace-Building Activities'. Available at http://www.un.org/esa/peacebuilding/Library/st_esa_246.pdf (accessed 10 February 2013).

United Nations (2003) *Women, Nationality and Citizenship*, UNDESA publication. Available at http://www.readbag.com/un-womenwatch-daw-public-jun03e (accessed 13 May 2014).

United Nations (2006) 'Integrated Disarmament, Demobilisation and Reintegration Standards'. Available at http://www.unddr.org/iddrs.aspx (accessed 9 June 2011).

United Nations (2008) 'Securing Peace and Development: The role of the United Nations in supporting security sector reform', A/62/659-S/2008/39. Available at http://www.un.org/Docs/sc/sgrep08.htm (accessed 9 February 2013).

United Nations (2009a) 'What is GAID?', *The Global Alliance for ICT and Development*, United Nations Department for Economic and Social Affairs. Available at http://www.un-gaid.org/About/tabid/861/language/en-US/Default.aspx (accessed 15 April 2009).

United Nations (2009b) 'Report of the Secretary General on Peacebuilding in the Immediate Aftermath of Conflict', A/63/881–S/2009/304. Available at http://www.unrol.org/doc.aspx?n=pbf_090611_sg.pdf (accessed 9 February 2013).

United Nations (2010) *Second Generation Disarmament, Demobilisation and Reintegration Practices in Peace Operations*, New York: United Nations.

United Nations (2011) *International Migration Report 2009: A Global Assessment* (United Nations, ST/ESA/SER.A/316).

United Nations Conference on Environment and Development (UNCED) (1992) *Agenda 21*. Available at http://sustainabledevelopment.un.org/content/documents/Agenda21.pdf.

United Nations Department of Economic and Social Affairs (UNDESA) (2006) *2004 World Survey on the Role of Women in Development: Women and International Migration*, New York: United Nations Publishing Section. Available at http://www.un.org/womenwatch/daw/public/WorldSurvey2004-Women&Migration.pdf (accessed 15 April 2009).

United Nations Department of Economic and Social Affairs, Population Division (2011), International Migration Report 2009: A Global Assessment (United Nations, ST/ESA/SER.A/316). Available at http://www.globalmigrationgroup.org/gmg/sites/default/files/uploads/UNCT_Corner/theme1/data-and-research/WorldMigrationReport2009.pdf (accessed 4 May, 2014).

United Nations Department of Peacekeeping Operations (DPKO) (2004) *Gender Resource Package for Peacekeeping Operations*, Best Practices Unit, New York: United Nations.

United Nations Department of Peacekeeping Operations (DPKO) (2005) *2005 Progress Report*, New York: United Nations.

United Nations Department of Peacekeeping Operations (DPKO) (2006) *Global Action Plan on Security Council Resolution on Women, Peace and Security*, New York: United Nations. Available at http://pbpu.unlb.org/pbpu/library/ Action%20Plan%20Brocure%20(sep%202006).pdf (no longer accessible).

United Nations Development Program (UNDP) (1995) *Human Development Report 1995*, New York: Oxford University Press.

United Nations Development Program (UNDP) (2006) 'Elaborating the Gender Dimensions of Democratic Governance', UNDP Democratic Governance Group. Available at http://www.un.org.vn/undp/projects/vie02007/PM_2006/gender_equality.htm (accessed 12 January 2008; no longer accessible).

United Nations Division for the Advancement of Women (2003) 'Women, Nationality and Citizenship', New York: United Nations.

United Nations Economic and Social Council (ECOSOC) (2004) 'Gender Mainstreaming in the United Nations Operational Activities', ECOSOC Panel discussion, 2 July 2004. Available at http://www.un.org/docs/ecosoc/meetings/docs/2%20July%20issues%20paper.pdf (accessed 15 April 2009)

United Nations Educational, Scientific and Cultural Organization (UNESCO) (2013) 'WSIS + 10: Towards Inclusive Knowledge Societies for Peace and Sustainable Development', 1st WSIS Review meeting, 25–27 February 2013. Available at http://www.unesco.org/new/en/communication–and–information/flagship–project–activities/unesco–and–wsis/wsis–10–review–meeting/ (accessed 1 September 2013).

United Nations General Assembly (2005) 'In Larger Freedom: Towards Development, Security and Human Rights for All', A/59/2005/Add.2. Available at http://www.un.org/largerfreedom/contents.htm (accessed 9 February 2013).

United Nations General Assembly (2000) *Millennium Development Goals*. Available at http://www.un.org/millenniumgoals/ (accessed 9 September 2013).

United Nations Global Initiative to Fight Human Trafficking (UN GIFT) (2008) *Human Trafficking: An Overview*, New York: United Nations. Available at http://www.ungift.org/docs/ungift/pdf/knowledge/ebook.pdf (accessed 17 April 2009).

United Nations High Commissioner for Refugees (2012) *UNHCR Global Report 2012: Statelessness.* Available at http://www.unhcr.org/51b1d61db.html (accessed 11 August 2013).

United Nations High Commissioner for Refugees (2013) *UNHCR Global Trends 2012: Displacement, The New 21st Century Challenge.* Available at http://www.refworld.org/docid/51c169d84.html (accessed 11 August 2013).

United Nations Integrated Regions International Network (IRIN) (2004) *Our Bodies – Their Battle Ground: Gender-Based Violence in Conflict Zones.* Available at http://www.irinnews.org/IndepthMain.aspx?IndepthId=20&ReportId=62814 (accessed 15 April 2009).

United Nations Integrated Regions International Network (IRIN) (2008a) *Africa-Asia: Rape as a Tool of War.* Available at http://www.irinnews.org/InDepthMain.aspx?InDepthId=20 andReportId=62817 (accessed 15 April 2009).

United Nations Integrated Regions International Network (IRIN) (2008b) *Africa-Asia: Definitions of Sexual and Gender-based Violence.* Available at http://www.irinnews.org/InDepthMain.aspx?InDepthId=20andReportId=62847 (accessed 15 April 2009).

United Nations International Research and Training Institute for the Advancement of Women (INSTRAW) (2007) *Virtual Discussion on Gender Training for Security Sector Personnel.* Available at http://www.un-instraw.org/en/gps/general/gender-training-for-security-sector-personnel.html (accessed 15 April 2009)

United Nations Peacebuilding Commission (2007a) 'Report of the Peacebuilding Commission on its First Session', A/62/137-S/2007/458. Available at http://www.un.org/peace/peacebuilding/docsandres.shtml (accessed 9 February 2013).

United Nations Peacebuilding Commission (2007b) 'Identical Letters Dated 21 June 2007 from the Chairman of the Burundi Configuration of the Peacebuilding Commission to the President of the Security Council, the President of the General Assembly and the President of the Economic and Social Council [Strategic Framework for Peacebuilding in Burundi]', PBC/1/BDI/4. Available at http://www.un.org/peace/peacebuilding/pbc-countrymtgs.shtml (accessed 9 February 2013).

United Nations Peacebuilding Commission (2008a) 'Background Note'. Available at http://www.un.org/peace/peacebuilding/Working%20Group%20on%20Lessons%20Learned/WGLLbackgroundpaper%2029.01.08.pdf (accessed 9 February 2013).

United Nations Peacebuilding Commission (2008b) 'Summary Notes of the Chair'. Available at http://www.un.org/peace/peacebuilding/Working%20Group%20on%20Lessons%20Learned/WGLL290108GenderPBCSummary.pdf (accessed 9 February 2013).

United Nations Peacebuilding Commission (2009) 'Strategic Framework for Peacebuilding in the Central African Republic', PBC/3/CAF/7. Available at http://www.un.org/peace/peacebuilding/pbc-countrymtgs.shtml (accessed 9 February 2013).

United Nations Peacebuilding Commission (2010) 'Emerging Lessons and Practices in Peacebuilding, 2007–2009'. Available at http://www.un.org/peace/peacebuilding/pbc-lessons.shtml (accessed 9 February 2013).

United Nations Peacebuilding Fund (2011) 'The PBF and Gender Equality'. Available at http://www.unpbf.org/news/pbf-gender-promotion-initiative/ (accessed 29 July 2013).

United Nations Secretary-General (2010) 'Women's Participation in Peacebuilding', A/65/354-S/2010/466. Available at http://www.un.org/ga/search/view_doc.asp?symbol=A/65/354 (accessed 29 July 2013).

United Nations Secretary-General (2012) 'Report of the Secretary-General on Women and Peace and Security'. Available at http://www.un.org/en/sc/documents/sgreports/2012.shtml (accessed 30 August 2013).

United Nations Security Council (2000) 'Resolution 1325', S/RES/1325. Available at www.un.org/Docs/scres/2000/sc2000.htm (accessed 9 February 2013).

United Nations Security Council (2005) 'Resolution 1645', S/RES/1645. Available at http://www.un.org/Docs/sc/unsc_resolutions05.htm (accessed 9 February 2013).

United Nations Security Council (2006) 'Security Council Resolution 1702: The Question Concerning Haiti'. Available at http://daccessdds.un.org/doc/UNDOC/GEN/N06/468/77/PDF/N0646877.pdf?OpenElement (accessed 15 April 2009).

United Nations Security Council (UNSC) (2009) 'Resolution 1889', S/RES/1889. Available at http://www.un.org/en/sc/documents/resolutions/2009.shtml (accessed 13 May 2014).

United States Department of Defense Office of Force Transformation (2003) *Military Transformation: A Strategic Approach*, Washington. Available at http://www.iwar.org.uk/rma/resources/transformation/military-transformation-a-strategic-approach.pdf (accessed 15 April 2009).

United States Department of Defense Office of Force Transformation (2005) *A Network-Centric Operations Case Study: US/UK Coalition Combat Operations During Operation Iraqi Freedom*, 2 March, Washington, DC. Available at http://www.dodccrp.org/events/9th_ICCRTS/CD/papers/023.pdf (accessed 15 April 2009).

United States Department of State (2013) *Syria: Numbers and Locations of Refugees and IDPs*, Humanitarian Information Unit. Available at https://hiu.state.gov/Products/Syria_DisplacementRefugees_2013July31_HIU_U876.pdf.

United States Government Accountability Office (GAO) (2006) 'Human Trafficking. Better Data, Strategy and Reporting Needed to Enhance US Anti-Trafficking Efforts Abroad'. Available at http://www.gao.gov/new.items/d06825.pdf (accessed 15 April 2009).

Valentine, D. and Wilchins, R. A. (1997) 'One Percent on the Burn Chart: Gender, Genitals and Hermaphrodites with Attitude', *Social Text*, 15(3/4): 215–22.

van Dijck, J. (2013) *The Culture of Connectivity: A Critical History of Social Media*, New York: Oxford University Press.

van Staveren, I. (2002) 'Global Finance and Gender', in J. Scholte and A. Schnabel (eds), *Civil Society and Global Finance*, London: Routledge.

Vepa, S. S. (2005) 'Feminization of Agriculture and Marginalization of Their Economic Stake', *Economic and Political Weekly*, XL.25.

Verloo, M. (2005) 'Displacement and Empowerment: Reflections on the Concept and Practice of the Council of Europe Approach to Gender Mainstreaming and Gender Equality', *Social Politics: International Studies in Gender, State and Society*, 12(1): 344–65.

Vertigans, S. (2010) 'British Muslims and the UK Government's "War on Terror" Within: Evidence of a Clash of Civilizations or Emergent De-Civilizing Processes?', *British Journal of Sociology*, 61(1): 26–44.

Veseth, M. (2005) *Globaloney: Unravelling the Myths of Globalization*, Oxford and New York: Rowman & Littlefield.

Via Campesina (1996) 'The Right to Produce and Access to Land', *Voice of the Turtle*. Available at http://www.voiceoftheturtle.org/library/1996%20 Declaration%20of%20Food%20Sovereignty.pdf.

Via Campesina (2007) *Nyéléni Declaration*. Sélingué, Mali: Forum for Food Sovereignty. Available at http://www.nyeleni.org/IMG/pdf/DeclNyeleni-en.pdf.

Villareal, A. S. and Yu, W. H. (2007) 'Economic Globalization and Women's Employment: The Case of Manufacturing in Mexico', *American Sociological Review*, 72(3): 365–89.

Volintiru, C. (2010) 'Towards a Dynamic Model of Terrorist Radicalization', EIR Working Papers No. 27. Available at http://ssrn.com/abstract=1747690 or http://dx.doi.org/10.2139/ssrn.1747690.

Volpp, L. (2001) 'Feminism versus Multiculturalism', *Columbia Law Review*, 101(5): 1181–218.

Votta, M. (2013) 'Tomb Raider 2013 Sales Figures are Deserved', *Inentertainment*, 8 March. Available at http://www.inentertainment.co.uk/20130308/tomb-raider-2013-sales-figures-are-deserved/ (accessed 30 August 2013).

Vuillamy, E. and Hinsliff, G. (2001) 'Bush's Star Wars Raises Global Arms Race Fears', *The Observer*, 14 January.

Wade, R. W. (2004) 'Is Globalization Reducing Poverty and Inequality?', *World Development*, 32(4): 567–89.

Wajcman, J. (1991) *Feminism Confronts Technology*, Cambridge: Polity Press.

Wajcman, J. (2004) *Technofeminism*, Cambridge: Polity Press.

Walker, R. B. J. (1992) 'Gender and Critique in the Theory of International Relations', in V. Spike Peterson (ed.), *Gendered States: Feminist (Re)Visions of International Relations Theory*, Boulder, CO: Lynne Rienner.

Walker, R. B. J. (1993) *Inside/Outside: International Relations as Political Theory*, Cambridge: Cambridge University Press.

Wallace, B. (2000) 'Canadian Aces Over Kosovo', *Macleans*, 27 March. Available at http://www.macleans.ca/topstories/article.jsp?content=32434#continue (accessed 25 April 2000; no longer accessible).

Waller, D. (1995) 'Onward Cyborg Soldiers', *Time Magazine*, 21 August.

Waller, M. R. and Rycenga, J. (eds) (2000) *Frontline Feminisms: Women, War, and Resistance*, New York: Garland Publishing.

Wallerstein, I. (1979) *The Capitalist World-Economy*, Cambridge: Cambridge University Press.

Walsh, M. (2007) 'Gendering International Justice: Progress and Pitfalls at International Criminal Tribunals', in D. Pankhurst (ed.), *Gendered Peace. Women's Struggles for Post-War Justice and Reconciliation*, New York: Routledge.

Walter, N. (2004) 'When the Veil Means Freedom', *The Guardian*, 20 January. Available at http://www.guardian.co.uk/world/2004/jan/20/france.schoolsworldwide1 (accessed 15 April 2009).

Waltz, K. (1959) *Man, the State, and War*, New York: Columbia University Press.

Walzer, M. (1994) *Thick and Thin: Moral Argument at Home and Abroad*, Notre Dame, IN: University of Notre Dame Press.

Waring, M. (1999) *Counting for Nothing: What Men Value and What Women are Worth*, 2nd edn, Toronto: University of Toronto Press.

Warner M. (2008) 'Evangelicals and Evangelicalisms, Sex in a Secular Age: The Ruse of Secular Humanism'. Available at http://blogs.ssrc.org/tif/2008/09/22/the-ruse-of-secular-humanism/

Warren, M. A. (1985) *Gendercide: The Implications of Sex Selection*, Lanham, MD: Rowman & Littlefield.

Watson, A. (2006) 'Children and International Relations: a New Site of Knowledge?', *Review of International Studies*, 32: 237–50.

Watson, A. (2007) 'Children Born of Wartime Rape. Rights and Representations', *International Feminist Journal of Politics*, 9(1): 20–34.

Watson, M. (2005) 'Towards a Polanyian perspective on Fair Trade: Market-Based Relationships and the Act of Ethical Consumption', *Global Society*, 20(4): 435–51.

Waylen, G. (2006) 'You Still Don't Understand: Why Troubled Engagements Continue Between Feminists And (Critical) IPE', *Review of International Studies*, 32: 145–64.

Weatherly, R. (1990) *The Discourse of Human Rights in China*, London: Macmillan.

Weber, C. (1994) 'Good Girls, Little Girls and Bad Girls: Male Paranoia in Robert Keohane's Critique of Feminist International Relations', *Millennium*, 23: 337–49.

Weber, C. (1999) *Faking It: US Hegemony in a 'Post-Phallic' Era*, Minneapolis, MN: University of Minnesota Press.

Weber, C. (2001) *International Relations Theory: A Critical Introduction*, London: Routledge.

Weber, C. (2005a) *International Relations Theory: A Critical Introduction*, 2nd edn, London, Routledge.

Weber, C. (2005b) 'Securitising the Unconscious: The Bush Doctrine of Preemption and Minority Report', *Geopolitics*, 10: 482–99.

Weber, C. (2008) 'Popular Visual Language as Global Communication', *Review of International Studies*, 34: 137–53.

WEDO (2013) *Women's Participation in UN Climate Negotiations: 2008–2012*. Available at http://www.wedo.org/wp-content/uploads/WomenUNFCCCParticipation2008-2012 FINAL2013.pdf.

Weedon, C. (1997) *Feminist Practice and Poststructuralist Theory*, 2nd edn, London: Blackwell.

Weinstein, B. (2006) '"They Don't Even Look Like Women Workers": Femininity and Class in Twentieth-Century Latin America', *International Labor and Working-Class History*, 69: 161–76.

Weiser, I. (2004) 'One Hundred Twelve Women Assaulted in Iraq, Afghanistan', *Common Dreams.org*, 18 May. Available at http://www.commondreams.org/views04/0518-06.htm (accessed 15 April 2009).

Weitzer, R. (2007) 'The Social Construction of Sex Trafficking: Ideology and Institutionalization of a Moral Crusade', *Politics and Society*, 35(3): 447–75.

Weldes, J. (1999) 'Going Cultural: Star Trek, State Action and Popular Culture', *Millennium*, 28: 117–34.

Weldes, J. (2001) 'Globalisation is Science Fiction', *Millennium*, 30: 647–67.

Weldes, J. (2003a) 'Introduction', in J. Weldes (ed.), *To Seek Out New Worlds: Exploring Links Between Science Fiction and World Politics*, New York: Palgrave Macmillan.

Weldes, J. (ed.) (2003b) *To Seek Out New Worlds: Exploring Links Between Science Fiction and World Politics*, New York: Palgrave Macmillan.

Weldes, J. (2006) 'High Politics and Low Data: Globalization Discourses and Popular Culture', in D. Yanow and P. Schwartz-Shea (eds), *Interpretation and Method: Empirical Research Methods and the Interpretive Turn*, Armonk, NY: M.E. Sharpe.

Werbner, P. (2002) 'The Place Which is Diaspora: Citizenship, Religion and Gender in the Making of Chaordic Transnationalism', *Journal of Ethnic and Migration Studies*, 28(1): 119–33.

Weston, K. (2002) *Gender in Real Time: Power and Transience in a Visual Age*, London: Routledge.

Whitaker, B. (1985) *Revised and Updated Report on the Question of the Prevention and Punishment of the Crime of Genocide*, the UN Whitaker Report, 2 July. Available at http://www.preventgenocide.org/prevent/UNdocs/whitaker/ (accessed 15 April 2009).

White, G., Howell, J. and Xiaoyuan, S. (1996) *In Search of Civil Society: Market Reform and Social Change in Contemporary China*, Oxford: Oxford University Press.

White, P. (2000) 'Feminism and Film', in J. Hill and P. C. Gibson (eds), *Film Studies: Critical Approaches*, Oxford: Oxford University Press.

Whitworth, S. (2000) 'Theory and Exclusion: Gender, Masculinity, and International Political Economy', in R. Stubbs and G. Underhill (eds), *Political Economy and the Changing Global Order*, 2nd edn, Toronto: Oxford University Press.

Whitworth, S. (2004) *Men, Militarism and UN Peacekeeping: A Gendered Analysis*, Boulder, CO: Westview Press.

Whitworth, S. (2008) 'Militarized Masculinity and Post Traumatic Stress Disorder', in J. L. Parpart and M. Zalewski (eds), *Rethinking the Man Question: Sex, Gender and Violence in International Relations*, New York: Zed Books.

Wichterich, C. (2000) *The Globalized Woman: Reports from a Future of Inequality*, London and New York: Zed Books.

Wiegman, R. (2000) 'Race, Ethnicity, and Film', in J. Hill and P. C. Gibson (eds), *Film Studies: Critical Approaches*, Oxford: Oxford University Press.

Wiegman, R. (2001) 'Object Lessons: Men, Masculinity, and the Sign Women', *Signs: Journal of Women in Culture and Society*, 26(2): 355–88.

Wiegman, R. (2004) 'On Being in Time With Feminism', *Modern Languages Quarterly*, 65(1): 161–76.

Wright, M. W. (2006) *Disposable Women and Other Myths of Global Capitalism*, London: Routledge.

Wiktorowicz, Q. (ed.) (2004) *Islamic Activism: A Social Movement Theory Approach*, Bloomington, IN: Indiana University Press.

Wilcox, M. M. (2012) '"Spiritual Sluts": Uncovering Gender, Ethnicity, and Sexuality in the Post-Secular', *Women's Studies: An Inter-Disciplinary Journal*, 41(6): 639–59.

Willett, S. (2010) 'Introduction: Security Council Resolution 1325: Assessing the Impact on Security', *International Peacekeeping*, 17(2): 142–58.

Williams, K. (2005) *Love My Rifle More Than You: Young and Female in the US Army*, London: Weidenfeld & Nicholson.

Williams, L. (ed.) (2004a) *Porn Studies*, Durham, NC: Duke University Press.

Williams, L. (2004b) 'Ready for Action: G.I. Jane, Demi Moore's Body and the Female Combat Movie', in Y. Tasker (ed.), *Action and Adventure Cinema*, London: Routledge.

Williams, L. (2008) *Screening Sex*, Durham, NC: Duke University Press.

Williams, R (1958) 'Resources of Hope', in N. McKenzie (ed.), *Convictions*, London: MacGibbon & Kee.

Williams, R. (1981) *Culture*, London: Fontana.

Willis, K. and Yeoh, B. (eds) (2000) *Gender and Migration*, Cheltenham: Edward Elgar.

Wilson, Z. (2005) 'State Making, Peace Making and the Inscription of Gendered Politics into Peace: Lessons from Angola', in D. Mazurana, A. Raven-Roberts and J. Parpart (eds), *Gender, Conflict and Peacekeeping*, Lanham, MD, and Oxford: Rowman & Littlefield.

Windfuhr, M. and Jonsen, J. (2005) *Food Sovereignty: Towards Democracy in Localized Food Systems*. Rugby: ITDG Publishing.

Wittman, H. (2011) 'Food Sovereignty: A New Rights Framework for Food and Nature?', *Environment and Society: Advances in Research*, 2(1): 87–105.

Wolf, D. (1990) 'Daughters, Decisions and Domination: An Empirical and Conceptual Critique of Household Strategies', *Development & Change*, 21(1): 43–74.

Women's Initiatives for Gender Justice (2007). *Gender Report Card 2007*. The Hague: Women's Initiatives for Gender Justice. Available at http://www.iccwomen.org/publications/resources/docs/GENDER_04-01-2008_FINAL_TO_PRINT.pdf (accessed 16 July 2013).

Wood, A. (1991) 'North-South Trade and Female Labour in Manufacturing: An Asymmetry', *Journal of Development Studies*, 27(2): 168–89.

Woodward, A. (2003) 'European Gender Mainstreaming: Promises and Pitfalls of Transformative Policy', *Review of Policy Research*, 20(1): 65–88.

Woolf, V. (1938) *Three Guineas*, New York: Harcourt Brace.

Woolgar, S. (2002) *Virtual Society? Technology, Cyberbole, Reality*, Oxford: Oxford University Press.

Worden, A. (1991) 'Despair and Hop: A Changsha Chronicle', in J. Unger (ed.), *The Pro-Democracy Protests in China: Reports from the Provinces*, Armonk, NY: M.E. Sharpe Inc.

World Bank (2001) 'Development Outreach Special Report: Women and Power'. Available at http://www.devoutreach.com/spring01/SpecialReport WomenandPower/tabid/1065/Default.aspx (accessed 15 April 2009).

World Bank (2002) *Globalization, Growth and Poverty: Building an Inclusive World Economy*. Washington, DC: World Bank/Oxford University Press.

World Bank (2006a) 'Vietnam Gender Assessment 2006'. Available at http://go.worldbank.org/7MIQQ147V0 (accessed 15 April 2009).

World Bank (2006b) *Global Economic Prospects: Economic Implications of Remittances and Migration*, Washington, DC: World Bank.

World Bank (2007a) 'Obstacles on the Road to Prosperity'. Available at http://go.worldbank.org/NXYIC0AKZ0 (accessed 2 July 2008)

World Bank (2007b) 'Gender in the World Bank: Bank Policy and its Implementation', *Gender and Development*, World Bank, 20 September 2007. Available at http://go.worldbank.org/GZXJ0EXNI0 (accessed 15 April 2009).

World Bank (2008a) 'Social Policy: Development in a Globalizing World', *Social Development*, World Bank. Available at http://go.worldbank.org/V17DL33HO0 (accessed 15 April 2009).

World Bank (2008b) 'Social Development: Concept Note', World Bank. Available at http://go.worldbank.org/CQTT183AY0 (accessed April 2008 and February 2009).

World Commission on Environment and Development (WCED) (1987) *Our Common Future*, Oxford: Oxford University Press.

World Health Organization (WHO) (2009) 'Post-Washington Consensus', World Health Organization. Available at http://www.who.int/trade/glossary/story074/en/ (accessed 15 April 2009).

World Internet Users and Population Stats. Available at http://www.internetworldstats.com/stats.htm (accessed 9 September 2013).

World Summit on the Information Society (WSIS) (2003) *Shaping Information Societies for Human Needs*, Civil Society Declaration to the World Summit on the Information Society, Geneva, 8 December 2003. Available at http://www.itu.int/wsis/docs/geneva/civil-society-declaration.pdf (accessed 15 April 2009).

World Trade Center (2006) Paramount Pictures, directed by Oliver Stone.

World Trade Organization (WTO) (2004) 'The Impact of Women in Small, Medium and Micro Enterprises on Increasing Trade under the WTO Agreements', Summary of Session, 12 July. Available at http://www.gwit.ch/.

Wyatt, S. (2008a) 'Feminism, Technology and the Information Society: Learning from the past, imagining the future', *Information, Communication and Society*, 11(1): 111–30.

Wyatt, S. (2008b) 'Technological Determinism is Dead; Long Live Technological Determinism' in E. Hackett, O. Amsterdamska, M. Lynch and J. Wajcman (eds), *The Handbook of Science and Technology Studies*, 3rd edn, Cambridge, MA: MIT Press.

Wyatt, S., Thomas, G. and Terranova, T. (2002) 'They Came, They Surfed, They Went Back to the Beach: Conceptualising Use and Non-Use of the Internet', in Steve Woolgar (ed.), *Virtual Society? Technology, Cyberpole, Reality*, Oxford: Oxford University Press, pp. 23–40.

Wyatt, S., Henwood, F., Miller, N. and Senker, P. (eds) (2000) *Technology and In/equality: Questioning the Information Society*, New York and London: Routledge.

Wyatt, S., Thomas, G. and Terranova, T. (2002) 'They Came, they Surfed, they Went Back to the Beach: Conceptualising Use and Non-use of the Internet', in S. Woolgar (ed.), *Virtual Society? Technology, Cyberbole, Reality*, Oxford: Oxford University Press.

Yanow, D. (1996), *How Does a Policy Mean? Interpreting Policy and Organizational Actions*, Washington, DC: Georgetown University Press.

Yeats, N. (2004) 'Global Care Chains: Critical Reflections and Lines of Enquiry', *International Feminist Journal of Politics*, 6(3): 369–91.

Yeoh, B. and Huang, S. (2000) 'Home and Away: Foreign Domestic Workers and Negotiations of Diasporic Identity in Singapore', *Women's Studies International Forum*, 23(4): 29–43.

Young, A. (1990) *Femininity in Dissent*, London: Routledge.

Young, I. M. (2003) 'The Logic of Masculinist Protection: Reflections on the Current Security State', *Signs: Journal of Women in Culture and Society*, 29: 1–25.

Young, I. M. (2005) 'The Logic of Masculinist Protection: Reflections on the Current Security State', in M. Friedman (ed.), *Women and Citizenship*, Oxford: Oxford University Press.

Youngs, G. (2004) 'Feminist International Relations: A Contradiction in Terms? Or: Why Women and Gender are Essential to Understanding the World "We" Live In', *International Affairs*, 80(1): 75–87.

Youngs, G. (2006) 'Feminist International Relations in the Age of the War on Terror: Ideologies, Religions and Conflict', *International Feminist Journal of Politics*, 8(1): 3–18.

Youngs, G. et al. (1999) 'Three Readings of G.I. Jane', *International Feminist Journal of Politics*, 1(3): 476–81.

Yuval-Davis, N. (1997) *Gender and Nation*, London: SAGE.

Yuval-Davis, N. (2006) 'Intersectionality and Feminist Politics', *European Journal of Women's Studies*, 13(3): 193–209.

Yuval-Davis, N. and Werbner, P. (eds) (1999) *Women, Citizenship and Difference*, London and New York: Zed Books.

Zalewski, M. (1996) '"All These Theories yet the Bodies Keep Piling Up": Theories, Theorists, Theorising', in S. Smith, K. Booth and M. Zalewski (eds), *International Theory: Positivism and Beyond*, Cambridge: Cambridge University Press.

Zalewski, M. (1999) 'Tampons and Cigars: (No) Escaping Sexual Difference in G.I. Jane', *International Feminist Journal of Politics*, 1(3): 479–81.

Zalewski, M. (2000) *Feminism After Postmodernism: Theorising Through Practice*, London: Routledge.

Zalewski, M. (2013) *Feminist International Relations: 'Exquisite Corpse'*, New York: Routledge.

Zalewski, M. and Parpart, J. (2008) 'Introduction: Rethinking the Man Question', in J. Parpart and M. Zalewski (eds), *Rethinking the Man Question: Sex, Gender and Violence in International Relations*, London: Zed Books.

Zalewski, M. and Parpart, J. (eds) (1998) *The 'Man' Question in International Relations*, Oxford and Boulder, CO: Westview Press.

Zarkov, D. (2007) *The Body of War: Media, Ethnicity and Gender in the Break-Up of Yugoslavia*, Durham, NC, and London: Duke University Press.

Zarkov, D. and Cockburn, C. (2002), 'Introduction', in C. Cockburn and D. Zarkov (eds), *The Postwar Moment: Militaries, Masculinities and International Peacekeeping*, London: Lawrence & Wishart.

Zarzycka, M. (2012) 'Madonnas of Warfare, Angels of Poverty: Cutting Through Press Photographs', *Photographies*, 5(1): 71–85.

Zhang, L. (2001) *Strangers in the City: Reconfigurations of Space, Power, and Social Networks Within China's Floating Population*, Stanford, CA: Stanford University Press.

Ziegler, J., Golay, C., Mahon, C. and Way, S. (2011) *The Fight for the Right to Food: Lessons Learned*, London: Palgrave Macmillan.

Zimbardo, P. (2007) *The Lucifer Effect: Understanding How Good People Turn Evil*, New York: Random House.

Žižek, S. (2008) *Violence*, New York, NY: Picador.

Zwarteveen, M. (1997) 'Water: From Basic Need to Commodity. A Discussion on Gender and Water Rights in the Context of Irrigation', *World Development*, 25(8): 1335–50.

Zwarteveen, M. (1998) 'Identifying Gender Aspects of New Irrigation Management Policies', *Agriculture and Human Values*, 15(4): 301–12.

Zwarteveen, M. and Meinzen-Dick, R. (1998) 'Gendered Participation in Water Management: Issues and Illustrations from Water Users' Associations in South Asia', *Agriculture and Human Values*, 15(4): 337–45.

Zylinska, J. (ed.) (2002) *The Cyborg Experiments: The Extensions of The Body in the Media Age*, London and New York: Continuum.

INDEX

Page numbers in *italics* refer to Figures.